W9-AQH-857

WITHDRAWN

Vermont Inns and Taverns,

Pre-Revolution To 1925-
An Illustrated and Annotated Checklist
By
John C. Wriston, Jr.

Academy Books

Rutland, Vermont

Illustration from the Broadside Collection, Vermont Historical Society.

ISBN 0-914960-75-X

Library of Congress Catalog Card Number preassigned is 91-073485

Copyright 1991, John C. Wriston, Jr.

* * *

All rights reserved. No part of this publication

may be reproduced, stored in a retrieval system or transmitted

in any form or by any means without the prior written permission

of the author, except for brief quotations in a review.

* * *

This project is funded in part

by the Vermont Statehood Bicentennial Commission

* * *

Manufactured in the United States of America at

Academy Books

Rutland, Vermont

Dedication

Dedicated to the memory of my parents, John C. Wriston and Hildreth Tyler Wriston, and my stepmother, Rhoda Orvis Wriston, Vermont inn-keepers all.

* * *

Table of Contents

* * *

Foreword

This book grew out of a long-term interest in Vermont post office history. Pictures of old inns began turning up along with those of post offices in boxes of cards at postcard shows; stories about taverns caught my attention during library searches for post office material; and the names of hotels began jumping out from the pages of Beers and Walton as post offices had done before.

It became apparent that while there was a great deal of information available about Vermont taverns and inns, it was widely scattered in directories and gazetteers, magazines and journals, town histories, and maps. A number of Vermont's more famous inns have been described, of course, but many quite respectable places still languish in relative obscurity; and there is no comprehensive list of the hundreds of smaller places that have come and gone with the years. It seemed worthwhile, then, to try to fill that gap, and at the same time to try to convey some sense of what these places were like at different times, and why they changed as they did.

This book is intended to meet two objectives, and serve two different groups. First, it is a listing by town of every tavern, inn and hotel in Vermont, from pre-Revolutionary days to 1925. Included in this list, which constitutes Appendix E, the bulk of the book, is information on location of the places within the towns; their history, insofar as it is known; name changes; names of owners or managers; and present status. It is hoped that this compilation will be of value to Vermont historians.

The second objective is more general, and the group intended to be served harder to define, but it is based on the assumption that many people interested in Vermont will find the subject of old taverns and inns as interesting as I have. Accordingly, the book begins with a number of chapters discussing various aspects of the hotel business in Vermont over the years--the tavern and stagecoach era, for example; alcohol, temperance and Vermont prohibition; the resorts, etc. Also interspersed among the lists of taverns and inns in Appendix E is anecdotal material on their history, their appearance, how they were run, their famous guests, and the like. Photographs of many of the places are included, dating back in some cases to the 1870s, and many photos not included in the book, but located while writing it, are cited.

A list of the sources examined while writing this book, and the methods used in compiling the lists of inns and taverns, may be found in Appendix A. Appendices B, C and D contain, respectively, a list of Vermont tavern signs; lists of Vermont hostelries based on their longevity; and lists of taverns once located on turnpikes. Appendix E is a chronological listing by town of every tavern and hotel known to have existed in Vermont, pre-Revolution to 1925--the "checklist."

* * *

v

Acknowledgements

I am grateful for the cheerful help I have received from staff members at three excellent libraries: Nadia S. Smith and J. Kevin Graffagnino, Special Collections, Bailey/Howe Library, University of Vermont; Karl ("Barney") Bloom and Reidun Nuquist, Vermont Historical Society Library; and Nancy Froysland-Hoerl, Cheryl Lee Thompson, and Dolores Altemus, Morris Library, University of Delaware. I also appreciate the assistance of Philip N. Cronenwett, Special Collections, Baker Library, Dartmouth College, in tracking down early almanacs; and that of Gregory Sanford and Kathren B. White, Vermont State Archives, in unearthing lists of early tavern licensees. I also made extensive use of the survey files at the Vermont Division for Historic Preservation in Montpelier, and am grateful to Curtis B. Johnson and his staff for their help and patience during my extended visits to their offices.

In particular, I want to acknowledge the help of the scores of Vermonters with whom I have corresponded over the last five years--members of local historical societies, authors of town histories, librarians, town clerks, or simply long-time residents with good memories. It has been a gratifying experience to discover how often busy people were willing to take the time to write long letters, often accompanied by maps, clippings or photos, or after research of their own on my behalf, to try to straighten me out on the history of the taverns and hotels in their towns. No book of this kind can even come close to being free of errors, but without this help there would be many more. I have tried to acknowledge individuals at the appropriate places in the book; this is a more general expression of thanks, and an apology to anyone whose name I may have neglected to mention.

The book benefitted at an early stage from helpful comments by Peter S. Jennison; and I also appreciate the early interest of Robert Sharp, my publisher, and his more recent help with the complexities of getting the manuscript ready for publication. I am very grateful to the Vermont Bicentennial Commission for a grant to help defray the cost of publication, and to my sister, Cynthia Massey, and my stepmother, Rhoda Wriston, for their financial help; finding the funds to publish a book of this kind is a daunting task, and the Commission's support came at a critical time.

I wish to thank my three daughters--Gail, Priscilla and Amy--for their contributions to illustrations and proof-reading; and my friends Mahendra Jain and Bob Minnehan for their patient help in teaching me how to use a personal computer.

Finally, I want to thank my wife, Tam Wriston, for gracefully accepting my absences, and my often preoccupied manner when present, over the last several years.

* * *

Chapter I

Introduction

In Vermont, as elsewhere, public houses reflected the changing society and surroundings in which they existed. In the beginning, in the settlement period, a tavern was generally no more than a log cabin home, made available to the traveling public by an enterprising or accommodating family. Travel was on foot or by horseback, along narrow blazed trails, and few people were on the road.

* * *

"It will be understood that in the early years, before 1800, the country was new, and the roads were bad at the best, and people traveled on foot and on horse back, so it was only the strong and vigorous who could travel at all, except, perhaps, in winter. People generally travelled with their own teams and it was not until about a century ago" (i.e., c. 1810) "that roads were good enough for wheeled vehicles, and there began to be a class of people who were willing to pay for being carried from place to place. About 1809, Silas May, who was then the mail carrier between Concord and Haverhill, began to convey it in a wagon, and any chance passenger as well." (1)

* * *

As settlements grew up and roads passable to wheeled vehicles were developed, more substantial structures began to appear, often built for the purpose, and the taverns became village social centers, where the local men would drop in for mail, news from the outside world, and companionship. (One of the oldest taverns for which a photo exists is the Aikens Stand, in Barnard; see photo, c. 1912, next page.) In many cases the local taverns also served as meeting-halls, courthouses, and places of worship.

* * *

"The most important public buildings were the inns. Business, politics, and social life took place mainly within the town's taprooms. John Fassett kept an inn from the first summer of settlement, and by 1782 Bennington had ten licensed innkeepers. Most inns, private simple farmhouses, had a few rooms open to travelers, paying guests, and the drinking public. Even the Fays referred to the Catamount Tavern as the 'family farm.' In the main village there were four large establishments, each profitable enough to put its owner among the town's financial elite. These innkeepers, John Fassett, Stephen Fay, Elijah Dewey, and Nathaniel Brush, dominated the village's commerce in many ways. In Bennington in the early days the storekeepers, innkeepers and merchants (wholesalers) were all housed in the inns under one roof. Along with lodging, liquor and food, Bennington's innkeepers sold paper, glass, lead, powder, dry goods, seed, tools, and some luxury items.

Much of the area's farm produce passed through the hands of the innkeepers...In an economy in which most people traded by credit or barter, the inns were among the few places where money regularly circulated, and the innkeepers functioned as primitive bankers." (2)

* * *

Aikens Stand (Barnard, A Look Back, 1982)

* * *

As the state continued to open up, with better roads and larger towns, more elaborate inns and hotels were built, some evolving from a tavern ancestor, others new. Also, the early nineteenth century saw the appearance of the first "resorts," places deriving most if not all of their business from "summer people," although commercial hotels in or near attractive locations also catered to summer visitors. The role of the village inn changed, too; it became less of a tavern in the present-day sense, and more of a place where local social functions were held.

The coming of the railroads, in the period from the late 1840s to the 1870s in different parts of the state, also had a marked impact on public houses, of course. Many taverns that had prospered and become famous as stopovers along stage routes went under, if they were in villages that were by-passed by the railroads, or along the roads between villages. Others, located in towns suddenly made more accessible by the railroads, flourished.

The automobile changed things again, from World War I on, although the transition from railroad to automobile was more gradual than that from stage-coach to railroad. The "drummers" began to make their rounds by car, from a base in the larger towns or their homes, instead of arriving in a town by train and setting up their displays in the local inns, or hiring a rig at the hotel livery to visit the outlying hamlets. With more flexible transportation available, summer visitors made shorter visits, instead of settling in for the season at the grand old lake resorts; and tourist cabins (later motels) made it difficult for the village inns to carry on.

One cannot readily assign definite dates to these periods. One merged into another, and some parts of Vermont were still unsettled when others had developed settled farms and villages. With these reservations, however, the following time-table can be adopted for the sake of discussion:

(1) Early settlement period: pre-Revolution to 1810;
(2) Stage-coach period: 1810-1850;
(3) Railroad period: 1850-1915;
(4) Automobile period: 1915-present.

To some extent, resort hotels are a special case, although here again, there was considerable overlap between resorts and commercial hotels or inns. Louise B. Roomet, in dealing with the history of Vermont as a resort area in the nineteenth century identified three periods: (1) Vermont resorts before 1850. The first were "watering holes" established at mineral springs, the earliest being Clarendon Springs near Rutland, where a frame hotel capable of accommodating a hundred people replaced a log house in 1798 (see Chapter V for a discussion of spas, and Clarendon Springs in Appendix E); other hotels followed; (2) Vermont resorts in the period 1850-75, when city hotels were booming, both for vacationers as well as businessmen, and when village hotels were beginning to attract middle class family vacationers; and (3) the period from 1875-1900, when, according to Roomet, Vermont's resorts lost ground to Maine (Bar Harbor), New Hampshire (the White Mountains), New York (Saratoga and the Adirondacks), etc., because they did not possess "the aesthetic of the 'picturesque and sublime' " that had taken root in the perception of the middle-class public of the time. (3)

Changes in the means of transportation, and the mobility of people, undoubtedly had the greatest influence on the development of taverns and inns, but there were other influences at work too. The emergence of a strong temperance movement in Vermont, culminating in a form of prohibition in 1852, had an obvious impact on the operation of public houses. Also, these old places burned at an appalling rate, and although one can hardly describe loss by fire as a social change, the sudden removal of a hotel often had a devastating effect on the life of the smaller communities. These topics and others are developed in more detail in the chapters that follow.

* * *

References

(1) Edward Miller and Frederic P. Wells, History of Ryegate, Vermont, 1774-1912 (St Johnsbury: Caledonian, 1913).

(2) John Page, "The Economic Structure of Society in Revolutionary Bennington," Vermont History 49 (Spring 1981): 69-84.

(3) Louise B. Roomet, "Vermont As A Resort Area in the Nineteenth Century," Vermont History 44 (Winter 1976): 1-13.

* * *

Pavilion Hotel, Hartland (William Orcutt stereo)

* * *

Chapter II

The Tavern and Stagecoach Period

The first roads in Vermont were no more than blazed trails, gradually widened by local settlers most interested in using them. The only exceptions were two military roads, the Crown Point Road from Charleston, New Hampshire to Ticonderoga (Crown Point) and Chimney Point (in Addison, across the lake), in about 1760; and the Bayley-Hazen road, built between 1776 and 1779 from Wells River to Hazen's Notch in Westfield. Most early roads were not suitable for wheeled vehicles, and until the 1780s, except in a handful of places such as Brattleboro and Bennington, and along the Crown Point Road, taverns were scarce indeed. Two examples of early taverns outside the larger settlements are Marshall's Stand on the Crown Point Road in Whiting, and the Chimney Point tavern in Addison. (1) The earliest listing of a road in Vermont, with the names of tavern-keepers along the route, seems to have been in 1771, in Nathaniel Ames' Almanack: "the road from No. 4 (i.e., Charleston, New Hampshire) to Crown Point." (2)

An organized system of roads only began to appear in the late 1790s, when the Vermont legislature authorized county committees to lay out public roads to connect some of the larger towns. James Kirkaldie's "Vermont Almanac and Register" for 1796 lists seven roads in Vermont, with tavern-keepers at the towns along the way: Rutland to Bennington, Rutland to Walpole, New Hampshire, Rutland to Canada (via Burlington and the islands), Rutland to Windsor, Windsor to Burlington, Windsor to St Johnsbury, and Windsor to Hartford, Connecticut. (3) This is apparently the first almanac to list anything for Vermont except the Crown Point Road.

The need for better roads outran these early public efforts, however, and starting about 1800, a large number of private turnpikes were built in Vermont, with a major influence on the development of taverns, of course. Over thirty turnpikes were chartered by the state and actually built during the period 1797 to 1867, most of them before 1830. Local people were usually allowed to pass free. Most of these turnpikes were still very rough--dusty in the summer and muddy in the spring, with holes, rocks, stumps and the like, and few bridges.

* * *

"We set out from Vergennes the next morning at three o'clock for Burlington, a distance of only twenty-two miles; yet the road was so very rough, that we did not arrive in that town until noon...For the most part the road lay through woods, where it required all the skill and dexterity of the driver to avoid deep ruts, huge stones, logs of wood, felled timber, and stumps of trees. The road was very narrow, and these obstructions continually obliged us to run in a serpentine direction." (4)

The journey made by Erastus Root in 1815 was typical of traveling conditions of the period: (1)

"He left Brattleboro by stage at 3 a.m. and had breakfast at Walpole, New Hampshire at 7:30. He spent the night in Rutland (good time, since it is about 75 miles from Walpole to Rutland) which he left at 2:30 the next morning. He breakfasted at 7 at Brandon, dined at 12 at Middlebury, and arrived in Burlington at 8 p.m."

* * *

These roads quickly became busy highways in spite of their shortcomings, both for stagecoaches, and for drovers with their herds and freight-carrying teamster's wagons as well. Turnpikes were not profitable in most cases, however, being expensive to maintain as well as to build, and usually reverted to the towns when the owners became discouraged.

As more roads were built and their quality improved, the amount of travel increased. More than 70 different stagecoach lines were serving Boston in 1826, and the number nearly doubled in the next decade. In the Farmer's Almanack for 1825, six of the many roads listed "from Boston to principal cities" traverse parts of Vermont. (5) The period 1820-40 was the "golden age" of the stagecoaches and the stagecoach culture, a term which includes not only stage lines and taverns, but the drivers, strongly independent and resourceful men; the mail system; changing designs in coaches, and their manufacture; and the livery stables, relay teams, hostlers, blacksmiths, etc. (6)

As travel increased, so did the number of taverns. (See Appendix D for a list of turnpike taverns). Specialization also became necessary, because the needs of drovers, freight wagon drivers and stagecoach passengers were quite different. Stage taverns were usually 10-14 miles apart, depending on the arrangements between the stage lines and the tavern-keepers, but in places where routes intersected or on main routes traveled by more than one stage line, they would be closer together than that. At one time, for example, there were 62 taverns on the Philadelphia-Lancaster turnpike, 63 miles long! Tavern-keepers themselves were often proprietors of stage lines. All the stage taverns had liveries, and the tavern-keepers would often provide relay teams, or a place for a driver with his own team to rest and care for his horses, before fitting into the schedule of a stage in the opposite direction. Taverns derived a good part of their income from boarding or leasing horses, and from boarding the drivers.

The early taverns were primitive indeed, as the following excerpts indicate.

* * *

"That was a rather pretentious house for those times. (i.e., Nathan Robinson's hotel in Stowe, c. 1798). It was built of logs 40 x 20 feet in dimension, one story high, and had two rooms. The kitchen had one bed; the "square room" had three; by

6

climbing a ladder one went "above," where there were three more beds. The house was heated by an immense stone fire place which would take in logs six feet long; and before which the guests would nightly gather with the neighbors who came in to hear the news." (7)

* * *

"All the strangers that happen to be in the house sat down to these meals promiscuously, and excepting in the large towns, the family of the house also forms a part of the company...If a single bedroom can be procured, more ought not to be looked for; but it is not always that even this is to be had, and those who travel through the country must often submit to be crammed into rooms where there is scarcely sufficient space to walk between the beds." (8)

* * *

Another traveler, who "found the taverns generally equipped with one large room upstairs containing more than a dozen beds so that we each had a separate one; a thing not always to be met with at every tavern in the States. But the practice of putting two or three in a bed is now little exercised, except at very indifferent taverns, and they are chiefly confined to the back parts of the country." (9)

* * *

Of Cephas Kent and his tavern in Dorset, "All records sing his praises; apparently his were the virtues which his contemporaries admired greatly."

In 1884, his grandson described him as follows: "Our ancestor kept the tavern on the great road from Bennington to Ticonderoga and Burlington and ...entertained the Vigilance Committee of the Green Mountain Boys and the Revolutionary Soldiers. He feared God and maintained the worship of God in his family. This practice he did not often allow his business as tavern keeper to interrupt. When a squad of soldiers called for an early breakfast he would put the large kettle with the potatoes over the fire and while they were cooking would throw open the door between the kitchen and the common room for guests who were invited to join in the devotions of the family...As he was justice of the peace it became his duty to detain persons traveling on the Sabbath without necessity. It was his custom to do this at his own expense as he made no charge for the Sabbath entertainment of those thus detained.

...the tavern was a small and humble affair, some twenty by thirty-two feet in dimensions, a story and a half high...It had a great central chimney and on either side of it a large room, the kitchen in front looking to the east and sitting-room in the rear facing the sunset. Over the kitchen was a bed-room. We cannot imagine how the ten members of the Kent family managed to pack themselves into this small abode and leave any room for the accommodation of travelers, let alone convention delegates" (i.e., to the 1776 convention of representatives from 31 towns). (10)

Stage coach travel was strenuous, not only because of the condition of the roads and the early departure times, but also because of the coaches themselves.

* * *

"The early stagecoaches were little more than covered wagons with three benches without backs set one behind the other, with the driver's seat outside...Women were generally given the rear seats because of the support for their backs afforded by the rear of the wagon...The coach with the egg-shaped body was introduced in 1818 and was a great improvement but in 1827 coach travel was revolutionized by the introduction of the Concord coach..." (11) (see photo below of a Concord coach; and photos following of two other short-run coaches).

Concord coach, Stowe and Morrisville stage

Jacksonville and Whitingham stage, c. 1909

"Coaches usually traveled at the rate of four or five miles an hour with a change of horses every ten miles. This gave passengers the opportunity to refresh themselves at the taverns along the way. It was customary for the stage to arrive at an inn at the hour of noon when a hearty dinner, the chief meal of the day, was ready for the travelers. When it came to overnight lodging, there was no such thing as a private room. All beds were big enough to accommodate at least two persons and frequently there were as many as three beds in a room...If a guest wanted a bath or a fire in the room, there was an extra charge...". (11)

* * *

Here is a description of the Pavilion Hotel in Hartland, built in 1795 by Isaac Stevens, and also known as Stevens' Hotel, Merritt's Pavilion, and the Hotel Hartland at various times:

"It stood in the center of the village ...At one time it housed the post office, store, meeting-house and caucus rooms, the court house, dining hall and dance hall. It had a spring floor for dancing. The original main hall was divided into bedrooms by swinging partitions when the place was remodeled in 1830, and these could be pushed back to make a hall when needed. While the hotel served visiting merchants and teamsters bringing goods from Boston, two barns were needed to stable the six and eight horse teams." (12)

Winter Stage, Williamsville and East Dover, c. 1910
(Mrs Porter Thayer)

"I remember when the stage with from four to six horses would come thundering into town with a toot of the horn and a crack of the whiplash and pull up to Merritt's Pavilion, change horses, all passengers into the bar-room and get a good drink of Santa Cruz rum and then continue the journey." (13)

* * *

It would be a mistake, however, to conclude from accounts like these that there were no places of comfort and distinction in early nineteenth century Vermont. Hyde's hotel in Sudbury, from 1801; Leland's Coffee House in Landgrove, on the Chester-Manchester turnpike, from about 1822; the Spring Hotel in Newbury, from

9

1800 (see photo); Ladd's Tavern in North Hero from 1803; the Eagle Tavern in East Poultney from before 1800; Painter's Tavern in Vergennes, later the Stevens Tavern, from about 1795; the Dewey House, later the Walloomsac Inn, in Bennington, from 1764; Aiken's Stand in Barnard, from the 1780s (see photo, Chapter I); and the Stage House in Brattleboro, these are only a few of the many places operating in the early 1800s that one wishes one could have visited. Contemporary descriptions of several of them follow.

Spring Hotel, Newbury (Special Collections, UVM)

Of Ladd's Tavern, in North Hero: Jedediah P. Ladd was North Hero's first postmaster (1817-26), with the office presumably in the tavern during that period; he operated the tavern until his death in 1845, and his son carried on for a few years more. "The building, facing the beautiful bay, then called Ladd's Bay, now City Bay, was a large, square sturdy wooden frame structure, massive hand hewn timbers. As time went on, additions were made, on the south side was a wing containing several chambers and a big kitchen room."

Described by Maria S. Ladd in 1864 as a time-browned, unpainted edifice, looking rather shadowy and mysterious...for many years the principal building in North Hero, "a place where hospitality in the form of bed, food, drink, warmth and good cheer was dispensed to the cold and weary traveler, to the driver going to market, and the gathering place on winter evenings before the glowing hearth, for the exchange of outside news and local gossip." (14)

* * *

Of the Eagle Tavern in East Poultney: The original Colonial era tavern "was too primitive for prosperous post-Revolutionary Poultney." It was razed to allow construction of a more impressive structure, still standing. "The Tap Room in the cellar, with its own outside steps...its rare brick floor and rough-beamed ceiling, its

10

broad fireplace and crane, and its huge oak 'coffee' table, must have provided the precocious young Greeley with a perfect 'hall' in which to hold forth" (Horace Greeley lived at the Eagle Tavern during his years in East Poultney).

"Three interesting rooms open off the main Entrance Hall...The Reading Room features a fireplace with native red slate hearth six feet long--in one piece...The Parlor with its old square piano and other antique furnishings gives no hint of its erstwhile function as a bar replete with swinging gates...A mahogany staircase leads to a spacious Upper Hall where the wide (23") floorboards and exposed (9 x 12) beams, one of which is forty-three feet long, speak eloquently of the timber indigenous to the region...The trapdoor in the floor of the windowless Gaming Room remains. The Ball Room, with arched ceiling, extends across the front. It served as a Masonic 'temple' until 1817 and was the scene of many festive social occasions." (15)

* * *

And the Stage House in Brattleboro, built by Samuel Dickinson in 1795. There were many proprietors over the years, and Simeon Leland, who became a great New York hotel magnate, once worked here.

"About the time of the last war with Britain it was the custom to roll into that big bar-room a hogshead of old West India rum and supply customers from the faucet. Years ago we heard Erastus Dickinson (nephew of Samuel Dickinson) say, 'I paid over $300 for a hogshead of old rum, and after it was on draft in the bar-room it was, by good judges, declared a superior article. It immediately acquired so excellent a reputation it would not stay with me, and in a little over one week, it all left me.'" (16)

* * *

When Asa Green was postmaster (i.e., in Brattleboro, 1811-41) the office was here in the old Stage House, and was open day and night, since it was a distributing office. Colonel Paul Chase had it for about twenty years, starting about 1827, during which period it was known as Chase's Stage House. "He was a man of distinguished and gracious presence who had exceptional social gifts, and was withal very handsome. He made an extended reputation for the house. Members of the best families throughout New England were innkeepers. The landlord was usually connected with the militia, often a justice of the peace or sheriff. As knowledge of current events came through hearing and talking rather than reading, the innkeeper was not only the well-informed man of the place, but influential in local affairs." (17)

* * *

The point has already been made that the taverns were the village social centers--places where the men would gather to hear news from outside and debate the issues of the day over a drink or two. They were also frequently the only available meeting place in town, and many taverns served for years as town hall, court house or even church meeting house or school. Examples of early taverns serving these roles are found in Groton and Lunenburg.

"Since Groton in its pioneer days was not located on any such highway (i.e., a stagecoach road) there was no demand for a spacious inn but there was a need for a kind of community center where the 'vendue' of the lands of tax delinquents might take place, or where an occasional traveler might find entertainment. Such a place was furnished by Dominicus Gray in 1798 when his new frame house...was ready for occupancy. So much has been written elsewhere...about the use of this inn in connection with town and proprietor's meetings, auctions, lawsuits, and June trainings that nothing further need be said except that before 1827 Gray's only rival was Aaron Hosmer, Jr, who operated an inn at the Orr Turn...from 1802 to 1809...Hosmer's inn was of hewn logs which made it rank somewhere between a house of unfinished logs and the frame house of Gray. Two or three early town meetings were held at Hosmer's Inn." (18)

* * *

"The Gates place (i.e., the Samuel Gates tavern in Lunenburg, built in 1792) soon became the center of town as it was a tavern for the weary traveler, a church on the Sabbath, and a place where meetings were held, including that of the first Essex County Court." (19)

* * *

As the century moved on, things changed. Along with better roads came more people, and the frontier settlements of the 1780s and 1790s became villages and towns. The log cabin taverns disappeared, and were replaced by substantial frame structures that were more often referred to as "hotels" or "houses" than taverns. The coming of the railroads from the late 1840s on in Vermont accelerated these changes, and signalled the end of the tavern period (see Chapter IV). Stages continued to operate until well into the 20th century, but on short, secondary routes serving towns not on the railroad, or as a way of bringing passengers from the depot to the hotel. As late as 1916, for example, the Bakersfield House was advertising a stage twice daily from the hotel to the railroad station in East Fairfield, several miles away. Many of the old places survived, of course, if they were in a town served by the railroad, or at locations attractive to the growing numbers of vacationers (see Chapter V) but in either case, their characters changed. They were still social centers, but in a somewhat different way. One of the most striking features of these places from the 1830s or 1840s on is how many of them had a dance-hall, and the extent to which they served as places where banquets, balls and oyster suppers (see photo) were held, and where traveling road-shows might perform, and not just as a corner men's club. Time and time again, one reads almost lyrical accounts of dancing on the "spring dance floor." A few examples are presented below.

* * *

The Morrisville House: "Here for many years its proprietor, F. L. Matthews, was a well-known figure and the hotel was the scene of many banquets, oyster suppers, dances and general good times as well as a home for the traveling public." (20)

* * *

Lovell's Hotel, in Rockingham: "The Lovell Hotel was a well-known hostelry since stage coach days with its dance hall which had a domed ceiling and spring floor, built over the stables. This was the only such floor of its kind except a similar one in Cambridgeport where they say the men took off their shoes and danced in their stocking feet. In Rockingham, many dances were put on by the Grange with supper served at midnight and dancing continuing until daylight." (21)

* * *

California oyster supper ticket (VHS Broadside)

* * *

Leland's Coffee House, in Landgrove: "The best bib and tucker was donned for a dance at 'Uncle Selah's' (i.e., Selah Warner, manager at the time). The men were given to standing collars, cutaway and swallow-tail coats and white vests. The ladies wore ball dresses of white or colored silks, low necks and short sleeves. The charge for supper, lodging and breakfast was $1.00 or $1.75 for man and wife. The victuals were set on the table and everyone helped themselves and each other, there being no bill of fare or waiters...The Inn was noted far and wide for its dances, people coming from miles around to attend them...". (22)

* * *

Downer's Hotel, in Weathersfield, in an account which appeared in the Vermont Tribune in 1902. (23) The paper had published a description of the old hotel (see photo, next page), and an elderly lady, living out of state, had been moved to write a long letter to the paper, describing her experiences as a girl:

"A ball at Downer's in those days was something to look forward to for weeks...What times we had getting ready!...A description of our dresses and jewels would not quite come up to the marvelous 'creations' that are exploited in the

13

newspapers nowadays; but under the more simple fabrics there beat as pure and loving hearts, and those capable of as much real innocent enjoyment as those robed in the more pretentious garments of the present day...It was a gay party that left Ludlow for the sleigh ride to Downer's. How merrily the bells jingled, how joyous the voices, and how smiling the faces of the occupants of those sleighs--tucked in, with plenty of warm buffalo robes around them, and hot freestones to their feet...How plain it all comes back to me today, as I think over the couples who participated in that sleigh ride and gathering at Downer's. The ride down over the glistening snow, the arrival, the great cheery fires, and the smiling face of our landlord; the dainty supper, and then the going to our rooms to make ready for the grand entrance into the ball room...

Downer's Hotel, Amsden

I shall never forget that scene as long as I remember anything, or those happy hours when our flying feet kept time to the music; and such music!...Over and over I have told the story of that night's enjoyment to my young friends, and tried to describe the music, the dancing, the supper, the ride home in the early morning--a sleepy, tired set; but oh, so satisfied and happy over our sleigh ride and Thanksgiving ball at Downer's. The old tavern, with its spacious rooms and comfortable piazzas, looks as it is--a veritable paradise for the weary dwellers in cities who drift to its friendly shelter in summer time."

* * *

Tavern Signs

Stella's Birthday

All travellers at first incline
Where'er they see the fairest sign;
And if they find the chamber neat,
And like the liquor, and the meat,
Will call again, and recommend
The Angel Inn to every friend:
What though the painting grows decayed,
The house will never lose its trade;
Nay, though the treacherous tapster Thomas
Hangs a new angel two doors from us,
As fine as dauber's hands can make it,
In hopes that strangers may mistake it;
We think it both a shame and sin
To quit the true old Angel Inn.

(Jonathan Swift, 1720-21).

* * *

Tavern signs in England and colonial America were in many cases an art form. There is an extensive literature on the subject, and the signs that have survived, in museums and private collections, are considered to be valuable examples of folk art. Vermont taverns appeared relatively late in the day compared to those in the colonies along the seaboard; and since it is probably true that the elegant and noteworthy signs reflect a settled community, and were more likely to be found in long established hostelries, then it is likely that there were few Vermont signs that would attract the attention of connisseurs.

One of the more elaborate Vermont examples was the sign for the Traveler's Home in Lower Waterford:

"The Traveler's Home had a plain square on which was painted a picture in color of a chariot, with a man standing up, waving a flag with an inscription on it, 'Traveler's Home'; the chariot was drawn by six prancing bay horses." (24)

Most Vermont tavern signs were far less elaborate than this; Capt Erastus Safford's sign, in Fairfax, was "Rest for the heavy laden and weary traveler" on a piece of paper nailed on a board, stuck in a hollow stump; and Amasa Brown's tavern in Worcester had as its sign a smooth board with letters in red chalk saying "Good cider for sale here." Signs were required by law, however:

"And it is hereby further enacted, That every person who shall keep an inn, or house of public entertainment, shall, within thirty days after his or her license, put up a proper sign, upon or near the front of his or her house with his or her name

15

thereon, and keep up such sign during the time he or she shall keep such house of entertainment, under penalty of forfeiting and paying two dollars for every month's neglect." (25)

A list of all Vermont tavern signs encountered, sophisticated or otherwise, may be found in Appendix B.

* * *

Hotel Post Offices

Post offices have been located in all kinds of places over the years--lawyer's, dentist's and doctor's offices, harness shops, drugstores, kitchens and sheds, churches and railroad stations. The two most common locations in the past, however, were general stores and taverns. Anyone familiar with Vermont, whether by hearsay or direct experience, can visualize the country store post office, even though it is steadily being replaced by the standard government issue building, or closed entirely. But taverns preceded stores in most places in settlement days, and were by far the most common location of the post offices, such as they were at the time.

The reasons for this are obvious. Taverns and early hotels were the focus of most of the town's social life, of course; but more importantly, stage coaches carried the mail, from the time when the roads first became passable to wheeled vehicles, and post riders vanished from the scene, until the stages themselves were overtaken by the railroads. It was in 1785, as routes were being reopened after the Revolutionary War, that Congress voted to use stagecoaches on established routes for this purpose. They were the main carriers for the next sixty years. Even as late as 1849, nearly 20% of the 400 Vermont hostelries listed in the New England Mercantile Union Directory were also post offices, including such well known places as the Barnes Tavern at Chimney Point, the Stage House in Brattleboro, the Clarendon House in Clarendon Springs, Stanton's Hotel in Essex, Selah Warner's Coffee House in Landgrove, the Magog House in Newport, and Beaman's Hotel in Poultney.

In those days, mail for all the towns along a route would be carried in a single bag, which had to be sorted by the postmaster at each stop. He also had to endorse a waybill, showing the arrival and departure time for the stage. Unless they were stopping for a meal or overnight, coaches tended not to linger. Indeed, the time spent at these stops was usually specified in the contracts between the stage lines and the Post Office Department--fifteen minutes in 1800, but only 7 by 1830! It was obviously convenient for all concerned, if not essential, that tavern and postoffice be one and the same, with the tavern keeper or one of his employees serving as postmaster as well.

Increases in the amount of mail reduced the number of passengers that could be carried, and stage companies began drawing a distinction between the "limited" stage (mail-carrying, and traveling rapidly) and ordinary stages that carried no mail, and could make longer stops. Some passengers were willing to pay higher rates to travel on the "limiteds," often saving the difference in tavern accommodations by traveling more rapidly, and well into the night.

The railroads began carrying mail in some parts of the country in the 1830s, but it was not until 1853 that the miles of mail-carrying stage routes actually began to decline. When mail was dropped off at the railroad depot to be picked up by the postmaster, it obviously made little difference where the post office was located, within reason. Also, more attractive general stores with a wider array of goods began appearing as settlements became established, and store-keepers soon realized that having the post office behind the counter brought people in. Finally, the hostelries themselves changed as the stagecoach culture declined, and although there are numerous examples of hotel post offices in the railroad era, and even into this century, especially at the summer hotels, the practice became less common.

* * *

References

(1)   Allan S. Everest, "Early Roads and Taverns of the Champlain Valley," Vermont History 37 (Autumn 1969): 247-255.

(2)   Nathaniel Ames' Almanack, Boston, 1771.

(3)   James Kirkaldie's Vermont Almanac and Register, Rutland, 1796.

(4)   John Lambert, in 1804, quoted in Everest (ref 1, above).

(5)   Farmer's Almanack, Robert B. Thomas, Boston, 1825.

(6)   Oliver W. Holmes and Peter T. Rohrbach, Stagecoach East (Washington, D.C.: Smithsonian Inst. Pr., 1983).

(7)   Walter J. Bigelow, History of Stowe, Vermont, from 1763 to 1934 (Hartford, 1934).

(8)   Isaac Weld, traveling along the Lake Champlain shore in 1796, quoted in Everest (ref 1, above).

(9)   John Lambert again, 1804, quoted in Everest (ref 1, above).

(10) Zephine Humphrey, The Story of Dorset (Rutland: Tuttle, 1924).

(11) Allan Forbes and Ralph M. Eastman, Taverns and Stagecoaches of New England, Vol II (Boston: State State Trust, 1953-54).

(12) Hartland--The Way It Was, 1761-1976 (n.p., 1976?).

(13) Nancy Darling, "History and Anniversary of Hartland," Vermonter 18 (November 1913): 221-234; (December 1913): 241-256.

(14) Allen L. Stratton, History, Town of North Hero, Vermont (Burlington: George Little Pr., 1976).

(15) East Poultney, Vermont's Cradle of Culture in the Wilderness (Poultney: Journal Pr., 1951).

(16) Henry Burnham, Early History of Brattleboro, Windham County, Vermont, Abby M. Hemenway, ed., (Brattleboro: D. Leonard, 1880).

(17) Mary R. Cabot, Annals of Brattleboro, 1681-1895 (Brattleboro: E. L. Hildreth, 1921-22).

(18) Waldo F. Glover, Mister Glover's Groton (Canaan, N.H.: Phoenix Publ. for the Groton Historical Society, 1978).

(19) Nellie M. Streeter, Town of Lunenburg, Vermont, 1763-1976 (Lunenburg: Stinehour Pr. for the Lunenburg Historical Soc., 1977).

(20) Anna L. Mower and Robert Hagerman, Morristown Two Times; a double

volume containing Mower's 1935 book with an update by Hagerman (Barre: Northlight Studio Pr. for the Morristown Historical Soc., 1982).

(21) Lyman S. Hayes, History of the Town of Rockingham, Vermont (Lynn, Mass.: Frank S. Whitten for the Town of Rockingham, 1907).

(22) Samuel R. Ogden, The Cheese that Changed Many Lives; Or, A Sentimental History of a Tiny Town High in the Green Mountains, Landgrove (Landgrove: Just-So Pr., 1978).

(23) Downer's: a brief historical sketch of an old Vermont Landmark; (Ludlow: Vermont Tribune, 1902).

(24) Charles E. Harris, A Vermont Village (Yarmouthport, Mass.: Register Pr., 1941).

(25) Vermont Statutes, Chapter 70, 1798.

* * *

Chapter III

Alcohol, Temperance and Vermont Prohibition

Early Vermonters were heavy drinkers. In the settlement era, and well into the 19th century, drinking was not only socially acceptable, but expected. Liquor was generally available at social events of all kinds, from barn-raisings to quilting bees.

* * *

"No occasion was ever perfect without it (i.e., cider and whiskey)... when the ladies had a quilting, every time they rolled the quilt all must take a little toddy, and when they had rolled it about four times, they were ready to drop work, tell stories and have a jolly time." (1)

* * *

"About the time Caledonia county was set off from Orange, Dr Greshom and Horace Beardsley entertained so sanquine an opinion that Cabot would be the shire town, that they proceeded to clear two acres of land...for the county buildings...On this site they raised the first frame house in town. This frame was all hard wood and two stories high, and it required a large force of men, and a corresponding quantity of rum, to raise it. All the men and women in Cabot, Peacham and Danville were invited to the raising, and two barrels of rum was (sic) provided for the occasion (to meet the threats that those invited 'would drink the Beardsleys dry') and all were invited to help themselves. The rum there imbibed lasted a great many two days, and in after years they enjoyed rehearsing the incidents of this 'raising'." (The Beardsleys did not realize their hopes in the location of the county site; the building was moved to the "Plain" and became the renowned "Yellow House," a favorite of travelers passing between the north and the Connecticut River). (2)

Liquor, at least in the form of hard cider, was also served regularly in many homes. Wells, for example, says that twenty to forty barrels of cider were considered necessary to support a family through the winter, and the special stuff would be brought out when the minister made his call. (3)

* * *

"Our early forebears started out as children taking of the liquid harvest. Children were given beer for breakfast...Beer and wine were considered temperance drinks and were encouraged to help cut down on the consumption of whiskey, rum and cider. Cabin raising, barn raisings, harvesting--all was indication for drink and plenty of the same. Men sything (sic) a field would follow each other around the field

19

cutting a swath and on each passing of a certain corner would take a healthy drink from the common jug set there for that purpose...Ministers did not frown on this practice and many a long sermon in an unheated meeting house was made more interesting by the flowing bowl passed at the tavern during the break periods." (4)

* * *

And from another source:

* * *

"Well, to begin, most of the clergy drank, and a family who failed to place before his pastor...the decanter of rum or cider brandy and bowl of lump sugar, chip'd off from one of those old-fashioned pyramids of snowy sweetness, was considered lacking in hospitality; and in these days of Auld Lang Syne, no one could be honestly born or spliced for life, unless all concerned were moved by the spirit. Raisings and movings, seed time, haying and harvesting, husking and paring bees, elections and turkey raffles, and even the bearers to a funeral, in some localities, had to be braced up with cider brandy...The minister's sideboard (at ordinations) took on the aspect of a public bar..." (5)

* * *

Every village had a still or two, and one of the reasons for the early establishment of apple orchards was to provide the raw material for cider and cider brandy. Other products produced locally included whiskey (from potato starch), New England rum (from imported molasses), and beer.

* * *

"Intemperance was a terrible scourge to this town, as was to have been expected--for the reason that the town (i.e., Charlotte) was cursed with three distilleries and beset with as extensive and fruitful orchards as any part of the state. It also contained about a dozen taverns, all floodgates of rum and ruin." (6) This viewpoint is reflected in the illustration on the next page, adapted from a drawing in an 1834 issue of the Temperance Recorder, Albany.

* * *

It is obvious that our settler forefathers were aware that it was possible to over-indulge; there were legal prohibitions against public drunkenness, and tavern-keepers were required, under penalty of fines and loss of licenses, to maintain orderly houses. Nevertheless, in spite of the huge amounts of liquor consumed, it does not appear that alcoholism and drunkenness were major problems in the settlement days. Whether this level of resistance was because the people were unusually young, unusually hard-working, or just plain tough, is hard to say now.

"The use of ardent spirits was not fatal to the hardy pioneers of the town. It was upon the younger generation that its effects were most disastrous, and it was by observing these effects that people began to think the use of ardent spirits as evil." (7)

* * *

Redrawn from an illustration in the Temperance Recorder, Vol III, No. 4, Albany, June, 1834. The original was accompanied by the following lines:

"But if the Ox were wont to push with his horn in time past, and it hath been testified to his owner, and hath not kept him in, but that he hath killed a man or a woman, the ox shall be stoned, and his owner also shall be put to death." (Exodus 21:29).

* * *

A large part of the early tavern-keepers income came from selling liquor by the drink. In the days when a place to stay overnight might cost fifty cents and a meal a quarter, and when a country tavern might only be able to accommodate a dozen men or so, mostly sleeping rough, it is obvious that revenue from toddy, sling, flip and the rest at ten cents or so a glass was important to the proprietor. For example, when Imry Perry, a drover, stopped at Cyrus Knapp's tavern in Dover in 1814, his bill included: "to 2 supers, .50; to 3 dinners, .60; to 2 lodgens, 113; to 4 glasses tod, .25; to 2 and 1/2 mugs tod, .25".

* * *

Even in the face of this economic reality, however, the point must be made about the early taverns (as it is by most people writing about them) that they were not primarily barrooms or beer halls, tempting the weak to stray, but places of respite to travellers and social centers for the village, where drink was always available because that was the custom of the times. Tavern-keepers and landlords were licensed by the town or county, and in general were leading and influential citizens; in the early days, in fact, many of them were veterans of the Revolutionary War and the War of 1812.

Attitudes towards drinking began to change in the early 1800s, and a strong temperance movement grew up in Vermont and other states, Maine in particular. The forces that lay behind the movement are complex, and have been dealt with by others (see, for example, references 8-10). For whatever reasons, the movement gained widespread support by the 1830s and 1840s. Temperance societies were formed in some Vermont towns in the 1820s, and even as early as 1817 (Ryegate); the American Society for the Promotion of Temperance was organized following an 1826 meeting in Boston, and soon had a number of influential Vermont members, and the Vermont Society for the Promotion of Temperance was organized in 1828 (see a temperance broadside of the period, below).

Temperance poster (Special Collections, UVM)

In the early days, reformers relied on persuasion and the moral force of their position. Leading citizens joined the local societies; meetings of a revivalist nature were held; people were urged to "take the pledge"; and delegations of citizens began to call on local tavern-keepers and merchants, asking them to foreswear the sale of liquor. In the second phase of the crusade, with progress slow and opinion closely divided, the crusaders turned to the state legislature, with the ultimate result that in 1853, Vermont adopted a form of prohibition, stringent at least in theory, based on the Maine liquor law, adopted by that state in 1851.

It is hard to know now how successful the earlier persuasive efforts were in the overall scheme of things. Certainly a number of places became "temperance houses," at least for a while (see list at end of chapter), and some new temperance places were established, but on the basis of the scanty information available for this period, temperance houses must have been few and far between. There probably were not too many men like Mr Torrey, for example, who ran a tavern on the road between Arlington and Stratton.

* * *

"When liquor began to be preached against as sinful, he laid aside his glass, took down his bar and sign and became thenceforth a farmer and lumberman." (11)

* * *

This reaction seems extreme, and there were probably more cases like that of Mrs Hill of Brandon, or Col Chester Carpenter of Derby.

* * *

"We are informed that Mrs Hill, who keeps a public house in Brandon, being convinced of the evil of retailing ardent spirits and that the advantages derived from it is (sic) not equivalent to the disadvantages, has taken all spirituous liquors from her bar, and resolved not to sell no more (sic) on any occasion." (12)

* * *

Col Chester Carpenter came to Derby in 1807, fought in the war of 1812, and later ran an inn in Derby. It became a temperance house after 1833, was sold to his son in 1845, and burned in 1884.

* * *

"(It) had a square chimney in the center to carry away the smoke from a big brick oven and three wide fireplaces. These fireplaces and two on the second floor all had broad granite hearths and were supported by the heavy brick walls of the ash bin and the storehouse. At the bar room door swung a 2 x 4 sign board with the eagle and shield on one side and a decanter and a half-filled glass of red brandy (on the other), and below these on each side the words, Carpenter's Inn, 1816.

In later times the inborn temperance principles of the owner sent the sign with the red glass and decanter to the dust of the attic, and other signs bearing no temptation to, or suggestion of evil, invited to the comforts and hospitality of 'Carpenter's Inn' weary travelers, friends and beggars. From Carpenter's Tavern the moneyless went after they were filled and lodged. Baptist ministers came, stayed and departed at their pleasure in welcome. Church members from remote parts of the town attending Sabbath or other meetings found open doors and hearts. Guests might have received slight attention compared with purest hotel life, but their horses were well-fed and cared for, the table and beds satisfactory for those days--clean at any rate." (13)

The old "Howard Stand" in Burlington, probably the best known place of its time in that city, is another example of a place that became a "temperance house," as announced by its proprietor in 1833 (see illustration, below; ref 14).

'TEMPERANCE IS HEALTH.'

Temperance  House.

H. LOVELY,

WOULD respectfully inform his friends and the public generally, that he is now fully prepared to accommodate Travellers, Parties of Pleasure, or Boarders, with every necessary luxury convenience to health or comfort, at the old "Howard Stand," north side of Court House Square, Burlington, Vermont.—*He has entirely discarded Ardent Spirits from his Bar:* believing its use not only detrimental to the health and morals of community, but unworthy a place in an orderly and well conducted House of entertainment. He will however, furnish to his customers, excellent WINES, of every description, PORTER of the first quality, and other harmless and refreshing drink.

In announcing the above facts to an enlightened public, the subscriber is not unaware of the existence of a diversity of opinion relative to the use of Spiritous Liquors: He has been influenced, however, to the adoption of his present course not only by a sense of duty to his fellowcitizens, but by a desire, to be ranked among that class of men whose efforts are directed to a reform in our civil society : and, in furtherance of his object, he would most respecfully request the co-operation of the citizens of this state and those from abroad.

His table will, at all times, be furnished with the best articles afforded by the markets : and no exertions will be spared to give satisfaction to those who may favor him with their custom.

Carriages will, at all times, be in readiness to convey people to and from the Boats ; and passengers can take Stages for any direction.

Burlington Sept. 13, 1833   tf

Mr Lovely's Temperance House

24

It is also hard to judge how successful the temperance houses were. In the prohibition period, in the 1860s, one S. K. Remick was operating the Passumpsic House in St Johnsbury.

* * *

"He felt that a hotel was not properly caring for its guests unless liquor was served and he opened a bar. In the lily white town that St Johnsbury was, this was about the worst thing he could have done. It was perfectly legal to get your weekly jug at the express office if you ordered it from Boston but drink in a hotel was sinful. He was apprehended several times and paid over a thousand dollars in fines. The last conviction came with a warning that he would have to go to jail on the next offense. He promised to conduct a temperance house, and, instead of losing money, he made twenty thousand dollars." (15)

* * *

To balance this optimistic account, consider the situation of the Tavern at Lyndon Center.

* * *

"The unprofitableness of the Tavern in its last years (i.e., the 1870s) was credited at the time to the fact that in 1870 the society known as the People's Practical Temperance Association, with I. H. Hall as president, was formed, and during the succeeding years the landlords maintained the hotel as a 'temperance house.' This was the end of the Tavern as a hotel." (16)

* * *

The Vermont prohibitory law took effect in March, 1853. It provided that liquor could be sold for "medicinal, chemical and mechanical purposes only" by an agent appointed in each town by the County Commissioner. Innkeepers could not be agents. This law, passed after a statewide referendum had shown only a narrow margin of support, was never as effective in eliminating drinking as it might have been. Certainly the law had the effect of closing down the bars in many taverns and inns, but it was still possible for individuals to bring liquor into the state for personal consumption, and many of the town agents interpreted very liberally the "medicinal use" clause in the law. Visitors to the state found the situation odd, to say the least.

* * *

"The one aspect of Vermont life which struck Englishmen as most strange was the anti-liquor legislation, the Maine law...originating with Neal Dow in Portland in 1851, then spreading throughout New England...As George Rose, a London businessman, stopped over in Rutland on his way from Boston to Niagara Falls in 1867, he discovered to his horror that no alcoholic refreshment was to be found.

Vermont, he complained, was 'under the dread rule of the Maine Liquor Laws.' Still, a closer acquaintance with the situation revealed to those foreign travelers that although the temperance laws were stern, they were easily and universally evaded. Landlords provided liquor for their tenants, and druggists sold spirits and wines 'as part of the medical pharmacopeia' in medicine bottles. In business offices throughout Vermont one could usually find a water bottle and glass openly displayed; but a bottle of whiskey was often discreetly hidden in the cupboard. Business transactions were frequently concluded with gulps of undiluted whiskey, followed by the chewing of cloves in order to conceal the aroma; and on the farms men drank fermented cider, thereby occasionally achieving 'almost maniacal forms of drunkenness.' " (17)

* * *

The struggles of the temperance societies continued throughout the second part of the century. The Vermont Society for the Promotion of Temperance, noting that liquor sales were increasing under one county commissioner, urged in 1859 "that all friends of humanity should strive to secure the absolute friends of the law as commissioners and agents." Temperance advocates also went after taverns selling liquor illegally. The Vermont chapter of the Women's Christian Temperance Union was formed in Montpelier in 1874, and the state Grange agreed to help the renewed reform effort, but the gains achieved in enforcement and general public support were usually transitory, and corruption and graft were widespread by the end of the century.

Enforcement was also apparently very uneven in different parts of the state, and the effectiveness of the law seems to have varied greatly from place to place. Attempts at enforcement were accompanied by all the difficulties and controversy encountered by Federal agents in the 1920s. According to Clifford:

"The years following the Civil War witnessed a dramatic increase in the violations of this law, particularly in the larger towns. Burlington, having come out strongly for prohibition in the 1850s, had become by the 1870s a testament to the measure's failure. The seemingly orderly town of six thousand had mushroomed into a city of twice the size where saloons and brothels flourished. In Rutland an attempt to crack down on the illegal sale of liquor in the winter of 1874 met with a mild outbreak of mob violence. The bustling railroad town of St Albans contained close to forty stores, restaurants and hostelries which dispersed liquor." (18)

* * *

The newspapers of the period are filled with stories of raids on hotels and taverns, and accounts of open defiance of the law in various places. One account of more or less open circumvention of the law comes from Brownsville (West Windsor).

* * *

Pierce Hulett's Brownsville distillery had long since closed down (i.e., by the 1860s). As the temperance movement flourished, drunkenness came to be deplored as strongly as it had been accepted at the turn of the century. The temperance supporters were elated when the General Assembly passed a state prohibition law in 1852 by a narrow margin, but there were plenty of irate citizens who didn't hesitate to show their disgust and outrage. Though the stills of Nathaniel Moulton, John Nichols and Mary Town had shut down, the town Liquor Agent saw to it that the community was reasonably well supplied with alcoholic beverages for "medicinal purposes only." This was evident by a $870.13 bill from Wm Edgar Bird and Company, Importers of Wines and Brandies, Etc, to A. L. Morgan, West Windsor's Liquor Agent, charging the town for one barrel of "Patent DR.D. Alcohol 95%," a barrel of Kentucky Bourbon Whiskey, one of old Rye Whiskey, one of Medford Rum, a half a barrel of Holland Gin and three gallons of Cognac brandy. (19)

* * *

There are numerous other examples of enforcement difficulty: in Bennington, the Putnam House and the Stark House were both closed briefly for liquor law violations in 1889; in Milton, beer was sold illegally at Austin's; in Northfield, liquor was sold in spite of the prohibitory law at Blood's Hotel; in Pownal, the Exchange Hotel closed in 1900 for liquor law violations, and burned under suspicious circumstances soon after; and in Springfield a well known but illegal bar existed in the basement of the Adnabrown Hotel.

A front page story in the Burlington Free Press for February 19, 1896, starts off, "Hotel Liquor Establishments Raided in St Albans," and goes on to describe a "general search and seizure" of the liquor dealers in town. Representatives of all the places in town (including the American House, the Grand Central Hotel, the Park View Hotel, the St Albans House, John White's "old place," the George Harris saloon on Foundry St, the Exchange Hotel, and Brennan's Elm Tree House) were arraigned in Municipal Court, found guilty of "keeping with intent to sell, and selling," and sentenced to fines of $40 each and costs. They all appealed, and the liquor was destroyed.

Then there is the defense offered by the Van Ness House, apparently to charges made publicly in the Rutland Herald that the hotel was serving liquor illegally:

"The management of the Van Ness House claim that all liquors purchased by them have been used for cooking purposes, it being a well-known fact that liquors enter into many modern hotel recipes. Any attempt, therefore, by the Rutland Herald to prove violations of the liquor laws by the printing of ledger accounts is in vain, especially since the figures show small amounts were purchased, such as would naturally be employed in the cuisine." (21)

* * *

The struggle between prohibitionists and anti-prohibitionists seems to have been waged especially fiercely in Rutland, leading at one point to a remarkable confrontation between the hotels and the authorities. On December 21, 1870, the four leading hotels in Rutland (the Bardwell, Bates, Central and Stevens), acting in concert,

27

discharged all their employees and locked their doors, in what was an attempt either to persuade the local authorities to ignore the operation of open bars in these hotels, or to lead the state legislature to repeal the 1853 prohibition law. This extraordinary action caused an uproar, naturally enough. Papers in other towns tended to poke fun at Rutland and its difficulties; leading citizens in Rutland opened their homes to travellers, and the Troy Times reported that railroad sleeping cars were being requisitioned. The Rutland Herald printed a long, indignant letter from a man who identified himself only as "Drummer," part of which is quoted below:

"Will you permit a traveler to protest against the outrageous abuse of the rights of man to which the public are exposed in this town. I came in on the night train, purposing (sic) to take the midnight train for Boston and found on arrival that the Hotels were all closed and I with many men, women and babies were left in the dimly lighted depot to make the best of it. To the citizens of Rutland this may seem a joke, but imagine yourself and wife turned out this cold night into a depot to pass several long hours.

To a strong man the injury is trivial, but a delicate woman, or man suffering perhaps already with incipient consumption might receive their death warrant from such exposure...

This is an outrage on the public and should not be allowed...The Rutland hotel-keepers are punishing the innocent travelers from east and west, from north and south...This is no question of liquor but is common justice..."[20]

* * *

The boycott was an ill-conceived move on the part of the hotels, of course, doomed to failure from the start, and they succumbed to the generally unfavorable public reaction some ten days later. The incident does serve, however, as a dramatic illustration of the difficulties hotels faced in trying to accommodate a public which supported only marginally the prohibition law of 1853.

The temperance laws were a major issue in the 1902 gubernatorial campaign. The Republican nominee, John W. McCullough of Bennington, was non-committal on the question, but his opponents, Percival W. Clement of Rutland, an irregular Republican, and Felix W. McGettrick of St Albans, a Democrat, were in favor of local option. McCullough won the election, but Clement did well, and the tide had finally turned. The legislature passed a local option law which was upheld by a narrow margin in a statewide referendum in 1903, and this has remained the system ever since, except, of course, for the period from 1920-1932 when the whole country was experimenting with prohibition. Local option was certainly a more liberal form of control than total prohibition, but still had an effect on the success of many inns, especially in the smaller towns where the "drys" were more likely to carry the day at town meeting time. Consider the case of the Union House in Cuttingsville, for example, established about 1830.

* * *

The place burned in 1903, and liquor was sold at a nearby tent or shed while a new inn was being built; but the town went dry in the interval, and the new inn was never used as such. (22)

* * *

The town of Johnson provides another example.

* * *

"...commercial travelers were numerous here in the horse and buggy days and a large livery stable was an important part of the hostelry...Mr Everett Wells...was one of the best remembered of many innkeepers, and from his day on the inn was called the Hotel Everett...the scene of many brilliant social events..."

In 1936 the town went dry and the proprietors of the time, the St Jock brothers, closed the hotel and boarded up the front with rough, weathered boards. The Burlington Free Press ran a picture...with the caption "Plenty of boards, but no board." It was soon converted to stores and apartments. (23)

* * *

In 1908 there were twenty-seven "license" towns in Vermont. There were twenty-nine in 1911 (with 111 "dry" towns) and 25 in 1920 (as opposed to 198 "dry" towns) but only a handful of places were consistently license towns. In towns where the vote was close, and the town would swing back and forth from one year to the next at town meeting time, the local option law probably created more problems for hotels than it did in towns that were predictably dry.

Vermont remained on local option after the end of national prohibition in 1932, but by 1937, there were 129 towns that permitted the sale of beer, and 71 of these permitted the sale of liquor as well. The local option law was amended in 1968, so that a vote on the licensing question is now held only in response to a petition filed by citizens seeking to change existing practice in their town.

* * *

Known Temperance Houses

Brandon, Mrs Hill, in the 1830s;
Brookfield, Norman Goodale, 1849;
Burlington, H. Lovely, the old Howard Stand, 1833-?;
Derby Center, Carpenter's Inn, from 1832 until at least 1849;
Enosburg (Center), Central Hotel, 1870s;
Essex, Butler's Tavern, Buell's Tavern, and the Page Tavern; "all closed their taverns to liquor in the same year" (c. 1830);
Ferrisburg, Nicholas Guindon's Tavern, by 1849 at least;
Hardwick, Alpha Warner's Stage House;

Montpelier, Mrs Safford's Temperance House on State St, 1842, 1843;

New Haven, Anson Bird's tavern, from 1816 or so until at least 1837;

Pawlet, Fitch's tavern, a temperance house at some point;

East Poultney, the Eagle Tavern, from 1838 through at least two proprietors;

St Johnsbury, the Passumpsic House;

Springfield, the Black River Hotel, became a temperance place in 1867;

Stratton, Torrey's tavern (mentioned in this chapter);

Winhall, Green Mountain Temperance House, 1873;

Woodford, Park's hotel, a temperance house, date uncertain.

* * *

References

(1) Vermont Historical Gazetteer, Abby Maria Hemenway, ed., Vol. IV, 1882 (Washington County, the Cabot chapter).

(2) Hamilton Child, Gazetteer of Orange County, Vermont, 1762-1888 (Syracuse: Syracuse Journal, 1888); the Cabot chapter.

(3) Frederic P. Wells, History of Newbury, Vermont, 1704-1902 (St. Johnsbury: Caledonian, 1902).

(4) "Reflections on Poultney's Past," Green Mountain Whittlin's 18 (1966): 20-29.

(5) Henry K. Adams, A Centennial History of St Albans, Vermont (St Albans: Wallace Pr., 1889).

(6) Rev. Bernice D. Ames, Vermont Historical Gazetteer, Abby Maria Hemenway, ed., Vol. I, 1867 (Addison County, the Charlotte chapter).

(7) Edward Miller and Frederic P. Wells, History of Ryegate, Vermont (St Johnsbury: Caledonian, 1913).

(8) David M. Ludlum, Social Ferment in Vermont, 1791-1850, 2nd edition, (N.Y.: Columbia University Pr., 1931; reprinted by Vermont Historical Soc., 1948, and AMS Pr., 1966).

(9) Hal S. Barron, Their Town: Economy and Society in a Settled Rural Community: Chelsea, Vermont, 1840-1900; Thesis (PhD), Univ. of Pa., 1980.

(10) Joseph R. Gusfield, Symbolic Crusade: Status Politics and the American Temperance Movement, 2nd edition (Urbana: Univ. of Ill. Pr., 1986).

(11) Vermont Historical Gazetteer, Abby Maria Hemenway, ed., Vol I (Bennington County, 1867, the Stratton chapter).

(12) Vermont Statesman, Castleton, August 15, 1832.

(13) Cecile B. Hay and Mildred B. Hay, History of Derby, Vermont (Littleton, N.H.: Courier Pr., 1967).

(14) Burlington Free Press, Oct 4, 1833: 3:4.

(15) Edward D. Asselin, "The Passumpsic House," Vermont Historical Society News and Notes 14 (April 1963): 57-58.

(16) Venila L. Shores, Lyndon, Gem in the Green, Ruth H. McCarty, ed. (Lyndonville: The Town, 1986).

(17) William J. Baker, "English Travelers and the Image of Vermont in Victorian England," Vermont History 42 (Summer 1974): 204-213.

(18) Deborah P. Clifford, "The Women's War Against Rum," Vermont History 52 (Summer 1984): 141-160.

(19) Mary B. Fenn, History of West Windsor (Taftsville: Countryman Pr. for West Windsor Historical Soc., 1977).

(20) Rutland Herald, Jan 2, 1871.

(21) Burlington Free Press, February 12, 1896: 4:1.

(22) Dawn D. Hance, Shrewsbury, Vermont: Our Town As It Was (Rutland: Academy Books, 1980).

(23) Margaret T. Smalley, History of Johnson, Vermont (Essex Jct: Essex Publ., 1961), who quotes from an earlier history: Mattie W. Baker, History of the Town of Johnson, Vermont, 1784-1907.

* * *

Chapter IV

The Railroad Era

The first railroad in Vermont was a 25-mile section of the Vermont Central between White River Junction and Bethel, opened in 1848. From that time on, the system expanded rapidly. By 1855, nearly a hundred towns were "on the railroad," and in 1880, there were about 185 towns being served. The number of towns accessible by rail continued to grow slowly until the 1920s, but it seems fair to say that the railroad era, at least from the point of view of passenger service and changes in the hotel business, extended roughly from 1850 until the end of World War I, when automobiles started coming into widespread use. "The railroad...the largest Vermont enterprise until well past 1900, reoriented everything it touched, and it touched nearly everything." (1) The nature of these changes has also been described by Meeks.

* * *

"Fully eighteen towns in Vermont went through population explosions as they were touched by the rails. Surprisingly, at least in population, neither Montpelier nor Randolph grew rapidly, but other communities more than made up for them. Readsboro, way down south on the HT and W, went from a population of 767 in the 1840 pre-railroad era to 1,107 in 1870 thanks to the expanding paper industry. St Johnsbury went from 1,887 to 4,665 during the same period, mostly because of the railroad junction the town had become, and the scale works...Burlington increased from 4,271 to 14,387 in thirty years, to become by 1870 Vermont's largest city by a considerable margin. St Albans, thanks to the railroad shops, grew from 2,702 in 1840 to 3,567 in 1870... Newport, another railway junction, went from 591 to 2,050 between 1840 and 1870...". (2).

* * *

The railroad history of Vermont is remarkably complicated, and full of human interest (see references 1,3,4). Slawson lists some 35 railroads that have served Vermont at one time or another, and even this list excludes a few freight-only systems and the more recent amalgamations. (5)

The expanding railroad system had an immediate impact on Vermont taverns and hotels. Many places that were flourishing in the 1840s disappeared within a short time, or found their custom much reduced as trains took over the main lines, and stages were relegated to short runs to towns the railroads didn't reach. The places affected most dramatically, of course, were those standing on turnpikes outside the villages, at some country crossroads. Their business effectively vanished. The Stratton Tavern in Brookfield, built on the Paine Turnpike about 1795 and operated as a tavern for about 50 years (c. 1800-1850) is an example.

Inns in a town reached by the railroad had only to adapt to the need to pick up their guests at the depot instead of having them deposited at the front door by the stage (see photo). Such places were not necessarily affected adversely, however;

The Island Villa "Turnout"

* * *

indeed, the ease of travel by rail compared to stagecoach often meant an increase in patronage. Inns in the villages not reached by the railroads could usually survive if there was still a reason for people to visit the place--drummers, for example, or vacationers, who would be brought by short-line stagecoaches from the depot towns.

* * *

"During Ridley's ownership (i.e., 1871-96), mainly two steady types of customers patronized the Bristol House. One group...the men who came once a week to catch up on the news and enjoy gentlemanly companionship. This was a carry-over from the days when once a week a horseback rider from Middlebury would arrive with the Bristol mail. The Bristol House was the distribution point...

The other main customers were the traveling salesmen, the 'drummers.' They would arrive by train, take the coach to the Bristol House, rent a horse and buggy from the livery stable there, and proceed on their rounds." (6)

* * *

In some places, new "depot houses" or "railroad hotels" were built (there have been at least seven "Railroad Houses," two "Depot Houses," and four "Junction Houses" in Vermont at one time or another). The whole center of business activity in Rutland shifted down the hill to the west to the depot area, and the Bardwell, built in the new business area in 1852, was part of Rutland's response to the increased business that the railroad brought (see photo, next page). In Pawlet, the railroad "made Mark's Corners, a hamlet of eighteen inhabitants, into West Pawlet, with new houses, new paint, a hotel, and a freight business of sixty dollars a week." (1) Island Pond was "nothing but the woods and water of Brighton when...(the railroad)...came in 1853. Lumbering started and within two years the village quickly boasted of twenty dwellings, two hotels, a school, a church and three saw mills..." (1)

Hotel Bardwell

The practice of hotels meeting the trains with their own coaches is illustrated by this example from Danville (see also photo, next page, of the Clarendon House stage).

* * *

"The train whistled for the nearby crossing and animated action began in the carriage barn of the old   Thurber Hotel where the 'depot hoss' was hitched to the two-seated fringed surrey.

The hostler snatched the light blanket off the horse. The driver leaped to his seat, unwound the reins from the whip-socket, and picked up the whip--someone unsnapped the hitchcord from the bit, rolled back the barn doors--and away they went hell bent for the depot...Many a nickel or cent changed hands among the village regulars who were usually on hand to see the trains come in and to see the winner of the first and coveted spot on the depot platform--the Thurber Hotel rig or the Elm House rig...

Four St Johnsbury and Lake Champlain passenger trains stopped at Danville each day, two up and two down...Both hotels met all trains...In winter the hotel drivers met the trains with a three-seated sleigh well equipped with buffalo robes." (7) (see photo, next page, of the Thurber House).

And there is this account, taken from an article in Vermont History.

* * *

"It took us all day to go to the big metropolis of Rutland (i.e., from Proctor)

34

taking the 11 o'clock train in the morning to ride the six miles, and then coming back on the 6 o'clock, when drunks were put off at the Double Roads junction. When we arrive in Rutland, there were two men, always fat, beating on tin pans, one yelling, "Come to the Bardwell," while the other tried to drown him out with, "Come to the Berwick!" Such a din." (8)

* * *

Clarendon House stage (Clarendon Historical Society)

Thurber House, Danville

* * *

As already mentioned, the places most adversely affected by the coming of the railroads were the country taverns which had depended almost entirely on stagecoach customers. They succumbed by the score. Some examples of the changes that occurred are presented below.

* * *

"We will not attempt giving a list of people who have kept public house at various times in town (i.e., Guildhall), for at one time, all through the country there was a tavern every few miles, but since the railroads have been constructed through the valleys of this region, we find the hotels have dropped off." (9)

* * *

"In the old stage-coach and teaming days, when this road formed an important part of one of the main lines of traffic...often as many as forty horses were stabled there in a single night (i.e., at the Huntley stand in Londonderry) while the house was well filled with guests. With the advent of the railroads...it long ago lost its public character and became a private farmhouse, finally to be abandoned..." (10)

* * *

The coming of the Rutland and Burlington Railroad "turned all travel from this route" (i.e., the turnpike from Sudbury through Hubbardton to Castleton and on). People were isolated, and three post offices, some getting mail but once a week, superseded the one kept before, "time out of mind," at the old Dewey stand in Hubbardton. (11)

* * *

Peter Matteson's tavern outside the village in Shaftsbury had operated since 1777, but closed when business declined in the 1850s with the advent of the Western Railroad.

* * *

Not all the news was bad, of course. The overall effect on the state was an increase in travel and accessibility, helping to make possible the dramatic increase in resort hotels in the latter part of the century (see Chapter V). Martell's Hotel, for example, built near the depot in Grand Isle in 1901, owed its very existence to the Rutland Railroad.

* * *

"For quite a number of years, this hotel existed at the Grand Isle railroad station...When the Rutland Railroad opened the line through the Islands in 1901, this depot location opened up possibilities for the need of a commercial hotel. Sensing the opportunity, he (i.e., Frederick A. Martell, who had been a blacksmith) sold out at the Corners and purchased about an acre of land at the railroad station. In 1901, he erected the front portion of his hotel. As the only commercial hotel in town, he received substantial patronage. About 1905, he enlarged and built the rear extension...This quite remarkable man, starting with nothing as a boy of thirteen, with initiative and perseverance, achieved substantial competence..." (12)

* * *

Martell Hotel, Grand Isle, Vermont.

Martell's Hotel, Grand Isle

* * *

The railroads also brought increased prosperity to many communities, accompanied by a great deal of political maneuvering and land speculation. One of the best known stories deals with Charles Paine and the Vermont Central. Paine owned a lot of real estate in his home town of Northfield, including the hotel, and continued adding to his holdings while working hard to achieve the route most favorable to his own interests. The engineering surveys seemed to favor a route through Williamstown Gulf, and on to Barre and Montpelier. When the railroad was built, however, it came over Roxbury Summit and through Northfield--five miles longer, with a steeper gradient, and connecting with Montpelier, the state capitol, only via a one-mile spur!

Paine's Northfield House faced the depot across the green, and sidings were built so that the trains could pull up directly in front of the hotel for overnight stops.

There are many other examples. White River Junction is a railroad town, and the Junction House, built in 1879, is another example of a "railroad hotel" (see photo). Passengers from New York arriving late at night in White River would often stay over at the Junction House before proceeding further north the next day. The St

Junction House, White River Junction

Johnsbury House was built by a local syndicate in 1850 as the entry of the railroad led to increased demand; Ira Gibbs built a public house in West Pawlet in 1851 when the railroad came through, on the site of the Indian River Valley Hotel of later years. In Newport, the Connecticut and Passumpsic Rivers Railroad company bought the old Memphremagog House soon after the railroad reached town in 1863, and remodeled it extensively for the summer tourist trade (see Newport in Appendix E). The first railroad terminal was in front of the hotel, and the station was in the basement. The depot in Highgate Springs was immediately across the road from the Franklin House, although in this case, the hotel preceded the railroad. The Franklin House in Vergennes is another place built in response to the coming of the railroad.

* * *

Hiram Adams built the Franklin House in 1848 when the railroad came through, and offered free shuttle service to all trains. "Fifteen bays wide, three and a half stories high, with double parapeted chimneys, its massive brick facade still dominates the downtown district. It survived Vergennes's wavering fortunes and hosted guests for nearly forty years, but in 1886, it underwent a metamorphosis. It has since housed commercial space on the ground floor, and apartments above." (13)

Franklin House, Vergennes (Special Collections, UVM)

One of the more dramatic examples of how the railroad affected communities has to do with Royalton.

* * *

"The coming of the railroad had brought a fever of speculation and rivalry.

38

North Royalton got a station first, but not for long; Royalton soon after, but it did not bring in business. It wrecked the pleasant village; buildings lucky enough to be left untouched had trains running just in front or in back. The stage quit and the inn was no longer busy...The busy people were just down the river (i.e., in South Royalton).

In 1848 the site of South Royalton was still just a grassy field, but Daniel Tarbell...and Lyman Benson were about to change all that." These enterprising gentlemen built a bridge in 1848, "leading the Chelsea road across the river to the new railroad. Then they built a combination store and station by the tracks and had a train stop: South Royalton. Tarbell built a hotel by the tracks (the South Royalton House)..."and the new village came up like a mushroom." (14) (See photo).

South Royalton House

The railroad changed the atmosphere of the hotels in the small towns, even in places that were not affected as dramatically as Royalton. Consider Troy, for example.

* * *

"The Old Frontier Hotel, built before 1878, stood on the present site of the Chittenden Trust Company bank. It was a large three story square building with a large entrance hall, dining room, office and display room in the main part of the house, with large kitchen space, pantries and storage rooms in the rear of the main part, and, over the entire kitchen area was a large assembly hall with an auditorium, stage, dressing rooms, and a spring dance floor, especially enjoyed by the many couples who attended the various special balls...For these formal dances, the ladies were resplendent in their beautiful evening gowns, long kid gloves and ornate fans. In those days, such dances were very formal, attended by the townspeople and many couples from up and down the Missisquoi Valley.

Besides dances, the hall was used for plays...minstrel shows, school graduations...Usually during a year several Traveling Road Companies, such as a series of melodrama plays, a glass blowing company, variety shows and a Kick-a-poo Indian Company, who entertained by skits, etc, meantime selling bottles of medicine...Charles A. Ramsdell was the popular proprietor during those early years...The display room which was on the main floor was used by the commercial travelers who came into town on the trains with their huge trunks of samples and used this room in which to display their wares, consisting of clothing, shoes, hats; in fact, a great variety of articles. The merchants could see and select the things they wished to buy, and the orders were shipped to them later by freight or express.

The office was a large room and could accommodate the men who wished to play cards if the day was too cool to sit on the large front porches...These chairs were filled on all pleasant days, as the sitters could enjoy the day watching the many activities on Main Street...The idle sitters found it very entertaining and often retained their favorite seat far into the evening when the North Troy Frontier Band gave a concert in the old bandstand." (15)

* * *

Trains stopped at the platform behind the hotel (i.e., the Isham House in East Fairfield), "giving passengers the choice of either eating dinner, then continuing on their way, or staying overnight for a little dancing on the wonderful spring dance floor which was made of boards put in on edge. When silent movies arrived, they were shown in this hall. Zea Mitchell played the piano to accomany them." (16)

* * *

The railroads also made possible the rapid expansion of the resort business that occurred in the second half of the nineteenth century, and the construction of a great many summer hotels. Martell's Hotel in Grand Isle, discussed above, is one example, and the grand old Memphremagog House in Newport another.

* * *

"The optimism that the owners of the Memphremagog House displayed in the late 1850s and early 1860s could only have come from the knowledge that the railroad was on its way to Newport...When the first train rolled into the village in October of 1863 it marked the beginning of a new era in Newport's history. The town's population nearly doubled between 1860 and 1870, then rose another 50 percent between 1870 and 1900...Nearly all of the growth occurred close to the lake...

Newport and the Memphremagog House prospered together after 1863. Lafayette Buck, "one of the greatest hotel keepers the United States has ever produced," ran the hotel for the Penders during and after the war. With the Passumpsic Railroad track running right by the Memphremagog, and the Railroad's first station located in the hotel's basement level, Buck had an obvious advantage in attracting guests who came to Newport on the trains...As the Memphremagog's reputation spread, the clientele increased to a point that more than justified the Penders' faith in what the railroads could do for their business." (17)

* * *

Resorts are discussed in Chapter V, and the only point that needs to be made here is that as the principal mode of transportation changed, so did hotel accommodations, and it was the railroads that made a vacation in northern New England a realistic possibility for the first time for many people.

South Alburg tourist cabins

The pattern changed once more, as automobiles became more generally affordable after World War I. The transition from the railroad era to the automobile era was more gradual than that from stage to train, but equally irresistible. The railroads began cutting back on passenger service during the 1930s, beginning with the branch lines. The major impact of the automobile would not be felt until roads improved after World War II, but by the 1920s the shift was well underway. In addition to such obvious effects as the challenge posed to commercial downtown hotels by tourist cabins and tourist homes (see photos), and later, motels, the resort places also experienced change. With the mobility provided by a car, people tended to give up spending a month or the season at a single lakeside resort, and made shorter stays at more places. This change was fatal to some places, for example, the Lake House (Lake St Catherine House) on Lake St Catherine, which lies partly in Wells and partly in Poultney.

* * *

"The Lake St Catherine Hotel, an attractive four-story building, was erected in 1859 and by 1880 had become a popular attraction for prominent social, political and theatrical leaders from the New York City area.

A large dining room contained 2500 square feet of floor space and charges to guests ranged from ten dollars a week up...

The popularity of the Lake St Catherine Hotel, usually called the Lake House, is evidenced by the names of some of the guests who registered there. They included Lillian Russell, the world-famous beauty and Broadway actress, DeWolf Hopper, one of the great actors of the American stage, Lew Dockstader of the famous minstrel troupe, and the noted Ott family. William K. Vanderbilt registered at the hotel on September 10, 1883, and requested to be furnished with fourteen horses for his party for an outing. In the summer of 1884 Jay Gould, the railroad magnate and reputed millionaire, registered, as did Charles Delmonico, well-known restaurateur, and Pierre Lorillard, the tobacco tycoon. Probably the hotel's most famous guest was President Grover Cleveland who came during his first term in office...Benjamin Harrison also vacationed here, but before he was elected to the presidency.

The popularity of the Lake House was of short duration, mainly between 1880 and 1890. This was partly due to the fact that transportation began to be revolutionized about that time, with the introduction of gasoline drive automobiles imported from Europe, very expensive at first but within the reach of the wealthier class. Then in 1908 Henry Ford came out with his Model T which took the country by storm. The horse and buggy days were at an end. Families took to the road and expensive hotels in summer resorts went out of business. The Lake House ...was torn down in 1908." (18)

* * *

Slack's Tourist Inn, Hartland

* * *

References

(1) T. D. S. Bassett, "500 Miles of Trouble and Excitement: Vermont Railroads, 1848-1861," Vermont History 49 (Summer 1981): 133-154.

(2) Harold A. Meeks, Time and Change in Vermont: A Human Geography (Chester, Conn.: Globe-Pequot Pr., 1986): 185.

(3) Robert C. Jones, The Central Vermont Railway: A Yankee Tradition (Silverton, Colo.: Sundance Publ., 1981, 6 volumes).

(4) Jim Shaugnessey, The Rutland Road (Berkeley, Cal.: Howell-North Books, 1964).

(5) George C. Slawson, Postal History of Vermont (N.Y.: Collector's Club, 1969).

(6) History of Bristol, Vermont (Bristol: Outlook Club, 1980).

(7) Tennie Touissant, in the Burlington Free Press, February 4, 1969.

(8) Bernice L. Wing, "Memories of a Vermont Quaker Farm" (excerpts from

correspondence), Vermont History <u>22</u> (April 1954): 151-2.

(9) Everett C. Benton, History of Guildhall, Vermont (Waverly, Mass.: 1886; 1985 facsimile ed., Univ. Microfilms).

(10) A. E. Cudworth, The History with Genealogical Sketches of Londonderry (Montpelier: Vermont Historical Soc., 1936).

(11) Vermont Historical Gazetteer, Abby M. Hemenway, ed., Vol III, 1877 (Hubbardton chapter).

(12) Allen L. Stratton, History of the South Heroe Islands; Being the Towns of South Hero and Grand Isle, Vermont (Burlington: Queen City Pr., 1980, 2 volumes).

(13) Vermont Division of Historic Preservation survey, 0120-9.

(14) Hope Nash, Royalton, Vermont (Royalton: The Town, South Royalton Woman's Club, Royalton Historical Soc.; Lunenburg: Stinehour Pr., 1975).

(15) Anne H. Butterfield, Memories of the Early Days in the Town of Troy, Vermont (n.p., 1977).

(16) Eleanor Ballway, Fairfield, Vermont Reminiscences (Essex Jct: Essex Publ. for the Fairfield Bicentennial Comm., 1977).

(17) J. Kevin Graffagnino, Vermont in the Victorian Age (Bennington: Vermont Heritage Pr.; Shelburne: Shelburne Museum, 1985).

(18) Iris Hopson Read, Lake St Catherine, A Historical Perspective (Wells: I. H. Read, 1979).

* * *

Chapter V

Resorts

It would probably be hard for most Vermonters to accept the suggestion that, except for the ski resorts in recent years, their state has not always been a leading resort area; the large numbers of people that descend on Vermont in the summer and during the foliage season seem to point to the opposite conclusion. It is certainly true that Vermont has attracted tourists ever since there were any, and that the resort business has been increasingly important to the Vermont economy, especially since World War I or so; but not until more recently has it been a major resort area as the New Jersey beaches were long ago, or Saratoga and the Adirondacks, or the White Mountains.

Roomet identifies three periods in the history of Vermont as a resort area in the nineteenth century: 1800-1850, 1850-75 and 1875-1900. (1) She goes on to suggest that the first represented Vermont's greatest resort era, from the point of view of its standing compared to other vacation areas in the northeast; that the second period saw a decline of the spas of the first period, and the beginning of a transition with respect to the clientele being attracted; and that in the latter part of the century, the third period, Vermont was no longer really competitive with New Hampshire, Maine and upper New York state. An 1875 tourist guide book, for example, devoted 140 pages or so to New England and upstate New York, but only 2-3 pages to Vermont. (2) The point is made by both Roomet and Rebek, writing about resorts in the same issue of Vermont History, that in the heyday of resorts, the 1880s and 1890s, Vermont did not quite satisfy the public expectation for "the picturesque and the sublime." Vermont was seen as beautiful, to be sure, but more pastoral. Its mountains were a little friendlier, perhaps, than Mt Washington in New Hampshire or Mt Marcy in the Adirondacks, and it had neither the ocean, as did Maine and New Jersey, nor the glittering resort communities like Saratoga, Bar Harbor and Newport, Rhode Island. (1, 3).

Graffagnino, in his beautifully illustrated book, Vermont in the Victorian Age, discusses the role of both landscape artists and lithographers in representing Vermont to the outside world. Although the landscape artists at first tended to emphasize the more picturesque features of the terrain, "by the end of the decade (i.e., the 1850s) the sublime started to give way to less rugged scenes better suited both to changing popular tastes and the pastoral look of Vermont's villages and rolling hills...this was the image of rural Vermont that drew seasonal visitors to the state between 1870 and 1900..." (4)

Vermont may not have been a leading tourist attraction during the period in question (nineteenth century, and the first quarter of the twentieth) but it certainly had resorts and resort hotels. In Roomet's first period, roughly the first half of the nineteenth century, Vermont resorts were mostly spas or "watering-holes," with the very first being Clarendon Springs, near Rutland.

These springs were known to the Indians and the early settlers, but according to legend, their exploitation began with the experiences of Asa Smith, the "strange mystic of Clarendon." (5) Smith dreamed, in 1776, of a spring in the western part of town which would heal his "scrofulous humor." He located the spring the next day after struggling through the wilderness, drank the water, made a mudpack for his aching limbs, and went home convinced that he was cured.

Development began with George Round, who moved to the Springs area in 1781 and began taking boarders in his cabin. This was expanded into a frame hotel, the American House, in 1798, the first of several at the Springs.

* * *

"George and Martha were hospitable people and gave shelter and food to these ailing travelers. First they added to their log home but soon other quarters were needed. Seventeen years after coming, George Round--farmer-turned-hotelman--built a frame two-and-a-half story 'hotel' on the level above the river to the west of the spring. At first this could accommodate some 20 guests, but two 'wings' were added and still they came. The American House must have resembled a clinic more than a hotel around the turn of the century." (6)

* * *

The Clarendon House, largest and most elegant of the hotels at the Springs, was built in 1835, and enlarged from three stories to five a few years later. It was an imposing brick building, with dormers on the top two stories, and verandas extending from the three bottom floors (see photo, next page). There were 52 guest rooms, and a large lobby, dining room and ballroom occupied most of the main floor. The hotel was set in a shady park, with a small pond and a decorative fountain, and spring water was piped from the well house directly to indoor baths in the hotel. There was also a bottling works in the basement, producing bottled water in various sized containers for the national market.

The peak of popularity for Clarendon Springs was probably in the late 1850s, although operations continued until 1898. (see Clarendon, Appendix E, for details.)

The immense popularity of spas in mid-century, and the extent to which many Americans believed in the miraculous curing powers of the mineral springs which were their central feature, is a phenomenon in its own right, explored, for example, by Meeks. (7) Meeks identifies 126 named mineral springs in Vermont in the late 1800s, of which thirty-one supported hotels.

"Some, such as Clarendon, Sheldon, Guilford, Highgate, and Middletown, were large and diverse recreation spas with bowling alleys, croquet lawns, bottling works, and livery stables. Others, such as Wheelock, Plainfield, Waterville, Barre, and Hartland, were much smaller..." (7)

Clarendon House (Special Collections, UVM)

A list of the thirty-one springs which supported hotels is presented at the end of this chapter. Most of these springs were recognized well before 1850, but only a handful had hotels by then. The railroads made it feasible to develop resorts at many of these places for the first time, and increased the patronage of those already established. Meeks points out that twenty-five of the thirty-one springs with hotels were within five miles of a railroad. Two of these places, Sheldon and South Hero, are described below.

* * *

Many Vermont towns had mineral spring hotels, and participated in the remarkable popularity these places enjoyed, mostly in the third quarter of the 19th century, but no town had so many hotels nor went through the cycle so quickly as Sheldon. In Sheldon, the boom began when a New York lawyer, C. Bainbridge Smith, "had occasion to pass through their town in 1865 in search of health. He was ill with an incurable cancer of the mouth, and was in such a condition that he could hardly speak. Finding the peculiar taste of the spring water delightful (i.e., from a spring discovered in Sheldon in 1817), and convincing himself that it was invigorating, he drank huge portions of it daily...in a remarkably short time he found himself entirely cured of his malady." (8)

Smith himself quickly developed the first of the springs, the Missisquoi (there were five springs eventually, within a few miles of each other) and began selling bottled water. In 1868, 14,792 boxes, each containing 24 quart bottles, were shipped from this spring alone.

* * *

"Then the people followed. They came in droves, from everywhere...Every housewife in town moved her family into the hayloft or the attic and gave up her featherbed to strangers. The price of board went skyhigh...The enterprising people of the town, not sold on the product themselves, were a little slow to sense the possibilities, but they finally began to realize the business opportunities..." (8).

* * *

Smith built the first and largest of the hotels, the Missisquoi Springs Hotel, in 1867; within a short time there were eleven hotels distributed over four of the five villages in the township. Some were new, like the Congress Hall (see photos), others simply enlarged and renovated private homes.

* * *

"The finest and largest was the Missisquoi. It contained over a hundred private rooms, furnished with imported regal splendor. The miracle water was piped to all rooms. Each hotel had its own bath house, a separate building with boilers to heat the water for baths taken several times a day by some of the guests.

The roads...constituted a problem. A plank highway was constructed from the nearest railroad (i.e., St Albans at the time)...This was a toll road. Extra stages were put on with six-horse baggage tenders. Two railroads finally hastened to the place" (i.e., the Missisquoi Railroad in 1871, built partly on the plank road right of way, and the Lamoille Valley Railroad, later the St Johnsbury and Lake Champlain, in 1877). (8)

* * *

Most of these hotels either burned, went out of business, or were carrying on marginally within five years or so. None of the original hotels are left, although the New Portland House, built to replace the original after a fire in 1901, is now in use as a nursing home. It has been estimated that nearly 300,000 people visited Sheldon during the boom era of no more than five years.

Frederick Landon owned a farm on Keeler's Bay in South Hero, including a well-known mineral spring. He built a handsome springhouse and a boarding-house nearby, and started doing business with city folk. He also shipped bottled water, but went bankrupt, and sold to Capt Warren Corbin in 1871.

* * *

"He was an enterprising and successful owner-operator, and his Iodine Spring

House became famous for its hospitality and beautiful location. To ensure the convenience of guests...(he) bought half interest in the stage line from Burlington to Grand Isle, making sure that passengers would find his place. Also, he was captain of the steamer 'A. Williams' from 1869-73. This steamer...made regular stops at the Iodine Spring House dock in Keeler's Bay." (9)

* * *

Congress Hall (St Albans Historical Society)

Congress Hall Spring (St Albans Historical Society)

The flavor of these places comes through in advertisements, with their overblown descriptions of the scenic wonders and the virtues of the mineral water, and their testimonials from satisfied patrons or medical doctors. Consider, for example, the following from an advertising brochure for the Alburg Springs House.

* * *

"The Alburgh Springs are among the oldest-known Medicinal Springs in America...Until the past four years no effort had been made to introduce the water to the general public. Not a word had been spoken or syllable written upon it by way of advertisement. Yet these springs can undoubtedly show today a longer and more interesting record of cures...than any others in this country...Their reputation...has steadily increased...until now thousands, who never saw the springs, drink the water daily at their homes, while the springs themselves are thronged with health-seekers from all parts of the country through the summer months...

Few inland water places offer more inducements to Summer Tourists than these springs...They are particularly alluring to those who prefer the healthful sports, beautiful scenery, perfect air and pastoral repose and simplicity of the country through the summer months to the bustle and glitter of more fashionable centers...

Among the mass of matter written upon this topic by the numerous artists and travelers who have visited here, the following extract from a letter clipped from the 'Boston Traveller' seems most pointed and truthful:

'Although the place at which I am at present sojourning may not be so familiar to many of your readers as Saratoga or Newport, yet it is certainly destined to become one of the most attractive of all our Summer Resorts. It has every natural requisite which a first-class watering place in the interior should possess...Of far greater importance to the health-seeker, it has the best mineral springs in America, and, if the repeated statements of the first physicians in Boston and New York are to be credited, the best in the world...I find parties here rowing and sailing in the bay, fishing, etc., seeming more like athletes than invalids, who assure me that for years they had been the victims, some of scrofula, some of kidney affection, and others of rheumatism, etc., and had sought relief in vain until they came here...'" (10)

* * *

The spas were Vermont's first resorts, and people came to them initially, often from great distances, for their health. The mineral spring resorts, however, with a few exceptions, had only a brief period of popularity. Sheldon's boom lasted less than ten years, for example, and the exceptions proved to be those places that had more to offer than springs, shaded paths, and a croquet pitch. The few that survived as resorts into the twentieth century were those that could appeal to the growing interest of vacationers in walking, golf, tennis, and water sports--swimming, boating and fishing. Meeks points out that if the Clarendon House had had a golf course, it might have continued to flourish like the Equinox House in Manchester and the Woodstock

Inn in Woodstock, both of which had them. These two places, at their respective peaks probably the most elegant in Vermont, are described below.

* * *

The Equinox, with its imposing pillared front and its air of being a transplanted Southern colonial mansion house, dominated Manchester's main street (old Route 7) for decades. The original building, modified and enlarged beyond all recognition, began as Munson's Tavern, built in 1801 on the site of a still earlier tavern. It became Vanderlip's Hotel in 1840, and the Taconic in about 1870, when it was acquired by A. J. Gray.

In the 1830s and 40s, Levi C. Orvis, scion of the Orvis family, owned two brick stores standing more or less where the north part of the Equinox House stands today. He tore down one of them and built a large house next to the other. When he died, his son, Franklin H. Orvis, combined the house and remaining store, enlarging and remodeling along the way, and opened the new structure as the Equinox House in 1853, with 125 rooms (including 60 in an "annex" across the street known as the Equinox Jr; see Manchester, Appendix E, for a photo and more information). He added the Taconic, which stood just south (with 75 more rooms) in 1880, connecting it to the Equinox with a second-story bridge over what was then Union Street. (It was also Franklin Orvis who built the stream-fed Equinox Pond in the 1870s, and stocked it with trout; and who built a carriage road to Lookout Rock on Mount Equinox. The Equinox House supplied special maps to its guests, showing the most attractive carriage drives in the area).

When Franklin Orvis died in 1900, Edward, one of his sons, carried on for a while. The place was incorporated in 1902, and purchased by George Orvis from his brothers in 1908. More remodeling and renovation followed, and garage facilities and quarters for chauffeurs had to be added; the Carsden Inn on Union St was built with this in mind in 1912. When George Orvis died in 1917, his widow, Anna Simonds Orvis, ran it until 1921, when she sold a controlling interest to Mrs V. H. P. Brown of New York. Andrew Martin, who had been with the inn for 46 years, mostly as manager, left then but came back when Mrs Orvis re-acquired the inn in 1922. The Equinox ran into trouble in the depression, however, and went into bankruptcy in 1938. It passed through several more changes of ownership, and was closed from 1973 until 1985, when it opened again after another major renovation.

Manchester has been described as "The Oldest Recreational Center in New England." Its flourishing development from the mid-nineteenth century on was undoubtedly accelerated by the railroad. Manchester got train service in 1852, when the line the Western Vermont (later the Harlem Extension) was building south from Rutland to Bennington reached Manchester. In 1871, Franklin Orvis, editor of the Manchester Journal as well as owner of the Equinox, noted that "nine hours and three-fourths from New York to Manchester is better than 'going afoot' but not exactly what we hoped for from 'the great northern' through route to Montreal." He asked for more and faster trains to accommodate visitors from New York, and a few weeks later put his own stage into operation from the doors of the Equinox to the

New York-bound trains at Shushan, New York, where connection was made with the Hudson River Railroad. The Harlem Extension put on another train, and Orvis's stage was withdrawn.

The flavor of the Equinox House, and Manchester itself, is described in "Manchester, Vermont: A Pleasant Land Among the Mountains." (11)

* * *

"The Equinox House in the nineteenth century catered to a clientele which came chiefly from New York City. Many guests came by rail with parlor and sleeping car accommodations. Some notable citizens spent the summer here, bringing not only their families, but also their stable of fine horses along with coachmen, footmen, grooms, stablemen and harnessmen. It was one of the events of the day to watch these elaborate turnouts start for an afternoon drive...

While the main hotel had the public rooms, the annex held the Music Hall...built...in 1868. Dancing and most entertainments, both for the town and the hotel, were held there...

Croquet and lawn tennis were played on the green in front of the hotel...Dining room service...was performed by trained men waiters from the best New York hotels...On August 23, 1865, the Equinox House menu carried twelve separate dishes and vegetables and twenty desserts and pastries..." (11)

* * *

Among the many distinguished guests entertained there were Mrs Abraham Lincoln and her son Robert, in 1863 and 1864. Robert Todd Lincoln, like so many other well-to-do men, fell in love with Manchester and built a mansion there later, Hildene, now a National Historic Site.

Manchester had a primitive golf course as early as 1894, due to the foresight of George A. Orvis, a later proprietor of the Equinox. This was replaced by an unusually attractive 18-hole course in 1900, the Ekwanok Country Club; and another course was built by Anna S. Orvis and the Equinox Company in 1925. The development of Manchester as a golfing center did much to maintain the Equinox House as a leading resort hotel well into the twentieth century.

Manchester was never really a "spa," although it did have a brief flurry of activity when a Dr L. H. Sprague operated the "Manchester Water Cure" in part of the Equinox Jr, from 1861-63. The Equinox Company also owned a bottling works, which sold bottled Equinox Springs water until about 1920.

* * *

Woodstock, like Manchester, was blessed with beautiful surroundings, and both villages were also fortunate in attracting a number of affluent people who built

51

substantial second homes there. Woodstock also had its share of early inns and taverns (see Appendix E) but its emergence as a leading resort is recent compared to Manchester. The Eagle Hotel, originally a two-story building facing the green, was built by Capt Israel Richardson in 1789, replacing an earlier tavern. Titus Hutchinson added a brick wing as a dining room and social hall in 1822. Porches and a third floor were added in 1828 or '30, and a fourth floor in 1867. The brick ell burned in 1885, but was replaced by F. B. Merrill, owner at the time.

In 1889, a group of local businessmen decided that Woodstock needed a first-class hotel, one that would establish Woodstock as a year-round resort, and the result was the Woodstock Inn, which opened in May, 1892, replacing the old Eagle Hotel. It was a four-story building, resembling a fashionable Newport "cottage," with a four hundred-foot veranda, a tower, and a hundred guest rooms, many of them connecting family suites. The building was steam heated and lit by gas, with bathrooms on each floor. Extracts from a contemporary description appear below.

* * *

"On entering the rotunda, what a contrast from the little, square dingy room of the old tavern (i.e., the Eagle Hotel)...A large and artistically furnished room now greets the traveller, with open fireplace, winding stairway, carved oak chairs...and a polished hard-wood floor, and mind you, no luggage is taken in and dragged across the floor, as is the common practice in most hotels, but is taken to a side luggage entrance where the baggage lift takes it to each floor.

Leading from the rotunda are the reception rooms, double parlor, ladies' writing room and music hall...A large open fireplace...a large oak sideboard with fine cut glass and other ornamental dishes occupies nearly the whole of one end of the (dining room)...A nurses' and children's dining hall...are connected." (12)

* * *

The new inn was an immediate success, attracting affluent guests by the score. It was open only in the summers until radiators were added in each room a few years later, but after that, the Inn became "Vermont's first winter-sports center for tourists, and for two decades its riotous winter parties were the talk of Boston and Montreal sportsmen." (12)

* * *

"Snowshoeing, skating, sleighing and tobogganing were the reigning sports. City visitors arrived to find the town gay and sparkling like a Tyrolese village. Met at the train (i.e., the Woodstock Railway, a 14-mile spur linking Woodstock to White River Junction, opened in 1875) by a six-in-hand and long red sleighs that could carry a dozen or fifteen, visitors were transported into a world of snow and rural glamour..." (12)

* * *

The place was managed for nearly 40 years by Arthur B. Wilder, brother of Frederick Wilder, one of the local business leaders responsible for raising the money for the inn. Arthur Wilder was an outstanding host to thousands of visitors and to villagers who used the Inn as their main social center, and has been described as "the patriarch of the movement that made recreation one of Vermont's principal industries." (12)

In another parallel to Manchester, the Woodstock Country Club was organized in 1895. A primitive golf course opened in 1896 on Mt Peg, rapidly expanded and improved over the next ten years, with the first clubhouse going up in 1899. A "winter sports center" with an electrically-lighted toboggan chute, toboggans, skis, snowshoes and sleds all available, was opened by 1910 under the joint auspices of the Inn and the country club.

Hard times and an aging physical plant led to the closing of the Inn during the winters from 1932 until 1943. The Beach family, who developed and operated the Basin Harbor Club in Ferrisburg, became majority stockholders in 1962, and made various improvements, but by 1967 it was obvious that drastic steps were necessary. The old inn was bought by Laurance Rockefeller, who kept it open while the new Woodstock Inn was under construction. A grand "Final Hop" was held in the old inn in March, 1969, and the new Inn opened soon after. (See Appendix E for photo of the old Woodstock Inn).

* * *

In the second half of the century, the surviving mineral spring resorts were undergoing changes, but more importantly, city hotels were booming, attracting vacationers as well as businessmen; and many of the smaller village hotels and inns "began to take a greater share of vacationers and to draw a clientele--the middle-class family--which was to become typical of all Vermont in the latter part of the century." (1) Danville provides an example.

* * *

"Charles W. Thurber came to Danville in 1879 and rented the Elm House of Dr Calvin Woodard for three years. He introduced a new idea in hotel business, catering to summer boarders. Business increased so much that an addition was made to the hotel. He continued to operate the Elm House alone for another three years, while operating several other hotels...He bought the Thurber House in 1888 and began fitting it up and opened it to the public in 1890. Business was so good he was unable to accommodate all the summer guests who applied. He continued to expand and finished off bedrooms in another building called the "annex"...Drummers were frequent guests and engaged teams and drivers to take them to nearby village stores not reached by the railroad. (See Chapter IV for a photo of the Thurber House, and more information).

Regulars or summer boarders usually...stayed all summer...The hotel could accommodate 20 or more regulars who paid $20 per week for board and room." (13)

Access to places like Danville was made practical by the railroad, of course, as was pointed out by Bachelder in 1875. (2)

* * *

"In days gone by, it was largely the custom, as a matter of course, to visit those popular localities of most convenient access; and so it happened that each succeeding year found the same familiar faces returned to the haunts of past enjoyment. But, with the remarkable improvement in railroad and steamboat travel, new resorts have been opened, and fresh wonders present their claims for examination...Experienced tourists no longer choose the shortest line to an objective point...but by judicious selection...can embody such routes as lie through new or pleasant places..."

* * *

The role that the hotels played in the life of the community was also changing in the second half of the century, as has already been pointed out. Consider, for example, the Caspian Lake House in Greensboro.

* * *

"By the turn of the century, Greensboro had been discovered by summer visitors and was changing as a town, and the clientele at the hotel reflected this change. During winter and early spring the guest list still consisted predominantly of business travelers from other towns in Vermont and of local people attending functions at the hotel...but the register of the summer months began to reveal a sprinkling of entries such as...Orange, N.J....and Washington, D.C.; by 1919, the hotel had closed for the winter and become exclusively a summer resort. On the spacious veranda...guests in comfortable wicker rockers sipped tea, watched the sunsets and made lasting friendships. For recreation they rode up Barr Hill in a wagon pulled by oxen. They sunbathed or canoed and rowed. Sometimes they rode horses from the stable behind the creamery..." (14)

* * *

In many cases, the hotel building dominated the town, and was a source of civic pride, because of its size and elegance.

* * *

"In larger communities, Vermont's hotels resembled mansions, rendered more public by porches heightened to two stories, piazzas broadened to 15 or 20 feet, and carriage houses expanded to liveries. Many, such as the original Island House at Bellows Falls and the Mansion House in Burlington, were converted mansions." (1)

* * *

Also, the distinction between a "resort," as being a hotel open only in summer (or winter), or offering some special recreational feature, and a "hotel" in the usual sense, broke down during this period. Given this assumption, many Vermont hostelries of this period could be considered resorts. This would be particularly true, of course, for places on or near lakes, or in the mountains, and much less so, or not at all, for the commercial hotels built near the stations in the larger places, or for hotels in towns not blessed with environmental niceties. Highgate Springs would always be a resort, for example, even when the "springs" lost their therapeutic allure, and the hotel at Maquam Bay in West Swanton a resort hotel; but Swanton itself, or St Albans city, attractive though these places undoubtedly were to their residents, still lacked the extra ingredient needed to lead anyone but a businessman to stay in their hotels.

The Bread Loaf Inn is another place distinctive enough to warrant description here. Situated in Ripton in the heart of the Green Mountains, and accessible in the early days only by a 13-mile stagecoach ride over a difficult road from Middlebury, the Bread Loaf offered a very different kind of vacation experience to its guests than the Equinox House or the Woodstock Inn. (See photo).

Bread Loaf Inn

Joseph Battell was a wealthy philanthropist who enjoyed a therapeutic weekend at a farmhouse in Ripton in the 1860s so much that he bought the place, and started inviting not only his friends, but their friends as well, to join him as "guests." The place developed into an inn in a haphazard fashion, apparently reflecting perfectly the host's approach to the hotel business, but it was immensely popular with people who fitted in, as described by W. Storrs Lee. (15)

* * *

"Within a few seasons (i.e., after Battell bought the farm) it became inevitable that the guests would crowd out the host if he did not act quickly. Carpenters were set to work building ells and porches, barns and bedrooms. He merely gave the builder a rough idea of the direction in which the ell was to extend and the number of stories...The bowling alley and music hall headed north, the immense dining hall east. Guests that fitted into Bread Loaf society particularly well were rewarded with custom-built houses or bungalows. Two annexes...with two- and three-story porches...were added. But as the establishment grew, it still retained its original atmosphere, that of an outsized family on a perpetual house party...

He ran a fabulous table...To provide vegetables out of season an immense hothouse appeared in the field south of the inn...The host knew no pecuniary standard of hospitality. He met the guests at Middlebury and drove them ...to Bread Loaf, handled their bags, escorted them to their rooms, lit their kerosene lamps, personally planned and supervised the sumptuous meals, and entertained them with reminiscences and homely wit around one of the numerous hearths. There were no bellhops, no tips, frequently no bills..." (15)

* * *

Battell had a wide variety of interests, too diversified to describe here, except to mention that he was one of the first forest conservationists, leaving thousands of acres to Middlebury College, which eventually became part of the Green Mountain National Forest; and that he fought a losing battle against the use of public roads by automobiles, going so far at one point as to close the Bread Loaf Road (the old Center Turnpike, the road from Middlebury over the mountains by way of Ripton) to all cars. Although he had the support of his neighbors in Ripton, this was clearly an illegal act, and Battell was forced to reopen the road. Battell died in 1915, and the Inn property, which he left to Middlebury College, became the home of a variety of college summer school programs.

Coming to Vermont for a vacation in the days before the automobile was a formidable undertaking for an out-of-state family, and one of the features of resorts in the latter part of the nineteenth century and the first part of the twentieth was the tendency for families to come back year after year to the same lakeside hotel and spend the whole season. An account of what this experience was like is presented below, from an article entitled "Willoughby Lake Sixty Years Ago--An Earlier Vermont Way of Life."

* * *

"Perhaps I see it all through the haze of charm with which one often invests the long past. Perhaps Willoughby was never quite as delightful as I have always pictured it. Perhaps I merely wish to 'be a boy again just for to-night.' But I cannot entirely accept these explanations. Though I have seen the place only twice since the summer of 1899, I still think of it with warm pleasure...

In the nineties Willoughby was a long day's journey from New York where I was born and brought up. One took the White Mountain Express which left Grand Central at 9 A.M. To a small boy the trip held absorbing interest: along the Sound to New Haven, up the Connecticut Valley, Hartford, Springfield, Greenfield, Brattleboro, White River Junction, and finally, about 5 P.M., Wells River. There we changed while the express went on into New Hampshire. Then supper, and presently the train from Boston and the last lap to St Johnsbury and West Burke, reached about

56

8:30. Followed then the final stage, a six-mile drive behind horses, with a lantern swung under the wagon, through the crisp coolness of a northern Vermont summer night, and arrival at the big lamplit hotel between nine and ten, pretty tired and sleepy. A long day indeed.

The Willoughby Lake House was a big, rambling, wooden structure, the type of old resort place now almost vanished from the American scene. It belonged to the pre-automobile age, when people traveled by train and spent their holidays, except for brief excursions by carriage, in one spot...Food was simple, but abundant and good...Upstairs were the rows of bedrooms, of course minus running water, but with good beds and plenty of quilts...Across the road...the barns and stables which housed the dozen or more horses needed for transportation and for working the big farm which was part of the establishment...Along the side of the building which faced the lake each floor had its roofed porch...There was much boating on the lake...Social activities...were exceedingly varied...dances, excursions to Burke Mountain ...charades, stereopticon views, baseball games, much music and singing, hay rides, card parties, walks..." (16) (See Westmore, Appendix E, for photos).

* * *

Attempts to promote Vermont tourism date from the last decade or so of the nineteenth century and were first carried out by the railroads and the state Board of Agriculture. (3) The state Publicity Department was established in 1911. Part of the emphasis was on the availability of abandoned hill farms, and the phenomenon of people owning second homes in Vermont, so prominent a feature of modern Vermont, probably dates from this period. A number of farms, working or otherwise, also began to take summer boarders at about this time, and it is often difficult to distinguish between these places and the more traditional inns (see photo, next page).

One other group of resorts that deserves mention is the "summit" houses, which enjoyed a brief period of popularity, mostly in the last forty years of the 19th century. Lee explains the remarkable appeal these places had by noting that this was "the age of American Romanticism...when nothing was more moving to a sensitive excursionist than a sunrise from a mountain top or a sunset across the ripples of a mountain lake. The railroads arrived in Vermont at just the right hour of the nineteenth century to allow the passengers to luxuriate in the national mood." (15)

There have been many "Green Mountain Houses" in Vermont, and a number of other "Summit Houses" or "Mountain Houses" too; but there were really only five mountain-top hotels that ever offered reasonable, if not luxurious, overnight accommodations. These were the Camels Hump Summit House; the Summit House on Mount Mansfield; Lincoln Lodge on Lincoln Mountain; the Killington Summit House; and Grand View Hotel on Snake Mountain, in Addison. The Camels Hump Summit House was the first, run in connection with Samuel Ridley's hotel in North Duxbury, which was on the railroad. Dating from the 1850s, and located just below the crest of the mountain, "the house was not intended to serve the fastidious--and did not" (ref 15, see photo); but it could accommodate thirty overnight guests who reached it, starting from Ridley's, by carriage to a halfway house, and by pony or on foot the rest of the way. Supplies were brought in by oxcart from the farm that Ridley ran in connection with his hotel in the valley.

* * *

Sunnyside Farm, Warren (Vermont Historical Society)

Camel's Hump Summit House

The Camels Hump Summit House eventually lost out to nearby Stowe and Mount Mansfield, which had both a bigger mountain to offer, and a much more luxurious base hotel as well, the Mount Mansfield Hotel. The Camels Hump place was abandoned in 1869 and burned in 1877.

In comparison to Camels Hump and North Duxbury, where guests could disembark from the train virtually in front of Ridley's hotel, and start their ascent of the mountain from that same point, Stowe was not on the railroad--guests had to drive ten miles by carriage from Waterbury, the nearest railroad station, and Stowe itself was still some five miles from the foot of Mount Mansfield. In spite of this handicap, there was a carriage road nearly to the top of Mansfield by 1858, and a small summit hotel as well. The preeminence of Stowe and Mount Mansfield as a mountain resort, however, really dates from 1864 and the opening in Stowe of the Mount Mansfield Hotel, one of the largest and most luxurious hotels of its day in the state (see Stowe, Appendix E). Business was good from the start, and an annex was soon added. By 1868, the carriage road to the top had been improved (although the trip was still apparently a hair-raising experience); and the Summit House bought by the owners of the main hotel in the village. The Summit House was enlarged, with porches, a good water system, and room for seventy-five guests--one of the most famous of whom was Ralph Waldo Emerson, in the summer of 1868 (see photo, next page). The Mount Mansfield Hotel in Stowe burned in 1889 in a spectacular fire that threatened the whole village, but the Summit House carried on. It was renovated and enlarged again in 1923, and is still in operation today, at the end of a toll road for automobiles.

Killington Summit House came later than these two, and lasted a comparatively short time. The carriage road to the top was built in 1879, and the hotel followed immediately. It was a more elaborate place than the summit house on Camels Hump or Mansfield, according to Lee, (15) with stables, sheds and annexes in addition to the main frame hotel structure, which had room for thirty to forty guests. It was well patronized for a few years, by dinner and overnight guests from nearby Rutland as well as by tourists, but it had the disadvantage of not being operated in connection with a "base" hotel; and its business fell off dramatically early in the automobile era when it was found that cars could not negotiate the mountain road. The ruins of the abandoned buildings burned in 1916.

* * *

Mt Mansfield Summit House

The Bread Loaf Inn was described earlier in this chapter. Far less well known was Battell's "summit house," built in 1899 on Lincoln Mountain, one of several mountains that he owned. It was a "story-and-a-half log cabin with dormitory-style sleeping accommodations and a suitable dining-room which doubled as 'parlor'"; located at the end of a carriage road, about a half-mile from the top of the mountain. (15) There is a Long Trail shelter close to the original site today. It is not known exactly when the place stopped operating, but probably soon after Battell's death in 1915. The Lodge was left to Middlebury College, along with the Bread Loaf Inn and most of the real estate, but all signs of the building itself were gone by 1930.

Grand View Hotel in Addison was different from the other summit houses. Snake Mountain is an isolated, detached mountain, not part of the main Green Mountain chain. Grand View's remarkable view of Lake Champlain and New York state beyond is due more to the gently sloping character of the land around it, and its proximity to the lake, than to its elevation, which is only some 1300 feet. Grand View was a small place, with a capacity of only fifteen guests or so, but it was said to be "much gayer than Bread Loaf, more colorful than Mansfield." (15) It was built in the early 1880s, and lasted until 1925; the flood of 1927 ruined the road to the top.

With respect to the kind of patrons it attracted, and the activities they pursued, Grand View really bears a closer resemblance to many other summer resorts of the period in Vermont than it does to the other summit houses; although the fact that it was on a mountain (albeit a small one), and had a view that it was justifiably proud of, clearly qualifies it as a summit house. (See Addison, Appendix E, for more information on Grand View; also, a photo of the Woodford Summit House).

The coming of the automobile changed the situation of Vermont hotels yet again, effectively from World War I on, although bad roads helped to make this change a more gradual one than the transition from stagecoaches to railroads had been. It was still a long trek from New York, of course, but with the increased flexibility in transport came increased flexibility in vacation arrangements. People tended to move around more, and the practice of spending the season at a single resort began to die out. Many of the village hotels that were at least partly dependent on businessmen arriving by train saw this source of business gradually disappear; the salesmen could cover a larger territory by car from their home-town base, or large city office; and the hotels in the larger cities also came under pressure, because of downtown congestion and the appearance, first, of tourist cabins, and later, the ubiquitous motels. (The effect of the automobile on one resort, the Lake St Catherine House, has already been described in Chapter IV).

Tourism is big business in Vermont today, but this more recent period is beyond the scope of this book. The Vermont summer resort scene today, however, is more one of cottages, camping, second homes and small-town inns than it is of large resort hotels.

* * *

Mineral Spring Hotels

(1) Alburg:	Mansion House, 1834; Missisquoi House, 1854;
(2) Barre:	Barre Spring House, East Barre, by 1873;
(3) Brattleboro:	Wesselhoeft's, 1845; Lawrence's, 1852;
(4) Brunswick:	Brunswick Springs Hotel, 1869;
(5) Clarendon Springs:	Clarendon Springs House, 1835; American House, Murray House, 1850s;
(6) Guilford:	Guilford Mineral Spring House, 1870;

(7) Hartland:	Spring House, c. 1860;
(8) Highgate Springs:	Franklin House, 1840;
(9) Manchester:	Equinox House, 1853;
(10) Middletown Springs:	Montvert, 1870;
(11) Newark:	Caledonia Spring House, 1875;
(12) Newbury:	Spring Hotel(?); another(?);
(13) Panton:	Elgin Spring House, 1871;
(14) Plainfield:	Mountain Springs Hotel (Plainfield Springs House), 1858;
(15) Sheldon:	seven hotels, 1860s (Sheldon, Appendix E;
(16) South Hero:	Iodine Spring House, 1868;
(17) Waterville:	Mountain Spring House, 1858;
(18) Wheelock:	Caledonia Mineral Spring House, 1830, renovated, 1860s;
(19) Whitingham:	Spring House, by 1887;
(20) Williamstown:	Gulf Spring House, 1847; and a second Gulf House, built later;
(21) Woodstock:	Sanatoga Spring, developed in a 15-acre park, apparently serving all of the hotels in Woodstock (not a hotel).

* * *

References

(1) Louise B. Roomet, "Vermont as a Resort Area in the Nineteenth Century," Vermont History 44 (Winter 1976): 1-13.

(2) Bachelder's Ill. Tourist Guide of the U.S.--Popular Resorts and How to Reach Them (Boston: J. R. Bachelder; N.Y.: Lee, Shepard and Dillingham, 1873).

(3) Andrea B. Rebek, "The Selling of Vermont: From Agriculture to Tourism, 1860-1910," Vermont History 44 (Winter 1976): 14-27.

(4) J. Kevin Graffagnino, Vermont in the Victorian Age (Bennington: Vermont Heritage Pr.; Shelburne: Shelburne Museum, 1985) 43-44.

(5) Louise E. Koier, "Those Wonderful Waters Brought the First Flood of Tourists to Vermont," Vermont Life 11 (Summer 1957): 56-60.

(6) Clarendon, Vermont: 1761-1976, Helen Rondina, ed. (Rutland: Academy Books, 1976).

(7) Harold A. Meeks, "Stagnant, Smelly and Successful: Vermont's Mineral Springs," Vermont History 47 (Winter 1979): 5-20.

(8) Enna Bates, "A Vermont Spring and a Cure for Cancer," Vermont Historical Society News and Notes 3 (March, 1952): 49-52.

(9) Allen L. Stratton, History of the South Heroe Island being the Towns of South Hero and Grand Isle, Vermont (Burlington: Queen City Pr., 1980).

(10) Alburgh Springs House, Lithia and Sulphur Water on Missisquoi Bay, Lake Champlain. On the Line of the Vermont Central Railroad at Alburg Springs, Vermont (pamphlet, 1875, Alburg, Vermont, Vermont Historical Society).

(11) Edwin L. Bigelow and Nancy H. Otis, Manchester, Vermont: A Pleasant Land Among the Mountains (Manchester: The Town, 1961).

(11) Edwin L. Bigelow and Nancy H. Otis, Manchester, Vermont: A Pleasant Land Among the Mountains (Manchester: The Town, 1961).

(12) Peter S. Jennison, The History of Woodstock, 1890-1983 (Woodstock: Countryman Pr. for the Woodstock Foundation, 1985).

(13) Tennie Touissant, in the Burlington Free Press, February 4, 1969.

(14) Peter D. Watson et al., The History of Greensboro: The First Two Hundred Years; Susan B. Weber, ed. (Greensboro: Greensboro Historical Soc., 1990).

(15) W. Storrs Lee, The Green Mountains of Vermont (N.Y.: Henry Holt, 1953).

(16) Cecil B. Dyer, "Willoughby Lake Sixty Years Ago--An Earlier Vermont Way of Life," Vermont History <u>24</u> (July 1956): 240-242, 247-250.

* * *

Chapter VI

Hotel Fires

Fire was a constant threat to Vermont communities in the old days. Buildings were more flammable then, the causes of fire more numerous, and fire protection primitive or non-existent in most places until late in the 19th century. Again and again, one finds descriptions of the "big fire" in town histories. Hotels were as vulnerable as the next place, of course, and burned by the scores, some of them two or even three times after being rebuilt. It is remarkable that only seven people are known to have died in Vermont hotel fires (through 1925), considering the tinder boxes most of them were, usually without fire escapes.

The log cabin taverns had huge fireplaces with wood and mud chimneys, obviously a major fire hazard in the early days. Later, though the chimneys improved, chimney fires were still common. Wood continued to be the main fuel, for both heating and cooking, with constant buildup of creosote; the virtually universal use of wooden roof shingles made every chimney fire a potentially major problem. Candles were another hazard, and whale oil and kerosene lamps were dropped or exploded. The fire that destroyed the old Franklin House in Rutland in 1868 was said to have been caused by an exploding kerosene lamp. Hot ashes carelessly deposited in a shed were another cause of fires.

In the smaller communities, there was virtually no fire protection at all until quite recent times. It was common practice in larger communities in colonial days for householders to keep leather water buckets, so that a bucket brigade could be organized when a fire was discovered, but whether this was ever required in any Vermont town is not known. The Civic Club of Bakersfield was buying water buckets for the town in the 1930s, and storing them in the home of a man who owned some long ladders.

Early protection was provided by force pumps, operated by hand and drawing water from a reservoir in the apparatus that had to be kept filled by a bucket brigade. Suction pumps that could draw water from a cistern or stream had to wait for the development of flexible hose. Some of these hand engines could be carried and operated by one or two men, but others were substantial pieces of equipment, drawn to the scene of a fire by a gang of men or a team of horses, and needing 8-12 men to operate the pumping handles. The photos on the next pages illustrate the kind of equipment available in the latter part of the 19th century. Few Vermont communities had city water systems with hydrants until late in the 19th century, although some places had cisterns at various locations in the village for the bucket brigades to draw water from. These would seem to have been of little value in a Vermont winter.

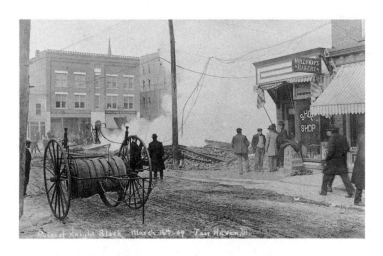

Fair Haven fire equipment, 1909

Rutland hand pumper
(Rutland in Retrospect, Robert E. West, 1978)

Steam engines (pumpers which expelled water by a steam engine) started coming into use in the late 1850s in the larger cities, some self-propelled and some horse drawn. Equipment of this kind usually required at least a skeleton staff of full-time paid firemen for efficient use, and paid forces were found in only a handful of places in Vermont in the 19th century. Many Vermont communities had volunteer companies, however, and the men were often paid by the town for time spent at obligatory drills as well as for time spent actually fighting fires. Bellows Falls' first volunteer company was organized in 1826, Windsor's in 1833, St Johnsbury's in 1844, and Burlington's in 1829, soon after the old Court House burned (major improvements in fire protection usually came only after a big fire!) but many places in Vermont had no organized

64

volunteers until quite recently. Organized companies from larger towns would respond to calls from the smaller places, of course (with the bills being sent later). In some of the major fires, special trains would bring men and equipment in. At the Scale Factory fire in St Johnsbury in January, 1876, for example, a special train brought relays of firemen from Lyndonville.

Northfield hand-drawn fire wagon, c. 1909
(Picture Northfield, 1985, Julia W. McIntire and Richard L. Cleveland)

* * *

At a fire in Belmont in 1946, "the only thing there was to fight the fire with were pack pumps and...soda acid fire extinguishers, which nearly all families in Belmont had possessed for years...The Ludlow Fire Company came with a pump and fourteen men...The Parmenter house was already burned..." The town bought a second-hand pumper in Long Island, and organized a volunteer fire company, soon after this fire.

Alarm systems took a long time to appear also. Church bells, of course, were used in many towns, and factory whistles in towns with a good-sized mill or factory. Locomotive whistles were even used on occasion. At the Center Village fire in St Johnsbury on July 1, 1876, 27 buildings, including the Armington Hotel, were lost. "As there was no telegraph station, a messenger had to drive his horse to the Plain...then the engines were dragged up three miles in the hot sun, the only local apparatus being pails and wet blankets."

A picture of the level of protection available in Vermont in 1879 is provided in a book by Clifford Thomson. (1) According to this source, Vermont had 40 communities with estimated populations of over 1000 in 1879. Twenty-seven of these had some protection, and five had none (eight communities failed to report). In most

65

cases, however, protection consisted of a hand-engine or two, and perhaps a hose carriage, if the village had a hydrant system. There were only 3 "steamers" in the whole state in 1879, two horse-drawn and one hand-drawn, and one "chemical" engine, while New Hampshire, with about the same number of communities of 1000 or more, had 22 steamers and 13 chemical engines.

There are some surprises when one looks at the larger places in Vermont in the tables in Thomson's book. (1) For example, Bellows Falls had hydrants, but only one hand-engine; Brattleboro was in relatively good shape, with one of Vermont's three steamers (hand-drawn) and 3 hand-engines. Burlington had hydrants and 300 volunteers, but no paid firemen. It had 2 hand-engines, a hook-and-ladder engine, and 9 hose companies--but no steamers. Bennington and Rutland had the two horse-drawn steamers in the state. Eight communities with populations of 1000 or more (including Poultney, with an estimated population at that time of 2500) had neither an organized volunteer force nor as much as a single hand engine. It is not surprising, given this kind of protection and the general level of flammability of buildings, that there were so many hotel fires.

As an approximation, based only on a survey of Hemenway, the Hamilton Child county gazetteers, and published town histories, some 230 Vermont hotels have been destroyed by fire, including 15 places that burned twice and 2 that burned three times, after having been rebuilt. There were several fires in which two or more hotels were lost at the same time; and four fires with a total of seven fatalities (the Glen Falls House at Lake Morey in 1912, 4 deaths; the second Northfield House in 1916, 1 dead; Carpenter's Hotel in Norton, 1904, 1 dead; and the old Passumpsic House in St Johnsbury, 1896, 1 dead). The photos below show a few of these hotel fires.

* * *

References

(1) Clifford Thomson, The Fire Departments of the United States--A Series of Tables Showing the Equipment of Various Cities, Towns and Villages (N.Y.: Fireman's Journal, 1879).

* * *

Hotel Burlington, 1910

Hotel Elliot, Cavendish

New Bardwell, Rutland, 1917
(Rutland in Retrospect, Robert E. West, 1978)

Hotel Windham, Bellows Falls, 1912

Fire in the Bethel Inn (Special Collections, UVM)

* * *

Appendix A

Sources Examined and Methods Used in Compiling the Lists of Inns and Taverns.

The lists in Appendix E are organized chronologically by township, and every place that ever had a post office (based on George C. Slawson's compilation of Vermont Post Offices, ref 1), and many that did not, is included. When there are several villages in a town, as is usually the case, they are all to be found as sub-headings under that township. For example, East Highgate, Highgate Center, Highgate (Falls), Highgate Springs and Saxe's Mills are all dealt with under Highgate. Established local names for places that differ from their official (i.e., postal) names, and early names that have been superseded, are also included (e.g., Newfane/Fayetteville) with Swift as the authority. (2) It was often the case, of course, that taverns and inns existed outside of towns (resort hotels on lakes, or taverns along the early roads linking towns, etc.). These situations are dealt with by giving resort lakes a sub-heading in their township (e.g., Lake Morey under Fairlee) and occasionally by using a sub-heading "Outside the Villages" to cover scattered taverns.

All places cited as "taverns" in the various sources are included here, even though it is certain that some of these places offered food and drink only, not lodging. For the more recent hostelries, an effort has been made to exclude "guest houses," "tourist cabins," and boarding-houses, although it is not always possible to tell the difference between a small country inn and a place that was no more than a summer boarding-house.

The lists were compiled by examining the sources listed below; the list is followed by a description of each source, and how it was dealt with.

Sources Examined.

(1) Walton, Vermont Register/Year Book.
(2) Vermont Business Directory.
(3) New England Mercantile Union Business Directory, 1849.
(4) Abby M. Hemenway, Vermont Historical Gazetteer.
(5) Hamilton Child, County Gazetteers/Directories.
(6) Walling, Beers and Other Land Ownership Maps.
(7) Sanborn Fire Insurance Company Maps.
(8) Town and county histories.
(9) Bassett references.
(10) Vermont Division of Historic Preservation.
(11) Local historical societies.
(12) Almanacs.
(13) Innkeeper's licenses, State Archives.

(14) Vermont Publicity Bureau.

* * *

(1) <u>Walton's Vermont Register/Year Book</u>. E. P. Walton began publishing this invaluable series in 1818. It has gone through a number of changes in title, publisher, and format, but still appears each year as the Vermont Yearbook, published since 1909 by Charles Tuttle of Rutland.

Walton provided not only statistical information (Town grand lists, voting records, stage and train accessibility, etc.) but also the names of town officials, post masters, merchants and artisans, doctors, and the like. This information was apparently compiled by relying heavily on returns filed by various state officials, and (for the Business Directory portion), merchants, postmasters and town clerks. Walton did not include hotels in its listings until 1870, except for a partial listing in 1855 and 1856, and the listing of hotels in a mere handful of towns in 1842 and 1843. An idea of the flavor of Walton's in the 19th century may perhaps be gained by examining a portion of the publisher's announcement from the 1872 edition.

* * *

"A word about the Business Directory--yes, more than a word. Very few persons are aware to what an expense of time and labor we are put to obtain the Information contained therein. That there are a great many inaccuracies therein, is not our fault. <u>The report of each and every town has been referred to a prominent man therein, generally a merchant or postmaster, within one month previous to the date of publication</u>. When the proofs have come back...corrections have been made, in every instance. We cannot go to every town ourselves, neither can we <u>pay</u> for the reports and sell the Register for any reasonable price. As it is, the Business Directory costs us more than any other portion of the book. It will be found more full, this year, than ever before, and, we trust, more accurate." (Emphasis in original).

* * *

In compiling the checklists, Walton was examined for the years 1870, '75, '80, '87, '92, '95, '98, 1905, '08-09 (recorded as 1908), '11-12 (recorded as 1911), 1913, '15, '20 and 1925 (in addition to 1855, '56 and 1842, '43)--in other words, at intervals of about five years.   The gaps are to a considerable extent filled by the Vermont Directory (see below) and it is unlikely that any significant number of hostelries of stature sufficient to attract the notice of the local chroniclers has been missed. However, these places changed owners and managers frequently, and there is no doubt that a number of these have been missed.

(2) <u>Vermont Business Directory</u>. (Title varies, see ref 3). This directory began appearing in 1870 at two-year intervals, and is similar to Walton in many respects. It apparently ceased publication in 1909. Each volume contains a list of hotels, and the lists for 1870-71, '73-74, '79-80, '83-84, '87-88 and '90-91 were incorporated into the checklists. (Hotels were not listed separately after 1900 in the Vermont Directory,

but as part of the write-up for each town.) In most cases, Walton and the Vermont Directory were in agreement, and an entry in the checklist without a citation may be from either source, or both; significant discrepancies (other than minor spelling differences) between the two directories are pointed out in the checklist.

(3) <u>New England Mercantile Union Business Directory: Part 3, Vermont, 1849</u>. (4) The publishers of this directory claimed that directories were available for each of the New England states, and that they would be revised annually, but it appears that this is the only one that was published for Vermont. It is very valuable, nevertheless, because it provides the earliest systematic list of Vermont hotels (396 of them, to be exact).

(4) <u>Hemenway's Vermont Historical Gazetteer</u>. Abby M. Hemenway's monumental series is too well known to call for a description here. The five volumes, covering every county but Windsor, appeared from 1867 to 1891 (the last being published posthumously) and were all scanned for references to taverns and hotels. "Scanning" does not mean reading line by line, and doubtless an occasional tavern reference was overlooked.

The town histories in these volumes were written by local people recruited by Miss Hemenway, and the coverage varies widely. Some of the contributions could almost stand alone (and some of the authors did, in fact, later expand their contributions into separately published town histories); others are a little thin. It is also unfortunately the case that not all of the contributors thought inns and taverns worth mentioning at all.

(5) <u>Hamilton Child, County Gazetteers/Business Directories</u>. All fourteen counties were covered in eleven volumes appearing from 1880 to 1889. In many cases, the histories appear to have been taken more or less directly from Hemenway. The Business Directory portion of each volume, however, contains a list of hotels for each town in the county. These lists were incorporated into the checklist, but usually only listed with a notation as to source when there was a discrepancy between Child and Walton or the Vermont Directory, or when Child covers a gap in the Walton/Vermont Directory coverage. Also, the descriptive portion of each volume (the town histories) was scanned for references to taverns and inns.

(6) <u>Walling, Beers and Other Land Ownership Maps</u>. The two leading sources for information about Vermont maps are "The Shaping of Vermont," by J. Kevin Graffagnino, 1983 (ref 5), and "Vermont Maps Prior to 1900: An Annotated Cartobibliography," by David A. Cobb (ref 6), to which the reader is referred for an overview of the subject.

Presdee and Edwards published detailed maps for several Vermont cities in the early 1850s, but the county land ownership maps are the most useful to historians.

"The county land ownership maps of Vermont, beginning with James D. Scott's <u>Scott's Map of Rutland County, Vermont from actual survey</u>, published in 1854, provide valuable research data for the genealogist, geographer and the historian. They not only show the entire county but also include in their margins inset maps of the individual villages, views of selected buildings, and statistics on agriculture, education and the population for each county. These county maps are of value since they indicate the owner or commercial function of each building on the map. Although most of them were published in the late 1850s, the last one was not published until 1878 when F. W. Beers issued his map of Essex County." (6)

* * *

All such maps that were available were examined for buildings marked "tavern," "hotel," and the like. The maps examined include all Presdee and Edwards city maps; Scott's map of Rutland County, 1854; Hosea Doten's map of Windsor County, 1855; McClellan's map of Windham County, 1856; Rice and Hardwood's map of Bennington County, 1856; all of the H. F. Walling maps (Addison; Chittenden; Franklin and Grand Isle; Caledonia; Orange; Washington; and Orleans, Lamoille and Essex combined, in the period 1857-59); and all of the F. W. Beers maps.

All of the maps referred to above except those of Beers are in the form of large wall maps; the Beers maps were published as bound atlases during the period 1869-78, except for Essex County, published as a wall map in 1878. Places found on a map of any kind are indicated on the checklist in Appendix E by an asterisk, with the particular map indicated with a notation. The scale in most of these maps is one inch to the mile, and the insets are at a larger scale still.

(7) Sanborn Fire Insurance Maps. The Sanborn Map Company was founded by D. A. Sanborn in New York City in 1867, and grew very rapidly. Its purpose was to provide detailed and specialized maps for fire insurance companies. The earliest copyrighted maps from Sanborn are said to date from 1883, but there are a number of Vermont Sanborn maps earlier than this, including Burlington in 1869. These maps are at a scale of 50 feet to the inch, and show all buildings to scale, including hotels, of course. The maps began coming out in large numbers from the mid-1880s on, and eventually covered a third or more of the towns in the state, including all of the larger places. Cobb provides a list of pre-1900 maps in the University of Vermont and Library of Congress collections; and the University of Vermont, Special Collections, has its own list, covering its entire collection. There is also a collection at the Vermont Historical Society in Montpelier, but there does not appear to be a single, all-encompassing list of the Vermont maps that Sanborn published. The maps are especially valuable because they were revised every five years or so for the larger towns. All Sanborn maps in the Library of Congress and University of Vermont collections were examined for hotels.

(8) Town and County Histories. All town histories listed in Bassett (ref 5), together with those published more recently that could be identified, were scanned for references to taverns and inns. Here again, coverage is very uneven. Some town histories contain an entire chapter devoted to taverns and hotels, and a handful even include maps; others, even some substantial volumes, ignore the subject entirely or mention a few places without dates or other details.

Also, six county histories were scanned: "History of Rutland County, Vermont," Henry P. Smith and William S. Rann, 1886; "History of Chittenden County, Vermont," William S. Rann, 1886; "History of Windsor County, Vermont," Lewis C. Aldrich and Frank R. Holmes, 1891; "History of Addison County, Vermont," H. P. Smith, 1886; "History of Bennington County, Vermont," Lewis C. Aldrich, 1889; and "History of Franklin and Grand Isle Counties, Vermont," Lewis C. Aldrich, 1891.

(9) <u>Bassett references</u>. Bassett's bibliography of Vermont history contains over six thousand entries. (7) In addition to entries for Hemenway, Child, town and county histories and the like, the bibliography covers what might be called the "periodical literature"--articles about Vermont history in journals and magazines, pamphlets, newspapers, town reports, etc. Bassett was first screened to identify entries which it was thought might contain material relating to inns and taverns, and then these selected entries (several hundred of them) were also examined, with certain rare exceptions for items hard to acquire.

(10) <u>Vermont Division of Historic Preservation</u>. Starting well over ten years ago, this state agency embarked on a statewide survey of all buildings of historic interest. While not yet complete, the survey had covered about 80% of the state by 1988. These surveys have not yet been published (except for Rutland county, ref 8) but are available at the agency's office in Montpelier. The information is organized by town within each county. The standard format includes date of construction of the building, and <u>original</u> use, when known; location, and present owner and use; and, in certain cases, especially for buildings in "historic districts," information on the history of the area and some of the buildings in it. There are also photographs and map locations for most of the buildings surveyed.

Buildings that have burned or been torn down are not included in this survey, obviously, but it nevertheless provides a wealth of information about the current status of one-time taverns, as well as revealing the existence of many old tavern buildings that did not turn up in the various directories, for one reason or another. These files were all examined for buildings identified as taverns, inns or hotels, now or in the past.

(11) <u>Local historical societies</u>. For various reasons, it was not practical to canvass all of the local Vermont historical societies, to invite them to examine the entry for their town in draft form. However, whenever questions arose in compiling the list of inns for a given town (e.g., disagreement between different sources; long gaps in the record; locations; present status of old places, etc.) assistance was sought from local sources. In most cases, this was the town historical society, when there was one, but in others it was the town clerk, or perhaps the author of a town history. Such assistance has been specifically acknowledged in every case, except when the local correspondent declined recognition.

(12) <u>Almanacs</u>. For a certain period, it was apparently the practice for many almanacs to include stage-coach routes. This section of an almanac usually carries a heading such as "Roads from Boston (or Bennington, Middlebury, etc, depending on where the almanac was published) to Principal Cities." There will then follow a series

of stage routes, listing the towns along the route, distance between these towns, and in many cases, names of the tavern-keepers for each town (see illustration, below).

* * *

An Aſtronomical Diary; Or, An

ALMANACK

For the Year of our LORD,

1773.

Being the firſt Year after Biſſextile or Leap Year.
Calculated for the Meridean of BOSTON, NEW-ENGLAND, Lat. 42 Deg. 25 Min. North.
Containing beſides what is common in Almanacks,— A Method of Planting Vineyards. — How a Nation may be *ruined* and *reformed*, &c. &c.

OUR great Forefathers, fir'd with virtuous Rage,
Did all the Perils of the Deep engage,
To fly thoſe Realms where proud tyrannic Sway,
And horrid Perſecution ſcout for Prey ;
Their native Soil and youthful Scenes they fled,
Where bounteous Nature all her bleſſings ſhed,
And ſiſter Art had ranſack'd foreign Shores,
Made every Dainty croud the Britiſh Stores,
Had rais'd the ample Dome and lofty Spire,
And ſpacious Theatre, where Crouds admire
The mighty Feats perform'd in ancient Days,
That ſpring to Life, reviv'd in Engliſh Plays.
Theſe Pleaſures all, our Fathers left behind,
But bro't the Seeds of Science in their Mind,
Here planted firſt fair *Freedom* with Applauſe,
Which gives the Reliſh to all other Joys :
Guard then the Plant,—this ſavage Land adorn,
This work they left their Children then unborn.

By Nathaniel Ames.

BOSTON: Printed and Sold by E. RUSSELL, and J. HICKS, next the Cornfield, Union-Street.

(XVII.) Road to Albany.

W[illegible], (N.X)	Brookfield,	63	63
Rice,	Ditto,	4	67
Chadwick,	Weſtern,	7	74
Patterſon,	Ware,	5	79
How,	Belchertown	5	82
Dwight,	Ditto,	3	84
[illegible]	Ditto,	4	88
Smith,	Amherſt,	4	92
Kellog,	Hadley,	4	96
Lyman,	Northampton	2	98
Tupper,	Cheſterfield	14	112
Miller,	Worthington	7	119
Marks,	Sandisfield	6	125
Gutridge,	Pittsfield	9	134
Hubbard,	Ditto	4	138
	Albany Ferry	25	163

(XVIII.) To Albany & Quebec.

Bliſs,(No. X.)	Springfield	96	96
Over the river	Ely's	2	98
Clap,	Weſtfield	7	105
[illegible]	Ditto	3	108
Knox,	Blandford	6	114
Pease,	Ditto	1	115
Rowley,	Greenwood	6	121
Young,	Ditto	4	125
Chadwick	Tyringham	7	132
R[illegible],	GBarington	9	141
Whiting,	Ditto	1	142
[illegible]	Egremont,	4	146
Cowles,	Nobletown	4	150
McKinltry,	Ditto	3	153
[illegible]	Ditto	3	156
[illegible]boom,	Stonehouſe	4	160
[illegible]neſs,	Kinderhook	2	162
[illegible]	Ditto	6	168
[illegible]	Ditto	1	169
Fitch,	Ditto,	12	181
[illegible] Ferry,		8	189
Half-moon,		12	201
Still-water,		13	214
Saratoga,		12	226
[illegible]		28	254
Ticonderoga.		44	298
Crown Point,		15	313
[illegible] Lake Champlain		12	325
[illegible]		16	341
[illegible]		6	[illegible]
Trois Rivieres		90	437
Quebec.		80	517

(XIX.) Road to No. Four or Charleſtown.

Winſlow(No. XV.)	Peter.	72	72
Morton,	Athol	6	78
Evans,	Warwick	9	87
Grout,	Wincheſter	11	98
Wyman,	Keen	14	112
Buterfield,	Weſtmorland	11	123
Phelps,	Walpole	9	132
Walker, or Haſtings,	*Charleſtown* or *No. Four.*	10	142

(XX.) Road to No. Four & Crown Point, over Charlſtown Ferry.

N[illegible]ell,	Cambridge	7	7
Buckman,	Lexington	3	10
Haywood, Barrett,	Concord	9	19
White,	Acton	5	24
Gilbert,	Littleton	5	29
Pierce,	Groton	8	37
Saxwell,	Shirley	4	41
Hutchins,	Lunenburg	5	46
Cowdin,	Fitchburgh	4	50
Foſter	Aſhburnham	8	58
Stimſon,	Winchendon	4	62
Nicholls,	Ditto	2	64
Darling,	Ditto	4	68
Deed,	Monadnock	8	76
Tiffany,	Swanzey	4	80
Hammond,	Ditto	5	85
Wyman,	Keene	6	91
Bellows,	Walpole	14	105
Phelps,	Ditto	3	108
Haſtins Walker	*Charleſtown*	11	119
Nott's Ferry,	Springfield	3	122
Springfield,	Stevens	5	127
Weathersfield	S[illegible]ord	2	129
Cavendiſh	Pain	6	135
Ditto	Coffin	5	138
Otter Creck,	Button	20	158
Rutland	Medes	6	16[illegible]
Pitsford	Waters	6	1[illegible]
Shoreham	Moor	20	19[illegible]
Breadport	Towners	8	19[illegible]
Over the Lake to C[illegible] Point	Lewis	2	20[illegible]

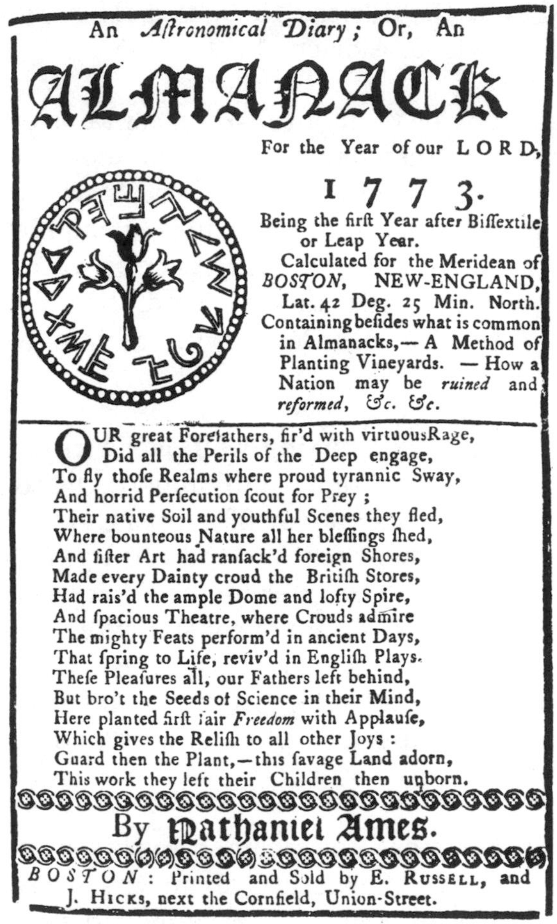

Cover, and representative page, from a Nathaniel Ames Almanack (Boston, 1773). Note entry XX, Crown Point Road, with Vermont taverns from Springfield on.

* * *

More than thirty almanacs representing a cross-section of Vermont and New England almanacs, were examined. No almanac earlier than 1771 was found which listed tavern-keepers, and the practice apparently died out about 1828, but aside from those few town histories which are based on actual searches of town records, the almanacs represent the only primary source of information on these early taverns, and are obviously of great value. Tavern-keepers changed frequently, however, and it was probably difficult for the almanac publishers to keep up, as illustrated by the following, taken from Nathanael Low's 1778 Almanack.

* * *

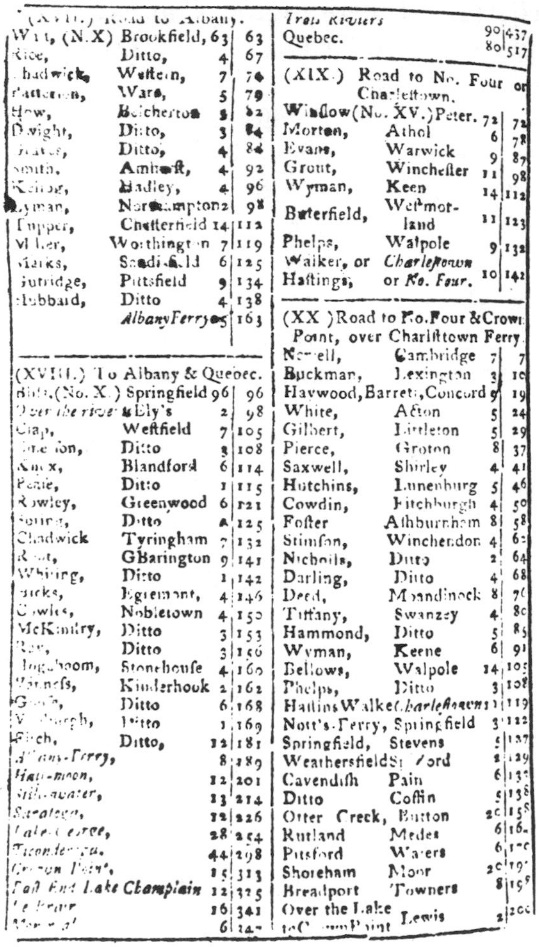

"It happens every year that some Tavern-keepers in one or other of the States

give up their license, and others are substituted in their room: It is therefore requested for the benefit of travellers as well as their own, that such new licensed persons would send a letter, free of charge, to either of the Printers hereof, that it may be printed the following years.--They must be particular in expressing the number of miles they are from the stages before and after them."

* * *

The almanacs examined are listed below: An Astronomical Diary or Almanack, Nathaniel Ames, 1771, 1775, 1786 (various Massachusetts publishers); An Astronomical Diary or Almanack, Nathanael Low, 1778 (Boston); Vermont Almanack, Eliakim Perry Jr, 1785 (Bennington); Weatherwise's Town and Country Almanack, Abraham Weatherwise, 1783 (Boston); The Massachusetts, New Hampshire, Rhode Island, Connecticut and Vermont Almanack, Abraham Weatherwise, 1794 (Boston); Bickerstaff's Boston Almanack, 1774; Thomas's New England Almanack, 1797 (Worcester); Vermont Almanac and Register, James Kirkaldie, 1796 (Rutland); Mower's New Hampshire and Vermont Almanac, 1805; Vermont and New York Almanac, Ebenezer Judd, 1811 (Middlebury); Curtis's Pocket Almanack, 1801 (Exeter) and 1802 (Walpole); The Gentlemen's and Ladies' Diary and Almanac, Asa Houghton, 1803, '05, '07, '10, '13 (various publishers); Leavitt's New England Farmer's Almanac and Agricultural Register, Dudley Leavitt, 1817, '20 (C. Norris publisher, 1817, Nathaniel Boardman, 1820); New England Farmer's Diary and Almanac, Truman Abell, 1815, '16, '23 (various publishers); An Astronomical Diary or Almanack, Thomas Spofford, 1820 (Exeter); The Farmer's Almanack, or an Astronomical Diary, Thomas Spofford, 1822 (Exeter); The Farmer's Almanack, Robert B. Thomas, 1802, '05, '25, '29 (various Boston publishers).

(13) Innkeeper's Licenses, State Archives. There are incomplete, but nonetheless helpful, records of tavern- and innkeeper's licenses (the terms are used synonomously) in the State Archives. These licenses were issued by the county courts, and for a brief period of time (approximately 1809-33) the court clerks for some but not all of the counties filed annual reports of licenses issued. Because these records are incomplete, they cannot be used to establish the span of years during which a particular tavernkeeper was operating, but they are still valuable, in some cases because they provide the only known date for a tavernkeeper, and confirmation (from a primary source) of his or her existence; and in others because they provide the names of tavernkeepers that were not turned up at all in the other sources examined.

It is possible that this source could be exploited more thoroughly by examining records at the various county courthouses, but this was not done.

(14) Vermont Publicity Bureau guides and Railroad guides. Vermont was the first state, in 1891, to establish a state publicity service, which became the Vermont Publicity Bureau (in the Department of State) in 1911. This agency has published numerous guides to places to stay in Vermont, and a number of them were consulted, as were several guides produced by the railroads (e.g., Heart of the Green Mountains, Rutland Railroad, 1897; and Summer Homes Among the Green Hills of Vermont and Along the Shores of Lake Champlain, Central Vermont Railroad, several issues); and

one or two guides issued by the State Board of Agriculture.

* * *

References

(1)   George C. Slawson et al., The Postal History of Vermont (N.Y.: Collector's Club, 1969).

(2)   Esther M. Swift, Vermont Place Names: Footprints of History (Brattleboro: Stephen Greene Pr., 1977).

(3)   Vermont Business Directory. Title and publisher vary; Vt State Bus Dir, 1870-71; Vt Bus Dir, 1873-74 to 1889; Vt State Dir, 1890-91. Published by Chase-Symonds, Boston, Wentworth and Co, 1871; Briggs and Co, 1873-74 to 1889; Union Publ Co, 1890-91 to 1903.

(4)   New England Mercantile Union Business Directory: Part 3, Vermont (N.Y.: Pratt and Co, 1849).

(5)   J. Kevin Graffagnino, The Shaping of Vermont: From the Wilderness to the Centennial, 1749-1877 (Rutland: 1983).

(6)   David A. Cobb, Vermont Maps Prior to 1900: An Annotated Carto-bibliography, Vermont History 39 (Summer and Fall, 1971).

(7)   T. D. S. Bassett, Vermont: A Bibliography of Its History (Hanover, N.H.: University Press of New England, 1981).

(8)   Vermont Division of Historic Preservation, Historic Architecture of Rutland County, Vermont, Curtis B. Johnson, ed., Elsa Gilbertson, asst. ed. (Montpelier: 1988).

* * *

Appendix B. List of Tavern Signs

(See Chapter II for a discussion).

(1) <u>Adamant</u>. Alpheus Bliss's tavern, 1820s; sign still exists, private collection.

(2) <u>Bellows Falls</u>. A photo of the sign for the Bellows Falls Stage House may be found in "History of Rockingham, Vermont," Lyman S. Hayes, 1907.

(3) <u>Bennington</u>. In "Taverns and Stagecoaches of Old New England," Volume II (Allan Forbes and Ralph M. Eastman), there is a photo of the sign for the E. Noyes tavern.

(4) <u>Bennington</u>. The Catamount Tavern had a stuffed catamount on top of a pole as its sign.

(5) <u>Brandon</u>. The McConnell tavern: "a large swinging sign between two uprights and on it was 'entertainment for Man and Beast,' with some decoration."

(6) <u>Brookfield</u>. There is a painted wooden sign with the words "Stratton Tavern" on both front and back at the Smithsonian Institution in Washington, believed to have come from the Stratton Tavern in Brookfield.

(7) <u>Calais</u> (Kent Corners). A. Kent tavern; there is a VHS photo of this.

(8) <u>Cavendish</u>. Dutton House, 1782, now in the Shelburne Museum. The tavern sign is said to have been painted on a little porch, "a picture representing the good dame of the house presenting a 'mug of flip' to a thirsty traveller." Painting obliterated a long time ago. (From the 150th Anniversary Celebration of Cavendish, Charles R. Cummings, Vermonter <u>17</u> (Aug-Sept 1912): 592-619).

(9) <u>Derby</u>. A 2 x 4 sign board with the eagle and shield on one side and a decanter and a half-filled glass of red brandy, and below these on each side the words, "Carpenter's Inn, 1816" (later removed when Carpenter's went temperance).

(10) <u>Fairfax</u>. Capt Erastus Safford's sign was "Rest for the heavy laden and weary traveler" on a piece of paper nailed on a board, stuck in a hollow stump (Hemenway).

(11) <u>Grafton</u>. Photo of a reproduction of the Old Tavern sign, in A Vermont Renaissance, Wilt Copping, Windham Foundation, Grafton, 1978.

(12) <u>Hardwick</u>. Alpha Warner's tavern, on the Hazen Road; the sign was a shield in a fancy frame, dated 1799, with the name Alpha Warner; the words "Stage House" were added later (Child).

(13) Jericho. The Bostwick House in Riverside, later the Dixon House; "A shield-shaped sign hung from a post in front... (it) read 'Bostwick House' in large gilt letters. The other side was adorned with a two-wheeled chariot, drawn by fiery steeds driven by a woman" (Lorraine S. Dwyer, Chittenden County Historical Society Bulletin, 4 #6 (June 1969).

(14) Manchester Center. Borland's Tavern: "The blue tavern sign measured four by six feet with a red border. Painted on it were a bush full of birds and a man holding a bird. The inscription read--'A bird in the hand is worth two in the bush'" (Edwin L. Bigelow and Nancy H. Otis, Manchester, Vermont, 1761-1961: A Pleasant Land Among the Mountains, 1961).

(15) Morristown. Boardman's tavern, an oblong sign bearing, besides the name Boardman's Inn, "the suggestive picture of a tankard and glasses."

(16) North Hero. Ladd's Tavern; "The prominent memory of Ladd's Tavern was the sign. At the northeast corner, near the roof, projected a short wooden arm, from which swung a square sign, bearing in the centre on either side, in large, black letters, the single word Inn. This sign seemed always moving with a melancholy creak; and after the demise of the old Proprietor, it might well have been the voice of the old Inn" (Allen L. Stratton, History of North Hero, Vermont, 1976).

(17) Panton. "On the farm of Truman Kent we found a hotel sign which was used for the old hotel kept here by Nathan Spaulding--"1810, Nathan Spaulding, Tavern" (Hamilton Child).

(18) Pomfret. The original sign for Abida Smith's tavern is in the possession of the Pomfret Historical Society.

(19) Reading. Sign for the Abel Amsden tavern is in the possession of the Reading Historical Society.

(20) Rochester. "E. D. Briggs' tavern sign has until recently hung in the lobby of the Inn" (E. N. Davis, Jr and Mary O. Davis, Rochester Remembers, Randolph, Vt, 1981).

(21) Rutland. Rutland Hotel (later Munn's Tavern), kept by Joseph Munn in the 1790s at the sign of the "Federal eagle."

(22) Rutland. The Tontine Coffee House, kept by Elias Buel in 1794 (later Page's tavern), at the sign of the "Bull's Head."

(23) Rutland. The Corner House, kept in the 1790s by Simeon Lester, at the sign of the "golden ball."

(24) Ryegate. The Vermont Historical Society owns a sign for the Robert Whitelaw tavern. The exact dates for this tavern are unknown, but Whitelaw had a tavern license in 1822. Painting on the sign is now illegible.

(25) <u>St Johnsbury</u>. Rice's Hotel; "On a high standard in front of the house hung and swung on creaking hinges the sign--A RICE HOTEL."

(26) <u>Shoreham</u>. The wooden sign for Chipman's Tavern in Cream Hill is in the possession of the Vermont Historical Society. Chipman ran the tavern from c. 1790 until he died in 1830. There is an eagle design on one side, possible Masonic emblems on the other, and the words "T. F. Chipman's Inn" on both sides. (See illustration, below).

Sign for the Chipman Tavern, Cream Hill
(Vermont Historical Society)

(27) <u>Shrewsbury</u>. Photos of the Gleason tavern sign and of the sign for the Finney tavern may be found in Dawn D. Hance, Shrewsbury, Vermont: Our Town As It Was, 1980. (See appendix E for a photo of the Gleason tavern sign).

(28) <u>Stowe</u>. Oliver Luce's tavern, c. 1794, had a large white ball as its sign (Walter J. Bigelow, History of Stowe, Vermont, from 1763 to 1934, 1934).

(29) <u>Wallingford</u>. In the History of Wallingford, Vermont by Walter Thorpe (1911), there is an engraving of the sign that once adorned the Deacon Mosely Hall tavern.

(30) <u>Wallingford</u>. A large square sign, with large gold foil letters starting at the bottom left; and a circle with the words "Temperance House"; said to be the first such sign, probably the John Ives hotel.

(31) <u>Lower Waterford</u>. Asa Grow's tavern; his sign was a kettle hung on an arm of the post.

(32) <u>Lower Waterford</u>. The Traveler's Home had a plain square on which was painted a picture in color of a chariot, with a man standing up, waving a flag with an inscription on it, "Traveler's Home"; the chariot was drawn by six prancing bay horses (Charles E. Harris, A Vermont Village, 1941).

(33) <u>West Brattleboro</u>. A photo of the tavern sign for the Hayes tavern ("R. Hayes, Entertainment") is found in Annals of Brattleboro, 1681-1895, Mary R. Cabot, 1921-22.

(34) <u>Worcester</u>. Amasa Brown's tavern, 1816; his sign was a smooth board with letters in red chalk saying "Good cider for sale here."

* * *

Appendix C

Hotel Longevity: The Oldest and the Longest-Lived

Descriptions of Vermont inns are often accompanied by statements about their age: what rank the place holds in terms of absolute age (date established), or in terms of years of continuous service. These statements are usually made cautiously, with qualification, because the writer is likely only to be familiar with the place under discussion; information about the ages of other places is not generally available.

An attempt is made here to provide two kinds of longevity lists, and since this may do as much to inspire controversy as to settle it, some explanation of the basis for these lists is called for.

First, the lists were compiled from the information contained in this book, and are thus based on sources already described in Appendix A. The only important sources left unexamined are the town and county land and licensing records, and it is thus entirely possible that some old taverns have been missed, and that the start-up dates for others not missed are in error.

Second, in order to be included in the longevity lists that follow, a place had to be listed <u>with a date</u> (or at least an approximate date) in one of the sources examined (Hemenway, almanacs, town histories, etc). There are many taverns and inns listed in this book with a question-mark for date, and even though it might seem reasonable in some cases, because of indirect evidence, to assign approximate dates, this was not done in compiling the lists.

With respect to the list of oldest places, there is only one Vermont tavern of record in the 1750s; there are 15 in the 1760s. These are listed individually below, but the numbers then go up so rapidly that listing by name becomes impractical: 50 more in the 1770s, 107 in the 1780s, and 215 in the 1790s. These numbers refer to start-up dates, and the total number of taverns operating in the 1790s, for example, would be 215 together with those founded in the earlier decades, except for those places that had closed in the interim.

The second list is based on years of continuous operation as an inn or tavern, insofar as it has been possible to determine. A place that was closed for renovation is not excluded, but if it stood empty for a year or so during an ownership change, or if an inn burned and was replaced on the same site, it was excluded. There is obviously room for error here too.

* * *

List 1. The Oldest Places.

1750s: Gould Tavern, Westminster, 1755

1760s: John Arms Tavern, Brattleboro, 1762
                Coffeen (Coffin) Tavern, Cavendish, c. 1769
                Dewey Stand/Walloomsac Inn, Old Bennington, 1764
                Stephen Fay Tavern/Catamount, Old Bennington, 1769
                Zadock Everest Tavern, Addison, 1765
                James Fassett Tavern, Old Bennington, c. 1762
                Abel Stockwell Tavern, Marlboro, 1763
                Robert Johnston Inn, Newbury, 1769
                John Sargeant Tavern, Dummerston, 1762
                Charles Wright Tavern, South Pownal, c. 1763
                Spaulding Tavern, Putney, 1766
                Waldo Tavern, Shaftsbury, 1765
                Martin Tavern, South Shaftsbury, 1769
                Stevens Tavern, Springfield, c. 1762
                Norton Tavern, Westminster, c. 1760

List 2. The Longest-Lived.

Rank	Establishment	Years
1	Dewey/Wallomsac Inn, Old Bennington	210
2	Shelburne Inn, Shelburne*	194
3	Dorset Inn, Dorset* (Note 1)	c. 194
4	Island House, South Hero*	c. 192
5	Old Tavern, Grafton* (Note 2)	189
6	Black Lantern Inn, Montgomery*	187
7	Equinox House, Manchester* (Note 3)	172
8	Stevens House/Painter's Tavern, Vergennes	c. 170
9	True Temper Inn, Wallingford*	c. 166
10	Vermont Hotel/Addison House/Middlebury Inn, Middlebury*	163
11	Rice Hotel/St Johnsbury House, St Johnsbury	c. 163
12	Kedron Valley Inn, South Woodstock*	161
13	Bristol Housel, Bristol	152
14	Barnes Tavern/St Frederick Inn, Chimney Point (Addison)	c. 150
15	Green Mountain House, West Wardsboro	c. 146

* * *

An asterisk (*) indicates the place is still operating.

Note 1: according to Resch, the Dorset Inn would be first here, operating since 1796 (ref 1); but the Dewey Stand/Walloomsac Inn was established in 1764, operated until a few years ago, and unless it was closed at some point in the past, a fact not known to this author, it would seem to be the leader.

Note 2: may have closed briefly in the late 1930s or early 1940s.

Note 3: closed for several years in the 1970s, but still had 172 years of continuous operation at that point.

* * *

List 3. Longevity by County.

County	Oldest	Longest Operating
Addison	Everest Tavern, Addison, 1765	Stevens Hotel/Painter's Tavern, Vergennes, c. 170
Bennington	Fassett's Tavern, Old Bennington, c. 1762	Dewey House/Walloomsac, Old Bennington, c. 210
Caledonia	John Gray Tavern, Ryegate, c. 1780; Brock Tavern, Ryegate, c. 1780;	Rice Hotel/St Johnsbury House, St Johnsbury, c. 163
Chittenden	Mallett Tavern, Colchester, 1770s	Shelburne Inn, Shelburne, 194
Essex	Gates tavern, Lunenburg, 1792	Heights House/Chandler House, Lunenburg, c. 70; West Concord House, Concord, 68
Franklin	Evarts Inn, Georgia Plain, c. 1788	Black Lantern Inn, Montgomery, 187
Grand Isle	Allen tavern, South Hero, 1783	Island House, South Hero, c. 192
Lamoille	Luce tavern, Stowe, c. 1794	Eagle/Boro/Hotel Cambridge/ American House, Cambridge, c. 100
Orange	Robert Johnston inn, Newbury, 1769	West Randolph Inn/Mansion House, West Randolph, c. 115

Orleans	Davison tavern, Craftsbury, 1795; a tavern, Newport, c. 1795	Valley House, Orleans (Barton Landing), 111
Rutland	Remington tavern, Castleton, c. 1770	True Temper Inn, Wallingford, c. 166
Washington	Beardsley's Yellow House, Cabot Plain, c. 1790; James Morse hotel, Cabot, c. 1790	Eagle Hotel/American House/ Montpelier House, Montpelier, 106
Windham	Whig tavern, Westminster, c. 1755	Old Tavern, Grafton, 189
Windsor	Coffin's tavern, Cavendish, c. 1769	Kedron Valley Inn, South Woodstock, 161

* * *

References

(1) Tyler Resch, Dorset (West Kennebunk, Maine: Phoenix Publ. for the Dorset Historical Society, 1989).

* * *

Appendix D

Turnpike Taverns and Inns

This list was begun while working on the index for this book, with the idea that there should be an entry under "Turnpikes, Taverns On" (or "Taverns, On Turnpikes"); but it grew so quickly as to make it impractical to include in the index. Basically, the list was prepared by examining a turnpike map contained in Wilgus's book (ref 1) and noting which towns the various routes passed through. This technique is clearly subject to error (it is not always easy to tell from the map if a village is on the turnpike or not), and undoubtedly there are places that have been missed, and perhaps a few included that were not actually on a chartered turnpike. For example, many of the taverns listed in Appendix E are described as being "stage" taverns; some of these will not appear on the lists below because no attempt was made to screen Appendix E for places so described. (For further information on turnpikes, see Chapter II). The turnpikes are listed in alphabetical order.

* * *

Bayley-Hazen Road

West Barnet: Walter Harvey tavern; Hardwick Street: Alpha Warner tavern, Warner's Stage House; Peacham: Elkins tavern; Ryegate: John Gray tavern (probable); Brock tavern, the "old Red Tavern"; Morrill stand; Whitelaw tavern; Warden tavern; (Note: probably others in Ryegate, since "at one period there were 7 inns along that road in this town"); South Walden, the Farrington stand (see Rte 15, Chap. II); Note: the Bayley-Hazen road went from West Danville through Walden, Walden Station and South Walden (more or less present Rte 15) and it seems likely that other Walden taverns were on it, but none of those known can be assigned with confidence except Farrington's, above.

Center Turnpike (Rtes 7, 12, 107 and 125, in part).

Bethel: Gardner-Wheeler Inn (probable); Lillie stand; Locust Creek Hotel (Lathrop stand); David Waller "hotel stand" (probable); Hancock: Joseph Butts tavern (Green Mountain House); Daniel Claflin inn (later the Mt Vernon House); East Middlebury: John Foot tavern (Waybury Inn); (Note: the northern terminus of the Center Turnpike was in Middlebury, where it met the Waltham Turnpike, present Route 7); so several of the Middlebury taverns, including the Vermont Hotel (later the Addison House) were probably on the Center Turnpike); Ripton: Lackey tavern; Ethan Owen tavern (probable); Stockbridge: a hotel (VDHP 1419-6).

Connecticut River Turnpike (Route 2 in part).

Hartford: Leavitt Inn; Hazen tavern; Richardson hotel; Hartland: Lull tavern; Pavilion Hotel (probable); Norwich: Burton tavern; Norwich Inn.

Crown Point Road.

Addison: Chimney Point Tavern; Brandon: a tavern "near the highway, where the old Crown Point Road crosses the Swamp road.."; several other Brandon taverns were also probably on the Crown Point Road, which came through the town; Bridport: Towner Tavern; Cavendish: Coffeen (Coffin) Tavern; Paine tavern; Clarendon: Joseph Smith Inn (probable); Butler tavern (listed in Bickerstaff's Stage Register as "Otter Creek," probably Clarendon); Center Rutland: James Mead tavern; Rutland: several old Rutland taverns on present Rte 7 (Main St) were surely on the Crown Point Road; Shoreham: Moore tavern; Cream Hill (Shoreham), Chipman tavern (probable); Shrewsbury: Page tavern; Gleason tavern; Buckmaster tavern; Springfield (town): a tavern (the Arthur Whitcomb house in 1922); Gaylord tavern; Whiting: the Marshall stand.

Fair Haven Turnpike (Rte 22A in part).

Benson: Smith Tavern (Mtn View Stock Farm, later); Joseph Gibbs tavern; Cramer tavern; Bridport: Benjamin Skiff hotel; a hotel, south of the village on 2A; Shoreham: Joseph Miller tavern; Hunsden tavern (?); Turrill tavern (probable).

Green Mountain Turnpike (Route 103 in part).

Proctorsville (Cavendish): the "Brick Tavern" (Stage House, Eagle Hotel); Sunset Tavern, Leonard Proctor; a tavern, Leonard Proctor; Chester: The Green Mountain Turnpike came into Chester via Gassetts and North Chester (present Rte 103), while Main St in Chester was the main road from Hanover, New Hampshire to Albany (not a named turnpike). Thus, most places in Chester village were probably not on the Green Mountain Turnpike, but those in Gassetts, North Chester and probably Chester Depot were; Hugh Henry tavern (probable); Star Inn (probable); Chester Depot: Sargeant Hotel (probable); Gassetts (Chester): J. Marshall hotel; North Chester: Holden tavern; Clarendon: Bowman tavern; Ludlow: Fletcher hotel; Bixby hotel; Locust Hill Inn (possible); Healdville (Mount Holly): the Green Stand; Mount Holly: Dickerman tavern; Clark hotel (probable, since Mount Holly was directly on the Green Mountain Turnpike); Cuttingsville (Shrewsbury): Cutting tavern (later the Union House); Bartonsville (Rockingham): Willard tavern; a second (unnamed) tavern.

Hubbardton Turnpike (Rte 30 in part).

Castleton Corners: Westover House; Hubbardton: Dewey stand; Webb tavern (probable); Sudbury: Mills hotel (south of Sudbury village, later the Hyde Hotel); Sawyer stand; Webster House (probable).

Mount Tabor Turnpike.

see Peru Turnpike, under Manchester.

Lamoille County Plank Road (Rte 100 in part).

Morristown: Boardman tavern (probable); Cady's Falls (Morristown): Boardman tavern; Stowe: Robinson hotel.

Paine Turnpike.

Brookfield: Experience Fisk tavern; Stratton Tavern (probably others); Northfield (town): William Jones tavern; (present) Williamstown: Flint tavern (on a road linking Williamstown to the Paine Turnpike); 1st Williamstown: Cornelius Lynde house; Judge Paine house; (these latter two are both probable, since the Paine Turnpike cut through this corner of the town).

Passumpsic Turnpike (Rte 5 in part).

Barnet: Gilchrist tavern; Stevens tavern; Passumpsic (Barnet): 3 taverns: the Passumpsic Inn, the Kendall (?) tavern, and the Cushman tavern; East Ryegate: "a stage stop."

Peru Turnpike (Rte 11 in part).

The eastern end of the Peru Turnpike was apparently in Peru, and was part of the main Manchester-Chester stage road (present Rte 11); so Landgrove, strictly speaking, was not on the Peru Turnpike; but Leland's Coffee House in Landgrove Hollow is listed here because it was so well known.

Manchester was the western end of the Peru Turnpike, and the southern end of the Mount Tabor turnpike too, and it seems virtually certain that several Manchester taverns were on one or the other or both of these turnpikes.

Peru: Butterfield Inn (actually in Landgrove Hollow; became Leland's Coffee House); Tuthill hotel (probable); Hillcrest Tea Room (possible).

Poultney Turnpike (Rte 30 in part).

Castleton Corners: Westover House; see Hubbardton Turnpike, which met the Peru Turnpike here; Poultney: Stanley (Beaman) hotel. Other early Poultney taverns are probables.

Randolph Turnpike (Rte 14 in part).

East Randolph: The Randolph turnpike came through here, and one or more of the four early taverns (Converse, Wheatley, Blodgett, Fish) must have been on it; South Randolph: Benedict tavern.

Royalton-Woodstock (Pomfret) Turnpike.

Barnard: Aikens stand; Tappan stand; "on the road from Barnard to Bethel down the Creek road there were at least four hotels..."; (the "Creek road" is present Rte 12, running west of the Royalton-Woodstock turnpike, but is described as being part of the "Woodstock-Montpelier stage road", this apparent discrepancy not resolved); the Duty and Graty Brown hotel, the Hammond House, the Wright tavern, and the Stewart stand are the four "hotels" referred to; Pomfret: Hutchinson inn; Jonathan Reynolds inn; South Pomfret: Winslow tavern; Royalton: Stevens tavern.

Rutland-Bridgewater Turnpike: same as the Sherburne Turnpike.

Rutland-Stockbridge Turnpike (Rtes 4, 100 in part).

Mendon: Richardson tavern; Pittsfield: Daniel Bow tavern; North Sherburne: Johnson tavern; Thrall Coffee House; Rutland: The Rutland-Stockbridge and the Sherburne (Rutland-Bridgewater) Turnpikes both had their western termini in Rutland (more or less at the intersection of present Rtes 4 and 7), and it seems likely that one or more of the old Rutland taverns on Main St would have been on these turnpikes.

Searsburg Turnpike (Rte 9 in part).

It is likely that the Searsburg Turnpike took over and rebuilt the western end of the Windham Turnpike, which see.

Woodford (city): William Park tavern; Luther Wilson tavern; H. P. Noyes tavern; Woodford Hollow: Elisha Lyon (sp?).

Sherburne Turnpike (Rtes 4, 100 in part).

Sherburne: Josiah Wood hotel; Nathan Eddy inn (probable).

Strafford Turnpike.

Chelsea: Phineas Dodge hotel; Hale tavern; Orange County Hotel.

Stratton Turnpike.

Arlington: Arlington was the western terminus of the Stratton Turnpike and it seems likely that at least one of the early taverns in Arlington, east of the village or in it, would be Stratton Turnpike taverns (taverns north and south of Arlington would have been on present Rte 7, not a named turnpike in this part of the state). The Hawley tavern, the Elnathan Merwin inn and the Stoddard tavern are all probables.

Stratton: Torrey tavern; Sunderland: Bradley tavern; the Kelly Stand; West Wardsboro: the West Wardsboro Hotel.

Weathersfield Turnpike (Rte 131 in part).

Cavendish: Dutton tavern; <u>Amsden (Weathersfield)</u>: Downer's Hotel; <u>Ascutney (Weathersfield)</u>: Colston tavern. Also, the Cook and Dean taverns were on present Rte 131 in Ascutney (more or less the Weathersfield Turnpike here) and they are probables.

<u>White River Turnpike</u> (Rte 14 in part).

Hartford: Delano hotel.

<u>Williamstown Turnpike</u> (Rte 14 in part).

The short-run Williamstown Turnpike had its southern terminus in Brookfield, as did the Paine Turnpike, and it is a moot point which turnpike the Brookfield taverns are on. See also Paine Turnpike.

(present) <u>Williamstown</u>: David Gale Inn; 1st Gulf Spring House.

<u>Windham Turnpike</u> (Rtes 9, 100 and 131 in part).

West Brattleboro: Mixer Tavern; <u>Marlboro</u>: Whitney Hotel (Marlboro Center Hotel, Whetstone Inn); <u>West Marlboro</u>: West Marlboro Inn; <u>Wilmington</u>: Lincoln Hotel (probable); Averill stand; Childs Tavern; Patch House (Vermont House); <u>Woodford</u>: Scott tavern; Lawrence tavern.

<u>Winooski Turnpike</u> (Rte 2 in part).

Burlington: Benedict tavern (Eldredge stand); Brown tavern; Ames tavern (probable; inns and taverns in downtown Burlington, e.g., the Howard Hotel, not included here); <u>Jonesville (Richmond)</u>: (Whipple) tavern; Hunt Hotel; <u>Richmond</u>: John Russell tavern; Farnsworth tavern; Whitcomb tavern; Russell's "old brick hotel"; Chequered House; <u>South Burlington</u>: Eldredge tavern; <u>Williston</u>: Calvin Morse tavern; Isaac French tavern; a tavern in Williston village (probable); Hull tavern (probable); Arnold tavern (probable); Eagle Hall (Going tavern); Chittenden tavern (probable).

* * *

References

(1) William J. Wilgus, The Role of Transportation in the Development of Vermont; maps by Earle W. Newton and the author (Montpelier: Vermont Historical Society, 1945).

* * *

Appendix E

An Annotated Listing of All Known Vermont Inns and Taverns, pre-Revolution to 1925.

The sources used to compile this list have been described in Appendix A. The lists are arranged alphabetically by town, first; when there are several towns or villages in the township, these are arranged alphabetically within the township. Finally, the places themselves are listed in approximate chronological order within each sub-heading.

Abbreviations used are as follows: VDHP, Vermont Division of Historic Preservation; VPB, Vermont Publicity Bureau; SBA, State Board of Agriculture; NEMU Dir, New England Mercantile Union Directory; VHS, Vermont Historical Society; VYB, Vermont Yearbook (Walton in recent years); CVRR, Central Vermont Railroad; UVM, University of Vermont. Short forms are also used in referring to several sources (e.g., Sanborn, Child, Hemenway, Beers, etc); the full names for these sources may be found in appendix A.

An asterisk after an entry indicates that that place was found on a map, and the particular map is cited in parentheses after the asterisk. The captions for the photographs indicate their source; when no source is shown, the photo came from the author's collection.

Paran Creek House, North Bennington
(Weichert-Isselhardt collection)

(1) **Addison** (Addison).

Several early innkeepers are referred to in Clark, (1) but it is often hard to tell where they were located; also, dates are not always provided.

(1a) Addison (including Grand View Mountain).

c. 1765:   a tavern, Zadock Everest; who came in 1765, and left when the war broke out; his log cabin was the first public house in the county (2); county court held here "On the west side of the road near where Mr and Mrs William Roberts live" (in 1976, ref 1); the place burned in 1890.

c. 1793:   a tavern, Seth Abbott; "an eating and drinking tavern" on land bought from Asa Willmarth; on what was the Theron Benedict place in 1976 (1); (Rte 22A);

c. 1814:   an inn, Aaron Jackson; on land purchased from William Whitford, probably on the Mountain Road; (1)

c. 1847:   a tavern, Amos Willmarth; "on the east side of the Mountain Road...presently owned by John Baker" (i.e., 1976, ref 1); there is an A. Willmarth on the 1871 Beers on the easternmost road in town, running under Grand View Mountain; this is VDHP 0101-7, building still standing.

1870, '72: --, C. H. Taylor* (Beers);

1874:   (a) Grand View Hotel, Jonas N. Smith;

* * *

Smith, descendant of an early settler, owned a lot of timber land on Grand View Mountain in the eastern part of town. In 1871 he bought a steam-powered sawmill and hauled it up the mountain. It was used there while the hotel, ice-house and barn were built, and then moved to a more convenient location. The hotel was finished in 1874, and included a 68-foot high observation tower (photo, Clark). It is said that one could see Lake George on a clear day, and a total of 42 church spires, including Plattsburg. The wooden tower was replaced with a steel one in the early 1880s. A covered roller-skating rink was built near the hotel, and many dances and church and school picnics held at the hotel complex.   Business was good until soon after the turn of the century, when the lakeshore resorts began to compete and the drive up the mountain discouraged users of the early automobiles. Regular operation stopped in 1920 except for pre-arranged parties. (See Chapter V, Resorts).

* * *

1883:   (a) as above;

1880s: The Poplars, Frank and Ermina Trimble; a 3-story hotel built in the early 1880s "toward the south end of Lake Street" (not clear where this is; listed under Chimney Point in 1903 SBA Vermont guide). Mrs Trimble continued operating after her husband's death, c. 1890, until about 1920, mostly as a summer place.

1890s: (a) Grand View Hotel, taken over by Mary Pond Smith and her son Seward;

1901:   --, Myron A. Smith;

1903:   (a) as above, -- (SBA Vermont guide);

1920, '25:   (a) as above, S. V. Smith.

(1b) <u>Chimney Point</u>. Northern terminus of the Crown Point Road.

1770s: (a) <u>Chimney Point Tavern</u>, Paine/Barnes place.

* * *

<u>Chimney Point Tavern</u>. The French built a fort at Chimney Point in 1690, which they burned when Ticonderoga fell in 1759 to the British. Benjamin Payne (Paine) was the first owner of this tract when Addison got its Wentworth charter (1761) and built a house on the old foundation, c. 1770; this place was operated as an inn for many years, sometimes referred to as the Capt. Hendee house during and after the Revolution. There is a reference in Bickerstaff's Boston Almanac (1774) to Lewis's tavern at the ferry to Crown Point. Place transferred to Asahel Barnes Sr in 1822 (<u>Barnes Tavern</u>) and to his son Asahel Jr a little later. Asahel Jr was a cabinet-maker who died in 1886; his son, Millard Barnes, took over the inn in 1890 and re-named it the <u>St Frederick Inn</u> (VDHP 0101-24). Asahel Barnes is listed as postmaster at Chimney Point from 1829-39 and 1847-86, presumably it was Barnes Jr during this latter period. Mostly a summer place in later years, but some ferry business. Closed c. 1920, made into a museum by the state in 1969.

* * *

1805: hotel (and store, PO), <u>Daniel Haskins</u>; first PM; somewhere on present (i.e., 1976, ref 1) George Marshall farm on Rte 125 on Lake Champlain; possibly in Bridport, since the Haskins store, tavern and PO are also mentioned in the Bridport town history; (3)

1841: (a) as above, B. Peach, who had it for 4 years and failed (2);

1849: (a) --, Asahel Barnes (NEMU Dir);

1871: (a) --, A. Barnes* (Beers);

1892: Walton lists an "Epsom Springs House," H. S. Foote, Chimney Point PO, but this is almost surely the <u>Elgin Spring House</u> in Panton, which see;

1899: (a) <u>Chimney Point Hotel</u>, -- (VHS photo);

1903: (a) <u>St Fredericks Inn</u>, -- (SBA);

1908: (a) <u>Hotel Fredericks</u>, --;

1920: (a) <u>St Frederic Inn</u>, M. F. Barnes.

1923: <u>Trimble House</u>, E. K. Trimble (VPB).

(1c) <u>Town Line</u>. No listings found.

(1d) <u>West Addison</u>.

1780s: a tavern, <u>Jonah Case</u>; built in 1780, first brick house in the county (owned in 1976 by Mr and Mrs J. J. Brady, ref 1); on a farm occupied in 1881 by William J. Conant, on road 36 near West Addison village (Child);

1790s: a tavern, <u>Isaiah Clark</u>; large building, an overnight stage-coach stop on the Burlington-Whitehall route (see photo, next page); burned in the early 1940s, replaced by dwelling of Francis Angier;

* * *

92

References

1. Erwin S. Clark, History of the Town of Addison, Vermont (Middlebury: Addison Pr., 1976).
2. H. P. Smith, History of Addison County, Vermont (Syracuse: D. Mason, 1886).
3. There's Only One Bridport in the U.S.A. (Bridport Historical Society, 1976).

* * *

Isaiah Clark tavern, 1870s (from Clark, ref 1)

(2) **Albany** (Orleans).

(2a) Albany (West Albany until 1865).

1804: a tavern, William Hayden; tavern license, 1817; until c. 1830; location unknown; "began on lot #4," Hemenway;

Note: tavern licenses to John Hayden, 1827, '28; Jonathan Fitz, 1828; Robert Rodgers, 1824-27; William Johnson, 1827, '32; Jesse Rodgers, 1824-30; and Ludovicus Lilley, 1829, locations unknown;

1849: --, L. Warren; --, N. H. Holt (NEMU Dir);

1870, '72: -- A. B. Shepard;

1878: (a) Darling's Hotel, --* (Beers);

1879: (a) as above; --, J. A. Dow; burned c. 1880, the Darlings moved to a nearby property and continued to operate for many years (see below);

c. 1880-1913: --, J. B. Darling; known as The Albany House, The Albany, Hotel Albany at various times;

1914: no hotel on Sanborn map;

1915: --, C. S. George; closed, and the building burned in January, 1967.

(2b) Albany Center.

1870-'78: --, Winthrop Howard.

(2c) <u>East Albany</u>.

1828: a tavern, <u>Levi Warren</u>; until c. 1850, probably East Albany; on the road from Irasburgh to Craftsbury (Hemenway).

(2d) <u>South Albany</u>.

1911: --, Mrs T. M. Rowell.

Note: the assistance of Ruth Lawrence, Albany, is gratefully acknowledged.

* * *

(3) **Alburg** (Grand Isle).

(3a) <u>Alburg</u> (2nd Alburg postally, formerly West Alburg).

1823: <u>Mott's Tavern</u>, Samuel Mott Jr; Mott Sr was licensed as an inn-keeper as early as 1807 at his home in Alburg, and his son from 1808 until at least 1829; prosperity evidently led to construction of this substantial stone building, built in 1823 as a stagecoach inn by Giles Mott, on the Montreal to Boston and New York route. Also known as the <u>Halfway House</u> (with respect to St Jean, Quebec and Burlington); Samuel Mott Jr died in 1854, the place changed hands several times. It was <u>Orange Spoor's Tavern</u> in the 1850s (see below), abandoned at the turn of the century, restored by Ray and Linne Poquette in 1932, still operating in 1968. On the west side of Rte 2 entering Alburg from the south.

* * *

In the 1850s, Jenny Lind stayed at Orange Spoor's Inn, a large grey fieldstone house overlooking Lake Champlain at Alburg. She came across the lake in a boat from Rouse's Point, and is said to have given a short, impromptu concert at the landing before proceeding to the inn.

* * *

Note: other tavern licensees, locations unknown, were Abel Phelps, 1826-29; Elijah Loomis, 1828, '29; Delancy Stoughton, 1829, '30; Benjamin S. Phelps, 1830; Abram G. Steel, 1828; and Robert and A. Ransom, 1825, '26;

1849: <u>Custom House</u>, John M. Sowles (NEMU Dir; location unknown);

1882: <u>Young's Hotel</u>, Nelson Young;

1905, '11, '13: --, O. O. Bell; --, N. K. Martin;

1908: <u>Lakeside</u>, --;

1915, '20: --, N. K. Martin; this is VDHP 0701-113, now a parish center in the St Amadeus church complex; the old inn (<u>Martin's</u>) was acquired by the church in 1965;

1925: <u>Alburg Inn</u>, Harold Webster (1940 Sanborn); formerly the "Y," connected with the railroad; it burned c. 1980, now a parking lot; <u>Maple Lawn</u>, --.

(3b) <u>Alburg Center</u> (1st Alburg postally, until 1865). No listings found.

(3c) <u>Alburg Springs</u>.

1849: (a) <u>Mansion House</u>, B. Carpenter (NEMU Dir);

94

1856: (a) as above, Chauncey Smith* (Walling); <u>Missisquoi House</u>, Niles and Hovey* (Walling); <u>Mansion House</u> and <u>Missisquoi House</u> both mentioned in Burt's Connecticut Valley Guide, 1867;

1870: (a) as above; (b) <u>Alburg Springs House</u>, - Sexton; opened in 1868; probably same as <u>Merritt House</u>, see photo; see also Chapter V;

Merritt House, Alburg Springs (Special Collections, UVM)

1871: (a) as above, C. Smith* (Beers); (b) as above, W. Sears* (Beers);

1870: (a) as above (Vt Dir); <u>Merritt House</u>, A. Keeler (Vt Dir; probably same as (b) above;

1872: (b) as above, - Cutting;

1873-'75: (a) as above;

1873: (a) as above, Vt Dir; (b) as above, W. Sears (E. H. Hudson listed as proprietor in Vt Dir);

1874: (b) as above, H. H. Howe;

1875, '76: (a) as above; (b) as above;

1879, '80: (a) <u>Mansion House</u>, C. Smith; (b) <u>Springs House</u>, C. C. Knapp;

1882: (b) as above;

1883, '84: (a) as above; (b) as above, W. Sears;

1887: (a) as above; (b) as above, L. E. Brooks;

1892, '95: (a) as above, H. A. Mills; (b) as above, H. H. Howe;

1916: (b) as above, Dr John S. Goodfellow (VPB);

1915, '17, '20: (b) as above, --;

* * *

Alburg Springs House. (from an early advertising pamphlet). "Few inland water-places offer more inducements to Summer Tourists than these springs. They are particularly alluring to those who prefer the healthful sports, beautiful scenery, perfect air, and pastoral repose and simplicity of the country through the summer months, to the bustle and glitter of more fashionable centres."

* * *

(3d) East Alburg.

1871:   (a) Ames House*, George W. Ames (Beers; also PO);

1872, '73:   (a) as above;

1874:   (a) as above, A. H. Harvey;

1879, '80:   Babbitt's Hotel, T. S. Babbitt;

1881, '84:   Bay House (Bayside), A. S. ("Sax") Hilliker;

1887, '92, '95: Atlantic Hotel, George Bremmer;

1890:   Bayside House, --; (see photo);

1898:   (b) American House, W. N. Phelps and son;

1901:   Atlantic House, James Collins;

1902:   (b) as above, (CVRR); Atlantic House, J. Lee Collins (CVRR);

Bayside Inn, East Alburg

1905, '08:   (a) as above;

1915:   The Club House, --* (Sanborn);

1915, '17, '20: Missisquoi Bay Fish and Game Club, J. D. Jarvis;

1923:   Club House Inn, J. D. Chamberland (VPB);

1925:   Collins Inn, J. H. Collins (also listed in 1923 VPB with C. B. Collins); The Tavern, --; both still operating in 1940; and a place called the Trestle Inn, possibly one of these, as late as 1955.

According to the Vermont Division of Historic Preservation, there is a building still standing (Perry Honsinger home in 1981, #8 in the East Alburg Historic District) that was originally a hotel, and then a store (Washburn's) at the turn of the century. This is not on the same site as the Ames House above, which is not shown on the VDHP survey. There is never more than one hotel listed at any one time here. The Ames House is last listed in 1874, and from 1879 on, four different names appear: Babbitt's Hotel, first listed in 1879; Bay House (Bayside), first listed in 1881; the Atlantic Hotel, first listed in 1887; and the American House, first listed in 1898. It seems likely that these are not four different places, but only two; the first one replacing the Ames House, and then being replaced itself "by the turn of the century," when it became a store (and later the Honsinger home) and the other being the one that replaced it, but it has not been possible to establish whether Babbitt's became the Bay House (Bayside) and then possibly the Atlantic, or was replaced by it.

* * *

(3e) South Alburg (never had a post office).

1911, '13, '15, '20, '25:   --, Allen Tracy; Traveler's Rest, --; Hazen House, --.

(3f) West Alburg, and (3g) Windmill Point, (PO, 1853-67), no listings found.

* * *

(4) **Andover** (Windsor).

Weston was split off from Andover in 1799, and many of the early settlers, and one of the early taverns, wound up in Weston after the split

(4a) Andover (known locally as Peaseville).

c. 1780:   a tavern, Frederick Rogers; where the first town meeting was held; on the west side of Markham Mountain, in present Weston township; (1)

* * *

"Coming west from Simondsville (sic), one comes to an ancient inn just before coming down into Weston Island. This building is marked by a marble stone in the front yard. Undoubtedly, the building once was much larger than the one now standing there, but internal evidence seems to support the view that it is a very old building, and doubtless did serve at one time as an inn. The stone in front is engraved with these words: Here Frederick Rogers, Revolutionary Soldier, Town Representative for five terms, built a Tavern. First Town Meeting held here March 27, 1780."

(This place cannot now be reached from the Andover side, via Rowell's Inn in Simonsville.)

* * *

(4b) Simonsville.

1770s: first tavern in town, John Simons Jr; in what was called "Weston Island"; (2)

c. 1828: (a) Simonsville Hotel, Edward L. Simons; first PM, also owned a store;

1849: (a) as above, Alva Haseltine; --, J. B. Manning; (NEMU Dir);

1855: hotel, Mrs Barnes* (Hosea Doten map, same site as Beers, below);

1869: (a) as above, B. F. Howard* (Beers); also 1870;

1890:   (a) <u>Peabody House</u>, Mrs H. M. Peabody (probably same as <u>Simonsville Inn</u>);

1901:   (a) as above, Col. H. O. Peabody;

1911, '13:   (a) <u>Rowell's Inn</u>, -- (same as <u>Simonsville Inn</u>, see photo); bought by Frederick Rowell in 1910; VDHP 1410-2;

1915, '17:   (a) as above, F. A. Rowell;

1920:   (a) as above, Mrs Etta Warner;

ROWELL'S INN, SIMONSVILLE, VT., CHICKEN, STEAK AND TROUT DINNERS

Rowell's Inn, Simonsville

1925:   (a) as above, Mrs Abbie Rowell; closed in 1957 after 47 years operation by Rowells, restored and reopened by Lee and Beth Davis in 1983.

Note: the assistance of Peter T. Farrar, Pioneer Memorial Society, Andover, is gratefully acknowledged.

* * *

References

(1) Thelma Kalinen and Lorraine Korpi, Historical Glimpses of Andover, Vermont, 1761-1961 (n.p., 1961?).
(2) Esther M. Swift, Vermont Place-Names: Footprints of History (Brattleboro: Stephen Greene Pr., 1977).

* * *

(5) **Arlington** (Bennington).

(5a) <u>Arlington</u>.

(?):   a tavern, <u>Abel Hawley</u>;

In November, 1773, one Jacob Marsh was arrested by Seth Warner and Remember Baker, and tried at Hawley's tavern, apparently for having accepted a commission as justice of the peace under New York, and of having claimed lands under New York jurisdiction. After the hearing, he was admonished to desist, under "pains of having his house burned and reduced to ashes, and his person punished at their pleasure."

c. 1780:   Deming's Tavern, Gamaliel Deming (early settler, selectman); northwest corner of Main St (Rte 7) and Rte 313; probably had only a brief existence as a tavern, stayed in the Deming family many generations; acquired by Henry S. Hard in 1864 (shown as Hard home on 1869 Beers), Austin E. Bartlett in 1881, who converted it to the Bartlett House hotel, adding a 3-story north wing. Bartlett had been proprietor of the 1st Arlington House/Inn on Main St (see below);

1785:   Stoddard's Tavern, -- (almanac);

1786:   Elnathan Merwin's Inn; first meeting of the Fairfax proprietors held here (Child); almanacs, 1785, 1796;

1812:   Hinsdale Tavern, -- (almanac);

1849:   hotel and stage house, Thomas Edie (NEMU Dir);

1856:   Union House, H. Gray and J. B. Lathrop* (Rice and Hardwood map; same site as Beers, below);

1869:   (a) Arlington House/Inn, A. E. Bartlett* (Beers);

1870, '73, '75, '78:   (a) as above, Austin E. Bartlett;

1879, '80:   (a) as above;

1883:   (a) Arlington House, Thomas H. O'Connor; --, A. E. Bartlett (this would be the Bartlett House, the old Deming Tavern);

1887:   (a) as above, E. P. Warren; (b) Bartlett House, W. C. Bartlett;

1890:   (a) as above, W. C. Bartlett; (b) as above, W. C. Bartlett (operating both, or is this an error?); last listing, date when it ceased operating as an inn not known, now a private home;

1901:   (a) as above, E. R. Pell;

1905:   (a) as above, John McCormick;

Arlington Inn

1905-present: Hill Farm Inn, one-half mile off Rte 7A, down the road from Sunderland church and Ira Allen cemetery; built from two old farm houses; summer place, 1905-38, year round since; one of the buildings may have been a tavern earlier (photo, VHS PC);

1908: (a) as above, --; Coolidge, -- (Bartlett House under another name?);

1911, '13, '15, '20, '25 (and 1916 VPB): (a) as above, -- (summer boarding);

1917: (a) Arlington House/Inn, --; later the Arco Inn (see photo); burned in the late 1950s, a bank now on the site;

1921: (a) Arco Inn, -- (Sanborn map, PC photo, same as Arlington House/Inn);

1925: Colonial Inn/2nd Arlington Inn, --; built as a large private home for Martin C. Deming, c. 1850, became the Colonial Inn in 1925; numerous owners since, became the 2nd Arlington Inn in 1976, Stephen Lundy, still operating; VDHP 0201-1; both (a) 1st Arlington House/Inn and (c) Colonial Inn (2nd Arlington Inn) are listed in 1935 VPB, 1955 VYB);

(5b) East Arlington.

This village is very close to the Sunderland border, and places in Sunderland town sometimes have East Arlington postal addresses.

(?): Hard's Tavern, --; VDHP 0201-10, built in 1778; west side of PO, near intersection of Schaefer Rd and Main St; Clark house in 1973;

1856: a hotel, E. Lyman* (Rice and Hardwood);

1869: (a) East Arlington Hotel, N. G. Hard* (Beers; same site as in 1856);

1870: (a) as above, Norman G. Hard;

1872, '75: Green Mountain House, N. G. Hard; probably same as (a) above;

1880, '82, '85: as above;

1880: Summit House, Franklin E. Lawrence (Child; see Sunderland);

1917, '20, '25: Pleasant View, --.

(5c) West Arlington.

1878: --, George Merworth.

Note: the assistance of Joyce A. Wyman, Town Clerk, is gratefully acknowledged.

* * *

(6) **Athens** (Windham)

(6a) Athens.

c. 1820: a tavern, James Shafter; a little west of the old brick church on the old county road (part of the McCusker residence, 1960).

* * *

(7) **Bakersfield** (Franklin).

(7a) Bakersfield.

c. 1797:   first hotel, <u>Samuel Cochran</u>; in the southern part of town (Child); probably VDHP 0601-2, on Rte 108 near the Fletcher town line;

c. 1797:   first tavern, <u>Stephen Maynard</u>; at the north end of town, Leonard Cropper place in 1975 (1); VDHP 0601-30;

Note: John Maynard was a licensed tavern-keeper in 1817, '20, '21, and John and Samuel Maynard, 1815, '17; other licensees, locations unknown, were Holbrook and Kellogg, James Smith, 1818; Haseltine Sanders, 1824; Samuel Maynard, 1822; Seneca Page, 1828; Robert Deane, 1832, '33; and O. T. Houghton, 1832;

c. 1825:   a tavern, <u>Elisha Barlow</u>; tavern license, 1824-30;

c. 1830:   a tavern, <u>Charles Stone</u>; replaced by or enlarged into <u>Beals Hotel</u>, which burned in 1944 (1); Start's garage on the site in 1975;

1849:   --, C. C. Stone; --, A. E. Parker (NEMU Dir);

1855, '56:   (a) <u>Beals House</u>, E. H. Beals* (Beers; photo, ref 1); (b) <u>Chadwick House</u>, W. Chadwick* (Beers; burned on Christmas Eve, 1871, rebuilt, present Murcury block); --, L. M. Warren;

1872, '75, '78: (a) as above; (b) as above;

1879:   (a) as above; <u>Hankinson House</u>, - Robbins (probably the <u>Chadwick House</u>);

1880:   (a) as above; (b) <u>Brigham House</u>, A. J. Robbins (same as <u>Chadwick House</u>);

1881, '82, '83: (a) as above; (b) as above, Mrs R. B. Hankinson;

1887:   (a) as above;

1890, '92:   (a) as above; (b) as above, I. V. Spooner;

1895:   (b) as above, J. G. Elder (used as Academy dormitory);

1898:   (b) as above, D. P. Moore;

1901:   (b) as above, --;

1905:   (b) as above, F. A. Baldwin;

Bakersfield House

101

1908:   (b) as above, --; (photo, ref 1; site of PO);

1911, '13, '17, '20:   (b) as above, --; <u>Bakersfield House</u> (see photo; also known as <u>Boutelle Hotel</u>); photo, ref 1, listed as boarding-house in 1915;

1915:   (b) as above, --* (Sanborn); <u>Bakersfield House</u>, --* (Sanborn);

1925:   <u>Bakersfield House</u>, --; burned in 1933.

* * *

References

(1) Elsie C. Wells, Bakersfield, Vermont: The Way It Was, the Way It Is, (Canaan, N.H.: Phoenix Publ, 1976.

* * *

(8) **Barnard** (Windsor).

(8a) <u>Barnard</u> (including Silver Lake).

c. 1790:   a tavern, <u>Moses Fay</u>; almanac, 1812; a long, one-story frame house plastered on the outside, north of the common, on what was Willis Paige's lawn in 1927 (1); burned years ago;

c. 1790:   <u>Aikens Stand</u>; on the old Turnpike road which ran from Woodstock to Royalton, passing between Barnard and present village of East Barnard (intersection of present Sears and East Barnard Roads);

* * *

Exact dates not known, land bought by Solomon Aikens in 1781. He and his son Elijah ran the tavern and maintained part of the turnpike. (2) A famous hostelry for years, visited by President Monroe in 1817; and Lafayette and his entourage in 1825, on their way to Montpelier, when "the old artillery company was out in force to greet the General." (2) Present owners are William and Judith Martin. The first post office in Barnard was located here. (Photo of building, c. 1912, ref 2.; see Chapter I).

* * *

c. 1790:   a hotel, <u>Shiverick Crowell</u>; stood beside the <u>Aikens Stand</u>, less well known;

(?):   Wright tavern, -- (almanac, 1812);

c. 1825:   <u>Farmers Hotel</u>, Luther Chaney; a large two-story house with ample lawns, the second place north of the Universalist church (1). Chaney was a blacksmith, owned a sawmill and built rental houses, and was town clerk and a justice of the peace. This place was partly burned, rebuilt by Chaney, and closed as a hotel when he died in 1848; a tenement at one point. Occupied in 1987 by the John Barnes family;

1832:   (a) <u>Silver Lake Hotel</u>, Rodney C. Caryl; in the village, at the foot of the lake. Place changed hands at least seven times in thirteen years, starting in 1837: Solon Danforth, Norman Dunham and Isaac Ayers; Danforth (with Zeb Twitchell running it); Albert H. Danforth; Solon Danforth again; Hiram Aikens, Warren Aikens and Russell Topliff as managers; bought in 1850 by William S. French for $2,000 and soon transferred to Celim E. French, under whose long reign (1850-88) the place became a famous summer resort (See photo, next page.) Henry O. French succeeded Celim, but it finally went out of business in the early part of the century. Last owned by Dorothy Thompson, author and newspaper columnist, but her remodeling plans were too expensive and the building was dismantled in 1936 (photos, refs 1-3);

1820s(?):   Tappan Stand; on the stage road to Woodstock (l);

1820s(?):   "On the road from Barnard to Bethel down the Creek road there were at least four hotels" (1); (see a to d below; creek referred to is Locust Creek, with present Rte 12 running along it, corresponding in part to the Woodstock-Montpelier stage road); (a) a hotel, Duty and Graty Brown; "where Frank White lately lived" (i.e., 1927); Deacon George Townsend also kept a hotel at this same place, built by Prince Haskell and Capt Edwin W. Haskell, his son; (b) "On the old Fort Defiance farm, the Hammond house was built for a hotel"; (1) home of Ralph and Andrea Ward in 1982 (photo, ref 2); c) "the brick house next north was the Wright tavern (see above, 1812), built by James Wright Sr c. 1820 and kept by his son, Thomas M. Wright"; on the Woodstock-Montpelier stage road, VDHP 1403-19, torn down about 1975, site of the Ariel Gilman home in 1982 (photo, ref 2); (d) "in the little hamlet of Newcombsville" (near the Bethel line on present Rte 12) "the two houses next south of the Albert Newton house (i.e., 1927) was the Steward stand (sic) where Lyman Steward and his wife Rocksalaney...cared for transients" (1);

Silver Lake House

1849:   --, H. Aikens (NEMU Dir);

1855, '56:   (a) Silver Lake House, Celim E. French* (shown as French Hotel on Hosea Doten map, 1855);

1869:   (a) as above, C. E. French* (Beers);

1870, '72-'87:   (a) as above;

1890, '92, '95, '98:   (a) as above, Henry O. French;

1901, '02, '05:   (a) as above, Ebenezer Holmes; Wayside Inn, H. French;

1908:   (a) as above, --; Wayside Inn, --;

1911, '13, '15:   (a) as above, Burt G. Cady;

1915:   (a) as above, Burt Cady* (Sanborn);

1917:   (a) Silver Lake House, a boarding-house; but the Lakeside Tavern, Charles M. Charlton, in 1923 (VPB);

(?):   Barnard Inn, --; the old Gayle house, once the Gay Winds Riding School, the

103

Barnard Inn since 1975; still operating 1987, on Rte 12, about one mile south of Silver Lake;

1925:   Foster Lodge, --; built around the Churchill place, on a hill overlooking Silver Lake; burned in 1972 (photo, ref 2).

(8b) East Barnard.

1839:   Tontine House, Chauncey Walcott; built by him, served as a tavern for some time; home of the Spencer Johnsons in 1982 (photo, ref 2);

1905:   --, M. E. Waters; --, F. M. Chase.

* * *

References

(1) William H. Newton, History of Barnard, Vermont, 1761-1927 (Montpelier: Vermont Hist. Soc., 1928).

(2) Barnard Historical Society, Barnard...A Look Back (Randolph Ctr: Greenhills Books, 1982).

(3) Alvin Peck, History of Barnard, 1927-1975 (Taftsville: Countryman Pr., 1975).

* * *

(9) **Barnet** (Caledonia).

(9a) Barnet.

1796:   Gilchrist tavern, --; listed in the Vermont Almanac and Register as a stage stop on the Windsor-St Johnsbury road, location unknown;

1797:   first hotel, Enos Stevens; almanacs, 1796, 1805; where W. S. Brock's house stood in 1923; (1) still the Brock house, across Rte 5 from the Barnet grocery store;

* * *

Stevens Tavern. Founded in 1791, according to Wyman Parker. (2) Place carried on by Enos's widow and then their son, Henry Stevens Sr, after Enos's death (tavern license for Henry, 1822-27). "In the latter's time...one of the best known inns in the North Country." (1) Henry Stevens was a farmer and mill-owner in addition to being an inn-keeper, and an antiquarian and book-collector. He was one of the founders of the Vermont Historical Society and a proprietor of the Passumpsic Turnpike. The tavern was called "The Sheaves" in his time; also PM from 1834-47, with the office in the inn. The tavern was kept by Phineas Stevens after Henry moved to Burlington, and burned with the Chappell Block in 1891.

* * *

(?):   a tavern, --; on the south corner of Main and Depot Sts; place destroyed by mud from Mill Hill during the flood of 1927, when John Robinson lived there;

Note: tavern licenses to John Duncan, 1823; Jazaniah Whitney, 1822; Brown and Emerson, 1824-27; and Clark Cushman, 1822-27, locations unknown;

1849:   Barnet House, Phineas Stevens; Railroad House, H. Quimby (NEMU Dir);

1849:   Green Mountain House, William Gleason; where Walker's Inn stood in 1927; (1) dedicated with a grand ball on January 9, 1849; "Mrs Gleason made it a rule to always grace the dining room with her person at meal time, and sat at the head of the table"; burned in 1863; George Greenbanks later built another hotel on the site, which was christened "Nilsson House" in honor of the Swedish singer, Christine Nilsson (see below); the place may have existed under another name between 1863 and 1874;

* * *

"In 1874 the hotel was owned by Robert Harvey, operated by Stillman Hazelton. Miss Nilsson was traveling with a large party, some of whom were in a great four-horse coach, and others were on horseback. The proprietor had notice of their coming and prepared a great supper. After it Miss Nilsson sang in the parlor and many of the citizens gathered on the piazza and at the open windows to hear her sing. After singing, the songstress drew a little child who was standing by the piano into her lap and kissed her, something which that lady recalls with pride. The party stayed at the hotel all night."

(?):   a tavern, Jonathan Wallace; building owned in 1923 by "Mr Douglas";

1855:   --, William Gleason Jr (this is the Green Mountain House);

1858:   --, W. Gleason Jr* (Walling; as above);

1870:   --, D. M. Clark;

1870:   Barnet House, Seth Ford;

1874:   (a) Barnet House, Robert Harvey; Dr H. J. Hazelton bought the tavern from the Harvey estate, sold it to his brother Lorenzo D. Hazelton; Charles Greenbanks was the next owner, and George Walker was the owner when it burned in the fall of 1913. Walker's Inn was built on the site next year, became the Dunbar Apartments, now (1988) a boarding-house for students at a meditation center;

1873, '75, '78: (a) Nilsson House, S. J. Hazelton* (Beers);

1879:   (a) as above, C. B. Hall;

1880:   (a) as above, C. S. (?) Greenbank;

1883:   (a) as above, C. T. Greenbank; (b) Traveler's Rest, Mrs S. Brock (VDHP 0301-68, #1, Brock's Inn, now a private home);

1887:   (a) as above, C. T. Greenbank; (b) as above, William S. Brock;

1890:   (a) as above, --; (b) as above; Wilson House, C. T. Greenbank;

1892:   (a) Nilsson House, A. H. Cheney; (b) Traveler's Rest, W. S. Brock; operated as Brock's Inn as late as 1955;

1895:   (a) as above, R. P. Lindsay;

1898:   (a) as above, W. M. Hunt;

1901:   (a) as above, Charles T. Greenbank; Shaw's Tavern, Charles E. Shaw;

1905:   (a) as above (burned in 1913); Cottage Hotel, W. P. Holton;

c. 1910:   Walker's Hotel, --; VDHP 0301-71, on the east side of Town Highway 99 where it intersects with TH 101; on the site of the Nilsson House, later an apartment house;

1915: Barnet House, --* (Sanborn, corner of Carter and Main); this must be a different place than the Barnet House of 1849, '70, said to have burned in 1891;

1917, '20:   Walker's Inn, G. A. Walker (built in 1914);

1925:   Old Homestead, Mrs C. E. Spafford; an overnight guest house at the north end of the village, still in use.

(9b) East Barnet (formerly Norrisville, McLerans).   No listings found.

(9c) McIndoes Falls.

1849:   (a) McIndoes Falls House, Flint and Whales; built c. 1830 (VDHP 0301-140, #13);

1870:   --, Frank Cowles;

1870:   --, Bibbie and Dewey (Vt Dir);

1872:   (a) McIndoes Hotel, --;

1873, '75:   (a) McIndoes Hotel, C. Dewey* (Beers);

1878:   --, S. F. Leighton;

1879, '80:   (a) as above, Van Dyke and Merrill;

1883:   --, George Van Dyke (probably McIndoes Hotel); (b) Bishop House, Ora Bishop; --, A. B. Perry;

1887, '90, '92: (b) as above;

1895, '98:   (b) as above; --, George F. Winch;

1919:   (a) McIndoes Hotel now a boarding house*; torn down about 1930; (Sanborn); Pleasant View Hotel, --* (Sanborn);

Note: There was a major fire in McIndoes Falls in 1923; perhaps the Bishop House burned at that time.

(9d) Passumpsic.

* * *

"The village was greatly assisted by the Passumpsic Turnpike, over which there was a vast amount of teaming. There were three taverns at that place all well patronized, for teamsters who came down from the towns above usually stopped over night there before beginning their journey on the 'pike'. " (1)

* * *

c. 1810:   (a) a tavern on the corner of Main and River Streets, Proctor Thayer or his son-in-law Ora B. Partridge, as an early landlord. This is the old Passumpsic Inn, VDHP 0301-9, now the Donald Merchant home. Operated by one of the Thayer family before and after 1850, and by Seth Ford for two to three years. "This tavern was quite a popular resort...serving refreshment for man and beast, sometimes transforming the man into a beast, to the edification of the small boys." (1) There is a building on the corner of Main and Mill Sts (perhaps River St earlier) labeled "M. Thayer estate" on the 1858 Walling; (b) another tavern across the street, possibly built by Jacob Kendall, burned c. 1850. "It was a great event...to see this huge Concord coach with its six or eight horses, swing up and stop in front of the tavern and see the hostlers rush out, unhitch the tired horses and hitch up the fresh ones, already harnessed. Meanwhile the great leather mail pouch was carried by two men into the same room where the Post Office is now (i.e., 1923, ref 1) and Levi P. Parks, the postmaster, and his clerk, emptied the contents of the bag upon a table, sorting out the letters and other matter belonging there. The balance of the mail was returned to the pouch and sent along as soon as the fresh horses were ready"; (c) a tavern, <u>Clark Cushman</u>; tavern license, 1822-24; in a large square brick house about one-half mile below the village, place now (i.e., 1988) owned by Bernard Willey;

1849: <u>Passumpsic Hotel</u>, Seth Ford;

Note: according to the St Johnsbury Republican in 1896, one Darius Harvey built the first hotel in Passumpsic...still standing in 1896; would it have been Ford's, above?

(9e) <u>West Barnet</u>.

(?): a tavern, <u>Walter Harvey</u>; tavern license, 1822-27; on the Hazen Road in the "Mosquitoville" area (southwest corner of the town); bought by William McPhee in 1850; where the Hazen Road crosses the line from Ryegate at the bridge over Jewett Brook (photo, ref 1).

Note: the assistance of the late Mr Robert Warden, Barnet Historical Society, and Mr and Mrs Elmer Faris, Groton, is gratefully acknowledged.

* * *

References

(1) Frederick P. Wells, History of Barnet, Vermont, 1760-1923 (Burlington: Free Press Pr., 1923).
(2) Wyman Parker, "The Young Henry Stevens," Vermont History News (May-June, 1986).

* * *

(10) **Barre** (Washington).

(10a) <u>Barre</u>.

c. 1802: a tavern, <u>Chapin Keith</u>; tavern license, 1822-30; on the Chelsea Turnpike east of the village, in the area known as Gospel village; a rambling white building, still standing at 172 Washington St, location #33 on map in ref 1; also photo;

* * *

Keith was "warned out of town" when he came in 1797, lest he become a charge on the town. He became high sheriff, probate court judge, and a well-to-do person, and he told the story that the tavern was built with the fees that accrued to him during just one year as sheriff. (Child)

* * *

Note: almanacs list <u>Worker and Davis</u> tavern in 1802, and <u>Worker</u> in 1807;

c. 1805: a tavern, --; in Gospel Village, a hamlet at the northeastern edge of Barre village (location #30 on map, ref 1);

Note: tavern licenses to James Paddock, 1817-24; Henry Keyes, 1820-23; Solomon Wheeler, 1822; John Hale, 1822-32; Mark Goss, 1826, '27; Richard F. Abbott, 1827; Laban Blodgett, 1830; Samuel Harrington, 1832; Joseph Brown, 1832; and J. P. Pinney, 1832;

(?): an early tavern, <u>Apollos Hale</u>; at the "Lower Village," later run by James Hale, tavern license 1822; Apollos licensed, 1817-21; not clear where this is, either Barre village or East Barre; but see below;

1849:   (a) <u>Twingsville Hotel</u>, Silas Town, Jr; (Twingsville was an early settlement at the north end of town); <u>Village Hotel</u>, James Hale (NEMU Dir);

1856:   (a) as above, - Nye; --, Mrs Eunice Hall;

1858:   (a) <u>Nye's Hotel</u>, S. Nye Jr (Twingsville hotel)* (Walling); (b) a hotel, H. Richardson* (Walling); close to location #15 in ref 1; this place apparently burned in 1857, since Child refers to a fire then destroying the hotel on the site of the "late E. E. French's residence," which is shown on Beers close to location #15;

* * *

When the Goddard Seminary was being built, there was no public house in Barre, and Leonard F. Aldrich's home was hotel for the workmen; Aldrich was very active in promoting and building the academy (1866-68); the seminary opened in 1870. (Child)

* * *

1870:   (a) as above, H. A. Peck;

1873:   (a) as above* (Beers, same location as Nye's in 1858); (b) <u>Cottage Hotel</u>, L. T. Tucker* (Beers, not the same site as <u>Richardson's</u> in 1858, but a little east of location #7 on map in ref 1);

Major Barre Hotels

(a) Twingsville Hotel (Nye's)	(e) Octagon House
(b) Cottage Hotel	(f) Central House
(c) 1st Hotel Barre	(g) City Hotel (Avenue)
(d) Avenue House (City Hotel)	(h) Northern Hotel
	(i) 2nd Hotel Barre

* * *

1875:   (b) as above, S. R. Ordway;

1879:   (c) 1st <u>Barre Hotel/Hotel Barre</u>, Elgin J. Gale; <u>Traveler's Home</u>, Crawford H. Jackson (may be in East Barre); <u>Evmar House</u>, E. J. Gale (may be in East Barre);

1880:   (c) as above; (d) <u>Avenue House</u>, M. Andrews; <u>Traveler's Home</u>, C. H. Jackson;

1883:   (e) <u>Octagon House</u>, O. H. Thompson;

1887:   (c) as above, H. A. Rugg; (e) as above, A. W. Spaulding; (f) <u>Central House</u>, Fred L. Hayden; <u>Park House</u>, Kimball Blanchard;

1889:   (c) <u>Barre Hotel</u>, --*; (f) <u>Central Hotel</u>, --*; (Sanborn);

1889:   (c) as above; (f) as above (N. Main); <u>Granite House</u>, George W. French (43 S. Main); <u>Park House</u> (16 N. Main);

1890:   (c) as above; (f) as above, George W. Jeffords;

1892:   (f) as above; <u>Union House</u>, M. J. Tierney;

1894:   (f) <u>Central</u>, --* (Sanborn); (d) <u>Avenue House</u>, --* (Sanborn, on Washington between Church and Elm Sts; became the <u>City Hotel</u> by 1900; see photo, next page);

1895:   (f) as above, J. D. Ryan; (d) Avenue House, A. D. Burgess;

1898:   (f) as above, --; (g) City Hotel, E. F. Gale; American House, George Gealse(?); Commercial House, Charles Johnson;

1900:   (f) Central, (g) City, and Phoenix, all on Sanborn;

1901:   (g) as above, K. W. Morse;

1905:   (g) as above; Windsor House, Amos R. Hall; (h) Northern Hotel, Norman and Drew;

1908:   (g) as above, --; (h) as above, --;

1911:   (g) as above, --; (h) as above, --;

1913:   (g) as above, William H. Snow; New Hotel Otis, --;

1915:   (i) Barre Hotel, - Buzzell;

1917, '20:   Buzzell Hotel, A. H. Buzzell; (i) Hotel Barre, J. V. Rowen (built in 1915; this is apparently the 2nd Hotel Barre);

1925:   (f) Central House, A. A. and E. T. Boyce; (i) as above.

(10b) East Barre.

1873:   (a) Barre Springs House, S. Bruce; VDHP 1205-254, built c. 1860, also known as Spring House Inn; now apartments; on the 1873 Beers as Spring House, S. Bruce Jr; on Rte 302, 1.5 miles east of Barre city line;

City Hotel, Barre

* * *

1879:   (a) as above, J. M. Hutchinson;

1890:   (a) as above, C. S. George; American Hotel, H. L. Doyle;

1892:   (a) as above, Frank Jones;

Note: an 1899 City Directory lists the Centennial House, Amos A. Hall, in East Barre;

1898:   (b) Riverside Hotel, W. E. Bixby* (1900 Sanborn);

1901: (b) as above, --.

(10c) Graniteville.

1898: Granite House, E. J. Woodbury;

c. 1903: Graniteville House, J. Chymowseth (VHS photo, c. 1893; presumably same as above).

(10d) South Barre.

c. 1802: first tavern, Major Ira Day; across the road from the Smith House (location #43, ref 1); "an imposing high building, no longer standing"; Badger and Porter's Stage Register, 1828;

* * *

Day was one of Barre's earliest and most successful entrepreneurs. His inn sheltered General Lafayette and his entourage during Lafayettte's tour of New England in 1826; Day is said to have had the interior of his tavern covered with a heavy paper, imported from Paris for the occasion, and to have furnished a coach and six white horses to carry the General over the turnpike through Williamstown Gulf. With Mr Cottrell of Montpelier, Day owned the first stage and mail route from Boston to Burlington; he also owned a number of local mills and stores.

* * *

(?): an early tavern, James Paddock (Hemenway); almanacs, 1825, '29.

(10e) Websterville. No listings found.

Note: the assistance of Verbena Pastor, Curator, Aldrich Public Library, is gratefully acknowledged.

* * *

References

(1) Carroll Fenwick, ed., Barre in Retrospect, 1776-1976 (Barre: Friends of the Aldrich Public Library, 1975).

* * *

(11) **Barton** (Orleans).

(11a) Barton (including Crystal Lake).

c. 1800: first tavern, Stephen K. Dexter;

Note: almanac lists a Pillsbury tavern, 1802, '05, location unknown; tavern licenses to James Pillsbury, 1817, '22; Stephen Thomas, 1827-30; Ellis Cobb, 1817; - Mansfield, 1827; Augustus Kimball, 1828; Thankful Smith, 1826; William B. Eastman, 1825, '26; Daniel B. Smith, 1817-25; George W. Kimball, 1817, '30; James Rugg, 1829; Moses Killen, 1830; Jonathan Killam, 1830, '32; Francis Way, 1832; and Norman Nye, 1833;

c. 1800: a tavern, Asa Kimball; his tavern said to be the first by Walbridge; (1) until 1816, but licenses 1823-'30;

1814: an inn, <u>Jonathan Robinson</u>; (3)

1849: --, C. Holman; --, H. Smith (see above); <u>Barton Hotel</u> (1st), F. W. Kimball (NEMU Dir; a George W. Kimball has a license in 1817);

1855: --, A. A. and L. Bucks (Walton);

1856: --, Hills and Merrill;

1858: <u>Hotel Barton</u>, run by Hill and Buck; and the <u>Railway Hotel</u>; both referred to in a Tourist's Handbook, 1859, the year after the railroad came through to Barton;

1859: --, R. H. Little* (Walling; this place does not correspond to any of the three hotel sites shown on the 1878 Beers map); --, H. Nye* (Walling; on the site of the <u>Crystal Lake House</u> in Beers, 1878; but probably replaced by it, since D. G. Hoyt, Orleans County Historical Society, has pointed out an 1860 newspaper reference stating that "Horatio Nye's Upper Inn burns");

1870, '72, '73: (a) <u>Crystal Lake House</u>, R. H. Little; (see photo);

1873: <u>Nelson House</u>, H. J. Haselton (Vt Dir);

1875: (a) as above, V. N. Spaulding;

1878: (a) as above* (Beers); (b) <u>Foster's Hotel</u>, E. H. Foster* (Beers; in what was originally Joseph B. Leland's home; Leland came in 1809; Foster's eventually became the <u>American House</u>); a hotel, --* (Beers; no name attached to this building on the square; it is probably the <u>Railroad Hotel</u>, at the intersection of Main and Church Sts);

1879, '80: (a) as above; (b) as above, N. P. Courser;

1883: (a) as above, H. E. Harris; (b) as above, E. H. Foster (Child);

1886: (a) as above, --* (Sanborn; shown also in 1892, '97, 1912, '22 and '28); (b) <u>American House</u>, --* (Sanborn; shown also in 1892, formerly <u>Foster's</u>);

1887: (a) as above, George E. Leith; (b) <u>American House</u>, George Haslett; both shown on an 1889 birdseye view; (5)

1890: (a) as above, Martin Dingman;

1892: (a) as above, Frank Shepard; (b) as above, H. L. Doyle;

Crystal Lake House

111

1895:   (a) as above, Charles Cheney; (b) as above, F. B. Lang; this place apparently burned or was razed at about this time; it is no longer listed, but replaced by the 2nd Hotel Barton (see below); see photo;

Hotel Barton

1898:   (a) as above, Howard Lindsay; (c) Hotel Barton, Elliott and Pattee; built in 1895 (1), operated until it burned in 1972; shown on Sanborn for 1897, 1904, '12, '22, '28;

1901:   (a) as above, H. G. Spaulding; (c) as above, H. F. Pillsbury and son;

1908:   (a), (c) as above, --;

1911:   (a) as above, John McAuley; (c) as above, John V. Rowan;

1913:   (a) as above, --; (c) as above, John V. Rowan;

1915:   (a) as above, -- (summers); (c) as above;

1920:   (a) as above, A. D. Seaver, operated until at least 1940; the Crystal Lake House building still stands as a bar and grill; (c) as above, Charles Darling;

1925:   (c) as above, G. I. Lincoln (burned in 1972, site now occupied by an apartment for the elderly);

(11b) Orleans (Barton Landing until 1909).

1833:   a tavern, Jesse Cook; in the second frame house in town; (2)

1834:   (a) Valley House, --; still operating (1988), said by present owner to have been built in 1834; on site of first tavern, kept by Jesse Cook; but the present Valley House was moved to this site at a later date;

1849:   --, H. Smith (NEMU Dir; who succeeded Cook in 1841);

1855:   --, Harris Smith;

1856:   --, Gilman Esty;

1859:   a hotel, --* (Walling);

1870:   (a) Valley House, John Colby;

112

1872, '75, '80, '83 (Child), '87, '90, '92:   (a) as above, J. H. Brown;

1878:   (a) --, J. Brown* (Beers, same site as 1859); Hygia, C. W. Cade* (Beers);

1879:   Riverside House, G. L. Gilman;

1887:   (a) as above, --* (Sanborn; also for 1895, 1900, 1905);

1895, '98, 1901, '05, '11, '13, '15, '17: (a) as above, E. H. Lathrop; who acquired it from Brown in 1891, continued until 1917; on 1910 Sanborn map;

1920, '25: (a) as above, F. J. Parlin (1922, '28 Sanborn);

1939:   (a) Valley House badly damaged by fire, its appearance drastically changed by rebuilding; still operating.

(11c) South Barton (became second Willoughby postally in 1909, for neighboring Lake Willoughby; no listings found).

Note: the assistance of Mr D. G. Hoyt, Orleans County Historical Society, is gratefully acknowledged.

* * *

References

(1) J. H. Walbridge, Barton--One Hundred Years, 1796-1896 (Barton: Orleans County Monitor, 1896).
(2) Benjamin F. D. Carpenter, "History of Barton Landing," Orleans County Historical Society Proceedings (1892): 1-14.
(3) Darrel Hoyt, Sketches of Orleans, Vermont, John Hayford, ed. (Brownington: Orleans County Historical Society, 1985).
(4) Darrel G. Hoyt, ed., Orleans, Formerly Barton Landing: Sesquicentennial, 1820-1970 (Enosburg Falls: Pel-Mac Pr., 1970).
(5) J. Kevin Graffagnino, Vermont in the Victorian Age (Bennington: Vermont Heritage Press, 1985).

* * *

(12) **Belvidere** (Lamoille).

(12a) Belvidere. No listings found.

(12b) Belvidere Center. No listings found.

(12c) Belvidere Corners.

1873:   --, O. Thomson;

1879:   --, Joseph Wescom;

1887:   --, Waldo Potter;

1890:   --, John Prince;

1892, '95, '98, 1901, '05, '08, '11, '13: Pond House, A. P. Brown;

1915, '17:   --, A. P. Brown.

* * *

(13) **Bennington** (Bennington).

      Bennington's first post office was established here in 1789, in the village on the hill now known as Old Bennington. It was just plain Bennington until 1849, by which time the "east village" (present day Bennington) had outstripped it. It then became West Bennington briefly, until protests lead to its being changed to Bennington Center. This name was also not popular with the residents of the older village, but it stuck until the office closed in 1889. Present Bennington (the second Bennington postally) was East Bennington from 1844-1849, before becoming Bennington. There is also a North Bennington.

      (13a) Bennington (Old Bennington).

      c. 1762:   a tavern, James Fassett; early town meetings held here;

      1764:   Dewey Inn, Elijah Dewey; became the Walloomsac Inn, see below; listed in the Vermont Almanac (1796) as a tavern on the Rutland-Troy road;

* * *

      Built by Elijah Dewey, son of Bennington's first minister, who ran it until 1796; women from the Dewey House cooked food for British and Hessian prisoners after the Battle of Bennington (1). Visited by Jefferson and Madison in 1791, and by Rutherford B. Hayes in 1877, by which time it was the Walloomsac House (see photo). Also visited by the abolitionist William Ellery Channing, who died there. See ref 1 for a portrait of Elijah Dewey and an 1890s picture of the Walloomsac House. VDHP 0202-12, probably the oldest inn in the state in terms of continuous operation (see Appendix C, Hotel Longevity).

      1769:   Catamount Tavern, Stephen Fay;

* * *

      Headquarters for Ethan Allen and the Green Mountain Boys in the 1770s, this place had a stuffed catamount on top of the signpost. Burned in 1871, the site is marked with a granite pedestal and bronze catamount. See ref 1 for 1861, 1869 photos.

* * *

      (?):   VDHP 0202-64, on the west side of Rte 7A at the intersection with Town Line Rd, near the Shaftsbury line; built c. 1800, reportedly once a tavern;

      (?):   VDHP 0202-90, west side of Rte 7, 0.2 miles south of Carpenter Hill Rd intersection, south of Bennington; built c. 1770, reportedly once a tavern.

      c. 1770:   David Harmon Inn; on the Vail Road, where Gen John Stark and his staff ate dinner Aug 14, 1777, on their way to the Battle of Bennington; see photo of ruins, 1919, below;

      1772:   Dimmick Tavern, --; on the West Road, near the five day encampment; once owned by Col Herrick, burned in 1869 (drawing in Resch);

      1780:   State Arms Hotel, --; its site was on the present Monument lawn; popular through the early 1800s (photo, ref 2);

      1797:   Thomas's New England Almanack lists Dewey's, Fay's, Hathaway's and Griswold's taverns; same for 1802, 1825, 1829; other almanac listings: M'Ewen, 1812; Billing, 1785 (see East Village); Hopkins, 1785;

      Note: there is a photo of the sign for an "E. Noyes" tavern in ref 3; this place is

114

unidentified;

Walloomsac Inn (Special Collections, UVM)

1822: tavern licenses to William Henry, George Gay, Henry Fassett, Charles Cushman, James Hicks Jr, Joseph House, Alanson Briggs, Jacob Lyon, David Weeks and Cyrus Hill, locations unknown;

1842: Walton lists eight hotels in Bennington this year without distinguishing between the three villages; only three of them can be clearly identified; they are all listed here with the understanding that some of the unidentified places were probably in present Bennington and North Bennington instead of Old Bennington:

State Arms, David Love (see above); Franklin House, M. Robinson (Bennington); --, S. Butler; --, J. Lyons; --, J. Loomis (probably Loomis House in North Bennington, which appears to be a predecessor of the Paran Creek House); --, James Hicks; --, D. Huling; --, T. J. Albro;

1849: Loomis Hotel, Jessie Loomis (probably North Bennington); --, G. W., F. W., and H. F. Robinson (NEMU Dir);

1855: --, J. Ranney;

1856: (a) Walloomsac House, --* (Rice and Hardwood);

1869: (a) as above, Alfred Robinson* (Beers); (b) Old Catamount Tavern, J. Fay* (Beers);

1870, '71, '73, '79, '80, '83, '87: (a) as above;

1890: (a) as above, Mrs J. Walter Longley;

1901, '05, '08, '13: (a) as above, W. H. Berry (summers); Berry bought the place in 1891, remodeled it, and it is still in the Berry family;

1917:   (a) as above, Mrs Harriet E. Twitchell;

Harmon Inn

1920, '25:   (a) as above, W. H. Berry; described by Resch (1) as belonging to the Berry family and still in business in 1975; not operating in 1987;

(13b) <u>Bennington</u> (East village, present Bennington).

(?):   a tavern, <u>Samuel Billings</u>; on the then main road to Pownal; building still standing, occupied by Thomas Jewett, c. 1880 (Child), west of road 68; a tavern in the 1760s-70s;

c. 1800:   <u>Crow Tavern</u>, Capt Hill; on the "Hunt place" (1); a Cyrus Hill had a tavern license in 1822;

early 1800s   (a) <u>Gates House/Hotel</u>, --; modernized in 1873, but mostly a boarding-house in its later years; burned in 1882;

1849:   (b) <u>Stark House</u>, Lewis Cady; (c) <u>Franklin House</u>, David Love; <u>Oregon House</u>, J. R. Gates (<u>Gates House</u> under another name?);

1852:   (c) <u>Franklin House</u>, D. Love* (Presdee and Edwards);

1855:   --, David Love (probably the <u>State Arms</u>); --, T. J. Albro; --, E. Wordsworth;

1869:   (a) <u>Gates Hotel</u>, R. Gates* (Beers); (b) <u>Stark Hotel</u>, Mrs Cady* (Beers);

1870:   (a) as above, John R. Gates; (b) as above, Mrs L. Cady;

1873:   (d) <u>Putnam House</u>, --; corner of Main and South Sts on the Franklin House site;

* * *

<u>Putnam House</u>. A large 3-story place built by Henry W. Putnam in 1873; on the site of the <u>Mt Anthony House</u>, an earlier hotel on the site which burned in 1868. It contained railway company offices and was a popular gathering place for men. Many rooms were rented on a long term basis to "lodgers." Leading hotel in its day. Vermont law between 1852 and 1903 prohibited the sale of liquor in inns, and according to Resch, both the <u>Putnam House</u> and the <u>Stark Hotel</u> were closed in 1889 after a raid. VDHP 0202--13, vacant in 1974; there is a UVM stereo of opening day. See photo.

1873:   (a) as above; (b) as above, William H. Cady;

116

1875:   (a), (b) as above; (d) <u>Putnam House</u>, --;

Putnam House

1878:   (a) <u>Gates House</u>, Lewis M. Gates; (b) <u>Stark House</u>, William H. Cady; (d) <u>Putnam House</u>, D. W. Wright; (e) <u>Elm Tree House</u>, M. Healy (later the <u>American</u>); (f) <u>Centennial House</u>, Cornelius Nolan (Dolan?; later the <u>Columbian</u>); (b), (d) and (f) shown on 1877 birdseye view; (4)

1879:   (a) <u>Gates House</u>, L. B. Ranney; (b) <u>Stark House</u>, C. F. Wilcox; (e) <u>Elm Tree House</u>, M. Healy; (f) <u>Centennial House</u>, Cornelius Nolan; (g) <u>O'Donnell House</u>, Daniel O'Donnell (all Vt Dir listings);

Major Bennington Hotels

(a) Gates House/Hotel   (f) Centennial (Columbian)
(b) Stark House/Hotel   (g) O'Donnell House
(c) Franklin House   (h) Godfrey House
(d) Putnam House   (i) Cottage (Burgess, Webster)
(e) Elm Tree House (American)

* * *

1880:   Hamilton Child lists: (a) <u>Gates House</u>, C. F. Wilcox (119 E. Main, burned in 1882); (b) <u>Stark House</u>, Luther B. Ranney (6-10 East Main); note that these first two managers are reversed from the Vt Dir for 1879, discrepancy unresolved; (d) <u>Putnam House</u>, L. Collins; (e) <u>Elm Tree House</u>, Michael Healy (northwest corner, North and River Sts); (f) <u>Centennial House</u>, Cornelius Nolan (southeast corner, Depot and River Sts, opp. depot); (g) <u>O'Donnell House</u>, C. J. Wheeler (corner of River and Railroad Sts); (Walton confirms);

1883:   (a) as above, I. Palmer Wood (burned in 1882); (b) as above, G. E. Town; (d) as above, L. Collins; (e) as above; (f) as above, --; (g) as above, C. J. Wheeler; (h) <u>Godfrey House</u>, J. M. Haley (sp?);

1885:   Note: Sanborn map shows (b), (d), (e), (f), (g) and (h) <u>Godfrey House</u> (on the west side of East Main St, across the river);

1887:   (b) as above, Geo. E. Towne; (d) as above, F. H. Deming; (e) as above; (f) as above, Mrs C. Nolan; (g) as above, (h) as above, J. H. Healy (sp?);

1890:   (b) as above, L. Collins; (d) as above, Lucius Collins (?); (e) as above, M. J. Guilfian; (f) as above;

1891:   Note: Sanborn shows (b), (d), (e), (f), (g), and (i) Cottage Hotel; (h) the Godfrey has become a paper box company;

1892:   (d), (e), and (f) as above; (i) Cottage Hotel, Hiram B. Fassett (later the Burgess, Webster);

1895:   (d) as above; (f) as above, J. J. Morrissey; (e) American House, M. Healy and son (formerly the Elm Tree House); (f) Columbian House, J. J. Morrissey (formerly the Centennial);

1896:   Note: Sanborn shows (b), (d), and (g); (e) Elm Tree now the American; (f) Centennial now the Columbian; (i) Cottage Hotel (on Main St, opp. the Putnam House and down the block) now the Burgess House ; and (h) Godfrey House still a paper box company;

1901:   (d) as above, L. Collins; (e) American, E. A. Shaw;

1901:   Note: the Sanborn shows (d), (e) American (formerly Elm Tree), (f), (g) and (i) Burgess (formerly Cottage, now Webster House);

1905:   (d) as above, Fred B. Howe; (e) American, J. H. Leahy; (f) Columbian, --; Prouty Inn, C. H. Prouty;

1906:   (d) Putnam; (e) American; (f) Columbian; (g) O'Donnell (again); (i) Webster/Burgess now the Cottage again;

1906:   Note: the Sanborn map shows (d), (e), (f), (g), and (i) Webster/Burgess, now Cottage again;

1908:   (d) as above, --; (e) as above, --; (f) as above, --;

1911:   (d) as above, P. C. Cornell; (e) as above, D. J. Cronin; (i) Cottage Hotel, John Leahy (later the Burgess, Webster);

1912:   Note: the Sanborn shows (f) Columbian as tenements; (e), (i) as before;

1913:   (d) as above, --; (e) as above, --; (i) as above, --;

1917:   (d) as above, P. C. Cornell; (e), (i) as above;

1920:   (d) as above, C. H. Stafford; (i) as above, --;

1921:   Note: the Sanborn shows (f) Columbian as hotel again; (d) Putnam and (e) American as before;

1925:   (d) as above, --; (f) as above, --; Hotel Bennington, --; Commercial Hotel, --; Leader House, --.

1925:   Note: Sanborn shows (d) Putnam House, and (f) Columbian; (e) the American is gone; also, there is now a Commercial Hotel on the south side of Main St, around the corner from Putnam, later the King Hotel; and the Hotel Bennington, northwest corner of River and North Sts. The Putnam House/Hotel Putnam operated until at least 1955.

(13c) North Bennington.

1842, '49:   see Loomis under (13a);

1855:   --, N. Loomis;

1856:   (a) Paran Creek House, N. B. Loomis* (Rice and Hardwood);

1869:   (b) as above, G. S. Wright* (Beers);

1870, '73:   (a) as above; (b) Bennington House, Josiah S. Carpenter;

1879, '80, '80 (Child): (a) as above, Charles Wright; (b) as above, C. D. Colvin;

1883:   (a) as above; (b) as above, J. Edward Walbridge; American House, J. Hitt;

1887:   (a) as above, G. S. Wright; (b) as above, W. H. Reed; Empire House, W. H. Reed, Vt Dir);

1890:   (a) Paran Creek House, -- (photo, ref 1); (b) as above, C. A. Myers;

1892, '95:   (b) as above, P. H. McCarthy; see photo, 1st page, Appendix E;

1898:   (a) Paran Creek has become the White Hotel, W. R. White; (b) as above;

1901:   (a) Hotel White, W. R. White; (b) (North) Bennington House, P. H. McCarthy;

1905:   (a) Hotel White, W. R. White (see photo); (b) as above;

1908, '11, '13: (a) Hotel White, W. R. White.

Hotel White

References

(1) Tyler Resch, Shires of Bennington (Bennington: Bennington Banner for the Bennington Museum, 1975).

(2) Park-McCullough House Association, "Those Were the Days": a collection of photographs (North Bennington: The Association, 1970-74). Volume 1, North Bennington.

(3) Allan Forbes and Ralph A. Emerson, Taverns and Stagecoaches of Old New England, Vol II (Boston: State Street Trust, 1953-54).

(4) J. Kevin Graffagnino, Vermont in the Victorian Age (Bennington: Vermont Heritage Press, 1985).

* * *

(14) **Benson** (Rutland).

The Whitehall-Vergennes stage road, just east of present Route 22-A, was finished in 1790, passed through Benson.

(14a) <u>Benson</u>.

c. 1790: a tavern, <u>Josiah Goodrich</u>; in Benson Village Historic District, bldg A27 (1); tavern license, 1817;

c. 1793: <u>Boardman Hill Tavern</u>, Simeon Goodrich (tavern license, 1821-23); until 1844; north of the village, VDHP 1101-4;

1795: <u>The Ark</u>, Chauncey Smith (tavern license, 1817-23); first physician, built a house in the village long used as a tavern (Hemenway, Child); Smith moved when the Fair Haven turnpike (present Route 22A) was built, c. 1810, kept a second tavern on what is now Mountain View Stock Farm, see below;

(?): an inn, <u>Reuben Nash</u>; an original proprietor, came in 1787, innkeeper, merchant and farmer, moved away in 1813, returned 1814, died 1846 (Hemenway);

(?): <u>Smith's Tavern</u> (later <u>Parson's Tavern</u>); on the Fair Haven turnpike in a place later known as Mountain View Stock Farm (VDHP 1101-35);

Note: tavern licenses to Joseph Stacy, 1817, '22, '23; Cyrus Ramsey, 1821; Orem Dickinson, 1821, '23; Dana Walker, 1822; Bishop Cramer, 1817;

c. 1840: <u>Miller's Hotel</u>, --; also known as <u>Village Hotel</u>; later bought by Jonas Reed, who sold it in 1869 to Amasa Briggs; Briggs used it as a residence until he died, when his son and daughter (John and Anna) re-opened it; sold to John Root c. 1887, burned soon after; no building on site now, which was the approach to a garage in 1927; "probably the best remembered hotel of Benson...at the northeast corner of Main and East Streets...a handsome two-story building with a west and south front with piazza extending the full length of both fronts" (2);

1849: <u>Village Hotel</u>, Jonas Reed (NEMU Dir);

1854: hotel, --* (Scott map);

1855: a tavern, <u>Joseph Gibbs</u>; on the lot occupied in 1927 by E. A. Gibbs; burned years ago; according to Everest, this place, on Rte 22A, dates from c. 1815, was enlarged in 1907 (3);

c. 1870: (a) <u>Union Hotel</u>, Jonas Reed; after selling the <u>Village Hotel</u> in 1869 (see above), Reed bought a small one-story building, moved it to site formerly occupied by Baptist church, added a second story and two wings; he had a shoe shop in the south wing; building occupied in 1927 by L. H. Kellogg as meat market, post office and residence;

1870: --, J. W. Adams;

1872, '75, '80: (a) <u>Union House</u>, Jonas Reed;

1883: (a) as above; (b) <u>Briggs House</u>, J. A. and A. J. Briggs;

1887, '89: (a) as above; (b) as above, Mrs A. J. Baily;

1890: (a) as above; (b) as above, J. Root;

1891: --, W. W. Ward;

1892: <u>Traveler's Home</u>, - Schofield;

1895: as above, P. E. Wilcox;

1898: <u>Hotel Belden</u>, (?) Charles Leonard;

1901:   --, Mrs P. E. Wilcox;

1905, '08, '11, '13:   Hotel Benson, John S. Carter;

1915, '16, '20: Hotel Wells, Joseph Wells* (Sanborn); burned in 1949.

(14b) Benson Landing.

(?):   Ladd's Tavern, Perry G. Ladd; on site of A. L. Hale's 1927 residence.

(14c) Outside the villages.

(?):   Cramer's Tavern, --; tavern license to Bishop Cramer, 1817; on the turnpike just north of the West Haven line; building known as the "Green Door" in 1927;

(?):   a tavern, Guy Wheeler; on the East Road approximately opposite C. W. Fay's 1927 residence;

(?):   Stiles Tavern, --; on the East Road about one mile north of Wheeler's (above); a part of this building still stands, known as "The Ranch" in 1927.

* * *

References

(1) Vermont Div. of Historic Preservation, Historic Architecture of Rutland County, Curtis B. Johnson, ed., Elsa Gilbertson, asst ed. (Montpelier: 1988).

* * *

(15) **Berkshire** (Franklin).

(15a) Berkshire (Center). No listings found.

Note: tavern licenses in 1816-27 to Elijah Phelps; 1819-33, Cromwell Bowen; 1817, David Thomas; 1819, David A. Nutting, Samuel Butler; 1819, '22, Elihu M. Royce; 1822, '24, '30 to Dan H. Benjamin; 1826-33, John Chaffee; 1824-26, Friend Hall; 1825, '26, Frederick A. Woodworth; 1822, '28-30, Dennis Sampson; 1829, George Woodworth; 1833, Caleb Royce, and French and Worthington; not known in which village any of these were.

(15b) East Berkshire.

1849:   --, I. C. and F. H. Stone (NEMU Dir);

1855:   --, J. C. Stowe;

1856:   --, H. Stowe;

1857:   --, O. J. Smith* (Walling);

1871:   Riverside House, H. S. Foster* (Beers; apparently the same site as in 1857);

1873:   (a) Central House, H. S. Foster;

1875:   (a) as above, D. P. Moore;

1879, '80, '82, '87, '90:   (a) as above;

1892:   (a) as above, George A. Best;

1898, 1901, '02, '05, '08:   (a) as above, B. L. Wilson;

1903:   (a) Central House, -- (SBA booklet, but listed for West Berkshire, presumably an error);

1911:   (a) as above, --;

1913:   (a) as above, A. D. Shannon; burned in 1913, rebuilt;

1916:   Avon House, Dick W. Paul (VPB); see photo;

1917, '20, '25: Avon House, --; but no hotel shown on 1915 Sanborn; Rhoda Berger, local historian, is of the opinion that the new place wasn't opened until 1923.

(15c) West Berkshire (once Union, briefly).

c. 1804:   a tavern, Comfort Chaffee; tavern license, 1817-25; on the road north out of West Berkshire (Potato Hill Rd); VDHP 0602-58;

1830:   --, C. Bowen (tavern license);

1849:   --, W. Page (NEMU Dir);

1855, '56:   --, B. B. Smith;

1857:   --, C. Burleson* (Walling);

1870:   (a) Phoenix Hotel, E. E. Hill* (Beers);

1875, '80:   (a) as above;

1878:   (a) as above, L. J. Squire; building built in 1835, has also served as Grange Hall, PO, now apartments; VDHP 0602-1, #11;

1882, '87, '92: (b) Franklin House, J. C. Davis;

1895, '98, 1901, '05, '11, '13:   (b) as above, C. R. Burleson;

1916:   (b) as above, Mrs C. R. Burleson; listed as Frontier in 1915;

1920, '25:   (b) as above, John Lawrence.

Note: the assistance of Rhoda Berger, Richford, is gratefully acknowledged.

* * *

(16) **Berlin** (Washington).

(16a) Berlin (Corners).

c. 1795:   a tavern, Capt Daniel Taylor: "for some time after he started his farm in the center of town, he kept a tavern and a small stock of things to sell" (Hemenway); a veteran of the Revolution and the war of 1812, died 1831;

c. 1800:   a tavern (and store), Jonas Parker; in a house later the residence of Israel Dewey (see below);

c. 1806:   a tavern, <u>Charles Huntoon</u>; in a building a little south of <u>Parker's</u>; a year or two later, he built a large square house on the opposite corner, used as a tavern for many years;

Avon House, East Berkshire (Rhoda Berger)

c. 1805:   a tavern, <u>Israel Dewey</u>; in the Parker place (above); Dewey was PM   in Berlin, 1825-50; according to Hemenway, he became a temperance man in 1830, moved to Lunenburg in 1851; not clear if he kept the tavern as a temperance house after 1830;

1816:   <u>Stiles Tavern</u>, -- (almanac); tavern license to an Abiel Stiles, 1817;

Note: tavern license to Paul Bailey, 1820-22, and Gershon Heaton, 1823, '26;

1887:   <u>Lake House</u>, C. H. Stewart.

(16b)   <u>Riverton</u> (West Berlin until 1918).   No listings found.

* * *

(17) **Bethel** (Windsor).

(17a) <u>Bethel</u>.

1803:   <u>Gardner-Wheeler Inn</u>, --; also known as <u>Tilly Parker's Hotel</u>; "a hostelry of local renown" (ref 1, also a photo); in the Bethel Mills Historic District (VDHP 1404-16); according to the VDHP, Main Street once ran 75-100' east of present location, and in front of the <u>Gardner-Wheeler Inn</u>; the hotel failed, and the road was re-located; once a favorite stopover for legislators;

c. 1810:   <u>Lillie Stand</u>, --; according to VDHP, the <u>Lillie Stand</u> was built for Gen Samuel Lillie, who founded the hamlet of Lilliesville, between 1802-12; still standing, a private home, VDHP 1404-24; also the <u>American House</u>, see below;

1812:   <u>Lathrop Stand</u>, John Lathrop; became the <u>Locust Creek Hotel</u> (see below); at the old junction of the Bethel-Woodstock and Bethel-Stockbridge roads; extensively modified between 1812-60, in almost continuous operation until c. 1902; now a private home (VDHP 1404-3);

1816: (a) Bethel House, Simeon Babbitt; he moved a barn to the village and built a hotel from it; (photo, c. 1890, ref 1; see Chap VI for a photo of this place burning; 1980, according to VDHP);

1817: "Hotel Stand", David Waller; until 1841, on land originally owned by Dr Joseph Gallup (photo, ref 1); on Rte 107, just south of Bethel village; now a bed-and-breakfast known as Eastwood House;

1849: (b) Depot House, H. A. Hatch; known as Wilson's Tavern later; burned in 1938; photo, c. 1920, ref 1; (c) Locust Creek House, J. C. Putnam;

1855: --, H. P. Bosworth; --, Asa Gaines;

c. 1855: American House, Azro Lillie; (see Lillie Stand, above); in Lilliesville, a hamlet west of Bethel (2);

1856: --, H. P. Bosworth;

1869: (a) Bethel House, --* (Beers); also known as the Bascom House for many years, and the Hotel Emery (according to VDHP; VDHP 1404-16, #5; see photo, next page); (b) Depot House, S. Archer* (Beers); (c) Locust Creek House, --* (Beers);

Note: VDHP says that there were three hotels in Bethel in the 1860s: the Bethel House (Hotel Emery, Bascom House), the Depot House, and the White River House. Unless this latter is simply another name for the Locust Creek House (outside the village), it doesn't show up on any of the directories or maps, and is unidentified.

1870: (a) as above, Carlos Newton; (b) as above;

1873, '75, '79: (a) as above, Samuel Archer; (b) as above, T. E. Wilson;

1879: (c) as above, J. J. Saltery; Spiller House, I. Thayer (Vt Dir, unidentified);

1880: (a) as above; (d) Wilson House, T. E. Wilson (former Depot House);

1883: (a) as above, George Gilson; (d) as above, A. L. Robinson;

1887: (a) Bascom House, Rollin Gilson* (Sanborn); also shown on Sanborn for 1891, 1901, '06, '14, '22, '29; a restaurant by 1962; (d) as above, J. D. Lawrence and Frank A. Holmes* (Sanborn); the Wilson House (above) became the Bethel Tavern/Inn about 1900, the Wilson House again in 1906 (Sanborn), and the Bethel Inn again in 1914, '22, '29; building gone by 1962; Bascom House and Wilson House both visible on 1886 birdseye view of the village; (3)

1890: (d) as above, M. E. Yarrington;

1895: (a) as above; (d) as above, A. C. Newell (1895 photo, VHS);

1898, 1902: (a) as above; (d) as above, B. C. Rogers; (c) Locust Creek House, VHS photo;

1905, '08: (a) as above, Harry Emery; (d) Bethel Tavern, G. L. Pratt (Sanborn, 1901; same as Wilson House);

1913: (a) as above; (d) as above, C. I. Church;

1915: (a) as above, H. L. and J. E. Emery; (d) as above, Pasquale Russo;

1917: (a) as above, --; (d) as above, H. L. and J. E. Emery;

1920, '25: (a) as above, H. L. and J. E. Emery (also known as Hotel Emery); (d) Bethel

<u>Inn</u>, H. J. B. Skern (Sanborn map, 1922, same as <u>Bethel Tavern</u>);

Hotel Emery

(17b) <u>East Bethel</u>.

(?):   a hotel, <u>Oliver H. Brooks</u>; who came "at an early date" (Child); carpenter, wheelwright, had control of the hotel for 21 years and was PM during part of that time (1842-57); the hotel referred to in Child is presumably <u>Thayer's</u>, <u>East Bethel Inn</u> (see below);

1849:   --, O. H. Brooks (NEMU Dir);

1855:   hotel, --* (Hosea Doten);

1869:   hotel, <u>Z. G. Thayer</u>* (Beers);

1879, '80, '87: <u>Thayer's Hotel</u>, Isaac Thayer;

1883:   <u>East Bethel House</u>, J. S. Thayer (Child);

1883, '87, '90: <u>Grand Central Hotel</u>, J. S. Thayer (Vt Dir);

1895, '98:   <u>Traveler's Rest</u>, K. Day;

1901:   as above, C. C. Carroll;

1905:   as above, --.

* * *

References

(1) Irene Cushing and Irene Stafford, Bethel: The Early Years (Bethel: Bethel Hist. Soc., Spaulding Pr., 1974).
(2) Wilmond W. Parker, "Lympus and Lilliesville in 1855," Vermont Historical Soc. Proceedings <u>9</u> (June 1941): 68-83.
(3) J. Kevin Graffagnino, Vermont in the Victorian Age (Bennington: Vermont Heritage Press, 1985).

* * *

(18) **Bloomfield** (Essex).

125

(18a) <u>Bloomfield</u> (Minehead until 1832).

1925:   <u>Bloomfield House</u>, George Couture; closed sometime between 1935-40;

(?):   <u>The Hillcrest</u>, -- (see photo).

(18b) <u>Nulhegan</u>.   No listings found.

The Hillcrest

* * *

(19) **Bolton** (Chittenden).

(19a) <u>Bolton</u> (also known as East Bolton and Bolton Station, at one time).

c. 1780:   a tavern, <u>John Moore</u>; "one of the first tavern-keepers...in the days when Vermont hotels were built of logs, and barroom, dining-room and kitchen were all in one" (Hemenway); it is James Moore in Child; the first town meeting was held here in 1794;

Note: Perhaps this is the place described by Levi Woodbury in 1819 as "a most unpromising Tavern to appearance, with a Canadian landlord, whom I found asleep on his barroom table..."; (1)

1790s: a tavern, "Mr Levaque" (Hemenway); almanacs, 1807-16; (about where the present trailer park is);

1823-29: <u>Whitcomb's Tavern</u>, -- (almanacs); tavern license to a James Whitcomb, 1820;

Note: tavern licenses also to Joseph Morse, 1820, '21 and Charles Nichols, 1821;

1849:   --, Joseph Smith (NEMU Dir); according to Rann, "Bishop's Hotel, at Bolton Station, was a public house forty years ago" (i.e., c. 1846); originally owned by Julius Hodges, bought by Solomon Bishop in 1866 (see below);

1855:   --, E. M. Bates;

1856:   --, E. M. Bates; --, M. L. Cotton;

1869:   (a) <u>Bolton Hotel</u>, S. and H. H. Bishop* (Beers);

1870:   (a) as above, --;

126

1873:   (a) as above, R. E. Wells;

1875:   (a) as above, S. Bishop;

1878:   (a) <u>Bishop House</u>, S. Bishop; <u>Bolton House</u> and <u>Bishop House</u> are one and the same, even though both places are listed in the Vt Dir in 1879 (see below);

1879:   (a) <u>Bolton House</u>, H. H. Bishop; (b) <u>Bishop House</u>, W. W. Bruce;

1880:   (a) <u>Bolton House</u>, W. W. Bruce;

1883:   (a) <u>Bishop House</u>, H. H. Bishop;

1887, '92, '95, '98:   (a) <u>Bolton House</u>, H. H. Bishop;

1901, '02, '05, '08, '11, '13, '15, '20: (a) <u>Bishop House</u>, C. S. Brush; (the CVRR booklet still lists H. H. Bishop in 1902; listed as a "farm" place in 1903 SBA booklet); there is a VHS photo of an unnamed hotel foundation, just west of the town clerk's residence, in "East Bolton"; probably the <u>Bishop/Bolton</u> House; a house put on this foundation in 1960. <u>Bishop House</u> said to have burned, 1918, across from present Bolton Store. See photo.

Bishop/Bolton House

(19b) <u>West Bolton</u>. No listings found.

Note: the assistance of Karen A. Stites, Chittenden County Historical Society Bulletin, and of Gardner Lane, is gratefully acknowledged.

References

(1) H. B. Fant, "Levi Woodbury's Week in Vermont, May 1819", Vermont History <u>34</u> (January 1966): 36.

* * *

(20) **Bradford** (Orange).

(20a) Bradford.

1790: (a) Vermont House, --; "at times more of a boarding house than it was a hotel" (2); on a site behind Dr Munson's dental office in 1968; burned in 1871, owned at the time by R. W. Chamberlin;

1796: Stebbins Tavern, --; listed in the Vermont Almanac and Register as a tavern on the Windsor-St Johnsbury road (also listed in 1801, '02, '05);

c. 1800: a tavern, Col John Barron; in the southeast corner of the town (the "Lower Plain"), Hemenway; in present day terms, this is just north of the Merry Meadow Farm, on Rte 5, south of Bradford; Barron died in 1813; originally on the west side of the road, later moved across the street to make room for the railroad; John Pearsons built a house on the same site in 1842, also a tavern (1);

Note: other almanac listings, locations unknown: May, 1801, '02, '05; Barnes, 1805;

c. 1815: Peletiah Corliss Tavern; on the stage road from Haverhill, N.H. to Montpelier; Harold Sinclair place on Rte 25 in 1968; photos in refs 2,3; still operating in 1849 (see below);

c. 1815: a tavern, Benjamin Baldwin; more recently the Ellis Shumway place, burned in 1915; near Baldwin's Bridge, Appleton farm in 1968; photo, ref 2;

1846: (b) Trotter House, Asa Low; built as a residence by Capt William Trotter, c. 1805, sold to Low, who converted it to an inn in 1846; known as the Bliss Hotel for a time, when it was owned by Ellis Bliss; later, H. B. Stevens and (last), A. B. Fabyan. Burned in 1887, site occupied later by Hotel Low, which was itself razed in 1960 to make way for the Bradford National Bank; 1887 Sanborn shows "ruins" on the site;

1849: Peletiah Corliss Tavern; (b) Bliss Hotel, E. Bliss Jr; --, S. Dickey (NEMU Dir);

1856: (b) Trotter House, H. B. Stevens; --, Ira W. Clark;

1858: (a) Vermont House, R. C. Johnson* (Walling); (b) as above* (Walling);

1870: (a) as above, R. W. Chamberlin (burned in 1871);

1873, '75: (b) as above, H. E. Harris;

1877: (b) as above, C. N. Stevens* (Beers);

1879, '80: (b) as above, E. S. Peaslee;

1883, '87: (b) as above, A. L. Fabyan (burned in 1887; photo, ref 3);

1890, '92: (c) Hotel Low, Libby Brothers* (Sanborn, also for 1892, '98, 1905, '12, '22); on the Trotter House site; see photo, next page;

1895: (c) as above;

1898: (c) as above, O. D. Johnson;

1901: (c) as above, Bishop Brothers;

1905, '08: (c) as above, H. L. Doyle;

Hotel Low

1913, '15:   (c) as above, M. A. Gale;

1925:   (c) as above, W. M. Gale; known in its later years as the <u>Bradford Inn</u>, razed in 1960; VHS photo;

(20b) <u>Bradford Center</u> and (20c) <u>West Bradford</u>, no listings found.

Note: the assistance of Phyllis Lavelle, curator of the Bradford Historical Society, is gratefully acknowledged.

* * *

References

(1) Katharine Blaisdell, Over the River and Thru the Years, Book Five, (N. Haverhill, N.H.: Blaisdell, 1979-84).
(2) Harold A. Haskins, A History of Bradford, Vermont (Littleton, N.H.: Courier Pr., 1968).
(3) Muriel Brainerd et al., A Picture Story of Historic Bradford Town (Burlington: Lane Pr., 1965).

* * *

(21) **Braintree** (Orange).

(21a) <u>Outside the Villages--Lower Branch Area</u> .

c. 1787:   a tavern, <u>Henry Brackett</u>; in the first frame house in town. (1) First town meeting here in 1788, place later owned by George Hutchinson (2); this place is shown on a 1970 map in Duclos as the Montgomery property (3);

<u>Outside the Villages--Braintree Center/Braintree Hill/Quaker Hill</u>.

c. 1795:   hotel (and store, later removed), <u>Samuel Bass</u> and <u>John French</u>; French moved to Randolph in 1806, Bass an absentee owner; building still stands, Laurence Benoir place in recent times (3);

(21b) <u>East Braintree</u>.

Changed to Snowsville in 1836, still the local name; then Braintree, then East Braintree in 1897; PO discontinued in 1920.

129

c. 1832:   a hotel, <u>Thomas Dutton</u>; "on the corner near present hotel" (referring to the <u>Snowsville House</u>, in 1883, see below; (2) this was East Braintree's first hotel, known later as the <u>Fan House</u> because of a decoration above the door, now apartments; Dutton also made harnesses at the same stand. Isaac Lothrop next manager;

1846:   (a) <u>Snowsville House</u>, Daniel Cram; built by Nathaniel Hutchinson Jr, Cram's father-in-law; operated successively by Hutchinson, A. B. Shedd, Stillman Moulton, James M. Warner (1855, '56), Vernon D. Partridge, Nathaniel Hutchinson again. He died in 1872, sold to William Blanchard in 1874, who ran it until his death in the late 1890s; a stagecoach stop;

1849:   (a) as above, A. B. Shedd (NEMU Dir);

1858:   (a) as above, --* (Walling);

1870, '73:   (a) as above, Nathaniel Hutchinson;

1875, '79, '80, '83, '87, '90:   (a) as above, William Blanchard* (Beers map, 1877) also shown on a map representing the village in 1876 (3);

1898:   (a) as above, Lucinda Jackson;

1901:   (a) --, Henry Jackson; sold this year to Lucy Williams and others;

1902:   (b) <u>Braintree House</u>, S. T. Farrington (probably same as <u>Snowsville House</u>); see photo;

1908:   (b) as above, --;

1911:   (b) as above, Solomon Williams;

1913:   (b) as above, Solomon Williams; he died in 1913 (1); bought by Alvin Williams;

1915:   (b) --, Salmon (?) Williams; <u>Hotel Bowman</u>, Carl Bowman;

1920, '25:   (b) as above, Alvin Williams (1); still standing (1988), converted to apartments in 1926; --, Carl Bowman (location unknown).

Braintree House

130

(21c) <u>West Braintree</u>.

Changed to Braintree by the Post Office Department in 1897, still referred to locally and on maps as West Braintree).

1870:   --, Manuel Haseltine;

1875:   --, Leonard Parker (Walton, but Vt Dir says Leonard Fish);

1873, '77, '79, '80: (a) <u>West Braintree House</u>, Leonard Fish* (Beers; place also known as <u>Valley House</u>, <u>Fish Hotel</u>);

1883:   (a) as above, H. Darnham;

1887, '88, '92; (a) as above, Leonard Fish; run as a boarding-house until at least 1926, became a store by 1930;

1895:   --, Paul Wagner;

c. 1900:   (a) as above; photo, ref 3; operated by the Bradburys, c. 1913; badly damaged by fire in 1953, made into apartments, burned by the fire department in 1985.

Note: the assistance of Gregory Storrow and Katherine F. Duclos, Braintree Historical Society, is gratefully acknowledged.

* * *

<u>References</u>

(1) Braintree Centennial, 1781-1881.
(2) H. Royce Bass, History of Braintree (Rutland: Tuttle, 1883).
(3) Katherine F. Duclos, History of Braintree, Vol II, 1883-1975 (Braintree: History Book Committee, 1976).

* * *

(22) **Brandon** (Rutland).

(22a) <u>Brandon</u>.

1789:   <u>Mr Flint's</u> (tavern), --;

* * *

"The Rev. Nathan Perkins of Hartford, Conn., on a preaching mission through the Vermont wilderness, writes: 'May 9--lodged at Mr Flint's of Brandon--meanest of all lodging, dirty--fleas without number.'" (1)

* * *

c. 1796:   a tavern, <u>Joshua Goss</u>; came in 1783, kept a tavern "for a long time" on the bank of the Neshobe River, where the town poor farm was in 1881 (Child); almanac, 1812-1822; 1950s photo of building, Everest;

1790s: a tavern, <u>Prince Soper</u>; in a house built by Joseph Larkin on the site of the Josiah Rossiter home (i.e., c. 1877, Hemenway);

(?):   tavern, --; "near the highway, where the old Crown Point road crosses the swamp road, stood the oldest tavern in Brandon, it is said" (1);

131

pre-1800: taverns kept by Capt Jacob Simonds (on site of the Brandon House and the Brandon Inn in later years, see below); Capt Abraham Gilbert (see below); and John Mott;

c. 1800:   Wayside Tavern, --; on the road to Forestdale; Stewart Jones place in 1961;

c. 1800-1810: four taverns on the Post Road outside the village (present Rte 7, approximately): (a) Willis Goodnow (Goodnough), south, near present (i.e., 1961) Valley View cabins (tavern licenses, 1817, '20, '22); this tavern later run by John Mott; (b) John Mott, north, some 40 rods east of Triangle Restaurant site in 1961; this place later run by Walter Sessions, who moved it when the road moved to its present location (Sessions listed in almanacs, 1812, '13; and a tavern license, 1817); also operated by John McConnell;

* * *

"Returning from Rutland we stayed overnight at the McConnell Tavern about two miles south of Brandon village. It was my first experience at a tavern and I well remember the big sign in front of the house at the joint of the two roads that met there. It was a large swinging sign between two uprights and on it was 'entertainment for Man and Beast,' with some decoration." (from Gov Ormsbee's autobiography, ref 2). Closed for many years when the McConnell family was growing up there, run as a home for retired teachers, c. 1924-40, restored and re-opened as the Century House in 1940, Mr and Mrs James Pate; it burned in 1947.

* * *

c. 1800-1810 (continued): (c) Gilbert's Tavern, a little further north, where George Baker lived in 1961; Abraham Gilbert is described in Smith and Rann as being "on the Stage Road nearly two miles east of the present village"; site of the first post office, and Gilbert was the first PM, until 1807; and (d) Joshua Goss, on the bank of Neshobe, below the Town Farm house (see above; almanacs, 1796, 1802, '07);

early 1800s: a tavern, Matthew Birchard (in the village, licenses, 1817, '22, '23); later the Penuel Child tavern (almanacs, 1825, '29); Howland's Jewelry store in 1961;

Note: tavern licenses in 1817 to Chester Goss; and in 1817, '21, '22 to Elijah Wood; 1821, Isaac Hill and James Whitcomb;

1818:   John Conant Tavern, --; on the stage road, closed in 1830; (4)

c. 1820:   Hillside Tavern, Isaac and Jemima Hill; in Conant Square "for many years"; tavern licenses to Isaac, 1821, '22; succeeded by Calvin Ide, Lucius Barker, - Gray, and William Field, who later built the Brandon House; followed by William Bates, and Dr Fred Schofield, who enlarged it; then Lewis Schofield, Steven L. Goodell, Julius Wallace, Samuel S. Skinner; then Capt J. W. Chase, who kept it as the Chase Hotel until 1862, when Capt A. S. Cook took over and named it the Eureka House; Cook was the last to operate it as an inn;

* * *

"On the death of Mr Hill, his widow, Jemima, a woman of remarkable energy and business capacity, kept the hostelry for some time..." (1)

"We are informed that Mrs Hill, who keeps a public house in Brandon, being convinced of the evil of retailing ardent spirits and that the advantages derived from it is not equivalent to the disadvantages, has taken spiritual liquors from her bar, and resolved not to sell no more on any occasion." (5)

* * *

1822:   (a) Brandon House, on the site of the Jacob Simonds tavern; bought by Drance (sic) June in 1822, who greatly enlarged and modified it into the Brandon House; then William Field (1832), who enlarged it in 1840; James Hastings, 1862-69; J. F. Stinson; then a stock company;

then Riley Deming, 1874; W. Merritt and D. Vail, 1876; Gardner brothers, 1881; F. Deming and L. Collins, 1883; John Higgins, 1885; A. E. Halsey, 1887; E. P. Warner, 1888. Burned in 1890 when owned by J. G. Parris and operated by F. M. Coxe and Zephaniah Hack, rebuilt as Hotel Brandon/Brandon Inn in 1892; (1888 photos, refs 1, 6);

1842:   --, William A. Field; --, F. Scofield, Jr;

1842:   a stagecoach inn, built by Orange Smalley, present (i.e., 1961) Marvin Parker place;

1843:   --, J. McConnell; --, A. S. Titus (Walton);

1849:   --, O. Smalley; --, L. F. Scofield; (a) Brandon House, William F. Fields (NEMU Dir); see photo;

1854:   (a) Brandon House, --* (Scott);

1856:   (a) as above, G. Allen; Eureka House, A. C. Cook (original Hillside Tavern);

1869, '70:   (a) as above, J. F. Stinson* (Beers);

Brandon House (Special Collections, UVM)

1870:   (b) Douglas House ; see photo, next page; built in 1850 by E. J. Bliss as a storehouse, who ran it only briefly as a hotel (Bliss House) in 1870, later kept by Albert Matthews, L. R. Barker, Frank Briggs, John Rutledge, Elroy Rogers, and H. C. Willard (1883); known as the Grand Union House briefly around 1910, John Lyon, proprietor;

1872:   (a) as above, David McBride; (b) Douglas House, A. W. Matthews; Churchill Tavern, Caleb Churchill and Nathan Hawley; on present Rte 73, between Brandon and Forestdale, on the banks of the Neshobe River; said by present owners to have been operated by the Churchill family for four generations; summer guests only by the 1940s-50s; sold in recent times to present owners who operate it as the Churchill House Inn; it is odd that this place doesn't appear in the standard directories at all;

1873: (a) as above, Riley Deming; (b) as above, A. J. Call;

1875: (a) as above; (b) as above, A. Matthews;

1878: (a) as above, F. H. Deming; (b) as above;

1879, '80: (a) as above, David McBride; (b) as above, John E. Rutledge;

1885: both the Douglas House and the Brandon House are shown on the 1885 Sanborn map; the Douglas was the Grand Union Hotel on 1892 Sanborn, back to the Douglas for 1897, 1901, '09; not operating in 1929, demolished in 1972; the Hotel Brandon/Brandon Inn, built after the Brandon House burned in 1890, is on Sanborn map in 1904, '09, 1929;

1883: (a) as above, E. P. Warner; (b) as above, E. J. Rogers;

1887: (a) as above, L. Collins/F. H. Deming; (b) as above, H. C. Willard/M. Doylan;

Douglas House (Special Collections, UVM)

1890: (a) as above, Coxe and Hack (burned this year); (b) as above, John Lyons;

1892: (b) as above, Hinckley and Cronan; (c) Hotel Brandon/Brandon Inn, (rebuilt), Frank E. Briggs and Charles H. Bliss; then Lawler Brothers; -- Mound, 1893; Schoff and Sauter, 1896; Henry Bissell, 1897; Daniel Sawyer, 1903; William Gardner, 1909; Charles Savery, 1910; Charles F. Moore, 1913-41; still operating; (VDHP 1102-8; an annex, VDHP 1102-7, was built in the 1850s);

1895: (b) Grand Union House (same as Douglas), as above; (c) Hotel Brandon, G. E. Towne;

1898: (b) Douglas House, John O'Connor; (c) as above, Schoff and Sauter;

1901: (b) as above; (c) as above;

1903:   (c) <u>Brandon Inn</u>. --; (SBA);

1905:   (b) as above, F. W. Johnson; (c) as above, E. E. Seeley;

1908, '13, '15: (b) as above, --; (c) as above,--;

1916:   (c) <u>Brandon Inn</u>, C. F. Moore;

Note: Walton sometimes lists <u>The Hortonia</u> (Lake Hortonia, Sudbury) and the <u>Silver Lake House</u> (Leicester) under Brandon;

1917:   (c) as above, --; <u>Echo Lake Farm</u>, --; <u>Pine Dale Farm</u>, --;

1920:   (c) as above, W. M. Johnson.

(22b) <u>Forestdale</u>.

1854:   --, --* (Scott).

Note: the assistance of John A. Read, Brandon Historical Society, is gratefully acknowledged.

* * *

References

(1) Leon S. Gay, Brandon, Vermont: A History of the Town, 1761-1961 (reprint edition, 1972).

(2) "Governor Ebenezer J. Ormsbee, 1886-1888," Vermont Quarterly <u>21</u> (Oct 1953): 273-278.

(3) Henry P. Smith and William S. Rann, History of Rutland County, Vermont (Syracuse: D. Mason, 1886).

(4) Vermont Div. of Historic Preservation, Historic Architecture of Rutland County, Curtis B. Johnson, ed., Elsa Gilbertson, asst ed. (Montpelier: 1988).

(5) Vermont Statesman, Castleton, issue of Aug 15, 1832, quoted in Gay (ref 1, above).

(6) Deborah S. Kirby and David R. Barker, Historic Photographs of Brandon and Forestdale, Vermont (Whiting: Research Applications, 1976)

* * *

(23) **Brattleboro** (Windham).

(23a) Brattleboro.

1762:   <u>John Arms Tavern</u>; where the Brattleboro Retreat farmhouse stood in 1921; Arms died in 1770 from the kick of a horse, place carried on by his widow Susannah and their son Josiah until the death of the latter; the first Brattleboro post office was in this tavern, in 1784; almanacs, 1785, 1796;

* * *

"During the Revolution this tavern became the rendezvous of Ethan Allen and the Green Mountain Boys and the headquarters of the officers of the state government. It was attacked and fired into by a party of Yorkers in 1784, wounding Maj Boyden and a traveler stopping there. The center of military strife, sheltering alike officers, soldiers, prisoners and travelers. Here military companies were 'warned to appear armed and equipped as the law directs' "; (1) there is a woodcut engraving of the tavern in "Annals of Brattleboro"; (2)

* * *

c. 1768:   a tavern (and store), Stephen Greenlief; in a log house where the American House later stood (Child);

1795:   Brattleboro Stage House, Samuel Dickinson; who built it and kept it until 1818 (almanacs, 1797 until 1825). Dickinson was followed by a Mr Palmer (a Seneca Palmer has a tavern license, 1821); John Blake (1822; tavern license, 1819, '20); and then Maj Henry Smith, when it was known as Smith's (almanac, 1829, and tavern licenses, 1822). For many years, the only hall available for public gatherings was associated with this place, dedicated in 1816 by "feasting and dancing" (Hemenway); Simeon Leland, who became a great hotel magnate, once worked here.

* * *

"About the time of the last war with Britain it was the custom to roll into that big bar-room a hogshead of old West India rum and supply customers from the faucet. Years ago we heard Erastus Dickinson (nephew of Samuel Dickinson) say, 'I paid over $300 for a hogshead of old rum, and after it was on draft in the bar-room it was, by good judges, declared a superior article. It immediately acquired so excellent a reputation it would not stay with me, and in a little over one week, it all left me.' " (Hemenway).

* * *

When Asa Green was postmaster (1811-41), the office was here, in the old Stage House, and was open night and day, since it was a distributing office. Col Paul Chase had it for about twenty years, starting about 1827, during which period it was known as Chase's Stage House. (Tavern license, 1829-33.)

* * *

"He was a man of distinguished and gracious presence who had exceptional social gifts, and was withal very handsome. He made an extended reputation for the house. Members of the best families throughout New England were inn-keepers. The landlord was usually connected with the militia, often a justice of the peace or sheriff. As knowledge of current events came through hearing and talking rather than through reading, the innkeeper was not only the well-informed man of the place, but influential in local affairs." (2)

* * *

Other proprietors were Salem Sumner, Erastus Dickinson (tavern license, 1817), Lemuel Whitney, William C. Perry, and Charles C. Lawrence. Liberty Rice had it in 1850, then Chase again. The name was changed to the Central House in 1853, place enlarged in 1855, name changed back to the Brattleboro House. William C. Perry had it in 1861, then Lawrence again, who had it when it burned in the great fire of October, 1869. It stood on the site of the present Crosby block.

* * *

1797:   Wickerton's Tavern, --; (Thomas's New England Almanac, on the road from Springfield, Mass., to Windsor, Vt);

c. 1811:   American House, Francis Goodhue; used as a home and store by John Holbrook until this year; known as the Phoenix House at some point in the early years; kept by Uriel Sikes, a hatmaker, from about 1820-35, as the Sikes Tavern or Sikes House (almanac, 1825, '29; tavern licenses, 1819-33); became the American House after Sikes left; proprietors immediately following were Ralph Herrick, a Mr Burnet, Edward Woodman; owned by the Goodhues (Joseph and Wells; Joseph had tavern licenses, 1816, '17) until 1860, then Charles F. Simonds; Stearns and Ray in 1862, Ray and Boyden in 1865; George A. Boyden was proprietor for 11 years; others were George A. Bugbee, Liberty Rice, T. H. Matthews, -- Shaw, Henry E. Nash, Rufus W. Rawson, J. S. Gates, C. Stearns, Henry Starkey, F. E. Reed. Site now occupied by a brick commercial block, the

American Building, built c. 1906. (Photos, ref 3).

* * *

Mr Sikes (i.e., one of the early proprietors) was a noted performer on the bass viol; he led a band of stringed instruments. On July 4, 1824, they rehearsed in the south front room of the hotel, then played a march at the head of the parade, escorting the main speaker of the day to the meeting-house.

* * *

Note: other tavern licenses to Simon Eaton, 1817; Franklin Jones, 1833; and Ebenezer W. Pomeroy, 1832;

1815: Rufus Clark's hotel (tavern license, 1816, '17). This house south of Whetstone Brook, bought by Capt Adolphus Stebbins in 1832, and owned in 1880 by his son, John Stebbins, was a hotel in 1815. The place was built in 1812 by Rufus's father, John Clark;

1829: Vermont House, Willard Pomeroy. In a house on Main St first owned by Dr Jonathan Allen, enlarged and opened as a hotel by Pomeroy. Razed in 1849, and a new three-story brick hotel built on the site by Capt Thomas C. Lord. This place burned in 1851, and the site was later occupied by the town hall and the Episcopal church. Willard's brother Chester was the first manager (tavern license, 1830), then Hiram and Alonzo Joy, and Capt T. C. Lord. A place called Wantastiquet Hall was built in the rear of the Vermont House by Calvin Townsley; it burned at the same time as the Vermont House, both places being then owned by Lord, who died a few weeks before the fire;

* * *

"Riding through the main street, we were surprised at the noise, bustle and city like appearance. On each side large blocks of brick stores and spacious hotels. 'Twas difficult to believe that we were in the back woods of 'Varmount' (sic) more than a hundred miles from the nearest sea shore. We found the hotel thronged with people, and considered ourselves fortunate in securing one out of a dozen beds made up in the Ball room..." (from a journal kept by a traveler in 1833, see ref 4; probably either Chase's Stage House or the Vermont House);

* * *

1842: Chase's Stage House, Paul Chase; Vermont House, - Lord (Main St); Phoenix House, - Bugbee (Main St); --, Roswell Goodenough (Walton);

1843: Stage House, Henry Smith; Temperance House, Uriel Sikes (American House), Walton;

1845: Wesselhoeft Water Cure, Robert Wesselhoeft; a hydrotherapy establishment on the corner of Church and Elliot Sts, where the Central Fire Station now stands;

* * *

In 1845, Dr Robert Wesselhoeft established an institution known as the "Wesselhoeft Water Cure," based on a form of treatment known as hydrotherapy. The benefits derived from the treatments and the stringent regimen that went with them were probably due more to psychology than physiology, but hydrotherapy was very popular for a brief period, and a second place, the Lawrence Water Cure, sprang up across the street from Wesselhoeft's in 1852. The majority of the patients were Southerners, however, with some well-to-do urban Yankees, and the Civil War brought an abrupt end to hydrotherapy in Brattleboro (see illustration, ref 5, next page). Harriet Beecher Stowe was once a guest at the Wesselhoeft. Became a boarding-house, eventually razed and replaced by the fire station; and the Lawrence site is now occupied by small commercial buildings.

Lawrence Water Cure
(Brattleboro: Selected Historical Vignettes, 1973, Houpis)

1849:   Revere House, James Fisk Sr; built by him at the southwest corner of Main and Elliot Sts (see photo); Fisk was also the first manager, 1850-56; "two upper floors of the adjoining stone building...were used in connection with the hotel, the second floor as a dining-room, and the third as Revere Hall, where public meetings were held before the erection of the Town Hall in 1855." (2)   Other proprietors were Henry Field, J. J. Crandall, Col H. B. Van Bibber, Asa Sanderson, George R. Cushing, the Knowlton brothers, Mr Stevens, L. V. H. Crosby, Henry C. Nash, George A. Boyden, and others; but Nash was owner and Henry Harris proprietor when it burned in 1877. After the fire the road was widened and the rest of the site occupied (i.e., 1880) by a brick bank block). (Photos, refs 3, 4, and a photo of the ruins after the fire, ref 3).

Revere House

"...a hostelry of great size and importance...four stories high. In appearance the Revere House resembled a Grecian Temple. Its windows claimed 24 lights. Granite accents throughout the facade made the building complete in all visual respects. It opened as a temperance house in 1850; but due to the relatively small demand for such institutions, became a hotel shortly there-after. To finance construction of the Revere House, Fisk peddled the equivalent of a department-store-on-wheels caravan throughout southern New England for many years previous to his Brattleboro venture." (5)

138

Fisk was the father of the legendary James Fisk Jr, railroad baron and high flyer, who was shot and killed in the Broadway Central Hotel in New York; his remains laid in state at the Revere House in 1872.

* * *

1849:   Stage House, Henry Smith; Phoenix House, Charles G. Lawrence; Vermont House, Thomas C. Lord (NEMU Dir);

1856:   (a) Central House, - Sanderson* (McClellan map, where it is listed as the Brattleboro House); (b) Revere House, --* (McClellan); American House, C. L. Whitney* (McClellan); --, H. C. Nash;

1869:   (a) Brattleboro House, C. G. Lawrence* (Beers); (b) Revere House, G. A. Boyden* (Beers); (c) American House, G. A. Boyden* (Beers); (d) Wesselhoeft House, P. B. Francis* (Beers);

1870:   Brattleboro House, --; second hotel by that name; on the south side of Whetstone Brook near the bridge. Building was first an organ manufactory built by Jacob Estey Co, fitted up as a hotel by Isaac Sargent in 1870 after the old Brattleboro House burned. Sargent went bankrupt; place reverted to Estey, and was being conducted in 1880 by Danton and Campbell. Razed in 1905, according to Houpis. (5) See photo.

Brattleboro House (Special Collections, UVM)

1870:   (a), (b) and (d) as above; (c) as above, H. Starkey; (but the Brattleboro House actually burned in 1869); Lawrence Hotel, John Knowlton;

1872:   (e) Brooks House, George J. Brooks; at the corner of Main and High Sts, a little north of the site of the old Brattleboro House, destroyed with other buildings in the vicinity in the great fire of 1869. An L-shaped building, fronting on both Main and High Sts;

"An architectural jewel...quintessential to the mid-Victorian period... The Brooks stands four, and in certain areas five stories tall... When first constructed, it boasted a 40-foot two-story veranda of Corinthian columns and iron railings, which matched beautifully the structure's sleek cornices, arcades and mansard roof." President Rutherford B. Hayes, with family connections in the area (see <u>Hayes Tavern</u>, West Brattleboro) stayed here in the summer of 1877. See photo.

The <u>Brooks</u> competed successfully for the White Mountain "carriage" trade for nearly six decades, essentially unchanged. In 1928 it was renovated by new owners, and re-opened as the <u>Hotel Brooks</u>, but declined from that point on. It closed in 1963, ignominiously bearing the name <u>Yankee Doodle Motor Inn</u>, and is now an office and apartment complex. (See ref 5, where may also be found descriptions of the original furnishings, and photos.)

Brooks House (Special Collections, UVM)

1873, '75:   (b) <u>Revere House</u>, H. C. Nash; (c) as above, G. A. Boyden; (f) (new) <u>Brattleboro House</u>, H. A. Morey; (e) <u>Brooks House</u>, C. G. Lawrence;

1878:   (c) as above; (e) as above, F. Goodhue; (f) as above, C. H. Morris;

1879, '80:   (c) as above; (f) as above, Danton and Campbell; (e) as above;

1883, '84:   (c) as above, J. H. Mathews* (Sanborn); (e) as above* (Sanborn); (f) described as a boarding-house in 1884, Child; (g) <u>Salisbury Hotel</u>, George H. Salisbury (41 Main St);

1885, 1891:   <u>American Hotel</u> and <u>Brooks House</u> both on Sanborn, 1891;

1890, '92:   (c) as above, F. K. Harvey; (e) as above, Crosby and Adams; <u>Bliss House</u>, G. A. Bliss* (Sanborn, 1891; Main St, c. of Bridge);

1895:   (c) as above, George E. Richards; (f) as above, Mrs J. A. Stafford; the <u>Bliss Hotel</u> of 1891 now the <u>Brattleboro Hotel</u>, Sanborn);

1896:   (c) <u>American</u>, --* (Sanborn); (e) <u>Brooks</u>, --* (Sanborn);

1901, '02:   (c) as above, C. C. Miller* (Sanborn); (e) as above, Crosby and Adams* (Sanborn); (f) <u>Hotel Brattleboro</u>, T. F. Turner* (Sanborn);

1905:   (c) as above, George Danyeau; (e) as above; (f) as above, Bissett and Sullivan; (but this was razed in 1905, according to Houpis; (5)

1906:   (c) <u>American Hotel</u> replaced by a new block, Sanborn; (e) <u>Brooks House</u> and (f) <u>Brattleboro</u>, shown, also in 1912 (Sanborn); <u>Brattleboro House</u> gone by 1919 (Sanborn), <u>Brooks</u> still there on 1925 map;

1908:   (e) as above; (f) as above, -- (razed in 1905?);

1911:   (e) as above, E. C. Crosby; (f) as above, Jennie E. Bushee; <u>The Palms</u>, E. E. Flagg;

1913:   (e) as above, --; (f) as above, --; <u>The Palms</u>, --;

1915, '17:   (e) as above, --;

1920:   (e) as above, --; <u>Hillrest</u>, --;

1923:   <u>Hotel Billings</u>, A. L. Billings (VPB);

1925:   (e) as above, --; <u>Hillrest</u>; <u>The Billings</u>,--; <u>The Billings</u> and the <u>Hotel Brooks</u> still operating in 1940.

(23b) <u>Waite</u>. PO, 1895-97. No listings found.

(23c) <u>West Brattleboro</u>.

1789:   <u>Hayes Tavern</u>, Rutherford Hayes; at the foot of Greenleaf St (now Western Ave); a two-story building with 24 rooms, ballroom, and shady veranda (turn-of-the-century photo in ref 5, where may also be found a reproduction of the original tavern sign). Hayes, a blacksmith by profession who came to Brattleboro in 1778, died in 1836; he was the grandfather of President Rutherford B. Hayes. The tavern ceased operating well over a hundred years ago, but the building stayed in the family until 1960, when it was demolished. It is now the site of the parking lot for the State Liquor Store on Western Avenue.

* * *

"In 1815 the old Brattleboro Light Infantry dined there, the day the mail coach--decked with flags-- brought here the tidings of peace after the War of 1812; the father of the president helped wait on table that day!" (Hemenway)

* * *

(?):   <u>Mixer's Tavern</u>, --; tavern license to a David Mixer, 1821-23; on the Windham County Turnpike (1800-32), on present Stark Road just east of Wright's Pottery Shop (6); L. and C. Mixer are shown on the 1856 McClellan map, on the western edge of Brattleboro, almost in Marlboro; this tavern was close to the high point of the eastern part of the turnpike; tavern licenses, 1821, '23;

(?):   <u>Glen House</u>, also built by Rutherford Hayes; his son Russell was proprietor, also Amasa Bixby, Henry Bassett (tavern license to Bixby and Bassett, 1820, '23), Timothy Root (tavern license, 1822), Phineas Stewart (the place was called <u>Stewart's Hotel</u> at one time, over fifty years ago, according to Hemenway, which would put it in the 1830s; tavern license to Stewart, 1823-32); also R. Goodenough, George Emerson, Mark Worcester, George A. Boyden, Henry Nash, C. C. Miller, L. D. Thayer, Mr Alden, William Warren, T. Clapp, Albert Smith, and John L. Sargent and

Seth Jones, owner and proprietor, respectively, c. 1880. "A favorite of the military of that day."

c. 1855: (b) Vermont House, Nathaniel Holland; "There is a hotel a few rods north of the Glen House, first set in operation by Nathaniel Holland some 20 years ago, and now owned by Charles Miller. Last public house in town before coming to the Marlboro line" (Hemenway);

1849: (a) Glen House, R. Goodnough; (b) Vermont House, Thomas C. Lord (NEMU Dir);

1856: (b) Vermont House, Nathaniel Holland;

1869: (a) as above, J. Sergeant* (Beers); (b) as above* (Beers);

1870: (a), (b) as above;

1873: (a) as above, L. P. Alden; (b) as above, Charles Miller;

1878: (a) as above, C. A. Clapp;

1879, '80: (a) as above, Seth W. Jones; (b) as above;

1883: (a) as above, E. J. Wood;

1901, '02: Melrose House, Sargent and Jones* (Sanborn; this place became a hospital some time after 1913);

1905: The Melrose, H. B. Haus;

1911: The Melrose, Mrs L. J. Strong;

1912: --, --* (hotel, Sanborn);

Note: the assistance of Harold A. Berry, Brattleboro Historical Society, is gratefully acknowledged.

* * *

References

(1) Grace F. Waters, "The Arms Tavern," Brattleboro Reformer, June 7, 1930.
(2) Mary R. Cabot, Annals of Brattleboro, 1681-1895 (Brattleboro: E. L. Hildreth, 1921-22).
(3) Harold A. Berry et al., Before Our Time: A Pictorial Memoir of Brattleboro, Vermont, from 1830-1930 (Brattleboro: Stephen Greene Pr., 1974).
(4) Charles W. Eldridge, "Journal of a Tour Through Vermont to Montreal and Quebec in 1833," Vermont Historical Soc. Proc. 2 (June, 1931): 53-82.
(5) John N. Houpis, Jr., Brattleboro: Selected Historical Vignettes (Brattleboro: Brattleboro Publ, 1973).
(6) Bernice Barnett and Lucie Sumner, "Border to Border Along the Windham County Turnpike," Cracker Barrel (Fall-Winter, 1987-88).

* * *

(24) **Bridgewater** (Windsor).

(24a) Bridgewater.

(?): a tavern, James Southgate; son of an original settler; in the village (Child); --, John Hawkins; --, Job Shaw (ref 1);

1834, '42:   --, John Woodward (1);

1849:   --, John Woodward (NEMU Dir);

1855, '56:   Woodward's Tavern, John Woodward (until 1858); --, C. C. Carpenter;

1858-60:   Woodward's Hotel, Samuel Dunbar and Columbus C. Carpenter (1);

1860-81:   Carpenter's Hotel, Columbus B. Carpenter;

* * *

From 1860 to 1881, Columbus Carpenter was the host, and many social events were held here. The Jackson Ball, commemorating Andrew Jackson's victory over the British at the Battle of New Orleans in 1815, was held annually on the 8th of January. "In 1869, one hundred and twenty-five couples attended, and in 1872, Hough's band furnished music" (1); badly damaged by fire in 1881, not used for some years.

* * *

1869:   Bridgewater Hotel, Bradford Chase* (Beers; presumably this is the same as Carpenter's);

1887:   Allard House, E. M. Allard;

1890:   Allard House, A. Edgerton; Waite House, Sarah Waite (probably a boarding-house);

1893:   Carpenter's Hotel (re-opened), Calvin Carpenter; he died in 1895;

1896, '98:   Carpenter's Hotel, George Bradley;

1901:   Bridgewater House, George Bradley (presumably this is the same as Carpenter's); Waite House, Mrs Waite;

1903-09:   Bridgewater Hotel, Ellen and Luther Forbes; (1)

1908-11:   as above, L. A. Barrows;

1911-19:   as above, Stevens and Farnsworth; became the property of the Bridgewater Woolen Co in 1919; VDHP says that the present Carpenter Hotel (i.e., 1973), formerly the Bridgewater Hotel, was built in the 1920s, operated by the Bridgewater Woolen Company, but that it is possible the building is earlier, and was expanded by the company. This seems to be the case, since local residents recall the first use of the hotel after its remodelling was in connection with a parade welcoming home World War I veterans. Vice President Coolidge's aides were staying here in 1923 when the news of Harding's death came through. Now an apartment building (VDHP 1405-13), referred to locally as the "Block."

1914:   Sanborn map shows hotel "being built"; there is a problem here: does this refer to the rebuilding, only now, after the fire of 1881, or the remodeling after the Bridgewater Woolen Company acquired the property? Neither answer wholly satisfactory, since Walton in 1893 refers to Carpenter's as being "re-opened"; and according to Adams, the hotel was not acquired by the company until 1919; (1)

1925:   Furman House, --.

(24b) Bridgewater Corners

pre-1840:   a tavern, --; on present Rte 4, across from what is now (i.e., 1976, Adams) the Junction Store; Ira Angell ran this tavern 1840-45;

143

1849: as above, Joel Willis (NEMU Dir, Child); building razed in the 1950s.

(24c) Briggs. No listings found.

(24d) West Bridgewater.

1883: Ottaquechee House, L. D. Spaulding;

1890: as above, Alonzo Madden.

Note: the assistance of Blanche C. King, Bridgewater, is gratefully acknowledged.

* * *

References

(1) Gladys S. Adams, Bridgewater, Vermont: 1889-1976 (n.p., 1976).

* * *

(25) **Bridport** (Addison).

(25a) Bridport.

1805: a hotel, Benjamin Skiff; until 1825; on present Rte 22A just north of Pratt's Store;

1814: a hotel, --; south of the village, at the intersection of Rte 22A and Hemenway Rd, where Jean Plouffe lives (i.e., 1976, ref 1); possibly the place kept by three brothers (John, Plinney and Ira Wickes) who came in 1814, kept a hotel where F. G. Converse lived in 1886, "taking turns at this, their farms and mechanical trades"; (2)

(?): a tavern, --; VDHP 0102-24, #22; built c. 1819 by John Brainerd, owned in 1977 by Ashley Dukette; "once a tavern, later a store"; burned years ago;

1820: hotel (and store), Daniel Haskins; on the Lake Road (Rte 125) near present John Krueger place (i.e., 1976, ref 1); Haskins was PM, 1805-10; sold to Hiram Smith in 1821;

1820: Sollace House, Calvin Sollace; built by him in the village on present Rte 22A; operated as a hotel by the grandson, George Sollace, 1895-1905; later the Hotel Bridport, razed in 1987; photo, ref 1;

(?): a hotel, Frank A. Nisun; "in the village" (2); probably Bridport House, see 1871 entry; no further information;

1849: --, D. Hill (NEMUir);

1856: Allen Hall, C. Allen; on Rte 22A where the Catholic church now stands; "one of the first hotels in Bridport" (photo, ref 1);

1871: Bridport House, Norman D. Phelps; who operated it until 1885; then Mrs E. B. Phelps, 1885-87; and Frank Nisun, 1887-92 (see above); on Rte 22A, just south of the Catholic church; now a small apartment house, Stephen Cook (current photo, ref 1); not to be confused with the Bridport Hotel/Hotel Bridport, which was in the Sollace House under another name; VDHP 0102-50;

1895, '98, 1901, '05: Hotel Bridport, G. F. Sollace (same as the Sollace House, above);

1897, 1901, '08: Mountain View Inn, T. W. Fletcher; annex added in 1897, when it opened as an inn; main building still stands; built c. 1808 by Samuel Buck; this may be the same as VDHP 0102-23, on Rte 22A at the intersection with Rte 125; said to have been built c. 1805, and extensively altered, once operated as the Grand View Inn;

1913:   --, Mrs A. L. Norton;

1914:   no hotel shown on Sanborn map;

1915:   --, Mrs A. L. Norton; --Mrs M. C. Townsend;

1917:   --, Mrs M. C. Townsend;

1925:   --, George Conn.

(25b) West Bridport. No listings found.

Note: the assistance of Wallace L. Payne, Bridport Historical Society, is gratefully acknowledged.

* * *

References

(1) Raymond H. Lounsbury, There's Only One Bridport in the USA (Bridport: Bridport Historical Society, 1976).
(2) Henry P. Smith, History of Addison County, Vermont (Syracuse: D. Mason, 1886).

* * *

(26) **Brighton** (Essex).

(26a) East Brighton. No listings found.

(26b) Island Pond (Brighton until 1853).

1853:   (a) Island Pond House, --; built when the Grand Trunk Railroad came through (Hemenway);

1850s: (a) Island Pond House, G. G. Waterhouse; 1st Vermont House, Diamond Stone;

1856:   (a) --, A. C. Jennings; --, (Green Mountain House), Gilkey and Hobbs;

Note: there is a problem here; both Hemenway and Hamilton Child say that the Green Mountain House, operated by J. D. and S. N. Gilkey, burned this year, and was not rebuilt; yet a place with this name is listed in Walton from 1870 into the 1890s; also listed in Bradford's Hotel Guide, 1875. Perhaps it was the Vermont House (see above) that burned, since no place with this name is listed again until 1879;

1870:   (a) Island Pond House, G. G. Waterhouse; (b) American House, H. B. Gilbert; (c) Green Mountain House, B. F. Powers;

1873:   (a), (c) as above; (b) as above, Moses Roberts;

1875:   (a) as above, Bartlett and Stone; (b), (c) as above;

1878:   (a) as above, - Stone; (b) as above, John Mulligan; (c) as above;

* * *

145

(a) Island Pond House
(b) American House
(c) Green Mountain House
(d) Village Hotel (also
City, Central, Vermont Hotel)

(e) Stewart House
(f) Brighton House
(g) 2nd Vermont House
(h) Essex House
(i) Lake View House

1879:   (a) as above, P. Hinman; (c) as above, L. F. Bigelow; (d) Village Hotel, H. Moore; it appears that this place was also known as the City Hotel, although in 1887 the Vermont Business Directory lists both the Village and the City; the City became the Central in its later days; it appears that this place was also known briefly as the Vermont Hotel, distinct from both the 1st and 2nd Vermont Houses; (e) Stewart House, P. Hinman;

1880:   (a) Island Pond House, Hinman and Mansur; given up as a hotel in the 1880s, after the Stewart House was built, and converted into apartments; it burned in a spectacular fire in November, 1905; (b) as above, G. Gilbert; (c) as above; (d) City Hotel, H. Moore;

1883:   (c) as above, N. Warren (on Lake St); (d) Village (City) Hotel, H. Moore; (listed twice in the Vermont Business Directory, with H. Moore, M. E. Percival); (e) Stewart House, W. A. Richardson; Richardson also managed a hotel in Orlando, Florida, in the winters while he was managing the Stewart House in the summers; he must have been one of the first resort managers to operate in this way; the Stewart was described as the town's finest hotel in 1887 (Child); (see photo); (f) Brighton House, J. D. Ruffe (?); (g) 2nd Vermont House, N. Warren (not to be confused with the Vermont Hotel, a name apparently used briefly for the Village/City Hotel);

Stewart House

1884:   (c), (e) as above; (d) the Vermont Business Directory lists both the City Hotel (H. Moore) and the Village Hotel (George A. Barney); (f) Brighton House, J. O'Keefe; French Hotel, L. Coutier;

1887:   (c) Green Mountain House, N. Warner (on Lake St); (d) Village (City), George D. Barney (Cross St); (e) Stewart House, W. A. Richardson (South St); (f) Brighton House, J. O'Keefe (Lake St; listed as F. Talbot in Vt Bus Dir); (g) 2nd Vermont House, N. Warren; (h) Essex House, M. C. Davis (Cross and Derby Sts, see photo); Canadian House, J. Belanger (possibly the same as the French Hotel, see above);

1889:   (d), (e) and (h) are shown on the Sanborn map; (c), (d), (e), (g) and (h) in Vt Bus Dir;

1890:   (d) Village, Smith and Moon; (e) Stewart, C. M. Dyer; Dyer bought it in 1889, the largest hotel in town at the time; (h) Essex, M. C. Davis;

1892:   (c), (e) as above; (d) as above, L. Riggie; (h) as above;

1895:   (d), (e) and (h) as above; (e) and (h) are on the Sanborn for this year, but (d) Village is now the Vermont Hotel, on Sanborn;

1898:   (d) as above, J. W. Skillen; (e), (h) as above;

1901:   (d) Central House, J. W. Skillen (same as Village, City); (e) as above; (h) as above, A. M. Stevens;

1904:   (e) and (h) on Sanborn, but Vermont (Village) is now the Central House; the Lake View is also shown;

Essex House

1905:   (d) as above; (e) as above, W. M. Buck; (h) as above; (i) Lake View (owned by the Fitzgerald Land and Lumber Co;

1909:   (e) and (h) on Sanborn; (d) Central now tenements; (i) Lake View as in 1904;

1908, '13:   (e) Stewart House, --;

1915, '17:   (e) as above, --; (h) as above, --;

1920:   (h) as above, and still on Sanborn, also in 1928; (i) Lake View has become a store with tenements above; and (e) Stewart is now a YMCA; (operated by Osborne Bros., 1916 VPB, as Osborne Hotel, probably same place, operating as late as 1955);

1925:   YMCA (former Stewart; burned, site shown as "to be hotel" on 1928 Sanborn).

Note: the assistance of John Carbonneau, Island Pond Historical Society, is gratefully acknowledged.

(27) **Bristol** (Addison).

(27a) Bristol. A wealth of information is available about the taverns and inns in Bristol due to the lengthy handwritten manuscript of Harvey Munsill, presumably written in mid-19th century (Munsill died in 1876) and published by the Bristol Historical Society in 1979 (ref 1); and the "History of Bristol, Vermont" (ref 2).

1788: a tavern, Henry McLaughlin; at what is now Daniel's Corner (intersection of Rtes 17 and 116, west of the village); McLaughlin was an original settler, and this first tavern was a log cabin; he continued the tavern in a brick house built near the original cabin in 1800 (first brick house in town); McLaughlin moved away in 1805, selling to David Ingraham, who carried on the tavern;

c. 1800: a tavern, Jacob Cadwell (Caldwell?); with his brother Isaac; in a log cabin four miles northeast of the village on the Starksboro road; the PO was here from 1804-15, and Jacob Cadwell was the first PM, according to Post Office Department records;

1808: a tavern, Robert Holley; at the corner of North and East (later Main) Sts; place acquired by Abraham Gaige in 1820, later expanded into the Bristol House/Inn;

(?): a tavern, Veris Miller; in Bristol Flats in a house built by Robert Dunshee;

(?): a tavern, Abraham Gaige; on the south side of the highway opposite the common, burned in 1817; Gaige rebuilt on the same site, but took over the Holley tavern (later the Bristol House) in 1820;

1820: (a) Bristol House, Abraham Gaige; who bought and rebuilt it this year; originally the Holley Tavern; Gaige was landlord from 1820-35, when his son, D. R. Gaige, took over; a number of landlords between then and 1871, when J. J. Ridley took over (including Samuel Eddy, 1840; Luman Munson; William Rutherford; Ransom Taft; Partch and Post; and David Brown, who sold to Ridley); Ridley was landlord until 1896, "except for a few months in 1893 between his sale...to Q. E. Grover and W. E. Frank and his repurchase of it"; Thomas Leonard, 1896; the Clement Burnhams bought it in 1906 and kept it until 1954; the place closed in 1960, when the north annex was moved to Mountain View Street for apartments and the main building, 139 years old, was torn down to make room for a Grand Union Store; see photo, next page;

* * *

"During Ridley's ownership, mainly two steady types of customers patronized the Bristol House. One group...the men who came in once a week to catch up on the news and enjoy gentlemanly companionship. This was a carry-over from the days when once a week a horseback rider from Middlebury would arrive with the Bristol mail. The Bristol House was the distribution point for the weekly mail delivery.

The other main customers were the traveling salesmen, the 'drummers.' They would arrive by train, take the coach to the Bristol House, rent a horse and buggy from the livery stable there, and proceed on their rounds." (2)

1835: a tavern, Henry Vradenburgh; in the village;

c. 1850: a hotel, --; in the O'Neill block, east end of Main St, north side; burned in 1929; Daniel Willard was the last manager; present site of McKinnon's filling station;

1849: --, Samuel Eddy (NEMU Dir; this is the Bristol House);

1855: --, William Rutherford (Bristol House);

1856: --, E. B. Howard;

1857: (a) Bristol House, --* (Walling);

1870: (a) as above, L. M. Crossman (UVM stereo view);

1871: (a) as above, J. J. and G. B. Ridley* (Beers);

1873: (a) as above, J. J. Ridley;

Bristol House

1875: (a) as above, --; --, C. P. Abernethy;

1878: (a) as above; Farr Hotel, J. R. Farr;

1879, '80, '81, '83: (a) as above;

1885: (a) as above, --* (Sanborn);

1880s: (b) Commercial Hotel, Ryland Hatch; in the Hatch block at the east end of Main St, south side;

1887: (a) as above; Ridley was also PM from 1885-89, a hotel PO; (b) Commercial House, R. F. Hatch; both shown on 1889 birdseye view; (4)

1890, '92, '95: (a) as above* (Sanborn); (b) as above* (Sanborn); there is a photo of the Bristol House, c. 1890, ref 3; both places on 1895 Sanborn;

1898: (a) as above, S. G. Morse; (b) as above;

1901, '05: (a) as above, Thomas Leonard* (on 1901, '06 Sanborn); Commercial House not operating in 1901 according to Sanborn map;

1908, '13, '15, '20, '25: (a) Bristol House, Clement A. Burnham; operating as late as 1955; Burnham was also PM, 1915-23, but the office was apparently not in hotel then; place shown on 1914, '27 Sanborn.

Note: the assistance of Helen M. Lathrop, Bristol Historical Society, is gratefully acknowledged.

* * *

References

(1) Harvey Munsill, The Early History of Bristol, Vermont (Bristol: Book Committee, Bristol Historical Soc., 1979?).
(2) History of Bristol, Vermont, 3rd edition (Bristol: Outlook Club, 1980).
(3) Harold Farnsworth et al., A History of New Haven in Vermont, 1761-1983 (Barre: Northlight Studio Pr., 1984; published by the Town of New Haven).
(4) J. Kevin Graffagnino, Vermont in the Victorian Age (Bennington: Vermont Heritage Press, 1985).

(28) **Brookfield** (Orange).

(28a) Brookfield.

c. 1790: first tavern, Experience Fisk; he came in 1790, lived where the MacAskill place now is (i.e., 1987), at the junction of Rte 14 and the hill road, once part of the Paine Turnpike, the stage road between Boston and Montreal;

* * *

The charter for the Paine turnpike conferred on him the right to build and operate a turnpike road "from Experience Fisk's in Brookfield, through Williamstown, Northfield, and Berlin, to the north side of Onion River." (2)

* * *

(?): other early tavern-keepers were Major Nathaniel Wheatley, on "the Branch" on Shubael Cross's land (listed in the Vermont Almanac and Register (1796) as a tavern on the Windsor-Burlington road; Wheatley also listed in almanacs from 1807-15); Ebenezer Stratton on East St (see below; almanacs, 1807-15); Major Reuben Adams, near the Randolph line on the central upland; Amos Humphrey in Brookfield Center; and Ebenezer Ainsworth north of Pond Village, where the road goes close to the Interstate (Ainsworth listed in almanacs, 1816, '25, '29); Capt J. S. Allen had a tavern north of that owned by Experience Fisk, on the Branch, after the private turnpike was built through Williamstown Gulf (i.e., after 1800). (1)

* * *

The Stratton Tavern still stands (home of Helen and Elizabeth Livingston in recent times, VDHP 0903-55). Built by Ebenezer Stratton c. 1795, on what was the Paine turnpike, opened in 1799, and functioned as a tavern from about 1800 until about 1850. On the west side of TH 10, 0.3 miles south of TH 13 junction. There is a tavern sign in the Smithsonian, with the words "Stratton Tavern" on both sides, that is believed to have come from this place. The opening of the Gulf Road (present Route 14) drove it out of business.

* * *

1810: a tavern, Amasa Edson; came c. 1796, settled near Brookfield Center; built a sawmill and put up houses in what is now Mill Village; (almanacs, 1823, '25, '29);

1849: --, O. Edson (NEMU Dir);

1855: --, N. Goodale;

1870: --, Mrs Clark;

1873, '75, '78: (a) Traveler's Home, Mrs E. Clark;

1877: (a) as above, * (Beers);

1879, '80, '83: (a) as above;

1887, '90, '92, '95: --, C. P. Fullam;

1898: --, S. Smith and son;

1901: Lake View House, J. J. Nye;

1903: Brookfield House, -- (SBA booklet; probably same as Lake View House);

1905:   --, O. F. Nichols;

1908:   Lake View House, --;

1911:   --, W. A. Ford;

1914:   no hotel on Sanborn map;

1915, '17:   --, R. R. (or H.?) Simmons.

(28b) East Brookfield.

1849:   --, J. S. Allen; Temperance House, Normus Goodale (possibly in Brookfield; NEMU Dir).

(28c) West Brookfield. No listings found.

Note: the assistance of Mrs Alice Wakefield, Brookfield Historical Society, is gratefully acknowledged.

* * *

(1) History of Brookfield, Vermont, Brookfield Historical Society (n.p., 1987).
(2) Frederic J. Wood, The Turnpikes of New England (Boston: Marshall Jones Co., 1919).

* * *

(29) **Brookline** (Windham).

(29a) Brookline.

(?):   first tavern (and store), Isaac Taft (Hemenway); "was built for a hotel; a public house here from earliest date" (settlements here in the 1770s); followed by Samuel Churchill, Benjamin Ormsbee (tavern license, 1820-27), Edson Higgins (license, 1829-32), Franklin Walker, Thomas Gordon, and Joel Codding "who took the sign down c. 1852"; a J. Codding is shown on the 1856 McClellan map at the same place as Walter S. Bennett on the 1869 Beers, and Hemenway says that one of the two early hotels was in the house later owned by Bennett; (second hotel mentioned by Hemenway not identified); this place (i.e., the Taft tavern) is VDHP 1303-2, the Codding Tavern; a boarding-house in the early 1900s, now a private home;

(?):   a hotel and two stores at the foot of Windmill Mountain in the early part of the 19th century (Child); the windmill was said to have pumped water for the hotel and other establishments, the hotel continued until 1850; Windmill Mtn is a long ridge running roughly north-south, on the east side of the town, partly in Dummerston, and beginning a little north of the hamlet of Brookline, so this place would appear to be different from Taft's, above;

1849:   Codding Tavern, J. B. Codding (NEMU Dir); (see Taft's, above).

* * *

(30) **Brownington** (Orleans).

(30a) Brownington.

1799:   a tavern, Maj Samuel Smith; almanac, 1802; on the place owned by C. N. Thrasher c. 1877 (Hemenway); Thrasher is shown on the 1859 Walling, at a different site from the Rice and Going Hotel, below;

(?):   a tavern, Judge Strong; almanac, 1805; tavern license to an Elijah Strong, 1817-30;

kept for many years at the place now occupied by Chester Gilbert (this may be Brownington Center);

(?):   a stagecoach inn, --; burned long ago, photo in ref 1;

1815:   a hotel, --; built in this year, known later as the Rice and Going Hotel; (photo, c. 1904, ref 1); probably started by Amherst Stewart (Hemenway); tavern license, 1822-30;

Note: tavern licenses also to George Nye, 1817; Samuel Chamberlin, 1817; and Thomas C. Stewart, 1833;

1849:   --, L. Bigelow; --, L. Ford (NEMU Dir); one of these places is probably the Rice and Going Hotel, the other probably at Brownington Center;

1855, '56:   as above;

1859:   Rice and Going Hotel, --* (Walling);

1870:   --, Phineas Wheeler.

(30b) Brownington Center.

1849:   see entry under Brownington, above;

1870, '73:   Central House, I. A. (or J. A.) Wyman.

(30c) Evansville.   No listings found.

* * *

References

(1) Ralph S. Swett, History of Brownington, 1799-1974: 175th Anniversary Booklet (n.p., 1974?).

* * *

(31) Brunswick (Essex).

(31a) Brunswick/Brunswick Springs.

There have been two post offices in the town, one at Brunswick (1825-26 and 1829-93) and one to serve the resort at the Springs (1892-94). Present-day maps show a hamlet on Rte 102 called Brunswick Springs, which was Brunswick in the old days; the springs themselves, accessible by a dirt road looping off Rte 102, are on the steep west bank of the Connecticut River, about two miles south of Bloomfield, Vermont and North Stratford, New Hampshire.

* * *

"In the heyday of the fashionable water places, when mineral water cures were fantastic, no story is more colorful or tragic than that of the Brunswick Mineral Springs.

Legend says that the Indians and early white settlers stripped their patients and held them under the flow of the 'Medicinal Waters of the Great Spirit,' and cured them of their ailments, which included consumption, dyspepsia, scrofula, kidney diseases, rheumatism, salt rheum, glandular troubles, lifeless limbs and loss of vitality.

The six springs are in the form of a semi-circle of not more than fifteen feet, and in correct order from right to left are: Arsenic, Bromide, Sulphur, Magnesium, Calcium and Iron. Compared with the celebrated Calybdeate Springs of Germany, the waters of Brunswick Springs are found to contain a greater variety of minerals and in larger quantities. The story is told that Indians from Lake Magog brought a British soldier with a wounded arm to the springs in 1784, and cured him with their method of holding him under the stream of water, all springs being conducted into one crude spout." (1)

* * *

1790:   a Major French is said to have been the first person to take boarders into his home for the mineral water treatments;

1800:   David Hyde opened his home to patients, and enlarged it in 1815; "there were as many as twelve families entertaining patients in their homes by 1820"; (1)

1805:   a tavern, - Cargill (almanac);

1816:   a tavern, William Marshall; said by Hemenway to be the only one except for one kept for a few years (no date) by Thomas G. French (see above); Marshall died in 1833, the place apparently carried on by his wife, see below;

1832:   John Schoff said to have built the first house over the springs;

1849:   --, Mrs William Marshall (NEMU Dir; see above); --, J. D. French (NEMU Dir; see above); photo of this place in ref 1, said to have been a stage stop on the River Road;

1860-c. 1900:   Brunswick Springs House, Charles Bailey; built in 1860 near the springs, various owners until Dr D. C. Rowell bought it in the late 1870s. "The doctor (a dentist) also operated a bottling plant where he offered the bottled water for sale" (1); bought by Henry Smith in 1894; he enlarged it and ran it for several years before it burned, exact date not established; photo, ref 1; also VHS postcard;

c. 1900-21:   Pine Crest Lodge (Brunswick Springs Lodge), Dr D. C. Rowell (see photo). Rowell bought the Brunswick Springs House property back after the fire, and built this place on a nearby elevation; John C. Hutchins acquired it in 1910 when Rowell died; this place also burned, in 1929; Hutchins attempted rebuilding twice more, fires both times (photo, ref 1);

* * *

"This last fabulous summer hotel and water resort was to be one hundred fifty feet long and four stories high, with broad verandas on all sides and plate glass windows overlooking tiny Silver Lake just across the road, the beautiful Connecticut River valley to the south and the White Mountains on the east. Sixty rooms, thirty with private baths, awaited the guests. Brunswick Springs water was piped to every room. No attempt has since been made to build another hotel.

Some people still believe an old Indian legend is true: 'Any use of the 'Water of the Great Spirit' for profit will not prosper'". So far it never has for any length of time." (1)

* * *

1878:   (a) Brunswick Mineral Springs Hotel, D. C. Rowell* (Beers);

1879:   (a) as above, --;

1883:   (a) as above, David O. Rowell;

1887:   (a) as above, Henry Smith (Child);

1908:   Pine Crest, --;

153

Brunswick Springs Lodge

1911: <u>Pine Crest Cottage</u>, D. D. and D. E. Rowell;

1915: <u>Pine Crest</u>, C. M. Bridgman (summers); also listed as <u>Brunswick Springs Lodge</u> (VPB), and as late as 1930 in Walton.

* * *

<u>References</u>

(1) Verne M. Hunter and Marjorie M. Carrier, The History of Brunswick, Vermont (Town of Brunswick Bicentennial Comm., 1977).

* * *

(32) **Burke** (Caledonia).

(32a) <u>Burke (Hollow)</u>.

c. 1802: a tavern, <u>Ebenezer Burrington</u> and his son Joseph (1); tavern licenses to an Asahel Burington, 1823, '24; and to J. and A. Burington, 1822;

(?): a tavern, <u>Abel Hall</u>; on part of the "present" (i.e., 1896) Theron Bell place;

(?): a tavern, <u>Bemis and Denison</u>; in a home occupied in 1896 by David Coe;

1830: <u>Bugbee Tavern</u>, --; two miles below the Hollow, built in this year;

1848: a tavern, <u>Daniel Denison</u>; who bought the house and store of Gideon Lamb, made it into a tavern; "succeeded by Clark Libbey, last tavern-keeper here" (1); property of Azro Kennerson in 1896; photo, ref 2;

1849: --, Daniel B. Denison; --, I. Thomas (NEMU Dir; this may be East or West Burke);

1855: --, A. Bugbee, Jr (see above); --, H. Colby (may be East or West Burke);

1870: --, Abel Bigbee (sp?);

1875: --, Mrs H. Bigbee.

(32b) <u>East Burke</u>.

(?): first tavern, <u>H. W. Belden</u>; in a house kept in 1896 by David Gilson;

154

(?):   a small house for visitors on top of Burke Mountain, built by Joseph S. Hale;

1858:   --, Evans Hall and Co* (Walling);

1870, '73:   --, Charles Webb;

1875:   --, C. Webb* (Beers; same site as 1858, above); probably the <u>Burke Mountain House</u>, see below;

1878, '80:   (a) <u>Burke Mountain House</u>, R. S. Pierce;

1883, '87:   (a) as above, C. C. Thurber;

1890:   (a) as above, N. L. Parker;

1892:   --, A. B. Colby;

1922, '28:   (a) as above, --* (Sanborn); said to have burned in 1976, still operating then.

(32c) <u>South Burke</u>. No listings found.

(32d) <u>West Burke</u>.

1858:   (a) <u>Trull's Hotel</u>, --* (Walling; became the <u>West Burke Hotel</u>, see below; names used interchangeably);

1870, '73:   --, Joel Trull;

1875:   (a) <u>West Burke Hotel</u>, David and J. Trull* (Beers, same site as 1858); David Trull also transported tourists to the <u>Willoughby Lake House</u>, 16 miles away;

1875, '78, '79, '80, '83:   (a) as above;

1887:   (a) as above, M. K. Colby;

1887:   <u>Smith's Hotel</u>, C. M. Smith (Child);

1888:   (a) as above, H. F. Foster; <u>The Arcadia</u>, E. B. O'Dell (Boston and Maine guide);

1890:   (a) as above, Francis Richardson;

1892:   --, C. A. Silver;

1895:   --, A. McGowen;

1905:   --, Charles Cheney;

1913:   --, A. C. Griffin;

1915:   --, A. V. Abar;

1916:   (a) <u>West Burke Hotel</u>, R. R. Davis (VPB);

1917:   (a) <u>West Burke Hotel</u>, -- (said to have burned, date not known); <u>Pisgah Lodge</u>, A. D. Abar.

Note: the assistance of Phyllis Burbank, Burke Historical Society, is gratefully acknowledged.

<u>References</u>

(1) St Johnsbury Republican, July 1, 1896.
(2) Past Views of Burke (Burke Historical Society, 1986).

* * *

(33) **Burlington** (Chittenden). Burlington (and Vergennes) were the first post offices north of Rutland, established in 1792 soon after Vermont joined the Union.

(33a) <u>Burlington</u>.

1788: an inn, <u>Gideon King</u>; who died in 1804, place carried on by son Joseph, who sold to Isaac Harrington in 1816; many subsequent lessees; on the northeast corner of King and Water (now Battery) Sts; first hotel in town, according to Child; almanac, 1802; 2-story building with a kitchen in the rear; court sessions held here in 1790, '91; the 1857 Walling shows the <u>Champlain House</u> at this site (see below) and the 1869 Beers shows a building labeled only "hotel" here; Child says the old <u>King hotel</u> was replaced by a brick house, c. 1840, but probably it was replaced by the <u>Champlain House</u>; Gideon King's brother Lyman built another inn later "on the square," later Col. Thomas's hotel (see below);

Note: the 1869 Sanborn shows a place called <u>Murphy's Hotel</u> at this site;

(?): a tavern, <u>Peter Benedict</u>; known later as the <u>Eldredge stand</u>, where the Winooski Turnpike (present Rte 2, Williston Rd, approximately) intersected the road from Hinesburg to the "high bridge" (at Winooski Park; this latter road is Eldredge St on the 1869 Beers, present Rte 116, approximately); for 50 years;

(?): a tavern, <u>Maj Ebenezer Brown</u>; one-half mile east of the Eldredge stand, above;

(?): a tavern, --; 2 miles south of the village on the Shelburne Road;

1790: a hotel, <u>Col Stephen Keyes</u>; on Water St (Battery St); listed in the Vermont Almanac and Register (1796) as a tavern at Burlington Bay on the Windsor-Burlington route;

1796: <u>Ames tavern</u>, --; listed on the Vermont Almanac and Register as a tavern on the Rutland-Canada, and Windsor-Burlington routes; also 1802, '07;

1800: a tavern, <u>Ebenezer Allen</u>; on the lake front, until 1806, when he died; see South Hero;

(?): a hotel, <u>Nathan Smith</u>; a Revolutionary War veteran who came in 1786, settled on the farm owned by D. Fisk in 1882 (Child) at the corner of roads 21, 22;

(?): a tavern, -; "the house on Colchester Avenue, just below the cemetery, long known as the Edgcomb place, was then a tavern stand" (about 1800; Child);

1808: (a) <u>American House</u>, --; south side of Court House Square, southeast corner of St Paul and Main Sts; a 4-story brick building; bought by Gov. Van Ness in 1824, who added the east wing on Main St, and the south wing on St Paul St in 1844; managers included Ira Shattuck from 1830 for about 6 years; Lemuel S. Drew from 1852-65; then Charles Miller; Drew again in 1878; from about 1886, the place was open only in the summers, in connection with the Van Ness, next door; for 60 years it was the leading hotel in Burlington; Presidents Monroe and Van Buren, and Henry Clay, were amongst its guests; it closed in the early part of the 20th century, and was replaced by the <u>Hotel Vermont</u> by at least 1911;

c. 1812: 1st <u>Howard Hotel</u>, John Howard; built by William Coit, building moved to the north side of Court House Square, used later as a hotel by Howard, for 35 years; (almanac,

1816, '23; tavern license, 1821); place also kept briefly after that by Royal Gould; Howard left in 1847, died in 1854; according to Rann, this place was sold by Sion E. Howard to Daniel Buckley, who leased it to Artemas Prouty in 1844 (1); it burned in January, 1846; place shown on map in Zadock Thompson, 1840 (2); Gen Lafayette banqueted here in June, 1825; Howard was distinguished for his heroism when the "Phoenix" burned on Lake Champlain in 1819; two of his sons established the Irving Hotel in New York City; there was a second <u>Howard House</u> at a different location later (see below);

* * *

"Busiest part...in the old days was at the head of Pearl St and around the square. The most popular resort for strangers and those who loved not the life of the soldier was the comfortable hostelry of 'Uncle John Howard.'" He came from Addison in 1812, exchanged his farm for the tavern with Azra Crane, preceding proprietor. The building was already old, could hardly be entitled to a more dignified appellation than that of a country tavern. Three stories in height, but not so high as many buildings now are at two stories. A framed building, it stood on the site now (i.e., 1886) covered by the store of B. Turk and Brother, next east from what was then the shoe shop of Lemuel Page. In the rear of the main building were two wings, one behind the other. The main entrance was on College; a broad covered piazza in front of the second story, and the roof topped by a platform with balustrade. Just east of the main building was a covered driveway separating the tavern from a little 2-story building just beyond; as early as 1825 a dancing-hall was built over this driveway. "What anecdotes were related and side-splitting jokes played in that old inn; what comedies of real life were enacted there; what laughter at the keen witticisms of Barty Willard came from the lips of the old time guests who arrived by the latest stage from Boston, Troy, Montpelier, or perhaps Canada, we can never know; but from the hearty genial nature of John Howard, and the smiles that illuminate the faces of the 'old settlers' whenever they hear or tell of the place, we are safe in assuming that a Boswell's life of Uncle John would be well worth the reading. The back yard of the inn took up nearly an acre of ground." (1)

* * *

(?):   <u>Green Mountain House</u>, --; built in 1789 by Frederick Saxton; on the northeast corner of Pearl and Prospect Sts; Rann described it as being at the "summit of its popularity" in 1827, then managed by Eli Barnard (1); tavern license, 1821; shown on an 1840 map (2); building shown as "vacant" on the 1889 Sanborn;

(?):   an inn, --; at a place later called the <u>Omnium Gatherum</u>, on the corner of Pine and Pearl Sts; this building still stands;

1827:   a tavern, <u>Capt Henry Thomas</u>; begun by Lyman King; on the northeast corner of Court House Square, converted into a commercial building (the Strong block) before 1846; kept earlier by Maj Abram Brinsmaid (tavern license, 1821); known at one time as the <u>Burlington Hotel</u>, not the same as the later <u>Hotel Burlington</u>;

1828:   1st <u>Howard Hotel</u>, --; listed as a stage terminus in Badger and Porter's Stage Directory;

Note: other almanac listings, unidentified: Crane, 1817-29; Brownson, 1802-16; Gould, 1825-29; Atwater, 1832 (also a tavern license to a Thomas Atwater, 1821); Hollister ("village,") 1832; Sawyer ("village,") 1812-15; Johnson ("village,") 1812-29 (also a tavern license to a Patrick Johnson, 1821); Bennett, 1812;

Note: other tavern licenses, all 1821, to David Giffin, Edward Washburn, Montgomery Olmstead, Josiah King and Silas Root;

Note: two other early taverns mentioned in Rann are listed together below; it seems possible, from their description, that they were little more than saloons. (1)

* * *

157

"Around the barracks (i.e., War of 1812) was a camping ground about two times as large as present Battery Park...a scene of greatest activity. The movement against the liquor traffic not having begun, soldier and civilian united in unconcealed successions of hilarious sprees. This thoroughfare (i.e., Water Street) was lined with little wooden buildings which had been converted into cheap boarding-houses, taverns and rum shops. One of the larger taverns, kept by one Chandonette, a Parisian, was a square framed house, two stories, painted white...on the northeast corner of Main and Water Sts, facing south... continually crowded with soldiers and camp followers, who spent their time in drinking and carousing. Another tavern on the east side of Water St, fronting west, on the present site of the building owned by Drew and Conger (i.e., 1886)...about 1821 Russell Harrington, brother of William C. Harrington, was the proprietor of this place..." (ref 1) (Harrington has an almanac listing, 1825, '29).

* * *

1840:   Pearl St House, --; on the southwest corner of Pearl and Prospect Sts; (2)

Note: The 1842 and 1843 Waltons list hotels for a few Vermont cities, including Burlington, and these are grouped together below. They are unnamed in Walton, and only a few of them can be even tentatively linked to the named hotels of a somewhat later time.

1842:   John Howard (College St; this is the 1st Howard's); Ira Shattuck (Main St, probably the American House, see below); J. S. Pierce (Pearl St); S. Broth, Jonas Hart, John Sarayan, J. A. Jenner (all on Water St; Jenner's is shown on an 1840 map) (2); Benjamin Bishop (Main St); M. Burdick (Church St); J. P. Maillet (Champlain St); Jeremiah Potter (College St); M. Russell (Pearl St); S. W. Taylor (Main St); one of the two places above on Pearl St was presumably the Green Mountain House/Pearl Street House;

1843:   John Howard, Benjamin Bishop, M. Burdick, J. P. Maillet, Jeremiah Potter, John Sarayan, J. A. Jenner, M. R. Russell, S. W. Taylor, as above; also M. S. Hart, (Water St; probably the Lake House, see below); and W. Root (Pearl St);

(?):   Franklin House, --; Riley Adams an early proprietor, followed by Lemuel Drew about 1849, who named it the 2nd Howard House; succeeded in 1852 by S. S. Skinner, then Sidney Smith after 3 years, then bought by D. C. Barber; it burned in June, 1867, and Barber built the Van Ness House on the site in 1870;

Note: the 1869 Beers shows a place called the Franklin at the northwest corner of Champlain and King Sts; apparently there were two Franklin Houses at different times;

(?):   (b) 2nd Howard Hotel,--; at the southwest corner of St Paul and Main Sts, formerly the Franklin House (see above); replaced by the Van Ness, after it burned in 1867;

(?):   (c) Champlain House, --; on Water St (Battery); Walling shows this on the old Gideon King site in 1857 (see discussion under Gideon King, above); it is a little puzzling that this place seems to drop out of Walton for about 15 years (1875-90) and is not listed in Child in 1882, but then reappears in 1890, and is listed more or less continuously until 1925; was there a second Champlain House? Shown on the 1889 Sanborn and subsequently, but not in 1885;

(?):   Exchange Hotel, --; on Water St (Battery); became the Lake House, c. 1858; according to Rann, a small tavern that had stood for years (i.e., the Exchange) was enlarged and named the Lake House at about the time of the opening of the Rutland Railroad; John Bradley was an early proprietor and others were Moses L. Hart, a Mr Curtis, and Z. G. Clark;

Note: there is a problem here; the Rutland Railroad came to Burlington about 1850, but this hostelry is listed as the Exchange until at least 1855 or so (Walton, 1855; Walling, 1857); Zadock Thompson (2) and Walling (1857) both show it as the Exchange; but Beers (1869) shows it as the Lake House (west side of Water St, between King and South);

(?):   (d) Lake House, --; the Exchange Hotel until about 1858 (see above); burned in

November, 1869);

(?):   (e) <u>Central House</u>, --; on Church St, between Bank and Cherry, opposite the jail;

(?):   (f) <u>Stanton House</u>, --; on the northwest corner of Church and Cherry Sts; became <u>Rowe's Hotel</u> by 1875 (see photo); built before 1800, but not clear when it became a hotel; according to Rann, <u>Rowe's Hotel</u> was an old landmark (i.e., in 1886), probably built before 1800, by Harvey Durkee; kept by his widow long after his death, followed by her son, Harvey Jr, and Robert Nulty, c. 1886; became the <u>Sherwood</u> by 1895 (Sanborn);

1840:   (a) <u>American House</u> *; (b) 2nd <u>Howard Hotel</u>*; <u>Pearl Street House</u>*; <u>Exchange</u>; <u>Franklin Hotel</u>*; <u>Jenner's Hotel</u>* (listed as J. A. Jenner in 1842, '43), and ref 2;

Rowe's Hotel (Special Collections, UVM)

1849:   (a) <u>American House</u>, William J. O'Dell; (b) 2nd <u>Howard House</u>, L.S. Drew; (c) <u>Champlain Hotel</u>, D. Cram; (d) <u>Exchange</u>, - Blodgett; <u>Eldrigh</u> (<u>Eldredge</u>) <u>House</u>, Z. D. Bishop (see above); <u>Church St House</u>, George W. Rhode (unidentified); <u>Hart's Hotel</u>, Moses L. Hart; <u>Traveler's Home</u>, C. F. Parsons; <u>Pearl St House</u> (formerly the <u>Green Mountain House</u>), John Edson; --, L. L. Skinner; (all NEMU Dir);

1855:   (a) <u>American</u>, Drew and Prouty; --, L. L. Skinner; (d) <u>Exchange</u>, - Blodgett; <u>Farmer's Hotel</u>, L. S. Hill (all Walton);

1856:   (a) as above; (b) 2nd <u>Howard House</u>, S. S. Smith;

1857:   (a) <u>American House</u>, L. S. Drew* (Walling); (b) 2nd <u>Howard House</u>, S. S. Smith* (Walling); (c) <u>Champlain House</u>, --* (Walling; Gideon King site); (d) <u>Exchange Hotel</u>, --* (Walling; <u>Lake House</u> site);

1868:   (a) as above, H. H. Have (Howe?); (c) as above, Edward Murphy; (d) <u>Lake House</u>, Z. G. Clark; (e) <u>Central House</u>, L. D. Turrill; (f) <u>Stanton House</u>, R. C. Rowe (all Walton);

1869:   (a) as above, H. B. (?) Howe and Co*; (d) as above*; (e) as above*; (f) as above* (Beers);

1869:   Sanborn map for this year shows (a) <u>American</u>; (d) <u>Lake House</u>; (e) <u>Central</u>; (g) <u>City</u> (see below); <u>Franklin</u> (northwest corner of Champlain and King); <u>Murphy's Hotel</u> (the <u>Lyman King/Champlain</u> site, northeast corner of Water and King); and a place called the <u>Allen House</u>, on the northeast corner, Main and Church;

1870:   (h) <u>Van Ness House</u>, D. C. Barber; named in honor of Gov. Cornelius Van Ness; a 4-story brick building on the southwest corner of Main and St Paul Sts, on the site of the old <u>Franklin House/2nd Howard</u>, which burned on June 11, 1867 (see above); west wing added in 1882 (see photo);

Van Ness House (Special Collections, UVM)

1870:   (a) as above; (d) <u>Lake House</u>, Z. G. Clark (listed as "burnt" in Walton); (e) as above; (f) as above; (g) <u>City Hotel</u>, Ray and Brooks; <u>Allen House</u>, Josiah P. Cutting (Orin Pelton in Vt Dir);

1873:   (a) as above, Cram and Stacy; (f) as above, Merritt and Stone; (h) <u>Van Ness House</u>, D. C. Barber;

1875:   (a) as above, H. H. Howe; (c) <u>Champlain Hotel</u>, William Deavitt; (h) as above; (i) <u>Rowe's Hotel</u>, R. C. Rowe (formerly <u>Stanton's</u>); (j) <u>Park House</u>, -- (later <u>Quincy House</u>); (k) <u>Lake View</u>, Abram Duguay (different from the <u>Lake House</u>, which burned in 1869; northeast corner of Battery and Cherry Sts, Sanborn, 1885; a boarding-house in the 1890s);

1879:   (a) as above, L. S. Drew; (h) as above; (i) as above, Henry Parker; (j) as above, C. O. Pettengill (NW corner, St Paul and Main); (k) <u>Lake View House</u>, Benjamin Lafond;

1880:   (a) as above; (h) as above; (i) as above; (j) as above, H. (?) O. Pettengill; (k) <u>Lake View House</u>, Abram Duguay;

1880s: Evart's House, --; on the north side of Main St, between Pine and St Paul (Sanborn);

Major Burlington Hotels

(a) American House (replaced by Hotel Vermont);
(b) 2nd Howard House (formerly the Franklin; replaced by Van Ness);
(c) Champlain Hotel (on the early Gideon King site);
(d) Lake House (formerly the Exchange);
(e) Central House;
(f) Stanton House (later Rowe's, the Sherwood; replaced by the New Sherwood);
(g) City (later New City and possibly La France);
(h) Van Ness House;
(i) Rowe's (formerly Stanton House);
(j) Park (later Quincy; replaced by Hotel Burlington);
(k) Lake View;
(l) Quincy (formerly Park);
(m) Hotel Burlington (formerly Quincy);
(n) Hotel Champlain;
(o) Sherwood (formerly Rowe's);
(p) Russell House (later Union Station Hotel);
(q) Hotel Vermont (replaced American House);
(r) Elmwood House;
(s) Arlington House (or Hotel Arlington; later New Arlington);
(t) Pitcher's Hotel (later Champlain Hotel);
(u) New Sherwood;
(v) New City; possibly became La France;
(w) New Arlington;
(x) Union Station Hotel (formerly Russell House);
(y) Champlain Hotel (formerly Pitcher's Hotel);

* * *

1882: (l) Quincy House, Diamond Stone; enlarged from a dwelling-house, first opened as the Park House by Charles Eaton in 1874; 3-story wooden building (Child); replaced by the Hotel Burlington by 1887;

1882: (a) as above; (h) Van Ness, Bowman, Woodbury and Clark, proprietors; (i) as above, H. S. Kimball; (k) Lake View House, John B. Forrant (Child; 32-34 Battery); (l) Quincy House, Diamond Stone (Child);

1883: (a) as above; (h) as above; (i) as above, Robert Nulty;

1885: Note: the 1885 Sanborn shows (a) American, (e) Central, (h) Van Ness, (i) Rowe's, (k) Lake View, and Evarts (on the north side of Main St, between Pine and St Paul Sts);

1887: (a) and (h), American and Van Ness, apparently combined, U. A. Woodbury, proprietor, L. S. Drew, manager; (g) City Hotel, J. A. Stone (Vt Dir; 143-145 Main St); (i) as above; (k) Lake View, J. B. Forant; Edmunds House, W. M. Fielder; Commercial House, E. M. Fulton (Vt Dir; 179 Bank St); Pearl Street House, J. Barnes (Vt Dir, 70 Pearl St); (m) Hotel Burlington, Delaney and Harrington (Vt Dir, St Paul opp. the Park); built in 1887 by George Delaney, first proprietor, according to Allen and replaced the Park; a 4-story brick building;

1889: Note: Sanborn shows (a) American, (c) Champlain, (g) Van Ness, (i) Rowe's, (k) Lake View (now a boarding-house), (m) Hotel Burlington, the Evarts ("in ruins,") and the Pearl St Hotel ("vacant");

1890: (a), (h) as above; (c) Champlain, John Donnelly (Vt Dir, 176 Battery); (g) as above,

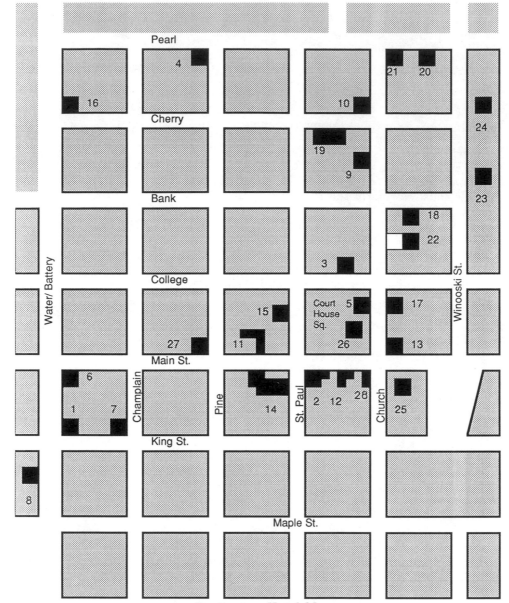

Burlington Hotel Map
(based on 1869 Beers)

* * *

1. Gideon King/Champlain House/ Murphy House
2. American House/Hotel Vermont
3. 1st Howard
4. Omnium Gatherum
5. Capt Henry Thomas tavern
6. Jenner's/Russell's/Union Station
7. Franklin House (not the predecessor of the Van Ness)
8. Exchange/Lake House
9. Central House
10. Stanton's/Rowe's/Sherwood/ New Sherwood
11. Evart's
12. City/New City
13. Allen House
14. Franklin/2nd Howard/ Van Ness
15. Park/Quincy/Hotel Burlington
16. Lake View
17. Hotel Champlain
18. Wayside Inn
19. Arlington/New Arlington
20. Gilbert Inn
21. Richardson
22. Traveller's Inn
23. Methodist church
24. Congregational church
25. US Customs/PO
26. Court House
27. New England Hotel
28. Pitcher's Hotel

* * *

162

Mrs James A. Stone; (m) as above; <u>Hotel Chittenden</u>, J. J. Thompson (Vt Dir, 35 Church);

1892: (a), (h) and (c) as above; (g) <u>City</u>, J. A. Stone; (k) <u>Lake View</u>, J. B. Forrant; (n) <u>Hotel Champlain</u>, W. B. Craven (different from the <u>Champlain House</u>); on Church St, east side, between Main and College Sts; on the 1906 Sanborn; (m) <u>Hotel Burlington</u>, Delaney and Harrington; <u>Crystal</u>, H. R. Coon; <u>Hotel Chittenden</u>, Clifford and Means;

1894: Note: Sanborn lists (a) <u>American</u>, (c) <u>Champlain</u>, (g) <u>City</u>, (h) <u>Van Ness</u>, (m) <u>Hotel Burlington</u>, and (o) <u>Sherwood</u> (formerly <u>Rowe's</u>);

1895: (a),(c) and (h) as above; (g) as above, Mrs C. (?) A. Stone; (k) <u>Lake View</u>, as above; (m) <u>Hotel Burlington</u>, as above; (o) <u>Sherwood</u>, T. K. Murphy (formerly <u>Rowe's</u>); <u>American</u>, Mrs M. Zottman (unidentified, but almost certainly not the same as the old <u>American</u>, still listed here above with the <u>Van Ness</u>); (n) <u>Hotel Champlain</u>, as above;

1898: (c) as above; (h) <u>Van Ness</u>, U. A. Woodbury; (g) <u>City</u>, as above; (k) <u>Lake View</u>, Mrs C. Galinas; (m) <u>Hotel Burlington</u>, G. M. Delaney; (n) <u>Hotel Champlain</u>, --; (o) <u>Sherwood</u>, T. K. Murphy; <u>Hotel Vendome</u>, S. F. Storrs; <u>Russell House</u>, C. Z. Brouillette; <u>Lafayette House</u>, Myron Barnes;

1900: Note: Sanborn lists (a) <u>American</u>, (c) <u>Champlain</u>, (g) <u>City</u>, (h) <u>Van Ness</u>, (m) <u>Hotel Burlington</u>, (o) <u>Sherwood</u>, and (p) <u>Russell</u>, on the northeast corner of Battery and Main Sts;

1901: (a) <u>American</u>, --; became the (q) <u>Hotel Vermont</u> by 1911, Sanborn); (g) <u>City</u>, J. T. Kelly; (h) <u>Van Ness</u>, U. A. Woodbury (Vt Dir); (m) as above; (n) <u>Hotel Champlain</u>, W. D. Craven (Vt Dir, 140 Church St; on the 1906 Sanborn, but missing in 1912); (o) <u>Sherwood</u>, T. K. Murphy (Vt Dir, 35 Church St); <u>Lakeside House</u>, Frederick Kean (Vt Dir, location unknown, almost certainly different from earlier <u>Lake House</u> and <u>Lake View House</u>); <u>Metropolitan House</u>, W. P. Perry (Vt Dir, 35 St Paul);

1902: <u>Riverside Park House</u>, W. R. Chambers (CVRR booklet);

1905: (c) <u>Champlain</u>, J. Mitchell; (h) <u>Van Ness</u>, U. A. Woodbury, prop., H. E. Woodbury, mgr; (g) <u>City</u>, F. J. Flanagan; (k) <u>Lake View</u>, Mrs C. Galinas; (m), (o) as above; (p) <u>Russell House</u>, --; <u>Lafayette House</u>, Fred Degree; <u>Riverside Park</u>, --; <u>American Hotel</u>, A. C. Green; <u>Hotel Exchange</u>, L. P. Levesque; <u>Crescent Beach Inn</u>, C. A. Wahlstrom;

1906: Note: Sanborn lists (a) <u>American</u>, (c) <u>Champlain</u>, (g) <u>City</u>, (h) <u>Van Ness</u>, (m) <u>Hotel Burlington</u>, (o) <u>Sherwood</u>, (p) <u>Russell Hotel</u>; also the (n) <u>Hotel Champlain</u> on Church St, east side, between Main and College Sts; and the <u>Wayside Inn</u>, on Bank St, south side, between Church and Center;

1908: (h) <u>Van Ness</u>, --; (m) <u>Hotel Burlington</u>, --; (latter missing from the 1912 Sanborn);

1911: (c) <u>Champlain</u>,--; (g) <u>City</u>, --; (h) <u>Van Ness</u>, --; (k) <u>Lake View House</u>, --; (o) <u>Sherwood</u>, --; (p) <u>Russell House</u>, --; (q) <u>Hotel Vermont</u>, -- (formerly the (a) <u>American House</u>); (s) <u>Arlington</u>, -- (Cherry St, south side, between St Paul and Church, 1912 Sanborn); (v) <u>Elmwood</u>, --; <u>Crescent Beach</u>, --; <u>Revere House</u>, --;

1912: Note: Sanborn lists (c) <u>Champlain</u>, (h) <u>Van Ness</u>, (g) <u>City</u>, (t) <u>Pitcher's Hotel</u> (southwest corner, Main and Church, just east of the <u>City Hotel</u>), (p) <u>Russell</u>, (q) <u>Hotel Vermont</u>, (u) <u>New Sherwood</u> (seems to be a different building, same site, than (o) <u>Sherwood</u>); the <u>Wayside</u>, (m) <u>Hotel Burlington</u> and (n) <u>Hotel Champlain</u> are gone; and a place called the (s) <u>Hotel Arlington</u> (Cherry St, between St Paul and Church, south side) is shown;

1913: (c), (g), (h), (o), (q), (s), and (v) as above; (k) <u>Lake View</u>, --; <u>Crescent Beach</u>, --; <u>Collins</u>, -;

1917:   (c), (h), (q), (r) and (s) as above; (v) <u>New City</u>, --; (j) <u>Lake View</u>, --; (t) <u>Pitcher's Hotel</u>, --; (w) <u>New Sherwood</u>, --; <u>Bay View Summer House</u>, --; <u>Revere</u>, --;

1919:   Note: Sanborn lists (q) <u>Hotel Vermont</u>, (c) <u>Champlain</u>, (h) <u>Van Ness</u>, (v) <u>New City</u>, (t) <u>Pitcher's</u>, (w) <u>New Arlington</u> (same location as the <u>Arlington</u>); (x) <u>Union Station Hotel</u> (formerly (p) <u>Russell's</u>); (u) <u>New Sherwood</u>; also the <u>Gilbert Inn</u>;

1920:   (c), (g), (q), (r), (t), (u), and (w) as above; <u>Bay View Summer House</u>, --;

1923:   (c), (h), (g), (q), (r), (t), (u), and (w) as above; <u>Ethan Allen Inn</u>, --; <u>Hotel Fotokas</u>, --; <u>La France Hotel</u>, --; (Pearl St, south side, between Church and Winooski, 1919 Sanborn); <u>Rock House</u>, --; <u>Gilbert Inn</u>, --; <u>Tremont House</u>, --; <u>Traveller's Inn</u>, --;

1925:   (c), (h), (g), (q) and (u) as above; (t) <u>Pitcher's</u> was (y) <u>Champlain Hotel</u> by 1926, Sanborn; (x) <u>Union Station Hotel</u>, --; <u>Ethan Allen Inn</u>, --; <u>Hotel Fotokas</u>, --; <u>La France Hotel</u>, -- (but according to Sanborn, the (v) <u>New City</u> became the <u>La France</u> by 1926); <u>Rock House</u>, --; <u>Traveller's Inn</u>, -- (later the <u>Hotel Breton</u>); <u>Silver Grey Inn</u>, --; <u>Lake Champlain Club</u>, -- (summers).

(33b) <u>Queen City Park</u>.

Site of a summer campground for the Vermont Spiritualist's Association, who stayed there first in tents, and later in a hotel. On Shelburne Bay, it was a stop on the Rutland Railroad at one time. There was a PO here from 1897-1932, with the last two postmasters, F. M. Hunt and D. H. Chapman, also being the innkeepers.

(?):   1st <u>Queen City Park Hotel</u>, --; between 1882, when the Association bought the site, and 1896, when a "new and elegant three story Hotel, capacity of 200, had been built to replace the original one which had burned." (4) The new one also burned, in 1939; see photo;

Queen City Park Hotel

1888:   <u>Queen City Park Hotel</u>, F. M. Hunt; Boston and Maine guide;

1905:   (a) 2nd <u>Queen City Park Hotel</u>, I. W. Hatch; see photo;

1908:   (a) as above, --;

1911, '13:   (a) as above, F. M. Hunt;

1920:   (a) as above, D. H. Chapman; listed in 1923 (VPB), and in 1935, '40.

Note: the assistance of Mr David Blow is gratefully acknowledged.

References

(1) William S. Rann, The History of Chittenden County, Vermont (Syracuse: D. Mason, 1886).

(2) Z. Thompson, History of Vermont (Burlington: The Author, 1853; Part Two, Gazetteer) 39.

(3) Charles E. Allen, About Burlington, Vermont (Burlington: Hobart J. Stanley, 1905).

(4) Lilian B. Carlisle, ed., Look Around Chittenden County (Burlington: Chittenden County Historical Soc., 1976).

* * *

(34) **Cabot** (Washington).

(34a) Cabot (village).

c. 1790: first hotel, James Morse; at "the center of the town" (exact location not clear; Hemenway); Morse said to be first settler, 1789, "later" opened the first hotel in a log house; also first justice of the peace and performed the first marriage in 1795; "the bar was in the square room and a bed in the same. This was in the early days of hotel-keeping" (Hemenway);

1833: a tavern, John Damon; (his 2nd, see under Cabot Plains); tavern license, 1823-27; kept his first tavern at his home in Cabot Plains, but moved "across the river" in 1833, present hotel is on the same site, later known as the Winooski House. Fisher was landlord four years, then Horace Bliss for ten "when it was known as a first-class hotel." Different proprietors until 1875, when it was renovated by William P. Whittier, who had it until 1881; then W. W. Buchanan;

1849: --, A. Webster; --, Calvin F. Cate (NEMU Dir; one of these is probably East or Lower Cabot);

1855, '56: --, G. O. Page; --, O. Underhill (probably East or Lower Cabot);

1858: --, G. H. Paige* (Walling);

1870, '73, '75, '78, '80: (a) Winooski House, W. P. Whittier* (Beers);

1883: (a) as above, Charles W. Cade;

1887: (a) as above, W. B. Fifield (M. H. Everett in Vt Dir);

1890: (a) as above, L. D. Smith;

1892: (a) as above, L. C. Cole;

1895, '98: (a) as above, R. J. O'Neill;

1901: (a) as above, A. V. Nelson;

1905, '11: --, E. M. Bliss;

1908: (a) Winooski House, --;

1914: (a) as above, --* (Sanborn); place burned about 1915, town hall now on the site;

1913, '15: --, H. W. Dane;

1917: (a) as above, H. W. Pond (?); (Dowd in VPB); a place called the Cabot Inn listed in Walton, 1930, '35, '40, no further information.

(34b) <u>Cabot Plains</u>.

First settlement here, 1783, but never a post office with this name. By 1810 or so, things were shifting to Cabot village (above) and Lower Cabot.

c. 1790: a tavern, <u>Horace and Gershom (sp?)Beardsley</u>; known as the "<u>Yellow House</u>," first frame house in town; a big two-story place, very busy, with an attached hall for meetings, sheds for teams, etc; this place was on the County road connecting Montpelier to the Bayley-Hazen road. The <u>Yellow House</u> was a focal point for smuggling activity during the War of 1812, declined thereafter, torn down in 1855;

* * *

"About the time Caledonia county was set off from Orange, Dr Greshom and Horace Beardsley entertained so sanguine an opinion that Cabot would be the shire town, that they proceeded to clear two acres of land...for the county buildings...On this site they raised the first frame house in town. This frame was all hard wood and two stories high, and it required a large force of men, and a corresponding quantity of rum, to raise it. All the men and women in Cabot, Peacham and Danville were invited to the raising, and two barrels of rum was provided for the occasion (to meet the threats that those invited 'would drink the Beardsleys dry,' and all were invited to help themselves. The rum there imbibed lasted a great many two days, and in after years they enjoyed rehearsing the incidents of this 'raising.' The Beardsleys did not realize their hopes in the location of the county site, and their building was not finished where it was raised. In about two years it was removed to the Plain, nicely finished, and became the renowned 'Yellow House,' and the favorite inn of the travelers passing between the north and Connecticut River. The Plain was the 'hub' of the town for about eighteen years...there now remains but a single farm house to mark the place of its departed glory." (Child, 1889)

* * *

c. 1805: a tavern, <u>John Damon</u>; (his 1st); Damon was an early settler on the plain, opened his house (where Mrs Joseph Lance's home stood, c. 1882, Hemenway) as a tavern, later built a hotel in the village (see above); tavern licenses, 1823, '24.

(34c) <u>East Cabot</u>.

c. 1820: a tavern, <u>John Clark</u>; opposite Molly Pond, later known as the <u>Pond House</u>.

(34d) <u>Lower Cabot</u>.

c. 1820: <u>Farmer's Tavern</u>, Elihu Coburn (Child; tavern license, 1822); he came in 1799, settled "in the valley where his son Elihu F. Coburn, now (i.e., 1889, Child) lives"; there is an H. and E. F. or E. E. Coburn on the 1873 Beers, a little south of Lower Cabot; he and his wife kept the <u>Farmer's Tavern</u> about thirty years; (VDHP 1204-31, the Gould Farm in 1879);

1836: a hotel, <u>Hector McLean</u>; who opened a store here in 1825; kept by various people.

(34e) <u>South Cabot</u>. No listings found.

Note: the assistance of Mrs Barbara Carpenter, of Cabot, is gratefully acknowledged.

* * *

(35) **Calais** (Washington).

(35a) <u>Adamant</u>.

1790s: a tavern, <u>Alpheus Bliss</u>; tavern license, 1823; a stage stop on the road from

Montpelier to Hardwick (corner of Fowler and Adamant Rds) until the route was changed and the Kent Tavern became the stopping place, c. 1823; the old tavern sign still exists (photo, Chapter II).

(35b) Calais (Maple Corners).

1849:   --, John Rich; --, John Morgan (John Rich is probably East Calais).

(35c) East Calais.

Note: tavern licenses to Shubael Wheeler, 1820, '22; Samuel Perry, 1823; and Lemuel Perry, 1822, locations unknown;

1849:   see entry for Calais, above;

1858:   --, I. S. Dwinnell* (Walling);

1870:   (a) Moscow House, James Morse;

1873:   (a) as above, Phineas Wheeler; burned in 1873, apparently rebuilt;

1875:   (a) as above, A. C. Slayton;

1878:   (a) as above, Clark M. Gray;

1879, '80:   (a) as above, Kelso Gray;

1883:   --, L. S. Dwinnell;

1887:   (a) as above, L. S. Dwinnell;

1890:   (a) as above, J. O. Lamb;

1892, '95, '98, 1905, '08, '13, '15:   (a) Moscow House, -- (but no hotel shown on 1914 Sanborn map); place burned, date unknown.

(35d) Kent Corners.

Never a post office with this name, although the Calais office was here at one time.

1837-49:   Kent Tavern, Abdiel Kent; a large brick tavern built in 1837 by this leading merchant and entrepreneur, in business for many years with his brother, Ira, as I. and A. Kent.

* * *

The building stayed in the family until 1918, when it was sold; it was later acquired by A. Atwater Kent, a grand-nephew of Abdiel, who transformed a tiny shop into what was once the world's largest radio business. The building was given to the Vermont Historical Society by Kent in 1944, restored to its original condition by volunteers, and is now a museum belonging to the Calais Historical Society. (1)

* * *

(35e) North Calais. No listings found.

* * *

References

(1) Hollister Kent, "The Story of the Tavern," Vermont Historical Soc. News and Notes 2

(November 1950): 1, 2.

* * *

(36) <u>Cambridge</u> (Lamoille).

    (36a) <u>Cambridge(boro)</u>.

    1805-31:   an inn, <u>Abner Brush</u>; tavern license, 1816-30; also license to a Silas Brush, 1832, '33; also PM, 1823-31, and a shoemaker by trade; Brush died in 1831. In 1813 a Mr Clapp, state representative from Montgomery, committed suicide by cutting his throat in Mr Brush's hotel;

    (?):   an old stage-coach house, --; built c. 1812, present Nye place (i.e., 1976, ref 1; photo); not clear which village this place is in;

    Note: tavern licenses to Elias Green, 1817-22; Thomas R. Hawley, 1807-28, and Thomas A. Hawley and son, 1829, '30; Alonzo Chadwick, 1826; Alonzo Shattuck, 1826; John Stevens, 1827; Henry and John Stearns, 1828; and John and Elias Stearns, 1830, '33;

    1828:   <u>Thomas Parker's Inn</u>; where the town meeting was held in 1828 (tavern license 1820-30); exact location unknown;

    1849:   --, E. W. Meach (NEMU Dir);

    1859:   hotel, H. Brewster* (Walling);

    1870:   --, Charles B. Waite;

* * *

    The latter-day hotel in Cambridge was built in 1826 by Peleg Stearns at the corner of Main and South Streets (Child); it was bought by Charles B. Waite in 1868, who changed its name from the <u>Eagle</u> to the <u>Boro House</u>. In 1882, Thaddeus S. Whipple became owner, and changed it to the <u>American House</u> (VDHP 0802-65, #30; now a private home); Child lists <u>both</u> the <u>Boro House</u> (C. B. Waite) and the <u>American House</u> (T. S. Whipple) for this year!

* * *

    1873, '75, '78, '79, '80, '83:   (a) <u>Boro House</u>, C. B. Waite* (Beers, 1878);

    1887: (a) as above, L. J. Knight;

    1890, '92:   (a) as above, G. P. White;

    1895: (a) as above, E. C. Wells;

    1898, 1901, '02, '05:   (a) <u>American House</u>, E. C. Wells (see photo, next page);

    1908, '11, '13, '15, '20:   (a) as above, --* (Sanborn, 1915);

    1925, '35:   <u>Hotel Cambridge</u>, R. R. McDougal (same as the <u>American House</u>); closed soon after this; a private home until the mid-1950s, then renovated and operated as <u>Cambridge Inn</u> and motel until c. 1982, now apartments.

    (36b) <u>East Cambridge</u>. No listings found.

    (36b) <u>Jeffersonville</u> (Cambridge Center until 1827). For Smuggler's Notch, see Stowe.

1849: --, George Carleton (NEMU Dir);

1859: --, George Carleton* (Walling);

1873, '75: (a) Central House, E. Chadwick;

1878: (a) as above, E. Chadwick* (Beers, same site as Walling, 1859);

1879, '80: (a) as above, M. Kay Campbell;

1883: Chadwick House, A. J. Lavigne;

American House (Jim Murphy)

1884: H. A. Chadwick licensed to keep a public house where Second Congregational Church now stands (i.e., 1976, ref 1); A. J. Lavigne also licensed;

1887: Cottage House, A. J. Lavigne;

1890: (a) Central House, A. C. Fletcher; Cottage House, --; probably same as the place later known as Smuggler's Notch Inn (VDHP 0802-66, #7), which was built c. 1860 on the south side of the intersection of Maple and Church Streets; later the Melendy House;

1892: (a) Central House, A. C. Fletcher;

1895, '98: (a) Central House, Irving H. Melendy;

1901, '02, '05: Melendy House, I. H. Melendy (see photo; intersection of Park St and Pleasant Valley Rd); not the same site as Central House (Carleton's) but same as Smuggler's Notch Inn; --, Harrington and Potter; see photo;

1908, '11, '13, '15, '20, '25: Melendy House, --*; (on Sanborn map, 1915); (Hotel Melendy, I. H. Melendy, 1923 VPB); listed as Smuggler's Notch Inn as late as 1955, Walton.

(36d) Cambridge Junction.

1898, 1901, '02:   Junction House, J. A. Farrell;

1905:   as above, R. A. Dickenson;

1910:   a license to D. F. Osborne "to keep a hotel and victualing house"; (1)

1911, '13, '15, '17, '20:   as above, --.

Melendy House/Hotel Melendy

(36e), (36f) North Cambridge and Pleasant Valley.

1840s-50s: Halfway House, a stagecoach inn on the road between Jonesville and St Albans; present Dan Reynolds place (i.e., 1976, ref 1).

Note: the assistance of Jane N. Porter, Town Clerk, is gratefully acknowledged.

* * *

References

(1) Winona S. Noble, The History of Cambridge, Vermont (Cambridge: The Town, 1976).

* * *

(37) **Canaan** (Essex).

(37a) Beecher Falls.

1898:   --, W. W. Sawyer;

1901:   Line House, W. W. Sawyer;

1905:   --, W. W. Sawyer;

1915:   --, Brooks and Brown; --, E. P. Chouinard;

1916:   Line House, E. P. Chouinard (see photo); there was a 2nd Line House here a little later, perhaps this one burned (see below); and another Line House in Canaan;

1924:   New Tourist Hotel (Line House), Art Bouchard (see photo).

(37b) Canaan.

170

1st Line House, Beecher Falls

2nd Line House, Beecher Falls

1849:   --, Charles Bailey (NEMU Dir);

1859:   --, M. Fletcher*(Walling);

1870:   Fletcher's Inn, Marvin Fletcher* (shown on an undated map in Holmes (1); frequent name changes for this place, Canaan House most of the time from 1873; date of construction not known, Holmes says "middle of the seventeenth century," presumably intended middle of the nineteenth;

(?):   Jacob's Tavern, --; referred to in Holmes; (1)

1871:   American House, Marvin Fletcher;

1872:   Essex House, Marvin Fletcher;

1873:   (a) Canaan House, Marvin Fletcher;

1874, '75, '79, '80, '87, '90, '92:   (a) as above* (Beers, 1878; photo, ref 1);

1883:   Union House, C. H. Weeks (presumably same as above);

1895:   (a) as above, G. A. Wiswell; who enlarged it, c. 1880;

1898:   (a) as above, C. H. Green;

171

Line House, Canaan

New Canaan House

1901, '05, '08: (a) as above, W. M. Buck (photo, ref 1);

1911, '13 , '15, '17, '20:   (a) as above, --;

(?):   Line House, --; see photo; no other information.

1925:   (a) as above, A. E. Stevens; the Canaan House burned in 1929; replaced by the New Canaan House (see photo), which also burned, in 1936; not rebuilt this time;

* * *

"All the traveling salesmen usually stayed there and on Mondays and Tuesdays a reservation was necessary to assure getting a room. Meals were served boarding house style.

An illustration of the practical jokes the salesmen used to play on each other constantly was the use a certain flag rope was put to; the flag rope stretched between the Canaan House and Green's Store (now Ray's store) and was used to display Canaan's World War I Liberty Bond flags (given to towns which exceeded their bond sales quotas--Canaan never missed making its quota). On a given morning it was never a surprise to see some salesman's missing nightshirt or pants hanging from the rope." (1)

(37c) South Canaan. No listings found.

(37d) Wallispond.

(?):   Wallispond Guest Cottage, --; (also known as Marshall's Tavern).

* * *

(38) **Castleton** (Rutland).

(38a) Castleton.

c. 1770:   a tavern, Zadock Remington, one-half mile west of Castleton village, probably the first in town (Hemenway); where the Allen brothers, Seth Warner, Benedict Arnold and others planned the attack on Fort Ticonderoga;

c. 1780:   a tavern, Reuben Moulton (and his son Reuben afterwards); two miles east of the village on the road to Rutland (Hemenway);

(?):   a tavern, Samuel Moulton; "near the center of the village" (1); also PM, 1810-38;

c. 1830:   a tavern, Arunah W. Hyde; in a former school building acquired by Hyde in 1830, who had a tavern there briefly before it again became a boarding school, Castleton Seminary; photo, ref 2;

1849:   (a) Mansion House, Charles Robbins (NEMU Dir); --, W. Colburn (location unknown, could be in another village in the township; NEMU Dir);

1854:   (a) Mansion House, --* (Scott map); (b) Westhour's (Westover's) Hotel, Hyde Westover* (Scott);

Note: Hyde Westover (like some of his relatives) was an entrepreneur; he probably built and sold several inns in the area (e.g., a Westover Hotel at Castleton, Castleton Corners and Hydeville);

1869:   (a) Sherman House, W. N. Bachelder* (Beers; same site as Mansion House on Scott, above); (b) Sanford House, Franklin Sanford* (Beers; same site as Westhour's (sic) on Scott, above, i.e., southeast corner of Seminary and Main Sts); local historians believe there was probably an earlier Sanford House, east of Elm St on south side of Main, opposite new PO;

1870:   (a) Bomoseen House, William N. Batchelder; presumably same as Sherman House, above; built in 1868, burned 1912; photo, ref 2;

1873, '75, '79, '80:   (a) as above; (b) as above, photo, ref 2;

1881, '83:   (a) as above, H. D. Ellis;

1887:   (a) as above, J. H. Witherell;

1890, '92:   (a) as above, Horace B. (?) Ellis;

1895:   (a) as above, Edward Mayo;

1898:   (a) as above, W. C. Mound;

1901:   (a) as above, D. A. Murphy;

1905, '08:   (a) as above, C. B. Webster; (b) as above, --; Sanford House burned in July, 1913;

1911, '13:   (a) as above, --; (c) The Maples, -- (the Adams-Brown-Shephard house in 1975); photo, ref 2;

1915:   (c) as above, --;

1916:   (c) The Maples, Charles B. Webster;

1920, '25:   (c) as above, -- (summer boarding; 1922 Sanborn).

(38b) Castleton Corners.

c. 1810:   Westover House, Hyde Westover; also known as the St Lawrence in later years; 1909 photo (2); Westover was a veteran of the War of 1812, and an early settler; he kept this place on the "old government turnpike" between Albany and Vergennes, heavily used in the War of 1812; Westover was also an assistant to Benjamin Carver, who kept a tavern on the opposite corner (see below, Child);

1869:   a hotel, W. Proctor * (Beers); revived as an inn in the 1950s, operated c. 10 years as the Westover House, razed in the 1970s;

c. 1870:   Carver's Hotel, Benjamin Carver; on the corner opposite the "present" (i.e., c. 1881) Westover Hotel;

Note: it is said that at one time there was a hotel and a saloon on each of the four corners at Castleton Corners: Proctor's (Westover House) on the northeast corner; Carver's Hotel, southeast; Barrow's House, northwest (1869, Beers); and a hotel run by A. W. G. Smith, southwest (also on Beers);

1879, '81, '83, '87:   Westover House, R. B. Westover; kept by Hyde Westover at one time;

1920:   Pleasant View House, --;

1925:   as above, John Whitney.

(38c) Hydeville.

1806:   a tavern, Arunah W. Hyde; in the Westover House, for many years; burned c. 1881 (Hemenway);

(?):   a tavern, Pitt Hyde; also PM, 1846-61; (1)

1849:   Hydeville House, Asa Gaines (NEMU Dir);

1854:   hotel, J. W. Bates* (Scott);

1869:   Hydeville Hotel, F. S. Heath* (Beers; same site as Bates hotel of 1854, possibly same building, at the lake outlet; many owners; on site of place known later at various times as O'Brien's Hotel (see photo, next page), Hotel Gibson, and Lake Bomoseen Inn, the latter still operating; photo, ref 2;

1879:   Russell House, R. W. Hyde; Arunah Hyde's home in 1869 (Beers); just west of Baptist church; operated at one time as the Mansion House, Amy Bates; a boarding house for slate company workers at least part of the time (1880s);

1883, '87:   as above, C. M. Hawkins;

1916:   two places are listed in the Vermont Publicity Bureau pamphlet: O'Brien's Hotel, D. E. O'Brien (the old Hydeville Hotel); and Burdett's-on-the-Lake;

1922:   Hotel Gibson, --* (Sanborn); old Hydeville Hotel.

(38d) <u>Lake Bomoseen/Bomoseen</u>.

Bomoseen is a village on the east side of Lake Bomoseen, but Bomoseen post office, operating since 1890, has been located at Castleton Corners since 1914; it was in the <u>Lake House</u> at Bomoseen at one time.

Lake Bomoseen developed as a major summer resort from about 1880. It is hard to keep track of the hotels, what with fires, rebuildings and name changes. Also, there are hotels mentioned that are not listed in the directories. (2)

O'Brien's Hotel

1869:   1st <u>Lake House</u>, J. Learned* (Beers);

1870, '73:   1st <u>Lake House</u>, D. L. Dawley;

1876:   (a) <u>Pic-Nic House</u> (later <u>Bixby's</u>), built in 1876 on the east side of the lake, connected by steamboat with the railroad depot at Hydeville;

1881:   (a) <u>Pic-Nic Hotel</u>, Marquis J. Bixby;

c. 1881:   (b) <u>Coffee House</u> (?), C. M. Coffee; on the east shore road (present Rte 30), north of the old ferry landing;

Note: a 1914 map of Lake Bomoseen shows C. M. Coffee's <u>Picnic House</u>, on east side of road, just north of <u>Cedar Grove</u> site (below); probably same as <u>Coffee House</u>, not Bixby's earlier <u>Pic-Nic House</u>;

1887:   (a) <u>Bixby House</u>, Marquis J. Bixby (VHS stereo view); same as <u>Pic-Nic House</u>, above; (b) (<u>Coffee House</u>), C. M. Coffee; (c) <u>Sheldon</u> House, - Hunter (location unknown); (d) <u>Taghkannuck</u> <u>House</u>, A. W. Barker (on the island); (e) 2nd <u>Lake House</u>, Richard H. Walker; built in 1882 (ref 2, also a photo) so the earlier hotel with the same name (see above, 1869) must have burned, fallen down, or changed names; the 2nd <u>Lake House</u> became part of the <u>Trakenseen Hotel</u> about 1920, still operating in 1980s as <u>Trak Inn</u>, much altered;

1890:   (a) as above, W. Hines; (c) as above, E. Monroe; (d) as above; (e) as above; (f) <u>Prospect House</u>, W. C. Mound (see photo); east shore, near ferry landing, on the lake side of the shore road; opened summer 1888, in continuous operation until 1989, but main building razed in 1972;

1891:   <u>Ellis Park</u>, --; built in 1891, burned in 1894; on the Avalon shore, on the west side of the lake (close to Cookville on Beers); <u>Del Monte</u>, --; built 1891, burned 1898, on the west side

175

of the lake, near Point of Pines; the <u>Glenwood</u> was built on the site (see below);

1892: (a) as above; (b) (<u>Coffee House</u>), C. M. Coffee; (c) as above, G. W. Scribner; (d) as above; (e) as above; (f) as above;

Principal Lake Bomoseen Hotels

1st Lake House
(a) Pic-Nic House, later Bixby's
(b) Coffee House
(c) Sheldon House
(d) Taghkannuck House
(e) 2nd Lake House, later part of
    Trakenseen
(f) Prospect House
    Ellis Park

Del Monte, same site as Glenwood
(g) Cedar Grove House (also Dunn's)
(h) Glenwood, on Del Monte site
    Wayside
(i) Trakenseen, 2nd Lake House
(j) Johnson's
(k) Lakeside
(l) Neshobe
    Grandview

Prospect House

1895: (a), (b), (e), as above; (d) as above, Timothy Clifford; (f) as above, H. B. Ellis;

1898: (b) (<u>Coffee House</u>), C. M. Coffee; (e) as above; (f) as above; (g) <u>Cedar Grove House</u>, Edward Dunn (also known as <u>Dunn's Hotel</u>, see photo; on the east side of the lake; built in 1898, demolished in 1971; operated by the Quinlan family, 1920-71; (photo, ref 2); its annexes survive as cottages;

Dunn's Hotel

1899: (h) <u>Glenwood</u>, -- (see photo) ; built on the <u>Del Monte</u> site (see above), also burned in 1912; photo in ref 2;

1901:   (e), (f), and (g), as above; (h) <u>Glenwood Hotel</u>, C. Mound; <u>Wayside Inn</u>, M. L. Faulkner (location unknown);

1905:   (b) (<u>Coffee House</u>), C. M. Coffee; (f) as above; (g) as above, Edward Dunn;

1908:   (e) 2nd <u>Lake House</u> , --; (f) <u>Prospect House</u>, --; (g) as above, --;

1913:   (b) (<u>Coffee House</u>), C. M. Coffee; (g) as above, Edward Dunn;

1915:   (e) as above, -- (post office here until 1914); (f) as above;

1916:   listed in the Vermont Publicity Bureau pamphlet: (f) <u>The Prospect and Cottages</u>, Horace B. Ellis; (g) <u>Cedar Grove</u>, Edward Dunn; (i) <u>Trakenseen</u>, E. D. Kennedy; (j) <u>Johnson's</u>, Hollis S. Johnson, at the head of Lake Bomoseen; north end, near Float Bridge; (k) <u>Lakeside</u>, O. I. Pond; (l) <u>Neshobe</u>, H. M. Redfield; (Neshobe Beach now a cottage colony, east shore);

Note: the original old house at <u>Johnson's</u> burned in 1934, replaced by a private home on same site and a second building nearby, operated as a summer hotel, 1934-World War II; sold in 1953 to Callahans, who ran it until 1960s when it burned in a fire in which they lost their lives;

Glenwood Hotel (Vermont Historical Soc.)

1920:   (f) as above, --; (i) <u>Trakenseen</u> (formerly 2nd <u>Lake House</u>); also 1923, VPB; <u>Grandview</u>, Edward Dunn (also 1923, VPB); (j) <u>Johnson's</u>, --; (k) <u>Lakeside</u>, --; (l) <u>Neshobe</u>, --;

1925:   (e) as above, --; (f) <u>Prospect House</u> (and Bomoseen Golf Course), still operating as resort but old hotel building razed c. 1970; (g) as above, L. P. Quinlan; (j) <u>Johnson's</u>, --; (k) <u>Lakeside</u>, --; (l) <u>Neshobe</u>, --; <u>Grandview</u>, --.

(38e) <u>West Castleton</u>. No listings found.

Note: the assistance of John and Florence Reil, and Margaret K. Onion, is gratefully acknowledged.

* * *

References

(1) George H. Beaman, "The Old Time Tavern," Rutland County Historical Society Proceedings <u>1</u> (1881): 77-81.
(2) Castleton Historical Society, Castleton: Scenes of Yesterday (Poultney: Journal Pr., 1975).

(39) **Cavendish** (Windsor).

Cavendish had a lot of taverns for a small town, because the Crown Point Road passed through; and it is hard to identify and locate them all. There is an unusual amount of material on their history (in addition to the usual sources) and it is not always easy to match up descriptions from the different sources. (1-5)

(39a) Outside the Villages.

The two earliest taverns (Coffeen's and the Paine Tavern) were on the Crown Point Road, which ran across the northern part of the town. These are both referred to in a 1784 almanac (Bickerstaff's Boston Almanack) which lists the towns, taverns and mileages from Boston to Crown Point.

c. 1769:   a tavern, Capt John Coffeen (Coffin); almanacs, 1771-1802; in the northwest part of town, on the Town Farm Rd a little north of the Center Rd intersection; Coffeen was a member of the state constitutional convention, and the town's first legislative representative;

(?):   Paine (Payne) Tavern, --; almanacs, 1771-1802; known locally as the "old Atherton place"; "on Tarbell Hill where the road divides, one way leading ...to Greenbush (i.e., Amsden), the other...to Reading" (2); building still stands (1988);

c. 1790:   Hiland Tavern, Jeremiah Johnson; a Revolutionary War veteran, died in 1847; on the east side of Rte 106, between Greenbush and Reading, in the far northeast corner of Cavendish; a small yellow house; "this house having been an inn for some time, it was not surprising to find a pipe that went under the road from the hillside where there was once a still"; (2)

1811:   a tavern, -; known locally as the Haven House, or Asa Spaulding house, on Twenty-Mile Stream (Stream Rd, northwest of Cavendish, just before the intersection with North Hill Rd);

1812:   Stiles Tavern, --; almanacs, listed until 1822;

(?):   Gordon's Hotel, Thomas Gordon; in Fittonsville, a hamlet that "began just south of the tracks" (4); "the present town hall was then the Baptist church," and the hotel, across from it, was where Mrs Anna Austin lived in 1940 (4); burned in 1882 (Child); kept by one Joseph Adams for 17 years;

(?):   a tavern, --; "on the Deacon Paine place on the hill road to Chester"; (3)

c. 1840:   Atherton Tavern, --; in Whitesville, a hamlet just northeast of Cavendish village on Rte 131; the Joseph S. Atherton farm in 1952; (1)

(?):   Snow Tavern, --; see note below; in Whitesville, on the north side of Rte 131, just east of where it crosses Twenty Mile Stream brook;

* * *

"The early taverns were the Dutton place on the corner built in 1782, Capt Coffeen's tavern on the old Crown Point Road, one on the same road where the Stedman Atherton house stands, one on the Deacon Paine place on the hill road to Chester, the Snow tavern and Atherton tavern in Whitesville (emphasis added). The tavern opposite the town hall was kept by Joseph Adams for 17 years." (3)

* * *

(39b) Cavendish.

1782:   Dutton House, Salmon Dutton (Samuel in some sources); who came this year and built the place, first building in the lower Black River valley (5); almanacs, 1796-1807;

* * *

Given to the Shelburne Museum in 1950, where it was reerected, by the late Sen Redfield Proctor, it having been the home of his great great-grandmother. Cavendish was first known as Duttonsville, after Salmon Dutton, a leading citizen who, amongst other things, surveyed the first road to Ludlow, which became part of the Green Mountain Turnpike (a toll-road from Rutland to Bellows Falls) in 1798. Used for many years as a hotel, but the exact dates are not known. "The old red house on the corner" (3); the tavern sign is said to have been painted on a little porch, "a picture representing the good dame of the house presenting a 'mug of flip' to a thirsty traveler." Painting obliterated c. 1832.

Another interesting anecdote is that "when the stage coach came to the top of Dutton Hill on the Green Mountain Turnpike en route to Rutland, the driver would sound on his horn a number of toots to indicate how many passengers he had who would wish food. This enabled the tavern-keeper to set the proper number of places at the table." (5)

* * *

1855:   hotel, S. Dulton (sic)* (Hosea Doten);

1856:   --, S. H. Burnham;

1869:   hotel, A. Walker* (Beers, same site as above);

1870, '75, '80: (a) Cavendish Hotel, Alfred Walker;

1887:   Black River House, E. E. Cross (UVM stereo view, unidentified; is this the Cavendish/Elliott?);

1892:   Hotel Elliott, also known as the Cavendish Inn; a stone building built as a store by Gen Davis and Daniel Wheeler in 1839, converted to a hotel in 1892 by George Mandigo; #37 in the Cavendish Village Historical District (VDHP 1406-22); just beyond where the Dutton house stood; burned in 1895, rebuilt, now a medical center; (see fire photo, Chapter VI);

1895, '98, 1901, '05:   (b) Hotel Elliott, George W. Mandigo;

1908:   (b) as above, --;

1913, '15:   (b) as above, --; (A. E. Ware in 1916 VPB);

1920:   (b) as above, W. A. Bean;

1925:   (b) as above, --; operating as Cavendish Inn in 1930, not in 1935.

(39c) Proctorsville.

Described by the Vermont Division of Historic Preservation as the best preserved mill village in Vermont. Together with Cavendish, it was on the original route of the Green Mountain Turnpike and the Champlain and Connecticut River Railroad (Rutland).

1783:   a tavern, Capt Leonard Proctor; built by him near where the Methodist church now stands, on Main St (i.e., 1964, ref 2); after many years, the place was divided, one part being moved north and becoming the Bassett House (later torn down); the other half was moved towards the canal, and came to be known as the Page House (i.e., 1988); kept at one time by Samuel Burbank (almanacs, 1825, '29);

1787:   Sunset Tavern, Capt Leonard Proctor; almanacs, 1812, '25, '29; the second house he built here (see above) on Main St, almost opposite the Page House; (this is #38 in the Proctorsville Historic District, VDHP 1406-2, still standing, 1988); Proctor died in 1827, place later called the "Town House" or the "Jenny House";

(?):   "Brick Tavern", --; kept by a Major Hyde for many years; also known as the Stage House and Eagle Hotel (#44 in the Proctorsville Historic District, VDHP 1406-2, still standing, 1988); on the Green Mountain Turnpike in Cavendish a little west of the Page house (above); a model landlord, "his place was celebrated for the good entertainment. It was a stage house, and the coaches stopped for dinner there. As many as 50 guests were frequently put up overnight, and perhaps 100 horses" (3); a commercial block, PO in 1973;

Note: The Proctor brothers, Jabez and John (Leonard's sons) kept the first store in Proctorsville, about 1798. It appears that Jabez sold his interest in the store to John and built the "brick tavern, now the Fraternal building." (3) This "brick tavern" is almost certainly the same as the one described above, kept later by Major Hyde, and built about 1800. Jabez Proctor was Sen Redfield Proctor's father;

1849:   (a) Stage House, Z. F. Hyde (NEMU Dir; this is the "brick tavern," above);

1855:   (a) --, Z. F. Hyde* (Hosea Doten);

1856:   (a) --, Z. F. Hyde;

1869:   (a) Eagle Hotel, H. A. Howe* (Beers, same site as the Stage House; A. S. Spaulding owner, Howe mgr);

1870:   (a) as above, Henry A. Howe;

1873, '75, '80: (a) as above, Joshua Tripp;

1883:   (a) as above, Asa W. Putnam;

1887:   (a) as above, H. E. Harris;

1890, '92:   (a) as above, G. D. Ordway;

1895:   (a) as above, M. J. Reagan;

1898:   --, Solon Densmore;

1905:   (b) Cottage Hotel, James Sheridan; see photo, next page;

1913, '15, '20, '25:   (b) as above,--* (shown on 1914 Sanborn, different from the Eagle Hotel).

Note: the assistance of Mr Carmine Guica, Cavendish, is gratefully acknowledged.

* * *

References

(1) Lois Wheeler, History of Cavendish, Vermont (Proctorsville, 1952).
(2) Cavendish Hist. Soc., Heritage and Homes, Cavendish, Vermont (Cavendish: The Society; Springfield: Hurd's Pr., 1964).
(3) Charles R. Cummings, "The 150th Anniversary Celebration of Cavendish," Vermonter 17 (Aug-Sept 1912): 592-619.
(4) Jane S. Butler, "The Passing of Fittonsville," Vermonter 45 (January 1940): 17-18.
(5) Leon Gay, "The Salmon Dutton House," Vermont Quarterly 18 (October 1950): 175-

Cottage Hotel

* * *

(40) **Charleston** (Orleans).

(40a) East Charleston (including Echo Lake).

1827:　a hotel, John Cushman (Hemenway); tavern license, 1829-32;

Note:　tavern licenses to Daniel Chadwick, 1825-30; Silas Gaskill, 1830; Winthrop Cole, 1832;

1849:　--, Oliver Warren (NEMU Dir);

1855, '56:　--, George Cole; --, William Buck;

1870:　--, M. C. Davis (Davis's Hotel in Walton); (a) Union Hotel, Charles Chase;

1873:　(a) as above, P. E. Davis;

1878:　East Charleston Hotel, M. C. Davis* (Beers; probably same as Union House);

1879:　--, M. R. (?) Davis;

1883:　--, J. G. Lang;

1883-84:　Riverside House, A. C. (?) Lang (Child);

1887:　--, A. D. Piper;

1890, '92:　(a) Union House, C. O. Goodwin; see photo, next page;

1895:　(a) as above; --, A. D. Piper; according to Hamilton, another hotel (i.e., besides the Union House) stood where the Nazarene Church stood in 1955; run by Frank Wilder;

1901:　(a) as above, C. S. Copp;

Union House

1911: (a) as above, --;

1914: Echo Inn, --* (Sanborn, same building as Union House, above);

1920: Echo Inn, A. C. Gallup; (also in 1916 VPB); place burned in a disastrous fire in 1921, and stood where Mrs Ernest Hudson's house stood in 1955;

(40b) West Charleston.

1822: first hotel, erected and kept by Ira Richard (Hemenway); tavern license, 1822-27, when the town was called "Navy";

1855: --, Isaac Bundy; --, Phineas Wheeler;

1856: --, Robert Wheeler;

1859: --, W. M. Ful-*(? rest of name illegible, Walling); --, P. Hinman* (Walling);

(?): a hotel once operated on a site to the left of Paul Gelineau's garage (i.e., 1955, ref 1); torn down before 1955;

(?): a hotel, Wilson Buck; present home of C. R. Durgin in 1955; (1)

1870, '73, '75: (a) 1st Clyde River Hotel, A. J. Morrill;

1878: (a) as above* (Beers);

1879, '80: (a) as above;

1883: (a) as above, J. M. Barrett;

1883-84: (a) as above, John M. Barrett (Child);

1887: (a) as above, W. H. Norton;

1890: (a) as above, J. O. Shedd;

1892: (a) as above, A. D. Piper;

1895: (a) as above, Harry Reuter;

1908: (a) as above, --;

1913, '15: (a) as above, Fred Hamblett; also 1916 VPB;

1920, '25: (a) as above, W. D. Allen; this was apparently the second Clyde River Hotel, according to Hamilton (ref 1; see photo); built by William Nelson after the first one burned (date not established); he bought the site and moved the old Universalist church there. This place also burned in the "big fire of 1924."

Note: the assistance of Richard A. Colburn, Sr., Charleston Historical Society, is gratefully acknowledged.

2nd Clyde River Hotel

* * *

References

(1) Esther Hamilton, History of the Town of Charleston, Vermont (n.p., 1955).

* * *

(41) **Charlotte** (Chittenden).

Charlotte has had three villages: (1) present Charlotte, just off Rte 7, the only one that still has a post office; formerly known as West Charlotte and Charlotte Four Corners; (2) East Charlotte, once known as Baptist Corners; and (3) Charlotte Center, on old Rte 7; no longer shown on most maps, but one of the original settlement sites. There are also cottage communities in the township, dating from the 1870s at Cedar Beach and from the 1880s at Thompson's Point; an early hostelry at Point Pleasant (McNeil's Ferry village, a busy place in the summer at one time, but never a PO); and there was once a summer hotel at Mt Philo as well.

(41a) Charlotte Center.

1783: a log tavern, Gen Hezekiah Barnes; who also established a store across the street, still operating in 1973; and a stone house built nearby in 1789, owned by the Alexander family in the 19th century, present William Pinney place (this is VDHP 0403-3, #2);

1785: a tavern, Ephraim Wooster; he was the first settler on the farm owned in 1934 by Lyman McNeil;

'c. 1786: a tavern, David Hubbell; for many years, on the site of S. E. Russell's home in 1882 (Child);

1790: a large frame tavern, Gen Hezekiah Barnes (again, see above; 1783, in another

183

source); almanacs, 1817-29; tavern license, 1821; near the old place when his custom outgrew the original log tavern; this building was moved to the Shelburne Museum as the Stage Coach Inn about 1950; Barnes was another innkeeper who died in an epidemic in 1813;

1806:   a tavern, Col William Williams; almanacs, 1796-1807; just north of the Jeremiah Barton tavern, see below; in 1806 he replaced his first cabin with a substantial building, opened a tavern which was an important stage stop between Burlington and Troy (1); this is VDHP 0403-39; "at this time there were eight hotels in Charlotte, all very well supported by the traveling farmers, who were hauling their produce to Albany and Troy" (Child);

Note: perhaps the place above was earlier, because a Williams tavern is listed in the 1796 Vermont Almanac and Register as a stage stop on the Rutland-Canada route;

c. 1810:   a stage stop, --; in the early 1800s, on old Rte 7; VDHP 0403-2, #9, the Rayta home in 1976;

c. 1812:   a tavern, --; as above, VDHP 0403-2, #8, the Swenor home in 1988;

Note: an 1812 almanac lists Beers, Martin, Hubert and Worcester taverns; Matthew Beer and Nathaniel Martin had tavern licenses in 1821; licenses also to Sawyer Curtis, Noble Lovely and Salmon Johnson in 1821;

* * *

"Intemperance was a terrible scourge to this town, as was to have been expected--for the reason that the town was cursed with three distilleries and beset with as extensive and fruitful orchards as any part of the state. It also contained about a dozen taverns, all floodgates of rum and ruin" (Hemenway).

* * *

1849:   --, C. C. Martin; --, E. D. Gifford; --, George Duran; Center Hotel, O. J. Baldwin (NEMU Dir; locations not known);

1849:   (a) Washington Hotel, B. F. Dickinson (NEMU Dir);

1869:   (a) Washington House, E. Mills* (Beers);

1870:   --, E. Mills (presumably the Washington House); --, William Bates;

1873:   Alexander House, Orson Alexander; it appears that the names Alexander House and Washington House were used interchangeably for a while;

1875, '78, '80: (a) Washington House, O. H. Alexander;

1882-83:   (a) as above, Henry Dorr (Child);

1897, 1908:   Eaton Hotel, --; (listed as "Charlotte" in directories, but probably at McNeil's Ferry, see below).

(41b) East Charlotte (Baptist Corners).

(?):   Echo Inn, -- (postcard photo);

c. 1820:   a tavern, William O. Baker; VDHP 0403-1, Sheehan home in 1976);

(41c) McNeil's Ferry (Point Pleasant).

A ferry was established here in 1790 by John McNeil. One of his sons, Charles, eventually took this over, and developed the ferry landing extensively. "There was such a volume of travel...that Charles built a tavern a few rods from his house. The tavern and bar proved quite popular, and he found it necessary to enlarge the building twice...McNeil's Ferry, with the cove, formed one of the most interesting attractions of Lake Champlain. Included in the little settlement was the ferry dock, the McNeil mansion, the tavern, the horse barns, and a little red house built for the captain of the horse boat" (i.e., horse-powered ferry. (2)

c. 1810: a tavern, Charles McNeil; at the ferry landing, Charlotte to Essex, New York; VDHP 0403-58;

1857: a tavern, C. McNeil* (Walling);

1869: a hotel, L. R. Eaton* (Beers);

1882-83: Monticello House, Charles H. McNeil (Child);

1890: Lakeview Hotel, T. C. Williams; Lake House in Rutland Railroad guide, 1897.

(41d) Mt Philo (North Ferrisburg mail address, but in the town of Charlotte).

1893: Cold Spring House, Frank and Clara Lewis; operating in the Smith-Jones farm at the base of Mt Philo;

c. 1896: Mt Philo Inn, Frank and Clara Lewis; built in stages, adjacent to the old farmhouse (above), which was torn down;

1908: Mt Philo Inn, --;

1920, '25: Mt Philo Inn, F. A. Lewis; see photo.

Mt Philo Inn

The Mt Philo Inn accommodated about 75 guests; the Lewises also operated a dairy farm and raised livestock and vegetables for the inn; a tent colony developed from c. 1900, which evolved into a series of cottages. Later operated by Walter Lewis, the son. Sold to Mr and Mrs Arthur Griggs in 1963, who ran it a few years; property dispersed now, and the old inn used in recent years as a cooperative apartment building (VDHP 0403-23; and ref 3).

* * *

(41e) Thompson's Point.

c. 1866: Charlotte Inn, --; in the days when the Ticonderoga docked here; now a garage and apartment building (VDHP 0403-6, #23);

Note: the above information is not in complete agreement with that contained in a booklet by Jessie S. Gibbs. (4) The dates provided there are 1896-c. 1921. According to Ms Gibbs, the Hotel Charlotte/Glenwood Inn (see photo) was built by William E. Hosford, later run by L. A. Van Bomel, and was later still a garage; it had room for about 40 guests; one room was a cigar and candy store, and also housed the Thompson Point post office, which operated as a summer office from 1899 until 1921. The inn was the social center of the Point. There is a photo in this brochure.

c. 1870s: a hotel, --- run by the Fields family, on Thompson Point Rd (VDHP 0403-61); house built about 1792; ceased operating as an inn by 1919.

(41f) West Charlotte (Four Corners, present Charlotte).

1811: a tavern, Jeremiah Barton; according to VDHP, it was on old Rte 7, between Thompson's Point Rd and Hinesburg Rd, now a home and apartment, 0403-37; there was also a Joseph Barton tavern, almost identical, for four years (1); at the Four Corners (the northwest corner, present Paul Oren place, photo in ref 3); both had tavern licenses in 1821, almanacs list a Barton tavern in 1824, '25;

1855: --, L. R. Hubbell;

1856: --, L. R. Hubbell; --, - Brown;

1857: a tavern, L. R. Hubbell* (Walling; on the site of Joseph Barton's tavern, above);

1869: --, L. R. Hubbell* (Beers; not indicated as a tavern, however).

Glenwood Hotel, Thompson's Point

References

(1) History of Charlotte, 1934 (Shelburne: Excelsior Pr., 1934).
(2) David J. Blow, "McNeil's Ferry, Charlotte," Chittenden County Historical Society Bulletin 4 (Sept 1968): 1-2.
(3) Lilian B. Carlisle, ed., Look Around Chittenden County (Burlington: Chittenden County Hist. Soc., 1976).
(4) Jessie S. Gibbs, Thompson's Point: A Few Facts and Fancies About A Favorite Summer Resort (n.p., privately printed booklet).

* * *

(42) Chelsea (Orange).

(42a) Chelsea.

c. 1796:   a tavern, Phineas Dodge; for a short time, serving a road, discontinued by 1812, that once lead west to Brookfield; house still stands (photo, ref 1);

pre-1800: Nathaniel Oak tavern, in the public building on the present (i.e., 1984) bank site;

c. 1810:   a hotel, Nathan Hale; on the corner of South Court St where Judge Keyser's house now stands (i.e., 1984, ref 2);

* * *

"On arriving in Chelsea Harry and Nathan continued to be 'in trade' together as they had in Windsor through the firm name of N. and H. Hale, and kept both a store and a tavern. Harry gave up the tavern after a short time, but Nathan owned and kept a hotel for many years while also making time pieces having learned the watch and clock making trade in Windsor." (2)

* * *

c. 1812:   a hotel, Phineas Dodge; a new place "at the Main St corner" when the Strafford Turnpike came through; W. S. Gilman has seen references to the Dodge House/Hotel (personal communication);

(?):   a stagecoach stop, on the Azariah Barnes farm; the Robert Edwards place in 1979 (photo, ref 1);

* * *

"The hotels have been spoken of, four of which were at one time in full operation, being sustained by home patronage and that of the traveling public, together with the income derived from the long and crowded terms of court then held, being nothing more nor less than a rally from all parts of the country; twice a year, when the judges, attorneys, sheriffs, jurors, parties, and witnesses came in a body to try and determine the various controversies in the county, and not only did they come but they staid four solid weeks at a time, saw the session through, and went home happy...From about 1835 to 1840 Chelsea was carrying on the largest business and was the most prosperous of any time in her history." (3)

* * *

1834:   Hale tavern stand leased to Elihu Norton, who also ran a livery; Chelsea was on the main Boston to Montreal stage route, and Norton also owned the Hanover-Montpelier stage line;

c. 1840:   Norton purchased a farm south of the Hale tavern stand (the Charles Titus place in 1984,) used it for stage passengers, operated his stage until 1864; and the Hale stand was sold to Daniel Tarbell in the 1840s, moved and became part of the 1st Orange County Hotel;

c. 1840:   reference to "two large hotels" in ref 2, these being the Hale-Norton tavern stand and the first Orange County Hotel;

1849:   Orange County Hotel, G. W. Graves (NEMU Dir);

1854:   Clark's Hotel; referred to in a reproduction of an advertisement in ref 1; must be either Hale's or the Orange County Hotel;

187

1857:   (a) 2nd <u>Orange County Hotel</u>, replacing the original that burned in January, 1857 (see photo); the second one also burned, in November 1916, and was never rebuilt. Not known exactly when the first one was built, but it was in service by at least 1840; there is a fire photo of this place, and other photos, ref 1. One John Pike was first manager of the second <u>Orange County Hotel</u>, but he "proved to be unpopular and was replaced by Ben F. Dickinson"; property sold to Edward Southworth; successive owners/managers included Chester Sanborn, A. W. Whitney, A. H. Powers, Ben Hyde, L. D. Humphrey, Charles Southworth, A. W. Whitney again; sold in 1887 to Elgin D. Barnes, who ran it for the next thirty years except for one five-year period by C. P. Dickinson.

2nd Orange County Hotel

"With three stage lines converging in the center of the village, and the Orange County Court holding at least two sessions a year, the hotel was the social center of the community. Here was the site of weddings, births, and funerals. Balls, oyster suppers, game suppers and annual stockholders meetings were held within its walls. In the 1890s before the building of the present town hall, town meetings were also held here. The hotel was a resting and dining place for travelers, summer visitors from the city, stage drivers, commercial salesmen, laborers working at local jobs, court judges and lawyers. Truly a hub of activities in the community, it is difficult to look back one hundred years and imagine the combined social and business atmosphere that was part of the Orange County Hotel in those years from 1857 to 1900. On the nights of February 17th and 18th in 1897, the Chelsea Dramatic Co. put on a show at the 'Opera House' (Town Hall.) Across the street at the hotel, Proprietor Barnes advertised that he would stay open all night, both nights, and that a supper would be served at 11:00 p.m. for $.75 per couple." (2)

* * *

1858:   (a) <u>Orange County Hotel</u>, John B. Pike* (Walling);

1870:   (a) as above, S. C. Sanborn;

1873, '75:   (a) as above, A. W. Whitney;

1877:   (a) as above, A. H. Powers* (Beers);

1878, '80:   (a) as above, Benjamin E. Hyde;

1883, '87:   (a) as above, A. W. Whitney;

1888:   (a) as above, E. D. Barnes;

1890, '92, '95: (a) as above; (b) <u>American House</u>, Ira Hood; apparently a name used when Hood opened his home on Main St as a boarding-house; still standing;

1898:   (a) as above; (b) as above, Mrs E. A. Hood;

1901, '05, '08: (a) as above, C. P. Dickinson; (b) as above;

1911, '13, '15: (a) as above, E. D. Barnes (but no hotel shown on the 1915 Sanborn; odd, since it did not burn until 1916);

1917:   <u>Chelsea Inn</u>, opened after the second <u>Orange County Hotel</u> burned, in the Nathan Hale house next to the new high-school, by Charles and Edith Dickinson; until 1929; 1925 photo, ref 1;

1920, '25:   <u>Chelsea Inn</u>, C. E. Dickinson; <u>Park View</u>, Mrs C. Flanders;

Note: the assistance of Mr W. S. Gilman, Chelsea Historical Society, is gratefully acknowledged.

* * *

References

(1) W. S. Gilman, Chelsea Album, 1863-1979 (Randolph: Herald Printery, 1979).
(2) W. S. Gilman, ed., A History of Chelsea, Vermont: 1784-1984. Chelsea Historical Soc. (Barre: Northlight Studio Pr., 1984).
(3) J. A. Keyes, "Among the early Chelseans: sketches, anecdotes, stories, legends, etc., connected with the early history of Chelsea" (Randolph: Herald and News, 1885).

* * *

(43) **Chester** (Windsor).

(43a) <u>Chester</u> (south village).

c. 1774:   a hotel, <u>William Atwood</u>; settled in this year "upon a farm where Chester village now is (Child); built a log house used as a hotel for some time;

c. 1780:   first tavern (?), <u>Hugh Henry</u>; came before 1780, settled on what is now (i.e., 1883, Child) the Henry homestead, about one mile east of Chester village; (an H. Henry place is shown in this vicinity on the 1869 Beers); also a store;

c. 1791-95:   <u>Star Inn</u>, Maj Abner Field; who died in 1791, his wife in 1811; at the fork of two old stage routes, off Rte 11 at the end of TH 54 (VDHP 1407-38); several miles west of Chester village;

* * *

"Early in its history Chester gained fame as the intersection of important stage coach lines. The major route from Boston to Montreal, known as the Green Mountain Turnpike, passed the Henry farm and came into the North village (i.e., North Chester) on what we now call North Street. The present Main Street was the route from Hanover, N.H. to Albany and Saratoga Springs, N.Y., and this road was considered as being '...the best passage of the Green Mountains in the state south of the Onion River.' Both routes brought commerce and heavy traffic into Chester, and as a result several stage taverns or inns were established here. The community of Gassetts bears the name of the proprietor of an inn located there. When Hugh Henry took over the present Henry property in 1780, it was thriving as a stage tavern and was also the station at which the horses were changed. The homes now (i.e., 1966) owned by Oswin Brooks, Henry Lackie and Paul Jeffrey were among the several inns operating prior to 1800..." (1)

* * *

Note: almanacs list the following Chester taverns, locations unknown: <u>Kimball</u> (1796, 1802, '07); <u>Ingraham</u> (1825, '29, see below); Seaman (1812, '13, '25, '29); and Folsom (1817-22);

1849:   <u>American House</u>, R. A. Deming (NEMU Dir);

1855:   <u>American House</u>, G. H. Hilton* (Hosea Doten; on the south side of Main St);

1855, '56:   --, Henry Ingraham; an <u>Ingraham Tavern</u> listed in almanacs in 1825, '29; but there is also an E. Ingraham in North Chester (see below), not clear which Ingraham tavern is referred to in the almanac; probably the North Chester one, since the Badger and Porter Stage Register for 1828 specifically cites Ephraim Ingraham Jr as proprietor;

1869:   (a) <u>Eagle Hotel</u>, A. K. Davenport* (Beers; on the north side of Main St); (b) <u>Ingraham House</u>, Henry H. Ingraham* (Beers, south side of Main St, but not the same site as the <u>American House</u>, above; see photo; not known what happened to this place;

1870:   (a) as above; (b) as above; (c) <u>Central House</u>, Nathan Abbott;

Ingraham House (Special Collections, UVM)

1871, '72:   (a) as above; converted to a bakery and apartments by at least the early 1900s, later razed, site now occupied by a grocery store; (b) <u>Ingraham House</u>, George H. Cole (UVM stereo view);

1873, '74:   (c) <u>Cole's Central House</u>, G. H. Cole;

190

1875:   (c) Central House, N. O. Johnson;

1879, '80:   (c) as above, H. O. Peabody;

1883:   (c) as above, N. O. Johnson;

1887:   (c) as above, H. R. Barney;

1892:   (d) The Fullerton, W. O. Chapin;

1895, '98, 1901:   (d) as above, Fred Rowell* (1900 Sanborn);

1905:   (d) as above, --* (Sanborn); also Maple House, across from the library, but not operating by 1912 (Sanborn), tenement by 1925);

1908, '11, '13, '15:   (d) as above, --;

1916:   (d) as above, F. M. Cleary (VPB); Clayton Inn, Mrs Fannie Clayton (VPB);

1920:   (d) as above, J. A. Rowell; (e) The Maples, the Misses Sargent; (also 1916);

1925:   (d) The New Fullerton, W. J. Cassin* (Sanborn; see photo); built c. 1920 to replace the Fullerton, which burned; #22 in the Chester Village Historic District (VDHP 1407-22); known as the Chester Inn in the 1950s-60s, extensively renovated recently, now The Inn at Long Last; (e) as above;

The New Fullerton

(43b) Chester Depot

1797:   a hotel, Jabez Sargeant Jr; VDHP 1407-18, on North St in Chester, the Jeffrey House;

1869:   (a) Chester House, Joel Todd* (Beers);

1870:   (a) as above;

1871:   (a) as above, John Thompson;

1873, '74:   (a) Chester House, H. H. Ingraham; apparently Mr Ingraham was no longer

191

operating the Ingraham House in the village;

1875: (a) as above;

1879, '80: (a) as above, Charles W. Abbott;

1880: (a) as above, C. P. Colton;

1887: (a) as above, John L. Sanborn;

1890: (a) as above, E. D. Barnes;

1892, '95: (a) as above, John Sanborn;

1897: (a) as above, Barnet M. Waite; burned before 1900, site now occupied by a diner.

(43c) Gassetts (known as Spafford, 1887-91).

1855: hotel, J. Marshall* (Hosea Doten; on the west side of the road at the four corners; a J. C. Marshall still at this site in Beers, 1869);

1856: --, C. C. White.

(43d) North Chester. (Stone Village Historic District (VDHP 1407-16).

c. 1800: Holden Tavern, --; (#14 in the Historic District);

1849: (a) Union House, E. Ingraham (NEMU Dir); see also Chester, 1855, '56 entry;

1855: (a) Union House, - Kelly* (Hosea Doten);

1869: (a) as above, John Kelley* (Beers); presumably Kelley's Tavern, built c. 1800, #7 in the Historic District, now a private home; but D. B. E. Kent refers to a Kelly's Tavern as "a sprawling old structure built before 1800, (which) takes up considerable space in Chester Depot."

1870: (a) as above.

Note: the assistance of Mr Paul H. Ballou is gratefully acknowledged.

* * *

(1) League of Women Voters of Chester, This is Chester, 1766-1966 (Chester: The League, 1966).
(2) Dorman B. E. Kent, Gazetteer of Vermont Heritage (Chester: National Survey, 1966).

* * *

(44) **Chittenden** (Rutland).

(44a) Chittenden.

1856: --, Henry J. Perry;

1881-82: Landon House, Wolcott B. Wing (Child; there is a W. B. Wing on the 1869 Beers, no hotel label); built c. 1858 as a store and tavern, Addison Spawn proprietor;

acquired by Walter Landon c. 1877, leased to Harry Stone as a hotel; Wing bought it in 1880; see photo;

Landon House (Chittenden Bicentennial, 1780-1976)

Note: There is a painting by James Hope (reproduced in ref 2) with the title "Tavern in New Boston, Vermont." There were several New Bostons in Vermont, but it seems likely that this is the one in Chittenden, since Hope lived for many years in nearby Castleton, and because this New Boston was once the last stop on the Rutland-Pittsfield mail stage before the pull east over the mountain to Pittsfield. (3) (This would have been the Rutland to Stockbridge turnpike.)

1898:   --, Henry J. Perry;

1901:   Landon House , H. J. Perry;

1905:   --, Kittridge Wing;

1915:   Landon House, Warren Austin; last proprietor, place razed in 1975.

(44b) Holden. No listings found.

Note: the assistance of the Chittenden Historical Society is gratefully acknowledged.

* * *

References

(1) Chittenden Bicentennial Committee, Chittenden Pictorial Review, 1780-1976 (Rutland: Academy Books).
(2) J. Kevin Graffagnino, Vermont in the Victorian Age (Bennington: Vermont Heritage Press, 1985).
(3) Esther M. Swift, Vermont Place Names: Footprints of History (Brattleboro: Stephen Greene Press, 1977).

* * *

(45) **Clarendon** (Rutland).

The Crown Point Road came through here in 1759, following the Otter Creek valley north after that.

(45a) Chippenhook (and Chippenhook Springs). No listings found.

(45b) Clarendon.

c. 1773:   Joseph Smith's Inn, at the intersection of the "Boston Road" and the main route to Albany; this is Pierce's Corner, present intersection of Rtes 7 and 103; Smith sold to his daughter and son-in-law, Sarah and John Bowman, in 1776, and they ran it as <u>Bowman's Tavern</u>, a Clarendon landmark, for fifty-one years; <u>Bowman's</u> is listed in the 1796 Vermont Almanac and Register as a stop on the Rutland-Boston road; also 1802, '07; sold to Edward Dyer, 1827; then Harvey Hawkins; and then Christopher Pierce, 1835; occupied by Pierces for four generations, but ceased operating as an inn by the late 1860s, perhaps somewhat earlier; burned in October, 1959; the Pierce place is shown on the 1869 Beers; (photo,ref 1);

* * *

"Joseph Smith's Inn...was very well known. Its location at the intersection of the Boston Road and the main route to Albany, New York made it accessible to travelers from both directions. The fact that Joseph Smith was known to be a loyal New Hampshire man led his inn to become a headquarters of sorts for Ethan Allen and his Green Mountain Boys...The story of Benjamin Spencer is well known. He lived in the south part of Durham (name originally given to Clarendon) and 'was active as a York justice and assistant judge'...To punish Mr Spencer for his activities against the interests of the New Hampshire grantees, Ethan Allen and a group of his followers moved against him in the autumn of 1773. He was captured and taken 'to the house of Joseph Smith of Durham, innkeeper.' Here he was held until he chose to be tried in front of his own home. He was convicted and punished by having the roof of his house removed." (1)

* * *

1774: <u>Butler's tavern</u>, -- (listed under Otter Creek, almost certainly Clarendon, in Bickerstaff's almanac);

1778: <u>Widow Potter's Inn</u>, --; (1)

1796: <u>Rice's Tavern</u>, --; listed in the Vermont Almanac and Register as a tavern on the Rutland-New York road, halfway between Rutland and Wallingford;

1808: <u>Nathaniel Crary tavern</u>; referred to in the Rutland Herald, 2/13/1808;

1843: <u>Caleb Hall's Inn,</u> --; referred to in the Rutland Herald, 1/3/1843; tavern license, 1823;

1849: --, C. B. Hall; --, G. Cheney (NEMU Dir);

c. 1850: a tavern, --; VDHP 1105-41, on old Route 7 between Pierce's Corner and North Clarendon, the DeZero house in 1976; owned by the Weeks family in mid-19th century, said to have been a coach stop;

1855: --, C. B. Hall* (Scott map; see above, Caleb Hall; also listed in Walton for this year);

Note: almanacs also listed these taverns, locations unknown: Parker's, 1807-22; Brown's, 1813-29 (a William Brown had a tavern license, 1817); Rice's, 1796; and Wilbur's, 1812;

Note: tavern licenses also issued to Constant (?) Barney, 1817; William Weeks, 1817, '21, '22; Seba French, 1817; Ebenezer Brooks, 1821; Benjamin Roberts, 1821; Oziel H. Round, 1821, '22; and Caleb Hall, 1823;

(45c) <u>Clarendon Springs</u>.

* * *

"An era of high hopes and grandiose dreams (i.e., the boom era of Green Mountain mineral springs) it was appropriately ushered in by a vision. Back in 1776, the strange mystic of Clarendon, Asa Smith, dreamed of a miraculous spring in the western part of town that would heal his 'scrofulous humor.' His vision included not only the spot in which the spring was to be found, but also a description of its chemical properties: 'chalybeate water impregnated with lime.'

194

Although greatly weakened by his affliction, the next day Asa tramped through the wilderness until he came to the place as he had divined it. There he drank the water, made a mud pack for his swollen limbs, and returned to his cabin in the eastern part of town--completely cured." (2) (There is also a chapter on Clarendon Springs in Graffagnino, ref 5.)

* * *

1781:   a hotel, George Rounds; Rounds was a neighbor of Asa Smith's (see above,) took a few boarders at his log cabin at the springs; in 1793 (Hemenway) he built a frame hotel, which was expanded over the years and became the American House (see below);

* * *

"George and Martha (i.e., Rounds) were hospitable people and gave shelter and food to these ailing travelers. First they added to their log home but soon other quarters were needed. Seventeen years after coming, George Round, farmer-turned-hotelman, built a frame 2 1/2 story 'hotel' on the level above the river to the west of the spring. At first this could accommodate some 20 guests but two 'wings'were added and still they came. The American House must have resembled a clinic more than a hotel around the turn of the century (i.e., the eighteenth century)." (1)

* * *

c. 1800:   the "Stone building"; a few rods west of the American House, used for service functions at the Clarendon Springs House (see below), to accommodate help, and possibly overflow guests too;

1834:   Clarendon House/Clarendon Springs House ; built by Thomas McLaughlin; the Rutland Herald for July 4, 1837, says it was "recently erected"; originally three stories, brick-walled, with 120 rooms, it proved inadequate to demand and two more stories were added in a few years; this, and the two other hotels bought by Byron Murray and his sons in 1866 (the American House, see above; and the Green Mountain House, see below), together with several smaller rooming-houses, could accommodate 500 guests; but the peak was past by the time the Murrays came on the scene; the American House was torn down, just before World War II; the Green Mountain House burned (see below); and only the Clarendon Springs House, which operated the longest, still stands (ref 1, photos; see photo, Chap. I); A4 in the Clarendon Springs Historic District. (3)

1825:   Green Mountain House, Silas Green; who built it; it was remodelled later by James Flowers, and burned in 1866; a place called the Cook House later built on the site (or Cobb House, so listed later in the Vt Dir, see below);

Note: There is a difficulty here: all sources mention three hotels in the boom days at Clarendon Springs (presumably the Clarendon House, the American House and the Green Mountain House) but the Green Mountain House is said to have burned in 1866, although Walton continues to list it until 1887, and the Vt Dir until the mid-1870s; and Beers lists the Murray House in 1869 (probably the Green Mountain House with a different name); perhaps the fire occurred in 1887; (photo, Green Mountain House,ref 1);

1834:   notice in the Rutland Herald (6/9/1834) that David Hodgman has taken over the house formerly occupied by O. H. Rounds; David Hodgman later reported at the "White House";

1844:   reference in the Rutland Herald (6/20/1844) to the Clarendon House (Col McLaughlin) and the Union Hall (D. Hodgman); the latter is presumably the American House;

1853:   Clarendon House* (on a sketch map in Zadock Thompson, ref 4);

1855, '56:   --, A. Lincoln; --, Thomas McLaughlin; McLaughlin's must be the Clarendon Springs House here; there are two taverns shown on the 1854 Scott map, no names;

1869: (a) Clarendon Springs House, B. Murray* (Beers); American House, B. Murray* (Beers); Murray House, B. Murray* (Beers); the Murray House is A3 in the Clarendon Springs Historic District; (3)

1870: (a) as above, Byron Murray; (b) Green Mountain House, James Flowers;

1873, '75: (a) as above; (b) as above, A. F. Style (Stile);

1878: (a) as above; (b) as above, A. N. Lyons;

1880, '87: (a), (b) as above; the Murray House closed in 1898;

1881-82: (a) as above, June-October (Child);

1890: (a) as above, George T. Murray (Vt Dir); Cobb House, A. H. Cobb (Vt Dir);

1898: (a) as above, George S. Fletcher;

1901: (a) as above, --;

1903: (a) as above, --; Wayside Inn, --; Powers House, -- (SBA);

1905: (a) as above, Robert Murray;

1908: (a) as above, --;

1920, '25: (a) Clarendon Springs House now a tea house; until c. 1930, now an antique shop.

(45d) East Clarendon.

1849: --, Calvin Crossman (NEMU Dir);

1855, '56: C. Crossman* (Scott map).

(45e) North Clarendon.

(?): Woods Bird Inn, - (VHS postcard photo);

1914: no hotel shown on Sanborn map for this year.

Note: the assistance of Mr David Potter, West Rutland, is gratefully acknowledged.

* * *

References

(1) David E. Potter et al., Clarendon, Vermont: 1761-1976, Helen Rondina, ed. (Rutland: Academy Books, 1976).
(2) Louise E. Koier, "Those wonderful waters brought the first flood of tourists to Vermont," Vermont Life 11 (Summer 1957): 56-60.
(3) Vermont Div. of Historic Preservation, Historic Architecture of Rutland County, Vermont, Curtis B. Johnson, ed., Elsa Gilbertson, asst. ed. (Montpelier: 1988).
(4) Z. Thompson, History of Vermont (Burlington: The Author, 1853; Part Two, Gazetteer).
(5) J. Kevin Graffagnino, Vermont in the Victorian Age (Bennington: Vermont Heritage Press, 1985).

* * *

(46) **Colchester** (Chittenden).

(46a) Colchester (including areas in the township lying outside Colchester village, Malletts Bay and Winooski village). There were also POs at Ft Ethan Allan (1902-17) and Champlain (1894-1901), no listings found.

c. 1800: four early taverns referred to in Wright (ref 1) without names: (1) on Porter's Point, where ferry travelers and winter sleighs passed; (2) at the intersection of the East Road with Town Road #27 (Severance Road on the Northern Cartographic map of Chittenden County); (3) at the intersection of East Road with Depot Road (town road 17); this is VDHP 0404-22, built c. 1810, now empty (i.e., in 1976); and (4) at the intersection of the West Road (present Rte 7) with Rtes 2A and 127; this latter place is probably the Munson tavern/homestead described in ref 2; built about 1843, operated by William H. Munson, building still standing and owned by Walter C. Munson in 1975 (VDHP 0404-4);

1830: a tavern, Arad Merrill; at the then intersection of the East Road with present Vt 15 (Winooski Park); this place became Dunbar's Hotel and later the Fanny Allen Hospital (see below); at one time the East Road connected the "high bridge" with Colchester village in a reasonably direct way; kept by Arad Merrill for 12 years, then his son Andrew J. Merrill (1849, NEMU Dir); sold to Dunbar in 1878 (VDHP 0404-29);

1856: --, Sidney Weston; --, Lucy Sharp; --, N. A. Austin; --, W. D. Ayers (locations not established, could be Colchester, Winooski, Malletts Bay or outside the villages);

1869: (a) Merrill's Hotel, A. J. Merrill* (Beers);

1870: (a) as above;

1879, '80, '82, '83, '87, '90: (a) Dunbar's Hotel, Frank J. Dunbar;

1892: (a) as above, A. B. Austin; converted to Fanny Allen Hospital starting in 1894;

* * *

"Dunbar's Hotel had a very good reputation. At one time there were 34 regular boarders for whom the Austin family served meals and filled dinner pails every day. Many of them were employed in the construction of Fort Ethan Allen. Transients too came to Dunbar's and the big ballroom in the right ell was the scene of many an evening party. To serve a midnight repast at such events, the hotel staff would go to bed right after the regular evening meal, then rise again in time to prepare the extra banquet, often in winter, an oyster supper." (2)

(46b) Malletts Bay.

"...a mysterious person by the name of Mallett, a Frenchman, resided on Mallett's Head...previous to the Revolution, and during its progress, claiming allegiance to no nation, but keeping a hotel for British and Continental, spy and smuggler alike. He died at an advanced age in 1790" (Child);

(?): Munson's Hotel, became the Malletts Bay House;

1869: Malletts Bay House, William D. Munson* (Beers; not the same as William H. Munson, early tavern-keeper in Colchester, see above); burned on Dec 22, 1891, apparently rebuilt on same site;

1870: (a) as above;

1873: (a) as above, L. Lirock (Liroch?);

197

1876: (a) as above, H. H. Howe;

1879, 1881: (a) as above, Frank Brownell;

1884: (a) as above, McKay Campbell;

1882-83, 1887: (a) as above, W. B. Craven;

1890, '92, 1901: (a) as above, F. F. Gokey;

1908: (a) as above, --;

1913, '15, '20: Vermont Inn, --;

1923: Lake Champlain Club, T. Russell Brown.

(46c) Winooski.

c. 1790-1810: Ichabod Brownell's tavern; built by Roswell Butler, at present 73 East Allen St; but Hemenway says Brownell, a blacksmith, came to the Falls in 1793, built the back part of the stone tavern home, "the only building still extant (i.e., c. 1867) put up in those times," where he kept tavern until about 1811; Butler was one of Ira Allen's partners in the lumber business here; several early Colchester town meetings held here, later a tenement building;

1796: Stanton's tavern, --; listed in the Vermont Almanac and Register as a stage stop on the Windsor-Burlington road; listed until c. 1816;

Note: almanacs also list a Hind's (or Hine's) tavern, location unknown; tavern license, William Hine, 1820, '21; other 1821 licenses to John Gove and Joseph Barnes;

1849: --, Cotton Fletcher; --, A. J. Merrill; Winooski Falls House, A. B. Stanton (all NEMU Dir);

c. 1850: a hotel, T. R. Fletcher; Fletcher's Hotel, then the River House Inn; now a residence (VDHP 0418-37, 81 East Allen St);

1857: a hotel, S. H. Weston* (Walling);

1869: (a) Stevens House, J. W. Celley* (Beers);

1870, '75: (a) as above;

1873: (a) as above, A. R. Pike;

1879, '80: (a) as above, C. P. Wing;

1882-83: (a) as above, James Evarts (Childs);

1883, '87, '90, '92, '95: (a) as above;

1898: Hotel American, --;

1908: Brunswick, --;

1911, '13: Hotel Brunswick, --; Allen House, --;

1915: Allen House, --; Hotel Oxford, --;

1920:   Hotel Brunswick, --; Oxford, --;

1925:   Hotel Brunswick, --; The House, --; Walton lists Allen House, Brunswick, and New City in 1930, none in 1935;

(?):   Winooski Hotel, -- (postcard photo).

Note: the assistance of Mr and Mrs Leon W. Germain, Winooski Historical Society, is gratefully acknowledged.

* * *

References

(1) Ruth E. Wright, History of the Town of Colchester, Bicentennial Edition (Burlington: Queen City Pr., 1963).
(2) Lilian B. Carlisle, ed., Look Around Chittenden County, Vermont (Burlington: Chittenden County Historical Soc., 1976).

* * *

(47) Concord (Essex).

(47a) Concord. Formerly West Concord, on Rte 2; this Concord is the second town of that name; postally, it was West Concord from 1850-1904, when it inherited the name Concord a year after the office at the "Corner" (the first Concord) closed.

1844:   (a) West Concord House, built by Levi Howe;

1849:   --, William B. Downing (NEMU Dir);

1855, '56:   --, Powers and Hill;

1859:   --, A. E. Bliss* (Walling);

1870:   (a) West Concord House, F. and W. A. Richardson;

1875, '80, '81: (a) as above, J. C. Spencer* (Beers, 1878);

1882:   (a) as above, J. D. Brigham;

1883:   (a) as above, G. V. Fraisine;

1885, '87:   (a) as above, J. C. Spencer;

1890, '92, '95, '98, 1901, '05, '09:   (a) as above, Frank Joslyn; photo, ref 1; this place burned in 1912;

1911:   (a) as above, --;

1914:   Cottage Hotel, --* (Sanborn; probably a private home fitted up as a hotel after the fire).

(47b) Concord (Corner).

c. 1798:   first tavern in town, Andrew Hardy; (2)

1805:   Hutchinson Tavern, --; almanac; a Jonathan Hutchinson was an early settler;

1849:   --, A. S. Howard (NEMU Dir).

(47c) East Concord.

1894:   hotel and boarding house, C. L. Pratt. (2)

(47d) Miles Pond. No listings found.

(47e) North Concord.

1877:   a hotel, Luther Russell, Jr* (Beers); Mr Russell built a structure that combined the functions of railroad depot, post office, store and hotel, all in one; photo, ref 2;

Note: the assistance of Mrs Bernice Payeur, Concord Historical Society, is gratefully acknowledged.

References

(1) William H. Jeffrey, Successful Vermonters: a modern gazetteer of Caledonia, Essex and Orleans counties (East Burke: Historical Publishing, 1904).
(2) Town of Concord, Vermont, 1781-1976, Then and Now (Concord: Concord Bicentennial Comm.; St Johnsbury: Troll Pr., 1976).

* * *

(48) Corinth (Orange).

(48a) Cookville.

Local name; town's first post office, called Corinth, established here in 1806, still operating.

c. 1800:   Daniel Cooke's inn; almanac, 1801, '02; surveyed by VDHP in 1977 (VDHP 0905-44, #9) who say it was built c. 1800 and is the focal point of the village today; on town highways 2 and 7; photo in ref 1;

* * *

The town takes its name from Daniel Cooke, an early settler and prominent citizen. "He had only $14 when he arrived in Corinth, and he immediately opened a store in one room of a neighbor's house. He married the neighbor's daughter, and when she died at the birth of their son, he married her sister, by whom he subsequently had six more sons and five daughters. In time Daniel built his own store and later added a potash plant, a tannery, a gristmill and a distillery. He also went into cattle trading, and kept a hotel at his home, which is still standing at the village. Two of his sons, Daniel and Henry, and a grandson, Daniel C. Cooke, were all postmasters at different times, and the grandson was town clerk for over twenty years."

* * *

1883:   (a) Riverdale House, M. J. Taplin; this is VDHP 0905-23, built c. 1810, now the Evelyn Richardson home (i.e., 1977); a little east of Cookville (Corinth) where Pike Hill Rd intersects TH #7; it is said that Mansfield Taplin, who came in 1832, used the place as an inn (Riverdale); still here in 1858, shown as M. Taplin on the Walling map, but VDHP says Ames C. Tenney, a mill operator, lived here in 1877; photo, ref 1;

1887:   (a) Riverdale/Riverside House (names apparently used interchangeably), W. B. Ladd;

1888:   (a) as above, Francis H. Frary; he and Mansfield Taplin were proprietors of this place "for a time"; (1)

1890:   (a) as above, W. B. Ladd.

(48b) Corinth Center.

c. 1800:   Robert Rowe tavern; still standing, across the road from Center church in 1964; this place was later (i.e., 1813) operated by John Bickford; photo,ref 1;

Note: almanacs list a Robinson tavern, 1801, '02, location unknown, but probably not Cookville;

(?):   Ainsworth's Tavern House, --; "near the center";

1845:   Rowe's tavern, Melitiah Willis;

1849:   --, M. Willis (NEMU Dir);

1883:   --, William Edwards (Vt Dir);

1887, '88, '90: Traveler's Home, W. M. Edwards; his father John also an inn-keeper, so this place must have been operating earlier; (1)

1901:   Avenue House, G. C. Hastings (village location uncertain, Vt Dir);

(48c) Corinth Corners (Heath, postally, 1896-1905).

(48d) East Corinth.

(?):   Stevens Tavern, --; shown on a map in ref 1 as "near the muster grounds, a little south of the village"; the Frank Emerson place in 1964;

(?):   Reuben Page's mansion "on the Newbury line"; (1)

(?):   a tavern, George Way; ref 1, see below, 1880);

1830-1905:   a village inn "for many years," no other identification; (1)

1853:   an inn, James C. Stevens; an inn, Nathaniel Andrews; (1)

1855:   --, N. Andros (probably Nathaniel Andrews, above);

1856:   --, James C. Stevens (see above);

1858:   Eagle Hotel, --* (Walling);

1870:   --, George Carrath (Vt Dir);

1873:   --, L. P. Foster (Vt Dir; also 1875); Ring's Hotel, Henry Ring;

1877:   --, L. P. Foster* (Beers);

1878:   --, W. J. Butterfield;

1879:   Cottage Hotel, John Butterfield;

1880:   --, W. J. Butterfield; --, G. F. Way;

1883:   --, J. L. Burgess; (a) Village Hotel, G. F. Way;

1887:   (a) as above, George Butterfield; (b) Saginaw House, S. F. Thompson;

1888, '90, '92, '95, '98, 1901:   (b) as above;

1890:   (a) as above, --.

(48e) <u>South Corinth</u>.   No listings found.

(48f) <u>West Corinth</u>.

c. 1886:   (a) <u>Maplewood Inn</u>, Eugene Darling; see photo; an expanded version of the family homestead, early 1800s; fell into disuse, finally burned in 1958; listed in Walton, 1935, '40;

Maplewood Inn

1901:   (a) as above, A. P. Cooke;

1916:   (a) as above, Hartwell E. Baxter (VPB).

* * *

References

(1) Town of Corinth History Committee, History of Corinth, Vermont, 1764-1964 (Corinth: The Town; West Topsham: Gibby Pr., 1964).

* * *

(49) **Cornwall** (Addison).

(49a) <u>Cornwall</u>.

c. 1774:   a tavern, <u>Nathan Foot Jr</u>; almanac, 1812; "for many years he kept the present house as a tavern, as it was well situated for the convenience of travelers" (1); Foot died in 1829; at the junction of Rte 30, Cider Mill Rd and Ridge Rd; "Lane House" in 1976 (VDHP 0104-15); the VDHP says that the ell was built c. 1785, the main block c. 1835;

c. 1784:   a tavern, <u>Ethan Andrus</u>; on a farm owned by W. H. and P. T. B. Matthews, c. 1886 (3); in a framed house; VDHP says the original Andrus place burned and Andrus left in 1808; this building was the James house on Rte 30 (VDHP 0104-8) in recent years;

c. 1795:   a tavern, <u>William Slade</u>; almanac, 1812; father of Gov Slade, whose birthplace is shown on the Beers map of Cornwall, a little south of the village (VDHP 0104-30); Matthews says it was c. 1786; Slade died in 1826;

202

c. 1796: a tavern, <u>Nathan Stowell</u>; almanac, 1812; on the east side of the road a little north of the church; original building replaced c. 1810 by one built by Chauncey H. Stowell, Nathan's son, and kept by him, Col Harmon Samson, and others, but not continuously; the Hugh Langey house in 1976 (VDHP 0104-20);

c. 1828: a tavern, <u>Col Benjamin Douglas</u>; the Robert Williams home in 1976 (VDHP 0104-38).

(49b) <u>West Cornwall</u>.

c. 1795: a tavern (and store), <u>Joshua Stockwell</u>; at Stockwell's Corners (the southeast corner), a place which became West Cornwall when the post office was established in 1859 (VDHP 0104-47).

* * *

References

(1) Beulah M. Sanford, Two Centuries of Cornwall Life (Rutland: Sharp Pr., 1962).
(2) Rev Lyman Matthews, History of the Town of Cornwall, Vermont (Middlebury: Mead and Fuller, 1862; reprinted 1975).
(3) Henry P. Smith, History of Addison County, Vermont (Syracuse: D. Mason, 1886).

* * *

(50) **Coventry** (Orleans).

The town was settled rather late, and very sparsely populated at first. As of 1821, there was no public house or store. Two villages acquired post offices: Coventry, or Coventry Falls; and East Coventry, or Coventry Station. Coventry Center was a significant community at one time, but never had a PO, and faded out in relation to Coventry.

(50a) <u>Coventry</u> (Coventry Falls).

1807: John Farnsworth licensed as a tavern-keeper; location not established (Hemenway);

1829: a tavern, <u>Dr Samuel S. Kendall</u>; tavern license, 1830; who opened his new house in the village for that purpose; with additions and alterations, it later became <u>Daniel Bean's Tavern</u> (see below) and later still the <u>Coventry House</u>; (1)

Note: tavern license for Sikes Sears, 1827-29, location unknown;

1849: --, Henry Thomas (NEMU Dir; location unknown, could be Coventry Center or East Coventry);

1855: --, Daniel Bean;

1856: --, Daniel Bean; --, M. Buck (location not clear);

1859: <u>Daniel Bean's Tavern</u>* (Walling; became the <u>Coventry House</u>);

1870: (a) <u>Coventry House</u>, M. N. Howland;

1873: (a) as above, W. W. Langmayd;

1875: (a) as above, G. S. Livingston;

1878: (a) as above, G. W. Cole* (Beers; same location as <u>Bean's</u>, above);

1879, '80:   (a) as above, George W. Mellon;

1883: --, C. Chamberlin;

1887, '90, '92, '95, '98:   (a) as above, B. F. Wiggin;

1901: (a) as above, H. W. Dam;

1908: (a) as above, --;

1911, '13:   --, W. F. Scott; a major fire in 1913 destroyed the hotel, Thurber's store and several houses (2); the hotel apparently was never rebuilt since no further listings are found. The hotel stood where the "Tin House" stood in 1977; #6 in the Coventry Village Historic District, VDHP 1005-22;

1914: no hotel on Sanborn map.

(50b) Coventry Center.

1823: Eber R. Hamilton built a large 2-story house in which Jacob Hurd lived in 1859 (ref 1; there is a T. Hurd on the 1859 Walling) and commenced keeping tavern there; tavern license, 1823, '25; this place is ascribed to "Heber" Hamilton in Child, said to be the first hotel in town;

(?):   a public house, Capt Plastridge (2); tavern license, Amasa Plastridge, 1826, '27.

(50c) East Coventry/Coventry Station. No listings found.

(50d) West Hill Region.

1823: Aretas Knight, at the first permanent settlement on West Hill, built a small house which "served as a house of entertainment for such as came to examine lands before purchasing, and a boarding house for settlers till they could build...His house was sometimes crowded to the utmost. It was inhabited several months by twenty-three individuals, eight of whom were married couples with fourteen children under seven years of age. The little building...is now one of Mr Cleveland's outhouses." (1)

* * *

References

(1) Pliny H. White, A History of Coventry, Orleans County, Vermont (Irasburgh: A. A. Earle, 1859; reprinted, Newport: Gilpin, Hunt, 1976).
(2) Thelma Wilcox, ed., Bits and Pieces of Coventry's History (Barre: Modern Pr., 1977).

* * *

(51) **Craftsbury** (Orleans).

There have been four settlements or villages in the town of Craftsbury, but the postal designations moved around so much that it is not always easy to know which village is which in directories and gazetteers. The "southern" village has been known as both South Craftsbury and just plain Craftsbury, as it is now; and the "hill" village was originally called North Craftsbury before settling down as Craftsbury Common. East Craftsbury was always East Craftsbury, but there was a tiny hamlet in the western part of town, usually called West Craftsbury, which had a post office called Branch for a while.

(51a) Branch. No listings found.

(51b) Craftsbury/South Craftsbury.

1795: a tavern, <u>Daniel Davison</u>; a veteran of the Revolutionary War, located in the southern part of town where he kept a hotel, and later at the Common (Child, locations unknown);

(?): <u>Eagle Hotel</u>, Amasa Scott; built by him, on Main St; various owners until 1864, when I. T. Patterson acquired it, and added another story; probably the same place in all listings below;

Note: tavern licenses to Thomas Tolman (?), 1822, '23, '25; Elijah Burroughs, 1829; Benjamin Clark, 1826; Oliver M. Hidden, 1830; and William Hidden, 1833, locations unknown;

1849: --, A. W. Hidden (NEMU Dir);

1850: a hotel, <u>Horace Andrus</u> (Anderson? see below); on road 40 for three years, and also at Craftsbury village for two (Child, locations unknown);

1855, '56: --, H. S. Anderson (Andrus?);

1859: <u>Hutchins Hotel</u>, --* (Walling);

1870, '73: --, I. T. Patterson;

1875, '78, '80: (a) <u>Eagle Hotel</u>, I. T. Patterson* (Beers, 1878);

1879: <u>Craftsbury House</u>, I. T. Patterson (listed this way only once, in Vt Dir for this year);

1883, '87: (a) as above, I. T. Patterson;

1890, '92, '95, '98, 1901: (a) as above, James Libbey;

Note: a place called the <u>Brewster House</u> is shown on the 1935 Sanborn, but it is on South Main St, south of the river, at a different site from the <u>Eagle Hotel</u>, above; the present day <u>Craftsbury Inn</u> operates in an old building that became an inn in 1935.

(51c) <u>Craftsbury Common/North Craftsbury</u>.

c. 1810: a tavern, <u>Dr William Scott</u>; the second doctor in town, "opened the first tavern, on the west side of the common, in a flat roofed house. About 1825 he built a new house, and is now occupied and owned by Bartlett Williams, he was a man that was well liked as a Doct and Tavern keeper..." (1)

1849: (a) <u>Orleans House</u>, E. Knight; --, W. I. Hastings (NEMU Dir); this is #20 in the Craftsbury Common Historic District (VDHP 1006-1); operated until 1957 (<u>Hearthside Inn</u>, Grace Rawson, in the 1930s, <u>Pikes Hotel</u> before that, see below, now Sterling College);

1855, '56: --, D. Andrews;

1859: (a) <u>Orleans House</u>, B. Carpenter* (Walling);

1870: (a) as above, A. R. Pike;

1873: (a) as above, William Hodgden;

1879, '80, '83, '87, '90: (a) as above, L. M. Washburn;

1883-84: (a) as above, Mrs E. J. Johnson (Child);

1892: (a) as above, G. K. Goodrich;

1895, '98, 1901, '05: (a) as above, A. B. Pike;

1908, '11, '13: (a) as above, --;

1915, '20, '25: (a) Orleans House, A. B. Pike; see photo;

Orleans House

1935: No hotel on Sanborn map for this year.

(51d) East Craftsbury.

(?):   --, Samuel E. Morse; Child says he was a distiller and hotel-keeper; died in 1834; this place was a hotel in 1929, not clear for how long; built in 1806 (#8 in the East Craftsbury Historic District, VDHP 1006-3).

(51e) West Craftsbury. No listings found.

* * *

References

(1) Amasa Scott, A Brief sketch of the first settlers of Craftsbury, Vermont (Craftsbury: Craftsbury Public Library, 1951?).

* * *

(52) **Danby** (Rutland).

There have been two villages in the town, Danby Four Corners and Danby village; the former was more prosperous at first, but it faded quickly when the railroad came through to Danby in 1851.

(52a) Danby.

1795: first tavern at the Boro, Rowland Stafford; near the "present" hotel (i.e., c. 1875, Hemenway); Vermont Almanac and Register, 1796;

1804: a tavern, William Webber; who built it on the site of the present hotel; succeeded by Dr McClure who left in 1808; then Elisha Southwick, Dr Augustus Mulford (c. 1810); the place burned in 1813 (see Rutland Herald, 3/24/1813), rebuilt by Mulford the same year, still standing (i.e., c. 1875, Hemenway); later the Danby House/Bond Hotel; Mulford succeeded by Hosea Williams (a Williams tavern is listed in an 1812 almanac), Rufus Bucklin Jr until 1820, then various; now (i.e., c. 1875) operated by Lytle Vance," the only hotel in town";

Note: tavern licenses to John Vaughan, 1817; Jabez Mattison, 1821, '22; and Isaac Southwick (Elisha, above?), 1823, locations unknown;

c. 1800: a hotel, Bradford Barnes; tavern license, 1817, '21; a little north of the village on the "present" (i.e., c. 1875, Hemenway) Austin Baker place (an A. S. Baker is shown on the 1869 Beers); succeeded by Samuel Dow in 1802 for a short time; no tavern at this site after that;

1824, '25: reference to town meetings at Arwin Hutchin's inn;

1832: town meeting at Bethuel Bromley's inn, at the west end of the village; place made out of the old Methodist meeting house by Barton Bromley; first kept by Arwin Hutchins, then N. Jenks (tavern license to Nicholas Jenks 1817, '21, '22), Samuel Harnden, Bethuel Bromley, Arnold Nicholson, Ephraim Gilmore, Ephraim Vail, Jephtha Frost, and others;

* * *

There are references to town meetings being held at Nicholas Jenks' inn in 1816 and 1826 and at Ephraim Gilman's tavern in 1828, both probably the same as Bromley's inn (above); and at Samuel Harnden's in 1829 and 1830 (also Bromley's). Harnden was also a shoemaker and a fiddler, one of the best in the state, according to Hemenway; and it is said that he cured a woman of fits by his fiddling, and later married her.

* * *

1849: --, Ephraim Chase; --, Levi Barrett; both NEMU Dir, not clear which village they are in;

(?): a tavern, Abraham Anthony; who kept a tavern "early, where the Phillips bros. now live" (i.e., c. 1875, Hemenway; not clear which village);

1869: --, E. Lewis* (Beers; same location as Bond's Danby House, below);

1870: (a) Danby House, Lytle Vance (see photo; this is the place rebuilt by Mulford in 1812); also known as Bond's Hotel, Ackert Hotel;

1872: (a) Bond's Hotel, William H. Bond;

1875-at least 1913: (a) as above, W. H. Bond; Bond was also postmaster, 1885-89 and 1893-1906, and is listed as operator of the Mount Tabor Hotel/House (in Danby) in 1897, 1901 (Vt Dir, location of this place unknown; and this name is not familiar to local historians; may refer to a place at Lake Griffith, see below); photo of Bond's hotel in ref 1;

1897: Grand View Terrace, --; (Rutland Railroad guide);

c. 1915-20: (a) Ackert Hotel (former Danby House/Bond Hotel); photo in ref 1; but according to the Sanborn map, this place was not operating in 1915;

1920: (a) --, Mrs Maude Baker;

1925: (a) --, Mrs Maude Baker Newton; destroyed by fire in 1934;

* * *

There is also reference in "Danby Two Centuries" to a hotel at Lake Griffith. (1) This is puzzling; the only body of water in Danby is called Danby Pond on Beers; the only Lake Griffith listed in Swift is half in Peru and half in Mount Tabor (called Mud Pond on Beers) and not in Danby town at all. (2) According to local historians, there was a place here called the Lake House, built by Silas L. Griffith for his personal use.

207

Danby House (Vermont Historical Society)

(52b) <u>Danby Four Corners</u>.

1775: first inn, <u>Capt John Burt</u>; "where the poor-house now stands...for many years" (c. 1875, Hemenway); the town farm (i.e., "poor-house") is shown on the 1869 Beers, about a mile north of the village;

* * *

John Hart, a land-jobber, went to Albany for relief in a dispute he was having with a business associate in Danby. He and a New York sheriff arrested Hart's associate in Danby, but the party was overtaken by the aroused settlers as they were making their way to Albany, and brought back to Danby, where Hart was tried by the Committee of Safety at <u>Burt's Tavern</u>.

"As soon as the shouts which burst forth on the arrival of the prisoner had subsided, and the echoes from the mountains had died away, the judges took their seats on the bench in the barroom, the prisoner was arraigned, and without loss of time convicted...and sentenced to receive thirty-nine stripes with the beach-seal on the naked back." John Hart did not long remain a citizen here after this event, but, disposing of his possessions, left for other parts." (Hemenway).

* * *

c. 1778-1800: a tavern, <u>Abraham Chase</u>; combination store and tavern about 1 1/4 miles south of the Corners ("near Alvah Risdon's place," Hemenway, c. 1875; this place is shown on the 1869 Beers); this tavern also operated by Henry Frost until 1810, then Jazaniah Barrett;

1810: two hotels at the Corners: (1) <u>Elisha Brown</u>, from 1800 "for many years"; and (2) <u>Henry Herrick Jr</u>, in a place known as the "Red House" a little north of the village; (1) town meetings held at the latter place for a while; succeeded by N. Jenks until 1823; in the first tavern above, Brown was succeeded by Herrick for 21 years; then David Kelley, Rufus Bucklin Jr, John Sweat, Ephraim Chase, - McCollister, Jephtha Frost, and others;

(?): a tavern, --; on the northeast corner at the Four Corners, before the building became the cheese factory (which is shown on the 1869 Beers); this place is probably the same as Elisha Brown's, above; a man was once sent to prison for accidentally killing another man in this tavern, but after a year the town petitioned his return; (1)

c. 1820: a tavern, <u>Rufus Bucklin Jr</u>; he also ran a tavern at the Corners for eight years (see above);

Note: no listings found for Danby Four Corners in Walton, Vt Dir or Child for the period 1855-1900;

1850:   a tavern, Seneca Smith; who "fitted up a tavern" kept by Oliver Sheldon, then John Croft, - Bates, Joseph Smith, others;

1905:   Hotel Nilox, G. H. Faxton;

Note: The assistance of Hugh G. Bromley and friends, associated with the Griffith Memorial Library, is gratefully acknowledged.

* * *

References

(1) Suzanne F. Crosby et al., Danby Two Centuries (Bennington: Hadwen, 1976).
(2) Esther M. Swift, Vermont Place-Names: Footprints of History (Brattleboro: Stephen Greene Pr., 1977).

* * *

(53) **Danville** (Caledonia).

Danville, the principal village, was once known as Danville Green; it was the shire town for Caledonia county until 1856, and it got a post office in 1799 which is still operating.

(53a) Danville.

1805:   the stage legislature met here in the fall of 1805, there being then two inns; the governor and his council met in the hall of Abel Morrill's tavern, just this side of the present cemetery (tavern license, 1822); and Col I. P. Dana bought "the old red tavern stand" which he improved; (1)

Note: almanacs list Baldwin's tavern (1802) and Page's tavern (1805), locations unknown; a Kelsea sp?) tavern is also listed in an 1802 almanac; (probably same as the Eagle Hotel, J. Kelsey, below);

Note: tavern licenses to Nahum Downs, 1824; Marmaduke Wait, 1822-26; Henry Hunt, 1822; Stutson (?) West, 1825,'27; and John Kelsey, 1827;

1812:   Cash's Tavern, in the village (Hemenway);

1849:   (a) Eagle Hotel, J. Kelsey; Caledonia Temperance House, Horace Evans (NEMU Dir);

1856:   --, Ira A. Preston;

1870, '73, '75: (a) Eagle Hotel, Aaron H. Smith;

1879, '80:   (a) as above; converted to Beehive (apartments, offices), c. 1883; (b) Elm House, Charles W. Thurber; (for an anecdote about the Thurber House and the Elm House in the railroad days, see Chapter IV);

1883:   (b) as above, Edward Warner;

1887:   (b) as above, C. W. Thurber (Walton, but J. C. Mooney in Vt Dir and E. Woodward in Child);

1888:   (b) Elm House, H. M. Osgood; (c) Thurber's Hotel, C. W. Thurber (Boston and Maine guide);

1890:   (b) as above, Charles Ingalls;

1892:   (c) Thurber's Hotel, C. W. Thurber;

1895, '98, 1901, '05, '08:   (b) as above, R. B. Gammell; (c) as above;

1911:   Danville Inn, --; (c) as above, Mrs S. O. Morse (boarding house);

1913:   Danville Inn, --; (c) as above;

1919:   (c) Thurber's Hotel, -- (see photo, Chapter IV);

1920:   (b) Elm House, --; (c) as above;

1925:   (b) as above, W. S. Cahoon; (c) as above, W. E. Worthen; razed in 1965.

(53b) Harvey (formerly Harvey's Hollow, and the first South Danville), and (53c), North Danville, no listings found.

(53d) South Danville (the second South Danville, postally; also known locally as Greenbank Hollow). No listings found.

(53e) West Danville (includes part of Joe's Pond).

1870:   (a) West Danville House, E. W. Huntoon; from this date until approximately 1879; burned at about that time;

1872:   (a) as above, C. H. Hall;

1873:   (a) as above, J. F. Laducer (Vt Dir);

1875:   (a) as above, Asa B. Mack* (Beers);

1879:   (a) as above, A. R. Pike;

1888:   Lakeside House, C. A. Gerry (Boston and Maine guide);

1901:   Lake Park House, Orman B. Flint (Vt Dir; probably same as above);

(?):   a hotel, --; VDHP describes a building (VDHP 0303-78, #3) built c. 1845, remodelled c. 1880 by G. W. Farrington, known at one time as Hasting's store, that was a stage hotel in the mid-19th century; not the same site as the place shown on Beers, 1875; has an interior post office dating from 1900.

Note: the assistance of Mary L. Prior, Danville Historical Society, is gratefully acknowledged.

* * *

References

(1) Charles A. Lawrence, "A legislative assembly at Danville in 1805," Vermonter 33 (Sept, 1928): 143-146.

* * *

(54) **Derby** (Orleans).

The town of Derby contains six places that have had post offices, three still operating; it also includes the eastern shore of the part of Lake Memphremagog that lies in the United States, and Salem Lake. There was once a town of Salem, but due to surveying errors when charters were being awarded, it was never a viable township. There was a Salem post office for a few years (1833-43) but part of the township was eventually absorbed into Derby and the rest into Newport city. What was once the village of West Derby became part of Newport city in 1917 (East Newport, locally). The town also includes two border villages, Beebe Plain and Derby Line.

(54a) Beebe Plain.

1878:   --, Mrs H. Bacon* (Beers);

1883-84:   Beebe Plain Hotel, Sarah J. Bacon (Child);

1914:   No hotel shown on Sanborn map.

(54b) Derby/Derby Center. Latter existed postally for only a month in 1850.

c. 1800:   a tavern, Capt Timothy Hinman; first settler in present Derby village area, where Charles Johnson lived c. 1883 (Child);

Note: almanacs list a Boardman tavern (1802, '05), location unknown;

1803:   a tavern, David Hopkinson (tavern license, 1817); he came in 1802, a little after Blake (see below) but his tavern license antedates Blake's by a year; the tavern was run by his family for over fifty years; (also a tavern license for a Noyes Hopkinson, 1817, 1822-32, under Salem, which was partly annexed by Newport in 1816, the rest by Derby in 1880);

1804:   a tavern, Ephraim Blake (tavern license, 1817, 1822-30); first settler, near the center of town in what was originally Salem (almanac, 1802); a road came through from Derby to Brownington, and Blake and Hopkinson were both on it, Blake near the center, Hopkinson at the extreme north; the Blakes were the only inhabitants until 1801; their farm now owned by Scott Warthin (i.e., 1977, ref 1); the tavern was still operating in 1822, when the first town meeting was held there;

Note: tavern licenses to William Salisbury, 1817, '22, '24, '25; Sampson Davis, 1817; Elijah Davis, 1823-30; Daniel Drew, 1823; Joseph Burroughs, 1823; Asa Kimball, 1827-29; Hoel Hinman, 1827; Benjamin Pomeroy, 1827; James Scott, 1830, '33; J. and R.V. Crane, 1832; Samuel Blake (Salem), 1830, '33; and Orra C. Bloss, 1826, locations unknown;

1816:   an inn, Col Chester Carpenter (tavern license, 1817, '22-33); original settler and later a leading citizen of Derby, he bought a farm with a small inn on it on the Clyde River, just south of the village; moved the inn to the main street of the village, a few years later moved it back to the farm property; this place later torn down, replaced by a "good-sized two-story tavern" (2); became a temperance place about 1832, stayed that way with the Carpenters and later, Jacob Bates;

* * *

Col Chester Carpenter (1787-1872) came from Randolph Center in 1807. He bought one hundred acres on the eastern shore of Lake Memphremagog for $100, built a barn and a house, and married Hannah Kendall in 1811. He fought in the war of 1812, and afterwards ran an inn and tavern in Derby. It became a temperance hotel after 1833, and was sold to his son Chester Carpenter Jr in 1845. The place burned in 1884 (photos of portraits of Carpenter, his wife, and son, ref 3);

* * *

211

This (i.e., Carpenter's second tavern) had a square chimney in the center to carry away the smoke from a big brick oven and three wide fireplaces. These fireplaces and two on the second floor all had broad granite hearths and were supported by the heavy brick walls of the ash bin and the storehouse. At the bar room door swung a 2 x 4 sign board with the eagle and shield on one side and a decanter and a half-filled glass of red brandy, and below these on each side the words, Carpenter's Inn, 1816.

"In later times the inborn temperance principles of the owner sent the sign with the red glass and decanter to the dust of the attic, and other signs bearing no temptation to, or suggestion of evil, invited to the comforts and hospitality of 'Carpenter's Inn' weary travelers, friends and beggars. From Carpenter's Tavern the moneyless went after they were filled and lodged. Baptist ministers came, stayed and departed at their pleasure in welcome. Church members from remote parts of the town attending Sabbath or other meetings found open doors and hearts. Guests might have received slight attention compared with purest hotel life, but their horses were well-fed and cared for, the table and beds satisfactory for those days--clean at any rate."

* * *

1849: --, C. Carpenter; --, Roswell Bates (NEMU Dir);

1855: --, J. Bates 2nd; --, H. E. Johnson;

1856: --, I. Bales 2nd (presumably a misspelling);

1859: --, Jacob Bates* (Walling);

1870: Derby Center Hotel, John M. Brigham;

1872, '73: Brigham's Hotel, G. (?) M. Brigham;

1875: Hinman's Hotel, W. H. Hinman;

1876, '78, '79, '80, '83, '84: Central House, W. H. Hinman* (Beers);

1887: Derby Lake House, J. G. Elder;

1887: Vt Dir still lists the Central House, although it burned in 1884; Walton does not;

1888: Derby House, A. C. Fellows (Boston and Maine pamphlet);

1890, '92, '95: --, A. D. Chandler, Mrs A. D. Chandler;

1898: Derby House, C. E. Twambly;

1898, 1901, '05: The Rickard, L. A. Rickard, Mrs L. A. Rickard;

1911, '13, '15: --, A. C. Fellows;

1916: Derby House, --* (Sanborn); now an apartment building;

1920: --, W. G. Coburn;

1920s: Kingsbury Farms Hotel, --; on the banks of the Clyde River, a short-lived summer hotel; photo, ref 1; owned by Kingsbury Foster, who also built a golf course and airfield there; listed until at least 1940;

1920s: Meadow Brook Club , Hiram Foster; another short-lived summer hotel.

(54c) Derby Line.

c. 1830: a tavern on the site of the later Derby Line Hotel (2); this place operated by Hannah Chase and her husband in 1837; "Mrs Chase often recalled that it was a common occurrence to serve dinner to 30 or 40 peddlers on a summer day." Among its last proprietors were Capt and Mrs Henry Foster.

1849: --, Timothy Winn (NEMU Dir);

1855, '56: --, A. B. Nelson;

1859: --, S. Foster* (Walling);

1870, '72: (a) Derby Line Hotel, Fred D. Butterfield; not known when the tavern was replaced by this place;

1873, '75, '78: (a) as above, H. B. Hanson* (Beers);

1879, '80, '83: (a) as above, J. K. Gilman;

1888: (a) as above, A. V. S. Cullins (Boston and Maine pamphlet);

1887, '92, '95, '98: (a) as above, H. E. Foster;

1897: (a) as above, H. E. Foster* (Sanborn; also 1904, '09, '19 and '25);

1901: (a) as above, J. E. Kelley;

1905: (a) as above, H. E. Foster (see photo, next page);

1911: --, J. U. Baxter;

1913, '15, '20, '25: --, A. V. S. Cullins; torn down in 1931, replaced by a US Customs and Immigration office; PO also in same building now (i.e., 1967).

(54d) North Derby. No listings found.

(54e) West Derby.

c. 1815: a hotel, Joseph Dane;

1849: --, J. G. Sinclair (NEMU Dir);

1855, '56: --, William Blake;

1859: --, William Blake* (Walling);

1878: no hotel shown on the Beers map;

1919: Hotel Elder, --* (Sanborn); Hotel West Derby, J. G. Elder, in 1916 VPB);

1925: Roeder's Inn, --* (Sanborn; Hotel Elder not operating in this year; Roeder's later became part of Broadview Hospital; the Hotel Elder building is now gone).

Note: the assistance of Mrs Pauline Glover, Town Clerk, is gratefully acknowledged.

* * *

References

(1) Emily M. Nelson, Frontier Crossroads, the Evolution of Newport, Vermont, Newport

History Committee (Canaan, N.H.: Phoenix, 1977).

(2) Cecile B. Hay and Mildred B. Hay, History of Derby, Vermont (Littleton, N. H.: Courier Pr., 1967).

(3) Edith Herrick, "History in towns: Brownington, Vermont," Antiques <u>114</u> (October 1978): 808-821.

(4) J. Kevin Graffagnino, Vermont in the Victorian Age (Bennington: Vermont Heritage Press, 1985).

Derby Line Hotel

* * *

(55) **Dorset** (Bennington).

"To begin with, we had five taverns: two on the West road, one in South Dorset, one in what we now call the village (then called West Dorset or Dorset corner) and one far up the Danby Mountain road, near the Danby line...then in Dorset Hollow a public house was presided over by one William Dunton..." (1)

(55a) <u>Dorset</u> (West Dorset or Dorset Corner locally).

1773: <u>Cephas Kent Tavern</u>; "south of the village on the West road, where a large stone marker stands now" (1); there is some disagreement as to whether this tavern was on the north or south corner of the West road and the road up the hill; the marker itself is a compromise, set between the two disputed locations, although the evidence seems to favor the south location; part of the structure is incorporated into the present Roland Beers home (VDHP 0203-3, 1973);

* * *

Of Cephas Kent and his tavern: "All records sing his praises; apparently his were the virtues which his contemporaries admired greatly." (1)

In 1884, his grandson Cephas recalled him in this way: "Our ancestor kept the tavern on the great road from Bennington to Ticonderoga and Burlington and received and entertained the Vigilance Commttee of the Green Mountain Boys and the Revolutionary Soldiers. He feared God and maintained the worship of God in his family. This practice he did not often allow his business as tavern keeper to interrupt. When a squad of soldiers called for an early breakfast he would put the large kettle with the potatoes over the fire and while they were cooking would throw open the door between the kitchen and the common room for guests who were invited to join in the devotions of the family...As he was justice of the peace it became his duty to detain persons traveling on the Sabbath without necessity. It was his custom to do this at his own expense as he made no charge for the Sabbath entertainment of those thus detained." (1)

In 1776 representatives from 31 towns met here, "taking the first firm step toward state independence." (2) And a description of the tavern:

"...the tavern was a small and humble affair, some twenty by thirty-two feet in dimensions, a story and a half high...It had a great central chimney and on either side of it a large room, the kitchen in front looking to the east and the sitting-room in the rear facing the sunset. Over the kitchen was a bed-room. We cannot imagine how the ten members of the Kent family managed to pack themselves into this small abode and leave any room for the accommodation of travelers, let alone convention delegates."

* * *

1796: Gray's Tavern, John Gray (tavern license, 1822); on Rte 30 at Dorset Green, now a library (VDHP 0202-13), across from the Dorset Inn; "The present inn (i.e., the Dorset Inn) was built before 1800, but was not used as a tavern until the Gray hostelry was discontinued"; (1)

c. 1796: (a) George Washington Tavern (Washington House); became the Dorset Inn in the 20th century; there is a c. 1915 photo in ref 1; in continuous use from 1796 until the present, according to the VDHP (0202-15) but this account seems to be at variance with Humphrey's (1); Resch says it is Vermont's oldest in continuous operation; (2)

1796: Deming's Tavern, --; listed in the Vermont Almanac and Register as a tavern on the Rutland-New York road; also listed, 1812; tavern license for Benjamin Deming, 1822;

Note: tavern licenses to Oliver Moore, Almond Curtis, Zachery Booth, 1822, and Peter Stannard, 1838;

(?): Asa Farwell tavern, location unknown; (1)

1849: --, J. H. Hodges (NEMU Dir);

1855: --, J. H. C. Hodges;

1869: (a) Washington House, L. Parris* (Beers);

1870: --, Levi Paris (Walton); (a) as above, Levi Barnes (?), Vt Dir;

1872, '73, '75, '80, '87, '92, '95: (a) as above, G. W. Baker;

1898: (a) as above, J. L. Obermaier;

1901: (b) Dorset Inn (formerly the Washington House), J. L. Obermaier; see photo;

1905: (b) as above, George H. Barrows; (c) Barrows House, E. W. Barrows; built by a Rev Jackson in 1784, opened as an inn in 1900 by William Barrows, who ran it until 1961; on the corner of Rte 30 and Dorset Hollow Rd, still in operation in 1987;

1908, '11, '13, '15, '20: (b) and (c) as above;

1914: Wade Inn, Charles Wade; across from the present PO, opened this year;

1916: (b) as above, V. T. Pratt; (c) as above, W. G. Barrows; Wade Inn, Charles A. Wade (VPB);

1921: (b) as above, --* (Sanborn);

1925: (b) as above, Miss A. A. Lapham; (c) as above, William G. Barrows; Wade Inn, C. A. Wade; (b) and (c) still operating, Wade Inn a boarding-house, by 1929, closed soon after.

(55b) East Dorset.

Dorset Inn

1852:   (a) Ira Cochran said to have built the first hotel at East Dorset this year; (3) the Mt Aeolus Inn, later the Wilson House (see below; see photo);

Mt Aeolus Inn (also the Wilson House)

1869:   --, B. Barrows* (Beers); same place as above, also known briefly as the Barrows House;

1870, '72:   (a) East Dorset Hotel, Blake Barrows;

1875, '78:   (a) as above;

1880:   (a) Wilson House, Barrows and Wilson; same as East Dorset Hotel, two names used interchangerably during this period;

1883:   (a) as above, William Wilson;

1887:   (a) as above, G. F. Griffiths;

1892, '95, '98: (a) as above, Wilson and Barrows;

1901:   (a) as above, G. B. Wilson;

216

1905, '08:   (a) as above, F. C. Williams;

1909:   (a) as above, --* (Sanborn);

1911, '13, '15, '20:   (a) as above, --; operated until c. 1970, then closed, reopened in 1987; this inn was the birthplace of William G. Wilson, co-founder of Alcoholics Anonymous (2); listed in Walton until at least 1940;

1921:   Mt Aeolus Inn, --* (Sanborn).

(55c) North Dorset.

1849:   --, Daniel Curtis (NEMU Dir);

1856:   --, D. Curtis* (Rice and Hardwood map); tavern license to David Curtis, 1822;

1869:   --, D. Curtis* (Beers);

* * *

This is "Uncle Daniel" Curtis, famous landlord of the hotel at North Dorset, according to Aldrich. (3) He followed his father, Elias Curtis, as landlord; and his son John followed him; but when stage travel ended, business declined; "so now only an occasional visitor" (i.e., 1889).

* * *

1870, '73:   North Dorset Hotel, John Curtis;

1875, '78, '79: Curtis House (same as North Dorset Hotel), John Curtis.

(55d) South Dorset.

(?):   "...the Sopers...kept a tavern at the east end of the road running across the valley to the west. For many years all town meetings were held here". (1) This is the West Road. (4)

Note: the assistance of Henry A. Chapman, Dorset Historical Society, is gratefully acknowledged.

* * *

References

(1) Zephine Humphrey, The Story of Dorset (Rutland: Tuttle, 1924).
(2) Tyler Resch, Shires of Bennington (Bennington: Bennington Museum, 1975).
(3) Lewis C. Aldrich, History of Bennington County, Vermont (Syracuse: D. Mason, 1889).

* * *

(56) **Dover** (Windham).

"Where they stopped at first (i.e., travelers passing through) we can only make a guess. Certainly, however, if their road passed a farmhouse of some size, they may have asked for a night's lodging there, even though a sign was not swinging above the door. Such houses gained the name of 'tavern' among the neighbors. Abner Perry, Dover's first settler, may not have planned it so, but by the time the present broad-porched dwelling was built, travelers along the public road to or from Wardsboro sometimes stopped there for the night, leading the neighbors to call the Perry house an inn." (1)

* * *

(56a) <u>Dover</u>.

  c. 1790:   a tavern, <u>Abner Perry</u> (see above);

  c. 1795:   first hotel, <u>Silas Johnson</u>; on the present (i.e., c. 1880, Hemenway) Joshua Parker farm on Estabrook Hill, south of the Center and near the branching of the road toward Marlboro and Wilmington; many town meetings were held there;

  1813: a tavern, <u>Cyrus Knapp</u> (tavern license, 1816, '17, '20, '22); Knapp came in 1793, and in 1813 built near the fork of the road from Dover to Marlboro and Wilmington, a large 2-story house as a tavern. He and his wife Thankful were popular and obliging, and their place became a "favorite place of public resort for many miles around" (Hemenway); kept it open for about 20 years, the building taken down in 1877 (but VDHP says it still stands as VDHP 1304-46). Knapp was also a cobbler, blacksmith, farmer, keeper of a livery stable, and a money-lender; his inn was across from Silas Johnson's tavern, on the "high corner of Estabrook Hill";

* * *

  "With the opening of the Knapp Tavern in 1813 the account books tell much of social interest. Page after page list the refreshments charged to the customers: the glass of 'biters,' or sling or 'wrum,' mugs of 'tod' (for toddy), or 'one sider twice,' sometimes followed by 'one segar,' and sometimes six, even seven, drinks in a single day to one customer. Many of these transactions were the charge accounts of local patrons, his hungry and thirsty neighbors for whom the tavern was the social gathering place as well as the public house." (1)

  1818: "Dover's third inn, built by Aaron P. Perry while the Knapp Tavern was in its prime, one-third of a mile toward the north, and on the corner across from the Common and meeting-house" (1); kept for "several years. Since it closed, no hotel in this part of town" (Hemenway; tavern license, 1821-27); the building was still standing in 1880, but said to be "ready for razing twenty years ago" (i.e., in 1924, ref 1); the Perry House was a political center of the town, and the town's first, and possibly only, Masonic meeting was held there; (1)

  1825: a tavern license to Justus Gale, location unknown;

  1855: --, Parley Whipple.

(56b) <u>East Dover</u>.

1901, '05, '06, '08, '11, '13, '20, '25: --, Mrs Mary A. Metcalf.

(56c) <u>West Dover</u>.

  (?): "the same may have been true of the present Shippee house on the hill southeast of the village of West Dover, which is said to have been a tavern even before Orville Corse lived there" (i.e., the same as was said of Abner Perry's place, see under Dover, above); (1)

  1846: an inn, <u>William H. Snow</u>; became the <u>West Dover House</u> a little later; frequent changes in ownership, including the Bogle brothers (1850); Parley Whipple ("Uncle" Parley); Ansel B. Collins; D. P. Leonard; Upton, May, Alexander, Jones and Fitzpatrick. "With its broad porch and gallery above, and thirty rooms to offer its patrons--among whom were buyers of lumber and chairstock, even of iron and Merino sheep--this inn continued, a thriving institution for seventy years and always an imposing structure" (1); VDHP 1304-4;

  1849: (a) <u>West Dover Hotel</u>, William H. Snow (NEMU Dir);

  1856: --, W. H. Snow* (McClellan);

  1869: (a) <u>West Dover Hotel</u>, A. B. Collins* (Beers);

218

1870, '73, '75: (a) as above; Ansel B. Collins kept it for nine years (Child); he was also deputy sheriff, constable, tax collector and selectman at various times;

1879, '81, '87, '90:   (a) as above, D. P. Leonard;

1901: --, W. L. Upton;

1902, '04, '05, '08, '11:   Green Mountain Inn, W. L. Upton (who was also PM); same as West Dover Inn; see photo; operating in 1990 as the West Dover Inn.

West Dover Hotel

* * *

References

(1) Nell M. Kull, History of Dover, Vermont (Brattleboro: Book Cellar, 1961).

* * *

(57) Dummerston (Windham).

(57a) Dummerston.

1762: a tavern, John Sargeant; said to have been the first Anglo-Saxon child born in Vermont, in 1732; built a home used as a tavern, the James Sargeant place in 1884 (Hemenway);

1775(?):   a tavern, --; in the north part of town, near Putney West Hill, on the present (i.e., 1884, Hemenway) Hosea Miller farm, owned previously by Dr Abel Duncan; the "present" dwelling was used as a tavern, pre-Revolution; refugees from Shay's Rebellion boarded there in 1787;

1790: a tavern, Daniel Taylor; next to his store; (1)

Note: almanacs list a Butler tavern (1805); a Miller tavern (1815, '16; tavern license to a Charles Miller, 1817, '20); and an unnamed tavern in "Fullam," original name for Dummerston, in 1785;

1832, '33:   a tavern, Peter Willard (tavern licenses); built by him in 1803 in District 3 (3); in the house now owned by James F. Baker; Willard said to have committed suicide when his brother had the road moved to favor business at his own tavern, Windmill Hill Tavern;

219

Note: tavern licenses also to Erastus Sargeant, 1817, '20; Seth Briggs, 1817, '20-23; Asa Black, 1821; Adim Thayer, 1822-26; Henry and Parker, 1823; Joseph Crosby Jr, 1823; Rufus Green, 1821; John Greenwood, 1824, '25; Lewis Henry, 1824-30; Justus Wrisley, 1822; Asa Knight, 1827-33; John Cone 2nd, 1832; Henry Babcock, 1829; David Reed, John M. Orris, 1833; George Fisher, Zebulon Goss, 1827;

1849: --, Luther Allyn (NEMU Dir); tavern license, 1832, '33;

1856: --, Salmon Howard (not known which village this was in).

(57b) <u>Dummerston Station</u> and (57c) <u>Dummerston West River</u>, no listings found.

(57d) <u>East Dummerston</u>.

c. 1800: the <u>Windmill Hill Tavern</u> referred to in the recent Dummerston town history (ref 2) seems to be the same as the <u>Butler</u> tavern (above, under Note). No listing for a "Windmill Hill Tavern" turned up in the directories, but the location is right (near Roger Birchard's store, shown on the 1869 Beers; the tavern building owned as a home by Nelson Willard in the late 1800s, also shown as N. Willard across the road from the Birchard store on the Beers map); the Windmill Hill name may be one assigned more recently, because of the windmill used for so many years to pump water to the tavern; the property was known as Windmill Hill farm in the 1950s, now the site of the Vermont-New Hampshire Veterinary Clinic, on Rte 5 in the vicinity of its intersection with the road from Dummerston Center (east of what used to be known as Slab Hollow); the old tavern was owned by a Capt Jabez Butler in 1802, who probably ran it before that date; other owners were Thomas Lewis, 1804, and Daniel Harvey, 1810;

(57e) <u>West Dummerston</u>.

c. 1795: <u>Taft's Tavern</u>; in District No. 2, "just north of an old store" (Hemenway); tavern license, Josiah Taft, 1820-30; a toll bridge used by stage coaches crossed the West River near this tavern (2); kept later by Josiah's son, Caleb, property in the Taft family until 1960s; site now occupied by Maple Valley Ski Area;

1849: <u>Emerson's Hotel</u>, G. W. Emerson;

1869: --, J. H. Austin* (Beers);

1870: --, N. J. Evans;

1873, '75, '79: --, S. W. Frink;

1880, '87: --, Mrs Lucy E. Frink;

1887: <u>Valley House</u>, Edward B. Russell (Vt Dir);

1905, '08: <u>Rogers Inn</u>, F. G. Rogers;

Note: the assistance of Mary Lou Carpenter, Dummerston Historical Society, is gratefully acknowledged.

* * *

References

(1) Caroline F. Stoat, "The Asa Knight Store of Dummerston, Vermont," Vermont History <u>53</u> (Fall 1985): 205-220.
(2) Alice C. Loomis and Frances W. Manix, editors, Dummerston, an "Equivalent Lands" Town, 1753-1986, Dummerston Historical Society (Brattleboro: American-Stratford, and Chelsea,

Michigan: BookCrafters, 1990).

* * *

(58) **Duxbury** (Washington).

(58a) Camel's Hump. Camel's Hump is on the line between Huntington and Duxbury, but closer to North Duxbury. Samuel Ridley, Jr (see below) built a carriage road to within 3 miles of the summit, and a bridle road almost to the peak; he also built a summit house for the "entertainment of those who made the ascent" (Child; mentioned in Burt's 1867 Guide of the Connecticut Valley; see Chapter V for more information on the Camels Hump Summit House, and other summit houses, and a photo). It was conducted "for some time" by Mr Wells and his wife Mary L., and they were the last proprietors; the house burned sometime before 1889. (See Huntington Center for Camel Hump's Inn.)

(58b) Duxbury (Duxbury Corners, formerly).

c. 1824:   Rev. Nathaniel Huntley, who was mainly a farmer, built and ran a hotel for a few years; tavern license, 1825-27; he died in 1858.

Note: tavern license to Horace Atkins, 1830, '33, location unknown.

(58c) North Duxbury/Ridley's Station.

(?):   in stage coach days, a hotel kept here by Samuel Ridley, Jr (Child, no date, but tavern licenses, 1826, '30, '32); at the mouth of Ridley Brook, place burned at some point;

1849:   --, Richard Lyman (NEMU Dir); not clear which settlement this was in;

1873:   Green Mountain House, W. R. Strickland* (Beers).

* * *

(59) **East Haven** (Essex).

(59a) East Haven.

1855, '56: --, Kittredge Hudson;

1870:   (a) East Haven Hotel, --;

1873, '75, '80, '83:   (a) East Haven Hotel, Kittridge Hudson.

* * *

(60) **East Montpelier** (Washington).

Created from the original town of Montpelier by the state legislature in 1848.

(60a) East Montpelier.

c. 1798:   first tavern, Freeman Snow; near where George Davis lived c. 1882, Hemenway (there is a G. Davis on the 1873 Beers); the place is described as being on the road to Marshfield, on what is now Snow Hill Road, below the Four Corners, near the Four Corners School, (1) which is shown on an excellent map contained in a brochure prepared by the East Montpelier Bicentennial Committee; (2)

c. 1814 until at least 1822:   a tavern, Jonathan Snow; who arrived before the town was organized, and "When Freeman's house closed" opened a large tavern further east on Snow Hill Rd, on site of the present (i.e., 1983) Anspach place; "when the War of 1812 broke out, he added a story to his house, opened it for a tavern, continued for about 28 years" (Child; this would be from c.

1812 until c. 1840); this place is #18 on the East Montpelier map referred to above;

* * *

"In 1819 Levi Woodbury described a stop at a tavern in Montpelier that may have been Snow's: 'Tonight I left a Tavern, where I was concluding to stop, because the Mistress wiped the inside of the tumbler, from which I was to drink water, with her hand. I could have quietly cured the difficulty by rinsing it; but she then filled it and presented it to me to drink. Of course I said nothing; but very calmly turned to my chaise and drove further'"; (1)

* * *

1811:   Morse Tavern, --; "Morse's Tavern, sometimes called 'People's Rest,' appears to have been the usual place for citizen's meetings, etc" (4); on County Rd south of the Morse School, VDHP 1207-80;

1820s-1836:   a tavern (and store), Merrill Williams; north of the mills in the village, on the east side of the road; Williams was also first PM, a tavern PO;

1836-44:   Williams place sold to Joseph Huntington, who leased it shortly before his death to Rensselaer Hammett;

1844-?:   Rensselaer Hammett, perhaps still part owner with John Mellen when the place burned (see below);

1847-49:   the Williams tavern burned in 1849, when owned by John Mellen;

1836-c. 1880:   Clough Tavern; opened this year by John Clough, in the former Joseph Wing house, occupied by the Coveys in 1981, on Center Road (ref 1, also photo); this place is #19 on the East Montpelier map referred to above; VDHP 1207-17; but the VDHP says it was built c. 1795;

* * *

"The floor boards still run diagonally in the old barroom section containing the original cupboard and money drawer in one corner. The tavern served as a meeting place in 1838 for a political group that discussed antislavery and imprisonment for debt. According to local lore, one of the Clough boys who had been drinking annoyed his brother, who in retaliation pulled the plug in the keg of whiskey and let it run into the cellar. The tavern remained busy as a stop on the stage route from Boston to Newport. The next stop north was the Bliss Tavern in Calais." (1)

* * *

c. 1840:   a tavern, --; at the "center," i.e., East Montpelier Center, a settlement that never achieved PO status; in the former Parley Davis house, known as Bruce's Inn in 1840; (photo, ref 1; #20 on the East Montpelier map);

(?):   an inn, David Gray; used mostly as a drover's inn, on "Horn of the Moon," a local name based on an Indian legend for a region in the northwest corner of the town; in the former Bradford Lane House; this place is #22 on the East Montpelier Historic Sites map; VDHP 1207-13;

1849:   Hammett's Tavern Stand, Rensselaer and Michael Hammett; who bought the East Village tavern or hotel from Gardner Steward (located between the present, i.e., 1983, Cate residence and Dudley's store); this is on the west side of the road, a different site from the tavern that burned in 1849; operated by "many innkeepers," must have existed prior to 1849;

1853:   Rensselaer sold his share to Michael, who hired Christopher C. Brooks to help manage it;

1855:   -, C. C. Brooks;

1856:   --, Michael Hammett;

1858:   Hammett's Tavern Stand* (Walling);

1870:   -, Michael Hammett; sold the Tavern Stand to Putnam MacKnight Cate;

1873:   --, P. M. Cate* (Beers; the place was also a store and PO); it burned in February, 1874;

1879:   --, J. B. Wells;

1898, 1901:   Wheelock House, J. S. Wheelock;

1903:   as above, -- (SBA pamphlet).

(60b) North Montpelier. Known locally in the old days as Rich's Hollow, for Samuel Rich, a farmer and millwright who settled in 1792.

1804:   Rich's Tavern. --; "a tavern and stage stop for the convenience of travelers on the stage line to Hardwick" (3); #19 in the North Montpelier Historic District (VDHP 1207-57);

* * *

"Samuel Rich's house...was considered one of the finest examples of Georgian architecture in the state. Much of the original charm and dignity was restored in 1966...In stagecoach days women used the ladies' parlor...to refresh themselves. The walls exhibit original stenciling...The barroom, right of the front hall, contains a small taproom door beside the fireplace. This convenience allowed the barmaid to serve her customers from the corner cupboard, where a secret money drawer provided a hideaway for the day's receipts...In the kitchen a large fireplace with double ovens spans half a wall...The ballroom, extending across the front of the second floor, is decorated with a ceiling molding of rope design...A fiddler' bench...provided a place for musicians to perform." (1)

* * *

1911-16:   a hotel, Mrs Lizzie Pray;

1914:   Kingsbury House, --* (Sanborn);

1923-36:   Twin Pine Farms, Mrs Murray C. Cutler; who housed tourists, but was issued an innkeeper's license; in the building used as the Tubbs Inn in the 1970s;

Note: the assistance of Ellen C. Hill, East Montpelier Historical Society, is gratefully acknowledged.

* * *

References

(1) Ellen C. Hill and Marilyn S. Blackwell, Across the Onion: A History of East Montpelier, Vermont, 1781-1981, East Montpelier Historical Soc. (Barre: Northlight Studio Pr., 1983).
(2) East Montpelier Bicentennial Comm., Historic Sites of East Montpelier, (East Montpelier, 1976?).
(3) Esther M. Swift, Vermont Place Names: Footprints of History (Brattleboro: Stephen Greene Pr., 1977).
(4) Marcus D. Gilman, The Bibliography of Vermont, George G. Benedict, ed. (Burlington:

Free Press, 1897).

* * *

(61) **Eden** (Lamoille).

    (61a) Eden.

    Note: tavern licenses to Jonas Stone, 1829; Edmund Clark, 1833; and William N. Smith, 1829, '30, locations unknown;

    1849:   --, Phil A. Matthews (NEMU Dir; could be Eden Mills);

    1855, '56:   --, E. Harrington;

    1859:   a hotel,--* (Walling);

    1870:   (a) Eden House, Jacob Harrington (also PM);

    1872, '75, '79: (a) as above;

    1878:   (a) as above* (Beers);

    1880, '83, '87: (a) as above;

    1883-84:   (a) as above, Child;

    1890, '95, '98, 1901, '05:   (a) as above, Albert O'Brien (also PM);

    1911, '13, '15, '20:   (a) as above, --;

    1915:   shown as Elm House on Sanborn map for this year, burned in 1931.

    (61b) Eden Mills.

    (?):   an inn, --; VDHP 0803-01, #9; built about 1850 on the North Rd/Mine Rd, originally the main road; now the Scott house;

    1859:   a hotel, B. F. Temple* (Walling);

    1870:   (a) Eden Pond House, George A. Hyde;

    1872:   (a) Pond House, Hill and Montgomery;

    1873:   (a) as above, Isaac D. Davis;

    1875, '79, '80: (a) as above, Benjamin Scott;

    1878:   (a) as above, A. Dwinnell* (Beers; same site as Walling, 1859);

    1883-84:   (a) as above, A. T. Scott (Child);

    1883:   (a) as above, D. B. (?) Robbins (Vt Dir);

    1887:   (a) as above, A. D. Robbins;

    1890:   (a) as above, William H. Hardy;

    1895:   (a) as above, E. H. Stone;

According to the VDHP, the building now on this site was built as a hotel about 1885 (0803-01, #5); but there has been a hotel on the site since at least 1859. Apparently the Pond House (above) burned or was razed soon after 1895, and was replaced by the Mount Norris (below).

* * *

1898:   (b) Mount Norris, E. H. Stone;

1901:   (b) as above, D. Kimball;

1905:   (b) as above, L. Sylvester;

1908, '11, '13, '15, '20, '25:   (b) as above, --; (listed until at least 1940).

* * *

(62) **Elmore/Lake Elmore** (Lamoille).

(62a) East Elmore. No listings found.

(62b) Elmore/Lake Elmore.

1813:   first hotel, Seth Olmstead; tavern license, 1823-32; on road 25, owned by the grandson, Samuel N. Olmstead in 1883, Child; however, the VDHP says the building dates from mid-19th century (0804-18); located on a hill facing Hill Tallman Rd (town highway 24), the road to East Elmore; three mail routes converged at East Elmore, which was a busy place in the latter half of the 19th century; now the Carl and Linda Tallman residence; shown on the 1859 Walling as S. Olmstead, and on Beers (1878) as S. N. Olmstead;

1856:   --, A. W. Averill;

1859:   --, A. W. Averill* (Walling);

1870, '75:   (a) Pond House, Seth Daniels;

1873:   (a) as above; (b) Mountain Lake House, Harvey Stone (Vt Dir);

1878:   (a) as above* (Beers);

1880:   (a) as above;

1883:   Lake House, S. B. Daniels (? Vt Dir);

1883-84:   (a) as above, Seth T. Daniels (Child);

1887:   Lake House, H. W. Fenn; S. D. David in Vt Dir).

(62c) South Elmore. No listings found.

* * *

(63) **Enosburg** (Franklin).

   (63a) Bordoville, and (63b) East Enosburg. No listings found.

   (63c) Enosburg (Center).

   c. 1798:   a tavern, Samuel Little; original settler; tavern license, 1817, '20-29;

   c. 1810:   a hotel, Charles Stevens; built at the Four Corners on the Boston Post Road; tavern license, 1815, '17, '18;

   Note: tavern licenses, Austin Fuller and Nathaniel Griswold, 1824; Alvin House, 1833; John Stevens, 1826, '27, '29; and Henry Lynch, 1822, locations unknown;

   1850:   Central Hotel, John Spooner; see photo; a stage stop on the Post Road from Boston to Montreal; until about 1900; not known if this was on the same site as Stevens' Hotel, above; there was an annex across the street; Mr Spooner also kept a dairy; part of the structure still stands; listed as a Temperance House in the 1870s; shown on Beers, 1871.

Central Hotel (Enosburg Historical Society)

(63d) Enosburg Falls.

   1857:   a hotel, P. Chadwick* (Walling); on the site of present A. J. Budd store on Main St;

   1870:   --, George Fassett;

   1871:   Chadwick House, Daniel Isham* (Beers); he became owner at this time;

   1873:   Eagle Hotel, Daniel Isham; he built a 3-story hotel on or near this same site, sold to Fernando C. Kimball Jr in 1876; it burned a year or two later;

   1875:   Eagle Hotel, Daniel Isham* (Beers);

   1878:   (a) Quincy House, Daniel Isham; who built it on Depot Street after the Eagle Hotel burned; leased to Burton H. Dickinson in 1880;

1882, '87, '92: (a) as above, B. H. Dickinson; Mr Dickinson also manufactured birch and ginger beer, operated the telegraph office in the hotel;

1895, '98: (a) as above; bought by H. H. and Charles Best in 1892; H. H. became sole proprietor;

1895: (a) as above, -- * (Sanborn); also, a place called the Central House is shown on the Sanborn map, but it is not operating by 1900;

1901, '02, '05, '08: (a) as above (photo, ref 1); shown on Sanborn for 1900, '05, '11, '20 and as New Quincy House in 1930;

New Quincy House

1911, '13: (a) as above, --;

1915, '20: (a) as above, L. H. Croft; (also VPB, 1916);

1923: A fire this year seriously damaged the third floor of the Quincy House. Other 20th century proprietors have been Floyd Lumnah, Francis Fox, William Wernert, Ellis Potter, Marcel Desnoyer, Hector Robert, James Page and his sister, Marta; still operating in 1990;

1925: (a) as above, R. G. (C.?) Gilpin.

(63e) North Enosburg.

1797: a tavern, Lewis Sweatland; probably on the site of the present (i.e., 1985) Hayes farm; (1)

(63f) West Enosburg.

1868: Coffee House, George Saxby; a stage stop on the road to St Albans; burned in 1942 "while Mr Lilly lived there" (ref 1; also a photo);

1871: --, G. H. Saxby; apparently this place was also known at one time as the Morning Star House (Vt Dir);

1872: --, G. W. Baker;

1873, '75: --, A. McNall (also PM);

1883, '80: --, A. McNall.

References

(1) Janice F. Geraw, ed., Enosburg, Vermont (Enosburg: Enosburg Historical Soc., 1985).

* * *

(64) **Essex** (Chittenden).

Page's Corner was the business center of the town from the time of the first permanent settlements in 1783, immediately after the Revolutionary War, until about 1820. The area known as Butler Corners was a challenger for a few years around 1820, but then things shifted to Essex Center until the railroad came through in 1850. From that time on, Essex Junction (originally known as Painesville, for Governor Paine, head of the Vermont Central) rapidly outstripped the Center. Painesville became Essex Junction officially in 1865.

(64a) Butler Corner.

c. 1794:   a tavern, Samuel Buell; on the county road to Burlington, at Butler Corner; VDHP 0405-10, the Fiske home in 1976;

(?):   a tavern, David Tyler; for many years, possibly either the same place or the same site as Buell's, above; Tyler also operated a tavern at the Center and one at the Junction, until he moved west; his chain was then managed by S. H. Boynton (1); a noted stopping place for travelers between Johnson and Burlington, given up after Boynton left; owned in 1963 by Fred Fiske (see Staunton House entry, Essex Junction, below);

Note: tavern licenses to Roswell Butler, 1821, and Benjamin Bennett, 1820, locations unknown;

(64b) Essex Center.

c. 1784:   a tavern, Joel Woodworth; probably the first in town, on what was (in 1963) the Harold Whitcomb farm, a short distance to the left of the bridge on the cross road leading to Bliss St; near Brown's River, near the Center but not in the village; later the site of Brown's Tavern, c. 1865, Hemenway;

(?):   a tavern, Joel Woodworth; second building at the Center, brought from its original location and rebuilt on the north side of the common; a part of Merle Wood Country Store in 1963; a remarkable house for its day, "pine logs, nicely hewn, set up endwise" (Child); also kept by Stephen Butler, and later by his son Billie Bishop Butler;

* * *

"It had been a cold stormy day. Weary with the buffetings of the wind, and the rush and roar of the city street, I was glad to see the welcoming light of home, and it was with a sigh of content that I sank into the comfortable depths of my old arm-chair.

It was early, and the lights in the library had not yet been turned on, only the ruddy glow of the dying embers in the grate suffused the room with a warm radiance.

Suddenly, it seemed to me, the round disk of the old pewter communion plate hanging over the fire-place seemed to expand, and I saw pictured on its smooth mirror-like surface, a long straggling village street. The houses were few and far between. Across from the village green stood a long, low, log house, with sheds at the back, in the shelter of which several teams were tied. The sign 'Tavern' swung on a cross-pole from the second story above the wide doorway.

By the dim light of tallow candles I discerned a number of figures moving about in the east wing, which I could see was used as an office or public room. In the living room beyond a huge hickory log blazed in the big brick fireplace. It was a scene of homely comfort, as Stephen Butler's pretty young wife Thankful moved briskly back and forth, stirring now and then the contents of a brass kettle suspended on a long crane, or basting a huge fore-quarter of venison hidden away in the big brick oven..." (2)

* * *

c. 1821:   B. B. Bishop's Hotel, referred to in ref 1; tavern license, 1821;

* * *

"It gained a noted reputation as a resort during the period of the War of 1812. It had a spacious hall, one so large for those days, it was used as a singing school by Mr Morgan and Harry Chittenden. The Masonic fraternity used it at times and it was hired for occasional festivities. In the early days of settlement, liquor was a common everyday part of the diet. Everybody, even the minister, took his 'sangaree,' his 'toddy,' his 'Santa Cruz,' his 'toads,' and thought no harm of it. Liquor was kept and sold in all taverns. Whenever one was on the road it was as common to stop at the tavern 'and wet one's eye' as one would stop today for any type of refreshment. Although the temperance idea was sounded by the circuit riders as early as 1805 in Essex, it did not succeed in converting the innkeepers till about 1830. Singularly, Mr Butler, Sam Buel and Col Page must have been reached by the same circuit rider of that time as they all closed their taverns to liquor in the same year." (1)

* * *

1849:   --, Israel Nichols; --, Ira Barney (NEMU Dir; not clear in which settlement these places were located);

1855:   --, P. Emery (location unknown);

1855, '56:   --, D. Tyler;

1857:   D. Tyler hotel* (Walling);

1869:   Essex Center Hotel, W. Scott* (Beers; appears to be at the same site as Tyler's, above);

1870:   Scott's Hotel, Wait Scott;

1870:   Essex Center House, Scott Williams (? Vt Dir);

1873:   Chittenden House, L. S. Mead (also 1875);

1879:   Chittenden House, H. D. Brown;

1882-83:   as above, Reuben Ferguson (Child);

1883:   Ferguson Hotel, R. Ferguson (almost certainly the same as above);

1887:   Chittenden House, R. Ferguson;

1887, '90, '92: --, Reuben Ferguson;

1895:   --, A. J. Lavigne;

1898, 1902, '05:   Ferguson House, Dwight J. Williams;

1911, '13, '15:   Ferguson House, --;

1920: Mountain View House, --* (shown on 1928 Sanborn); on north side of Seminary St, listed until at least 1940.

(64c) Essex Junction/Painesville.

(?):   an early tavern at a crossroads near the falls; (3)

c. 1820:   Stevens House, Abram Stevens; a brick building, later known as the Staunton House (sometimes Stanton), the Junction House, and finally Lincoln Hall (VDHP 0405-78). Henry Staunton sold it in 1858 to David and Samuel Tyler who operated it with the taverns they ran at the Center and at Butler Corners; the Junction House changed hands intermittently, 1893-1911, when Henry Root sold it to the village of Essex Junction; a frame tavern preceded this brick building on the same site; the Staunton House was the site of the first PO in Painesville, established in 1844 with Henry Staunton as PM (a tavern PO); he served in this dual capacity for 11 years, followed by other members of the family, the PO not being moved until Norman Brownell became PM in 1865, coincident with the name change to Essex Junction. There is also a reference in Child to the "old Sawyer tavern," built by Abram Stevens, used as a hardware store c. 1882 by Strong and Co; is this the same place?

1849:   Stanton's Hotel, H. Stanton (NEMU Dir);

1856:   --, H. Kimball (listed as "Parisville" in Walton!);

1857:   H. Stanton hotel* (Walling; same site as the Junction House on Beers, below; the Walling map also has an etching (ambrotyope) showing the Staunton Hotel and PO);

Note: There are two photos in Bent's book which, according to their legends, are of the same inn at different times, that inn said to be the Junction House/Central House. (1) In fact, these two inns were not the same, and the photos are of the Central House, which later became the Johnson Hotel (see below).

1869:   (a) Central House, R. G. Kimball* (Beers; near the depot). Not known when this place was built, but it is not on the 1857 Walling. There is another problem: Child says this place was opened by Edward O. Joslyn in 1882; did this earlier Central House burn, or is Child in error? (b) Junction House, D. G. Wells* (Beers; at the Five Corners);

1870:   (a) Central House, R. G. Kimball; (b) Junction House, Samuel Tyler;

1873, '75:   (a) as above, G. P. Howe; (b) as above, R. B. Spaulding;

1879:   (a) as above, E. C. Winnie;

1880:   (a) as above; (b) as above, Samuel Tyler;

1882-83:   (a) as above, E. O. Joslyn; (b) as above, Truman A. Hunt (Child);

1883:   (a) as above; (b) as above, C. E. Demerett;

Note: the 1884 Sanborn shows the Folsom House at the Junction House site, and a place called Johnson's Hotel at the Central House site;

1887:   (a) as above, Eugene F. Leet; (b) as above, Zephaniah Hapgood;

1890:   (a) as above, F. F. Shepard; (b) as above, W. S. Bennett;

1892:   (a) as above, Mrs Alvina R. Fisher; (b) as above, --;

1895:   (a) as above, W. B. Johnson; (b) as above, Zephaniah Hapgood;

Note: both (a) and (b) on 1899 Sanborn; (a) still operating in 1904, but (b) has ceased;

1898, 1901, '02, '05, '08: (a) Johnson's Hotel, W. D. Johnson (photos, in refs 1, 4; see photo); also listed in 1902 CVRR booklet;

Johnson's Hotel

1911, '13: (a) as above, -- (photo, ref 4); legend on this photo says that Johnson's was on the site of the present PO parking lot);

1916: Lincoln Inn, G. I. Lincoln (VPB); listed until at least 1955, now a restaurant;

1920: Lincoln Inn, G. I. Lincoln (see photo);

Lincoln Inn

Note: 1922 Sanborn shows Lincoln Inn; but the old Johnson Hotel is gone; Junction House still stands, not operating;

1925: as above, --;

(?): Murray's Tavern, --; originally a stables, built c. 1880, VDHP 0405-43, #4).

(64d) Pages Corner.

1790: a tavern, John Redd; on the northwest corner; became the Colonel Page tavern; Page arrived in 1812, bought from Reed; there were two taverns on this corner (see below), a major stop on the Rutland-Highgate stage route;

1790s: a tavern, <u>Curtis Holgate</u>; on the southeast corner; he sold out, operated the "Old South Wharf" in Burlington (1); the tavern was continued by Samuel Farrar (see below) who was PM when Vermont was a republic; then Adonijah Brooks as tavernkeeper. Early town meetings held here, in particular the historic meeting in 1804 when the town tried to come to grips with Ira Allen's tangled land affairs; (1)

* * *

"Most of the town meetings were held at one of these taverns until 1821. During the Embargo Act connected with the War of 1812, the taverns featured prominently as rendezvous points for smugglers making plans for shipments of potash and lumber up Lake Champlain to Canada. The maze of roads and trails leading from the Corners offered numerous escape routes to contrabandists in case of discovery-another reason for the popularity of the taverns during this period." (3)

* * *

<u>References</u>

(1) Frank R. Bent, History of the Town of Essex (Essex: The Town, 1963).
(2) Sarah Butler Northrup, "A Vision relative to the Tavern, 1787, and the First Congregational Church, 1797, Essex, Vermont," Vermonter <u>21</u> (March, 1921): 76-77.
(3) Lilian B. Carlisle, ed., Look Around Chittenden County (Burlington: Chittenden County Historical Soc., 1976).
(4) Harriet F. Powell, Yesterday in Essex (Essex Jct: Essex Publ, 1977).

* * *

(65) **Fairfax** (Franklin).

(65a) <u>Beaver</u> (PO, 1892-1901), and (65b) <u>Buck Hollow</u> (PO, 1850-1901). No listings found.

(65c) <u>Fairfax</u> (including area once known as Fairfax Falls).

1790s: a tavern, <u>Capt Erastus Safford</u>; the second in town; "his sign was 'Rest for the heavy laden and weary traveler' on a piece of paper nailed on a board, stuck in a hollow stump" (Hemenway); probably near the bridge at the Falls;

(?): a tavern, <u>Robert Barnett</u>; on the river near Safford's, probably at what was once called Fairfax Falls;

c. 1800: a hotel, <u>Stephen England</u>; he came in 1788 (referred to as "Shen" England in Child, who also says he came in 1794) and died in 1810; he built the first hotel some time after he came, in the village near where the <u>Fairfax House</u> now stands (i.e., c. 1882, Child); soon sold to Hampton Lovegrove, and the "old stand yet remains a house of public entertainment" (Hemenway, c. 1871, referring to the <u>Fairfax House</u>, below); Lovegrove was the first PM, thus a tavern PO; tavern license, 1817, '20, '24-32;

Note: tavern licenses to Joseph Felton, 1816, '21; George Buck, 1815; John Richardson, 1817; Benjamin Richardson, 1821, '22, '24-33; Daniel Fuller, 1824; Smith Brush, 1821; Joshua Brush, 1825; Reuben Dewey, 1833; L. and J. Wells, 1832; Edwin Hard, 1829-32; and Caleb F. Hull, 1828-33, on "Fairfield Plain";

late 1820s: "a hotel or tavern on the plain across the river--(at Fairfax Falls)--and a hotel kept by Reuben Lovegrove on the same side of the river as the toll house"; (1)

c. 1835: <u>Shedd's Hotel</u>, --; Everest has a 1950s photo of this building, probably the

Valley House; (2) (Shedd's/Shield's, see below);

(?):   "a tavern kept some years opposite the store," Bradbury Blake; Gen Grout's home, c. 1871;

1842:   a hotel, Ira Farnsworth; a tanner, who built it and kept it about 8 years; innumerable proprietors since, Samuel Randall in 1871; photo, ref 1; shown on both the Beers and Walling maps;

1849:   --, Ira Farnsworth; --, Silas W. Brush (both NEMU Dir, not known in which settlement Brush's place was);

1857:   (a) Mrs Dunbar's hotel* (Walling, became the Fairfax House, below); (b) L. A. Hyde's hotel* (Walling; became the Valley House, then a tenement in the early 20th century; VDHP 0604-43);

1862:   (a) Fairfax House, Mrs Whitney; opened by her "on the old stand first occupied by Stephen England";

1870:   (a) --, Abraham Foss; (b) --, Richard Flinn;

1870:   (a) --, A. Foss* (Beers, same site as Mrs Dunbar's; (b) a hotel, --* (Beers, same site as Hyde's above);

1872, '73, '75: (a) Fairfax House, A. Foss;

1872:   (b) Valley House, William Pitcher;

1873:   (b) as above, James Shehan;

1875:   (b) as above, E. J. Pease;

1880:   (a) as above, F. P. Levigne; (b) as above, C. D. Currier;

1882:   (a) Temperance House, M. V. Hicks (Child; same as Fairfax House, above); (b) as above, C. D. Carrie (Currier ?) (Child);

1883:   (a) Fairfax Hotel, M. V. Hicks (Vt Dir; still a temperance house); (b) as above, Frederick Woodworth;

1887:   Cleveland House, L. Cady (probably the same as the Fairfax Hotel); (b) as above, J. D. Shield (Shedd elsewhere);

1890, '92, '95, '98, 1901, '02, '05:   (b) as above, J. D. Shedd (photo, ref 1);

1908:   (b) Valley House, --;

1911:   --, J. D. Shedd;

1915:   no hotel shown on the Sanborn map;

1920:   --, Mrs Mayo Despart;

1925:   (b) Fairfax Inn, G. W. Burleson; same as the Valley House; listed in 1930, not '35.

(65d) Huntsville. (PO, 1893-1901). No listings found.

(65e) North Fairfax.

c. 1790:   first tavern, <u>Hampton Lovegrove</u>; came in 1787, began his tavern a few years after that on a farm owned in 1871 (Hemenway) by Harman Johnson; there is an H. T. Johnson in the area on the 1871 Beers, in school district #9;

c. 1796:   a hotel, <u>Joseph Brush</u>; (1)

c. 1870:   an inn, --; on the south side of Rte 104, North Fairfax, just east of Nichols Rd; VDHP 0604-58;

(?):   a public house, <u>Nathaniel Gove</u>; came in 1800, kept a tavern many years on a farm owned c. 1881 by Charles Brush; location uncertain, but probably not in either Fairfax or North Fairfax village; there is a C. H. Brush on the 1871 Beers in school district #11, a little northwest of Fairfax.

Note: the assistance of Mrs Gene L. Cain, Fairfax Historical Society, is gratefully acknowledged.

* * *

References

(1) Bicentennial Committee, Fairfax, Its Creation and Development. Town of Fairfax (St Albans: Regal Art Pr., 1980: 22-24); quoting the recollections of one Nathan Woodward, born in Fairfax in 1818.

(2) Allan S. Everest, who donated a collection of tavern photos to Special Collections, UVM.

* * *

(66) **Fairfield** (Franklin).

(66a) <u>East Fairfield</u>.

(?):   a place, built c. 1830, later the <u>Ritchie Hotel</u>, date of first use as a hotel not known; see below;

1849:   --, N. W. Isham; --, J. Brown; (NEMU Dir; the former is probably a precursor of the <u>Isham House</u> (see below), the latter possibly in Fairfield);

1857:   --, S. Weston* (Walling);

Note: tavern listings (almanacs) to William Hops, 1824-33, Chellis Montague, 1826, '27, Hubbel Mitchell, 1821, and Hubbard Barlow, 1828-30, locations unknown;

1870:   (a) <u>Ritchie's Hotel</u>, Thomas Ritchie; built about 1830, according to VDHP (0605-15), overlooks the millpond on Black Creek; not used as an inn after 1880, now the Marshall True home (1981);

1871:   (a) --, T. Ritchie* (Beers; same location as <u>Weston's</u>, above); (b) --, H. S. Isham* (Beers);

* * *

Built about 1870 by Henry S. Isham, who lived there until his death; trains stopped at the platform behind the hotel, "giving passengers the choice of staying overnight for a little dancing on the wonderful spring dance floor which was made of boards put in on edge. When silent movies arrived, they were shown in this hall. Zoa Mitchell played the piano to accompany them"; burned in January, 1923. (1)

234

1873: (b) --, Henry S. Isham;

1875: (a) <u>East Fairfield Hotel</u>, Thomas Ritchie (<u>Ritchie's</u>, above); (b) --, H. S. Isham;

1879, '80, '82, '83, '87, '90: (b) <u>Isham House</u>, H. S. Isham;

1892, '95: (b) as above, Mrs H. S. Isham;

1898: (b) as above, H. S. Isham (?);

1901, '05, '11, '13, '15, '20: (b) <u>Isham House</u>, Mrs Eunice Isham* (Sanborn);

(66b) <u>Fairfield</u>.

1855: --, M. Hall (?);

1857: --, G. W. Ball* (Walling);

1870: <u>Driscoll's Hotel</u>, J. G. Driscoll; <u>Sherwood Hotel</u>, B. Sherwood;

1871: <u>Driscoll's Hotel</u>, J. Driscoll* (Beers, at the Ball location, see above);

1873: --, E. G. (?) Driscoll;

1875: --, John Driscoll;

1878, '79: (a) <u>Franklin County House</u>, E. C. Soule; probably same as <u>Ball's</u>, <u>Driscoll's</u>, above, on same site);

* * *

The <u>Franklin County House</u> was owned by the Soule family for several generations. It was built about 1836 by Edwin Soule, sold to his father Solomon; then to S. Allen Soule Sr, Horace W. Soule, James Farrell, Mrs E. J. Montgomery (H. W. Soule's daughter); the last owner to operate it as a hotel was Henry D. Shannon. The north wing, which contained the spring dance floor, was removed c. 1916; the rest of the building still stands (VDHP 0605-8, #24, 1986). (1)

* * *

1880, '83, '87, '90, '92: (a) as above, S. A. Soule;

1898, 1901: (a) as above, H. W. Soule (also PM);

1905, '08: --, J. A. Farrell;

c. 1900: a tavern, --; built c. 1860, possibly by Nathan Gilbert; VDHP 0605-9, on Rte 36, 4 miles east of Fairfield Center;

1911: --, H. Shannon;

1915: no hotel on the Sanborn map.

(66c) <u>Herrick</u>. (PO, 1899-1902). No listings found.

* * *

References

(1) Eleanor Ballway, Fairfield, Vermont Reminiscences (Essex Jct: Essex Publ, for the

Fairfield Bicentennial Committee, 1977.

* * *

(67) **Fair Haven** (Rutland).

(67a) Fair Haven.

c. 1780-88: a tavern, Philip Priest; who built a log house in the west part of town near the Poultney River, where Hiram Hamilton lived c. 1875, (Hemenway), kept tavern there;

1784: a tavern, Silas Safford; Safford was an employee of Matthew Lyons, built a 20 x 30 house where Henry Green's house stood in 1870 (1); he was here when the first road came through, keeping a tavern; this is presumably the Lyons tavern, later the Mack/Cutler tavern, etc;

Note: this place was occupied by Col Lyons himself at first, kept by him as a public house; he built a second house opposite where the Vermont Hotel stood c. 1870, and moved there, leaving the tavern to Nathaniel Dickinson, 1795; sold to David Mack in 1795, who kept it until 1798; then Dr Simeon Smith owned it, with John Brown running it; Smith sold to Isaac Cutler in 1803; he sold it in 1809 to Thomas Wilmot, Cutler never kept it himself; Royal Dennis kept it, 1807-09. Wilmot enlarged it, 1811-12, but died in 1813; kept until 1817 by John Beaman; Mrs Wilmot leased it in 1829 to Moses Colton for 5 years; she also bought (and promptly closed) the old "Dennis" tavern, then run by James Greenough; Mrs Wilmot leased the old Lyons stand to her son-in-law, Spencer Ward, in 1834; he gave it up in 1836, and she sold to John D. Stannard in 1838; he kept it until 1850, sold in 1853 to Joseph Adams, the owner in 1870; re-modeled, kept for several years by David B. Colton; (1)

1785: Brush tavern, --; almanac, location unknown;

1790: a public house, Silas Safford; he bought the place where Mr Barnes now lives (i.e., 1870) and opened another public house, sold in 1814 to James Y. Watson;

1809: a hotel, Royal Dennis; who had been keeping the tavern stand of Isaac Cutler for 2 years, in 1809 bought 1 1/2 acres where the Graves block now stands (i.e., 1870), including the old Hennesey store; remodeled the store, made a "nice" hotel, kept by him for several years; well-known place, transferred to his brother Samuel in 1822; kept by Moses Beaman for several years; he was landlord in 1825, James Greenough in 1828-29, bought by Lucy Wilmot in 1829 (see above), who banned a tavern at this (the old Dennis) site. Sold in 1838, tavern still prohibited for 15 years, it was a store; never re-opened as a tavern, site occupied in 1870 by the printing plant of the Fair Haven Journal. (1)

1849: --, J. D. Stannard (NEMU Dir);

1854: J. Adams hotel* (Scott);

1855: --, D. B. Colton;

1858: (a) Vermont House, Served Fish; built by him in this year, a 3-story brick building on the Mathew Lyon home site, corner of S. Main and Liberty Streets, where an earlier tavern had stood (see above); Mr Fish kept it until 1866, then David Offensend, David McBride, sold in 1870 to Charles C. Knight; "not adequate to the needs of the village" (i.e., c. 1875, Hemenway); the back wing of this place was the house built by Lyons;

1869: (a) Vermont House/Hotel, D. McBride* (Beers);

1870, '72, '73: (a) as above;

1875, '79, '80: (b) Knight's House, C. C. Knight; this place burned in November, 1879, not clear if it is the Vermont House under another name;

1878:   (b) as above; <u>Eusty House</u>, R. W. Pitts and son;

1881-82:   <u>Traveler's Home</u>, William S. Streeter; on Marble St (Child);

1883:   (c) <u>Hyde Park View House</u>, Russell W. Hyde; on the site of the old <u>Lyons Tavern</u> (2); (d) <u>Woods Hotel</u>, L. E. Wood;

1885:   (c) <u>Park View House</u>, --* (Sanborn, on the west side of S. Main, facing the park, later the <u>Hotel Allen</u>); Sanborn also shows (g) <u>Cottage Hotel</u>, not listed as such in Walton until c. 1898; must have operated earlier under a different name; the <u>Cottage</u> is also shown on Sanborn in 1897, 1904, but as a boarding-house in 1892;

1887:   (c) <u>Park View House</u>, Rutledge Brothers; (d) <u>Wood's</u>, L. E. Wood; --, D. O. Jones;

* * *

Fair Haven Hotels

(a) Vermont Hotel
(b) Knight's
(c) Hyde Park View House
(d) Wood's Hotel
(e) Hotel Rutledge

(f) Kelly's
(g) Cottage
(h) Hotel Allen (New Castle Inn)
(i) Fair Haven Inn

* * *

1892:   (c) <u>Park View</u>, D. J. Rutledge; (also on Sanborn map for 1892, '97, became the <u>Hotel Allen</u> by 1904, according to Sanborn); (d) <u>Wood's</u>, L. E Wood; --, W. L. (?) Jones;

1895, '96:   (c) as above, J. E. (?) Rutledge; (d) as above; (f) <u>Kelly's</u>, John J. Kelly;

1898:   (c) as above; (d) as above; (g) <u>Cottage Hotel</u>, A. H. Merriam; see photo;

1900:   (d) <u>Wood's Hotel</u>, L. E. Wood; (g) <u>Cottage Hotel</u>, A. H. Merriam; <u>Lewis House</u>, Mrs E. H. Lewis;

1901:   (e) <u>Hotel Rutledge</u>, D. J. Rutledge (corner of Main and River Streets); (g) as above;

1902:   (d) <u>Wood's</u>, L. E. Wood; (e) as above; (g) as above; <u>Lewis House</u>, Mrs E. H. Lewis;

Cottage Hotel

237

1904:   (d) as above; (e) as above; (g) as above; <u>Lewis House</u>, Mrs E. H. Lewis; (h) <u>Hotel Allen</u>, F. E. Allen (former <u>Park View</u>); see photo;

Hotel Allen

1905:   (e) as above; --, D. O. Jones; (h) as above, F. E. Allen and C. R. Allen; also known as the <u>New Castle Inn</u> at some later date);

1906:   (e) as above; (g) as above; (h) as above;

1908:   (e), (g), and (h), as above, --;

1909:   (g) <u>Cottage</u>, --* (Sanborn); (h) <u>Hotel Allen</u>, --* (Sanborn);

1911, '13, '15:   (g) as above, --; (h) as above,--;

1916:   (h) <u>Hotel Allen</u>, David Rutledge (VPB); (i) <u>Fair Haven Inn</u>, --;

1920:   (h) as above, G. R. Bush; (i) as above, --;

1925:   (h) as above, --; the <u>Hotel Allen</u> is listed until at least 1955, building razed soon after that; (i) as above, summer only, --;

* * *

<u>References</u>

(1)   Andrew N. Adams, A History of the Town of Fair Haven, Vermont (Fair Haven: Leonard and Phelps, 1870).

* * *

(68) **Fairlee** (Orange).

Originally included present West Fairlee, which was split off as a separate township in 1797. Fairlee post office opened in 1808, South Fairlee in 1872; the latter became Ely (the second PO with that name) in 1927, to match the name of the railroad station there, serving the copper mine at Vershire. The township also includes two bodies of water: Fairlee Pond, as it was known until the 1880s, now Lake Morey (for Samuel Morey, considered by many to be the true inventor of the steamboat); and Lake Fairlee, in the southern part of the town, lying partly in Thetford and partly in West Fairlee.

(68a) <u>Fairlee.</u>

1796:   <u>Freeman's tavern</u>, --; listed in the Vermont Almanac and Register as a stage stop on the Windsor-St Johnsbury road; almanacs also list the <u>Freeman tavern</u> and a <u>May tavern</u> in 1805;

1807:   a tavern (and store), <u>Capt Lancelot H. Granger</u>; who, "soon after coming to town" (in 1801, according to Hemenway) built his place on the present site of Saladino's Garage and the PO (i.e., 1957, ref 1); Granger was also the first PM (1808); he sold the tavern to Solomon Mann, and the store to George Mann, and both were taken over by Phineas Bailey in 1821;

1821:   <u>Bailey's Hotel</u>, Phineas Bailey (see photo); he came from Orford, and "took up hotel-keeping in the old hotel building run by several others before then" (Hemenway); his son Jerome ran it later, was also PM (1831-45), and then the grandson Frank M. Bailey; Jerome died in 1868, and the place was sold c. 1870 to Benjamin Driggs, who only lasted a year or two before selling to Albert Newcomb; he had it until 1888, the name being changed to the <u>Fairlee House</u> during this period;

Bailey's Hotel (William Orcutt stereo)

1849:   --, G. W. Powers (NEMU Dir);

1870:   <u>Bailey's Hotel</u>, Frank M. Bailey;

1879:   --, Albert G. Newcomb;

1883, '87, '88, '90:   <u>Fairlee House</u>, Albert G. Newcomb;

1888:   <u>Fairlee Inn</u>, W. M. Gale (Boston and Maine booklet);

c. 1888:   <u>Fairlee House</u> sold to Herbert Warren, became known as the <u>Wynona House</u>;

* * *

"Named by a Mrs Wheeler of Orford who paid for one-half the cost of a new sign for the privilege. The name was taken from a poem called 'Minnehaha' by Henry W. Longfellow." (1)

* * *

1892, '98:   --, H. P. Warren (also PM);

1897, 1900, 1901:   Wynona House, H. P. Warren; sold in 1901 to Manus Gale;

1901:   Fairlee Inn, Manus Gale; became Gale's Inn, but the place was now on a downhill slope; sold to a syndicate in 1905, and six months later sold again to W. H. Daniell, who re-named it the Cliff House; sold again in 1906 to William Church, became Church's Tavern (see photo); Church continued as proprietor until 1911, when it was sold to William Gale, and then in 1913 to another syndicate; it burned on September 18, 1914, and the site stood idle until the garage and PO were built on it (1930 and 1934, respectively);

Church's Tavern

1905:   Gale's Inn, Maurice (?) Gale;

(?):   Cliff House, Mrs E. L. Wallace; (2)

1911:   Church's Tavern, --;

1915:   Fairlee Inn, -;

1925:   Silver Maple Lodge, --; in a remodeled farmhouse built in 1855, on Route 5 south of Fairlee, still operating;

1927:   Wayside Inn, --* (Sanborn).

(68b) Lake Morey (no post office).

1888:   (a) Glen Falls House, George Spear; who built it as a summer resort, 30 rooms, on Middle Point on the east side of the lake; see photo;

1888:   (a) Glen Falls House, W. M. Gale; Kaulin, G. H. Kendall; The Bungalow, Mrs K. W. Millican (Boston and Maine pamphlet);

1889:   (a) Glen Falls House sold to S. S. Houghton, who began building cottages;

1905:   (a) as above, C. F. Pierce and Son; (b) Lake Morey Summer Hotel (also known as the Lake Morey House, not to be confused with the Lake Morey Inn); the Lake Morey House was converted from the George Sampson farm at the head of the lake by one Crocker;

1908:   (a) as above;

1910:   Kaulin, George Kendall (predecessor of the Lake Morey Inn/Club); photo, ref 1; enlarged subsequently, sold to Robert Cookman in 1918, became the Lake Morey Club in 1920, the Lake Morey Inn in 1924; an annex was added in 1926; photo, ref 1; shown on 1927 Sanborn; still operating, Mr and Mrs Borden Avery;

Glen Falls House

1911:   Kaulin, George Kendall; (a) Glen Falls House, C. F. Pierce; Pavilion, F. H. Griffin; Lake Morey Summer Hotel;

1912:   (a) Glen Falls House burned, with 4 deaths; the injured taken to Hanover Hospital by a special train; never rebuilt, the site eventually converted into a tea room and picnic area; it is still listed in Walton in 1913;

1915:   Bunaglo, --; Kaulin, --; (also 1916 VPB, George H. Kendall);

1916:   Bonnie Oaks, Dr E. H. Page; evolved into a group of cottages with a main dining room; listed as Bonnie Oaks Inn as late as 1955, Lake Morey Inn also;

1917:   Rutledge Inn, --; the Rutledge home became a summer inn after putting up guests displaced by a fire at the Kaulin, still operating;

1923:   Lake Morey Club, R. C. Cookman, prop., A. B. Dickey, mgr (VPB);

1920s: The Accomac, William and Ruth Rutledge; guest house, later some cottages added.

(68c)   South Fairlee (became (2nd) Ely postally in 1927). No listings found.

Note: the assistance of Hester C. Gardner, Curator, Fairlee Historical Society, is gratefully acknowledged

* * *

References

(1) Philip G. Robinson, The Town Under the Cliff: A History of Fairlee, Vermont (West Topsham: Gibby Pr., 1957).
(2) Souvenir of Lake Morey, Fairlee, Vermont (Woodsville, N.H.: Geo. H. Kendall, 1908 (?)).

* * *

(69) **Fayston** (Washington).

(69a) North Fayston. No listings found.

Ferdinand (Essex).

Granted by Benning Wentworth in 1761, followed a day later by the adjoining town of Wenlock. Wenlock was divided betwen Brighton and Ferdinand in 1853 by the Vermont legislature. Ferdinand never had a PO with this name, but the name Wenlock was used for the first PO in town, which operated at the Beattie lumber-mill from 1881 until 1887. Another office, appropriately called Millsite, existed at the same location from 1918-23.

No tavern or hotel listings were found for Ferdinand, Millsite or Wenlock, but Ferdinand was inadvertently omitted when the list of towns for Appendix E was first compiled.

* * *

(70) **Ferrisburg** (Addison).

Most of the early taverns in this township lay on the old stage road from Vergennes through North Ferrisburg, the approximate route of present Rte 7. Mt Philo lies in North Ferrisburg but has a Charlotte mailing address (which see); the township also includes Basin Harbor.

(70a) On the old stage road, going south from North Ferrisburg:

(?): "North of the watering trough and up under the bank, Roswell Hopkins kept a tavern. Wing Rogers was inn-keeper here at one time" (1); (tavern license to Hopkins, 1812); the precise location of this tavern not known, probably in North Ferrisburg village;

(?): "James Aiken owned the John Wheeler farm, now (i.e., c. 1897) belonging to Lucius B. Martin. This house was a tavern"; there is a Martin place on the 1871 Beers, halfway between North Ferrisburg and Ferrisburg, that is probably the place referred to, since the author of this quotation, in his account, is moving south along the old stage road, a farm at a time; (1)

1794: In "the Old Yellow House," close to the Wheeler place (see above), a tavern; shown on the 1871 Beers as "academy ruins," but tavern use of this building apparently preceded its use as an academy; tavern keepers included William Gage, George Pease, Calvin C. Martin, Asa Hemenway; but Child says (apparently referring to this place) "the old hotel building now (i.e., c. 1882) standing near Dr Crane's was kept by William Gates (Gage?) as early as 1794--and later by George Pease"; Pease is listed in almanacs as a tavernkeeper in 1825, '29;

1796: Burt Tavern, --; listed in the Vermont Almanac and Register as a stage stop on the Rutland-Canada road, also almanacs in 1802, '07;

(?): "the old Keene place, afterwards occupied by Capt Gideon Hawley, who luxuriated in tavern keeping, making the third tavern in about a mile" (1); this place thus close to Aiken's and the "old Yellow House", above); almanacs, 1817-29;

(?): "Cyrus Collins built up the George Field place, and this was a tavern" (1); there is a George Field store a little south of the four corners in Ferrisburg on the 1871 Beers;

(?): "The brick house on the hill known as the Bragg place, stands on the farm formerly owned by Alpha Tupper and here was another tavern" (1); owned by Joseph Birkett, c. 1879; there is a Bragg place on the stage road partway between Vergennes and Ferrisburg on the 1871 Beers;

1849: Temperance House, Nicholas Guindon (NEMU Dir);

1850s: a temperance tavern, Nicholas Guindon; "about where George Palmer lives" (i.e.,

c. 1897); Guindon was an ardent abolitionist, and his house was a station on the underground railway, precise location not known.

(70b) Basin Harbor.

1791:   a tavern, Gen Platt Rogers; who acquired land on the north point of Basin Harbor, built the first permanent residence and a shipyard; he apparently kept a tavern from the beginning; (2)

c. 1800:   Homestead, the Winans family; Ida Rogers, Platt's daughter, married James Winans, and they inherited part of Platt's land; Winans built the first steamboat to operate on Lake Champlain, in 1809; the Winans family continued to operate the inn, known as the Homestead; Lt Thomas MacDonough was a guest in 1811, while building the U. S. fleet at Vergennes before the Battle of Plattsburgh; this inn was heavily used, not only by guests from the various boats that stopped there, but also by farmers and merchants crossing the lake on the ice in the winter; the original building burned, c. 1820, and was replaced; it eventually became part of the Basin Harbor Club (see below);

1887:   The Lodge, the Beach family; see photo; developed into an inn from a farm at Basin Harbor acquired by the Beach family in 1882; developed into "the largest club resort on the shore of Lake Champlain," (2) with cottages, golf course, etc; became the Basin Harbor Club (Harbor Homestead), managed by Allen P. Beach from 1910 into the 1950s; VDHP 0105-42;

The Lodge at Basin Harbor

1920:   (a) The Lodge, H. F. Beach; (b) The Homestead, J. G. Walker;

1925:   (a) as above.

(70c) Ferrisburg.

c. 1783:   a tavern, Zuriel Tupper; who built a frame house in which he "fitted up" a room for a place of worship, and town meetings; this was also the first tavern, precise location not known; Tupper came to Ferrisburg in 1783; (Everest photo);

1849:   Temperance House, Mrs Aurelia Collins (NEMU Dir);

1856:   --, Mrs A. Collins;

1857:   Union House, --* (Walling);

1875:   Fort Cassin Hotel, -- (in Bradford's Hotel Guide); Fort Cassin Point, near MacDonough Point, was the site of a small fort built to protect MacDonough's ships; there is a

243

small cottage community there now, but this is the only reference found to this place; shown on Beers, between Basin Harbor and Long Point.

(70d) <u>Long Point</u>.

(?):   VDHP notes a building at Kingsland Bay, now owned by the state and used for storage, built c. 1790, "<u>MacDonough Lodge</u>"; on MacDonough Point overlooking the bay, "one of the few extant remains of the early history of the Lake Champlain region"; Kingsland Bay was a favored protected spot where MacDonough moored his ships; the stone house served as an inn and ferry stop for the commercial trade across the lake; VDHP 0105-41.

(70e) <u>North Ferrisburg</u>.

1830s: "In the stage-coach days, and indeed some time after, John and Carlos C. Martin, sons of Squire Martin, kept a public house where Stoddard Martin now lives (i.e., c. 1897, ref 1); the PO was there at one time, a tavern PO; place was built by an earlier Stoddard Martin in 1830 (Child, and VDHP), stood on the site of Jimmo's Motel in 1975 at the intersection of Rte 7 and the road to North Ferrisburg; according to Smith (3); the first Stoddard left the hotel in 1841; he was followed by his son, John W. Martin for 14 years; then Aaron B. Webb, Calvin Martin, Benai Thompson, Absalom Wheeler, Martin F. Allen, and James Mooney, proprietor c. 1885;

1849:   --, J. and C. Martin (NEMU Dir);

1856:   --, C. C. Martin;

1870:   (a) <u>Martin House</u>, James Jones;

1871:   (a) as above, S. B. Martin* (Beers);

1873, '75:   (a) as above;

1878:   (a) as above, M. L. Richardson;

1879:   (a) as above, W. and S. Martin (Vt Dir);

1880, '81, '83, '87, '92, '95:   (a) as above, Stoddard Martin;

1887, '92:   (b) <u>Brookside Inn</u>, M. C. (?) Richardson;

1901:   (a) as above, Stoddard B. Martin;

1898, 1905:   (a) as above; (b) as above;

1908, '13:   (a) <u>Martin House</u>, -- (see photo, next page);

1915:   no hotel shown on Sanborn.

* * *

References

(1) Paulena Hollenbach and Ronald W. Slayton, Ferrisburgh: A Scrapbook of Memories (Ferrisburgh: Ferrisburgh Bicentenial Comm., 1976).
(2) Allen P. Beach, Basin Harbor Story (Burlington: Queen City Pr., 1963).
(3) H. P. Smith, History of Addison County, Vermont (Syracuse: D. Mason, 1886).

* * *

(71) **Fletcher** (Franklin).

(71a) <u>Binghamville</u>.

c. 1840: a hotel, --; "probably" a hotel, first half of the 19th century; at the southwest corner of the intersection of School River and Lapointe Rds, 1.9 miles south of Binghamville; VDHP 0606-30, the Walter Cross place in 1981;

(71b) <u>East Fletcher</u>. No listings found.

(71c) <u>Fletcher</u>.

c. 1800: Zerah Willoughby opened the first store in his home on a farm owned c. 1891 by O. O. Carpenter (1); also a tavern known as the <u>Willoughby House</u>; "in these days the travel through the Lamoille valley was all on the early road on the north side of the river"; there is a Carpenter place on this road in the 1871 Beers;

1820: tavern license to Elias Blair;

c. 1835 an inn, <u>Col A. Scott</u>; on the early stage road (north side of Rushford Rd, 1.4 miles east of Fletcher, VDHP 0606-06); Isador Fox lived here in 1981.

(71d) <u>West Fletcher</u>. No listings found.

* * *

References

(1) Lewis C. Aldrich, History of Franklin and Grand Isle Counties (Syracuse: D. Mason, 1891).

Martin House, North Ferrisburg

* * *

(72) **Franklin** (Franklin).

(72a) <u>East Franklin</u>.

1857: --, M. E. Lindsay* (Walling);

(?): an inn, --; VDHP 0607-2, #1; same site as <u>Lindsay's hotel</u> on Walling; also known at one time as the <u>Stage Coach Spa</u>, according to Towle (1); built by a Mr Smith when East

Franklin was known as "Smithville"; also operated by E. L. Hibbard, and Charles and Mabel Scott, now a rest home.

(72b) <u>Franklin</u> (Huntsburg until 1823).

c. 1790: first public house, <u>Samuel Peckham</u> (Hemenway); tavern license, 1817, '20, '22; and to Widow Sophia Peckham, 1824-28;

c. 1795: tavern stand, <u>Clark Rogers</u>; "he settled early at Franklin village" (Child, who says that this was the first tavern stand);

Note: tavern licenses, locations unknown, to Asa Haskins, 1815, '20, '21, '24; Elizabeth Haskins, 1825-29; Josiah Randall, 1825, '28; Isaac Carr, 1828-30; Dan Rublee, 1829, '30; Samuel Smith, 1832; Charles Gallup, 1833; and Lewis Bascomb, 1833;

c. 1795: a tavern, <u>Thomas and Uri Foot</u>; in Franklin "Center," (?) Hemenway;

1849: <u>Brick Tavern Stand</u>, Orin Manson (NEMU Dir);

1856: --, Orin Manson;

1857: --, O. Manson* (Walling);

1870: (a) <u>Franklin House</u>, Thomas Bolac; see photo, next page;

* * *

The <u>Franklin House</u> was built by Manson in 1845, changed hands frequently until 1875 when it was bought by Guy Chaplin, owned by Chaplin and then his son "Hobe" until it burned in the disastrous fire of 1925.

"It was a large building, standing on the lot where Dick Wright Inc (i.e., the Ford Agency) now is located, with eight guest rooms upstairs, two small back bedrooms for the help and a master bedroom downstairs. A large stove stood in the hall upstairs. This stove in one room heated that floor. One bathroom served the upstairs. The lobby, office and bar, two dining rooms, kitchen and store room completed the downstairs. All this was heated by two coal stoves in the lobby and kitchen. The most popular room in the house was the so-called 'wash room'; here was the bar where hard liquor was sold. Adjoining this was a semi-bath, so called the washroom. Thus the name! A vine covered veranda surrounded the front and side. The usual array of tavern chairs welcomed the hot and weary traveler who could sit and watch the small town business carried on, the air filled with dust as the horses stopped at the town tub for a cool drink of fresh spring water.

Hobe, with his wife, and daughter, Clara, and one hired girl ran this--making butter, cooking, laundering and serving. Hobe had a livery stable...

In the days of 'drummers' every small town had a hotel. Some drummers drove into town with their own rigs to be put up in the barn. Others coming by train into Sheldon, came up on the Franklin stage. Hobe rented out horses to take the drummers to nearby towns. What uproarious laughter there was when the drummers got to swapping their newest stories. Other guests came from afar and a few students had their dinners there. Teachers were boarders. For twenty years twice a week the poker game took place..." (1)

1871, '73: (a) as above, Jed P. Clark* (Beers, same site as 1857 Walling);

1875, '79, '80, '82: (a) as above, Guy C. Chaplin;

c. 1880: an inn (and store), --; present PO moved in 1907 to make room for library next to it; VDHP 0607-1, #29; inn is not on the same site as Beers, Walling sites, above;

c. 1890:   Patton Farm, --; built c. 1855, took summer guests in 1890s; overlooking Lake Carmi (Franklin Pond), VDHP 0607-71;

Franklin House (glass plate negative)

1883, '87, '90, '92, '95:   (a) as above, Guy and H. B. Chaplin;

1898, 1901, '02, '05:   (a) as above, Hobart ("Hobe") and Louise Chaplin;

1911, '13, '15, '20, '25:   (a) as above, --; (still H. B. Chaplin in 1916, VPB, burned in 1925).

(72c) Morses Line, and (72d) South Franklin. No listings found.

* * *

References

(1) Martha H. Towle, A History of Franklin: Past and Present, Fact or Fancy, Legend or Folksay, 1789-1989, Franklin Historical Soc. (Burlington: Queen City Pr., 1989).

* * *

(73) **Georgia** (Franklin).

(73a) Carman (became Oakland, 1897).

1857:   an inn, --; close to the former Oakland station, it "may have been an inn at some point" (VDHP 0608-2, the Gates home in 1980, north of the tracks).

(73b) East Georgia.

1857:   a hotel, B. C. Barney* (Walling);

1870, '71:   Depot House, Phineas Spencer* (Beers, same site as above);

1873, '75:   as above;

1879:   as above, G. P. Spencer; building gone;

1916:   reference is made in the 1975 Georgia Town History to Asahel Hyde's hotel, where the young people went dancing and where "Economos later bought" (precise location unknown, but there was a view of the river); and to "the other old hotel on the river bank...just above the bridge," run by a Mr Woodruff.

(73c) Georgia.

c. 1790:   (a) Franklin House Tavern, Col Benjamin Holmes; early public meetings held here; owned in early 1800s by Albert Bliss, probably the place cited by NEMU Dir in 1849 (see below); the Franklin Hotel of 1870; VDHP 0608-31, #10, now apartments, much altered; this place was run by Thomas Page in 1826 (2); tavern license, 1817-29; sold to his son, Ansel Page, who sold it in turn to Levi Shepard, father of Reuben Shepard (presumably the R. S. Shepard, below);

Note: alamancs list the following taverns, locations unknown: Post (1807, '10); Doane (1813, '15, '16); Hyde (1812; an Alvan Hyde has a tavern license, 1820-27; Stannard (1812); and Merritt (1823; an Ansell Merritt has a tavern license, 1816, and a Samuel Merritt, 1820-22);

Note: tavern licenses also issued to Philo Fairchild, 1815; Frederick Cushman Jr, 1817, '18; George Cushman, 1815; Ralph Grinnell, 1818; Esbon Ward (Weed?), 1820, '22, '25; Laban Fairbanks, 1824, '25; Jonathan R. Danforth, 1817; Roswell Hutchins, 1819; Nathaniel M. Torrey, 1820-22; Fanny Torrey, 1829, '30; Elijah Loomis, 1830; Seymour Eggleston, 1827-33; Thomas Thomas, 1829; Samuel Bartlett Jr, 1821;

1849:   --, R. S. Shepard; (a) --, Albert Bliss (NEMU Dir);

1857:   Mudgett Hotel, --* (Walling);

1870:   (a) Franklin House, R. S. Shepard;

1871:   (a) as above, --* (Beers; also the PO);

1873, '75:   (a) as above;

1879, '80:   (a) as above, James Evarts;

1882, '83:   (a) as above, Patrick Shehan;

1887:   (a) as above, W. Cleveland;

1887, '90:   (a) as above, George Kimpton (? Vt Dir);

1892, '95, '98, 1902:   (a) as above, W. A. Caldwell; operated into the 1950s as a tourist house, the Pitcher Place.

(73d) Georgia Plain. No listings found.

(73e) Lakeside (PO, 1898-1901).

c. 1788:   an inn, Reuben Evarts; one of the earliest houses in Georgia, at the north corner of the intersection of Cline and Stone Schoolhouse Rds (VDHP 0608-63; Duranleau house in 1988; shown as M. Chase on Beers); served travelers coming ashore at Melville Landing, about a mile to the west;

c. 1796:   a tavern, Capt Brown Torrey; a veteran of the Revolutionary War, and a merchant; an early tavern at the north corner of the intersection of Stone Schoolhouse and Georgia Shore Rds (Melville Landing); VDHP 0608-57; shown as M. H. Torrey on Beers; a stone house, still standing (photo and description, ref 1; a Nathaniel Torrey has a tavern license, 1820, '22.

(73f) <u>West Georgia</u>.

c. 1840:   an inn, --; on Sodom Rd, believed to have been a stagecoach stop (VDHP 0608-73, the Schuler home in 1980); on the 1857 Walling as the Menton Pierce place.

Note: the assistance of Peter S. Mallett, Georgia Historical Society, is gratefully acknowledged.

<u>References</u>

(1) Herbert W. Congdon, Old Vermont Houses (Peterborough, N.H.: 1940; 1946 revised edition).

* * *

(74) **<u>Glastenbury</u>** (Bennington).

There was a post office in Glastenbury for only 4 years, 1873-77; there is no settlement there now, no people, and no roads, except for a short loop off Route 7 on the western edge of the township. There were logging settlements there in the latter part of the 19th century, however: one in the northern part of town (Fayville), and another in the southern part of Glastenbury, at the forks of Bolles Brook. A logging camp was established at this latter place a few years after the Civil War, and in 1872, a 9-mile mountain railroad was built linking it to Bennington (the Bennington and Glastenbury Railroad). This line stopped running when the timber ran out in 1889, but was reopened in 1894 as the Bennington and Woodford Electric Railroad; the original workman's dormitory became a "pavilion," serving as a clubhouse, dance hall and dining-room; and the old company store became the <u>Glastenbury</u> Inn (see photo). The railroad stopped running in 1897 after a severe washout, but in its day, it ran excursions every 45 minutes from 9 A. M. to 8:15 P.M. in the summer.

Glastenbury Inn (Weichert-Isselhardt collection)

(74a) <u>Glastenbury</u> (Bennington).

249

1875, '78:   --, T. Harbor (location unknown).

References

(1) Ruth Levin, Ordinary Heroes, Story of Shaftsbury, Tyler Resch, ed. (Shaftsbury: Shaftsbury Historical Soc., 1978).
(2) Tyler Resch, Shires of Bennington (Bennington: Bennington Museum, 1975).

* * *

(75) **Glover** (Orleans).

Post offices existed briefly at three settlements in this town besides the two listed below, namely, Gloverton, Maples and South Glover, but no listings have been found for them.

(75a) Outside the Villages.

1799:   a tavern (and store), Ralph Parker; on lot 116 near the Hinman Road, put through Glover in 1791 or 1792, at the southeast end of Hinman Pond (present Lake Parker); Parker was town clerk, and the town's first representative to the state legislature, 1802-14; the location of this early tavern is shown on a sketch map in ref 1, representing the "Parker settlement" in 1810;

c. 1800:   a tavern, James Vance; "for quite a number of years," in his second house, a frame house on the east side of the Hinman Road, just south of the present West Glover-Glover village road; (see photo, c. 1950, of the Vance tavern building, still standing, oldest house in town, present Clark home;

Vance tavern building
(History of the Town of Glover, Vermont, 1983)

c. 1803:   a tavern, Nathan Norton; at the south end of town on the Hinman Road; his son kept the place after him; a Jeremiah Norton had a tavern license, 1823-26, Nathan Norton in 1817, '22;

250

(?): a tavern, in the Dopp/Schumann house; on the road to Sheffield (1); still standing, and the barn on this property houses the Bread and Puppet Museum;

c. 1820: a tavern, Silas Clark; in the valley "after the pond ran away" (i.e., after June 6, 1810, ref 1); tavern license, 1828, '33; this place is in the southeast corner of the town, where there is a marker on present Rte 16; Clark ran this tavern until his death in 1836; carried on by Charles A. Clark, became the Pond (or Dry Pond) Hotel (see photo of the Clark or Dry Pond Hotel, c. 1920); the original house stood north of Clark's (formerly Tildy's) Pond on Vt 16 until the early 1950s;

Clark's Old Hotel, Dry Pond, Glover, Vt.

Dry Pond Hotel
(History of the Town of Glover, Vermont, 1983)

(75b) Glover village.

1817: Mr Dan Gray came in 1817, "kept the hotel for several years" (Hemenway); tavern license, 1825-33;

Note: tavern licenses, locations unknown, to - Randall, 1817; Josiah N. Stevens, 1833; Samuel Bean Jr, 1827; and Benjamin Starkey, 1828;

1820s: Glover Hotel/Inn, --; on the east side of Main St, just south of what is now called Dexter Hill or Mountain Rd; shown on sketch map, ref 1, which represents the village in 1840; razed c. 1960; also a photo of the old Glover Hotel/Johnson House/Hen House, c. 1890; it is odd that the Glover Hotel isn't listed in Walton most of these years; still standing, private home;

1830: Union House, --; "the largest hotel in Glover, catering to travelers and business men for many, many years" (1); became a nursing home in early 1950s; see photo, next page; also shown on sketch map in ref 1; VDHP 1008-3; the desk from the old hotel is preserved in the Glover Room in the Old Stone House Museum in Brownington;

* * *

"Dan Gray built the Union House with the help of Moses Goodwin and was the first proprietor; John Jenness was the second, and Ethan Foster the third owner. The Sherburnes then purchased Union House, with first 'Uncle John' and 'Aunt Maria' running it for many years and then Henry and Rosette Hall. Rosette was the daughter of Uncle John and Aunt Maria. The Halls lived at the Union House all their married life, as did their daughter, Mamie, and her husband...with their children.

When 'Uncle John' bought the place, there was a large barn ...which could care for about 30 horses at a time. When the stage coach was within a few miles of town, a horn would be blown at intervals, loud and clear, warning the countryside of its approach. The sound would carry a long distance, so by the time the coach arrived, four fresh lively horses would be circling nervously around, ready and willing to replace the tired and sweating ones who had made the long run over the Vermont hills.

There was a short delay during which some of the passengers might make a hasty trip to the bar room inside...When road conditions were real bad, the pasengers would often spend the night there.

The Union House was noted for its wonderful balls at New Year's, Thanksgiving, Fourth of July, and other holidays...On many occasions there were two bands. As soon as one dance ended, the other band started to play and a new set formed. People came from everywhere, many from a long distance for teams, which of course was the only transportation in those days.

It must have made quite a picture: the big hostelry with many lights, the high-spirited horses drawing sleighs, many bells on the teams making music in the frosty air, buffalo robes and warm freestones, pretty girls and everywhere the sound of gaiety." (2)

Union House
(History of the Town of Glover, Vermont, 1983)

1855:   --, James Russell; --, C. A. Clark;

1856:   --, C. A. Clark;

1859:   --, I. Dwinell* (Walling);

1870, '73, '75:   (a) Union House, Ethan E. Foster;

1878:   as above, J. Sherburne* (Beers; same site as Walling, 1859);

1879, '80, '87, '92, '95, '98: (a) as above;

1883-84:   (a) Union House, -- (Child);

1875, '83, '87, '90:   (a) Union House, A. H. Hall (? Vt Dir);

1901:   (a) Union House, A. H. Hall;

1903:   (a) <u>Hall's Hotel</u> (the <u>Union House</u>); a rest home since c. 1953, but date when it ceased operating as an inn not known; <u>Hotel Richardson</u> (SBA pamphlet);

1905:   <u>Hotel Richardson</u>, E. Richardson;

1908:   <u>Glover Inn</u>, -;

1911:   --, Lillian McQueen;

1913:   --, E. Richardson;

1914:   no hotel on Sanborn map;

1915:   --, Mrs Lillian McQueen;

1916:   <u>Glover Inn</u>, Lillian McQueen; <u>Riverside Inn</u>, Mrs E. Richardson (VPB; <u>Hotel Richardson</u>?) see photo.

Riverside Inn (Vermont Historical Society)

(75c) <u>Maples</u> (PO, 1898-1903). No listings found.

(75d) <u>West Glover</u>.

1878:   --, E. Cook.

Note: the assistance of L. Marguerite Histed, Town Clerk, and Richard Evans, is gratefully acknowledged.

* * *

References

(1) Glover Bicentennial Committee, History of the Town of Glover, Vermont (Burlington: Queen City Pr., 1983).
(2) from an article by Daisy Dopp, quoted in the town history, ibid: 24-25.

* * *

(76) **Goshen** (Addison).

(76a) <u>Goshen</u>.

1849:   --, C. Phillips;

Note: Blueberry Hill Farm has operated as an inn only since the 1940s.

* * *

(77) **Grafton** (Windham).

(77a) Grafton.

c. 1785:   "from earliest times Henry Bond had run a store and hotel in his two-room log dwelling" (1); "located where widow Nancy Fisher's house now stands" (i.e., c. 1884, Child);

c. 1785:   tavern licenses to David Stickney, Job Gleason, Jonathan Gleason;

1801:   an inn, Enos Lovell; who converted his 2-story house for this purpose; the building still stands as part of the Old Tavern (see below); doubled in size, c. 1820; earliest known photo, before addition of third floor in 1865, in ref 2;

* * *

The present tavern in Grafton was originally the Burgess homestead. It is not known when it was first used as a hotel (a Hyman Burgess had a tavern license in 1823).

Turner and Warner were proprietors of it, also Chaffee and Turner. They were there in 1841. At one time it was run by Henry Wilcox; at another time John Ayers was the landlord (see 1849 entry, below). William and Sophina Stratton operated it during the Civil War years, and were probably the last landlords before it was remodeled by the Phelps brothers (see below). Managers since the Phelpses include: Harlan Leonard, Judson Rickett, Walter Walker, Daniel Bond, Ernest Lawrence, Harry and Cecilia Dutton, Kingsley Perry, Clarence and Phyllis Dettmer, and John and Hildreth Wriston. (VDHP 1306-21). See photo, next page.

* * *

Note: There is an excellent description of the Tavern in a booklet called "Innkeeping in Grafton 100 Years Ago" (see ref 3), from which the following excerpts are taken:

"There is no evidence that the Tavern at this time (i.e., the 1870s) was in any sense a resort or tourist hotel. Obviously it was well known...about this pleasant hostelry in a village of great natural charm...

But during the 1860s, the guest list clearly identifies the Tavern as essentially a so-called commercial hotel...This was the era of the Yankee peddler, and the hard core of Phelps' clientele, year round (Phelps was then the proprietor) was a constant stream of agents, drummers, commercial travelers, and itinerant practitioners of all sorts who came back to Grafton repeatedly on their business rounds, using the Tavern as their base of operations as they plied their trade, house to house, with pack or by wagon...

They brought to Grafton such diversified products as boots and shoes, brooms and brushes, buggy whips...ready made clothing, coffee mixers, crackers, dry goods and notions, garden seed, hardware, horse nails and medicines, knitting and sewing machines, shirts and drawers, soap, spectacles, tea and spices, umbrellas, washers and wringers...There was the dentist who came...from Factory Point (now Manchester Depot), a daguerrotype artist and a clock repairer from Fayetteville...and a photographer from South Royalton... Also there came buyers of sheep and horses, accompanied by drovers to take the livestock to other markets."

1841:   Eagle Hotel, Thomas Davis; in the Alexander house just below the present (i.e., 1978) Historical Society building; for a number of years. Davis added porches, and otherwise enlarged the original building (1); ran it until at least 1869; also the Temperance Hotel at one point; VDHP 1306-3;

Note: tavern licenses to John Bassett, 1820, '21; John Goodridge, 1820; Abel Burditt,

1822; and Nathan Wheeler, 1823;

The Tavern at Grafton

1849: --, John Ayres (NEMU Dir);

(?): "at an early date a Mr Park had a hotel on the Edson lot"; (1)

1855: --, William Stratton;

1856: --, W. Stratton* (McClellan; on the <u>Phelps Hotel/Old Tavern</u> site);

1865: <u>Old Tavern</u> bought by two brothers, Francis and Harlan Phelps, operated by them and their wives for 48 years; capital provided by Francis Phelps, who returned from gold-hunting in the west with a considerable fortune, for those days. They greatly enlarged the hotel by adding a third story and porches;

* * *

"Harlan was a good businessman and managed The Tavern. Brother Francis, aided by his wife, Achsa, did everything else.

Francis was a big man, famous for his feats of strength. He also doubled as liveryman, sheriff, legislator, town officer and 'music man.' He organized the Grafton Band which celebrated its 100th anniversary in 1967. It still plays regularly on the village green.

While The Tavern was popular among the literary set (Kipling was a visitor in 1892) and was the 'in' place for local social events, it was still basically a commercial hotel patronized mostly by commercial travelers who knew it as a 'good place to stop.'

There were notable exceptions. Ulysses S. Grant came to the Tavern on December 19, 1867, while campaigning for his first term as President. The Tavern has played host to other famous guests: Daniel Webster, Oliver Wendell Holmes, Theodore Roosevelt, Woodrow Wilson, and Ralph Waldo Emerson" (ref 2; in addition to the Tavern photo, there are photos of Francis and Achsa Phelps; a reproduction of the register page signed by Grant; and a photo of Kipling and others on the porch).

* * *

1869:   Grafton Hotel, F. and H. Phelps* (Beers);

1870:   --, F. and H. Phelps;

1875-1901:   Grafton Hotel/Phelps Hotel, frequent listings in Walton; the list of managers in ref 2 is not in complete agreement with Walton;

1905:   Grafton House, J. D. Rickett;

1908:   Hotel Grafton, - Phelps;

1911:   The Tavern, W. E. L. Grafton;

1913, '15, '20: The Tavern, --; (E. A. Lawrence in 1916 VPB);

1915:   shown on Sanborn;

1925:   as above, H. C.(N.?) Dutton.

(77b) Houghtonville. No listings found.

* * *

References

(1) Helen M. Pettengill, History of Grafton, Vermont, 1754-1975, and Sidelights on Grafton History (Grafton: Grafton Historical Soc., 1975).
(2) Wilf Copping, A Vermont Renaissance, Grafton and the Windham Foundation (Grafton: Windham Foundation, 1978).
(3) Stuart F. Heinritz, Innkeeping in Grafton 100 Years Ago (Grafton: Grafton Historical Soc., 1969).

* * *

(78) **Granby** (Essex).

(78a) Granby. No listings found.

* * *

(79) **Grand Isle** (Grand Isle).

Originally part of the town of Two Heroes, granted by the state of Vermont in 1779; divided in 1798, with the northern island becoming North Hero, and the southern Middle and South Hero, sharing a representative to the state legislature. Divided again in 1810, when Middle Hero gained complete autonomy, and the name Grand Isle. The township included the villages of Pearl and Adams (at Adams Landing, a steamboat stop) which both had POs, briefly; and Gordon's, on the west side of the island, present-day terminus of the ferry to New York state, which never had a PO.

(79a) East Shore (Adams, Adams Landing).

c. 1890-1910:   --, Maria ("Mattie") Adams; summer boarders at the brick house at Adams Landing, place known as the Arbor Vitae; and at an associated cottage known as Vantine's (Vantine Manor) VHS PC photo; Vantine Manor still listed in 1955, but listed in 1923 VPB as Vantine's, Vantine Brothers;

256

(?):   Corbin Lodge, --; at the "draw" between Grand Isle and North Hero; VHS PC photo;

1912-50:   Hurlburt's Lodge, --; built by Victor Hurlburt in 1894; on US 2, east side, about two miles north of the Corners; known more recently as Sportsman's Inn, Hitching Post, Island Cove; see photo; listed as Hillcrest Farm House in 1916, '23 VPB;

Hurlburt's Lodge

Note: the Vermont Historical Society has photos of two other places, not located: Center's Hotel, 1897; and Great Elm Inn, 1922.

(79b) Grand Isle ("Corners").

c. 1795:   a tavern, Timothy Nightingale; near the present Grand Isle Corners (1); Nightingale was committed to debtor's prison in 1800;

c. 1800:   Samson's Inn, Daniel Samson/Sampson; about a mile and a quarter north of the Corners on the main road (1); site occupied in recent years by Superior's Diner-Restaurant, later owned by Mr and Mrs Mark Howrican, Jr; the original inn burned long ago; Samson died in 1820 (1824, according to Hemenway) and his son Reuben continued it until 1847, when it closed; (tavern license, 1825-30); celebrated, according to Stratton, "for the amount of patronage it received as well as for the large number of balls and other entertainments held there";

Note: Stratton lists other tavern licensees from the town records, locations unknown: Adon Ames, 1806; Alexander F. Hyde, 1810, '11; Andrew Hazen, 1816; James Tobias, 1816; and the State Archives list Henry C. Boardman, 1829, '30, and Elisha Boardman, 1828, locations also unknown; (1)

1901: Martell's Hotel, Frederick A. Martell; see photo, Chap IV; built near the depot in Grand Isle by Martell, enlarged in 1905; became the Belmont Hotel; Martell died in an automobile accident in 1925;

* * *

"For quite a number of years, this hotel existed at the Grand Isle railroad station. It stood on the east side of the tracks and station, and south side of the highway. In more recent years, the building was mainly torn down.

When the Rutland Railroad opened the line through the Islands in 1901, this depot location opened up possibilities for the need of a commercial hotel.

Sensing the opportunity...he (i.e., Martell, who had been a blacksmith) sold out at the

Corners and purchased about an acre of land at the railroad station. In 1901, he erected the front portion (photo, ref 1) of his hotel. As the only commercial hotel in town, he received substantial patronage. About 1905, he enlarged and built the rear extension.

...This quite remarkable man, starting with nothing as a boy of thirteen, with initiative and perseverance, achieved substantial competence..." (1)

* * *

1915, '20, '25: --, F. A. Briggs; --, F. A. Martell.

(79c) <u>Pearl</u>.

1903:   <u>Island Villa Hotel</u>, Frank A. Briggs; at Robinson's Point on the east shore, near Pearl Bay; a popular summer place, considered a luxury hotel with the highest advertised rates in the islands; Briggs died in 1922, and his wife Mattie in 1925; their son Malcolm A. continued operating the place for some time (still listed in 1955); it became a Catholic girls' summer camp, c. 1956, still standing; the VDHP regards it is "a premier example of a large, turn-of-the-century resort hotel...well maintained because of successful adaptive-use" (VDHP 0702-6, #1).

(79d) <u>West Shore</u> (Gordon's Landing, Ladd's Point).

c. 1789:   a tavern, <u>Alexander Gordon</u>; at Gordon's Landing (later Ladd's Point); Gordon established a ferry to North Hero before he opened the tavern, and committed suicide in 1802; his wife probably ran the place until c. 1808, when it was sold to Ephraim Beardsley and Ebenezer Hatch; Hatch ran it until at least 1812 (tavern license in 1816); almanacs, 1796 until at least 1829;

c. 1798:   a tavern, <u>Benjamin Bell</u>; until 1802, at his ferry landing on the west shore, "same location as the landing for present Grand Isle-Cumberland Head ferry" (1); same statement about <u>Gordons</u> (above);

c. 1800:   a tavern, <u>Capt David Wilcox</u>; also on the west shore, about three-quarters of a mile north of Bell's; site then known as Allen's Bay, now Wilcox Point or Cove; there was considerable rivalry between the two tavern-keepers and ferry operators, Bell and Wilcox, described in detail in ref 1.

Note: the assistance of Mrs Linda Smith, Grand Isle Historical Society, is gratefully acknowledged.

* * *

References

(1) Allen L. Stratton, History of the South Heroe Islands; Being the Towns of South Hero and Grand Isle, Vermont (two volumes) (Burlington: Queen City Pr., 1980).

* * *

(80) **Granville** (Addison).

(80a) <u>East Granville</u> (Sandusky, 1857-68). No listings found.

(80b) <u>Granville</u> (Kingston until 1835; also known as Granville Center, Upper Village).

Modern maps show two villages on Rte 100, Granville and Lower Granville, about a mile and a half south. The upper village was once Granville Center, and the lower one Granville; the post office was in the lower village until "recent times." (1) Since several Granville inn-keepers were also PMs, Granville inns of uncertain location are shown as being in the lower village, where the PO was.

1871: Central Hall, W. Ellis* (Beers, in Granville Center; there is also a D. H. Whitney residence on Beers in Granville Center, and he was proprietor of this place a little later;

1878, '80:   Corner Hotel, H. (?) H. Whitney (probably Granville);

1881: Central House, D. H. Whitney and Sons (Child);

1883, '87:   Central House, L. L. Udall;

1890, '98, 1901, '11:   Central House, H. C. Hubbard;

Note: listed as Hubbard Hotel, H. C. Hubbard, village not specified, in 1902, '05, '13, '20, '25, almost certainly the same as the Central House. Local authorities say that the Central House stopped operating in 1920, although still listed in 1925; building still standing, but vacant.

(80c) Lower Granville (but no PO by that name, see above).

(?):   first tavern, Eleazer Kendall; in house occupied in 1886 by Royal H. Bostwick (2); not clear which village this is;

c. 1840:   an inn, --; present "Christmas Tree Inn" (VDHP 0107-1, on Rte 100); built about 1840, used as an inn;

1855, '56:   --, Warren Hayden (PM, 1839-45 and 1849-53);

1857: --, W. Hayden* (Walling);

1870: --, F. B. Dimick (also PM);

1871: --, H. C. Vinton* (Beers; appears to be the same site as in 1857, Walling; VDHP 0107-3, now a home);

1872, '73:   Granville House, Henry C. Vinton;

1875: Granville House, D. W. Rodgers;

1908: Capitol, --; Granville Hotel listed until at least 1955.

Note: the assistance of Kathy Werner, Assistant Town Clerk, is gratefully acknowledged.

* * *

References

(1) Esther M. Swift, Vermont Place-Names: Footprints of History (Brattleboro: Stephen Greene Pr., 1977).
(2) Henry P. Smith, History of Addison County, Vermont (Syracuse: D. Mason, 1886).

* * *

(81) **Greensboro** (Orleans).

(81a) East Greensboro. No listings found.

(81b) Greensboro (including Caspian Lake).

In 1792, there were two roads in Greensboro: the Bayley-Hazen Road, running west of the lake, and the Hinman Road, passing by the southeast end of the lake where the village developed, and on to Glover. The first two taverns were built on this latter road, one (Huntington's, see below) north of the village; the other kept in the village by Timothy Stanley and his wife, Eunice (see below).

1790s: a tavern, Timothy and Eunice Stanley; in their log house in Greensboro village; a tavern at this same site in the 1820s, in a new frame building, by R. B. Ewen (site shown on a map, ref 1, present J. B. McIntyre);

1797: Huntington's Tavern, Dr Samuel Huntington; on what is now (i.e., 1990) the Lumsden farm on Baker Hill, on the road to Barr Hill; the building burned c. 1977; became the old Stagehouse, run by Col S. Baker in the 1830s; (1)

(?): a hotel (and store), --; once owned by George C. Glosten, now a home, #35 in the Greensboro Historic District (VDHP 1009-85); hotel date unknown;

1832: (a) Caspian Lake House, Col Levi Stevens;

1849: --, Josiah N. Stevens (NEMU Dir); tavern license to Jos. N. Stearns (sp?), 1833, State Archives;

1859: (a) --, B. S. Wilson* (Walling); the Caspian Lake House;

1870: --, B. C. Burpee; --, D. McFarland; this latter is probably Duncan McFarland, who came from Scotland in 1848, settled on a farm near Greensboro Four Corners, and conducted a hotel, on the "old stage road from Montpelier to Newport...until after the railroad reached Greensboro Bend, when it became unprofitable." (1)

1872, '73, '78, '79, '80: (a) Greensboro Hotel, Anson B. Cook* (Beers, 1878); same location as Walling, 1859; same as Caspian Lake House;

1883: (a) as above, B. F. Wiggins;

1883-84: (a) Caspian Lake House (also known as Sawyer's Hotel), William B. Sawyer; Child says he had it from 1880;

1886: (a) Caspian Lake House, S. Hill; also, the Boston and Lowell Railroad Guide lists a place called the Lake View House, Charles L. Conant; VDHP says there was a Lakeview Inn, built as a home c. 1870, a boarding-house c. 1900, then a tea room, and finally an inn, until 1976 (VDHP 1009-43); now a private home; but the town history says the place began as the Goss boarding-house, built in 1907; (1)

1887: Cottage Hotel, A. Smalley;

1888: (a) Caspian Lake House, F. H. Dunfur; Lake View House, J. A. Goss (Boston and Maine Railroad Guide);

1890: as above, N. C. Dunklee;

1887, '90, '92: (a) as above, Samuel Hill;

1892: Cottage Hotel, E. A. Townsend;

1895: (a) as above, E. A. Townsend;

1898, 1901: (a) Caspian Lake House, W. A. Stone; see photo, next page;

1905, '13, '15: (a) as above, F. H. Dufur;

Lake View House

1908:   (a) as above, --;

1914:   (a) as above, --* (Sanborn map; PO in same building);

1916:   (a) as above; <u>Lake View</u>, Charles F. Richards (VPB); see photo, above;

1920:   (a) as above, A. W. Webb; <u>Caspian Lake House</u>, listed in 1935, razed in 1937; <u>Lake View House</u> listed until at least 1955;

1925:   (a) as above, F. H. Dufur;

Note: the present <u>Highland Lodge</u> is a home converted to an inn in 1926 (VDHP 1009-48).

(81c) <u>Greensboro Bend</u> (formerly Greensboro Station). Said by the Vermont Division of Historic Preservation to be an outstanding example of a northern Vermont railroad village. Created by the railroad, which came through in 1872.

Caspian Lake House (History of Greensboro, 1990)

1879: Folsom's Hotel, A. P. Folsom; built by him in 1877 to accommodate workers at the mill, but later made into a regular hotel (Child), operated by the Hopkins family;

1883: Hopkin's Hotel, A. D. Hopkins;

1883-84: (a) Greensboro Bend Hotel, W. E. and A. D. Hopkins (Child);

Published by L. S. Collins   Hotel, Church & Schoolhouse, Greensboro Bend, Vt.

Greensboro Bend Hotel

1887: --, John Denning (Deming in Vt Dir);

1890: (a) as above, W. M. Blair;

1892: --, A. A. Brown;

1895: --, A. B. Pike;

1898: --, J. and A. McGowan;

1901: (a) as above, T. T. Beanlee; the hotel gradually evolved into a tenement house and was finally torn down;

1905: --, W. Barton;

1908: Lake View, --; this is almost certainly an error; Greensboro Bend is not on Caspian Lake; there is also a Lake View House at Greensboro, of course (see above);

1913: Summer Hill, --;

1914: Graham's Hotel, --* (Sanborn); this place burned; it stood next to #27 in the Greensboro Bend Historic District (VDHP 1009-86);

1915: --, William Graham;

1920: The Lake View, C. P. Reynolds; (Lake View House in a VPB booklet, 1935; see comment under 1905, above).

(81d) Greensboro Four Corners/Mills. No listings found.

(81e) North Greensboro. No listings found. However, according to Watson et al., Aaron Hill operated a tavern in North Greensboro, some time after 1809; and his son Samuel also operated a hotel, location unknown.

Note: the assistance of Janet L. Lang, Assistant Town Clerk, and Wilhelmina Smith, is gratefully acknowledged.

* * *

References

(1) Peter D. Watson et al., The History of Greensboro: The First Two Hundred Years, Susan B. Weber, ed. (Greensboro: Greensboro Historical Society, 1990).

* * *

(82) **Groton** (Caledonia).

Includes Lake Groton (or Groton Pond) and Ricker's Pond, and several short-lived post offices at hamlets that were really only lumber camps or sawmills (Peabody Station and Ricker's Mills). There was also a post office at West Groton for a short time, known as Westville; and one at Groton Pond. No listings were found for (82b) Groton Pond, (82c) Peabody Station, or (82e) Westville (West Groton).

(82a) Groton.

1790s: reference in Hemenway to "the old county road" (from Peacham to Orange) passing the "Massey hotel and store, since the Pillsbury farm" (in Groton);

1798: a tavern, Dominicus Gray; about one and a quarter miles north of the present village, where three roads converged; a frame building, VDHP 0304-51; Gray died in 1833; tavern license, 1822-27;

* * *

"Since Groton in its pioneer days was not located on any such highway (i.e., a stagecoach road) there was no demand for a spacious inn but there was need for a kind of community center where the 'vendue' of the lands of tax delinquents might take place, or where an occasional traveler might find entertainment. Such a place was furnished by Dominicus Gray in 1798 when his new frame house, begun in 1797, was ready for occupancy. So much has been written elsewhere in this book (i.e., ref 1) about the use of this inn in connection with town and proprietor's meetings, auctions, lawsuits, and June trainings that nothing further need be said except that before 1827 Gray's only rival was Aaron Hosmer, Jr, who operated an inn at the Orr Turn near the present Harry Welch place (i.e., c. 1978) from 1802 to 1809. According to H. N. Welch, Hosmer's inn was of hewn logs which made it rank somewhere between a house of unfinished logs and the frame house of Gray. Two or three early town meetings were held at Hosmer's Inn."

* * *

1802:   an inn, Aaron Hosmer, Jr; at the Orr Turn (see above); until 1809;

1824:   tavern license to Nathan H. Downs;

1827:   Randall's Inn; Samuel Randall built an inn in the village; Randall sold to Samuel G. Clark in 1831; inn-keepers changed often in the ensuing years, although not necessarily the owners; known as "Moulton Heath's Inn" in 1831; run by B. Brickett in 1834, Erastus Baldwin in 1835; George Welch was innkeeper and owner at this stand from 1850-54 and 1859-65; he died in 1865; the place was operated by Calvin Clark, son of Samuel G., 1854-59, when George Welch was operating the other place in town (see below); Charlotte Welch, George's widow, operated the place from 1865-93, joined in this effort by Aaron Welch, George's brother, whom she married; Aaron died in 1893; their son Alexander carried on for a year or two, when the place was sold to James

S. Weed; from about 1873 on, the place carried a colorful sign with "Railroad House" on it; it was also known as Weed's Hotel"; this is VDHP 0304-18, #16, a store and apartment in 1980;

c. 1840:   Marshall's Tavern, McLane Marshall; a second tavern in the village, just east of the ell of the Darling store; Marshall was innkeeper until 1854, except for two years when Jesse Page was in charge; George Welch had it from 1854-59 (see above, as an early operator of Weed's as well); Almun L. Clark owned it from 1859-67, with Azro J. Bailey as innkeeper in 1859, '60; William B. Jones proprietor from 1867-77; the building was then moved and converted to a private home (VDHP 0304-20); it was known as the American House at some point, but more often as Marshall's Tavern;

1849:   --, McLane Marshall (NEMU Dir; see below);

1856:   --, George Welch; --, Calvin Clark;

1870:   --, Aaron Welch;

1872, '75, '78: (a) Railroad Hotel, Aaron Welch* (Beers); (b) --, W. B. Jones;

1873:   (b) American House, William B. Jones;

1879, '80, '83, '90, '92, '95:   (a) as above;

1901:   Cliff House, George Webber (not known if this is Weed's (the Railroad Hotel) in its last days, or an earlier name for the Groton House, which came into operation about this time);

1898, 1901:   (a) Weed's Hotel, J. S. Weed;

1905:   --, R. D. Sherry (this is the Groton House, owned by Ralph Sherry; he was also PM fromn 1905-11, so this was probably a hotel PO; also known as Moulton's briefly; torn down in 1954 to make way for the new PO);

1908:   --, Weed;

1911, '13, '15: Groton House, Mrs Helen Welsh;

1920:   as above, G. S. Welch;

1925:   as above, J. T. Darling.

(82d) Rickers Mills.

1860:   Lake House, McLane Marshall;

* * *

"License is hereby granted to McLane Marshall to keep a Tavern or Inn in the Lake House, so called, in Groton, for the term of one year from date, of which all the good people will take notice and govern themselves accordingly. June 4, 1860." (1)

The Lake House was a commodious two-story building with double piazza commanding a fine view of Ricker Pond"; a resort, in contrast to the two places in the village; William H. Hubbard took over, 1864-67; and I. N. Hall (or Hall and Darling), 1867-c. 1880; Leverett Page was the last person to operate it as an inn, until about 1894, when it was converted to a summer home."

* * *

1875:   Lake House, --* (Beers);

1887:   Lake House, L. H. Page.

Note: the assistance of Mrs Alice L. Goodine, Groton Historical Society, is gratefully acknowledged.

* * *

References

(1) Waldo F. Glover and the Glover Historical Society, Mister Glover's Groton (Canaan, N.H.: Phoenix Pr., 1978).

* * *

(83) **Guildhall** (Essex).

(83a) Central. No listings found.

(83b) Guildhall.

c. 1800:   a tavern, Nathan Cass; "we believe Mr Nathan Cass was the first regular hotel keeper, for in the year 1800, he obtained from the County Court a tavern license, and we think he had already kept tavern some years, but it seems that others were also keeping public places..."; (1)

1801:   David Hopkinson and John Dana also received tavern licenses; "we will not attempt giving a list of people who have kept public houses at various times in town; for at one time, all through the country there was a tavern every few miles, but since the Railroads have been constructed through the valleys of this region, we find the hotels have dropped off...until now we have only one" (i.e., the Essex House, see below; ref 1); Hopkinson listed in an 1805 almanac, also a "Haw" tavern;

early 1800s (?): photo of the Wayne Judge residence, early 1900s, believed to have been a stagecoach inn; (2)

1849:   --, Morse Woods (NEMU Dir);

1855, '56:   --, John Dodge (also PM, 1854-57 and earlier);

1859:   hotel (and Union store), M. Wood* (Walling);

c. 1867:   "two public houses in the small village in the northwest corner of town, where the county buildings are" (i.e., Guildhall village; Hemenway);

1870, '73, '75: (a) Essex House, W. H. Hartshorn (also PM);

1879, '80:   (a) as above (but Mr Hartshorn no longer PM);

1883:   (a) as above, C. E. Hartshorn and J. M. Poole;

1886:   (a) Essex House, Charles E. Hartshorn; "which is very pleasantly located in the village...one of the best hotels in this section of the state..."; (1) a resort, but not exclusively so; burned in 1892; photo, 1870s-80s, ref 2;

* * *

"In 1892 fire destroyed the hotel and on Oct 27, 1892 the townspeople petitioned the selectmen to exempt from taxation for a period of 10 years a good modern hotel if Mr Hartshorn would rebuild. A special town meeting was held...voting the exemption. However, Mr Hartshorn

265

chose not to rebuild and held the land until 1900." (The site is now occupied by the library and Masonic building).

* * *

1887, '90:   (a) as above, Charles E. Hartshorn; (Child says that Jonathan Cummings was proprietor at one time for 11 years, hard to see where this fits in);

1892:   (a) as above, Frank Harris (burned September, 1892);

early 1900s: Ramsdell House, George Ramsdell; (also known as the Central Hotel); a boarding house, located where the Stanley Hall residence is now (i.e., 1975);

* * *

"When Essex County Court convened, the jury, judge, lawyers, etc., stayed at the Ramsdell House and a 'taxi,' a two horse surrey ran between the Court House and the Ramsdell House, and also the Nelson Call Farm if there were too many boarders for the Ramsdell House, around 1912. It burned down in February, 1912." (2)

* * *

1901:   (b) Central Hotel, George Ramsdell;

1905, '08:   (b) as above, --;

1914:   no hotel on Sanborn.

* * *

References

(1) Everett C. Benton, History of Guildhall, Vermont (Waverly, Mass.: 1886, 1985 facsimile edition, Univ. Microfilm).
(2) Patricia Rogers, History of Guildhall, Vermont (Guildhall: Guildhall Bicentennial Comm., 1975).

* * *

(84) **Guilford** (Windham).

(84a) Algiers.   Also known as East Guilford. Swift calls this Guilford's "most southerly village." (1) It never had a PO, and is not shown on the Vermont Road Atlas, Northern Cartographic).

c. 1776:   Gale Tavern, Ephraim Gale, Sr; who came to Guilford c. 1776; a stage tavern, used "until the building of the railroad in Brattleboro," taken down in 1850; listed in an 1817 almanac as a stage tavern on the road from Springfield, Massachusetts to Hanover, New Hampshire;

1802:   "a new tavern", --; (Hemenway, who also calls this place East Guilford).

(84b) Green River (once Greenwater).

1829:   Pratt tavern, --; almanac, location unknown; a Solomon C. Pratt has a tavern license, 1820, '21;

1849:   (a) Green River House/Tavern, M. E. Nelson; owned by Jonah Cutting and run by James M. Stafford in 1845; VDHP 1307-9, just south and east of the intersection of Green River and Stage Rds;

266

Note: The 1849 NEMU Directory lists both the Green River House (above), and a place called the Railroad House, John Reed; the latter has not been identified, although it may be the Gale Tavern in Algiers;

1855: --, Stephen Smith;

1856: Smith's Hotel, S. Smith* (McClellan map; the place is labeled West Guilford on this map but is at the Green River location on later maps); other owners include Barney Gallup, D. M. Thompson (1863), Nathan B. Hadley; Cushman Wilcox (1864), A. W. Putnam, Park. W. Shearer (1868), Fred H. Stowe (1890) and W. Edward Benson (1917), ref 2; other tavern licenses to Cyrus Martin, 1817; William Goodnow, 1823; and Russell Hyde, 1826-33, locations unknown;

1869: a hotel, J. W. Reid* (Beers);

Note: It is hard to be sure, because there is no large scale insert for Green River (West Guilford) on the McClellan map, but this place does not appear to be at the same site as Smith's Hotel, above;

1870: (a) Green River House, --;

1880: (a) as above, Park W. Shearer; also 1884 (on road 37, Child);

1887: (a) as above, Charles Clisbee;

1895: (a) as above, Fred Stowe;

1905, '11, '13, '15: (a) as above;

(84c) Guilford.

1817: Broad Brook House/Inn, Solomon C. Pratt; who built it, sold to Arad Hunt in 1820; numerous owners, several of whom operated it as an inn, including Elihu Field (tavern license, 1825-33) and Erastus Burt (license, 1824); operating as recently as the 1920s, later a grocery store;

1849: --, D. Jacobs (NEMU Dir, under East Guilford); this is the Broad Brook Inn, owned 1839-55 by D. Jacobs;

1855: --, Mrs Lucretia Jacobs;

(?): "the house in which Horace W. Tafts now lives (i.e., 1884, Child) was built about a hundred years ago, and was used as a hotel";

1860: a passing reference to the Broad Brook House in ref 2;

1869: --, R. Wright* (Beers);

1870: (a) Broad Brook House, A. R. Wright;

1872: (a) as above, T. S. Stockwell;

1873, '75, '80: (a) as above, A. R. Baker;

1884: (a) as above, C. S. Miller;

1887: (a) as above, - Chatfield;

1892: (a) as above, - Shepardson;

1895: (a) as above, J. L. Squires;

1898:   (a) as above, H. Chatfield;

1901:   (a) as above, S. S. Taylor;

1905:   (a) as above, W. H. Barrett;

1908, '13, '15, '20, '25:   (a) as above, --.

(84d) <u>Guilford Center</u>.

c. 1800:   <u>Elisha Chase tavern</u>; "The old tavern property at Guilford Center village was built in the corner of the crossroads next south of the present Grange Hall (i.e., 1961) about 1800..."; property sold in 1802 to Elisha Chase, who may have built the tavern as the first reference to it is that year. Numerous owners, including John Barnard, Edward Houghton (1806, see also below), Edward Houghton Jr (1823); leased by Loring Kingsbury, 1820-31 (tavern license, 1820, '21, '24); Thomas Lynde, Brutus R. Merrill (1835), etc. Building used as the town clerk's office, 1900-1904, razed in the early 1930s. (2)

c. 1800:   on original lot 105, where the mineral springs were found, "Edward Houghton built a large structure, which was used as an inn and hotel." (2) This is VDHP 1307-3. (Houghton apparently also ran the <u>Chase tavern</u> at one time, see above).

* * *

"Even today (i.e., c. 1961) there is a trap door leading to the cellar where the owner kept his supply of cider and hard liquor. The building itself is a monstrous thirty-seven room affair, with many of the rooms having a private staircase leading to the chambers...In the corridors...the walls were so made that there are perfectly rounded corners at every meeting of the walls...The rambling house stands on a small hill overlooking the quiet town of Guilford Center, a small community, even during the 1800s, of about fifteen buildings. The site of the structure is in an ideal place...these facts, plus the mineral springs, probably contributed greatly to the success of the development.

The popularity of other water cures in the state...may have contributed much to the development of the Mineral Springs in Guilford...No matter what caused it, the Guilford Mineral Springs Company was founded. The existence of mineral springs on the Houghton farm has been common knowledge for many years...James Dalton, Joseph Burnett, W. B. Potter, and John Knowlton bought the buildings and land on August 4, 1868...The company ...enlarged the grounds and built several new buildings, among them the spring house, bottling house, and pavilions and bridges near the springs. Trees were planted, drives were cleared, and the property became the most attractive in town. The springs house, bottling house and springs were all located about one-half mile from the central house, beside a winding brooklet...Although the cure was doubted by many citizens, the water must have had some effect on its users as indicated by the success of the company from 1868 to 1875...In treating the various patients...the treatment consisted of taking baths in the mineral water and drinking large quantities of the same...

Almost all the guests at the Mineral Springs Farm were accommodated in the spacious rooms of the huge, centrally-located inn. The cost was low for the stay..." (2)

* * *

1770s: <u>Stowell tavern</u>, Hezekiah Stowell; "...one of the most noted of all the many historic spots of old Guilford. This farm was (on lots)...whereon the old White Meeting House stood, about one half mile to the north, on the hill road between Guilford Center and East Guilford...probably settled (by Stowell) in 1772...Stowell's house was the rendezvous of the Guilford Yankees..." Stowell moved away in 1786.

1849:   --, N. Conant* (NEMU Dir); there is an N. Conant on the 1856 McClellan map;

1855: --, - Cobb;

1869: <u>Central House</u>, H. R. Chase* (Beers);

1870: <u>Central House (Mineral Springs House)</u>, H. R. Chase.

(84e) <u>Hale</u> (known locally as Hinesburg; had a PO from 1896-1903). No listings found.

(84f) <u>Packers Corners</u>.

c. 1784: <u>Packer Tavern</u>, --; probably built by James Packer, the family came to Guilford in 1774; a tavern as early as 1784, south central part of town, very close to the Massachusetts border; where the old county road from Guilford Center to Leyden intersects the town road from South Hollow to Green River. (2)

Note: the assistance of Mrs Virginia Fitch, Brattleboro, is gratefully acknowledged.

* * *

References

(1) Esther M. Swift, Vermont Place Names: Footprints of History (Brattleboro: Stephen Greene Pr., 1977).
(2) Broad Brook Grange, Guilford, Official History of Guilford, Vermont, 1678-1961 (Guilford: The Town, 1961).

* * *

(85) **Halifax** (Windham).

Includes two hamlets that had POs for a few years (Grove, 1884-1919; and Valley, 1899-1921) and one that didn't (Reid Hollow, in the northeastern part of the township) as well as West and South Halifax.

(85a) <u>Grove</u>. No listings found.

(85b) <u>Halifax</u> (Center).

Note: tavern licenses to Isaac Day, 1817, '20, '23; Benjamin Henry, 1820, '21, '23; and Samuel Goodnow, 1820-30, locations unknown;

c. 1770: a tavern (and store), --; now Crosier's Store, residence and antique shop (VDHP 1308-9); on the west side of the road at the intersection in Halifax village;

1911, '13: <u>Maplehurst Lodge</u>, -- (summers);

1915: as above, E. S. Niles; Niles was a dentist; the place deteriorated after Dr Niles gave it up, and was razed in the 1950s;

1920: as above, E. J. Niles;

1925: as above, J. F. R. Hanson.

(85c) <u>Reid Hollow</u>.

1869: a hotel, --* (Beers).

(85d) <u>South Halifax</u>.

1849:   Temperance House, James L. Stark (NEMU Dir); tavern license, 1830, '32, '33;

1856:   --, James L. Stark; Stark was a Yale graduate and a prominent citizen, died in 1868;

1870:   Stark's Hotel, Jed Stark (James L.'s son; also PM until 1888); this place was on Rte 112, just on the Vermont side of the state line; also known as the South Halifax Hotel; the Stark homestead dates from 1792;

* * *

"Stark's Tavern became famous as a hostelry throughout the area. The grounds were beautifully landscaped. The stage coach horses were sheltered here and it had quite a reputation as a mecca for eloping couples from Massachusetts and Vermont to come to be married here as the line went through the parlor and the couples would stand one in Vermont and the other in Massachusetts." As a matter of fact, when the property was accurately surveyed it was found to be entirely in Vermont. (Personal communication from Mrs Ada W. Wilcox, a daughter of the family who lived on the place after it closed; courtesy of Mrs Clara Barnard and the Halifax Historical Society).

* * *

1873, '75, '79, '80:   Stark's Hotel, Jed Stark.

Stark's Hotel, South Halifax (Bernice Barnett, Halifax)

(85e) Valley. No listings found.

(85f) West Halifax.

1901:   --, Noah Bate;

1908:   --, - Larrabee;

Note: the assistance of Mrs Clara Barnard and the Halifax Historical Society is gratefully acknowledged.

* * *

(86) **Hancock** (Addison).

(86a) Hancock.

270

Hancock was on the route of the Center Turnpike, finished in 1808 between Woodstock and Middlebury; it was also on an earlier north-south route along the valleys of the Tweed, White and Mad Rivers. A hotel at the intersection of Rtes 100 and 125 was in continuous use from at least 1814, when Charles Church came, until the 1960s; it was the central point of Church's stage operations (see below).

1808: first tavern, Joseph Butts; for 19 years; this place became the Green Mountain House (the "old hotel"); list of owners provided by Mrs Julia Kinsley, based on town records; Whittier et al., quoting from Zadock Thompson, has the initial date as 1808, but this seems to be when Esias Butts obtained the place and enlarged it (1); Esias was followed after 4 years by Nathan Dolbear, who kept it only 4 years and sold it back; Charles Church came in 1815, "in the hotel business for many years" (Child; actually 12 years); Church followed by Colonel John Hackett in 1827, for 21 years, until 1853; the ownership was shared when Col Hackett died, and changed hands frequently in complex ways until 1866, when it was acquired by John and Marietta Wright; Wright died in 1881, place run by his widow until 1892 (the Wright Hotel during this period); Arthur Miller and his wife then ran it as the Green Mountain House until 1907 (also listed as the Miller House), sold to Helen Richardson; William McCray, 1911, and the McCrays ran it for 12 years, until 1923; then Robert Groves, Rinaldo Whittier, and the Comes family in 1929; who ran it first as a hotel, later a store, until 1971. Now apartments above, shops below. This is VDHP 0108-1, #1.

(?): "Daniel Claflin commenced on the mountain farm, on the road to Middlebury, in a very early day, and kept a public house for many years, a really convenient place for travelers who had to pass over the mountain...from East Middlebury to Hancock. Mr Manning later owned it...still later it was called the Mt Vernon House, and was owned by the Turnpike Co. and operated by a Mr Packard" (Hemenway); however, according to ref 1, "another old history states that Mr Solomon Dunham also ran the Vernon House for the Turnpike Company. One oldtimer said that Mr Manning's tavern was on the right of the old road, and Mr Dunham's was just below him, on the left, about where the ski area is, and that there was considerable rivalry between the two." Building gone.

1812: Sprague Tavern, --; almanac, location unknown, probably Claflin's;

(?): an early tavern in the village, John Lord; later run by Dr Darius Smith in the house owned in 1988 by Mrs Rama Taylor;

(?): still another tavern, kept by Reuben Lamb (almanac, 1812), on the place later occupied by Solomon Dunham (see above); just below the present (i.e., 1964) Dan Dunham house;

1849: --, John Hackett (NEMU Dir);

1870: (a) Green Mountain House, John E. Wright;

Hancock Village, Showing the "Miller House" Hancock, Vt.   Stockwell Bros. Co. Series, Rights Reserved

Miller House, Hancock Village

1871:   (a) as above* (Beers);

1873, '75, '79, '80:   (a) as above;

1881, '83, '87, '90, '92:   (a) as above, Mrs E. C. Wright;

1881:   (a) as above, Mrs Etta C. Wright, corner of roads 5 and 10 (Child);

1895:   (a) as above, A. L. Miller;

1898:   (a) as above, C. B. Guptil;

1905:   (as) as above, A. L. Miller (Miller House); see photo, previous page;

1914:   no hotel on Sanborn map.

Note: the assistance of Mrs Julia Kinsley is gratefully acknowledged.

* * *

References

(1) Belva C. Whittier, et al., The Story of Hancock, Vermont, 1780-1964, (n.p., 1964).

* * *

(87) **Hardwick** (Caledonia).

"Probably no other town in Vermont has moved the name of its main village around as Hardwick has--one needs to have a schedule showing what post offices were open when, in order to be certain which village was called Hardwick at any given time." (1)

Settlement occurred in Hardwick in three areas in the early days: Hardwick Street, on the Bayley-Hazen road in the northeast corner of town; at Stevens Mills, or Stevensville, which became East Hardwick; and at Lamoilleville, or South Hardwick, which is present-day Hardwick. The 1858 Walling map shows these areas clearly. The first post office called Hardwick was in the Street area, in 1810; this place became North Hardwick postally for a brief period before being changed back to the (2nd) Hardwick (1846-49). The Stevens Mills area got a PO in 1846 (Stephens), which ultimately became East Hardwick. The Lamoilleville area got its PO (Lamoilville) in 1827; it became South Hardwick in 1842, and the (3rd) Hardwick in 1867.

(87a) East Hardwick (Stevens Mills, Stevensville, Stephens).

Settled by Samuel Stevens, who gave land for a temperance hotel which was known as the Montgomery Hotel in 1849 (see below).

Note: tavern licenses, Daniel French (1822-24) and Eph. Cushman, 1823, locations unknown;

1849:   (a) Montgomery Hotel, Harvey Montgomery; who built it on land donated by Samuel Stevens, kept it for 14 years as a temperance house; Montgomery was also PM, 1846-49, when the place was called Stephens;

1858:   (a) Hardwick Hotel, H. Montgomery* (Walling);

1870:   --, O. C. Osgood;

1873:   --, O. N. Burnham;

272

1875:   --, O. R. (?) Burnham* (Beers);

1879:   (a) East Hardwick Hotel, J. and A. F. Dow (same as Hardwick Hotel, above);

1880:   --, J. F. Dow;

1883:   (a) Hardwick Hotel, A. and C. R. Wicher;

1887:   (a) as above, C. Witcher (sp?);

1890:   (a) as above, Mrs A. Stone;

1892:   --, H. Stone;

1895:   --, S. Lafleur;

1898:   --, H. Bonett;

1901:   (a) East Hardwick Hotel, --;

1903:   Valley House, --; SBA guide, presumably same as above;

1905:   --, J. B. Fisk;

1915:   no hotel shown on the Sanborn map; the East Hardwick Hotel now a boarding-house.

(87b) Hardwick (Lamoilville, South Hardwick).

1858:   a hotel, A. S. and M. T. Whipple* (Walling);

1870:   --, G. Bill (sp?);

1870:   --, Bill Gilman (Vt Dir, presumably same person as above, with one of the names garbled);

1873:   (a) Hardwick Hotel, Drennan Brothers (Vt Dir; became the Centennial House, recently restored for offices and shops);

1875:   (a) as above, Drennan Brothers* (Beers);

1875:   --, J. S. and R. F. Drennan (according to Child,the Centennial House was built by J. Drennan in 1876;,but this date appears to be in error;

1879:   (a) Centennial House, E. Joslyn;

1880:   --, O. E. Joslyn;

1883:   (a) as above, C. W. Thurber;

1887:   (a) as above, Ira F. Batchelder; (b) Maple Park House, A. R. Pike (Main St, Child; building destroyed);

1890:   (b) as above, A. D. Hopkins;

1892:   (a) as above, S. A. Pierce; visible in 1892 birdseye view of the village (2); (b) as above;

1895:   (a) as above, I. F. Batchelder;

1898:   (a) as above, H. G. Spaulding* (Sanborn map);

1901:   (a) as above, George E. Cookin;

1905:   (a) as above, F. H. Daniels (shown as the <u>Hardwick Inn</u> on Sanborn, and in the 1903 SBA guide);

1911:   (a) as above, --;

1913, '15:   (a) <u>Hardwick Inn</u>, --; shown as the <u>New Hardwick Hotel</u>, W. H. Snow, on 1915 Sanborn; also shown on the 1912, '22 and '29 Sanborns); see photo;

1919:   (a) as above, --* (Sanborn; there is also a <u>Dew Drop Inn</u> at the southwest corner of Wolcott and Main Sts on this map, torn down by 1956);

1920:   (a) <u>New Hardwick Inn</u>, F. A. Worthen;

1925:   (a) <u>New Hardwick Hotel</u>, Eileen Benjamin; still standing.

New Hardwick Hotel, Hardwick, Vt.

New Hardwick Hotel

(87c) <u>Hardwick Street</u>.

(?):   a tavern, <u>Col Alpha Warner</u>; who came about 1790, settled on the Bayley-Hazen road (the "Street") and built a log tavern; torn down when he built a large tavern in 1799 (see below);

1799:   <u>Warner's Tavern</u>, Col Alpha Warner; tavern license, 1822-24; later the Delano mansion, still standing and known as the <u>Stage House</u>; the original tavern sign is in the possession of the present owner, and a copy of it hangs outside in the summers;

1849:   <u>Stage and Temperance House,</u> Alpha Warner (NEMU Dir);

(?):   according to the St Johnsbury Republican in 1895, Lewis H. Delano (who married two Warner daughters) kept a regular hotel for many years on Hardwick Street in a large mansion owned in 1895 by Mr J. R. Delano; Lewis H. Delano was the PM at the 1st Hardwick PO, from 1828-46; however, a member of the Greensboro Historical Society doubts that the Delanos continued the <u>Stage House</u> as an inn after Warner left, and there are no directory listings to support the St Johnsbury Republican.

(87d) <u>Mackville</u>.

There was once a hamlet a little south of present Hardwick known as Mackville, a possible location for the place mentioned below; this suggestion does not meet with the approval of a local historian, who says that 1795 was too early for Mackville.

1795: a hotel, <u>Capt John Bridgewater</u> (Bridgeman?); "in the south part of town" (St Johnsbury Republican, 1895);

References

(1) Esther M. Swift, Vermont Place Names: Footprints of History (Brattleboro: Stephen Greene Pr., 1977).
(2) J. Kevin Graffagnino, Vermont in the Victorian Age (Bennington: Vermont Heritage Press, 1985).

* * *

(88) **Hartford** (Windsor).

(88a) <u>Hartford</u>.

1794: <u>Leavitt's Inn</u>, Freegrace Leavitt; "at the center of the town"; VDHP 1408-20;

* * *

"The church or meeting house was nearby. On Sunday, between services, the men would wander over to the Inn for a bit of spirits. It is reported that many of them did not return for the afternoon services. During the War of 1812 Mr Leavitt operated a very successful distillery producing potato whiskey. From 1808 until 1819 proprietor's meetings were held at the Inn...The old Inn is still standing and is now a private dwelling" (i.e., 1974; ref 1).

* * *

"Prior to the completion of the Central Vermont railroad, the main route of travel between the eastern portion of Hartford and Woodstock passed directly by Leavitt's Inn. Mr Leavitt was...not long in learning the fact that a great majority of those who went to court at Woodstock to obtain justice, found themselves in the end, in the condition of the man who went for wool and returned home shorn. Mr Leavitt...hit upon a novel way of pointing a moral for all those who traveled to and from the county seat. On the sign board ...in front of his house, he caused to be painted two pictures. One represented a genteelly-dressed man mounted on a spirited-looking, finely caparisoned horse, on the road to Woodstock. Below this figure was the legend, 'I'm going to court!' The picture on the reverse side of the sign, represented a man returning from Woodstock, and in a pitiable plight. His face wore an expression of sullen despair; his hat was awry; his garments were threadbare.. Under this picture was the apt and instructive legend, 'I've been to court!' (2)

* * *

1795: an inn, <u>Samuel Tilden Jr</u>; "on the river road about four miles from White River Junction, and a few rods west of the present dwelling house of William Dutton" (i.e., 1889, ref 2); proprietor's meetings were held here until 1800; in another place, however, Tucker says this public house was in Hartford village on the south side of the river near the railroad station; (2)

1790: <u>Hazen's Tavern</u>, --; listed in the Vermont Almanac and Register as a tavern on the Windsor-St Johnsbury road (14 miles from <u>Lull's</u> in Hartland, 2 miles from <u>Bunton's</u> in Norwich, precise location unknown);

1801: a hotel, <u>Asa Richardson</u>; on the north side of the river in the village; sold to William Strong in 1812; listed as <u>Richardson's</u> in almanacs, 1815, '16;

1812: --, William Strong; sold to Noah Ashley in 1815, and the place was sold twice more within the year, to Consider Bardwell and Theodore Cooley; "on the old Woodstock road west of the James Udall place"; (2)

1820: --, George and Bani Udall; bought this place, and Bani moved it to the site of what became the <u>Pease Hotel</u> (also known as the <u>White River Hotel</u>). The place changed hands twice more and was sold to Luther Pease in 1848;

1848: <u>Pease Hotel</u> (<u>White River Hotel</u>), Luther Pease; he died in 1876, and the hotel became the property of Horace C. Pease, then Charles W. Pease; it burned on January 24, 1889, and while a new hotel was under construction, Pease used his home on School St as a hotel (ref 1; also photos of the old <u>Pease Hotel</u>, the ruins after the fire, and the new hotel); see photo;

White River Hotel (probable; William Orcutt stereo)

1849: (a) <u>White River Hotel</u>, N. M. Thompson (NEMU Dir);

1855: (a) as above, L. Pease;

1869, '72:   (a) as above, L. Pease and Son* (Beers);

1870, '73, '75, '80, '87:   (a) as above, Charles W. Pease;

1878: (a) as above; --, G. W. Cone;

1879: (a) as above, H. E. Harris (Vt Dir);

1883: (a) <u>Pease's Hotel</u> (<u>White River Hotel</u>), C. W. Pease;

1887: (a) as above, M. S. Davis (Vt Dir);

1893: (b) <u>New Pease Hotel</u>, Allen L. Pease; leased to various managers; sold in 1908 to Addison Ely, who changed the name to the <u>White River Tavern</u> and went bankrupt in 1912; building razed in 1919; see photo, next page;

1901: (b) as above, W. H. Flint;

1902: (b) as above, A. H. Silver;

1905: (b) as above, M. R. Courser;

1908: <u>Hartford Inn</u>, -- (probably <u>White River Tavern</u>);

1911, '13, '15, '20:   <u>White River Tavern</u>, --; (W. E. Coleman, 1916 VPB);

(88b) Quechee.

c. 1783:   Burch's Inn, Benjamin Burch (or Burtch); probably near Quechee village, but location uncertain; (2)

(?):   "On the site of Channing William's store in Quechee village, there once stood a hotel, which was destroyed by fire in --. Among the proprietors of this hotel were George Udall, the builder of the house together with a store, Daniel Cushing (1838), William E. Eastman (1839), Lester Richardson (1841);" (2)

White River Tavern

1883:   --, Frank J. Osmer.

(88c) West Hartford.

c. 1790:   a hotel, Francis W. Savage; built, and kept by him until his death in 1817;

1838:   a hotel, Alvan Tucker; kept until 1840, then a series of proprietors: Samuel C. Sawyer, C. C. Rowell, Stephen S. Downer, James Merchant, Joseph Morill, Albert E. Williamson, Charles H. Thurston, Harry M. Cutting, Alpheus Kempton, and finally Frank Wheeler, who made improvements in 1888; it burned in 1924. This place was "on the south side of the highway, opposite F. F. Holt's store (i.e., 1889)...one of the oldest houses in the town. It was built for a brewery..."; (2)

1849:   --, Christopher C. Rowell (NEMU Dir);

1855:   --, A. E. Williamson* (Hosea Doten map);

1855, '56:   --, Albert Williamson;

1870:   West Hartford House, C. H. Thurston;

1872, '75, '78, '80:   Union House, H. M. Cutting;

1901, '02:   Wheeler House, F. P. Wheeler;

1913:   --, Mrs F. P. Wheeler.

(88d) White River Junction.

This community sprang up when the railroads came through, three of them intersecting here. It didn't get a post office until 1850, and grew slowly until 1867, when a new highway bridge was built across the White River.

1811:   a hotel, <u>Consider Bardwell</u>; "on the site of the elegant mansion recently erected...by William Roberts, Esquire, there once stood a hotel..." (2); sold to Noah Ashley in 1815, and by him to Elias Lyman in 1817; it is odd that Consider Bardwell and Noah Ashley were both also involved in buying and selling the inn in Hartford at about this same time; later proprietors were Luther Delano and Ahira Gilbert (1825 for the latter);

* * *

"Consider Bardwell was an eccentric man, irascible in temper...But, though prone to quarrel, he loved a good joke...and seldom let slip an opportunity to indulge this propensity. On one occasion, after an altercation with one of his customers, over their cups, they mutually agreed to settle their differences by a duel with shotguns. At the appointed hour his adversary put in his appearance, armed with a shotgun. Being busily engaged... Bardwell said to the man: 'Tom, I'll tell you what I'll do; you go out and set up a board about my size, and shoot at it, and if you hit it, I'll acknowledge myself killed and treat the crowd.' This ludicrous proposition had the effect of oil upon troubled waters, and ended the farce, much to the satisfaction of the crowd who drank all round at the expense of both parties to the quarrel." (2)

* * *

1850:   1st <u>Junction House</u> (first), Col Samuel Nutt;

* * *

Nutt was one of White River Junction's outstanding personalities. He left home at an early age, saved his money, and became a boatman on the Connecticut River. He was an early subscriber to the Vermont Central Railroad, which operated near one of his farms, and saw the need for public accommodation in White River Junction. Accordingly, he bought the Grafton House in Enfield, New Hampshire, had it torn down and moved to White River Junction, and opened it as the <u>Junction House</u> in 1850 (photo, ref 1). He also became White River Junction's first postmaster that year (photo, ref 1) with the office in his house next to the hotel. Nutt died in 1871.

* * *

c. 1852:   a hotel, <u>Elizur Southworth</u>; on the site occupied by N. P. Wheeler's store in 1869; bought by John P. Williams in 1853, sold to one of the Barrons in 1854; soon moved and united with the <u>Junction House</u>.

* * *

"On the 10th of August, 1878, this hotel was entirely destroyed by fire. It was a den of wickedness and its destruction should have been regarded by the senior proprietor thereof as the natural sequence of the unrestricted looseness that characterized his system of running this public house." (These strong words from William H. Tucker, ref 2; the proprietors at the time were A. T. and O. F. Barron, according to Walton.)

* * *

1854:   (a) <u>Junction House</u> (1st), sold to Isaac B. Culver;

1855:   <u>Hartford House</u>, --* (Hosea Doten map); (a) <u>Junction House</u>, --* (Hosea Doten);

1855, '56:   --, Samuel Nutt;

1869:   (a) as above, A. T. and O. F. Barron* (Beers); (purchased by them in 1859);

1870, '72, '75, '78:   (a) as above;

1879:   (a) Junction House (1st), rebuilt after the fire by Ballard and Andrews; the new hotel (2nd Junction House) had 200 rooms; the proprietors since then include Charles Ballard; Van Ness Spaulding; and Lavender and Eddy; in 1889; see photo, Chapter IV;

The new Junction House was the center of activity in the town, noted for its fine service and hospitality. Gate's Opera House stood next door. In its peak years, the hotel accommodated more than 38,000 guests. In the late winter of 1920, Lillian Gish appeared in White River Junction to film the ice scenes for the movie "Way Down East."

* * *

1880s: a building erected in this decade as the Smith-Bagley Block, later the Waverly House, the American House, the Adams House, and Teddy's Hotel; burned in 1849;

1879:   Grover House, A. J. Grover; (a) as above;

1883:   (b) 2nd Junction House, Charles Ballard (Child);

1887:   (b) as above, S. E. Nutting;

1892:   (b) as above, N. S. Eddy;

1895:   (b) as above, St George Waverley; (c) Maple Tree Inn, --;

1897:   (b) as above, --; (c) as above; (d) American House, --;

1901, '05:   (b) as above, Gibbs and Wheeler;

1901:   (b) 2nd Junction House, William Barron; sold to Lyman Gibbs and Nathaniel Wheeler, and flourished for years; became the Hotel Coolidge in 1924;

1908:   (b) as above, --;

1911:   (b) as above, Gibbs and Wheeler; (d) as above, J. W. Burton;

1913, '15:   (b) as above, --; (d) as above, --;

1916:   (b) as above, Gibbs and Wheeler; (d) as above, Angus McDonald (VPB);

1920:   (b) as above, --; (d) as above, --;

1925:   (b) Hotel Coolidge, --; Adams House, --; (listed until c. 1935); Smith House --;

1925:   (b) Hotel Coolidge, Nathaniel P. Wheeler; destroyed in White River Junction's worst fire on Jan 29, 1925 (photos, ref 1); rebuilt as the New Hotel Coolidge, and opened in the summer of 1925 as a 2-story building; 2 towers and a third floor were added later. The place had 160 rooms. This is building #4 in the White River Junction Historic District, VDHP 1408-30; still operating in 1986.

(88e) Wilder (Olcott until 1897). No listings found.

(88f) Outside the Villages.

(?):   "Zebulon Delano kept a hotel for a number of years at the junction of the White River turnpike and the Jericho road, where Fred Huse resides" (i.e., 1889, ref 2);

(?):   "Joshua Ryder kept a hotel two miles from White River village on the hill road to

Windsor"; (2)

Note: the assistance of Mr Cameron Clifford, West Hartford, is gratefully acknowledged.

* * *

References

(1) John W. St Croix, Historical Highlights of the Town of Hartford, Vermont, 1761-1974, 2nd edition (Hartford: Imperial, 1974).

(2) William H. Tucker, History of Hartford, Vermont (Burlington: Free Pr., 1889).

(3) John W. St Croix, An Album of the Town of Hartford, Vermont, 1761-1969, (White River Jct: Right Pr., 1969).

* * *

(89) **Hartland** (Windsor).

(89a) Hartland. (known locally as Hartland Three Corners at one time).

(?): first tavern, Timothy Lull Sr; first settler, he came in 1763; near the middle of the present village; listed in the Vermont Almanac and Register, 1796, as a tavern on the Rutland-Windsor road, and the Windsor-St Johnsbury road; almanac listings until 1816;

1807: (a) Pavilion Hotel, Lyman Childs; almanacs, 1807-29;

* * *

Built on land deeded to Isaac Stevens in 1774, no firm date for its construction; but Atwood says this place (known also at various times as Stevens' Hotel, Merritt's Pavilion and the Hotel Hartland) was built by Isaac Stevens "around 1775, probably later than that date." (1) (The VDHP says c. 1795). It stood in the center of the village until replaced by Damon Hall in 1914 (see photo). At one time it housed the post office, store, meeting-house and caucus rooms, the court house, dining hall and dance hall. It had a spring floor for dancing. The original main hall was divided into bedrooms by swinging partitions when the place was remodeled in 1830, and these could be pushed back to make a hall when needed. "While the hotel served visiting merchants and teamsters bringing goods from Boston, two barns were needed to stable the six and eight horse teams" (ref 2; also photo);

* * *

"I remember when the stage with from four to six horses, would come thundering into town with a toot of the horn and a crack of the whiplash and pull up to Merritt's Pavilion (i.e., Stevens Hotel, the Pavilion Hotel), change horses, all passengers go into the bar-room and get a good drink of Santa Cruz rum and then continue the journey." (3)

Note: almanacs also list a Webster Tavern (1813, '16) and a Bates Tavern (1812), locations unknown;

1849: (a) Pavilion House, Lewis Merritt (NEMU Dir); --, Mrs M. Gilson (NEMU Dir);

1855: --, D. H. Summer* (Hosea Doten; close to the railroad east of the village; presumably this is the Central Railroad House (see below);

1856: --, George M. Mason;

1869: (a) Pavilion Hotel, --* (Beers; not named as such on the map, but shown in the village); (b) Central Railroad House, D. F. Alexander* (Beers; shown in the Business Directory portion); (see photo, end of Chapter I);

1870: (a) as above, B. F. Hoisington; (b) as above;

1872: (b) as above (Vt Dir);

1873: (b) Railroad House, Frank Dunbar;

1875, '78: (a) as above, R. L. Britton; (b) as above, George Chatfield;

1879: (a) Pavilion House, R. L. Britten; (b) Railroad House, - Cummings;

1880: (a) as above; (b) as above, --;

1883: (a) as above, W. R. Sturtevant;

1887: (a) Pavilion Hotel, J. W. Reed;

1890: (a) as above;

1901: (a) Hotel Hartland, Bennett and Eldridge (Vt Dir);

1902: Snow's Hotel, J. H. Snow; (a) Hartland Hotel, Bennett and Eldridge (same as Pavilion); Three Pines Inn , F. B. Daniels (all listed in the CVRR guide);

1905, '08: (a) Hotel Hartland, C. B. Wheeler; replaced by Damon Hall in 1914;

1911, '13, '15: Hotel Three Pines, C. A. Daniels; building still standing on the Quechee Road;

1925: The Maples, --* (Sanborn).

(89b) Hartland Four Corners.

1796: Page tavern, --; listed in the Vermont Almanac and Register as a tavern on the Windsor-Burlington road;

c. 1800: "...an old brick tavern near the present hall and post office--in fact the hall is said to have been part of the old tavern" (1); this is the Gilson Tavern, see below); "In 1822 there was a score of buildings in this village, among them four taverns..." (a quotation ascribed to one Miss Sturtevant in ref 1; "The Gilson Tavern stood on the southwest corner of the crossroads and its wing is the present town hall...built about 1800, and taken down in the early 50s" (i.e., 1850s);

1807: "...no buildings except the tavern, which stood on the southeast corner (a conflict here with Atwood, ref 1, above) a gambrel-roofed house occupied by Dr Friend Sturtevant"; (2)

(?): "the house now (i.e., 1948) owned by Warren Field was also once a tavern many years ago."

(89c) North Hartland. (changed to Evarts, 1909-11, then back again).

1849: Quechee House, William Minor (NEMU Dir);

1914: no hotel on the Sanborn map.

(89d) Outside the villages.

<u>Fieldville</u>. There is a photo in ref 2 of a "Spring House" in this hamlet; "around 1860 there were many Spiritualists who 'took the water' here; sometimes religious services were held, attended by as many as 200 people." The building shown may have served as a hotel.

(?):   the <u>Burk Stand</u>, --; on the county road to Woodstock, now (i.e., 1976) the home of John W. Samuel; photo, ref 2;

(?):   a public house, <u>Alexander Campbell</u>; on the road over Hartland Hill (photo, ref 2); buildings and road now gone, this place was at one time the home of Edgar Spear.

Note: the assistance of Mr Frank L. Motschman is gratefully acknowledged

* * *

References

(1) Howland F. Atwood, "Notes for a history of Hartland," Vermont Quarterly <u>16</u> (July 1948): 96-123.
(2) Hartland--The Way It Was, 1761-1976 (n.p, 1976?).
(3) Nancy Darling, "History and Anniversary of Hartland," Vermonter <u>18</u> (November 1913): 221-234; and December 1913: 241-256.

* * *

(90) **Highgate** (Franklin).

(90a) <u>East Highgate</u> (Powell's Falls until 1832).

(?):   --, James Cutler; who used his house as a tavern (Hemenway, 1871);

1857:   --, A. H. Spear* (Walling; a hotel on this site since at least 1857, but not clear if the present building (VDHP 0609-16) is that building);

1871:   --, J. L. Gibbs* (Beers; same site as in 1857);

1892:   --, A. A. Bates;

1905, '13, '15: --, Richard Bridge;

1915:   no hotel on Sanborn map.

(90b) <u>Highgate</u> (became Highgate Falls in 1936).

Note: tavern licenses to the following, locations unknown: Arwin P. Herrick, 1817, '20; Harvey Dibble, Samuel Keys, 1815; Widow Charlotte Dibble, 1817, '19; Newcomb Lampkins, 1819; Charles Hull, John Averill, 1818; Boardman and Dixon, 1818; Smith Farrand, 1833, '36; Ebenezer Stockwell, 1820-22; Edmond Wait, 1820, '22; Andrew Clowe, 1822, '24; E. A.(?) Haskins, Olive Herrick, 1824; Dewey and Co, 1825; Thomas Webster, 1827; Stephen P. Hollenbeck, 1829; Peter Shetles, 1829, '30, '36; Henry Morton (Martin?), 1830, '32; Abel Drury, 1818, '19, '22;

(?):   --, F. N. Johnson; "tavern-keeper at the old stand on the north bank of the river" (Hemenway, 1871); location unknown, apparently by the bridge linking Highgate and Highgate Center across the Missisquoi River;

1849:   --, C. R. and H. Jenison (sic) (NEMU Dir); built c. 1830, probably by Israel Jenison; Jenison family ran this place as the <u>Champlain House</u> for visitors to the local mineral springs (Charles H. Jennison has a tavern license, 1826-28 and 1830-36); Horace Greeley stopped here; VDHP 0609-28, at the southeast corner of Main and Spring Sts, owned by Maynard Beyor in 1982;

Maynard Beyor in 1982;

1855, '56:   --, G. Cursow (sp?);

1857:   --, S. Casson* (Walling);

1870:   (a) <u>Green Mountain House</u>, --; (see photo); (b) <u>Champlain House</u>, Jed P. Clark;

1871:   (a) as above, Johnson and Briggs* (Beers); (b) <u>Champlain House</u>, I. S. Jenison* (Beers);

1873:   (a) as above, C. Johnson; (b) as above, J. Osborne;

1875:   (a) as above, F. N. Johnson;

1878, '80:   (a) as above, Byron Tuller (Fuller in Vt Dir);

(?):   <u>Manor Mayfair</u>, --;

1911:   --, Richard Bridge; <u>The Manor</u> is listed until at least 1955;

1915:   two "old hotel" buildings, not operating, on the Sanborn map

Green Mountain House (Special Collections, UVM)

(90c) <u>Highgate Center</u>.

1833-38:   <u>Stinehour Hotel</u>, Henry Stinehour; a tanner who gave it up (Child) and established this place at the northeast corner of present Rte 78 and St Armand St; VDHP 0609-93, vacant in 1982;

1849:   --, H. Stinehour (NEMU Dir);

1855, '56:   --, H. Stinehour;

1857:   --, H. Stinehour* (Walling);

1870, '71, '75, '80, '82, '87:   (a) Stinehour House, the Misses Stinehour* (C. C. and F. M. Stinehour, in Vt Dir; Beers, 1871); see photo;

1887:   (b) Commercial House, William H. Mitchell;

1892, '95:   (b) Commercial House, Arthur Sheltus (Philip Shelton in Aldrich; (1)

1898, 1901, '05, '11, '13, '15:   (b) as above, Mrs Abbie L. Redding (shown on the 1915 Sanborn);

1920:   (b) as above, R. S. Grieb;

1925:   --, Mrs Grace Fisher.

Stinehour House (St Albans Historical Society)

(90d) Highgate Springs.

c. 1835:   (a) Franklin Hotel, S. S. and S. W. Keyes; "built nearly 50 years ago" (i.e., 50 years before 1882, Child); sold to Judson L. Scott in 1868, who kept it as a summer resort about 9 years; sold to an outside group, leased back to Mr Scott; "it has, in connection with the cottages adjoining it, accommodations for 125 people" (Child); see below;

* * *

According to Florence M. Beebe, it was built about 1818 by the Keyes brothers; owned by the Averill family in 1861, who sold to Judson L. Scott about 1868.

"The spring of mineral water, having valuable medicinal qualities, has attracted thousands of guests to come here for their health from distant places; this is enclosed in a small house a short distance from the hotel, and was originally a deer-lick. Before the days of the auto many hundreds of excursionists would come to Highgate Springs by train for a day's outing as these grounds were fitted up for recreation with swings, board walks, and pavilion for dancing."

1857:   (a) <u>Franklin House</u>, F. N. Johnson* (Walling);

1871:   (a) as above, L. S. and J. L. Scott* (Beers);

1875, '80:   (a) as above;

1882, '87, '92, '95:   (a) as above, J. L. Scott (also PM, 1869-95 and 1901);

1902:   (a) as above; <u>Park View Cottage</u>, E. H. Warner;

1898, 1905:   (a) <u>Franklin House</u>, --; see photo;

Franklin House

1908:   (a) as above, --; (b) <u>Lakeside</u>, --;

1911:   (a) as above, Frank Cadorette;

1913, '20:   (a) as above, Frank Cadorette; (b) as above, --; <u>Lake View House</u>, --;

1916:   (a) as above; (b) as above, D. M. Hatch; <u>Lakeview House</u>, E. A. Platt; (all VPB);

1925:   (a) as above; (b) as above; <u>Lake View House</u>, --; see photo, next page;

(?):   <u>Highgate Springs Hotel</u>, --; unidentified;

1936:   (a) as above, --* (Sanborn); closed for two years during World War II; the <u>Franklin House</u>, operating in its later days as part of the Tyler and Wriston Place, and then the Tyler Place, burned on September 4, 1974, just after the season had ended. Rebuilt on a different site.

(90e) <u>Saxes Mills</u>.

The first settlements were in the northwest part of the township, including an area known as Saxe's Mills; there was a post office here from 1832-58.

1801:   first tavern (and store), <u>Matthew Godfrey</u> and <u>Peter Saxe</u>.

* * *

<u>References</u>

(1) Lewis C. Aldrich, History of Franklin and Grand Isle Counties, Vermont (Syracuse: D. Mason, 1891).
(2) Florence M. Beebe, "The Franklin House," Vermonter <u>46</u> (May 1941): 113.

* * *

Lake View House (Jim Murphy, George Gilbert collection)

* * *

(91) **Hinesburg** (Chittenden).

(91a) <u>Hinesburg</u>.

1794:   a tavern, <u>Elijah Peck</u>; on the site now occupied by Lantman's store; site of the <u>Hinesburg Hotel</u> (see below); first 2-story building in town; according to Carpenter, it was built in 1788; (1)

(?):   an inn, --; built by Jedediah Boynton in 1825, and used as an inn; VDHP 0407-18, #8, the Russell home in 1977, a going farm;

1849:   <u>Burrett's Hotel</u>, Andrew Burrett (NEMU Dir);

1855:   --, L. C. Ray;

1856:   --, R. W. Post;

1857:   --, R. W. Post* (Walling);

1860:   (a) <u>Hinesburg Hotel</u>, Royal Wright Post; built by him on the site of the original tavern, a 3-story frame building; (see photo; also, photo, ref 2); frequent ownership changes, including Nathaniel Miles, Baldwin, Crandall, Lewis and Ray (Lewis Ray, according to Rann (3); probably the L. C. Ray listed for 1855) and Reuben Wickware;

Hinesburg Inn (Special Collections, UVM)

1869:   (a) <u>Wickware Hotel</u>, Reuben Wickware* (Beers; same site as above);

1870:   (a) as above (Vt Dir);

c. 1870:   an inn, --; on Baldwin Rd a little west of Hinesburg; VDHP 0407-19, the Eddy farm in 1977;

1870:   (a) <u>Hinesburg Hotel</u>, George W. Flanagan;

* * *

"His tenure was notable for the dances held on the third floor, so popular that people drove out from Burlington to attend. For these galas, Flanagan hired professional musicians, printed programs for the guests and served a supper at midnight, ending another night of "The Portland Fancy" and other popular contras and square dances." (2) Flanagan was still manager in 1886; later owners included Carpenter, Degree, Parker and Palmer. Converted to a store by William E. Lantman in 1926, still in use in 1977; this is VDHP 0407-18, #10.

* * *

1872, '75, '78, '80:   (a) <u>Flanagan's Hotel</u>, H. C. and George W. Flanagan;

1882:   (a) <u>Hinesburg Hotel</u>, George W. Flanagan (Child);

1887, '92:   (a) as above;

1895, '98:   (a) <u>Carpenter House</u>, C. J. Carpenter (same place); also in 1897 Rutland Railroad guide;

1901:   <u>Parker House</u>, F. C. and F. S. Parker;

1905:   <u>Palmer House</u>, H. P. Palmer;

1908:   --, - Carpenter;

1915:   store building, labeled "formerly old hotel," on Sanborn map; this is in disagreement with the date of conversion of the hotel to the store cited above.

(91b) <u>South Hinesburg</u>.

c. 1793:   a tavern, <u>Epaphras Hull</u>; tavern license, 1821; on the site occupied by Charles Wright in 1886; described as being "one mile north of the lower village," which probably refers to South Hinesburg; Hull committed suicide, and was buried in a roadside lot on his land, according to Carpenter. with a marble marker which can be seen from the road; (1)

1825:   a tavern, <u>Robert Beach</u>; "in the south part of town where Edgar Degree now lives" (i.e., 1886), location unknown.

* * *

References

(1) Leonard E. Carpenter, Hinesburg, Vermont, from 1762 (Burlington: Sheldon Pr., 1961).
(2) Lilian B. Carlisle, ed., Look Around Chittenden County (Burlington: Chittenden County Historical Soc., 1976).
(3) William S. Rann, History of Chittenden County, Vermont (Syracuse: D. Mason, 1886).

* * *

(92) **Holland** (Orleans).

(92a) <u>Holland</u>.

1853:   town records indicate that George Davis was licensed as an inn-keeper. (1) The building still stands, at the intersection of roads 32 and 33 in the southwest corner of town, according to long-time residents; used now as a summer home.

(92b) <u>Tice</u>, and (92c) <u>West Holland</u>. No listings found.

Note: the assistance of Evelyn S. Page, town clerk, is gratefully acknowledged.

* * *

References

(1) Ella Farrow, History of Holland (Burlington: Queen City Pr., 1979).

* * *

(93) **Hubbardton** (Rutland).

Includes the northern end of Lake Bomoseen and the southern half of Lake Hortonia.

(93a) <u>East Hubbardton</u>.   PO, 1855-1907; no listings found.

(93b) <u>Hortonia</u>. Hortonville until 1963, on Lake Hortonia; Hortonville had a post office from 1858-1913, Hortonia never had one.

c. 1810:   a tavern, <u>Daniel Horton</u>; on present Route 144, just west of the village; shown as A. Gibbs on 1869 Beers; Gibbs bought the place in 1855; originally VDHP 1108-1, but removed from register because of alterations.

(93c) <u>Hubbardton</u>.

(?):   a tavern, <u>Capt Reuben Webb</u> (tavern license, 1821-23; the village blacksmith; in a house occupied by Hiram Linsley c. 1886 (1); later involved in alleged violations of the 1851 prohibition law, which led him to leave town at an advanced age;

1811: the "old Dewey stand," first operated by Daniel Meeker, who died in 1821 (almanac, 1812); Hemenway gives no date for the opening of this place, but Meeker was PM from 1811-22, and Hubbardton's PO opened in 1811, so the tavern was open by 1811 at least;

* * *

"Building of a turnpike from the present site of Hyde's Hotel in Sudbury to Castleton, and so on, opened a thoroughfare to Troy, etc" (Hemenway; this was the direct mail and stage route from Troy to Burlington, passing through Hubbardton). The coming of the Rutland and Burlington Railroad (in the early 1850s) "turned all travel from this route"; people were isolated, three post offices, some getting mail but once a week, superseded the one kept before, "time out of mind," at the old Dewey stand." (Hemenway).

* * *

1821: Dewey Stand, Ebenezer B. Dewey; tavern license, 1822, '23; Dewey was Meeker's son-in-law, succeeded him in the tavern, which he kept until 1848, when he went west; frequent changes since; Dewey was also PM, 1822-31 and 1838-48, so the place was a tavern PO through most, if not all, of its early existence;

1849: --, A. Walker (NEMU Dir);

1856: --, M. J. Walker;

1869: a hotel, M. J. Webster* (Beers);

1870, '72, '75: --, Martin J. Webster;

1879: Howard House, Z. H. Howard;

1879, '81, '83, '90: Howard House, Z. H. Howard (Child, 1881);

1903: Mott House, -- (SBA guide).

* * *

(94) **Huntington** (Chittenden).

(94a) Hanksville.

(?): a tavern, John Derby; "at the south end of town, long discontinued" (Hemenway; location unknown, but it was probably near present day Hanksville).

(94b) Huntington ("north village.")

1826: (a) Green Mountain House, Gordon Taylor; opened this year (1); first tavern in the north village, enlarged in 1840, became the Huntington House (the two names seem to have been used interchangeably). Landlords who followed included Sanford Eddy, Alexander Ferguson, Jonathan Dike, Charles Lovekin, John Cook, Hiram Cook, Truman Wood, James Wood, Daniel Hill, Ansel Eddy, Solomon Johns, Edward Irish, Melvin Heath, and the "present proprietor," Edmond T. Collins, who took over in 1865 (i.e., 1886, ref 2);

1849: --, Truman J. Wood (NEMU Dir);

1855, '56: --, John Derby (but see entry under Hanksville); --, John Cook;

1869: (a) Huntington House, Edmond T. Collins* (Beers);

1870, '75, '78, '80, '87, '92:   (a) as above;

1882:   (a) Green Mountain House, E. T. Collins (Child, same place);

1895, '98, 1905, '08, '11, '13, '15:   (a) as above, E. A. Fuller (Fuller House in Vt Dir, 1902);

1916:   (a) as above, Norman A. Jones (VPB);

1920:   (a) Green Mountain Inn, E. A. Fuller (photo, ref 1; razed in 1940); Riverside Inn, Jennie B. Sweet;

1925:   Riverside Inn, Jennie B. Sweet; listed in 1935, not in 1940; now a private home, "just before the iron bridge to Bridge St."

(94c) Huntington Center ("south village"; includes Camel's Hump).

c. 1800:   first tavern, Jabez Fargo; tavern license, 1820, '21; in his new frame house. Fargo died in 1827.

Note: This place was in the east central part of town (Hemenway), and the first PO was also here, with Fargo as PM, according to Hemenway, but there is a conflict here with the official records. According to Slawson, Huntington didn't get a PO until 1827 (Huntington Center not until 1861, ref 3); but the Post Office Department records show Jabez Fargo as PM from 1805-27. Hemenway says the office was briefly discontinued (perhaps in 1827, when Fargo died), re-opened at the "south village" (probably Huntington Center) and moved to the "north village" in 1829;

1828:   (a) Camel's Hump Inn, Benjamin Allen; opened this year (1); sold to John Derby in 1839, and to Abel Turner in 1843; then Joseph Rounds, Gershom Conger (for 9 years), and George Conger (1 year); not to be confused with the Camel's Hump Summit House;

1869:   (a) as above, A. McGee* (Beers);

1870:   (a) as above;

1875, '78, '80, '82:   (a) as above, Gershom Conger;

1887, '92:   (a) as above, M. J. Ellis;

1895, 1902:   (a) as above, R. L. Delong;

1905, '08:   (a) as above, Thomas Dupont (photo, ref 1); the building was razed about 1943.

Note: The assistance of Lorraine J. Jones, Huntington Historical Society, is gratefully acknowledged.

* * *

References

(1) Bertha B. Hansen, Huntington, Vermont, 1786-1976, Olga M. Hallock, ed. (n.p., 1976?).
(2) William S. Rann, History of Chittenden County, Vermont (Syracuse: D. Mason, 1886).
(3) George C. Slawson, The Postal History of Vermont (N.Y.: Collector's Club, 1969).

* * *

(95) **Hyde Park** (Lamoille).

(95a) <u>Centerville</u> (PO, 1895-1903), and (95b) <u>Garfield</u> (PO, 1890-1903). No listings found.

(95c) <u>Hyde Park</u>. Became the shire town for Lamoille County in 1836, obviously beneficial to innkeepers.

c. 1808: a tavern, <u>John McDaniel</u>; the first settler; "on the Torence Finnegan place, a mile and a half down the Lamoille towards Johnson" (Hemenway); tavern license, 1822, and in 1824, '28, '29 to McDaniel and Taylor; McDaniel came in 1787, according to Child;

Note: tavern licenses to Hiram Hyde, 1824; Breed Noyes and Co, 1826-30; Gamaliel Taylor, 1826; and Daniel and Taylor, 1825, locations unknown;

1840: 3 hotels in Hyde Park (Zadock Thompson);

1849: --, W. Matthews; --, J. Perkins; --, H. S. Kelsey; (a) <u>Dutton's Hotel</u>, Thomas Dutton (all NEMU Dir; <u>Dutton's</u> probably became the <u>Village Hotel</u>, below);

1859: (a) --, T. Dutton* (Walling); (b) <u>American House</u>, Dutton and Hyde* (Walling; but W. P. Keeler is listed as proprietor in the Business Directory part of Walling);

* * *

There were two substantial hotels in Hyde Park for some time, from at least 1859 until the 1890s, but it is difficult to sort them out unambiguously. The older of the two was built in the early 1830s, at the east end of Main St (1) and is probably the one shown on the 1859 Walling as T. Dutton's hotel; this is also probably the one that was called the <u>Village Hotel</u> in the 1860s. The newer one was built in 1861 by H. F. Keeler and called the <u>American House</u>, according to the town history. (1) It was built in 1858, according to Child, which seems a better date since the 1859 Walling map shows a second hotel in Hyde Park (also at the east end of Main St, but on the north side of the street) labeled the <u>American Hotel</u>. It seems likely that this place was built a few years earlier than the town history indicates, although it is possible, of course, that there was an earlier place with the same name. The <u>American House</u> passed through a long series of owners, was burned and rebuilt, and was known as the <u>Hotel Phoenix</u> and the <u>Hyde Park Inn</u> at various points in its career.

Later proprietors included Soshina and John Childs; L. N. Noyes; Dr Randall (presumably C. F. Randall, listed in Walton as the proprietor in the 1880s); Waterman and Libbey, 1868; J. J. Nesmith, 1869; and E. B. Sawyer, 1871.

There was a disastrous fire in Hyde Park in 1910 that destroyed 20 or so buildings in the center of town.

* * *

1870: (a) <u>Village Hotel</u>, Nehemiah Waterman; (b) <u>American House</u>, J. L. Nesmith;

1873: (b) as above, E. B. Sawyer;

1875: (a) as above, J. F. Kelley; (b) as above;

1879: (b) <u>American House</u>, J. F. Kelley* (Beers);

1880, '83, '87, '90: (b) as above, C. F. Randall; this place burned in 1891, and was rebuilt; sold to N. Keeler, who named it the <u>Hotel Phoenix</u>; see photo; sold again, became the <u>Hyde Park Inn</u>; later owners were Charles Savery, Richard Grant, and the Maust family in 1926; it was a furniture store and apartment building in 1976;

1888:   Hyde Park Inn, C. E. Savery (Boston and Maine guide);

1892, '95, '98: (b) Phoenix House/Hotel Phoenix, F. N. Keeler* (Sanborn map for 1896, 1909);

1901:   (b) as above, William Emery (C. H. Crane in Vt Dir);

Hotel Phoenix (Vermont Historical Society)

1905, '08:   (b) as above, A. G. Spicer;

1911:   (b) as above, --;

1913:   (b) Hyde Park Inn, -- (same place);

1915, '16:   (b) as above, Charles E. Savery;

1920:   (b) as above;

1922:   (b) as above, --* (Sanborn);

1925:   (b) as above, R. W. Grant; listed until at least 1940.

(95d) North Hyde Park.

1840:   a hotel, David Holton; an original settler (c. 1815), he built this place at a later date, used it for six or seven years as a hotel (Hemenway); became the Valley Hotel;

1870:   (a) Union House, --; Walton consistently lists the Union House as being in North Hyde Park, but the Vt Dir lists it as being in Hyde Park in 1870 and 1873; this ambiguity has not been resolved;

1873:   (a) as above, D. Randall; (b) Valley Hotel, Poteus (Porter?) Butts (Vt Dir; this is VDHP 0805-23, #26);

1875:   --, L. P. Butts;

1878:   (b) Valley House, L. P. Butts* (Beers);

1880:   (a) as above, J. F. Kelley; (b) as above;

1883, '87, '92: (b) as above;

1895, '98:   (b) as above, A. W. Lampher;

1901:   (b) as above, William Emery;

1905, '08:   (b) as above, Martin Wilkins;

1911, '13, '15, '20, '25:   (b) as above, S. W. Beardsley (also on the 1915 Sanborn); ceased operating c. 1930, present Merle Stewart home.

Note: The assistance of Dexter M. Stewart, North Hyde Park, is gratefully acknowledged.

* * *

References

(1) Hyde Park--Shire Town, Bicentennial Committee, 1976.

* * *

(96) <u>Ira</u> (Rutland).

(96a) <u>Ira</u>.

1807:   --, <u>Capt Daniel Graves</u>; tavern license, 1817, '21-23; a tavern where Clark Potter lived, c. 1926 (1); established c. 1794, according to Child, but 1807, according to the town history (1); on the main Rutland to Troy road; sold in 1833 to his sons, George and Harvey, who continued it (photo, ref 1); the railroad changed things, and the place changed hands; Julia A. Fish, 1854; Enos C. Fish, 1867, used it as a farm. Building #9 in the Town of Ira Historic District map; (2)

(?):   Peck also refers to a tavern in a building owned in 1926 by E. S. and Hiram Merithew (photo, ref 1);

c. 1815:   a tavern, --; #25 on the Town of Ira map (2); built c. 1815, updated in the 1840s, no other information;

1852-55:   --, John Mason; tavern-keeper (also PM, 1852-53 and 1855);

1925:   --, C. A. Cramton.

* * *

References

(1) Simon L. Peck, History of Ira, Vermont (Rutland: Tuttle, 1926).
(2) Vermont Div. of Historic Preservation, Historic Architecture of Rutland County, Curtis B. Johnson, ed., Elsa Gilbertson, asst ed. (Montpelier: 1988).

* * *

(97) **Irasburg** (Orleans).

(97a) <u>Irasburg</u>.

c. 1804:   first tavern, <u>Capt James Richardson</u>; he settled on lot #80 in 1803, owned c. 1877 by Daniel Houghton (Hemenway); when the roads came through a few years later, he kept a tavern at the four corners (of roads running from Barton to Coventry, and Glover to Brownington); an important stopping place at one time, "is now an old pasture, with no road within a half mile" (Hemenway); Richardson died in service in the War of 1812;

c. 1805:   a hotel, <u>Eban Burton</u>; in the first framed house in the village; used for many years as a hotel, other proprietors were Jesse Rolf (tavern license, 1817), Ezekiel Little (license, 1828-30), and George Nye (Nye having it from 1828 for several years, license, 1822-33);

Note: tavern licenses also to Leonard Brown, 1817; Jacob Babbitt Jr, 1824-28; Nathan Fisk, 1822, '23; Jonas Cutting, 1828; N. B. Dodge, 1833; and Sabin Killam, 1829, '30, '33, locations unknown;

1849:   --, John Fuller (NEMU Dir); probably this is the <u>Irasburgh House</u>, below, said to have been built before 1850; the <u>Nye tavern</u> (above) became the ell of the hotel; reproduction of a drawing of this place in the 1988 town report;

1855:   --, A. S. Whipple; --, T. T. Bruin;

1856:   --, A. S. Whipple;

1859:   --, J. W. Mason* (Walling);

1870:   (a) <u>Irasburgh House</u>, Levi F. Edgerton;

1873, '75:   (a) as above, E. W. Powell;

1878:   (a) as above, B. G. Pike* (Beers);

1879:   (a) as above; (b) <u>Black River House</u>, Samuel Stanford;

1880:   (a) as above;

1883:   (a) as above; (b) as above (Child);

1887:   (a) as above, G. K. Hill; <u>Valley</u>, S. Stanford (listed as <u>Black River House</u> in Vt Dir, so this is apparently an alternate name for the same place);

1892:   (a) as above, John Ord; (b) as above;

1895:   (a) as above, R. F. Drenan; (b) as above;

1898:   (a) as above, John S. Miller;

1901:   (a) as above, T. B. Caples;

1905:   (a) as above, David Prance;

1908:   (a) <u>Irasburgh House</u>, --;

1911:   --, R. N. Baldwin; --, T. C. Fisher; --, B. H. Wilson;

1913:   --, D. T. Chaffee;

1915:   --, B. (?) T. Chaffee (but no hotel on the 1914 Sanborn map); burned in 1934.

* * *

(98) **Isle La Motte** (Grand Isle).

(98a) <u>Fisk</u>. No listings found.

(98b) <u>Isle La Motte</u>. (Vineyard until 1853).

1805: a tavern, <u>Caleb Hill</u>; at his home; tavern license, 1805; (1) Hill died in 1814, his license was renewed each year until then; this is VDHP 0703-2;

* * *

Caleb Hill, 33 years old, bought land on Isle La Motte and built a stone house at the north end of it in 1803, 35 x 45 feet, two stories; a notable house for the time. In 1805, he was licensed "to keep a tavern at his present residence"; in 1806 the legislature granted him a charter for a ferry from Isle La Motte to Alburgh; he became part of the local militia, a captain in 1811; he was an assistant judge of county court, and town treasurer, and town representative, 1812-14.

At one point during the War of 1812, MacDonough's fleet lay off the north end of Isle La Motte, within sight of Hill's place, guarding the entrance to the lake from the British, lying in the Richelieu. Hill was a purveyor to the fleet, but sailors from the American fleet kept coming ashore, stealing chickens and garden stuff; and under pretense of being British soldiers, would enter homes and by threats or violence, compel the inmates to prepare suppers, etc.

By August 1814, inhabitants were terrorized to the limit; and MacDonough asked Hill, in his capacity as a militia officer, to arrest them if possible. A group of seven men entered Hill's Tavern a day or two after this conversation, and Hill was killed in a struggle. People were outraged, and MacDonough held a trial of sorts, at which four men were found guilty. MacDonough moved the fleet away soon after, abandoning the northern end of the lake to the British, who came in and occupied Isle La Motte; the four convicted American sailors escaped from the fleet. (2)

* * *

1808: a tavern, <u>Nathaniel Douglass</u> (no license renewals);

1815: a tavern, <u>John Clark</u>; who continued renewing for some time; also, tavern license in 1828, State Archives;

1816: a tavern, <u>Cyrus Wait</u> (no renewals);

1818: a tavern, <u>Samuel Fisk</u> (also in 1821, but Fisk got in a little trouble a year later);

* * *

"Samuel Fisk being of evil mind, not having the fear of God before his eyes, at Vineyard on November 10, 1822, not regarding the Sabbath did break the same by Selling Spirituous Liquor..." (this quote from Stratton, cited above, and ascribed to William Wait, Justice of the Peace, who fined Fisk 50 cents plus $2.66 cost for "evil doings.")

* * *

c. 1829: an inn and tavern, <u>Ira Hill</u>; "in his Stone House at the 'Corners' which he continued for many years" (1); tavern license, 1829; Hill also kept a store and was postmaster, 1829-44 and 1849-53.

* * *

This well-known place was built by the Scottish stone mason James Ritchie, in 1822. Hill operated it as a combination residence, inn-tavern and store for many years, with a ballroom on the second floor. There is a day book in existence covering day-to-day transactions in the inn and store for the period 1829-38 (excerpts, ref 1). There was also an attached cider mill. Hill apparently ceased his activities as an inn-keeper in later life, died in 1887 (photo, ref 1); this is VDHP 0703-13, #9, at the southwest corner of the Ferry Rd and Rte 129 intersection).

According to a grand-niece, Ira's son, Henry H., didn't keep the tavern but continued living there until his own death; but there is a problem here, because Walton lists the place until at least 1908 with H. H. Hill as proprietor. It is not clear when the place finally ceased operating.

* * *

1887, '90:   (a) <u>Island House</u>, H. H. Hill (same as Ira Hill's tavern);

1898:   (a) as above, O. H. Parker;

1901:   (a) as above, R. W. Hill;

1908:   (a) --, - Hill; <u>Lake View</u>, --;

1911, '13:   (b) <u>Bright View Cottage</u>, C. W. Brown;

1915:   (a) <u>Hill House</u>, Josie A. Duba* (see photo; also shown on the Sanborn map); (b) as above; <u>Gardehille</u>, W. P. Gordon;

1916:   (a) as above, Joseph (?) A. Duba; <u>Owl Hill</u>, Arthur H. Hill; <u>Parkers-on-Lake-Champlain</u>, O. A. Skeels (VPB);

1920:   (a) as above, Josie A. Duba; (b) as above, C. W. Brown;

1925:   (a) as above; listed until at least 1955.

Note: the assistance of Mrs Edith O. Andrews, Isle La Motte Historical Society, and Mrs Edith LaBombard, Isle La Motte, is gratefully acknowledged

* * *

<u>References</u>

(1) Allen L. Stratton, History of the Town of Isle La Motte, Vermont (Barre: Northlight Studio Pr., 1984).

(2) Mrs Frank B. Severance, "An Episode in United States History," Vermonter <u>42</u> (July 1937): 147-50.

Hill House

* * *

(99) **Jamaica** (Windham).

(99a) <u>East Jamaica</u>. Abandoned in 1961, and now under water, as a result of the Townshend dam on the West River.

1793: first tavern, <u>John Wellman</u>; (name given as Williams in Worthen, ref 1); near the bridge across the West River, and the road to Wardsboro; location shown on a map, c. 1815, ref 1;

(99b) <u>Jamaica</u>.

1803: first inn in the village, <u>Roger Howe</u>; near the log bridge over the Ball Mountain Stream at the foot of North St (now Depot St); location shown on a map, c. 1815 (1); Mr Howe's sign was a rough board nailed to a tree, "Pay today and trust tomorrow." (Photo, ref 1);

* * *

There is a confusing account in Hemenway of a second early hotel in Jamaica, apparently also run by Howe; "a small building now used for a pig-sty by Deacon James (John?) Muzzy (same in size then as now) was once the hotel in Jamaica." This bizarre account is strongly discounted by Mr Worthen and a descendant of Mr Muzzy (personal communication).

* * *

1814: (a) <u>Jamaica House</u>, Nathaniel Cheney; (tavern license, 1820-27); at the midpoint between Brattleboro and Manchester, an important stagecoach stop;

* * *

"It was an imposing building, three stories high, with a flexible dance floor on which many generations of Jamaicans were to enjoy themselves. Jamaica House is still functioning in 1976" (photo, ref 1); other proprietors were Samuel Hastley; Moses Chamberlain (tavern license, 1829-32); Ezra Wilder (license, 1833); S. Newell in 1840; Horace Howe; J. S. Knowlton, who sold it to S. E. Ransom in 1867; O. F. Knowlton; H. E. Sawyer (1868); E. R. Prior; William Barns (1880); Henry A. and Frank B. McLean, 1883; H. A. Stockwell, 1884; Mr Taylor; William F. Gleason, 1891; W. B. Clark, 1910; C. C. Allen, 1913; B. G. Wilder, 1914; still in use (1988) but there may have been a break in the continuity since Booker says it was not in operation at that time (2); VDHP 1309-6; listed in Walton in 1940, 1968, but not in 1955.

* * *

Note: tavern licenses to John T. Sumner, 1826, '27, location unknown;

1849: --, J. E. Knowlton (NEMU Dir);

1855: --, J. E. Knowlton;

1856: --, E. Knowlton* (McClellan map);

1869: (a) <u>Jamaica House</u>, Hiram E. Sawyer* (Beers);

1870: (a) as above;

1872: (a) as above, E. W. Prior;

1873, '75: (a) as above, S. E. Rawson;

1878, '80: (a) as above, E. W. Prior;

1883: (a) as above, H. A. Stockwell;

1884:   (a) as above, McLean brothers;

1887, '90:   (a) as above, D. F. Taylor (Vt Dir);

1887:   (a) as above, F. B. McLean;

1888:   <u>Crystal Lake Farm</u>, W. S. Shepardson (Boston and Maine guide);

1892, '95, '98, 1905, '08:   (a) as above;

1901, '02:   (a) as above, W. F. Gleason;

1910:   <u>Brookside Inn</u>, -- (once the Cheney residence);

1911, '13, '15: (a) <u>Jamaica House</u>, --* (see photo; 1915 Sanborn);

Jamaica House

1920:   (a) as above, C. C. Allen;

1925:   (a) as above, B. G. Wilder.

(99c) <u>Rawsonville</u>. No listings found.

Note: the assistance of Mr Mark Worthen is gratefully acknowledged.

* * *

<u>References</u>

    (1)   Mark Worthen, Hometown Jamaica, A Pictorial History of a Vermont Village (Brattleboro: Griswold Pr., 1976).
    (2) Warren E. Booker, Historical Notes: Jamaica, Windham County, Vermont (Brattleboro: E. L. Hildreth, 1940).

* * *

(100) **Jay** (Orleans).

(100a) <u>Jay</u>.

1870:   --, M. R. Currier;

1878:   (a) <u>Mountain House</u>, J. W. Phillips* (Beers); (G. G. Stevens in Walton for this year); located along present Rte 242, just east of the entrance to the Jay Peak Ski area;

1883:   (b) <u>Jay Peak House</u>, Henry D. Chamberlain (Child, who says the place is being built "at this time"; the PO and town clerk's office were in this building); in Jay village on the crossroad just north of the Rte 242 intersection;

1887, '92, '95:   (b) <u>Jay Peak House</u>, H. D. Chamberlain (also PM);

* * *

An excellent example of a hotel post office. Chamberlain was PM three times for a total of about 20 years (1865-67, 1873-84 and 1889-97); and one Ermina S. Chamberlain, presumably his wife or sister (although conceivably his mother or aunt) was PM twice during the same period (1884-86 and 1896-1905).

* * *

1898:   (b) as above (but Chamberlain no longer PM);

1901:   (a) <u>Mountain House</u>, H. G. Banister; what happened to this place not established, but the building is gone; (b) <u>Jay Peak House</u>, H. D. Chamberlain; a private home since the late 1920s;

Note: the assistance of Reed Cherington, Director, Old Stone House Museum, Brownington, is gratefully acknowledged.

* * *

(101) **Jericho** (Chittenden).

(101a) <u>Jericho</u>. (also known at one time as Jericho Four Corners).

1787:   first tavern, <u>David Stanton</u> (Hemenway); location unknown, not necessarily Jericho village. From a 1787 diary, quoted in Hemenway: "Crossed the Onion River into Jericho (from Governor Chittenden's), called at Stannard's (Stanton's?) for breakfast";

1801, '02:   <u>Russell Tavern</u>, --; almanacs, location unknown;

1817:   (a) <u>Barney's Hotel</u>, Truman Barney; built by him before 1817 (1); many landlords, including (not necessarily in order) John Delaware, Erastus D. Hubbel (tavern license, 1821), James McNasser for several years before 1852, Martin C. Barney and his wife Maria (1852-70), Solomon Barney, c. 1870-1880; Albert Martin, C. N. Percival, Fred Gibson (Gilson?), J. H. May, Zeph Hapgood, Ferdinand Beach (who re-named it the <u>Beach House</u>); and William Folsom. It burned in 1904, when owned by Folsom. William Folsom then bought the house across the street from the <u>Barney Hotel/Beach House</u> site, ran it as a hotel until he died in 1909; both sites are shown on a detailed map in ref 1;

1821:   tavern license to Moses Billings, location unknown;

1849:   --, Albert Barney (listed at Jericho Corner in the NEMU Dir); --, Elias Bartlett (listed at Jericho in the NEMU Dir); confusing, locations unknown, probably one is <u>Barney's Tavern</u> in Jericho, the other <u>Bostwick's</u> in the Riverside/Underhill Flats area (see below);

1855:   (a) <u>Barney's Hotel</u>, J. H. Ransom (M. C. Barney's son-in-law);

1856:   --, Fordyce Lathrop;

1857:   a hotel, <u>F. Lathrop</u>* (Walling map, on the same site as <u>Barney's Hotel</u>);

1863: --, Martin C. Barney (license from the town); Martin C. Barney (presumably the same man) also ran a tavern in Underhill Flats for many years, according to Carlisle (2); it would have to have been before he moved to the village of Jericho; Underhill Flats actually lies partly in the town of Jericho;

1863: a hotel, Luther S. Prouty; "in a brick house on Church Street where Hiram Tilley now lives" (i.e., c. 1916); the hotel mentioned is shown on the map in ref 1; Prouty sold to L. M. Stevens in 1867, building still standing, but how long this place continued as a hotel is not known;

1869, '73, '79: (a) Barney's Hotel, M. C. Barney* (Beers);

1875, '80: (a) as above, S. M. Barney;

1882, '83: (a) Beach House, C. N. Percival (Child; but listed as F. D. Gilson (Gibson?) in Vt Dir; same place as the Barney House;

1887: (a) as above, F. D. Gilson (but listed as H. L. Maloney in Vt Dir);

1890: (a) as above, J. H. May;

1892: (a) as above, Z. F. Hapgood;

1895: (a) as above, J. H. May;

1898, 1901, '02, '05: (a) Hotel Jericho, William Folsom (still the same place);

1908: (b) Hotel Jericho, -- (this place, with the same name as above, is at a new location after the fire; see above);

(?): Chapin House, --; location unknown.

(101b) Jericho Center.

1868: a summer guest-house, Edgar and Ann Barber; who took in summer guests here (VDHP 0409-21, on Barber Farm Rd; until 1913;

(101c) Nashville. No listings found.

(101d) Riverside. Including that part of the village of Underhill Flats which lies in Jericho.

1786: a tavern, Elijah Benedict; said to be in Underhill Flats, but may have been Riverside; (3)

1851: (a) Bostwick House, Rufus Brown (licensed by the town of Jericho for about 20 years, ending in 1862; (1) built in 1803, burned in 1891;

1855: --, R. Brown;

1857: (a) Bostwick House, Rufus Brown* (Walling);

* * *

Arthur Bostwick built the original place, called the Bostwick House until its sale to Leonard Dixon about 1866. It began as a 2-story building, enlarged by Bostwick and later by his son-in-law, Rufus Brown, who added an ell. In the old days, it was an important stopping place for the teamsters with their four, six or eight-horse rigs. It had its period of greatest popularity in the 1870s and 1880s, however, under the management of Leonard Dixon, who added a large 3-story addition and a dance hall, and made it into a popular summer resort, Dixon's Hotel.

"...the Dixon House was an impressive structure with porches extending the full width of the facade, a porch on each of the three floors, a large ell with porches extended to the rear. It was said that 300 guests could be accommodated...This might be a slight exaggeration as the Hotel Register records rooms only to No. 45.

From the rear porches, the Adirondacks could be seen, and...the front porches faced Mt Mansfield. The grounds were nicely landscaped with old-fashioned gardens enclosed by picket fences.

A shield-shaped sign hung from a post in front...(it) read 'Bostwick House' in large gilt letters. The other side was adorned with a two-wheeled chariot, drawn by fiery steeds driven by a woman.

The popularity of the hotel received a great boost in 1877 when the Burlington and Lamoille Railroad began its daily trips between Essex Junction and Cambridge Junction...the Hotel thrived mightily. The railroad passed close to the Hotel, and indeed, made a special stop for the convenience of the Hotel patrons. The Dixon House even had its own post office...

Riverside, the little community of houses and stores which surrounded the Hotel, benefited from the success of the hostelry in various ways."

Dixon died in 1886 at the age of 76; the railroad ran a special train to Underhill for the convenience of those wishing to attend the funeral. The place continued under the management of S. M. Barney until January 13, 1891, when it burned to the ground. (4)

* * *

1862: (a) as above, L. M. Dixon (a "selectman's license"); also known as <u>Dixon's Hotel;</u>,

1869: (a) as above, L. M. Dixon* (Beers); the place has an Underhill PO address but is well across the line in Jericho;

1870: (a) <u>Bostwick House</u>, S. M. Bostwick;

1875, '79, '80, '83:   (a) <u>Bostwick House</u>, L. M. Dixon (listed as <u>Dixon House</u> in Child, 1882; and Vt Dir, 1883);

1873: (a) as above, L. M. Dixon;

1887: (a) <u>Dixon House</u>, L. M. Dixon;

1890: (a) <u>Dixon House</u>, J. L. Knox;

c. 1890:   <u>Hotel Sinclair</u>, Edward Sinclair; built by him, and operated as a hotel by Mr Sinclair and his wife Ruth for nearly 50 years; photo, ref 2; its location shown on the map in ref 1; Mr Sinclair died in 1933, the place becoming first a nursing home, then a private dwelling; VDHP 0409-69, #1, on Rte 15, almost on the town line.

Note: the assistance of Mrs Elinor Merle, Jericho Historical Society, is gratefully acknowledged.

* * *

References

(1) Chauncey H. Hayden et al., History of Jericho, Vermont (Burlington: Free Pr., 1916).
(2) Lilian B. Carlisle, ed., Look Around Chittenden County (Burlington: Chittenden County Historical Soc., 1977).

(3) Loraine S. Dwyer, History of Underhill, Vermont (Underhill: Underhill Historical Soc., 1976).

(4) Loraine S. Dwyer, "The Dixon House," Chittenden County Historical Society Bulletin 4 (June 1969): 1-3.

* * *

(102) **Johnson** (Lamoille).

(102a) East Johnson. No listings found.

(102b) Johnson.

c. 1800 (?):   Allen Stand; an old stagecoach house next to the cement bridge on Rte 15, still standing (i.e., 1961, ref 1; known as the "West Tenement";

1812:   a hotel, Capt Thomas Waterman; tavern license, 1816-32; built by him "prior to the War of 1812" (1); a 2-story place on Main Street;

* * *

"Mrs Baker's history recounts that while Captain Waterman, the hotel proprietor, and many of the able-bodied men of the town were participating in the Battle of Plattsburg in 1814, a squad of British officers rode through the village and stopped at the Hotel for dinner which was served them with trepidation and no recompense. Thomas Waterman ...built the hotel and ran it for forty years...(photo, ref 2).

This place had a succession of owners and names. About 1887, George Saxby moved it back from the original site, turned it a little, and built the present (i.e., 1961) three-story structure in front. Twenty-five years later (i.e., c. 1912) the third story was added to the original part. This is VDHP 0806-1, #87; the narrow rear part is a remnant of 1812 original; now a commercial building).

"...commercial travelers were numerous here in the horse and buggy days and a large livery stable was an important part of the hostelry. Through many changes Johnson Village Water and Light Department occupy the old Livery Stable. Mr Everett Wells...was one of the best remembered of many innkeepers, and from his day on the inn was called the Hotel Everett...the scene of many brilliant social events and the ladies left their wraps in the large 'bridal chamber,' now Ethel Hill's living-room" (i.e., 1961, ref 1).

In 1936 the town voted dry and the proprietors, the St Jock brothers, closed the hotel and boarded up the front with rough, weathered boards. The Burlington Free Press ran a picture...with the caption "Plenty of boards, but no board." It was soon converted into stores and apartments.

* * *

Note: tavern license to Simeon Lyman, 1829-32, location unknown;

1849:   --, O. Allen* (Nemu Dir; presumably this is the Allen Stand; it is shown on a map of the 1840s in ref 2);

1856:   --, O. Allen; --, R. A. Weed;

1859:   Meig's Hotel, --* (Walling; Dr Meigs helped run the Waterman Hotel (2); this place is also shown on the 1840s map referred to above;

1870:   Parker's Hotel, Frank Fisk;

1872:   Parker's Hotel, C. S. Stanley;

1873:   Village Hotel, George H. Saxby;

1875, '80, '87: --, George H. Saxby (Walton);

1879, '83, '87: (a) Johnson House, G. H. Saxby (Vt Dir);

1878:   a hotel, G. H. Saxby* (Beers);

1883:   (a) Johnson House, G. H. Saxby (Child);

1887:   (a) as above* (Sanborn);

1890, '95:   (a) as above, A. D. Robbins;

1897:   (a) as above* (Sanborn; same site as 1887, but different building, enlarged (see above); also on Sanborn for 1904, '09, '25 but a store there by 1936);

1898:   (a) as above, W. M. Morris;

1901:   (a) as above, F. C. Kimball;

1905, '08:   (a) as above, E. E. Wells; the hotel was known as the Hotel Everett from this time on (see photo); but since Wells apparently owned it twice, perhaps this change occurred during his second period of ownership;

Hotel Everett (Vermont Historical Society)

1911, '13, '15, '16:   (a) as above, A. B. Chapman; (Hotel Johnson in 1916 VPB);

1920:   (a) The Everett, E. E. Wells (see above); listed as Johnson House in 1930, The Everett in 1935, not listed in 1940;

1925:   (a) as above, James Learie.

* * *

References

(1) Margaret T. Smalley et al., History of Johnson, Vermont (Essex Jct: Essex Publ, 1961).
(2) Oread Literary Club, History of the Town of Johnson, Vermont, 1784-1907 (Burlington: Free Pr., 1907).

(103) **Landgrove** (Bennington).

(103a) Landgrove Hollow. Never a post office with this name. Postally, the 1st Landgrove was discontinued in 1865; and North Landgrove, with a PO in its own name from 1863-70, became the 2nd Landgrove in 1870. Landgrove Hollow is where present Rte 11 crosses the north-south Landgrove road, south of North Landgrove. The Chester-Manchester stage road went through the south end of Landgrove, intersecting the Peru Turnpike 5 miles west of Landgrove, completed c. 1820.

(?): a tavern, Daniel Tuthill; tavern license, 1822; first town clerk, kept a tavern "on place now occupied by Leroy Woodward" (i.e., 1889, ref 1); until 1816, when he moved to Peru and built the Bromley House there with his son, Russell;

c. 1822: Leland Coffee House (Green Mountain Coffee House), Simeon Leland; tavern license, 1822; who opened a store in Landgrove Hollow about 1820 and a tavern soon after (Badger and Porter Stage Register, 1828); he also established a stage-coach line which ran daily in each direction from Charleston, New Hampshire via Chester to Manchester, Vermont. This was probably the most popular route over the Green Mountains, and Leland's Coffee House was a famous hostelry. It was the birthplace of the Leland brothers, Charles and Warren, who with their own sons became internationally recognized hotel-keepers. (2) (See also Peru.)

* * *

"In the days of the Old Stage coach, and 'flip' at three cents a glass...on what was formerly the stage road leading from Troy to Boston, stands all that remains of the once famous 'Old Coffee House,' kept at first by the Lelands and bought later by Selah Warner in about 1831. The main building was seventy-five feet long. In the forties Selah Warner erected a dance hall...It was called the Leland Stand when Selah Warner bought the place and was proprietor up until 1857...

The visitors at the Coffee House under the management of Selah Warner would compare favorably with the present day. The 'best bib and tucker' was donned for a dance at 'Uncle Selah's.' The men were given to standing collars, cutaway and swallow-tailed coats and white vests. The ladies wore ball dresses of white or colored silks, low necks and short sleeves. The charge for supper, lodging and breakfast was $1.00 or $1.75 for man and wife. The victuals were set on the table and everyone helped themselves and each other, there being no bill of fare or waiters. The house was full of guests every night and the landlord was frequently called up after he retired to get supper for some belated guest...The Inn was noted far and wide for its dances, people coming from miles around to attend them...The music consisted of ...two violins, a flute and a harp--come from Troy and cost $25.00 for the dance...at the opening ball Thanksgiving Day over one hundred and fifty tickets were sold. The dancing began at one o'clock in the afternoon continuing until daylight the next morning. The whole bill including a meat supper at 10 P.M. and a cake supper at 1 A. M. cost $2.50. Much teaming was done, the principal freight being flour and salt, and Mr Warner kept a large number of horses as his store house was the distributing point." (2)

There is a painting in "Shires of Bennington" which "purports to show Simeon Leland's Green Mountain Coffee House as it was in 1818." (3) (There is a small discrepancy in dates here.)

* * *

(?): there is a house in Landgrove Hollow, near Flood Brook, that was built by R. Roeselle for use as an inn, occupied by the Manats (i.e., 1976, ref 4);

c. 1829: Utley's Tavern, --; referred to in ref 5; no date or other information, location unknown; the Utleys were the original settlers in Landgrove, settling there under the mistaken impression that it was part of Peru. It turned out to be a "gore," lying between Peru on the west and Weston and Londonderry on the east, and was chartered to the Utleys in 1780 as a very small township; (6)

1849:   --, Selah Warner (NEMU Dir);

1870:   (a) Landgrove Coffee House, Charles and Warren Leland (this is confusing; did the Lelands buy the place back from Selah Warner in later life, and have it as part of their chain, or is Walton in error?);

1873:   (a) Green Mountain Coffee House, David Howard.

(103b) North Landgrove.

1870:   Landgrove Hotel, --.

* * *

(1) Lewis C. Aldrich, History of Bennington County, Vermont (Syracuse: D. Mason, 1889).
(2) Augustus St Clair, The Lelands and American Hotels (N.Y.: 1877).
(3) Tyler Resch, Shires of Bennington (Bennington: Bennington Museum, 1975).
(4) Samuel R. Ogden, A Short Account of the Early History of Landgrove, Bennington County, Vermont (Rutland, 1976).
(5) Ira K. Batchelder, History of Peru, Vermont (Brattleboro: Phoenix Pr., 1891).
(6) Esther M. Swift, Vermont Place Names: Footprints of History (Brattleboro: Stephen Greene Pr., 1977).

* * *

(104) **Leicester** (Addison)

Includes the southern part of Lake Dunmore, Fern Lake, and Silver Lake.

(104a) Fernville (Silver Lake).

1881:   (a) Silver Lake House, Frank Chandler; also 1903, SBA;

1905, '08, '16, '17:   (a) as above; burned, date not established;

1913, '20:   summer boarding-houses only.

(104b) Leicester.

c. 1790:   an inn, Capt John Smith; at the corner of Middle and Fern Lake Rds (Middle Rd is Shackett Rd on the Vermont Road Atlas); this is VDHP 0109-2, "an elegant mansion for its day," and a stagecoach stop;

c. 1795:   a tavern, --; possibly built for John Bullock, who was an early proprietor and distiller; this is VDHP 0109-08, on Shackett Rd a little north of the place mentioned above;

c. 1828:   a tavern, --; present Ray Lamoreux home (VDHP 0109-12, 1977); at the northeast corner of the intersection of Rte 7 and Fern Lake Road;

(?):   a tavern, Joseph Woodward; "in the old red house on the east road now owned by Frank Chandler" (1); almanac listings, 1796-1829; "a tavern stage-house in the old days--but he was not successful"; location unknown;

c. 1830:   Stagecoach Inn, --; at the intersection of US Rte 7 and TH 2 (Leicester Four Corners); originally a store, but Dr William Giles kept hotel there many years. (Giles was PM, 1838-42 and again in 1857; he is shown as owner on the 1857 Walling map); Silas Johnson followed him about 1845, for 4 years; Jehiel Griswold, 12 years; Edward Fales, about 1 year; Lucius Cramton, a number of years; became a store and PO, then a private dwelling; on the National Register of Historic Places;

1849:   --, - Cramton (NEMU Dir; this is apparently the place listed immediately above, because "Cramton" is listed as a proprietor; the "corners" is almost certainly Leiceister.

(104c) Leicester Junction (Whiting Station until 1872).

1873, '79, '81: (a) Junction House, Oliver C. Huntley (PM, 1876-1908); this place, also known as Huntley's Hotel, was built by L. E. Higgins, c. 1872, as a hotel and PO; bought by O. C. Huntley in 1876 (Smith, cited above);

1883, '87, '90, '98, 1901, '05, '11, '13, '15:   (a) as above.

(104d) Otter Creek. PO from 1850-52; no listings found.

* * *

References

(1) Henry P. Smith, History of Addison County, Vermont (Syracuse: D. Mason, 1886).

* * *

(105) **Lemington** (Essex). No listings found.

* * *

(106) **Lincoln** (Addison).

A hamlet called Lincoln Center never had a post office.

(106a) Lincoln.

c. 1796:   first hotel, Thomas Goodrich; "owner and landlord of first hotel, for many years" (Child); according to Smith, however, he came in 1799 and his hotel "was not a success although quite well patronized by the fun lovers and dram drinkers" (1); his place was on the present Goodyear farm (VDHP 0110-04), on the north side of TH 2, 0.1 mile southeast of the intersection with TH 27;

1849:   --, Almond C. Allen (NEMU Dir; location unknown);

c. 1880:   The Long Run Inn, James F. Burke; this place is said to have been the Lincoln House (2); if it was, there were two such places, the other being in West Lincoln (see discussion below under West Lincoln); the Long Run Inn is VDHP 0110-02, #1; and the VDHP cites a 1907 postcard photo of it; it was a boarding-house at one point, now the Conway place (i.e., 1977).

(106b) South Lincoln. No listings found.

(106c) West Lincoln.

1870:   (a) Lincoln Hotel, John Ring;

1871:   a hotel, C. E. Varney* (Beers);

1872, '73, '75, '78:   (a) Lincoln Hotel, Charles E. Varney;

* * *

There is some confusion here in the directories, and perhaps the town history too. Both the Vermont Business Directory and Hamilton Child list the Lincoln Hotel as being in West

Lincoln most of the time (in 1881, in Child; in 1883, '87 and '90 in the Vt Dir, although there it is put in Lincoln in 1873, '79 and 1901); while Walton always lists the hotel as being in Lincoln. Then there is a map (ref 2) which puts the <u>Lincoln House</u> (as a forerunner of a place called the <u>Long House</u>--probably <u>Long Run House</u>) in Lincoln, and one might think that would settle it--but Beers calls present day West Lincoln, Lincoln village, and puts <u>Varney's hotel</u> (the <u>Lincoln Hotel</u>) there!

It does not seem likely that Beers would put a hotel building in the wrong village. Also, the VDHP describes a building in West Lincoln, now the Atkins home (VDHP 0110-01, #12, 1977) as being a hotel run by C. E. Varney in 1871, built c. 1840, and this seems definitive. It is also a fact, however, that the <u>Long Run</u> (see above) was in Lincoln, so either the town history is wrong when it says that the <u>Long Run</u> was formerly the <u>Lincoln House</u>; or there were two places known as the <u>Lincoln House/Hotel</u>, one in each village, perhaps overlapping in time. The fact that Beers refers to West Lincoln as "Lincoln village" may also have added to the confusion. (See photo).

For the reasons above, all listings for the <u>Lincoln House/Hotel</u> that appear in Vt Dir, Walton and Child have arbitrarily been put under West Lincoln.

Lincoln House

1879, '80, '81, '83:   (a) as above, Rollin M. Frank;

1887:   (a) as above, M. A. Gove;

1890, '92, '95: (a) as above, C. G. Butterfield;

1898:   (a) as above, W. H. Bean;

1901:   (a) as above, T. Dupont (Vt Dir);

1905, '08:   (a) as above, I. A. Colby;

1911, '13:   (a) as above, H. E. Shattuck.

* * *

References

(1) Henry P. Smith, History of Addison County, Vermont (Syracuse: D. Mason, 1886).
(2) Lincoln Bicentennial Committee, Memories of a Mountain Town (Middlebury: Addison Pr., 1976).

(107) **Londonderry** (Windham). Includes Lowell Lake.

Patented by New York in 1770 as Kent, including both Londonderry and Windham, changed to Londonderry by Vermont in 1780; when the towns were divided in 1795, North Windham wound up in Londonderry township.

(107a) Londonderry   ("north village").

c. 1780:   a hotel, Arrington Gibson; one of the first two, according to Child; "for a time, while this road extended through that part of Londonderry now (i.e., 1936, ref 1) the 'Middle-of-the-Town'; Arrington Gibson was licensed as an Inn Keeper and his inn was his farm house, still standing on what is now (i.e., 1988) the Elinor Janeway farm on the Middletown road about halfway between North and South Londonderry;

c. 1780:   a hotel, Samuel Sherburg; (the other "first," ref 1); this place was "just back of the present hotel at the north village" (Child);

1799:   an inn, Jonathan Aiken; annual town meeting held here in 1799 (1); the same place as Sherburg's, referred to above; Hemenway says that Major Jonathan Aiken had it before the division of the town, i.e., before 1795; he sold to John Miltimore in 1799, and the place has been the site of a public house down to at least 1936) (1); many different proprietors, and several buildings and names;

(?):   Huntley Stand, Salmon Willard; tavern license, 1822-27; "at the top of the mountain on the stage road to Chester" (1); torn down in 1929, it stood on the present (i.e., 1988) Claude Crossman property on Rte 11, on Huntley Mountain; the Vermont Marble Co used it as a dormitory for lumber-jacks, 1915-18;

* * *

"In the old stage-coach and teaming days, when this road formed an important part of one of the main lines of traffic from southern New Hampshire and Massachusetts across to the Hudson River, often as many as forty horses were stabled there in a single night while the house was well filled with guests. With the advent of railroads and resulting changes in methods and lines of transportation and travel it long ago lost its public character and became a private farm house, finally to be abandoned, and recently the buildings have been dismantled entirely" (i.e., 1936, ref 1).

* * *

Note: tavern licenses to Silas Davis and Lyman Harrington, 1819-28; Simeon Leland, 1816, '17 (for more on Leland, see Landgrove); Sylvester W. Sheldon, 1832, '33; Joseph Crosby Jr, 1828; Liman Hewes, 1828-30; John Aikens, 1828-33; Jonathan Melendy, 1829; Samuel Arnold, 1826, '27; Alfred Pierce, 1833; John Emerson, 1829; Tyler and Pierce, 1829; and Fairbanks and Crosby, 1825, '26, locations unknown;

1843:   a tavern (and store), Josiah Stowell; not kept long as a tavern, replaced by the present (i.e., 1936) dwelling and store of Fred H. Leonard;

1849:   --, Peter Dudley; --, J. T. G. Hartley (both NEMU Dir; locations unknown);

1855:   --, H. A. Howe;

1856:   --, Wait and Parker; Wait's Hotel, B. S. Wait* (McClellan map; in North Londonderry, on the map of the entire town; however, on the detailed inset map for North Londonderry, a building on the same site is listed as E. Lyman's hotel; Albert B. Waite was another operator of this place, which changed names and owners frequently (see below, 1869);

1869:   --, R. Todd* (Beers map, same site as Lyman's, above; Todd's Hotel, Lyman's Hotel, the Londonderry Hotel and the Hotel Wantastiquet (and perhaps the Green Mountain House) were all different names for the same place; the Hotel Wantastiquet (see below) was the last hotel to occupy the site; it burned in April, 1932, and the site is now occupied by the Shoe Barn (i.e., 1988);

1870: (a) Londonderry House, Charles H. Allen (George Allen in Vt Dir);

1872: Green Mountain House, A. Howard;

1873: (a) as above, Joel Todd;

1875, '79: (a) as above, Joseph Larrabee;

1880, '83: (a) as above, John Sanborn;

1884: (a) as above, George O. Davis (Child; at the corner of Main and North Sts);

1887: --, Luther Knight (Walton);

1887: (a) as above, E. P. Barney (Vt Dir);

1890: (a) as above, John Farwell (Vt Dir);

1892: --, John Farwell (Walton);

1895: --, E. P. Barney;

1901: (a) as above, A. F. Leffingwell; see photo;

1902: Gibson Inn, Alvarado C. Gibson; same place, burned in 1902, promptly rebuilt;

1911, '13: (a) Carleton House, J. E. Carleton; see photo, next page;

1915: (a) as above, Mrs E. P. Barney* (Sanborn map); (but still J. F. Carleton in the 1916 VPB);

1920: (a) as above, O. D. Parker;

1925: (a) Hotel Wantastiquet, A. Shroeder;

(?): Highland House, --; a summer boarding-house on the Waite family farm, Rte 100; operated by Ana Waite in the 1930s and before; a Highland House operated by C. S. Wait is listed in the 1888 Boston and Maine guide and 1916 VPB; and as Hiland House in 1915 Walton; still operating.

(107b) Lowell Lake (no post office with that name).

1880: a summer hotel, George H. Hilton; at the outlet of what was then known as Derry Pond; re-named Lowell Lake at this time for Mrs Hilton's father, one Abraham Lowell (1); managed in 1936 by D. H. Hilton, son of the founder;

1883, '84, '87, '92, '95, '98: (a) Lowell Lake House, George H. Hilton;

1905, '11, '13, '15, '16: (a) as above, D. H. Hilton; see photo;

1915: summer boarding houses: Stowell House, F. Stowell; Aldrich House, A. Aldrich;

1920: (a) as above, --;

1925: (a) as above, D. H. Hilton; in Walton until at least 1940; razed by the state of

Vermont about 1982 when the site became a state recreation area; Carleton Lake House, J. E. Carleton; so listed in Vt Dir, but this is almost certainly the Carleton in the north village, and Walton puts it there.

Londonderry House

Carleton House

(107c) North Windham, No listings found, but see also Windham.

(107d) South Londonderry.

(?):   first tavern, on the east side of the main street, "nearly, if not actually, upon the lot now (i.e., 1936, ref 1) occupied by the Riverside Inn"; the building also housed the village store, and the site continued to be used for a public house;

1849:   --, Benson Aldrich (NEMU Dir);

1855, '56:   --, C. Maynard* (McClellan map);

1869:   --, C. R. Brown* (Beers, same site as above);

1870:   (a) West River House, Charles R. Brown;

1873:   (a) as above, Thomas Evans;

1875:   (a) as above, S. D. Curtis;

1879, '80:   (a) as above, Thomas Evans and son;

1882: the original building or its modified successor, the West River House, burned this year and was replaced by the present (i.e., 1936) Riverside Inn;

Lowell Lake House

1883, '84: (b) Peabody House, Col H. O. Peabody;

1887: (b) as above, H. P. Snow (Walton);

1887: (b) as above, Jerome Converse (Vt Dir; which also lists a second place: (c) Edge Water Park Hotel, --;

1890: (b) Peabody House, John Farwell; (c) as above, --;

1901, '02: (b) as above, L. J. Strong;

1905: --, G. O. Davis;

1908: Hunt's Tavern, Walter L. Hunt (see photo); who enlarged his home on the west side of Main St; it burned in 1920; (b) Peabody House, --;

Hunt's Tavern

1913, '15: Riverside Inn, D. A. Boynton (see photo); Hunt's Tavern, W. L. Hunt; also in 1916 VPB, with the Fairmount, H. A. Babbitt;

1920: Riverside Inn, D. A. Boynton (until 1940); Hunt's Tavern, Howard Burke;

1920: Fairmount, Hugh Babbitt; summer boarders.

311

Note: the assistance of Mr Robert H. Trask, Londonderry Historical Society, is gratefully acknowledged.

* * *

References

(1) A. E. Cudworth, The History with Genealogical Sketches of Londonderry (Montpelier: Vermont Historical Soc., 1936).

Riverside Inn

* * *

(108) **Lowell** (Orleans). Kellyvale until 1831.

(108a) Lowell.

(?):   Caldwell's Shanty; according to Hemenway, this place "came to be as celebrated as any hotel in the state"; Caldwell began a clearing a half-mile east of the present village; his house was "logs and poles on 3 sides, open on the fourth, covered with bark"; for several years the only "hotel" in the valley;

Note: tavern licenses to Asabel (Asahel?) Curtis, 1817, '22-30; John Harding, 1822, '24, '26; and Varnum Spaulding, 1825, '26, locations unknown;

1838:   --, Amasa Paine; kept a hotel in the village for 12 years, also PM (1841-45);

1859:   a hotel, S. Work* (Walling);

1870:   Brigham's Hotel, Levi Brigham;

1873, '75:   Lowell House, H. C. Brown;

1878:   Brown Hotel, J. Martin* (Beers; at the same four corners as Work's in 1859, but not the same site);

1880:   --, Leonard Austin;

1883:   --, Hart Stannart; --, George H. Watson;

1883:   --, George R.(?) Watson (Child);

1887:   --, George H. Watson;

1890, '92, '98: --, Ferdinand Sawyer;

1901: --, L. O. Cox; --, A. P. Sweet;

1905: --, C. W. Greenwood;

1908: Lowell Hotel, --;

1911, '13, '20: --, William Kelly (also on 1914 Sanborn);

1915: --, G. E. Curtis; --, William Kelley;

1916: Lowell Hotel, William Kelley (VPB); apartments later, then vacant, burned in the mid-1950s.

* * *

(109) **Ludlow** (Windsor). Includes Lake Rescue.

(109a) Ludlow.

c. 1788: Green Stand, Joseph Green; "where W. B. Hoskinson's family lived (i.e., 1931, ref 1); now in Mt Holly, due to the transfer of a large tract from the west side of Ludlow to help make up Mt Holly when it was created in 1792;

1790: a tavern, E. A. Goodrich; on the site of the present (i.e., 1931) Willard Johnson house, east of the village;

* * *

"In those days, there were not many roads in town, and the amount of travel was very limited. Therefore, Mr Goodrich had but little business as an inn-keeper. We are told...that the first mails brought to town were distributed here. Avery Denison ran the house for a few years after Mr Goodrich went out. There were less than a hundred people in town at that time, and the stage lines had not been opened. Travelling was done on horse-back. This tavern went out of existence about 1800." (1)

* * *

Note: almanacs list several Ludlow taverns, locations unknown: Dennison, 1817-22; Reed, 1802, '07; Page, 1825, '29; Burbank, 1825, '29; and Bowen, 1812; Levi Woodbury stopped at Brown's Tavern in 1819 (Bowen's?), place not identified; (2)

c. 1798: a hotel, Thomas Bixby; on the farm now owned by Julia Ranta, west of the village (i.e., 1988; this is #134 on a map, ref 1; this farm was at a toll-gate on the Green Mountain Turnpike;

1808: a hotel, Nathan P. Fletcher; listed as Fletcher's in the Vermont Almanac and Register (1796), a tavern on the Rutland-Boston road; on the north side of the village park; the barns stood on the site later occupied by the first Universalist church; Abel Woodward in 1814, Andrew Johnson in 1822, then Elijah Scott until 1853 (Scott's Tavern); later, summer boarders only. It burned in 1888, and a house was built on the site by Henry Scott. Site now occupied by a laundromat with apartments above (i.e., 1988);

* * *

"This old stand was for many years the only hotel in town, and did a flourishing business before the railroad was built. All the stage-drivers with their cargoes of travelers, put up here, as well as all the teams that transported products to and from Boston. The old stand did a lively business while the railroad was being built. The liquor traffic increased rapidly, so a Mr Franklin Riggs opened a bar in his house, which stood on the site now occupied by the residence of Hon. W. W. Stickney. The lovers of new rum would first sample Mr Scott's offering, then Mr Riggs's supply would be sampled. New rum was sold at three cents a glass, or six cents a pint. The reader can imagine ...what an effect this must have had on the community. In the spring of 1845, Mr Riggs being about to paint his house, asked the Rev. Wattos Warren, a Congregationalist clergyman who was passing by, what color he had better use, and received the reply that the color of West India rum would be appropriate. Mr Riggs, being offended, replied with an oath that he would paint it the color of Mr Warren's character, and the house received a coat of black paint." (1)

* * *

1830:   a hotel, <u>Emery Burpee</u>; south of the river in Ludlow village; built by Burpee as a private home, opened as a hotel "soon after" by John Howe (1); later a factory boarding-house;

1842:   (a) <u>Green Mountain House</u>, later the <u>Ludlow House</u>; Moses Haven and his son Augustus built the western part of this place in 1830 as a double residence, but Mr Haven died soon after. It was opened as a public house in 1842 by Isaac Johnson, who stayed about 3 years; then John R. Smith; C. C. White; G. R. Richardson; White and Augustus Maynard; George Wood in 1855. The PO was here, in the <u>Ludlow House</u>, from August, 1844 until May, 1845, with John R. Smith as PM; it was acquired in 1856 by Luther Wright, who put on a wooden addition including a dance hall with a spring floor, and changed it to the <u>Ludlow House</u>; Warren Adams had it from 1857-64, followed by George H. Cole; Lawson Dawley (1867); Henry A. Howe and C. A. Moore, 1870; Henry A. Green and his wife Louisa, 1872-82; Hiram L. Warner; E. P. Warner; C. P. Colton, who stayed until 1900; and C. F. Knowlton.

1843:   a hotel, <u>Harvey H. Dyer</u>; "by the Branch bridge at Grahamsville, known by some as the Archer place" (1); (Grahamsville is north of Ludlow village). Used as a hotel for several years, housed the help during the building of the railroad; became a public nuisance and stopped operating as a hotel when the railroad was done;

1849:   a hotel, <u>Abram Adams</u>; in "the large house facing the upper end of Main Street, now occupied by the Woodward school house" (i.e., 1931, ref 1; Adams expected that the railroad depot would be built near the Goodspeed crossing, west of the village, putting his hotel in an advantageous spot; but it was built where it now stands, and this building was never used as a hotel; became a school, later Benson's garage (VDHP 1410-9);

1853:   <u>Smith's Hotel</u>, --* (Presdee and Edwards map);

1855:   <u>Vermont Hotel</u>, --* (Hosea Doten; same site as above);

1855, '56:   --, G. Wood (this is the <u>Green Mountain House</u>, see above); --, R. Scott;

1869:   (a) <u>Ludlow House</u>, L. Dawley* (Beers; formerly the <u>Green Mountain House</u>; apparently the same site as <u>Smith's Hotel</u> and the <u>Vermont Hotel</u>, above);

1870:   (a) as above;

1873:   (a) as above, Starkey and Jenison;

1875:   (a) as above, D. A. Jennison;

1879, '80:   (a) as above, H. A. Green;

1883:   (a) as above, H. L. Warner (Child);

1885:   (a) as above, --* (Sanborn);

1887:   (a) as above, H. L. Warner;

1890:   (a) as above, G. W. Mandigo; Traveller's Rest, Mrs Martha Giddings;

1892:   (a) as above; (b) Goddard House, A. P. Pollard; built in 1891 by Charles W. Goddard; also operated as The Goddard, Riverside Inn and Okemo Tavern; on the north side of Main St, west of the intersection of Main and Depot; such notables as Calvin Coolidge and Thomas Edison stayed there; demolished in 1936, and a gas station built on the site;

1894:   (a) as above, --* (Sanborn); (c) Okemo Hotel, --* (Sanborn; not the same as the later Okemo Tavern; the Okemo Hotel was built by J. S. Gill on High Hill for a summer hotel but never used as such; Gill gave the place to the Odd Fellows in 1895 as a home for needy members of the order;

1895:   (a) as above, C. P. Colton; (b) as above, M. F. Buckminster;

1898:   (a) as above; (b) as above, H. A. Thorndike;

1900:   (a) as above, --* (Sanborn); (b) Riverside House, --* (Sanborn; same as the Goddard House, above);

1901:   (a) as above, C. F. Knowlton; (b) Riverside, L. W. Shattuck;

1905, '08:   (a) Ludlow House, James Sollace* (see photo; 1905 Sanborn); (b) as above, D. K. Butterfield;

Ludlow House

1911:   (a) as above, G. H. Raymond; (b) Goddard House, G. W. Goddard and Son;

1912:   (a) as above, --* (Sanborn); (b) Goddard Hotel, --* (Sanborn);

1913, '20:   (a) as above, --; (b) as above, --;

1915:   (b) Goddard House, --; Leffingwell Inn, --;

1921:   (b) Okemo Tavern, --* (Sanborn; formerly the Goddard); the old Ludlow House by now an annex to the Okemo Tavern;

1925:   (b) Okemo Tavern, A. E. Taylor;

Note: a place called Locust Hill Inn, said to have been a stage stop on the Green Mountain Turnpike (the Tyson road, c. 1900) was built as a private home c. 1810, and run as a family style summer resort from the 1920s through World War II (Lawrence and Helen Barton); became the Okemo Inn in 1962, a year round resort, still operating (VDHP 1410-23); also,

315

Governor's Inn, Charles and Deedy Marble; at 86 Main St, built as a private mansion c. 1895, date when it became an inn uncertain.

(109b) Lake Rescue. No post office.

1920, '25:   Lake Rescue House, --; summers only (1916, '23, VPB). Also known as the Wilder House; on Rte 100, on the road to Plymouth; a private home for the past 40 years or so.

Note: the assistance of Mrs Hazel H. Petty, Ludlow, is gratefully acknowledged.

* * *

References

(1) Joseph N. Harris, History of Ludlow, Vermont (Charleston, N. H.: I. H. Harding, 1949?).
(2) H. B. Fant, "Levi Woodbury's Week in Vermont, May 1819," Vermont History 34 (January 1966): 36.

* * *

(110) **Lunenburg** (Essex).

(110a) Gilman (Fitzdale until 1921).

(?):   a hotel here burned and was replaced, and the second one later razed (1); no further information, no other listings found.

(110b) Lunenburg.

1792:   first tavern, Samuel Gates; (almanac, 1805); "about one-half mile east of present village on a hill along what is now US Rte 2" (1); Gates was an original grantee and a Revolutionary War veteran; photo, ref 1. This place burned in 1849.

* * *

"The Gates place soon became the center of town as it was a tavern for the weary traveler, a church on the Sabbath, and a place where meetings were held, including that of the first Essex County Court." (1)

* * *

(?):   a tavern near the old town hall (ref 1; no other information);

1849:   on July 13 of this year, the "tavern of Silsby and Brooks" burned, not rebuilt;

1850s: (b) Maple Grove Inn, --; "a small hotel in the 1850s" (1); this place became Fred Powers' home, and later burned;

(?):   (a) Heights House, --; also known as the Chandler House; built by Myron Chandler for his son, James B. S. Chandler; operated for years by the Whites, and later by the Albert Newmans (photo, and copy of early register page, in ref 1);

1870, '73, '78: (a) Chandler House, James B. S. Chandler;

1875:   (a) as above, L. B. Hartshorn;

1878:   (a) as above, J. B. S. Chandler* (Beers);

1879: (a) as above, Damon Snow (Vt Dir);

1880: (a) as above, D. D. Snow (Walton);

1883: (a) Lunenburg Heights House (same as Chandler House), W. A. White; (b) Maple Grove House, R. Thomas;

1887: (a) as above; (b) as above, Stephen J. Powers (Child);

1888: (a) as above, A. J. Newman (Boston and Maine guide);

1890: (a) as above;

1892: (a) as above, Mrs William A. White;

1898: (a) Heights House, as above; (b) as above, A. N. Nichols;

1905, '08: (a) as above, Miss Julia R. White; see photo;

Heights House

1911, '13, '15, '16: (a) as above, A. J. Newman; Cottage Hotel, C. W. Turner (location unknown);

1914: (a) as above, --* (Sanborn);

1920: (a) as above;

1925: (a) as above; Hillcrest House, E. L. Balch; The Woodbine, Frank Corliss.

(110c) South Lunenburg. No listings found.

Note: the assistance of Mr Evan Hammond, Lunenburg Historical Society, is gratefully acknowledged.

* * *

References

(1) Nellie B. Streeter, Town of Lunenburg, Vermont, 1763-1976 (Lunenburg: Town Historical Soc., Stinehour Pr., 1977).

(111) **Lyndon** (Caledonia).

Settlement occurred first in what was once called Lyndon Corner, or the Corners, which became Lyndon officially. The village of Lyndon Center developed later; it still has a post office, but has been more or less absorbed by Lyndonville, the present commercial center of the town. Lyndonville was established by the Connecticut and Passumpsic Rivers Railroad in 1866, when their shops in St Johnsbury burned. There was also a hamlet of East Lyndon; and another, now gone, called Red Village. Neither of these places had post offices, but Red Village had a hotel!

(111a) Lyndon (Lyndon Corner).

1790s: reference in town records to Daniel Reniff as an inn-keeper; town meetings held there, 1791-96, location unknown; also references to Joel Fletcher, same circumstances, 1800;

1807: (a) The Tavern (Hotel Lyndon), built by Capt Alfred Fletcher for John Johnson on the southwest corner of present Main and York Sts; Fletcher took a lease for five years as his pay;

* * *

Businesses developed rapidly near the Tavern, and as a result Lyndon Corner became the real metropolis of the 19th-century town of Lyndon and the marketplace of the neighboring towns. It may have reached the peak of prosperity in 1874..." (1)

* * *

The Tavern was apparently the first framed house in town; square, two-story red building with a hip roof and a swing sign at its northeast corner. The place went through a great many owners over the years. Fletcher ran it for five years, and sold to Ephraim Chamberlain, who kept it until 1823 or 1824. Then Isaac Cutler until 1832 (tavern license, 1823-25); Epaphras B. Chase for a couple of years, then Bunker Hubbard as manager until 1845; then T. B. Brickett, Jonathan Dow, Dr Edward Mattocks, and A. W. Titus, all for short periods. W. H. Watson had it from 1847-52; then the old stage-driver, Daniel Clough, 1852-54; J. M. and W. H. Hoyt, 1854-58; John A. Darling until 1866, when it was sold to Curtis Stevens; J. McHubbard a year later, then Stephen McGaffey until 1877, when Curtis Stevens bought it again; then George Warner, in 1896, who leased it to Al Breakwood in 1897; it burned almost at once, and Breakwood lost heavily. (See photo, next page.)

The place was remodeled extensively in the 1840s, with the hip roof being replaced with a pitched roof, a double piazza on the front, and a large ell on the west. It did a thriving business for most of its lifetime, a major overnight stop for stagecoaches from Boston to Montreal. "Even after the stagecoaches were discontinued, it never failed to be profitable when well kept. The hall over the carriage shed was well known to dancers..." (ref 1, also a photo).

* * *

Note: tavern licenses to Isaac Prescott and Ira Evans, 1824; Asa Goodwin, 1822-25; Aaron Quimby, 1823; Martha Harris, 1822; Willard Stevens, 1826, '27; and Samuel Hoyt, 1826, '27, locations unknown;

1843: --, N. H. Fletcher; --, B. G. Hubbard (these are both Walton listings, one of the very few listings this early in Walton; location of the first place unknown, the second is the Tavern;

1849: (a) --, William S. Watson (NEMU Dir);

1855: (a) --, W. H. Hoyt;

1858: (a) a hotel, --* (Walling; the Tavern);

1870, '75: (a) Lyndon House, S. R. McGaffey* (Beers; same as the Tavern);

1879, '80, '87, '92, '95:　　　(a) as above, Curtis Stevens;

1884:　(a) as above, -- * (Sanborn; also shown in 1889, 1895, but building gone by 1900);

1895:　(a) as above; --, Don H. Gray.

Lyndon House
(Hotel Lyndon, The Tavern; Special Collections, UVM)

(111b) <u>Lyndon Center</u>.

1790s:　<u>Welch's Tavern</u>, Jacob Welch; in Squabble Hollow, near the foot of Mathewson Hill (once Pudding Hill), north of Lyndon Center; Shores quotes a newspaper account of its destruction by fire in 1923 as follows:

"...erected by Jacob Welch and later on his two sons Jacob and Charles, owned it and conducted a well-known wayside tavern that was very popular with coaching parties before the days of the railroad. These two brothers sold the property to Alfred Baldwin who sold it to Lang Welch. The next owner was Silas Dunton and he sold to N. G. Simpson in ...1909." (1)

c. 1800:　　　first hotel, <u>Josiah C. Willard</u>; tavern license, 1822-27; "a long low building known as the Willard residence, and Willard was referred to as the village landlord at the time of his death (1830)"; (1)

* * *

"In the fall of 1839 Lewis Davis, alias George McAlllister, went to the hotel for some rum, and, being refused, chopped down the signpost and was taken to jail. Soon afterward Mrs Willard closed the house as a hotel. The building continued to exist until 1876, when C. K. Hubbard tore it down." (1)

* * *

1831:　(a) <u>The Tavern</u>, Stephen McGaffey and Deacon Samuel Hoyt; (not to be confused with the <u>Tavern</u> at the Corner, with which both McGaffey and Hoyt were briefly associated); on the east side of the road between Burke and Lyndon, on the site of the building long used as the post office (and just south of the present Lyndon Center post office); Hoyt kept it until 1837; then Howard Fletcher, until 1844; Erastus Woodruff until 1850; Nathan Ruggles until 1854; Hiram Hill, with Saul Simond as manager; followed shortly by Lafayette Buck, a Mr Blanchard, and Ruggles again; C. Felch in 1865; W. F. Ruggles bought it in 1865 and went broke four years later. John B. Hoffman bought it, leased it to his son Charles E. in 1873, and to Alanson Fletcher in 1874. Sold then to Caleb Garfield, who leased it to Charles Hall in 1874 "for three years at $300 per year." (1)

Other owners/managers until the place finally closed for good in 1879 were L. M. Hall, Luke Farley and his son Oscar, and A. D. Massey. The building was converted into tenements in 1879, and acquired in 1912 as part of the "Lower Campus" of Lyndon Institute.

* * *

"The unprofitableness of the Tavern in its last years was credited at the time to the fact that in 1870 the society known as "The People's Practical Temperance Association," with I. H. Hall as president, was formed, and during the succeeding years the landlords maintained the hotel as a 'temperance house.' This was the end of the Tavern as a hotel." (1)

* * *

1849: (a) --, E. Woodruff (NEMU Dir; listed as Lyndon, but Lyndon Corner is listed separately in this directory, and this is Lyndon Center; also, Woodruff was a proprietor of the Tavern (see above);

1855: (a) --, N. W. Ruggles;

1858: (a) --, N. W. Ruggles* (Walling; this is the Tavern);

1870: (a) Lyndon Center House, W. R. Ruggles (same place);

1873: (a) as above, C. E. Hoffman;

1875: --, J. M. Hoffman* (Beers; same site);

1875: (a) as above, C. G. Garfield;

1879: (a) as above, --.

(111c) Lyndonville.

1866: (a) Walker's Hotel, George B. Walker; on the southeast corner of Main and Depot Streets; Walker bought the first lot that the railroad company made available, and began construction of his hotel just five days after the building of the railroad shops had begun, in August, 1866; his place burned a year later and was immediately replaced; another wing was added soon after.

* * *

"The hotel was 60 feet square, 3 stories high surmounted by a cupola...on the west and north sides it had a two-story piazza...Each story was provided with earth closets and all the large rooms had water connections... There were about 60 bedrooms...The whole house was warmed by a furnace." (1)

* * *

1871: Walker went bankrupt, and sold to G. H. and J. M. Weeks, and L. K. Quimby, who were the owners when it burned again in 1874. It was not rebuilt this time, but replaced a few years later by the Webb Hotel (see below).

1877: (b) Webb Hotel, Charles Webb; on Depot St, extending east from the corner of Elm (one block east of the site of Walker's); 36 rooms. This place also burned, in a major fire of Nov 27, 1894, and reopened the following June. It became the Hotel Lyndon a few years later;

1870, '73, '75: (a) Walker's Hotel, George B. Walker (burned in 1874, see above);

1875: (a) as above* (Beers);

1877: (c) Centennial House, L. F. Shonyo; soon leased to a Mr Gilmore, followed by Steven Wiggin, who renamed it the Union House. It reverted to Shonyo in 1879, and was sold to O. G. Chase in 1888, who enlarged it. Chase kept it 23 years, selling to J. J. Neagle in 1911 (see below);

1879: (b) Webb's Hotel, Charles Webb (on site of the later Hotel Lyndon); (c) Union House, L. F. Shonyo (originally the Centennial);

1880: (b) Lyndonville Hotel (same as Webb's), Charles Webb; (c) as above;

1883, '87: (b) as above; (also 1884 Sanborn); (c) as above;

1888: (b) Hotel Lyndon, H. N. Doyle (Boston and Maine guide); (c) Pleasant View House, J. J. Neagle (Boston and Maine guide);

1889: (b) Webb Hotel, --* (Sanborn); (c) as above, --* (Sanborn); both of these places are also shown on the Sanborn maps for 1895, 1900 and 1905;

1890: (b) as above; (c) as above, O. G. Chase; also known as Chase's Hotel (see photo);

Chase's Hotel (Vermont Historical Society)

1892: (b) as above; (c) as above;

1895, '98, 1901: (b) as above, W. N. Webb; (c) as above;

1905: (b) as above; (c) as above;

1910: (b) Webb Hotel becomes the Hotel Lyndon, D. I. Grapes (see photo, next page); leased almost at once to H. L. Doyle, then Guy Harris, and in 1915, J. J. Neagle, who also owned the old Union House; it next belonged to E. D. Thompson and his wife, and then S. S. McDowell, who was owner and manager when it burned again in 1924;

1911: (c) Pleasant View House, J. J. Neagle; formerly the Union House, renamed by Neagle; when he leased the Hotel Lyndon in 1915, he moved there, and made the Pleasant View into a tenement house. After Neagle died, S. S. McDowell became owner, and reopened it as a hotel in 1925. It passed through several more owners, being known as Gracie's Inn in the late 1950s; burned on June 3, 1979;

1912: (b) Lyndon Hotel, --* (Sanborn, formerly Webb's); (c) Pleasant View House, --* (Sanborn, formerly the Union House);

1913: (b) Hotel Lyndon, --; (c) Union House (?), --;

1916: (b) Hotel Lyndon, Joseph J. Neagle (VPB; this publication lists a second place with the same name, G. H. Harris as manager, both in Lyndonville; location unknown); (c) Pleasant View, Joseph J. Neagle;

Webb Hotel/Hotel Lyndon

1915, '20, '25: (b) Hotel Lyndon, --; (c) Pleasant View, --;

1922: (b) Hotel Lyndon now apartments for Lyndon Institute; (c) as above* (Sanborn);

1928: following the 1924 fire (when the Webb Hotel/Hotel Lyndon burned for the second time), the Lyndonville Hotel Corporation was formed by a group of local business leaders. The result was the Darling Inn, named for E. A. Darling, president of the company and donor of the site. The Darling Inn, occupying the original Webb Hotel/Hotel Lyndon site, and the site of the Eaton block, opened in 1928 (shown on Sanborn map for that year). For some 35 years it served the region with distinction, but gradually ran onto hard times. It was often closed during the mid-winter months, and changed hands and managers frequently. It was converted into a convalescent and retirement home in 1964.

(111d) Red Village (see introduction).

1820s: a hotel, Major Pierce; Shores says that the last proprietor of whom she found record was one Deacon Samuel Hoyt, no date provided. (1)

* * *

"Its major patronage consisted of farmers on the way to or from Portland or Boston with commodities for sale...Pierce's Hotel was probably typical of its period. In those days taverns--usually located some five or six miles apart--provided meals for both man and beast as well as lodging, cigars, rum and even stronger drinks. Most convenient, all these services could be had without any limitation of time schedule." (1)

* * *

References

(1) Venila L. Shores, Lyndon, Gem in the Green, Ruth H. McCarty, ed. (Lyndonville: The Town, 1986).

* * *

(112) **Maidstone** (Essex).

(112a) Maidstone (including Maidstone Lake).

c. 1800:   first tavern, Isaac Stevens;

1805:   almanac listing for a Hall tavern and a Smith tavern, locations unknown;

1905, '08:   Maidstone Lake House, -- (summers).

* * *

(113) **Manchester** (Bennington).

"Manchester has always been a town of inns and taverns."

(113a) Barnumville.

c. 1825:   the Brick Tavern, --; a stagecoach inn located below the toll gate at the foot of the Peru Turnpike; owners included Mattison (a Johnson Mattison had a tavern license in 1822), Bailey, Upton, Hicks, Cook, and Benedict (VDHP 0206-37); private home (Christopher Swezey) in 1988; for architectural details, see ref 1;

(113b) Manchester.

1770:   Marsh's Tavern, Col William Marsh; where the south end of the Equinox House now stands;

1774:   Eliakim Weller's Tavern; on the east side of the "Street" near Dellwood Cemetery (the Capt H. McConkey house in 1961, ref 2); meetings of "Committees of Safety" and the early Vermont legislature were held here; also known as Anna Weller's;

(?):   a tavern, Truman Purdy; tavern license, 1822; also on the east side of the Street, on present (i.e., 1961) site of the Equinox Jr; later Straight's Tavern (Union House, Abram Straight); this building housed a courtroom and jail before the Court House was built;

(?):   Allis Tavern, --; in the same general vicinity, also on site of the later Equinox Jr; listed in the Vermont Almanac and Register, 1796; in 1812, Joshua Raymond had this place; (3)

1788:   Munson Tavern/1811 House, Jared Munson; he bought the place in 1788, enlarged and remodeled it in 1811; it was in the Munson family "for many years until John Moffat, naming it the "Munson House," turned it into a year-round hotel" (2); other owners include John Boynton, O. Cushman and Charles Isham, who made it into his private home in 1905; it was reopened in 1939 as the 1811 House by Henry B. Robinson;

c. 1795:   Pierpont Tavern, Robert Pierpont; almanac, 1812; tavern license, 1822; "in which neither drinking to excess or any gambling were allowed" (4); the present (i.e., 1961) Elizabeth P. Harris home; also operated briefly by Capt Peter Black; the 1828 Badger and Porter Stage Register refers to Black's Hotel, probably this place;

Note: the Rutland Herald for March 5, 1817, has an advertisement in which Pierpont is trying to sell the tavern "lately occupied by Capt Peter Black"; same thing ten years later (3/11/1828), Pierpont selling or letting the tavern and store "lately occupied by Rufus Lemon";

(?):   "Israel Roach came soon after (i.e., soon after 1795) bought the house formerly kept as a tavern by John Pierce, kept an orderly house" (4); tavern license, 1822;

1805:   Keys tavern, --; almanac, location unknown;

1822:   other tavern licenses to Major Hawley, Lydia Black, Elisha Tryon, John P. Roberts, Christopher Roberts, and William Smith, locations unknown;

c. 1830:   Leland Tavern, Alexander and Simeon Leland; on the "Street" south of the Equinox House; Simeon kept the Leland Coffee House in Landgrove, while William managed the Manchester place; these brothers later founded a world-famous hotel chain (see under Landgrove);

c. 1833:   Orvis Inn, with "five owners before Dr Ezra Francisco bought it in 1851" (2); passed to J. M. Shattuck, bought by Charles F. Orvis from William B. Thomas in 1883. It was operated as a summer place until 1937 by this branch of the Orvis family, and was one of the first local places to stay open year-round, starting in 1937, for skiers.

1840:   (a) Vanderlip's Hotel, Martin Vanderlip; the Taconic from about 1870-80, it evolved into the Equinox House, see below;

* * *

Complex History of the Equinox House

The Pride of Manchester, and a world-famous hotel--had its beginnings in the first hotel in Manchester, standing about 1770 about where the south end of the present hotel stands. This was Col William Marsh's tavern (already cited), later kept for him by Martin Powel. The Council of Safety met here in 1777, and the Vermont legislature in 1788. It was a rather modest building, described in some detail in Bigelow and Otis.

Marsh was a Tory, and his holdings, including the Tavern, were confiscated, the tavern being taken over by Thaddeus Munson. This place fell into disuse, however, after a few years, and Munson built another tavern close by in 1801. The "raising" took place on March 4, 1801, Jefferson's inauguration day, and "Munson's Tavern, with its colonial front and elegant round pillars was not only the showplace of Manchester but the largest and finest inn for its time in Vermont." For a while, however, it was open only when court was in session.

J. P. Roberts ran the place briefly, and it was sold in 1816, after Munson's death, to Capt Peter Black, who enlarged it and added sheds and barns on the site of the old Marsh Tavern. In 1840, the property was transferred from James Pierce to Martin Vanderlip, and it became Vanderlip's Hotel for about thirty years. He enlarged it still further, and sold it about 1870 to A. J. Gray, who renamed it the Taconic.

During this same period (the 1830s and 40s) Levi C. Orvis, scion of the Orvis family, came into possession of two brick stores standing more or less where the north part of the Equinox House now stands. He tore down one of them, and built a large house adjacent to the remaining store; and when Levi died, his son Franklin H. combined the house and remaining store, enlarging and remodeling along the way, and opened the whole shebang as the Equinox House in 1853, with 125 rooms, including 60 in the "annex" (the Equinox Jr across the Street). He added the Taconic, which stood just south, in 1880 (with 75 more rooms), connecting the two with a second-story bridge over what was then Union Street.

When F. H. Orvis died in 1900, Edward, one of his sons, carried on for a while. The place was incorporated in 1902, and purchased by George Orvis from his brothers in 1908, with Andrew E. Martin as manager. More remodeling and renovation was carried out, and garage facilities and quarters for chauffeurs had to be added: the Carsden Inn on Union Street was built with this in

324

mind in 1912 (see photo). George Orvis died in 1917; his widow, Anna Simond Orvis, ran it until 1921, when she sold a controlling interest to Mrs V. H. P. Brown of New York. Andrew Martin, who had been with the place 46 years, mostly as manager, left the following year, but came back when Mrs Orvis re-acquired the inn in 1922. It ran into trouble in the depression, however, and went into bankruptcy in 1938. It passed through several more changes of ownership, but was closed from 1973 until 1985, when it opened again after a major renovation.

Carsden Inn

1842:   (a) <u>American House</u>, Martin Vanderlip (apparently another name for <u>Vanderlip's Hotel</u>); (b) <u>Union</u>, A. B. Straight (<u>Straight's Tavern</u>, originally <u>Truman Purdy's Tavern</u>); --, E. M. Curtis; --, - Edson;

1843:   (a) as above; (b) as above; --, E. M. Curtis; <u>Temperance Hotel</u>, John L. Roberts;

1849:   (a) as above; (b) as above (NEMU Dir);

1855:   (a) <u>Vanderlip's</u>, M. Vanderlip; (b) <u>Straight's Tavern</u>, Abram B. Straight; (c) <u>Equinox</u>, F. H. Orvis;

1856:   <u>Vermont House</u>, --* (Rice and Hardwood map; this name not mentioned in ref 2; it could be <u>Straight's Tavern</u> (<u>Union House</u>), above; (a) <u>Vanderlip's Hotel</u>, --* (Rice and Hardwood); (c) <u>Equinox</u>, --* (Rice and Hardwood);

1869:   (a) as above, Mrs E. M. Vanderlip* (Beers); (c) as above, F. H. Orvis* (Beers); <u>Manchester House</u>, F. H. Orvis* (Beers; according to Bigelow and Otis, Charles F. Orvis had this place); (2)

Leading Manchester Hotels

(a) Vanderlip's (American; formerly Munson's Tavern, became the Taconic, and then part of the Equinox)
(b) Union (Straight's Tavern)
(c) Equinox (original)
(d) Elm House
(e) Equinox (combined with the Taconic, 1880)
(f) Munson House
(g) Orchard Park (later Worthy Inn)

* * *

1870:   (a) as above; (c) as above; <u>Manchester House</u>, F. H. Orvis; (d) <u>Elm House</u>, William

325

Brownson;

1873: (a) as above; (c) as above; (d) Elm House, C. F. Orvis;

1875: (c) as above; (d) as above;

1879: (a) Taconic Hotel, Henry Gray (formerly Vanderlip's); (c) as above; (d) Elm House, C. F. Orvis;

1880: (a) Taconic House, A. J. Gray; (c) as above; (d) Elm House, C. F. Orvis;

1883: (e) combined Equinox-Taconic; (d) as above; (f) Munson Homestead, Mrs C. B. Munson;

1884: Fiske's Summit House, Mr and Mrs Benjamin Fiske; on the west side of US Rte 7, south of the village; a comfortable farmhouse accommodating fifty guests. (2) It became Macnaughton's about 1900, and closed in the early 1940s after a fire. Now Seth Warner's bed-and-breakfast;

1885: (e) Equinox, with Taconic addition* (Sanborn); Manchester Cottage* (Sanborn); (f) Munson House* (Sanborn);

1887: (e) as above; (f) Munson House, John Moffat;

1890: (e) as above; (f) as above;

1892: (e) as above; (f) as above, Z. Boynton;

1895: (e) as above; (f) as above, L. L. Munroe;

1897: (e) as above* (Sanborn);

1898: (e) as above; (e) as above, F. C. Williams;

1901: (e) as above, E. C. Orvis (summers); (f) as above;

1904: (f) as above* (Sanborn);

1905: (e) Equinox House, E. C. Orvis (see photo);

1907: (g) Orchard Park, Charles H. Willard and Co; became the Worthy Inn in 1919, and was bought by Snow Valley Inc in 1945, basically to serve the growing volume of skiers; operating since 1985 as the Village Country Inn, Anne and Jay Degan;

1908: (e) as above, --;

1911: (e) as above, George Orvis; (g) Orchard Park, J. V. Newman;

1913, '15: (e) as above, George Orvis; (g) Orchard Park, J. V. Newman (later the Worthy Inn);

1916: (e) as above, George Orvis (A. E. Martin manager); (2463 cars registered in 1914, according to the VPB);

1920: (e) as above, A. E. Martin; (g) as above, C. H. Willard (shown as Worthy Inn on 1921 Sanborn; see photo);

1925: (e) as above; (g) Worthy Inn, J.T. Brown; Orvis Inn, R. J. and A. C. Orvis (see photo); Macnaughton's; still listed in 1935 (VPB): Macnaughton's, Manchester Inn, Orvis Inn,

Worthy Inn, <u>Equinox</u>; in 1955 and 1968 (VYB): <u>Orvis</u>, <u>Equinox</u>, <u>Worthy Inn</u>.

Equinox House (Special Collections, UVM)

Worthy Inn

(113c) <u>Manchester Center</u> (Factory Point until 1886).

(?):   first tavern, <u>Martin Mead</u>; on the site of the present (i.e., 1961) <u>Colburn House</u>;

1790:   the "<u>Old Tavern</u>", --; built by Aaron Sheldon, known as the <u>Stagecoach Inn</u>, 1846; <u>Lockwood's Hotel</u>, 1856; <u>Thayer's Hotel</u>, 1860; and the <u>Fairview, 1900</u> (5); (VDHP 0206-31, #8); an inn until recent years (The Old Tavern, 1934), now a restaurant only, Ye Olde Taverne, on Rte 7A;

1790: <u>Briggs House</u>, John Roberts; tavern license, 1822; once owned by Eben Curtiss, Russell Dean, Dr Claude Campbell, and James B. Campbell; now a private home (VDHP 0206-31, #37);

c. 1814:   <u>Brooks Tavern</u>, David Brooks; on the corner of Harry Adams house and what is now (i.e., 1961) the Battenkill Locker;

c. 1815:   a tavern, <u>James Borland</u>; in the building that became Estabrook's Opera House; William Ames took over in 1821. Sold by Julia Ames Hill to W. H. Fullerton in 1867, who

327

sold to Dr Ezra Edson; converted to an opera house and home in 1884, burned in 1893, rebuilt in 1896 on the site now occupied (i.e., 1961) by the Factory Point National Bank; "The blue tavern sign measured four by six feet with a red border. Painted on it were a bush full of birds and a man holding a bird. The inscription read--'A bird in the hand is worth two in the bush' "; (2)

Orvis Inn, Manchester

1849:   --, Alfred Briggs (NEMU Dir);

1855:   --, M. Lockwood;

1856:   Lockwood Hotel, --* (Rice and Hardwood);

1869:   (a) Thayer's Hotel, --* (Beers; this was Lockwood's);

1870:   Earle House, Edwin Earle;

1872:   (b) Colburn House, Cyrus Roberts; the building was apparently once a house "on the farm of Martin Slocum, Josiah H. Bartlett, and E. A. Jameson" (2); presumably the building was moved to the present site. The third floor became a dance hall. Managers included John Vanderlip, John Moffat, John Angel, Henry Davis, Lorenzo Shaffner, Mrs Shaffner, Bernice Weed, Perry Bond, David Rutledge, H. W. Mattison, William Caulstone, and Frank Bond, who ran it from 1905 until he died in 1947. Operated until c. 1980, now shops, office, apartment; VDHP 0206-1; see photo, next page;

1873, '75:   Cliffdale House, G. W. Utley;

1873:   (a) Fairview, H. W. Davis; (b) Colburn House, John M. Vanderlip (listed until at least 1968);

1875:   (a) as above; (b) as above, John Angell;

1879, '80:   (a) as above, S. E. Thayer; (b) as above, H. W. Davis;

1883:   (a) as above; (b) as above;

1885:   (a) as above* (Sanborn); (b) as above* (Sanborn);

1887, '90, '92, '95:   (a) as above; (b) as above, L. Shaffner;

1892, '97:   (a) as above* (Sanborn); (b) Colburn House, --* (Sanborn);

1898:   (a) as above, S. E. Thayer; (b) Colburn House, D. Rutledge; --, M. (?) W. Utley (this

328

is probably Cliffdale House, above);

1901:   (a) as above, Charles Phalen; (b) as above, H. W. Mattison;

1905:   (a) Fairview, H. K. White (same as Thayer's); on the 1904, '09 Sanborn; (b) as above, William Caulstone (also 1904, '09 Sanborn);

1908:   (b) as above, --;

1911, '13, '15, '20:   (a) Fairview, Burt and Lakin (also 1921 Sanborn); (b) as above, F. E. Bond (also 1921 Sanborn);

1916:   (b) as above, F. E. Bond (VPB); Orvis Cottage, C. F. Orvis (VPB; but this is in Manchester village);

1925:   (a) Fairview, C. A. Mattison; (b) as above.

Colburn House

(113d) Manchester Depot.

1905:   (a) Battenkill Inn, Robert Batchelder; he managed it until 1909; near the depot, it was "a convenient stopping place for visitors getting off the trains" (2); known as Mt Equinox Lodge in the 1940s, and the Town Tavern in the 1950s; it was again the Battenkill Inn in 1961, now Grabber's Restaurant and Pub (VDHP 0206-22);

1908:   (a) Battenkill Inn, -- (shown as "being built" on 1904 Sanborn); see photo;

1911, '13:   (a) as above, A. L. Carpenter;

1915, '20:   (a) as above, S. W. Baumgardner (1921 Sanborn);

1925:   (a) as above, C. F. Williams (also 1923 VPB).

Note: the assistance of Mrs Mary Bort, Manchester Historical Society, is gratefully acknowledged.

References

(1) Herbert W. Congdon, Old Vermont Houses (N.Y.: Knopf, 1946).
(2) E. L. Bigelow and N. H. Otis, Manchester, Vermont: A Pleasant Land Among the Mountains (Manchester: The Town, 1961).

(3) Lewis C. Aldrich, History of Bennington County, Vermont (Syracuse: D. Mason, 1889).

(4) John S. Pettibone, "The early history of Manchester," Vermont Historical Society Proceedings 1 (Dec 1930): 147-166.

(5) Manchester Historical Soc., Town of Manchester, Vermont, Mary H. Bort, ed. (Rutland: Sharp Offset Pr., 1976?).

Battenkill Inn, Manchester Depot

* * *

(114) **Marlboro** (Windham).

(114a) Marlboro.

c. 1763:   first tavern, Abel Stockwell; almanac listings, 1797 until 1829; first settler, in the eastern part of town, on a farm once known as the Ames place (erroneously "Arms" in Child, 1884); near the high point on Ames Hill Rd; the Ames farm is shown on the 1856 and 1869 maps, very close to the Brattleboro line; tavern building no longer standing;

c. 1772:   a hotel, Gen Jonas Whitney; same as the Marlboro Center Hotel, below; now the Whetstone Inn;

* * *

This place was established by one Jonas Whitney, an early settler, on the southeast corner at the crossroads in Marlboro (Center). Gen Jonathan Smith, Whitney's son-in-law, moved into the place in 1812, and left in 1834 (tavern license, 1820-26). It was on the Windham County turnpike, which ceased operating about 1831. Other proprietors included Nelson Hawkins, 1840; Perley Ballou, 1842; L. D. Keyes, 1850; Cotton Mather Haughton, 1857 ("probable"); and Fosdic Prouty, 1859. This is VDHP 1311-3; the VDHP says the place was built in 1803. Almanac listings, 1797-1829.

Note: tavern licenses to Pulsipher Hatch, 1817; James Hatch, Sr, 1820-23, and Whitney and Lyman, 1817, locations unknown;

1849:   --, L. W. Snow (NEMU Dir);

1856:   a hotel, Absalom Snow* (McClellan map; a little west of the village); also known as the Union House;

330

1869:   Marlboro Center Hotel, A. M. Prouty* (Beers; this is not the same site as in 1856);

1870:   --, Amos M. Prouty; --, Amos (?) Snow;

1879, '83:   Union House, A. Snow;

1884:   Union House, Absalom Snow (on road 31, Child).

(114b) West Marlboro.

c. 1772:   West Marlboro Inn , Samuel Whitney; at the Adams crossroad in the western part of town; on the northwest corner across from the Methodist church, shown on both the 1856 and 1869 maps as I. Adams, but the tavern gone by 1861; there were militia musters at Capt Ira Adams' "West Marlboro Inn"; Adams settled on this farm and tavern stand in 1821 (1); it too was on the Windham County turnpike.

1785:   Granger tavern, --; almanac, location unknown;

Note: Mr John P. Nevins, Marlboro Historical Society, has provided two other tavern listings, as follows (next two entries):

(?):   a tavern, Cotton Mather Houghton; who is referred to in Newton as "merchant and tavern-keeper." (1)   Houghton was born in 1826, died in 1858; perhaps this is the Gen Smith/Marlboro Center Hotel above, where Houghton is a "probable" innkeeper;

1836:   the Marlboro militia met this year at the "Higley Inn, Luke Higley"; there is a Higley Hill and a logical crossroads in the northwest corner of the town; and the 1856 McClellan map shows Higleys in the area.

Note: the assistance of Mr John P. Nevins and the Marlboro Historical Society is gratefully acknowledged.

* * *

References

(1) Ephraim H. Newton, History of the Town of Marlborogh, Windham County, Vermont (Montpelier: Vermont Historical Soc., 1930).

* * *

(115) **Marshfield** (Washington).

(115a) Lanesboro. No listings found.

(115b) Marshfield.

1805:   first tavern, Joshua Pitkin; "for many years" (Child); tavern license, 1822, '23, '27; Dudley Pitkin, his son, carried on from about 1824 for a few years (Hemenway); (tavern license, 1825-32); just past the Town House on road to Plainfield;

pre-1811:   second tavern, Charles Cate; tavern license, 1820, '21; "where Erastus Eddy now lives" (Hemenway, apparently written in 1869); Joshua Smith bought out Cate, continued for 17 years (Hemenway; tavern license, 1820-27); place described in Child, 1889, as being "where Mrs Ormsbee now lives";

c. 1811:   a tavern, Capt James English; "where Obed Lamburton now lives" (i.e., c.

1869, Hemenway; on road to Plainfield, shown as O. Lamburton on Beers); Capt Jacob Putnam bought him out in 1820, and ran the tavern for some time with his son, "first at the old stand, later in the village" (Hemenway); became the Halfway House (see below);

1826: a hotel, Eli Wheelock; tavern license, 1827; who enlarged a house built in 1821 by Daniel Wilson on the site of the present (i.e., 1869, Hemenway) hotel; still in use, with numerous additions and alterations; owners include Horace Bliss, Lyman Clark, Jabez L. Carpenter; A. F. Putnam for 6 years, who sold to P. Stevens; owner c. 1869 was P. Lee;

c. 1843: Half Way House, Alonzo F. Putnam; for six years (Child; photo, ref 1);

1849: (a) Eagle Hotel, J. L. Carpenter; Halfway House, Jacob Putnam;

1859: a hotel, A. H. Dow* (Walling; the Eagle);

1870: (a) Marshfield House, Perry Lee; although listed in Vt Dir as Marshfield House, may well still be the Eagle;

1873: (a) Eagle Hotel, W.C. Goodwin* (Beers; same site as hotel on 1859 Walling); (b) Marshfield House, W. H.Smith; just west of the Eagle on site of a house built by Daniel Spencer; operated by H. H. Meader for most of its existence, burned in 1905 (but see below, 1913); another operator was Wallace Lamburton;

1875: (a) (Eagle Hotel), William C. Goodwin;

1879: Spencer House, H. H. Meader; but Meader operated the Marshfield House, so this is probably an error in the Vt Dir; perhaps referred to as the Spencer House because it was built by Daniel Spencer, 1873;

1880, '83: (b) (Marshfield House), H. H. Meader;

1887: --, D. W. Bancroft (probably the Eagle);

1889: (b) Marshfield House, Horace H. Meader (Child);

1890: (a) Eagle Hotel, -- (burned in 1893); (b) as above, Bancroft and Preston;

1892, '95, '98: (b) (Marshfield House), H. H. Meader;

Marshfield House

1901: Commercial House, H. H. Meader (presumably this is the Marshfield House) ; Spencer House, E. V. Spencer; (both these places also listed in 1903 SBA); see photo;

332

Spencer House, E. V. Spencer; (both these places also listed in 1903 SBA); see photo;

1908:   Hotel Spencer, --;

1913, '15:   (b) Marshfield House, -- (also 1916 VPB, C. B. Slayton); Shady Dell, --; both on 1914 Sanborn; the Shady Dell is a boarding-house; but there is a problem here, since the town history says the Marshfield House burned in 1905. (1)

Note: the assistance of Mr Caleb Pitkin, Marshfield, is gratefully acknowledged.

* * *

References

(1) Fred E. and Ozias C. Pitkin, History of Marshfield (unfinished, portions appearing in the Plainfield County Journal in 1975-76; mimeograph version, N. Andover, Mass., 1941).

Spencer House

* * *

(116) **Mendon** (Rutland).

(116a) Mendon.   Chartered as Medway; Parkerstown, 1804-27.

c. 1810:   first public house, Johnson Richardson; near East Creek, on the turnpike over Sherburne Pass to Bridgewater and Woodstock, exact location not clear; (in District No 1, on a farm occupied in 1886 by Reuben Ranger, a little west of his home) (1); kept later by his son Rufus (tavern license, 1817, '21-23) and others (A. B. Campbell, Ira Seward) "until it burned." (2) There is an 1829 Rutland Herald reference to Richardson's Tavern; and an 1843 reference to this place (with Rufus Richardson) in Sherburne Center.   This farm was later occupied by Reuben Ranger;   Ranger's name appears in this vicinity on the Beers map, as does that of R. Richardson, the latter at a fork in the road which seems a likely spot for the tavern; Hemenway lists an Edson Johnson as a proprietor after Rufus Richardson;

* * *

"While Johnson Richardson was keeping the public house at Mendon, it was necessary for Mrs Richardson to keep a servant.   On one occasion this happened to be a bright, smart lass, by the name of Lydia Fales.   Mrs Richardson's son, Rufus...paid numerous little attentions to the pretty Lydia, and...they soon became very much in love with each other...neither liked to spare time to go to Rutland to get married...Thus affairs stood, until one day Esquire Williams of Rutland, while on his way to Woodstock, stopped at Richardson's to bait his horse.   Lydia was washing that day, and had finished all but mopping the floor.   She was right in the middle of this healthful exercise, when Rufus came rushing in and informed her a justice of the peace was in the house, and they could be married immediately. This Lydia agreed to, and she dropped her mop, the Squire came and performed the ceremony, after which she resumed her work." (Child).

* * *

(?):   second tavern, <u>Asa and Josiah Hale</u>; original proprietors; bought by Thomas Hooker, who sold it in 1810 to Elisha Esterbrooks (tavern license, 1817, '21); then Ebenezer Mussey moved it to a house he bought "across from where the Mendon church now stands" (i.e., 1976, ref 2); he ran this inn (the <u>Mussey Tavern</u>) from at least 1828 until 1853, and also had the post office there (he was PM from 1844 to 1853); it was bought then by William Ripley as a private dwelling. There is a W. Y. Ripley at the appropriate spot on the Beers map; and a photo of the building in ref 2. Later the summer home of Gen Edward H. Ripley, building long gone;

Note: the account in Smith and Rann differs from that in Ruth, above. "The original proprietors were Asa Hale and Josiah Hale...Thomas Hooker bought it of them, and sold it to John and William Shaw. As early as 1810 they sold to Elisha Estarbrooks (sic), who remained a number of years. Ebenezer Mussey purchased it of Estarbrooks, and Edward Mussey, his son, bought it of him in 1831. He kept this house for ten years. Then he purchased of Alanson Munson, Ambrose Brown and James Barrett the house now occupied by General Edward H. Ripley (i.e., 1886)...continued the entertainment of guests in this house until January 19, 1853, when he sold the property to William Y. Ripley. It was thereafter never used for hotel purposes."

Note: tavern license to David Stewart, 1822;

* * *

The <u>Killington House</u> at the base of Killington Peak actually lies in the town of Sherburne (which see) although the approach to this place was from Rutland, "over the Mendon Road to Brewer's Corner following the ridge top to the hotel at the base of the mountain"; (2) the road is shown on the Northern Cartographic Vermont Road Atlas).

* * *

1849: --, E. Mussey; the Rutland Herald has E. Mussey selling this place in 1846; described as "three and a-half miles east of Rutland, two stories, painted, mostly new, 38' x 63'"; --, Rufus Richardson (NEMU Dir);

1870:   --, J. E. Johnson;

1872:   <u>Green Mountain House</u>, J. E. Johnson;

1887:   <u>Pomeroy House</u>, Edward Pomeroy;

1890:   <u>Pomeroy House</u>, --.

* * *

<u>References</u>

(1) Henry P. Smith and William S. Rann, History of Rutland County, Vermont (Syracuse: D. Mason, 1886).
(2) Mary E. Ruth, History of Mendon (Rutland: Mendon Bicentennial Comm., 1976).

* * *

(117) **Middlebury** (Addison).

(117a) <u>East Middlebury</u>.

1810:   a tavern, John Foot; a large place built by Foot for his workmen (1); followed by Royal D. Farr, then his son Frank; became the Waybury Inn, still operating (i.e., 1991); VDHP says it was built by Jonathan Foote, on the Center Turnpike (VDHP 0111-10); exterior shots of this inn were used on the "Bob Newhart Show";

1870:   (a) Farr House, Royal D. Farr;

1871:   (a) Glen House, R. D. Farr* (Beers; same as Farr House); the stage line from Hancock to Middlebury, connecting with trains there, passed by this place; the fare from the Glen House to Middlebury was 25 cents;

1873:   (a) as above;

1875:   (a) as above, - Smith;

1880, '83:   (a) as above, Will Allen;

1887, '90, '92: (a) as above, Frank A. Farr;

1895:   (a) as above, J. F. Goodro;

1897:   the Rutland Railroad guide lists two Glen Houses! The first, Frank Farr, 3 1/2 miles from the station, 10 guests only; the second, 5 miles from station, 50 guests; the latter must be the Farr House above, but is the other an "annex"? Guide also lists a Mountain View Inn, 7 miles, 50 guests, location unknown;

1898, 1901:   (a) as above, Frank Farr;

1905:   (a) as above, J. Goodro;

1908:   (a) as above, --;

1911, '13, '15, '20:   Green Mountain House, C. W. Tisdale (same place; on the 1920 Sanborn, 1923 VPB with M. H. Tisdale, not operating in 1927); it was the Glen Tavern in 1929, '40, reopened by Chester Way in 1945 as the Wayside Inn; Waybury Inn in 1955, still operating; National Register of Historic Places.

(117b) Middlebury.

c. 1783:   a tavern, Capt John Chipman; a brick house, 4-5 miles from the village at the falls on Otter Creek (2); this place burned about 1830;

c. 1783:   a tavern (and ferry), John Hobson Johnson ("Hop" Johnson); "at the head of the rapids on the west side of the creek, then in Cornwall ...a little below present (i.e., 1859) railroad bridge...until 1789"; his wife kept the place after he died;

c. 1785:   a tavern, "old Mr Blodgett" (2); "in that part of Cornwall which is now in Middlebury...convenient for the travel on the ice";

c. 1786:   a tavern, Col William B. Sumner; (ref 2, no other information);

c. 1787:   a tavern, William Goodrich; "on Otter Creek, easterly...on site of present (i.e., 1859) Austin-Johnson house";

1790: a tavern, John Deming; on the site of the present (i.e., 1859) Congregational church; courts held here in 1792, 1793; Samuel Foot followed until 1803, then sold to Loudon Case; Foot's tavern is listed in the Vermont Almanac and Register (1796) as a tavern on the Rutland-Canada route;

"One night...his guests numbered 25, all wanting breakfast the next morning which must have caused consternation in the primitive hotel...He built a new house in 1790...". (3)

* * *

c. 1795:   Mattocks Tavern, Samuel H. Mattocks Jr; listed in the Vermont Almanac and Register (1796); also almanac listings 1802, '07; and a Nixon and Mattock, 1825, '29; courts held here also; on the site of the Addison House, later the Middlebury Inn (see below); Mattocks carried on until 1804, then Nathan Rosseter; Loudon Case; Artemus Nixon until 1812; Harvey Bell until 1814; the place burned in 1816, but was promptly replaced; the site has always been occupied by a hotel;

1797:   a tavern, Capt Ebenezer Markham; north of Solomon Foot's house until his death in 1813; (almanac, 1812);

c. 1797:   "another tavern, next north of place now (i.e., 1859) occupied by Dr Allen" (2); run by Dr Joseph Clark, later owned by Dr William G. Hooker, Charles Bowen, others; now (i.e., 1859) Mr Bellows;

(?):   a tavern, Darius Tupper; almanac, 1812; on a lot just south of house lot 66, a large house; he died in 1828, house later torn down; (3)

Note: other Middlebury taverns listed in almanacs, locations unknown: Nixon's, 1812, '13; Kinsley, 1825, '29; Boardman, 1812; and Griswold, 1812; also, a tavern license in 1808 to Daniel Chaffin;

1805:   a tavern, Harvey Bell; who bought "Amasa Stowell's tavern lot," kept a public house there (until he leased the Mattocks Tavern in 1812...and died there in 1844) (3); almanacs list a Bell tavern, 1812-22;

1811:   a tavern, Paul Reed; on the east side of the street leading south from the Court House; Reed died in 1836, place later run by Harry Moore; it became the Middlebury House and then the Pierce House (see below);

1816:   a tavern (temporary), Samuel Mattocks; in a brick house built by Ep Miller; until a new brick hotel was built on the old tavern stand site by Nathan Wood in 1826; opened in 1827 as the Vermont Hotel; it became the Addison House in 1852, and the Middlebury Inn in 1925;

Note: Smith mentions 2 other places hard to locate: (a) the old "Ep Miller" house, taken down to make room for the town hall, converted into a hotel when the "Vermont Hotel" burned in 1816; reference is to the predecessor of the Vermont Hotel, used as such for twenty years; so apparently the Ep Miller building (see above, 1816) continued in use after the Vermont Hotel replaced the Mattocks tavern; (b) "the dwelling house of L. R. Sayre...used 30 years" (as a public house);

* * *

Principal Middlebury Hotels

(a) Vermont Hotel (Addison House, Middlebury Inn)
(b) Reed's Tavern (Moore's Hotel, Union House, Middlebury House, Pierce House)
(c) Park House
(d) Logan House (Hotel Logan)
(e) Hotel Sargent

* * *

1842: (a) <u>Vermont Hotel</u>, Lucius Shaw (became the <u>Addison House</u> in 1852); --, J. C. Huntington; (b) --, Paul A. Reed (became the <u>Middlebury House</u>, then the <u>Pierce House</u>);

1843: --, J. C. Huntington; (a) as above; <u>Addison County Temperance Hotel</u>, B. B. Brown;

1849: (a) as above, S. P. Damon (NEMU Dir); --, H. Moore (NEMU Dir; this is the <u>Middlebury House</u>); --, Jehiel Griswold (NEMU Dir);

1853: (a) <u>Addison House</u>, --* (Presdee and Edwards); (b) <u>Moore's Hotel</u> * (Presdee and Edwards; this is the <u>Middlebury House</u>);

1856: (a) as above, George R. Orcutt; (b) <u>Middlebury House</u>, H. Moore;

1857: (a) as above* (Walling); (b) as above, Moore and Bros* (Walling);

1870: (a) as above, Darwin Rider; (b) <u>Union House</u>, George Nichols (same as <u>Middlebury House</u>, so listed in Vt Dir);

1871: (a) as above* (Beers); (b) <u>Middlebury House</u>, T. B. Smith* (Beers);

1873, '75: (a) as above, C. N. Scoville; (b) <u>Union House</u>, T. B. Smith (<u>Middlebury House</u>);

1879, '80: (a) as above, D. Rider; (b) <u>Middlebury House</u>, F. W. Pierce; (c) <u>Park House</u>, J. M. Ring; see photo;

1881, '83: (a) as above; (b) <u>Pierce House</u>, Fuller W. Pierce (Court St, Child; formerly the <u>Middlebury House</u>; see photo); (c) as above, Mrs Phebe H. Batchelder (Court St, Child);

1885: (a), (b), both on Sanborn map;

1887: (a) as above; (b) as above, F. W. Pierce; (d) <u>Logan House</u>, J. H. Sargent (next door to the Sheldon Museum, building erected in 1801);

1890, '92: (a) as above; (b) as above, John Higgins; (d) as above; all three on Sanborn for 1892;

1895: (a) as above; (b) as above; (d) <u>Logan House</u>, D. Sawyer;

1897: <u>Bartlett Hall</u>, --; (Rutland Railroad guide, 1/4 mile from railroad, 11 guests, location unknown);

1898: (a) as above, H. E. Bissell; (b) as above; (d) as above;

1901: (a) as above, John Higgins; (b) as above, E. W. Train; (d) as above, J. H. Sargent;

1905: (a) as above (also on Sanborn); (b) as above (also on Sanborn as the <u>Hotel Pierce</u>); the <u>Pierce House</u> became a wing of the new <u>Sargent House</u> in 1905, J. H. Sargent, proprietor (formerly proprietor of the <u>Logan House</u>); (d) as above, D. Sawyer (also on Sanborn as <u>Hotel Logan</u>);

1908: (a) as above; (d) <u>Logan House</u>, --; (e) <u>Sargent House</u>, -- (incorporating the former <u>Pierce House</u>); <u>Allen House</u>, --;

1910: (a), (d) and <u>Hotel Allen</u> on Sanborn;

1911: (a) as above, John Higgins; (d) <u>Logan House</u>, John Sargent; (e) <u>Sargent House</u>, J. J. O'Connell; <u>Allen House</u>, E. W. Train;

Park House (Special Collections, UVM)

Pierce House (Sheldon Museum)

1913: (a) as above, --; (d) as above, -; (e) <u>Sargent House</u>, --; <u>Allen House</u>, --;

1915: (a) as above, John Higgins; (d) as above, J. H. Burns; the <u>Logan House</u> now shops below, apartments above, from the late 1920s; also the Maison Francaise, headquarters of Middlebury College's French school, in the early 1920s; (e) <u>Hotel Sargent</u>, J. J. O'Connell; <u>Middlebury Inn</u>, C. N. Bosley (this was the first place with this name, formerly the <u>Hotel Allen</u>; shown as closed on the 1920 Sanborn);

1916: (a) as above; (e) as above, J. J. O'Connell;

338

1920:   (a) <u>Addison House</u>, John Higgins; (also Sanborn; see photo); (d) as above, J. H. Burns (also Sanborn); (e) as above (also Sanborn);

Addison House

1923:   1st <u>Middlebury Inn</u>, D. D. McHugh (VPB); not to be confused with the present <u>Middlebury Inn</u>, which the <u>Addison House</u> became in 1926; precise location unknown, described as close to the station, and accommodating 30 guests; see photo;

1925:   (a) as above, G. P. Bitner; Walton also lists the <u>Middlebury Inn</u>, J. H. Mack, presumably the 1st (not present) inn of that name (see immediately above); (e) as above, Mrs J. J. O'Connell;

1st Middlebury Inn

1927:   (a) <u>Addison</u> now the 2nd <u>Middlebury Inn</u> (Sanborn), after extensive renovation; John C.Wriston, manager; still operating; <u>Hotel Douglas</u> (Sanborn); (e) <u>Sargent</u> (Sanborn); listed in VYB in 1940, not in 1955; main building still stands, now an apartment house.

Note: the assistance of Polly C. Darnell, Librarian, Sheldon Museum, is gratefully acknowledged.

References

(1) J. T. Fenn, "In and around East Middlebury," Green Mountain Whittlin's <u>13</u> (n.d.): 28.
(2) Samuel Swift, History of the Town of Middlebury in the County of Addison, Vermont (Middlebury: A. H. Copeland, 1859; reprinted, Tuttle, Rutland, 1971). Samuel Swift, 1859.

(3) Henry P. Smith, History of Addison County, Vermont (Syracuse: D. Mason, 1886).

* * *

(118) **Middlesex** (Washington).

(118a) <u>Middlesex</u>.

(?):   first tavern, <u>Col Solomon Hutchins</u>; an early settler (Hemenway); almanacs, 1801, '02; tavern license, 1817-33;

Note: tavern licenses to Thomas Stowell, 1825-32, and Joseph Chapin Jr, 1832, locations unknown;

1839:   a fire destroyed the tavern "that stood where B. Barrett's store and tavern now stand" (i.e., c. 1882, Hemenway); <u>Barrett's</u> is the <u>Washington</u> House, see below;

* * *

This place was owned in 1835 by a man named Mann; and Simeon Edson, who kept tavern where J. O. Hobart "now lives" (i.e., c. 1882) was arrested as an arsonist. At a justice trial, the jury found him guilty. He was put in jail to await county court trial, but got bail, and never appeared at the trial; and as there was "lack of good proof, his bonds were never called for." (Hemenway).

* * *

1849:   --, C. Hastings (NEMU Dir);

1855:   --, H. Bruce;

1856:   --, A. C. Chamberlain;

1858:   --, A. S. (?) Chamberlain* (Walling);

1870, '75:   (a) <u>Washington House</u>, Benjamin Barrett and son;

1873:   (a) as above* (Beers; same site as 1858);

1878, '80, '83: (a) as above, Frank A. Barrett;

(?):   <u>Middlesex House</u>, --; presumably this is the <u>Washington House</u> (see discussion below) but the only direct evidence for a place with this name is two photos (VHS) labeled <u>Middlesex House</u>, one c. 1880, the other c. 1895;

1887, '90:   (a) as above, Noah Fisher; (b) <u>Village Hotel</u>, William Holden;

* * *

Ward Knapp refers to two hotels in Middlesex, across the street from each other, but doesn't name them. The older (and smaller) one, "located on Vince O'Neill's station site," was run at one time by Homer Nichols, and torn down about 1929. The second one was described as a long building with verandas, which burned (no date given). Walton lists two hotels in Middlesex for a few years starting in 1887, when the <u>Village Hotel</u> joined the venerable <u>Washington House</u>, so the latter is the older of the two that Mr Knapp remembered. It was the <u>Washington House</u>, presumably, that was also known as the <u>Middlesex House</u>, and the <u>Village Hotel</u> must have gone out of business, apparently in a fire, before 1900.

* * *

340

1889: (a) as above, A. R. Fisher; (b) as above;

1892: (a) as above;

1898: --, W. H. Farrar;

1901: --, C. C. Ainsworth;

1908: (a) Washington House, --.

(118b) Putnamville.

1807: Putnam tavern, --; first town meeting held here, in Seth Putnam's home in 1790; a Putnam tavern is listed in almanacs, 1807, '10, location unknown.

* * *

References

(1) Ward Knapp Remembers Middlesex (Middlesex: The Town, c. 1976).

* * *

(119) **Middletown** (Rutland).

(119a) Middletown Springs (changed from Middletown in 1875).

1780s: first tavern, Luther Filmore "and one of the Brewster family, until about 1810" (Hemenway); tavern license to a Jonathan Brewster Jr in 1817, '21, '23;

1810: Hemenway says there were two taverns in the village at this time;

(?): a hotel, Jeremiah Leffingwell; in a building built by Amasa Squires about 1800, owned c. 1877 by M. E. Vail (Hemenway); private home for many years; kept by a Mr Monroe in 1867; currently operating as the Middletown Springs Inn;

Note: tavern license to Erastus S. Munroe in 1817, '21, '22, location unknown;

1849: --, Samuel Andrews (NEMU Dir);

1856: --, Samuel Andrus (sp?);

1869: A. W. Gray and Sons hotel, A. Thompson* (Beers);

1870: --, T. G. Hoyt;

1872: (a) Montvert, Edward Rickcord; (b) Valley Hotel, J. H. Fenton;

"The village is also noted for the mineral springs...situated on the north bank of the river, and are said, in tradition, to have been used by the red man as far back as were those at Saratoga. Be that as it may, a century ago they were found by the first settlers...and were used with great benefit; but being off the line of any great thoroughfare, and the country at that time a wilderness, their use was local. But in the great freshet of the year 1811, the great storm flooded the Poultney River, and it overflowed its banks, cut a new channel and left these springs buried deep under hundreds of tons of dirt and debris. Their history was almost lost, and they existed only in tradition. Young men and women grew to manhood and womanhood--to old age; saw their grandchildren rise up to take their places, and after more than half a century in 1868, another flood sent the Poultney River over its banks, and by a freak of nature it undid what it had done before, and so cutting through the deposit of dirt and gravel, these healing fountains were again uncovered. Now the country is cleared. The woods have been swept back to the hill tops, and a numerous and busy population surrounds them, while hundreds come many miles each year to drink of the healthful waters." (Child; a sketch of this place appears in an 1874 advertisement in ref 1; also a stereopticon view, 1870s, in Special Collections, UVM).

Following this, the Mountain Springs Hotel Corporation was formed and a large hotel built (the Montvert), opened in the summer of 1871; five stories high, including basement and attic, with 137 rooms, and managed (c. 1877, Hemenway) by J. J. Joslin, William H. Poor and James Clark (see photo). Hemenway also reports that "the old hotel" (presumably the Valley) was fixed up, and that Dexter Adams has a boarding-house; the latter is presumably the Adams House, below. A Rutland Railroad guide of 1897 gives a daily rate for the Montvert as $3.50, while the Valley and the Adams are only $1.50.

1873, '75:　　(a) Montvert, Dwight Doolittle; (b) Valley Hotel, Alonzo Gates; (c) Adams House, G. D. Adams;

1879:　(b) as above; (c) as above, O. J. Gates;

1880:　(b) as above; (c) as above, G. D. Adams;

1881:　(a) as above, T. R. Wilson; (b) as above, Alonzo Gates (East St, Child); (c) as above, Adams and Son (North and Park Square, Child);

1890:　(a) as above, G. W. McAvoy; (b) as above; (c) as above;

1892:　(a) as above, A. E. Dick; (b) as above; (c) as above;

1895:　(a) as above, J. Eager; (b) as above, D. A. Parker; (c) as above;

1898:　(a) as above, --; (b) as above; (c) as above, G. D. Adams;

1901:　(a) as above, --; (b) as above, D. A. Barker (Parker?);

1905:　(a) as above, --; (the Montvert was torn down in 1906); (b) as above, D. A. Barker(?);

Montvert Hotel (Special Collections, UVM)

342

1908, '11, '13, '15:   (b) <u>Valley Hotel</u>, --; (see photos below, one from the 1870s, the other 1910);

Valley Hotel, 1870s (Vermont Historical Soc)

1916, '20:   (b) as above, E. M. Leffingwell;

1925:   <u>Eaglewood</u>, A. W. Gardner; <u>Cottage Hotel</u>, Mrs Orson Thomas.

Note: the assistance of Mr Herbert M. Davison, Middletown Springs Historical Society, is gratefully acknowledged.

References

(1) J. Kevin Graffagnino, Vermont in the Victorian Age (Bennington: Vermont Heritage Press, 1985).

Valley Hotel, 1910

* * *

(120) **Milton** (Chittenden).

Four villages in Milton have had post offices, but only Milton itself (the "Falls") is still operating.

(120a) <u>Milton</u> (Falls).

343

c. 1785: a tavern, <u>Elisha Ashley</u>; in a house owned c. 1886 by Rev John H. Woodward (1); location unknown;

(?): a large public house, <u>Truman Fairchild</u>; "just west of Snake Hill" (1); this is now called Arrowhead Mountain, and the place would have been on the road paralleling present Rte 7, close to the northern edge of town. It was probably on the old Stage Road, because it is stated that "the Old Stage Road from Checkerberry crossed the Lamoille River at Miner's Falls (Poor Farm Falls) and continued past the Town Farm (this is is shown on the 1869 Beers) to Georgia and St Albans." (2) The article also says there was once a tavern at these lower falls, but this would not have been Fairchild's;

(?): a tavern, --; present Jack Howard place, on the southeast corner of Main St and East Rd (i.e., 1976, VDHP 0410-13); said to have been a stage stop, early 19th century;

c. 1815: a tavern, <u>Moses Ayres</u>; built by him on site of the "present" (i.e., 1886) hotel of Patrick Maxfield, the <u>Elm Tree House</u>, on the west side of the river; this place was also known as the <u>Glen House</u> at one time (Beers, 1869); Ayres leased it to Judge Edmund Wellington, who was followed by Solomon Cushman, Warren Sibley, Sylvester Ward, and others; Maxfield succeeded William Landon "after a vacancy";

* * *

There was once an even earlier tavern on this same site. (3) Charles F. Skeels, who kept the <u>Glenwood</u> (i.e., the second <u>Austin's Hotel</u>, see below) bought the <u>Elm Tree House</u>, and changed its name to <u>Skeels Hotel</u>. The building is now abandoned but still standing (i.e., 1975).

* * *

Note: tavern licenses to Thomas Garlick, Jacob Davis, Caleb Lathrop, Timothy Pearl, and Eliakim S. Fairchild, 1821, locations unknown;

1849: --, S. Ward; --, Proctor Adams;

c. 1855: a tavern, --; for several years (VDHP 0410-17, #1);

1855, '56: --, S. Ward;

1857: --, S. Ward* (Walling; on the site of the <u>Glen House</u>, see below);

1867: (a) 1st <u>Austin's Hotel</u>, A. N. Austin; Austin built two hotels, of which this was the first, on Main St in Milton, about halfway between the river and the railroad depot; Austin kept this place for about 10 years; it was later called the <u>Central House</u>; (photo, ref 2); this is VDHP 0410-17, #22, still standing);

* * *

Principal Milton Hotels

(a) 1st Austin's Hotel (later the Central House);
(b) Ward's Tavern (later Glen House, Elm Tree House, Skeel's Hotel);
(c) 2nd Austin House (later the Glenwood).

* * *

1869: (a) 1st <u>Austin Hotel</u>, A. N. Austin* (Beers); (b) <u>Glen House</u>, A. L. Witter* (Beers);

1870: (a) 1st <u>Austin House</u>, A. N. Austin; (b) <u>Glen House</u>, A. L. Witters (became <u>Elm Tree House</u>);

1873: (a) as above; (b) as above, William Landon; (c) Eagle Hotel, H. P. Seegar; (unidentified, possibly Miltonboro);

1875, '78: (a) as above; (b) as above;

c. 1879: (c) 2nd Austin's Hotel, A. N. Austin; built as a hardware store in 1879, but soon converted into a hotel close to the railroad station; Charles F. Skeels was proprietor later for 8 years, when it was called the Glenwood; its site is VDHP 0410-17, #8);

* * *

"There were 26 bedrooms. The new hotel maintained its place as the center of Milton's social life and entertainment activities. During the summer months, visitors from as far away as New York City came to spend the season there. The Austins were notable hosts and splendid entertainments took place in their public hall and in the recreation room where many of the businessmen gathered to play billiards. Milton was a "dry" community, but the stimulating beverage known as beer was unlawfully and openly sold at the counter. The Austin family lived on the premises in a separate annex. Colonial Apartments, on upper Main St just east of the tracks and across from the Post Office, occupy the site of the former Austin Hotel." (3)

* * *

1879: (a) Central House, R. D. Wheeler (the old Austin House); (b) as above; (c) 2nd Austin House, A. N. Austin (later the Glenwood);

1880: (b) as above; (c) as above, Sprague and Salisbury;

1883: (b) as above; (c) as above, A. N. Austin;

1887: (b) as above; (c) as above, P. M. Mansfield;

1890: (c) as above; Proctor Hotel, William Landon (is this the Elm Tree House under another name?);

1892: (b) Elm Tree House, P. M. Mansfield; (c) 2nd Austin House, A. N. Austin (see photo); Proctor Hotel, William Landon;

1895, '98: (b) as above; (c) as above;

1901, '05: (b) as above; (c) Glenwood, Charles F. Skeels (formerly the second Austin House);

1911: (b) as above, C. F. Skeels;

1913, '15, '20, '25: (b) Skeels Hotel, -- (formerly Elm Tree House; still C. F. Skeels in 1916 VPB; Everest photo, 1950s).

(120b) Miltonboro (the summer camp area on Lake Champlain).

1913: Camp Rich; developed in 1874 by Charles Rich, main house a boarding-house (VDHP 0410-30, #5); Camp Watson (see photo, next page); Algonquin;

c. 1915: Eagle Tavern, --; VDHP 04110-31, on the lake shore at the south end of the road south from Bean's Point (Camp Rich area); now Eagle Mountain Harbor Camp, consisting of a main building and cabins; (could this be the same as Eagle Hotel, listed in Vt Dir for 1873? probably not); also known as the Eagle Mountain Inn (Walton, 1915);

1916: Camp Rich, David R. Bean (accommodations for 100 guests, plus cottages, VPB); Algonquin Inn, Mrs A. H. Martin, 50 guests (VPB); Hillside Farm, Charles H. Howard (25 guests,

guests, VPB); <u>Camp Watson</u>, George L. Morse, 50 guests (VPB);

1920:   <u>Camp Rich</u>; <u>Camp Watson</u>; <u>Algonquin</u>; <u>Hillside Farm</u>;

1925:   <u>Camp Rich</u>; <u>Camp Watson</u>; <u>Hillside Farm</u>; listed in 1930, not 1935;

Camp Watson

(120c) <u>Milton Center</u>.

Known locally as Checkerberry, in the early 1800s this village rivaled Milton, but the railroad went through Milton, and put Checkerberry into a long decline. In recent years, however, this area (on Route 7 at the "bend," several miles south of Milton village) has grown again, in a sprawling way, while the falls village has declined.

1796:   <u>Mansfield's Tavern</u>, --; listed in Vermont Almanac and Register as a tavern on the Rutland-Canada road (via the Islands); location unknown; also listed in 1802, '07;

Note: other Milton taverns listed in almanacs, locations unknown, are: Hulgate's, 1807-29; Hyde's, 1813, '16; Burrall's, 1813, '16; and Platt's, 1812;

c. 1800:   <u>Checkerberry Hotel</u>, John D. Gale; said to have been built before 1800, always used as a hotel; known as "<u>The Rest</u>" in later years; VDHP 0410-18, #18, the Robert Paquette home in 1977;

1807:   a tavern, <u>N. N. Manley</u>; said by Rann to have been one of the first, by 1807 at least; almanac, 1807-1816;

(?):   two taverns in Checkerberry, one kept by <u>Eaton Smith</u>, the other by <u>William Lacey</u>, but no dates given; (1)

1855:   --, C. L. Burke (probably Drake);

1856:   --, C. L. Drake (listed as being in West Milton in Walton; but so is the <u>Rest Hotel</u>, below; Walton must have confused the two villages, because the Walling map shows <u>Drake's hotel</u> to be in Milton Center);

1857:   a hotel, <u>C. L. Drake</u>* (Walling);

1869:   <u>The Rest</u>, J. D. Gale* (Beers; same site as on Walling);

1870, '75, '80:   <u>Rest Hotel</u>, J. D. Gale;

1882:   <u>Checkerberry Hotel</u>, John D. Gale (Child); see photo; also an Everest photo, 1950s;

Checkerberry Hotel (Milton's Story, 1976)

(120d) <u>West Milton</u>. Area first settled.

c. 1825:   an inn, --; a stagecoach inn, business from a barge landing (VDHP 0410-34, the "Granger place", owned by Ronald Morgan in 1977);

c. 1849:   <u>Willow Bay Tavern</u>, Heman Allen; at intersection of present Rte 2 and Bear Trap Rd, a stopover after crossing the Sand Bar Bridge, also built in 1849. This is VDHP 0410-36, the Thompson farm in 1977.

* * *

References

(1) William S. Rann, History of Chittenden County, Vermont (Syracuse: D. Mason, 1886).
(2) Barbara F. Hollenbeck et al., Milton's Story (Milton: Milton Bicentennial Committee, 1976).
(3) Lilian B. Carlisle, ed., Look Around Chittenden County (Burlington: Chittenden County Historical Soc., 1976).

* * *

(121) **Monkton** (Addison).

(121a) East Monkton.

(121b) Monkton (Monktonboro).

c. 1780:   first hotel, Samuel Barnum; on the corner of roads 35 and 36, in a building owned by Asahel Dean in 1881 (Child); a whipping-post and pillory stood nearby. This is in the Barnumtown district, a hamlet a little southwest of Monkton that never achieved post office status; it was named for Barnabas Barnum; Samuel Barnum also an early settler, and the first town clerk. This is VDHP 0112-2; they say the tavern was built c. 1800; the Arthur Stearns house c. 1977; Everest photo, 1950s.

c. 1780:   a hotel, Hezekiah Smith; "just north of the Borough," where Harvey Potter lived c. 1886 (1); Hezekiah Smith died in the epidemic of 1813, as did a lot of innkeepers; William Niles married his widow and kept the place for several years;

(?):   a tavern, Luman V. Smith; in the house occupied by F. H. Dean c. 1886 (1); he was followed by Chauncey Hutchins, L. C. Keeler;

c. 1845:   a tavern, James Miner; converted from a home built c. 1798; place owned by Donald Oatley in 1977 (this is VDHP 0112-28, #1); this tavern is almost surely the place shown on the 1871 Beers as P. R. Gage's, which became the Colfax House/Florona Hotel; other early managers were L. C. Keeler, Reuben Wickware, Daniel Isham, George Tobey, Platt Gage, Elmer Collins, Lewis Osier (for 6 years); M. F. Muzzey in 1885;

1849:   --, M. R. Bates (NEMU Dir; an M. B. Bates is shown on the 1857 Walling map);

1870:   --, G. R. Tobey;

1871:   --, P. R. Gage* (Beers);

1873:   (a) Colfax House, Elmer D. Collins;

1875, '80:   --, E. D. Collins;

1881:   (a) Florence Hotel, Lewis Osier; this name is spelled several different ways; according to Swift, it was the Florona Hotel, named for Mount Florona;

1883:   (a) Florovina Hotel (see above), Lewis Osier;

1887:   (a) --, M. F. Muzzey;

1890:   (a) Florona Hotel, M. P. Bull;

1901, '05, '08: Ladd House, J. E. Ladd.

(121c) Monkton Ridge.

c. 1830:   a tavern, --; owned by O. Skiffin in mid-century, now Theodore Meader (i.e., 1977; VDHP 0112-20, #1).

Note: there is an Everest photo (1950s) of a former tavern in Monkton Ridge, said to be c. 1815.

* * *

References

(1) Henry P. Smith, History of Addison County, Vermont (Syracuse: D. Mason, 1886).
(2) Esther M. Swift, Vermont Place-Names: Footprints of History (Brattleboro: Stephen Greene Pr., 1977).

Monkton Ridge hotel (unidentified)

* * *

(122) **Montgomery** (Franklin).

(122a) Averys Gore, (122b) Black Falls, (122c) Glendale (Hectorville until 1899) and (122d) Hillwest, no listings found.

(122e) Montgomery.

1803: the place that became Samson's (see below) and is now the Black Lantern Inn (i.e., 1991); this is VDHP 0610-1, #8), said to have been built in 1803; (1)

Note: tavern licenses to Samuel Lusk, 1818-32, and Alvin House, 1824, '25, locations unknown; (a Lusk tavern is referred to in a report to the state legislature in 1821, in the Hazen's Notch area; ref 1);

1856: --, W. Williams (could be Montgomery Center);

1857: --, Tolman Sampson* (Walling);

1871: --, A. S. Samson* (Beers; same site as in 1857);

1870, '75, '80: --, A. S. Samson;

1883: (a) Samson House, A. S. Samson;

1882, '87: (a) Montgomery House, A. S. Samson; still listed as Samson House in Vt Dir in 1887, '90;

1898, 1901: (a) Mansfield House, W. G. Mansfield; almost surely the same as above;

1902, '05: (a) Mansfield House, George M. Patterson; see photo;

349

The Mansfield
House
Montgomery, Vermont

Mansfield House

1909:   (a) as above, --* (Sanborn);

1911:   (a) --, G. M. Patterson;

1913:   --, Simon Coon;

1916:   (a) as above, G. M. Patterson (VPB);

1920:   (a) LaPlant House, A. LaPlant* (Sanborn; formerly the Mansfield House);

1925:   --, G. B. Fuller; this place has also been known as the Gilbert Hotel, the Trout River Inn, and the Village Inn (1); shown as the Trout River Inn on the 1930 Sanborn; now the Black Lantern Inn;

(?):   there is a photograph in ref 1, taken about 1870, showing a place called the Checkerboard Square Hotel; later rebuilt and used as a parsonage for the Union Methodist church, which it stood next to; it is odd that it doesn't seem to turn up in any of the directories.

(122f) Montgomery Center.

1849:   --, O. L. Kelton (NEMU Dir); location uncertain, but probably Montgomery Center since Kelton had a mill here later;

1870:   --, George Baker;

1871:   a hotel, C. C. Martin* (Beers; on the same site as VDHP 0610-2, #9, Puffer's Hardware and apartments in 1982; built c. 1820);

1875:   --, C. C. Martin;

1880:   --, H. O. Rowley;

c. 1880:   a tavern (and store, PO), --; local name was Gardyne Hall; VDHP 0610-2, #16;

1882, '87, '92, '95, '98, 1905, '11, '13: (a) Martin House, Horace O. Rowley; also known as Rowley's Hotel; made into apartments in the 1960s; it was called the Central House in 1902 in the CVRR guide; and the Martin House in 1901 in Vt Dir, but with L. D. Rowley as manager; see photo;

350

Hotel, Montgomery Centre, Vt.

Martin House, Montgomery Center

1909, '20:   (a) <u>Montgomery Inn</u>, --* (Sanborn; this is the <u>Martin House</u>);

1915, '16:   (a) as above, J. J. LaFrank (VPB);

1920:   --, A. B. Chappell;

1925:   --, H. I. Meterier; listed as a "lodging-house" on the 1930 Sanborn.

References

(1) W. R. Branthoover and Sara Taylor, Montgomery, Vermont: The History of a Town (Montgomery: Montgomery Historical Soc., 1976).

* * *

(123) **Montpelier** (Washington).

(123a) <u>Montpelier</u>.

1793:   (a) <u>Union House</u>, Col Jacob Davis; first tavern in town, exact location unknown; on the southeast bank of the North Branch, near the present (i.e., 1976) Unitarian Church (1); built by Thomas Hawkins, first blacksmith, about 1792; kept by Houghton, Taft, Cottrill (before he took the <u>Pavilion</u>), Lamb, Mann and others (Hemenway); kept for some time by David Wing Jr; burned in 1834 and rebuilt (see Rutland Herald, 2/16/1835); burned again in 1859, and rebuilt at a nearby but different location (see "new" <u>Union House</u>, below; map location #6, see photo); Davis is listed as a tavernkeeper in almanacs from 1796 until c. 1823; Wing is also listed in 1801, '02; Mann and Cottrill are both listed in 1825, '29; burned for good in 1930;

Note: according to Gridley, the first tavern was on the <u>site</u> of the <u>Union House</u> and was kept by David Wing; (2)

* * *

Col Davis was an original settler, regarded as the father of the town; he accommodated many travelers and settlers in his house, the first frame house in town, built in 1790, prior to the opening of the <u>Union House</u>; one such guest was Prince Edward, father of Queen Victoria, in the winter of 1790-91.

* * *

c. 1800:   <u>Hutchins Tavern</u>, William Hutchins; later the <u>Shepard Tavern</u> and the <u>Farmer's Hotel</u>; on Main St opposite Barre St, in the general vicinity of map location #1; burned

351

in 1875;

1807-08: (b) <u>Davis Tavern</u>, Thomas Davis; tavern license, 1820-22; became the <u>Pavilion</u>; built as a place for legislators to stay; on the north side of State St, just east of the capitol grounds; location #2 on the map; M. Cottrill is listed in Badger and Porter's Stage Register, 1828, as a tavern-keeper, probably at this place;

1807, '10: <u>Gore tavern</u>, -- (almanacs, location unknown);

Union House (Special Collections, UVM)

1810: a hotel, <u>Obadiah Eaton</u>; (almanacs, 1825, '29; tavern license, 1820-24); where the old Central Vermont depot was later built (map location #3); this building was moved to Elm St, became a private home, now offices for doctors and dentists; not found in Walton;

Note: tavern licenses, locations unknown, to Parrit Blaisdell, 1817, '22, '23, '25; Samuel Cornforth, 1817; Michael Hammett, 1817-24; Jonathan Snow, 1817-32; Jonathan Shepard, 1821-30; Reuben Lamb, 1820-22; Oliver Perry, 1817; Calvin Hubbard, 1821, '22; Solomon Mann, 1823; Merrill Williams, 1825-33; Mahlon Cottrill, 1825-32; Calvin Fullerton, 1827, '30; Ebenezer Coleburn, 1830, '33; Chester W. Houghton, 1817, '20; Sally Hutchins, 1817; John Rich, 1830; Joseph Wing, Dudley Pitkin, 1830; William Mann, 1833; Lyman Hawley, 1827; George S. Mann and Ralph McIntire, 1825; Samuel Campbell, 1826;

1824: a hotel, <u>Rufus Campbell</u>; tavern license, 1825, '26; on the south side of State St, a little west of Main, exact location unknown; later a store; not found in Walton; also kept by Hugh Gonsley and William Rogers;

(?): (g) <u>Burnham House</u>, Lewis Burnham; built as a dwelling on State St by Henry Y. Barnes, operated by Burnham as a temperance hotel; across from the post office, became <u>Bishop's House</u> (Hemenway); also known as the <u>Montpelier House</u>, <u>Exchange Hotel</u> (see discussion in box below); <u>Bishop's</u> is shown on the 1873 Beers in the right area, location #4 (see photo, next page);

(?): <u>Cadwell House</u>, --; on site of the present Blanchard Block (i.e., 1976, ref 1, near the corner of Main and State Sts); plaque on building referring to <u>Cadwell House</u> and Lafayette's visit, so it was in existence in 1825; not found in Walton; built by James Hawkins; "the favorite boarding place of governors and other dignitaries" (Hemenway);

(?):   (c) Eagle Hotel, --; enlarged and became the American House, date uncertain, but after Rufus Campbell's (see above); location #5; also the Montpelier House;

1826:   Montpelier House, John Davis; on the site of the later Montpelier Tavern; run by Davis until 1834; Henry Young and Lewis Greeley were owners in the period between then and 1860, possibly others; from 1860 until 1880, owners were Lewis Burnham, J. W. Andrews, Chester Clark, Erwin M. Irish, George Wheeler and Albert Sparrow (same as Eagle, American; see discussion in box below); the place was sold to the Waldo Farrars and Pearl Cleveland in 1926, badly damaged in the 1927 flood, reopened in 1932 as the Montpelier Tavern Hotel;

1841:   Gouchier Hotel, --; village meeting held here this year; not identified;

1842, '43:   (a) Union House, J. Kelsey (original location, but second building; address on Main St); a temperance place in 1843; (b) the Pavilion, M. Cottrill; (c) Eagle, S. Kimball (a temperance place in 1843); (f) --, Jonathan Shepard (presumably Shepard's Hotel); Temperance, Mrs Safford (on State St, location unknown); Village, William Rogers (on State St, location unknown); Winooski, H. Campbell (on State St, location unknown);

Bishop's House (from Montpelier, 1976, Perry H. Merrill)

* * *

Principal Montpelier Hotels

(a) original Union House (1st and 2nd, same site);
(b) Davis Tavern, became the Pavilion;
(c) Eagle, became the American; also the Montpelier
House (see discussion in box below); Montpelier Tavern Hotel;
(d) "new" Union House (3rd, new site);
(e) Montpelier Hotel; there was both a Montpelier House
and a Montpelier Hotel (see discussion in box below);
(f) Hutchins-Shepard tavern;
(g) Burnham's, became Bishop's; also later the Montpelier Hotel, Exchange Hotel;
(h) Hotel Kempton, became the Vermont Hotel, and the Lennox;
(i) Exchange, became Adams by 1899 (originally the Montpelier Hotel);
(j) Miller's Inn;

353

(The Riverside was listed only briefly in Walton, not given an initial here; a rooming and boarding house).

* * *

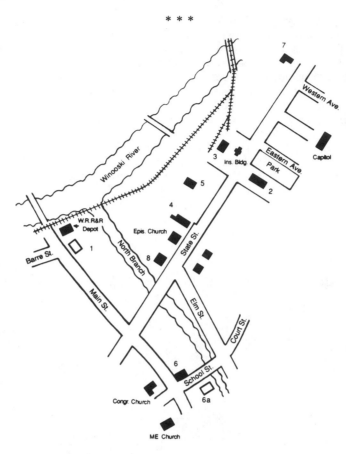

Map of Montpelier (based on Beers, Walling)

* * *

<u>Map Locations</u>

#1:   Hutchins Tavern/Shepard Tavern, etc; not listed in Walton;
#2:   Davis Tavern/Pavilion;
#3:   Eaton Hotel, where the CV depot was;
#4:   Burnham/Bishop/Montpelier Hotel;
#5:   Eagle/American/Montpelier House
#6:   "new" Union House;
#6a: original Union House;
#7:   Riverside;
#8:   Hotel Kempton;

* * *

There are a couple of problems with the location and identity of several Montpelier hotels. The first has to do with <u>Burnham's</u>, which became <u>Bishop's</u>, according to Hemenway.

There is a <u>Bishop's Hotel</u> on the 1873 Beers, on State St more or less across from the present post office (map location #4), which fits Merrill's description. On the 1859 Walling, however, the site seems to be occupied by a place called the <u>Montpelier Hotel</u>, but it is hard to be certain. Both Beers and Walling show only two hotels on the south side of State St between the

354

depot area and the river: for Walling, it is the Eagle (well established as the predecessor of the American; this building, built in 1826, was also known as the Montpelier House at one point, confusing things still further) and the Montpelier Hotel; for Beers, it is the American and Bishop's.

The simplest explanation is to say that Burnham's/Bishop's and the Montpelier Hotel are one and the same. The arguments against this are that earlier writers have not suggested it; and that both places are listed in the Directory part of the 1859 Walling. The directories are not infallible, however, and there was another place with a very similar name (Montpelier House), as mentioned above.

The arguments in favor of the suggested identity are the fact that no other place is shown in the right area on the Walling/Beers maps; that the two places are not listed together in the directories (except for the sole example mentioned above); that the Montpelier Hotel was owned by Lewis Burnham at some point in the period 1860-80 (he is listed as such in 1865, '67, and '68); and finally, that a comparison of the 1884 and 1889 Sanborn maps shows the American changing to the Montpelier Hotel.

A second difficulty is the identity of a hotel shown on the 1859 Walling map, on the west side of Main St just south of where the new Union House was built (i.e., just south of map location #6). It is clearly marked "hotel", but the name of the owner cannot be made out. The same map shows four other hotels clearly (Eagle, Pavilion, Union, Montpelier) so there is no established hotel unaccounted for--and no hotel on this site in 1873 (Beers).

* * *

1849:   (a) as above, Levi Boutwell; (b) as above; (c) as above, P. Kimball; (f) as above; Temperance House, E. G. Strong (location unknown); --, Julius Y. Dewey (unidentified); --, H. P. Darling (unidentified);

1850s: the VDHP says there was a hotel known as the Coffee House, off East Montpelier Rd; the Barre Road ran behind it then; (VDHP 1211-154, probably built by Jacob Davis Jr);

1855:   (a) --, Levi Boutwell (presumably the Union House); (b) --, M. Cottrill (the Pavilion); (c) --, Mrs P. Kimball (presumably the Eagle); (g) -, I. (?) Burnham (presumably Burnham's, Lewis Burnham);

1856:   (b) as above; --, A. Kellogg (unidentified); (g) --, I. Burnham (Burnham's); --, A. H. Davis (unidentified);

(?):   (b) Pavilion Hotel, Mahlon Cottrill; who doubled the size of the place, added piazzas and renamed it the Pavilion (formerly the Davis Tavern); he sold to Col Levi Boutwell in 1856; the place was acquired by Theron O. Bailey in 1874, who razed it and built a "modern 90-room luxury hotel"; sold to the State of Vermont in 1969, replaced by the Pavilion Office Building, closely resembling the old Pavilion; see photo;

1859:   (from the Directory portion of Walling): (a) Union House, A. Redway; (b) Pavilion, Levi Boutwell; (e) Montpelier Hotel, C. Clark; (g) Burnham's Hotel, - Burnham;

c. 1860:   (d) "new" Union House, --; on the corner of Main and School Sts, on the opposite side of the street from the old Union House (map location #6);

1865:   (b) as above; (c) American House, C. Newcomb; (e) Montpelier Hotel, Lewis Burnham;

1867:   (b) as above; (c) American House, Chester Clark; (d) Union House, J. S. Lee; (e) as above;

1868:   (b) Pavilion, Dunton Brothers; (c) as above; (d) Union House, George P. Foster ("New" Union); (e) as above;

1870: (b) Pavilion, Levi Boutwell; (c) American, J. W. Andrews (S. W. in Vt Dir); (d) Union House, George P. Foster; (g) Burnham's, D. W. Dudley;

1873: (b) Pavilion, R. T. Aldrich; (c) American, Clark and Coffey; (d) as above; (g) Bishop's Hotel, H. H. Bishop (Vt Dir);

Pavilion Hotel (Montpelier, 1976, Perry H. Merrill)

1873: (b) Pavilion, Levi Boutwell* (Beers); (c) American, Clark and Coffey* (Beers); (d) Union House, George P. Foster* (Beers); (g) Bishop's Hotel, J. H. Bostwick* (Beers);

1875: (b) Pavilion, --; (c) American House, Chester Clark; (d) as above; (g) Bishop's, H. H. Bishop;

1879, '80: (b) Pavilion, T. O. Bailey; (c) as above; (d) as above; (g) Bishop's, R. J. Coffey and H. X. Fales; Central House, Mrs M. M. True;

1883: (b) as above, A. J. Sibley; (c) as above; (d) as above, Irish and Sparrow; (g) as above, H. Fales;

1884: (c) American House, --* (Sanborn); (h) Hotel Kempton, --* (Sanborn, location #8);

1887: (b) as above, Jesse S. Viles; (d) Union House, George Wheeler; (e) Montpelier House, Irish and Sparrow; Central House, F. (?) W. Kempton (is this the same as the Hotel Kempton, above?);

1888: (b) Pavilion, T. J. Heaphy (Boston and Maine guide);

1890: (b) as above; (d) as above, J. A. Kelton; (e) "New" Montpelier House, George Wheeler;

c. 1890: (j) Miller's Inn, William Miller; at 118-120 State St, sold when he died in 1916 to Edward and Julia Meigs; later owners were Farrar and Burbank, Lena Heimiller, Elmer Pierce and William J. Sykas, who converted it into the "Lobster Pot";

1892: (b) as above; (d) as above, H. E. Bliss; (e) as above; (h) as above; (i) Exchange Hotel, Kelton and Sparrow* (just west of Episcopal church, on State St, 1894 Sanborn);

1895:   (b) as above* (on 1894 Sanborn); (d) as above, Worthen and Griswold; (e) as above; (h) as above* (on 1894 Sanborn); (i) as above, Ross and Hyde;

1898:   (b) as above; (d) as above, Griswold and Kendall; (e) Montpelier House, A. S. Sparrow (see photo); (h) Vermont House, F. R. Hayden (formerly Hotel Kempton (i) as above, Charles Hubbard;

Montpelier House

Note: in addition to (b), (e) and (i) above, the 1899 Barre City Directory shows (for Montpelier) a place called the Phoenix House, Thomas Smith, at 59 S. Main;

1901:   (b) as above; (d) as above, H. C. Holmes; (e) as above;

1905:   (b), (d), and (e), as above; (j) Miller's Inn, William Miller;

1908:   (b) as above; (d) as above; (e) as above;

1911:   (b) as above, T. J. Heaphy; (d) as above, H. C. Holmes; (e) as above, A. S. Sparrow; (j) as above;

1913:   (b), (d), (e), and (j), as above;

1915:   (b), (d), (e), and (j), as above;

1920:   (b) as above; (d) as above; (e) as above; Jewett Inn, A. C. Blanchard (lower State St; a boarding and rooming house behind the library, fronting on School St); The Kellogg, Mary C. McAvoy (unidentified); Riverside, C. L. Parmenter (128 State St); it is puzzling that this place only shows up now in Walton; it is shown on the 1873 Beers, and when it closed in 1946, it was said to be a hundred years old; there is a state office building on the site now; see photo, next page;

1925:   (b) Pavilion, as above, listed until c. 1930; (d) as above, H. C. Holmes; (e) Montpelier House, Mrs A. S. Sparrow; became Montpelier Tavern by 1928, so listed until at least 1968; (j) as above, Farrar and Burbank, listed until at least 1940.

(123b) West Montpelier.   No listings found.

Note: the assistance of Mr Robert N. Cleveland is gratefully acknowledged.

References

(1) Perry H. Merrill, Montpelier, the Capital City's History, 1780-1976 (Barre: Northlight

357

Studio Pr., 1977).

    (2) John Gridley, History of Montpelier (Montpelier: E. P. Walton, 1843).

The "Riverside," State Street. Montpelier, Vt.   810

Riverside

* * *

(124) **Moretown** (Washington).

    (124a) Moretown.

    1823: Cobb tavern, --; almanac, location unknown; also listed in almanacs in 1825, '29; tavern license to Silas W. Cobb, 1820-23;

    Note: tavern licenses to Joshua Luce, 1817; Elijah Winship, 1821-27; David Johnson, 1825-27; Simon Stevens, 1826; and Abner Child, 1830, locations unknown;

    1835: first hotel, Joseph Sawyer (Hemenway);

    1849: --, Joseph Sawyer (NEMU Dir);

    1856: --, George L. Noyes;

    1858: --, G. L. Noyes* (Walling);

    1870: -- B. F. Perry (B. L. in Vt Dir);

    1873: Village Hotel, G. Fisher* (Beers; same site as Walling, above); this is VDHP 1212-36, a minimart on the site in 1978;

    1873: --, D. Bruce (Vt Dir); Village Hotel, Noah Fisher (Walton);

    1875, '79, '80, '83:   --, Noah Fisher;

    1887: --, Peter L. Gay; (Central House, E. E. Joslyn, in Vt Dir);

    1889: Central House, B. N. and D. S. Phillips (Child);

1890:   Central House, D. S. Phillips (Vt Dir);

1892:   --, D. S. Phillips (Walton);

1895, '98, 1901, '05:   --, Gustavus Sherman;

1902:   Sherman House, H. G. Sherman (CVRR booklet);

1908:   Moretown, --;

1911:   --, Mrs Mary Sherman (same as Sherman's, above?); --, P. E. Griffith;

1914:   Moretown House, --* (Sanborn);

1913, '15:   --, Mrs Mary Sherman;

1920:   --, Daniel Irish;

1925:   --, A. L. Kingsbury.

* * *

(125) **Morgan** (Orleans). Includes Echo and Seymour Lakes.

(125a) Morgan.

1911, '15:   Lake View, --.

(125b) Morgan Center.

1883:   Seymour Lake House, F. C. O. Bush (Child); built before 1880 and burned about 1940 (1); it was 3 stories high, and had large verandas. The same account also mentions several summer lodges on Seymour Lake: Seymour Lodge, Gilliam Lodge, Vinton Lodge and the Quananichie Inn, all operating in the first part of the century, only Seymour Lodge still operating (i.e., 1990); Quananichie Inn operated until at least 1955, now a private dwelling; see photo;

Quananichie Inn

1887, '90:   Seymour Lake Lodge, F. Bush;

1901: The Alpine, F. L. Holmes; location unknown, could be Morgan.

* * *

<u>References</u>

(1) A. P. Hunt and V. Cobb, History of Morgan (Morgan: Morgan Bicentennial Committee, 1976).

* * *

(126) **Morristown** (Lamoille).

(126a) <u>Cadys Falls</u>.

(?):   a tavern, <u>Elisha Boardman</u>; north of Cadys Falls, where the road forks, one leading to Johnson, the other to Hyde Park (Hemenway); see discussion of Boardman under Morristown;

1849: --, E. Town (NEMU Dir); but Mower and Hagerman say that Town didn't build his place in Cadys Falls until 1853 (1); this is puzzling; listed as Morristown in NEMU;

1853: a hotel, <u>Edmund Town</u> (1); used as such for about 30 years, later a home (Fred and Ullie Dow in 1883); this was a 2-story building with an ell, and a dance hall in the ell;

1859: hotel, <u>E. Town</u>* (Walling);

1870, '75:   <u>Morrisville House</u>, Edmund Town (called the <u>Cadys Falls House</u> in Vt Dir, 1873).

(126b) <u>Morristown</u> (Morristown Corners).

c. 1800:   first tavern, <u>Elisha Boardman</u>; tavern license to an Opiah (Ozias?) Boardman, 1824-33;

* * *

"There is no doubt that the first tavern keeper in town was Elisha Boardman, but some question has been raised as to where his hotel was located. His descendants maintain that it was north of Cadys Falls...(which see)...This was the point at which the Boardmans located upon coming to town and unquestionably a house of entertainment for man and beast was kept there and is so reported in Hemenway...But according to...other authorities, Mr Boardman first settled at the Center (see below) opposite the cabin built by Jacob Walker, where his hotel served as town house and schoolhouse for a time as well as a hostelry. Here was hung out the oblong sign bearing, beside the name Boardman's Inn, the suggestive picture of a tankard and glasses."

The "Center" referred to here is the geographical center of the town, where Jacob Walker settled; it was on a road surveyed in 1800 that ran from Waterbury through Stowe past Walker's door and on to Hyde Park. (This would appear to be the road called Stagecoach Road in the Vermont Road Atlas, Northern Cartographic). Boardman subsequently moved north of Cadys Falls and opened another tavern there, if the account above is correct. (1)

* * *

Note: tavern licenses to Robert Kimball, 1817, '22; Joseph Noyes, 1822-25; William Gay (Joy?), 1822; Truman Tenney, 1825-30; Daniel Parsons, 1826; and David P. Noyes, 1827-29, locations unknown;

(?):   a hotel, <u>Joseph Sears</u>; tavern license, 1823-30; first at the Corners, in the house owned in 1935 by Eli Fisk; (1)

(?):   <u>Call-and-See House</u>, William Clement; on the Laporte Road (present Rte 100) "which diverted the Stowe travel from the Corners"; later sold to Lyman Woodworth, who kept the dance hall going; then a dwelling-house until about 1935, when it was again used for overnight lodging;

1850: Judge West's Tavern; there is a reference in Hemenway to Judge West's tavern burning in the winter of 1850; unidentified, no other reference found to this place.

(126c) Morrisville.

(?):   first hotel, E. V. Herrick; tavern license to Noyes, Bridge and Herrick, 1824-27; and to an Elias B. (?) Herrick, 1827-29;

(?):   Morrisville House, F. L. Matthews; "before 1853," on the site of the later Randall Hotel;

* * *

"Here for many years its proprietor, F. L. Matthews, was a well known figure and the hotel was the scene of many banquets, oyster suppers, dance (sic) and general good times as well as a home for the traveling public. Perhaps Mr Matthews' successors lacked his capacity to serve as a host, at any rate for many years there was an almost annual change of managers." (1) Among them were A. S. and M. T. Whipple; E. O. Hammond in 1870; Munroe Jocelyn in 1871; George Orcutt in 1872; B. S. Wilson in 1873; the Foster Brothers in 1875; and E. C. Carpenter in 1878. The place burned in 1879 when owned by a Mr Robbins, but was rebuilt; for several years, L. B. Boynton was owner and sometimes manager as well.

* * *

(?):   (b) Vermont House, A. G. West; West came in 1837, "served his apprenticeship...as proprietor of the Morrisville House"; built and managed the Vermont House on Portland St, on the site of the Kelley Block, now (i.e., 1935) occupied by the Ben Franklin store; this place catered primarily to railroad patrons, burned in a major fire in 1893;

1849: --, A. G. West (NEMU Dir);

1859: (a) Morrisville House, --* (Walling);

1870: (a) as above, --;

1873: (a) as above, Orcutt and Boynton;

1875: (a) as above, B. S. Wilson;

1878: (a) as above, L. B. and C. M. Boynton* (Beers);

1879: (a) as above, E. C. Carpenter;

1880, '83:   (a) as above, L. B. Boynton; (b) Vermont House, A. G. West; (both shown on 1889 birdseye view, ref 2);

1883: (a) as above (Child);

1887: (a) as above* (Sanborn, on the southwest corner of Summer and Main Sts intersection, called the Hotel Boynton, also listed that way in Vt Dir);

1888: (a) The Randall, C. F. Randall; (Boston and Maine guide);

1890: (a) Hotel Boynton, L. B. Boynton (Vt Dir); (b) Vermont House, --;

1891: (a) Randall House, Carroll F. Randall; "his genial personality making him an ideal landlord"; Randall bought the Morrisville House in 1891, moved it back to serve as the dining room and kitchen of a new, 3-story structure, facing Main St; he continued as proprietor for over 30 years. The property changed hands several times after his death in 1925; there was a damaging fire in 1928, and the building was razed in 1956;

1892: (a) <u>Morrisville House</u>, Carroll Randall* (Sanborn; it is still listed as the <u>Morrisville House</u> in Walton, but was the <u>Randall</u> from 1891); (b) as above* (also on Sanborn, but not operating by 1897, Sanborn); (c) <u>Union House</u>, S. W. Bolac* (Sanborn);

1895: (a) as above; (c) as above;

1897: (a) <u>Randall</u>* (Sanborn); (c) <u>Exchange</u>* (Sanborn; formerly the <u>Union House</u>);

1898: (a) as above; (c) <u>Exchange</u>, George Tillotson;

1901: (a) <u>The Randall</u>, C. F. Randall (see photo); (d) <u>Hotel Lamoille</u>, E. G. Foss; occupied the building where Aiken's Market and the Quality Restaurant were housed in 1935; burned in 1909, not rebuilt as a hotel;

1902, '04: (a) as above; (d) <u>Lamoille House</u>, E. A. Hill;

1903: (a) as above* (Sanborn); (c) <u>The Avalon</u>, --* (Sanborn; this is the former <u>Exchange/Union</u>);

1905: (a) as above; (c) <u>The Avalon</u>, E. G. Foss* (1903 Sanborn; closed by 1922, building standing); (d) <u>Lamoille House</u>, E. A. Hill;

1908: (a) as above; (c) as above;

1913, '16, '20, '25: (a) as above, --;

The Randall

1922, '28: (a) <u>Hotel Randall</u>, the only hotel operating (Sanborn). Carroll F. Randall, proprietor for over 30 years, died in 1925, and his funeral was held at the hotel; severely damaged by fire in 1928; several ownership changes, the last being Erwin D. Miller, place razed in 1956, gas station/parking lot now on the site.

Note: the assistance of Mr R. N. Terrill is gratefully acknowledged.

<u>References</u>

* * *

(1) Anna L. Mower and Robert Hagerman, Morristown Two Times (Barre: Northlight Studio Pr., for the Morristown Historical Soc., 1982). Note: this is a double volume, containing Mower's 1935 contribution with an update by Hagerman.

(2) J. Kevin Graffagnino, Vermont in the Victorian Age (Bennington: Vermont Heritage Press, 1985).

* * *

(127) **Mount Holly** (Rutland).

This mountain town includes three villages that have had post offices: Belmont, known as Mechanicsville until 1911, also including Star Lake; Healdville; and Mount Holly itself. The latter two places were on the old stage coach route across the mountains from Rutland to Ludlow. The township also has three hamlets that never achieved post office status: Bowlville, Hortonville and Tarbellville. No listings have been found for any of these latter places.

(127a) <u>Belmont</u> (Mechanicsville).

1810-16:   a tavern, <u>Nathan T. Sprague</u> (precise dates for the tavern not known, but he was PM during the period indicated; almanac, 1825, '29; tavern license, 1821-23 (under Mt Holly); listed in ref 1;

Note: local historians doubt that Mr Sprague had his tavern here; instead, it is believed that he had the <u>Clark tavern</u> in Mt Holly until 1833, when he sold to Rufus Crowley;

1873: --, Harvey Livingston; also 1878;

1887: <u>Chase House</u>, E. R. Chase; opened in 1883, a brick house on Main St; (2)

1888: <u>Lakeview-in-the-Mountains</u>, Mrs E. E. White; (Boston and Maine guide; probably same as <u>Lakeview Cottage</u>, below);

1892: <u>Trask House</u>, G. E. Trask;

1890s: "after the factory closed in 1889 (i.e., the Chase Toy Factory)...the town became something of a mecca for tourists. There were two summer hotels--one, <u>Green Mountain Cottage</u>, owned by A. B. Chadburn and the other, <u>Lake View Cottage</u>, owned by E. E. White." (3) <u>Green Mountain Cottage</u> was in Belmont village, the <u>Lake View</u> a little north on Belmont Rd; the 1897 Rutland Railroad guide lists <u>Green Mountain Cottage</u> (2 1/2 miles from the station) and the <u>Elms</u> (20 guests, 1/2 mile from the station, unidentified but presumably in Mount Holly);

1895, '98:   (a) <u>Green Mountain Cottage</u>, A. B. Chadburn (see photo, next page);

1901: (a) as above;

1905: (a) as above; --, E. E. White (this would be the <u>Lake View</u>);

1914: (a) as above* (Sanborn; listed as a boarding-house, also 1916 VPB);

1911, '15:   hotel and summer board, A. B. Chadbourne (sic), E. E. White;

1920: (b) <u>Lake-View-in-the-Mountains</u>, E. E. White; (also 1923 VPB);

1925: (a) <u>Green Mountain Cottage</u>, E. E. Chadburn (A. B.'s son); (b) as above, Mrs A. S. Hawes; the <u>Green Mountain Cottage</u> operated until c. 1963, <u>Lake View</u>, c. 1925; both now private homes.

(127b) <u>Healdville</u>.

c. 1786:   the <u>Green Stand</u>, Capt Joseph Green; the first hotel in town; almanacs, 1802-29; tavern license, 1807; across Branch Brook from the Green Cemetery; (4) Green was a veteran of the Revolutionary War; the tavern was "a large square, two-story house. It was taken down about 1919. There was a large barn across the road with a large floor with doors at each end to allow

363

stage coaches to enter with their teams in inclement weather...". Site occupied by Pratt's Antique Shop (i.e., 1982); (see also 109a, Ludlow); see photo;

Green Mountain Cottage

c. 1786:   second hotel, <u>David Bent</u>; "at the junction of the Lake Ninevah Road and the Shunpike, possibly Mrs Myrtle LeBrun now lives there, or across the road." (4) Almanacs, 1796, 1802, '07.

(?):   "the home of Mrs James Clifford was at one time a tavern with a large dance floor... about 1 mile west of the old Mt Holly PO on the old road to East Wallingford." (4)

(127c) <u>Mount Holly</u>

Note: tavern licenses, locations unknown, under Mt Holly, for Darius Green and John White, 1817, '21, '23; Horace Newton, 1821, '22; and Homer East, 1823;

c. 1786:   third hotel in town, <u>Stephen Clark</u>; near the Mount Holly Baptist Church where Raymond Maglione now lives (i.e., 1988); Clark was an original settler, said to have moved away in 1815, but listed in almanacs as a tavern-keeper, 1812-22; he was also the first PM, at a store in North Mount Holly kept by Lyman Clark and Martin Carviner, according to Child; but he is not listed in official Post Office records as having been a PM at any time; Tarbell says that this tavern was later kept by Nathan Sprague (see Belmont) (4); then Rufus Crowley (1833), D. T. Huntoon (1841), George E. Bingham (1843), Merritt H. Dickerman (1852);

Note: the Rutland Herald in 1838 (Oct 30) reports that "Rufus Crowley (see above) wants to sell the <u>Mt Holly Tavern</u>, once occupied by Judge Sprage (sic) and for past five years by Crowley";

c. 1800:   a toll stop, <u>Simeon Dickerman</u> (5); "in the northwest corner of town, on the turnpike, probably a tavern";

1844: an inn, <u>George E. Bingham</u>; "in the north part of the town near the meeting house" (4); this is the <u>Clark tavern</u>, see above;

1849: --, D. F. Huntoon (NEMU Dir; the old <u>Clark</u> tavern, above); there is a Rutland Herald reference to <u>D. T. Huntoon's Inn</u> (1/23/1838); --, A. Johnson (NEMU Dir, location unknown, could be Belmont or Healdville);

1854: --, --* (Scott map);

1897: <u>The Elms</u>, -- (see 1890s entry under Belmont).

The Green Stand
(History of Mount Holly, 1987, Carroll Tarbell)

Note: the assistance of Mr Carroll R. Tarbell, Mt Holly Historical Society, is gratefully acknowledged.

* * *

References

(1) George H. Beaman, "The Old Time Tavern," Rutland County Historical Society Proceedings <u>1</u> (1881): 77-81.
(2) Henry P. Smith and William S. Rann, History of Rutland County, Vermont, (Syracuse: D. Mason, 1886).
(3) James F. Holden, Mount Holly, Its Early Days (n.p., 1982?).
(4) Carroll R. Tarbell, History of Mount Holly, Vermont (n.p., 1987).
(5) Vermont Div. of Historic Preservation, Historic Architecture of Rutland County, Curtis B. Johnson, ed., Elsa Gilbertson, asst ed. (Montpelier: 1988).

* * *

(128) **Mount Tabor** (Rutland). Re-named Griffith in 1891.

1817: a tavern license to Edward C. Tabor;

(?):   <u>Clark Hunting Lodge</u>, -- (see photo).

* * *

(129) **Newark** (Caledonia).

(129a) <u>East Newark</u>.

No longer shown on most maps. It was a little north of East Haven, on what is now Rte 114, until 1842, when the East Haven-East Newark road was opened, the only way north in this area was through Newark.

1875: <u>Caledonia Springs House</u>, C. H. Ladd* (Beers).

(129b) <u>Newark</u> (also known as "Newark Street ").

(?):   first hotel, <u>Philomen Hartwell</u> (Child);

1849: --, Lauren M. Sleeper (NEMU Dir);

(?):   a hotel, <u>Daniel Smith</u> (Child).

* * *

(130) **<u>Newbury</u>** (Orange).

"When all the travel went along the public roads, taverns were common...Nearly all the taverns in Newbury were on the river road" (present Rte 5, more or less; from Wells, ref 1).

(130a) <u>Boltonville</u>. No listings found.

(130b) <u>Newbury</u>.

1769: first inn, <u>Robert Johnston</u>; according to the VDHP, it was on the site of a barn at either location #3 or #5 in the Newbury Village Historic District (0907-1), east side of Main St (Rte 5) just north of the turn-off for Haverhill, New Hampshire;

Clark Hunting Lodge, Mt Tabor

* * *

"Mr Perry says that the first tavern in Newbury was opened by Col Thomas Johnson after he built his new house in 1775, but it is certain that Col Robert Johnston kept an inn three or four years before that time." (1) The Mr Perry referred to above is the Rev Clark Perry, who preserved the early documents, kept notes.

* * *

1775: a tavern, <u>Col Thomas Johnson</u>; at the "oxbow," a little north of Newbury village; almanacs, 1796, 1802, '05; Johnson was PM when Vermont was a republic and also the first PM after Vermont joined the union; kept later by his son, Moses; this is VDHP 0907-38, #4; <u>Johnson's tavern</u> is listed in the 1796 Vermont Almanac and Register;

1785: an inn, <u>Col William Wallace</u>; possibly in the place which later became the <u>Spring Hotel</u> (see below) since Wallace was keeping that place in 1800;

1788: a tavern, Joseph Smith; in the house where E. H. Farnham and his sister lived in 1902, ref 1;

c. 1790:   a tavern, --; VDHP says that a building at site 0907-1, #62 (North Main St, east side) is believed to have been a tavern from c. 1790;

(?):   VDHP surveyed a building (0907-1, #2) on the west side of Route 5, a little north of where it crosses the railroad; built c. 1790, owned by Roy Bixby in 1977, a "possible" inn;

c. 1790:   Sawyer House, Capt Nehemiah Lovewell; almanac, 1796, 1805; (this was its name in 1902, ref 1); Lovewell kept tavern there until he died in 1801, and his widow continued until 1825; converted to a seminary boarding-house in 1833; on the curve on Rte 5 opposite the common; the site was occupied by the Hamlin house in 1977 (VDHP 0907-1, #31); there is a Lovell Tavern listed in the 1796 Vermont Almanac and Register, possibly the same place;

* * *

"Mrs Lovewell had trouble with Col Thomas Johnson over a barrel of rum, which she bought of him, and which she averred was more than half water. The colonel stoutly affirmed that it was rum, and nothing but rum, when it left his premises. The affair made much talk, and the colonel sued the widow for slander. It came out in the trial that the barrel had taken a whole night to travel the mile which lay between the two taverns, a circumstance which Mrs Lovewell's hired man, and two others, were very backward about explaining. But peace was restored." (1)

1796: Mill's tavern, --; in the Vermont Almanac and Register;

1800: Ingall's Inn, Jeremiah Ingalls; in a large house on what was called Ingall's Hill in 1902, ref 1; for about 10 years;

1800: Spring Hotel, Col William Wallace; originally a square, 2-story house; enlarged by Edward Little in 1810, who added a 3rd story; Little was followed by Barnard Brickett (Brickett's Inn); Peter Wheelock from 1833-1836; then Joseph Atkinson, and Tappan Stevens ("Judge" Stevens,) who enlarged it again, and had it for a long time. Run in connection with the sulphur springs which were discovered about 1782. Kept by Nelson B. Stevens after his uncle, Judge Stevens, retired. See photo, Chapter II.

* * *

"The hostelry was one of the noted inns of the north country, and always enjoyed the reputation of being a well-kept hotel, with a good run of custom, and was a popular summer resort in connection with the sulphur springs. About 1868, it came into the hands of Samuel L. Kendall, who added, in 1869, a fourth story with a French roof and cupola, and a wing containing thirteen rooms. He introduced gas, manufactured upon the premises. The main building then contained about forty rooms, was painted white, and was a very conspicuous landmark. In that house, as originally constructed, there was a secret apartment, known only to the proprietor, reached by a winding passage around one of the great chimneys, and fitted up with huge chests for the concealment of smuggled goods." (1)

* * *

(?):   Montebello House, James Spear; this was its name in 1902, when Wells was writing, original name unknown; enlarged several times, most recently by Rev William Clark in 1873;

1834: Newbury House, Timothy Morse; who added the brick part of it to the original wooden structure, which was a store owned by Moses Wallace; "across the street and northeast of the library, where Harlie Slack now lives" (i.e., 1978, ref 2); many owners, including Nelson B. Stevens, Hiram Hill, and Ezekiel Sawyer from 1854 to 1856; converted into apartments about 1889, burned in 1906; site is shown as VDHP 0907-1, #64, on North Main St; the VDHP says it was a boarding-house;

1849: (a) <u>Spring Hotel</u>, Tappan Stevens; (b) <u>Newbury House</u>, Elijah Austin (NEMU Dir);

1855, '56:   (a) as above; --, J. S. Appleton (probably the <u>Newbury House</u>);

1858: (a) <u>Spring Hotel</u>, T. Stevens* (Walling); (b) <u>Newbury House</u>, N. B. Stevens* (Walling);

1870: --, Kendall and Demerritt (Vt Dir);

1870: (b) as above, S. A. Kendall (Walton; this is confusing, since Wells has Kendall at the <u>Spring House</u> in 1868); (1)

1873: (a) as above, R. W. Chamberlain; (b) as above, also R. W. Chamberlain (Vt Dir); there is a photo, c. 1875, of "Montebello Springs" with a hotel, presumably the <u>Spring House</u>, in the background; (3)

1875: (a) and (b) as above, both listed as being managed by R. W. Chamberlain in Walton;

1877: (a) as above, R. W. Chamberlain* (Beers);

1879: (a) as above, A. L. Fabyan;

1883: (c) <u>Sawyer House</u>, George A. Sawyer;

1888: (c) as above (Child, and Boston and Maine guide); <u>Montebello House</u>, Joseph E. Wesener (Child);

1887, '92, '95, '98: (c) <u>Sawyer House</u>, George A. Sawyer;

1898: --, M. A. Gale (unidentified);

1901: <u>Gale House</u>, Maurice Gale (Vt Dir, unidentified); (c) as above;

1908: (c) as above; --, M. A. Gale;

1911:   (c) --, G. A. Sawyer;

1905, '13, '15:   (c) as above; no hotel shown on the 1914 Sanborn, and the <u>Sawyer House</u> burned in a major fire on June 14, 1913;

1920s: <u>Newbury Inn</u>, Mr and Mrs Charles White; VDHP 0907-1, #34, on the south side of the common; built in 1856, first used as a boarding-house for seminary students; listed until at least 1946, now a real estate office.

(130c) <u>Newbury Center</u>.

(?):   a tavern, <u>Samuel Gibson</u>; who "kept store, many years ago, in a wing of the tavern-house built by him, and afterward long used by John Wood at the Centre" (i.e., 1902, ref 1); burned in 1899.

(130d) <u>South Newbury</u>.

(?):   a tavern, <u>Col Remembrance Chamberlain</u> and his son, Col Moody Chamberlain; on the place called Riverside Farm in 1902 (1); the old building burned in 1876.

(130e) <u>Wells River</u>.

(?):   first hotel, <u>Benjamin Bowers</u>; almanac, 1802, '05; who came before 1796 (1); where the

Baldwin Block was situated in 1902; a small place, and when Joshua Hale succeeded Bowers it became an ell to the larger place that Hale built, which came to be known as the <u>Wells River House</u>, and later, <u>Hale's Tavern</u>;

(?): <u>Wells River House</u>, - Johnson; Johnson was the proprietor in 1902; the place was built by the Hales (see above) for Mrs Hale's sister, Mrs Barstow; the Hales kept the place many years, and were followed by one Pickett, Justus Gale, Jesse Cook, Simeon Stevens, Young and Hobbs, Sawyer and Chaplin, Jacob Kent, and Harry B. Stevens;

c. 1830: <u>Coosuck House</u>, --; "where the new hotel now is" (i.e., 1902, ref 1); built by Col Jacob Kent; kept by Henry Slack and William R. Austin, and later Slack alone; later still, Slack returned, "kept it until he died, having bought it of Colonel Kent" (1); it has been kept by one Hartshorn; by Durant and Adams; and by one Fry; it burned in 1892, and the present one (i.e., 1902) was built on its site by Col Kent; (1)

(?): an inn, <u>Henry F. Slack</u>; after he left the <u>Coosuck House</u>, in a house north of S. S. Peach's present dwelling (i.e., c. 1902, ref 1); burned some time ago; Slack went back to the <u>Coosuck House</u> (see above); Slack leased his place to John A. Bowen at one point;

* * *

In the Wells River Historic District (VDHP 0907-110), #14 is the site of the <u>Coosuck House</u> (burned in 1892) and of <u>Hale's Tavern</u> (burned also, date not established, still listed in the VPB in 1955); a Gulf station was on the site in 1978; site #78, the Durant-Adams block, is on the site of the <u>Wells River House</u>, first hotel in the village, according to VDHP, and kept by Ezekiel Sawyer, 1838-1950 (this is not in agreement with other information).

* * *

1849: <u>American House</u>, H. F. Slack; (b) <u>Wells River House</u>, Chaplin and Sawyer; (both NEMU Dir);

1870: (a) <u>Coosuck House</u>, U. Durant;

1873: (a) as above, Durant and Adams; <u>Private Hotel</u>, M. S. Slack (Vt Dir; unidentified);

1875: (a) as above, U. Durant; --, M. G. (?) Slack;

1877, '79: (a) as above, Durant and Adams* (1877 Beers);

1883: (a) as above, Union H. Durant; <u>Cottage Hotel</u>, W. B. Johnson;

1887: (b) <u>Wells River House</u>, W. P. (?) Johnson; -, F. P. Danforth;

1888: (b) as above, William P. Johnson (Child);

1888: (c) <u>Hale's Tavern</u>, J. F. Hale (Boston and Maine guide);

1890: (b) as above, George M. Frye;

1892: (b) --, George F. (?) Frye;

1895, '98, 1901: (b) <u>Wells River House</u>, William P. Johnson; (c) <u>Hale's Tavern</u>, Jerome F. Hale; see photo;

1905, '08, '11, '13, '16, '20: (c) as above;

Jerome Hale came to Wells River in 1895 as proprietor of <u>Hale's Tavern</u>, which he owned for 40 years. "Hale's Tavern became one of the best known hotels in the North country, and its owner, Jerome Hale, took a great deal of interest in his fellowmen and that helped to make him a good hotel proprietor. He used to notice heavy men particularly, and make them weigh themselves. He listed them if they weighed over 200, and finally the New England Fat Men's Club was formed. It held meetings twice a year, usually in Wells River, and Mr Hale took great pride in putting on a 'big feed'...<u>Hale's Tavern</u> became headquarters for the New England Fat Men's Club, an organization in which every member must tip the scales at 200 pounds. A great deal of fun was derived from this unique organization. Among these was the choosing of officers by their weight-- the president weighing the most." (1)

Hale's Tavern

1925: (c) as above, W. F. Burleigh; until at least 1955, razed c. 1960.

Note: there is an excellent photo, said to be of the "Parker House" (Special Collections, UVM) in Wells River. Unfortunately, no "Parker House" turned up in the usual sources for Wells River, nor does this place (a substantial 3 and 1/2 story building) seem to correspond to any of the other "Parker Houses" in Vermont, nor to the <u>Coosuck</u> or <u>Hale's Tavern</u>; it is possible that it is the <u>Wells River House</u>.

(130f) <u>West Newbury</u>.

c. 1804: a tavern, <u>John Smith</u>; on a farm owned by his grandson, John Smith in 1902, who had the old tavern sign when Wells was writing; (1)

(?): a tavern, <u>Gideon Tewksbury</u>; "for a long time, on what is now called the Cunningham place, near the Bradford line" (1902, ref 1).

* * *

References

(1) Frederic P. Wells, History of Newbury, Vermont, 1704-1902 (St Johnsbury: Caledonian, 1902).

(2) Selectmen, Town of Newbury, History of Newbury, Vermont, 1900 to 1977 (Bradford: Fox Publ., 1978).

(3) J. Kevin Graffagnino, Vermont in the Victorian Age (Bennington: Vermont Heritage Press, 1985).

* * *

(131) **Newfane** (Windham).

Became the shire town in 1787, when the courts were moved from Westminster to the settlement on Newfane Hill (first Newfane). Court buildings moved to the valley settlement (Fayetteville) in 1825, because of difficulty of access to the hill during the winter, and the rest of the village soon followed. Name changed from Fayetteville to 2nd Newfane in 1882.

(131a) Newfane (Fayetteville).

(?): a tavern, Col Ephraim Holland; before the Revolutionary War, about one mile southeast of the settlement on Newfane Hill, on north side of the road to Brattleboro; Holland died in 1822, the building was moved to Fayetteville in 1840; (1)

1787: first tavern, Luke Brown; a tavern and store combined, in partnership with Luke Knowlton, an original settler; partnership soon dissolved, and Knowlton took in Ezekiel Knowlton; later proprietors included John Holbrook, 1785-90; Capt Adams; Dr Brooks; Oliver Chapin and Zatter Butterfield; Joseph Ellis; David W. Sanborn; and Anthony Jones (Jones Coffee House or Tavern); tavern license to Jones, 1817, '20-30;

Note: tavern licenses also to Josiah Willard, 1817, '20-23; Calvin Townsley, 1820-25; Asa Knight, 1824, '25; David Reed, 1821-24; Henry Wheelock, 1822-33; David Johnson, 1828; Williams and Sanborn, 1817; James Blake, 1827; Benjamin Ormsbee; 1828-30; David Hayward, 1829; Austin Birchard, 1826, locations unknown;

c. 1830: Jones Tavern, Anthony Jones; brought down from the Hill about this date; also known as Fayetteville Inn, Pratt's Inn, Bowles Hotel, Vermont Hotel, Newfane Inn. A Birchard store opened on Newfane Hill in 1822, and moved to the new village in 1825. DeWitt Leonard says that Anthony Jones "began" soon after the Birchards, suggesting that he built the original Fayetteville House on the Hill in the 1820s. (1) This was moved to the new village and is the central block of the Newfane Inn, still operating. It is possible, however, that Jones began his brief career as an innkeeper in Brown's Tavern (see above), where he is known to have been a late proprietor; and that this is the building moved;

Note: Mr Robert L. Crowell, Windham County Historical Society, has compiled a list of owners of the Newfane Inn from land records. This list is not in complete agreement with information from other sources, probably because the owner of record was not always the proprietor. The land record list is: Anthony Jones, who sold to Samuel N. Adams in 1832 (tavern license, 1833); transferred to Edson Higgins, then Arad Burnett until 1841; Ezra Purple until 1845; William H. Williams until 1857; Charles and Eunice Wakefield until 1866; Wallers and Ingrams until 1867; Francis D. Sawyer until 1870; Stillman and Jane Worcester until 1894; Harrie G. E. Pratt until 1897; Hattie and Eugene N. Augier, 1897; Newton A. Dickinson, 1903; Samuel G. Brown, Frank A. DeWitt, then the Newfane Hotel Co, 1905-16; Elmer A. and Augusta E. Whitcomb, until 1942; Eric and Gundela S. H. Weindl as of 1978;

1849: (a) Windham County House, William H. Osgood (NEMU Dir; built about 1825, VDHP 1312-11, enlarged in 1854); #14 on a 1983 historic district map of Newfane; (b) Vermont Hotel, W. C. Perry (NEMU Dir); this is almost surely the Fayetteville House/Newfane Inn, built by Anthony Jones "on the hill," brought down and enlarged in the late 1820s; VDHP 1312-3; #37 on a 1983 historic district map of Newfane;

1855: --, E. Wheelock; --, J. W. Perry;

1856: --, E. Wheelock; --, F. G. Knapp;

1856: (b) Vermont Hotel, --* (McClellan map);

1869: (a) hotel and jail, Thomas Evans, proprietor and jailer* (Beers; this is the Windham County House, although not so labeled on the map); a second unnamed hotel is shown on the Vermont Hotel site; presumably the Newfane Inn;

There is a ditty about the County House, by James Ray, printed in 1848:

Wm. H. Osgood, Jailer and Innkeeper.

Says William H., I keep fresh steak
Good pies, and Oyster soup;
And ham and eggs, two kinds of bread,
And cupboard stuff to boot.

* * *

1870: (a) Windham County House, Thomas Evans;

1873, '75: (a) as above, C. P. Stone; (b) Fayetteville House, Charles Bowles (Jones Tavern, Bowles Hotel, Vermont Hotel, Newfane Inn);

1879, '80:   (a) as above; (b) as above, S. and C. S. Worcester (also spelled Wooster);

1883: (a) as above, H. G. Underwood; (b) as above, S. Wooster and son;

1884: (b) as above, Stillman Wooster (Child);

1888: (b) Newfane Inn, J. E. Smiley;

1887, '90, '92, '95: (a) as above, George W. Underwood; (b) as above;

1898: (a) as above, H. A. Kilburn; Burke's Inn, H. M. Burke (presumably still the Newfane House);

1901: (a) as above, F. E. Davis; (b) Newfane House, H. M. Burke;

1902: (a) as above, M. F. Spencer (CVRR guide); (b) as above;

1905, '08:   (a) as above; (b) as above, C. H. Minchen;

1911: (a) County House, M. F. Benson; (b) Newfane Inn, J. E. Smiley; see photos;

1913, '15, '20, '25: (a) as above, --*; hotel portion razed in 1956; (b) as above, --* (same site as the Vermont House, 1856; the Newfane Inn is still operating in 1988 as the Old Newfane Inn); both of these places are on the 1915 Sanborn map;

Note: a place operating from 1936-50 as the Vermont Inn and from 1950-c. 1966 as the West Valley Inn (when it became a private home) was listed in Walton for "summer board" by 1915; (#53 on a 1983 historic district map of Newfane).

(131b) South Newfane (originally known as Pondville).

1869: --, --* (Beers).

(131c) Williamsville.

c. 1815:   an inn, David Reed; tavern license, 1823, '24; main part built earlier as a home by Ebenezer Morse; proprietors who followed Reed were Emory and Asa Wheelock, 1829; Henry Wheelock, 1829-35 and 1837-39; George A. Morse, 1835-37; Luke A. Wright, 1839-46; Clark Adams and Samuel Hall, 1846-51; Richmond Dunklee, 1851-56; A. L. Howard, 1856-58; Fred Thompson, 1858-60; Lucius Halladay, 1860-70; H. E. Harris, 1870-72; S. W. Bowker since 1872; (1)

1849: --, Samuel Hall (NEMU Dir);

County House

1869: a hotel, <u>L. Halladay</u>* (Beers);

1870: --, L. Halladay;

1873, '75:   (a) <u>Williamsville House</u>, S. W. Bowker;

1879, '80:   (a) as above, H. O. Bowker;

1883: (a) as above, H. P. Hendricks;

1884: (a) as above, Frank B. Plimpton; (J. G. Hall in 1885 in Vt Dir);

1887: (a) as above, Shipman and Brown; this building still standing as a private home in 1988;

1898: --, Dewitt Fisher;

Note: the assistance of Mr Robert L. Crowell, Newfane, and the Windham County Historical Society, is gratefully acknowledged.

References

(1) Centennial Proceedings and other historical facts and incidents relating to Newfane, the county seat of Windham County, Vermont, 1774-1874 (Brattleboro: DeWitt Leonard, 1877).

Newfane Inn

(132) **New Haven** (Addison).

(132a) <u>Beldens</u>, (132b) <u>Brookville</u>, and (132c) <u>Dana</u>, no listings found.

(132d) <u>New Haven</u>.

(?):   a tavern, <u>Capt Matthew Phelps</u>; probably about 1800; Phelps was the first PM (1802-04) and his son, Matthew Jr, was PM from 1804-08; the office was in this tavern "more or less regularly until the mid-1800s" (1); taken over by James Saxton some time after 1816, and run by his son-in-law, Anson Bird, for many years; "Bird was commended in 1837 for operating his establishment 'on temperance principles'; this place became the <u>New Haven Hotel/Partch Hotel</u> (see below);

1796: a tavern, <u>Moses Stow</u>; location shown on map in ref 1, on Town Hill, along present Rte 7 south of New Haven Junction, on the north side; the place stayed in the Stow family until 1963, not clear how long it was a tavern; it was owned by Loyal W. Stow in 1846, and until at least 1856, and Edson A. and Alice Stow Doud, 1866-1913;

1825, '29:   <u>Gage tavern</u>, --; (almanac, locaton unknown);

1849: --, L. W. Stow (NEMU Dir; see immediately above); <u>Townhill House</u>, E. L. Caldwell (unidentified);

1855, '56:   --, L. W. Stow;

1856: a hotel, <u>Loyal W. Stow</u>* (Walling);

1870, '73, '75, '79: (a) <u>New Haven Hotel</u>, William M. Partch; also known as the <u>Partch Hotel</u>; same as the <u>Phelps Tavern</u>, see above; map in ref 1 shows the location of this place, same as on 1871 Beers; and the same as a place occupied by Mrs Anson Bird, a later proprietor, on the 1857 Walling; proprietors following Matthew Phelps were James Saxton, 1816; Betsey Saxton Bird, 1857 (Mrs Anson Bird, presumably); Timothy Smith, 1859; James T. Hyde, 1861; Charles E. Varney, 1866; William M. Partch, 1868; Frederick M. and William H. Partch, 1891; Frederick M. Partch, 1894; the place burned in 1920, and a private home was built on the site, owned by Harvey and Gail Smith in 1984;

1871: --, William M. Partch* (Beers);

1880: (a) as above, H. S. Langdon (Walton, ?);

1881: (a) as above, William M. Partch (Child);

1883, '87, '90, '92: (a) as above, William M. Partch;

1895, '98, 1901:   (a) as above, F. M. Partch; burned in 1920;

1915: no hotel shown on the Sanborn map.

(132e) <u>New Haven Junction</u> (Depot). No post office.

c. 1840:   a hotel, --; on Rte 7, about 1 mile south of New Haven Junction; "for farmers taking stock to market in the 1840s-50s" (VDHP 0113-26, apartments in 1975).

(132f) <u>New Haven Mills</u>.

c. 1820:   a tavern, <u>Peter Bradley</u>; a map in ref 1 shows a tavern site, c. 1820-50, with proprietors being Peter Bradley, 1822; John Howdin, 1825; Andelotia Pier, 1823; Rodman Chapman, 1825; William Granger, 1830; Benjamin Walker and Hiram Rider, 1839;

1901: --, George A. Summer.

* * *

References

(1) Harold Farnsworth and Robert Rodgers, A History of New Haven in Vermont, 1761-1983 (New Haven: The Town, 1984).

* * *

(133) **Newport** (Orleans).

On Lake Memphremagog. First chartered as Duncansborough, but in 1816, when the state was straightening out conflicting surveys and grants, part of the old town of Salem was added and the name was changed to Newport. The part that was added included West Derby (East Newport, locally) and the Lake Bridge area, which became part of Newport city when it was incorporated in 1917. The rest of Salem became part of Derby in 1880, including the sites of two old taverns described in Nelson (1); see Derby for a description of the Hopkinson and Blake taverns.

(133a) Newport.

c. 1795: a tavern, --; in the Adams Bay area, where the first settlement in Duncansborough was made by James and Martin Adams in 1793; they came down the Barton River, settled near where it runs in to Lake Memphremagog; there was a tavern there soon after, on present Lake Road; (1)

(?): Lane's Tavern, Seymour Lane; tavern license, 1823-32; at the intersection of the "Burlington Road" (Rtes 100, 105) and City Farm Rd, in Newport town; reference to a meeting here in 1831; also a reference to this tavern and its location, c. 1800, in Currier. (2) The tavern apparently moved (or Lane moved and re-established himself) to the Lake Bridge area, around 1838: "This area referred to as Lake Bridge till the post office was brought down from Seymour Lane's Tavern (1832) and brought the name of Newport with it." (1) Nelson says the PO was established in 1832, the Post Office Department says 1834; Lane was the first PM (1834-40); it is not clear if Lane reestablished himself as a tavern-keeper in the Lake Bridge area after the move;

1824: tavern license to Ira Richards, location unknown;

1835: a hotel, Horatio N. Wright;

1836: first hotel in West Derby, William Blake; Blake apparently kept a tavern on his farm east of the village until one James Dane built a 2-story hotel at what is now (i.e., 1977, ref 1) the corner of Main and Sias Sts in Newport city; this became the Magoon Block, still standing in 1977; not clear if this is the date when Dane built the hotel, or when Blake kept the tavern on his farm;

1836: a tavern, George W. Smith; he sold the place to Isaac Ramsdell in 1837, and proceeded to build a new 2-story tavern on the north side of the street (see immediately below);

1837: Smith's Tavern (second), which became the Memphremagog House, George W. Smith; built on the north side of the street, just past the log bridge on the Newport side; not clear when it was first called the Memphremagog House, certainly by the time it was acquired by Phineas Page in 1851; he built a 2-story addition on the east end in 1854; see photo;

* * *

"Mrs Page was an excellent landlady, and she added as much to the reputation of the house as her husband; her fish dinners of 'lake trout' were known as far as the Memphremagog House...Mrs Page was a very benevolent and philanthropic woman, several families in destitute circumstances were fed not wholly from the crumbs of her table, but with full loaves.

375

One thing she did...she learned that teams occasionally dropped through the ice into the lake and she obtained a long rope and kept it in a secure place, in readiness to be used especially on such occasions.

West of the hotel there was a long open horse shed with a dance hall in the second story, extending to the hotel stables. These two buildings stood exactly on the land where now (i.e., 1912) stands the brick block of E. Lane and Son." (1)

* * *

"Mr Page was a shoemaker and he kept his bench in the bar room and did shoemaking when his attention was not required at the bar." (2)

* * *

The Memphremagog House was sold to Samuel and Simon Pender in 1858; they remodeled the old parts and built a 2-story central part; the railroad bought the place soon after it (the Connecticut and Passumpsic Rivers Railroad) came through to Newport in 1863; the old parts were torn down in 1869 and 1870, and the place was expanded again, for the summer tourist trade. There were a number of managers, but W. H. Bowman was manager when the hotel was in the height of its glory; the most imposing hotel in Newport, it could accommodate four hundred guests "and often was so full that extra rooms were rented elsewhere." (1)

Memphremagog House (Special Collections, UVM)

* * *

"This famous house entertained royalty. June 17, 1866, Sir Hugh Allan escorted here His Royal Highness, Prince Arthur of England and Sir John Young, Governor of Canada...later when Mr Bowman was proprietor, the house was run as a summer resort by...the Passumpsic Railroad, guests coming each year from Philadelphia, New York and Boston...The railroad ran excursions in here from all down the line and they had an opera company from Boston who played here a week at a time such light operas as 'H.M.S. Pinafore', 'The Mikado'... the afternoon matinee was in the old dance pavilion at Bayview Park on the east lake shore just opposite the Mountain House below Owl's Head. There would be such crowds on the boat that Captain Fogg would stand on the upper deck warning people not to rush from side to side for fear the boat would capsize. If the railroad did not have enough passenger cars...they sometimes used the common platform cars with benches nailed to the floor and evergreen trees put around the sides to make the cars look better. They had band tournaments at Lake Park and fireworks on the lawn of the hotel in the evening. Newport was some gay place at that time." (1)

The first railroad terminal in Newport was in front of the <u>Memphremagog House</u> for a few years, with the station in the basement. The hotel burned on May 15, 1907, and was not replaced. (See also Chapter IV).

* * *

1849: (a) <u>Magog House</u> (<u>Memphremagog House</u>), P. Page (NEMU Dir); this predates by 2 years the time when Nelson says Page acquired it; --, Horace N. Wright (NEMU Dir; this place unidentified);

1855, '56:   (a) --, Phineas Page;

1859: --, --* (Walling; the <u>Magog House);</u> see cover illustration;

c. 1865:   <u>Lake House</u>, B. Beloyd; built after the railroad came, about where the freight office and Poulin's Grain Store now stand (1977, ref 1); later moved across the street at Railroad Square, burned about 1901 or 1902;

1873: (b) <u>Bellevue Hotel</u>, Horace Bean; on Main Street, opposite the <u>Memphremagog House</u>; a 3-story brick building with a long, 2-story veranda on the front; Bean kept it for 5 years, with E. Knowlton as manager; the PO was in an ell of the building; sold in 1878 to Jerry and Ellen Drew, former owners of the <u>St Johnsbury House</u>; in 1886, Drew changed its name to <u>Newport House</u> (second place with that name; see below under <u>Newport House</u>, 1891); both the <u>Bellevue</u> and the <u>Memphremagog House</u> are shown in a birdseye view of the period; (3)

1870, '73:   (a) as above, W. F. Bowman; <u>Lake House</u>, Horace Bean;

1873: <u>Newport House</u> (first), N. C. and A. J. Cole;

1875: (a) as above; (b) <u>Bellevue House</u>, Horace Bean; <u>Newport House</u>, Cole Brothers;

1878: (a) as above, Bush and Robinson* (Beers); (b) as above, H. Bean* (Beers); <u>Newport House</u>, N. C. Cole* (Beers);

1879, '80:   (a) as above, C. A. Gleason; (b) as above;

1883: (a) as above, W. F. Bowman; (b) as above, Jerry Drew;

1883: (a) as above (Child); (b) as above, Emery Knowlton (Child);

1885: (a) as above, --* (Sanborn); (b) <u>Bellevue House</u>, --* (Sanborn);

1887: (a) as above, W. H. Witt; (b) 2nd <u>Newport House</u>, Jerry Drew (formerly the <u>Bellevue</u>); <u>Lake House</u>, C. M. Cade (C. W. in Vt Dir); <u>Arlington House</u>, B. W. Lee; <u>Central House</u>, Eugene E. Joslyn (Vt Dir, unidentified);

1889: Sanborn shows <u>Memphremagog House</u>, the <u>Newport House</u> (formerly the <u>Bellevue</u>) and the <u>Lake Hotel</u>; all three are also shown in 1895, 1906;

1890: (a) as above; <u>Central House</u>, Eugene E. Joslyn; <u>Lake House</u>, A. A. Brown; (b) 2nd <u>Newport House</u>, H. W. Bishop;

1891: (b) 2nd <u>Newport House</u>, Jerry Drew; he was also leasing the <u>Memphremagog House</u> this year; Drew converted the first <u>Newport House</u>, which had stood just beside the <u>Bellevue</u>, into a business block (the Drew Block; see photo, next page); it became the <u>Hurst Hotel</u> later, was razed in 1973 (see below). Drew died in 1892, but the family kept the <u>Newport</u> several more years; A. A.

377

Vallee was manager in 1893; sold in 1902 to Harry Stewart, who owned it 17 years; sold then to A. M. Bowen and Grace Bowen; Fred Sisco and Frank Hapgood were managers in the 1920-25 period; place sold to Fred Hall and Kathryn McLean in 1925, Hall sole owner in 1933. Completely renovated during Hall's 20-year tenure. Other owners, the last being Robert and Marie Keroack; site now occupied by a Chittenden Trust Company bank;

1892: (a) as above; (b) as above; Arlington House, B. W. Lee;

1895: (a) as above, G. F. Goode; (b) as above, A. H. Valley; Arlington House, W. L. Lindsey; Lake House, A. A. Brown;

1898: (a) as above, Campbell and Holbrook; (b) as above, J. H. Gaines; Lake House, D. W. Sisco;

1901: (a) as above, Sisco and Holbrook; (b) as above, Sisco and Holbrook; Central House, S. G. Scott (unidentified); Lake House, R. C. Sisco;

1903: Raymond Hotel, Fred Sisco; on the old Lake House site; D. W. and Louisa Sisco proprietors in 1906, H. L. Doyle in 1916; burned before World War II, last operated by Earl M. and Louvian Goddard; a big hotel, close to the lake and the station, popular with travelers (photo, ref 1);

1905: (a) as above, G. F. Goode; (b) as above, Frank Hapgood; Hotel Raymond, D. W. Sisco (all three also on Sanborn);

1908: (a) as above; (b) as above; Lake House, D. W. Sisco; this is puzzling, and unresolved, because the Raymond Hotel is said to have been built on the Lake House site about 1903 (see above);

1911: (b) Newport House, F. E. Hapgood; The Raymond, D. W. Sisco; see photo;

1913: (b) as above; The Raymond, D. W. Sisco; Hotel Elder, J. G. Elder;

1909, '13: (a) Memphremagog House now gone from the Sanborn map; (b) Newport House and the Raymond both shown;

1915: (b) Newport House, H. L. Doyle; The Raymond, D. W. Sisco;

1916: The Raymond, H. L. Doyle; --, C. A. Ramsdell;

1919: (b) as above* (Sanborn); New City Hotel* (Sanborn; formerly the Raymond);

1920: (b) as above, F. D. Burns; Hotel Elder, J. G. Elder; New City, Earl Goddard;

1923: (b) Newport House, A. M. Bowen; Hurst's Hotel, Richard Hurst; Hotel Raymond, E. M. Goddard; Roeder's Inn, Albert Roeder (on the lake, one-half mile from the station);

1925: (b) as above, A. M. Bowen (also on Sanborn, still listed in 1968); The Raymond, Earl Goddard (also on Sanborn, with its name changed back from New City); Hotel Elder, Mrs J. G. Elder (listed in 1930, not in 1935); Hurst Hotel, Richard Hurst (also on Sanborn, but gone by 1958; see photo);

(?): Hurst Hotel, Richard Hurst; in the building that was the first Newport House, then the Drew Block; between the second Newport House and the tracks, "the basement facing the tracks held the restaurant and offered easy access to railroad men and travelers to eat or sleep. On the Main St side were several stores with rooms above"; (1)

1st Newport House and Bellevue House
(Special Collections, UVM)

The Raymond

* * *

There were also a number of summer hotels on that part of Lake Memphremagog lying in Canada, including the <u>Mountain House</u> at Owl's Head (see photo, next page). The following account of this popular resort, accessible by lake steamer from Newport, is from the Township Sun for August, 1984.

"One of the most attractive summer hotels ever built on Memphremagog was the Mountain House, built in 1855 on the bay at the base of Owl's Head. It burned a few years after it was completed but a larger one was immediately constructed and was so successful that it was soon enlarged to accommodate 100 people. It reached the zenith of its popularity in 1889 and a new owner added another ell which gave the hotel a total of 400 rooms. Ideally situated at the foot of the towering Owl's Head Mountain, and with an unsurpassed view of the lake, it had 500 acres of mountain, woodlands and gardens with well-kept tennis courts as well as bowling and croquet greens. There was a large separate pavilion for dancing in addition to boathouses and stables. The hotel had its own steam launch 'Owl' for the exclusive use of guests and it connected with early morning trains as well as taking visitors on excursions around the lake. Other guests arriving by train at Magog or Newport were able to board the 'Mountain Maid' or 'The Lady of the Lake' at the quays close to the stations...This beautiful summer hotel flourished until 1899 when a second disastrous fire destroyed it completely and it was never rebuilt."

Hurst Hotel

Mountain House (Special Collections, UVM)

(133b) Newport Center.

1870: Newport Center House, H. M. Deane;

1873: Spring House, A. R. Gilner;

1875: (a) Newport Springs House, A. L. Soper;

1878: Sleeper's Hotel, G. L. Sleeper* (Beers; PO in the hotel); there is a problem here, because Nelson says that Sleeper ran "the hotel in Newport Center from 1866 to 1885 except for three years" (1); were there two hotels during much of this time? The Sleeper Hotel burned on August 20, 1886, in a major fire, shortly after Sleeper had leased it to Frank Decatur;

1880: (a) as above, George L. Sleeper;

1883: Newport Center House, J. Buzzell (probably same place as above);

1883: Austin House, A. Chandler Austin (Child; not identified);

1887: (a) as above, F. Decatur;

1887: Jenkins Hotel, S. W. Jenks (Vt Dir);

1898: Hotel Niles, Elmer Niles; Cottage House, M. A. Phillips;

1914: no hotel on Sanborn map.

(133c) South Newport. No listings found.

(133d) West Newport (East Troy, locally). No listings found.

Note: the assistance of Emily W. Nelson, Newport, is gratefully acknowledged.

References

(1) Emily M. Nelson, Frontier Crossroads, the Evolution of Newport, Vermont (Canaan, N.H.: Phoenix Publ. for the Newport History Committee, 1977).
(2) John M. Currier, "Sketches in the early history of Newport village," Orleans County Historical Society Proceedings (1888): 48-51.
(3) J. Kevin Graffagnino, Vermont in the Victorian Age (Bennington: Vermont Heritage Press, 1985).

* * *

(134) **Northfield** (Washington).

Three villages in the town have had post offices: Northfield itself, also known as Depot Village; Northfield Falls (Gouldsville until 1905); and South Northfield. The first two are still operating. There is also a section just south of Northfield on Route 12, known as Center Village in the old days, which once dominated the town but never had a post office. The coming of the railroad to the "depot village" in 1848 changed things almost overnight, especially since the offices and shops of the Vermont Central were located there for many years. (Charles Paine, its president, was a Northfield man).

(134a) Center Village (no post office).

1818: Center Village Hotel, Capt Abel Keyes; with his son, Joseph, for about 5 years; they both had tavern licenses in 1820;

1820s: a tavern, Ebenezer Frizzle; location unknown; Frizzle came in 1823, died in 1849;

Note: tavern licenses   to Elijah Smith, Jr, 1822, '30, and John Starkweather, 1821, '22, locations unknown (not even which village);

1837: a hotel, Isaac W. Brown; bought out his father, carried on for a number of years; moved to Depot village in 1855 (which see);

1849: --, Isaac W. Brown (NEMU Dir);

1855: a hotel, Isaac W. Brown; (possibly Depot Village);

(?): Blood's Hotel, --; also known as the National and Brown's Hotel; built by Capt Abel Keyes in 1818, and almost certainly the same as the Center Village Hotel (see above; ref 1); McIntire also says that Joel, and then Isaac, Brown owned the place after Keyes, when it was known as Brown's Hotel (see above also); on present Rte 12, facing the Center park;

* * *

"During the long tenure of Bill Blood as proprietor it was an oasis for the thirsty souls in the Sahara...during Neal Dow's Prohibition Law under which Vermont suffered for fifty years...Just what manner of man this Mr Blood was, I do not know, but I know the whisperings and mutterings of the Center folk when they carried the body covered with a white sheet across the road, struck terror to my soul...Yes, Blood's Hotel! Many a community housewife waited supper many a night while her better half tarried at Blood's Hotel where good cheer, good talk and surcease from care were always to be had. No need for the wife to ask where her errant spouse had been. One knew she knew by the way she rattled the tins and pans on the back of the stove when she put the 'warmed-over-vittles' on the table...Nevertheless Blood's Hotel (before Bill Blood's tenure and afterwards) played a big part in community life..." (2)

* * *

It was leased by Mrs Blood for a year or two after her husband died, about 1883; bought by Col Francis Voltaire Randall, who re-named it the Randall House. It was advertised as a hotel in 1887, but whether this was part of an offer to sell, or as an advertisement for an operating hotel, is not clear. Sold to Norwich University in 1904, used for a while as a drill hall, later torn down. (Photo, ref 3).

* * *

1855: --, J. B. Brown;

1856: (a) Central House, --;

1858: --, W. Brown* (Walling);

1867: (a) Central House, Perry Lee;

1870, '75, '79, '80: (a) Central House, William Blood (but better known as Blood's Hotel within a few years);

1873: (a) National House, William Blood (Vt Dir, same place);

1892: (a) as above;

1895: (a) as above, H. E. Burnap;

1903: (a) as above, --* (Sanborn);

1905: (a) as above, J. C. Donahue.

(134b) Northfield (Depot Village).

1836: 1st Northfield House, William Rogers; built by Charles Paine, at the east end of the common. Paine was the son of Elijah Paine of Williamstown, a turnpike magnate and leading citizen of the area; Charles Paine was governor of Vermont, 1841-42, and head of the Vermont Central railroad for many years; it was Paine who was responsible for the line coming through

Northfield, by a route that many thought less practical than other choices available. Managers following Rogers were George Robinson, 1854; a Mr Burnham, until 1859; John L. Batchelder, until about the time that the railroad offices and shops moved to St Albans, when E. A. Webb became host. He was succeeded by Mrs Perley R. Downer, and then her son, Mr R. Wright; in 1867, the property was bought by Hartshorn and Hayward, and resold soon after to Hiram Fales. It was during this time "that the south wing was moved around to front on Main Street, and the overhead connection with Paine Block (so called) was removed." (4) The place was bought by J. H. Ransom about 1874, and he had it when it burned in 1879.

The second Northfield House was built next year by George M. Fisk, a little south of the first site (see photo, next page), with W. H. Morris as the first landlord, followed by Lucien Keith, and then A. J. Robbins. J. C. Fletcher came about 1884, and M. E. Yarrington in 1891; he was followed by F. A. Sanderson, a Mr Raymond, F. K. Sawyer, and Mr Fifield, who was landlord when it burned again (see below).

* * *

"The writer recalls very vividly the little shady park in front of the original house which included two elms now standing and the stream of water that kept the rubber ball in the air...also the pole from which the swinging sign hung and on top of which was the house filled with martin birds every summer. I remember distinctly how ten years after the Vermont Railroad came to Northfield the passenger trains came across the common from the north and the south and stopped at the long platform at the south side of the Northfield House for refreshments and that it was no uncommon thing for the house to have 50-100 guests. I can see today in my mind's eye the fish pond...near the Fuller barn maintained by the hotel, full of trout. It was a popular resort for boys as well as grown people." (4)

1849: --, H. Nye; --, Chester Gilman (locations unknown, NEMU Dir); (a) Northfield House, E. A. Webb (NEMU Dir);

1855: --, W. T. Burnham;

1856: --, George Robinson; (a) Northfield House, J. W. Brown;

1858: (a) as above, E. A. Webb* (Walling);

1867: (a) as above, Hartshorn and Heywood;

1870: (a) as above, Hiram Fales;

1873, '75:   (a) as above, J. H. Ransom* (Beers, 1873); Bradford's Hotel Guide also listed the National House in 1875; (Northfield Center?)

1879: (a) as above (burned this year); (b) Avery House, Lewis W. Avery;

1880: (c) 2nd Northfield House, George M. Smith; this place also burned, in October 1916, with the death of one person who lived in the hotel; it was never rebuilt, in spite of many studies and proposals; other owners in the years before it burned were G. H. Raymond, Fred K. Sawyer, and Ernest Fifield, who bought it in 1915 and was the proprietor when it burned. (photos, ref 3).

* * *

"Its architecture was very different from the former colonial-type structure. Four stores high, flat-roofed, box-shaped, the hotel had double porches running the length of the front of the building--favorite spots for guests to sit where they could look out over the Common. Awnings over the windows in the two upper stories gave the building an attractive appearance. The hotel opened with a large ball and W. H. Morris assumed management of the establishment. For years it was well patronized. In good weather the ladies took the upper deck while the men sat out in front on

383

the street level, chewed tobacco and told stories. About the 1890s it was the fashion for more affluent couples of the town to live at the hotel. It was a day when wives or grown daughters of men who could afford and encouraged such practices either had maids to do their housework or boarded out." (2)

* * *

2nd Northfield House
(Picture Northfield: McIntire and Cleveland, 1985)

1883: (b) as above; <u>Morris House</u>, W. H. Morris;

1885, '92:   (c) as above, --* (Sanborn; 2nd <u>Northfield House</u>);

1887, '89:   (b) as above; (c) as above, J. C. Fletcher; <u>Morris House</u>, W. H. Morris;

1890: <u>Morris House</u>, W. H. Morris;

1892, '95:   (c) as above, M. E. Yarrington;

1898, 1901, '02:   (c) as above;

1903: (c) as above, --* (Sanborn); <u>Central Hotel</u>, --* (Sanborn);

1904: <u>West Side Hotel</u>, --; built by the E. B. Bliss Granite Co; at the corner of Union and Pearl Sts; a 3-story boarding-house with "forty-five sleeping rooms, a toilet and bathroom on each floor and a dining room which seated 200. It was equipped with steam heat and electric lights. Mr and Mrs Church came from Skowhegan, Maine, to run it." Built for the granite company workers, sold in 1914 to local people who ran it briefly, but damaged by fire in 1915 and closed as a hotel. It was cut in half and converted into two separate buildings, still standing (see photo);

1905: (c) as above; <u>Broggi's Hotel</u>, M. Broggi (not identified);

1908: (c) as above;

1910: (c) as above, --* (Sanborn);

1911: (c) as above, F. A. Sanderson;

1913, '15:   (c) as above, --; (F. K. Sawyer proprietor in 1916, VPB);

1919: 2nd Northfield House gone (Sanborn); Park Inn*, (Sanborn) but this building gone by 1926;

(?):   Avery Hotel, L. W. Avery; at 9 South Main St, a few rods south of the Northfield House (sketch, ref 2);

1919: Park Hotel, --; established by a group of Northfield citizens and businessmen, at the corner of S. Main and Slate Ave; the hotel was apparently the former Gilbert Andrews House, with limited facilities and frequent changes in managers. It closed in 1924, converted back to a double dwelling.

(134c) Northfield Falls.

1819: a tavern, Elijah Burnham; where John Fisk formerly kept tavern (Hemenway; but in another place in the same volume, Hemenway says that Fisk was born in 1783, kept tavern in the Falls village c. 1825); tavern license to Fisk, 1827, '30, '33;

Note: the Northfield Falls Inn, now closed, was in a building built in 1875, and was not an inn until fairly recent times.

West Side Hotel
(Picture Northfield: McIntire and Cleveland, 1985)

(134d) South Northfield. No listings found.

(134e) Outside the Villages.

1811: a tavern, William Jones; tavern license, 1817-32; "on Judge Paine's turnpike, near the toll-gate." (VDHP 1213-11, on Berlin Pond Road just inside the Williamstown town line, near the Deming home; tollgate, inn and tavern known as the Half-Way House (photo, ref 3);

(?):   a tavern, Albijence Ainsworth's father; "the well-known "Ainsworth tavern on the hill road to Cleaveland village" (Hemenway, site not identified); but Cleaveland village is Brookfield,

385

so this must be Rte 12 or a dirt road leading south from Rte 64.

Note: the assistance of Mrs Julia W. McIntire, Northfield Historical Society, is gratefully acknowledged.

* * *

References

(1) personal communication, Julia W. McIntire.

(2) Julia W. McIntire, Green Mountain Heritage: The Chronicle of Northfield, Vermont (Canaan, N.H.: Phoenix Publ, for the Town of Northfield, 1974).

(3) Julia W. McIntire and Richard L. Cleveland, Picture Northfield, A Photographic Study (Northfield: Northfield Historical Soc.; Barre: Northlight Studio Pr., 1985).

(4) J. L. Moseley, "History of the Old Northfield House," Heart of Vermont 1 (May 1917): 8-9.

(5) Esther M. Swift, Vermont Place-Names: Footprints in History (Brattleboro: Stephen Greene Pr., 1977).

* * *

(135) **North Hero** (Grand Isle).

(135a) <u>LaGrange</u>. No listings found.

(135b) <u>North Hero</u>.

1803: <u>Ladd's Tavern</u>, Jedediah P. Ladd; tavern license, 1825, '28-30; "a substantial building located several home-lots south of the Court House,and approximately where Mrs Genia (Ernest) Way now lives" (i.e., 1976, ref 1). Ladd was North Hero's first PM (1817-26), presumably with the office in the tavern; he ran the tavern until his death in 1845, and his son Abner carried on for a few years more (tavern license, 1825, '28); torn down in 1857; the site is #17 in the North Hero Village Historic District (VDHP 0704-31);

* * *

"The building, facing the beautiful bay, then called Ladd's Bay, now City Bay, was a large, square, sturdy wooden frame structure, massive hand hewn timbers. As time went on, additions were made, on the south side was a wing containing several chambers, and a big kitchen room." (1) Described by Maria S. Ladd in 1864 as a time-browned, unpainted edifice, looking rather shadowy and mysterious. It was for many years the principal building in North Hero, 'a place where hospitality in the form of bed, food, drink, warmth and good cheer was dispensed to the cold and weary traveler, to the driver going to market, and the gathering place on winter evenings before the glowing hearth, for the exchange of outside news and local gossip.'

Here at his Tavern, the Selectmen met, Town meetings were held, it was frequently the Justice Court for Civil cases, Church meetings were held here in the Tavern-Room.

Aside from its basic function as a tavern, the most remembered use was as the Court House for the County of Grand Isle, newly incorporated in 1802, and organized in 1805, with North Hero as the Shire Town. Here at Ladd's Inn all County Court matters were transacted from 1806 until 1825, when the new Stone Court House was built...

Here at Ladd's Tavern was the Gaol or Jail. The upper northwest Chamber room was used for keeping prisoners, there being no Jail in North Hero until 1825.

The old time Tavern or Inn is not to be associated with the impression of a bar or saloon. The Tavern was formally approved by the selectmen, the Keeper had to be nominated by the town officials 'as fit and suitable to keep an inn or house of public entertainment.' This nomination was presented to the County Court and the Court would then grant a license, but again, only if the

Court saw fit.

The Innkeeper was a man of good standing in the neighborhood and thoroughly respected. By state law, the Inn 'shall at all times be furnished with suitable refreshments, provisions, and accommodations for travellers, their cattle and horses; that he shall put up a proper sign; shall erect and keep in good condition a shed for horses, with a suitable trough or manger.'

The prominent memory of Ladd's Tavern was the sign. At the northeast corner, near the roof, projected a short wooden arm, from which swung a square sign, bearing in the centre on either side, large, black letters, the single word Inn. This sign seemed always moving with a melancholy creak; and after the demise of the old Proprietor, it might well have been the voice of the old Inn."

* * *

Note: tavern licenses, Paul B. Torrey, 1826, and Samuel Webster, 1829, locations unknown;

1845: <u>Knight's Inn</u>, John Knight, Jr; probably built by him in this year; on Knight's Point at the south end of North Hero; the remains of Knight's Landing for the old North Hero-Grand Isle ferry still there across the road; the building was purchased by the Vermont Forest and Parks Department in the 1970s (photo, ref 1);

1849: --, Benjamin Wright (NEMU Dir, unidentified);

1873: <u>County House</u>, R. R. Hathaway (unidentified);

1896: (a) <u>Irving House</u>, James H. and Nellie Dodds; named after their son, with a ferry stop across the street; built in response to increasing numbers of tourists in the Islands; a 3-story square wooden structure, on the west side of the road near the center of the village, just south of the M.E. church, looking out on City Bay; it had the first bathroom in town. Dodds also kept a store and was PM, town clerk and senator from Grand Isle County; he died in 1944, and his son Donald and his wife Eva ran it until 1967, when Donald Dodds died; Eva ran it alone until 1970, when the place was sold to Roger Sorg, who renovated and expanded it; it operates now as the <u>North Hero House</u>, John C. Apgar; this is VDHP 0704-31, #6; see photo;

"At the time it was built, there was a regular lake Steamer service, the boats stopping in the summer, at the Landing right across the road...Two or three Steamers would stop here daily, bringing guests to the Island and to the Irving House...They would come to stay, with their steamer trunks, and entourage...the full-length, double decked front veranda with the numerous wicker rocking chairs, was a particular pleasure summer evenings.

With the advent of the new Rutland-Canadian Railroad through the Islands, the Irving House benefited by more travelers coming to the Islands. The railroad was opened for passenger business January 7, 1901...a listing of Summer Boarding Houses, dated 1902, tells that the Irving House has accommodations for twenty guests at $2.00 per day or $10.00 per week...these rates included three meals per day...

The combination of the railroad, then followed by the automobile, gradually diminished the lake Steamer business. More convenient and flexible transportation tended to shorten the stay of the Irving House guest and a more transient type of business prevailed." (1)

* * *

1901: (a) <u>Irving House</u>, J. H. Dodds;

1905: (a) as above; (b) <u>Parker House</u>, J. N. Parker (see photo; location unknown);

1908: (a) as above, --; <u>Island House</u>, -- (probably <u>Parker's</u>);

Irving House

1911: (a) as above, J. H. Dodds; (b) as above, A. V. Sheek;

1913, '16:   (a) as above, J. H. Dodds; (b) as above, J. N. Parker;

1920, '25:   (a) as above, --; still operating; (b) as above, --, until c. 1935.

* * *

References

(1) Allen L. Stratton, History, Town of North Hero, Vermont (Burlington: George Little Pr., 1976).

Parker House, North Hero

* * *

(136) **Norton** (Essex).

(136a) Averill. There is a town of Averill, but Averill PO is actually just over the line in the town of Norton. Averill contains three lakes, Great and Little Averill, and Forest Pond, and there have been summer resort establishments on Great Averill and Forest.

(?):   Lakeside, later Quimby's Inn (see photo); on the northwest shore of Great Averill; a lumber camp in the 1870s, with a 3-story boarding house which became the inn about the turn of the century; porches on both the 1st and 2nd floors (sketch, ref 1); owners include George

Fitzgerald, 1898; Louisa West, 1899; Paul West, 1901; George Butterfield, 1903; Lucy Lea, 1905; Frank Baldwin, 1907; the name Lakeside Inn appears on the deed accompanying this last transfer; Baldwin added cottages. The place was bought by Hortense Quimby in 1928, who named it Quimby's Inn; run for years in conjunction with the Cold Spring Club on nearby Forest Lake (see below; photo, ref 1); more cottages were added, and the place became a private summer home complex in 1970;

Lakeside Inn (Quimby's)

(?): Cold Spring Club, or Cold Spring House, or Quimby's Cold Spring Club; acquired by Charles M. Quimby in 1884, the property consisted of a few cottages and a main building; run as a resort for fishermen and hunters at first; Quimby died in 1919, and his daughter Hortense expanded it greatly (photo, ref 1); became a guest-owned corporation, Quimby Country, in 1965, still operating;

1908: Cold Spring Camp, --;

1916: Lakeside Inn and Cottages, Carpenter and Cameron (VPB); Cold Spring Camp, C. M. Quimby;

1920, '25: --, C. M. Quimby, until at least 1968, also a W. H. Carpenter; --, F. W. Baldwin.

(136b) Lake. No listings found.

(136c) Norton (Norton Mills until 1932).

1871: (a) Norton Mills House, J. F. Davis* (map, ref 1);

1870, '73: (a) as above;

1875, '80: (a) as above, S. Cleaveland;

1878: (a) as above, --* (Beers);

(?): (b) Stetson House, A. M. Stetson; built before 1885, probably by Andrew Stetson; not clear if this might have been the same place as the Norton Mills House later replaced by Carpenter's Hotel, operated by William Carpenter and his son, J. W. (see below); the Stetson House burned in a major fire on May 4, 1904, with the death of Katie Pelletier who lived in the hotel (photo, ref 1);

1883: (b) Stetson House, G. Clantier;

1884: (b) as above, William and J. W. Carpenter; J. W. moved back to Norton to run this place

389

with his father until 1893; J. W. Carpenter later bought the place now known as <u>Carpenter's Hotel</u> (i.e., in 1986, ref 1);

(?):   (c) <u>Carpenter's Hotel</u>, William Carpenter (see photo); built before 1870 as a boarding house, across from the Canadian Customs House, bought by J. W. Carpenter in 1904, run by him until his death in 1934; his son Hanford carried on until he died in 1972; there is a building right at the border in the 1878 Beers, labeled PO and store; Andrews says this map shows a PO "in the building we now know as Carpenter's hotel" (i.e., in 1986) so this building, built originally as an A. M. Stetson Co boarding house, must have become <u>Carpenter's Hotel</u>;

1887: (b) as above, William Carpenter (J. C. Carpenter in Vt Dir);

1892: (b) as above, W. J. Cheney (Chesney in Vt Dir; also known as <u>Carpenter's Hotel</u>, 1st);

1895, '98:   (b) as above, W. W. Lindsay;

1901: (b) as above, A. A. Lyons;

1908: (c) as above, --; this must be the 2nd <u>Carpenter's Hotel</u> (see above);

1913, '20, '25:   --, J. W. Carpenter;

1915: --, Carpenter and Griffith;

1916: <u>Hotel Carpenter</u>, J. W. Carpenter (VPB).

* * *

References

(1) Lydia C. Andrews, Three Towns: Norton and Averill, Vermont and Stanhope, Quebec (Littleton, N.H.: Sherwin/Dodge, 1986).

Carpenter's Hotel

(137) **Norwich** (Windsor).

(137a) <u>Lewiston</u>, (137b) <u>Pompanoosuc</u>, and (137d) <u>West Norwich</u>, no listings found.

(137c) <u>Norwich</u>.

1796: <u>Burton's Tavern</u>, --; listed in the Vermont Almanac and Register as a stage stop, Windsor-St Johnsbury road; also in 1805; not clear if this is the <u>Norwich Inn</u> (see below);

390

1849: (a) Union House, J. T. Burnham (NEMU Dir); Temperance House, Mrs Mary Partridge (NEMU Dir);

1855: (a) Union House, --* (Walling);

* * *

The Norwich Inn was built in 1797 by Jasper Merdock as a stagecoach stop. "The original building was a long narrow structure with a Carriage House, located behind the Inn, to house...animals." Sold to the Curtis family in 1800, who renamed it the Curtis Inn. Acquired by a Dr Bowles in 1840, when it became the Union Hall. Burned to the ground on December 18, 1889 in a major fire that also destroyed the general store and PO, and a house on the other side of the inn where the proprietors had usually lived. Rebuilt in 1890 as the Newton Inn. The store (and PO) next door was also rebuilt, and a second-floor passageway connected the inn with a dancehall (also known as the Union Hall) on the second floor of the store building. Sold to the Walkers in 1919, who changed the name back to the Norwich Inn. The Walkers ran it for some 25 years, and the place has changed hands several times since then. It is now operating as The Inn at Norwich. (From a brochure for the current inn.)

* * *

1855: --, M. H. Brackett;

1856: --, Pascal Hatch;

1869: --, --* (Beers);

1870, '73:   (a) as above, D. S. Brigham; listed as Rural Home, D. S. Brigham, for 1879, '83 in Vt Dir;

1887: (a) as above, W. S. Bowles; also listed in the Boston and Maine guide;

1887, '90:   (a) Norwich Hotel, W. S. Bowles (Vt Dir); burned in 1889;

1892, '95, '98, 1901, '05, '08, '13, '15: (a) The Newton Inn, W. S. Bowles (rebuilt, after the fire);

1920: (a) as above, --;

1925: (a) Norwich Inn, Charles Walker (see photo, next page); also shown on 1939 Sanborn.

Norwich Inn

(138) **Orange** (Orange).

(138a) East Orange.

1851: --, Enoch Sargent; granted a license by the town of Orange; his place is on the 1858 Walling, but not shown as an inn at that time.

(138b) Orange.

1839: an inn, Orange Fifield; record of a town meeting held there;

1849: --, L. Lane (NEMU Dir);

1851: an inn, S. G. Fisher (record of a town meeting, probably same as above);

1855: --, G. (?) G. Fisher;

1858: Orange Fifield's hotel* (Walling).

* * *

(139) **Orwell** (Addison).

(139a) Chipmans Point.

c. 1810:   Sholes Tavern, Joseph Sholes; tavern license, 1817, '21-23;

* * *

The settlement at Chipmans Point, first called Sholes Landing, was once the largest in the town, established by Joseph Sholes. He built a tavern, and later the second store; Walter Chipman built the first store, and was the first postmaster. It was a relay station for freight coming up the lake from Whitehall, N.Y., as well as for lake passengers, and Sholes Tavern was a busy place.

"It accommodated stage coach passengers and other persons traveling about. When the main line of the Delaware and Hudson Railroad was built on the other side of the Lake, the engineers, surveyors, etc., made the Sholes Tavern their headquarters. A grandson of the original Sholes (Joseph) ran the place; 'hard money' was plentiful; two bar tenders were in constant service; games of 'seven-up' were always in progress; and a two or three day session of poker was common. (1)

The hotel itself was an impressive structure, painted white in a neo-Grecian style with a high pillared portico and many large windows fronting the lake with a spacious dining room and large airy guest rooms...

The warehouses belong to the era before the railroads. In those days steamers traveled up and down the lake from Whitehall to Plattsburgh always stopping at Chipmans Point to load and unload freight. The heyday of Chipmans Point was during the 1840s. It was then the terminus of a stage line which ran from the Point to Brandon connecting with the steamboats. The stage was the pumpkin shell variety drawn by four horses. It left the Point on Tuesdays, Thursdays and Saturdays for Rochester with connections at Brandon, Burlington and Boston. It returned on Mondays, Wednesdays and Fridays in time for passengers to take the boats." (2) The place declined after this period, and was sold in 1883 after three generations of Sholes' ownership. Run for a while as a summer hotel by Plin Phelps as the Phelps Hotel (see photo, next page); owned by Mrs Ida M. Hall after 1900, but fell into a state of decay a few years after that. Bought by Philip W. Smith, owner of the IGA store in Orwell, in 1933, renovated, and sold to Rev Jusserand deForest, who opened it as a boy's camp. Bought by Mr and Mrs William Gray in 1946, modernized, and opened as the Chipman Point Inn, with an associated marina; burned in 1949, but the marina and a restaurant in the old store building still continue (photos, ref 4).

* * *

1856:   --, J. Sholes;

1857:   --, J. Sholes* (Walling);

1871:   --, Mrs D. Sholes* (Beers);

1870, '72, '73, '75, '80:   --, C. C. Sholes;

1881:   Lake House, Charles C. Sholes (Child);

1883:   Lake House, A. P. Cutting;

1884:   --, A. P. Cutting;

1890, '92, '95: --, R. C. Crammond;

1898, 1901, '05:   Phelps House, P. S. Phelps (same as Sholes Tavern, see above; burned in 1949, its foundations serve as "environmental sculpture" for the Chipmans Point Marina (VDHP 0114-11).

Phelps Hotel

(139b) North Orwell. No listings found.

(139c) Orwell (Center).

1798:   a tavern, Lt Jonas Rice (Royce, in Child); a tavern for many years, in the Rice (Royce) family until 1888, building still standing (i.e., 1963, ref 1);

c. 1800:   an inn, Willis Abell; tavern license, 1817, '21; at Abells Corners; the ell of the present house was built in 1800, main part a few years later (1); C. E. Abell's place at Abell's Corners, a little east of Orwell village, shown on the 1871 Beers;

(?):   a tavern, Clark Sanford; early settler, kept a hotel several years on farm occupied by one Irving c. 1882 (Child);

(?):   a tavern, Joseph Sanford; an early settler; on a farm owned in 1886 by Addison

393

Kimball (3); for several years;

Note: tavern licenses to James Q. McFarland, Chauncey Chittenden and Josiah Austin, 1817; Alpheus Rice, 1817, '21-23; William Higley, 1820, '21; John Wickes, 1821, '23; B. P. Wickes, 1821; Jesse Boynton, 1821; and Jeremiah Boyden (Boynton), 1817, '23, all unknown locations;

(?):   a tavern, <u>Brinsley Peters</u>; known as "Old Father Peters," a small tavern in the eastern part of town, about one mile west of Joab Smith's (i.e., 1886, ref 3);

1816:   <u>Eagle Hotel</u>, Jeremiah Boynton; tavern license, 1817, '21, '22; kept by him for about 25 years, then by his son Joshua until 1887 (<u>Boynton's Inn</u>), when the place was sold to Fred B. Kimball, who had been an innkeeper at Larabees Point. Burned in 1897, rebuilt by Kimball as the <u>Eagle Inn</u>, with a soaring eagle on a pole pointing skyward from the front. The <u>Eagle Inn</u> was primarily a summer hotel, but part of it was kept open year round. Dennis J. Leonard was manager in the early 1900s; place bought by Ira LaFleur in 1915, leased to Frank Sheldon for a while, sold again in 1923 to Mrs Isobel Woodall; operated as late as 1930, demolished in 1969, site now occupied by town office; (photo, ref 4);

1849:   --, J. Boynton (NEMU Dir);

1855, '56:   --, J. W. Boynton;

1857:   a hotel, <u>J. W. Boynton</u>* (Walling);

1870:   --, Joshua W. Boynton;

1871:   (a) <u>Boynton Hotel</u>, J. W. Boynton* (Beers; see photo);

Boynton Hotel (Orwell Historical Society)

1873, '75, '79, '80, '81, '87:   (a) <u>Eagle Hotel</u>, J. W. Boynton (same as above);

1887:   (a) as above, F. B. Kimball (Vt Dir);

1888, '92, '95, '98, 1901, '05:   (a) <u>Eagle Inn</u>, F. B. Kimball (see photo); the 1897 Rutland Railroad guide also listed a place called the <u>Crammond House</u> (25 guests, 5 miles from the station);

Eagle Hotel, 1891 (Orwell Historical Society)

1908, '13, '20, '25:   (a) as above, --; shown on 1915 Sanborn;

1911:   (a) as above, D. J. Leonard.

* * *

References

(1) Doris S. Bishop, A History of the Town of Orwell, Vermont (Orwell: The Town; Poultney: Journal Pr., 1963).
(2) Muriel T. Hyzer, "The Town That Was," Green Mountain Whittlin's 20 (1968): 18-21.
(3) Henry P. Smith, History of Addison County, Vermont (Syracuse: D. Mason, 1886).
(4) Orwell Historical Soc., A History of the Town of Orwell, Vermont, Past and Present (1988).

* * *

(140) **Panton** (Addison).

(140a) Panton.   Panton lost out in a land-grant dispute with Weybridge in the very beginning, and lost more land when Vergennes city and Waltham town were formed.

c. 1788:   a hotel, Gideon Spencer; who lived "in the part of town set off to Vergennes" (i.e., in 1788; ref 1); "near the creek on the west side";

(?):   a hotel, Abner G. Holcomb; "kept a hotel for a time"; (1)

c. 1790:   a hotel, Friend Adams; at Arnold Bay, at a place once known as Adams Ferry; Adams was a large land-owner at one time, and owned the ferry, dock and boats, a store and store-house, and a farm as well as the tavern; he died in 1839. An Adams place is shown on the 1857 Walling, not marked as a tavern; this is VDHP 0115-3;

c. 1800:   a hotel, Aaron Bristol; once known as Bristol's Inn; a log structure, on a farm owned c. 1881 (Child) by Norman W. Bristol; there is an N. W. Bristol place on the 1871

Beers, just southwest of Vergennes city; two Bristol buildings are listed by VDHP, 0115-2 and -13, but no mention of early tavern use;

1810: a tavern, Nathan Spaulding; "on the farm of Truman Kent we found a hotel sign which was used for the old hotel kept here by Nathan Spaulding--"1810, Nathan Spaulding, Tavern" (Child); just south of where Henry Wightman lives today (i.e., 1961, ref 2);

(?): a tavern, Isaac Havens; referred to in Smith as being on the road from Vergennes to Addison meeting house, in the east part of town, two "places" north of the Elgin Spring House "of later years"; (1)

c. 1848: Elgin Spring House, --; VDHP 0115-8; according to the VDHP, this place was built about 1848 for Solomon Adams; from the mid-19th century until its end, he and his son Hiram ran a popular summer resort here, the Elgin Spring House; the spring is on the hill east of Rte 22A, near the Addison line; they once shipped bottled water; place owned in 1977 by Frederick Noonan;

1871: Elgin Spring House, H. Allen* (Beers).

* * *

References

(1) Henry P. Smith, History of Addison County, Vermont (Syracuse: D. Mason, 1886).
(2) William T. B. Kent and Alberta Kent, Concerning the Town of Panton: Two Hundred Years Old, 1761-1961 (Burlington: Sheldon Pr., 1961).

* * *

(141) **Pawlet** (Rutland).

(141a) North Pawlet.

c. 1800: a public house, Bethel Hurd; (dates from c. 1780, according to Smith and Rann (1); became the Vermont Hotel, also known as the Bigart Tavern; after Hurd, it was kept by Joel Simonds, William Stevens (licensed in 1807-09, replaced by Joel Simonds Jr), Willard Cobb, Jeremiah Arnold, James Bigart and "perhaps some others" (2); closed in 1852, no tavern since;

(141b) Pawlet.

c. 1775: first hotel, Jonathan Willard; on site of the brick house now (i.e., 1981, ref 3) owned by Merritt J. Mars; followed by Timothy Strong (tavern license, 1807-11) who left c. 1816;

1776: a tavern, Joseph Armstrong; in the northeast part of town, "where the widow of Curtis Reed now lives" (i.e., 1886, Smith and Rann, ref 1) for 25 years; licensed in 1807, no record thereafter;

1784: taverns also kept by Benoni Smith, Elisha Clark, and Martin Smith, according to town records cited in Offensend; (3)

1785: a tavern (and store), Col Stephen Pearl; "settled early in the south part of town" (1); moved to Burlington in 1794; almanac listing, 1785;

1808: a tavern, Ephraim Fitch; son of an original settler, he built and kept the brick tavern in the village (licensed in 1807-11); he was killed in 1813, cutting ice from his mill (1); followed by Lemuel Barden until 1830 (licensed 1817, '21, '22), who "would not serve his customers rum after he thought they had enough"; (there is a Rutland Herald reference to Samuel Barden's tavern (3/31/1829); also a tavern license, 1823); this place was the precursor of the 1886 Franklin

House; Barden was followed by his son, John T. Barden; place acquired by Col Ozias Clark, rented to various parties and kept as a temperance house by Harry Griswold, Robert Clark, Ephraim F. Clark; then kept by others, including Henry Bostwick, Harrison Vail, Chapin Andrus, William Blossom Jr, Dewitt Hulett (proprietor in 1867, ref 2); D. W. Bromley took over then; converted to a store by the turn of the century; C11 in the Pawlet Village Historic District; (4)

c. 1812: a tavern, Reuben Smith; tavern license, 1821; where B. F. Giles lived in 1867; for some 20 years, closing in 1832; (2)

(?): a tavern, --; "the Red house owned by Orla Loomis, has been used as a tavern stand"; (2)

Note: tavern licenses also "approbated" for John Penfield, 1821; A. Henry and E. Aspinwell, 1807, '08; Minor Branch, 1807-10; Isaac Sheldon, 1808-10; and Peter Stevens, Joseph Upham, 1810, locations unknown;

1869: (a) Franklin House, Daniel W. Bromley* (Beers; see history above);

1870, '73, '75, '80, '83, '87, '92, '95: (a) as above (see photo);

1882(?): (b) Crescent Valley House, Amos G. Leach and John R. Crapo (see photo, next page); built by them about this time, across from the town hall; mainly a summer hotel; its proprietors claimed it was the best summer resort in the county, with accommodations for 140 people in the main structure and an annex; it had "well ventilated rooms, modern appliances, bath rooms on all floors, was lighted with gas, and furnished in the latest and most elegant style"; the Elite Cornet Band, a group of Pawlet musicians, gave an open air concert in front of the hotel every week (3); Upton Sinclair, author of 'The Jungle', clerked there one summer. Yet this place closed after seven seasons or so, about 1889; the furnishings were sold at a sheriff's sale, the building sold later, and had been torn down by 1911.

* * *

There is a problem here with dates. Offensend, working with local accounts and articles in the Granville Sentinel, is of the opinion that the place only lasted about 7 years, from about 1882-1889, and this may well be correct. However, the Crescent Valley Hotel is listed in Walton in 1895, 1898 and 1901 (see below) and it is odd that Walton would continue to list it for more than ten years after it closed.

* * *

Franklin House

1883, '87: (b) Crescent Valley House, Leach and Crapo;

1895: (b) as above, --;

1897: Rutland Railroad guide lists both (a) and (b), each "40 rods" from the station;

1898: (b) as above, E. J. Brown;

1898, 1901:   (a) as above, --;

1901: (b) as above, --;

1905, '08:   (a) as above, C. E. Denio;

1911: (a) as above, A. C. Mason;

1913, '15:   (a) as above (shown as "closed" on the 1915 Sanborn);

1916: (a) <u>Franklin House</u>, George H. Murray (VPB);

1920: (a) as above, --; <u>Allen's Inn</u>, -- (see photo);

Crescent Valley House (Vermont Historical Society)

Allen's Inn

1925: <u>Allen's Inn</u>, --.

(141c) <u>West Pawlet</u>.

1807:   a tavern (and store), <u>Eleazer Lyman</u>; kept by Joseph Ackley (licensed, 1817, '21), James S. Brown (licensed 1817, '21), and others; (2)

1817:   Seeley Brown, tavern license;

(?):   a tavern, --; kept now (i.e., 1867, ref 2) by Capt James Johnson; earlier by Elisha Marks, Innis Hollister, Ira Gibbs, and "perhaps others";

1851:   a public house, <u>Ira Gibbs</u>; built by him when the railroad came through, on the site of the "present" (i.e., 1867) hotel; sold to David Woodard after several years; it burned in 1858 and was replaced by "the present commodious house which is called the Indian River Valley Hotel"; (2) a large dance hall was associated with this place; Woodard kept it until about 1878, it was closed by 1886;

1854:   a tavern, --; there is a place labeled "tavern," with no name attached, at Marks Corners (West Pawlet) on the 1854 Scott map; presumably this is the same as the tavern above, precursor of the <u>Indian River Valley House</u>;

1869:   (a) <u>Indian River Valley Hotel</u>, David Woodard* (Beers);

1870, '73, '75, '80:   (a) as above;

1879:   (a) as above, A. Thompson (Vt Dir);

1881:   (a) as above, David Woodard (Child); <u>Avenue Hotel</u>, A. E. Phinney (Child; listed as <u>Phinney's Hotel</u> in 1880 in Walton);

1884:   (a) as above, G. W. Peck;

1892:   (b) <u>Bethesda House</u>, J. B. Powell (also referred to as <u>Powell House</u>; not known if this is the same as the <u>Indian River Valley House</u> that was said to have been closed by 1886;

1895:   (b) as above;

1901:   (b) <u>Powell House</u>; <u>Union House</u>, J. J. McDenner (location unknown).

Note: the assistance of Dorothy B. Offensend, Pawlet Historical Society, is gratefully acknowledged.

* * *

<u>References</u>

(1) Henry P. Smith and William S. Rann, History of Rutland County, Vermont (Syracuse: D. Mason, 1886).

(2) H. Hollister, Pawlet for One Hundred Years (Albany: Joel Munsell, 1867; reprint edition of 1976).

(3) Dorothy B. Offensend, The Hub of a Community, the Pawlet Town Hall (Rutland: QuickPrint, 1981).

(4) Vermont Div. of Historic Preservation, Historic Architecture of Rutland County, Curtis B. Johnson, ed., Elsa Gilbertson, asst ed. (Montpelier: 1988).

* * *

(142) **Peacham** (Caledonia).

(142a) <u>East Peacham</u> and (142b) <u>North Peacham</u>, no listings found.

(142c) <u>Peacham</u> (and Peacham Hollow).

1787: a tavern, <u>Jonathan Elkins</u> (see photo; but not clear if this place, or the <u>David Elkins</u> tavern of 1806 (below) is the building in the photo); on the Bayley-Hazen road; for 15 years the only one, operated in 1803 by Jonathan Elkins Jr (almanac, 1802; Elkins and Hall, 1805); described as "commodious and handsomely built" (1); busy in the early days, but isolated by the re-routing of the road; National Register of Historic Places;

(?):   <u>Varnum Tavern</u>, Adam and Dolly Varnum; location unknown; tavern license to an Abraham Varnum, 1826, '27;

1801: a tavern, that became known as the <u>Clark-Martin</u> house; in Peacham Hollow, a little north of the main village; a two and a half-story building with a ballroom on the second floor, an important place in the first half of the 19th century until stage traffic dropped away. It fell into decay, and burned in 1936. Some of its proprietors were John Spencer, 1801-04; Noah Martin, 1805; Reuben Hand, 1806; Sam Bruce, c. 1850; Tom Clark; and Jim C. Clark;

1802: a tavern, <u>Dr Solomon Heaton</u>; briefly, until he moved away;

1803-07: a tavern, <u>Timothy Hall</u>;

Elkins Tavern (Vermont Historical Society)

1803: tavern licenses also issued to William Scott, David Elkins, Luther Bayley, Dr William Scott;

1804: a tavern license, <u>Timothy Chamberlin</u>; taken over later in the year by Silas Barnard after Chamberlin died;

c. 1803:   an inn, <u>Joel Walker</u>; turned over in 1806 to David Elkins, who announced that he was opening a "House of Public Entertainment, where the weary traveler may find refreshment, and the thirsty pilgrim every kind of liquor the county affords to please his palate and moderately to satisfy the calls of an intemperate appetite"; (1)

1807: a tavern, <u>Joel Walker</u>; back in business, apparently at a new stand;

1812: <u>White House Tavern</u>, S. Hall (see below);

Note: tavern licenses to Walter Stuart and John Elkins, 1824; Zena Crossman, 1822-27; Ashbel Martin, 1823; and Isaiah Silver, 1821-25;

1834: <u>White House Tavern</u>, John Brown; tavern license, 1826, '27; there is apparently a gap in the town records, according to Bogart, and this place is described as "opening" this year, with no indication as to what happened to it between 1812 and 1834; on the site of a house later occupied by C. A. Bunker; Brown's son Abram continued from 1845 until 1851, when the place burned;

1848:   Wheeler's Tavern, --; (1)

1849:   --, A. A. Wheeler; Clark-Martin House, Samuel Bruce (NEMU Dir);

1853:   an inn, L. F. Strobridge; in a building occupied by Mrs Mary Mackay in 1948; this place was occupied successively by Joshua O. Morse, David Merrill (as the Hillside Inn) and Paul F. Ferguson (as Traveler's Rest) in the 1860s; it was continued until about 1900 by John Atwell, then became a private home (Mackay) and burned later;

1855, '56:   (a) --, L. Strobridge;

1870:   (a) Hillside Inn, David Merrill (originally Strobridge's);

1872:   (a) Traveler's Home, Paul F. Ferguson;

1873:   (a) as above, John Atwell;

1875:   (a) as above* (Beers);

1879, '80, '83, '87, '90, '92:   (a) as above;

1887:   Peacham Hotel, John Atwell (Child; presumably the Traveler's Home); Prospect House, Clare Bailey (Child, location unknown);

1890:   (b) Mountain View House, W. H. Bayley; built by William Mattocks c. 1847, converted into a hotel by Bayley in 1890, run by him and his wife until 1919, when they moved away; became a private home, then the Alumni House for Peacham Academy, now a private home again (VDHP 0309-72, #27, Hilary Smith);

1895, '98:   (b) Mountain View House, W. H. Bayley;

1901:   (b) as above, Mrs W. H. Bayley;

1905, '08, '11, '13, '15, '20:   (b) as above;

1908:   Hillcrest Lodge, Ellen G. Prentiss; reverted to a private home in 1921;

1916:   (b) as above, Walter H. Bayley (VPB);

1920, '25:   Hillcrest, --;

1931:   Choate Inn and Annex, Elsie A. Choate (see photo); in the old law offices of John Mattocks, and the printing office of Farley and Goss; shown on 1937 Sanborn, listed until at least 1940; VDHP 0309-72, #11, now a private home.

(142d) South Peacham. No listings found.

Note: the assistance of Edmund A. Brown, Peacham Historical Society, and of Mrs Agnes M. Farrow and Mrs Eloise B. Miller, Peacham, is gratefully acknowledged.

* * *

References

(1) Ernest L. Bogart, Peacham--Story of a Vermont Hill Town (Montpelier: Vermont Historical Soc., 1948).

Choate Inn, Peacham

(143) **Peru** (Bennington).

(143a) Peru.

1803:   Butterfield's Inn, in Landgrove Hollow, which became the famous Leland stand (Green Mountain Tavern, or Green Mountain Coffee House); a short distance from Peru, on the Peru Turnpike; see Landgrove;

c. 1807:   a tavern, Reuben Bigelow; tavern license, 1822; until the turnpike came through, about 1816;

1814:   an inn, Benjamin Barnard; tavern license, 1822; until 1839;

1822:   a hotel, Russell Tuthill; built by Daniel Tuthill and his son Russell, the only brick building in Peru; kept by them until 1835, when it was sold to L. McMullen, who kept it a year or two (1); then leased to Mr Smalley, F. Lyon, L. Howard, and Hiram Messenger, finally sold to Charles Lyon; then R. Gibson, who sold it to Leonard Howard; then Edward Batchelder, finally sold in 1870 to George K. Davis, who named it the Bromley House; sold to Robert I. Batchelder in 1898; later acquired by Marshall Hapgood (Hapgood's store in Peru), his daughter Della and her husband Perry Warren; burned in 1974 (VDHP says 1976), replaced by a new structure;

1831:   a hotel, Hiram Messenger; "on the height of land on the turnpike road...for ten or twelve years" (1); Alexander Leland rented it for two years, and J. G. Mellendy owned it later; he sold to a Mr Dickinson, whose heirs occupied it in 1891; (1)

1849:   (a) --, Reuel Gibson (Tuthill's, later the Bromley House); --, Amherst Messenger (location unknown); both NEMU Dir;

1856:   (a) --, L. Howard (Tuthill's);

1856:   (a) a hotel, A. Clark* (Rice and Hardwood map; same site as on Beers, below);

1869:   (a) Peru Hotel, E. Batchelder* (Beers);

1870:   (a) --, Edward Batchelder;

1873, '75, '79, '80:   (a) Bromley House, George K. Davis (originally Tuthill's; Davis was PM, 1873-83;

1883:   (a) as above, P. T. Wyman;

1887, '90, '92, '95, '98:   (a) as above, George K. Davis (see photo);

1890s: Richardson Lodge, George Richardson or Marshall Hapgood (referred to in Samuel R. Ogden's book on Landgrove, cited there); "high on the eastern slope of Stiles Peak, on the North Road out of Peru, at the end of the traveled road...now hard to locate for the Forest Service has torn the buildings down"; see photo;

c. 1900:   Russell Inn, Effie L. Russell; built in 1841 by Oliver P. Simonds, lifelong resident of Peru, who was a shoemaker, town clerk and PM; acquired by the Russells after he died about 1898, and converted into an inn; this place is not listed in Walton until c. 1935, still listed 1968; listed in 1923 VPB;

c. 1900:   Hillcrest Tea Room, Will and Ellen Burroughs; on Rte 11, one mile east of Bromley Mountain and one-half mile west of Peru village; described as a tea room/stage stop at the turn of the century, the Wiley Inn since 1943; built in 1835; listed in 1923 VPB;

1901:   (a) Bromley House, R. I. Batchelder;

Bromley House

Richardson Lodge

1905, '08:   (a) as above, M. J. Hapgood;

403

1913, '15:   (a) as above, Della Hapgood;

1916, '20, '25: (a) as above, Perry Warren.

* * *

References

(1) Ira K. Batchelder, History of Peru, Vermont (Brattleboro: Phoenix Pr., 1891).

* * *

(144) **Pittsfield** (Rutland).

(144a) Pittsfield.

c. 1786:   first tavern in town, Capt Daniel Bow (or Bowe); tavern license, 1823; in a one story log building "at the foot of the mountain just off the old turnpike past Townsend's"; (1) described in Davis and Hance as being at the junction of Rte 100 and Tozier Hill Road; (2) Bow had expanded into a large framed dwelling by 1797;

c. 1803:   a tavern, Zebedee Sprout; he died in 1810, and the place was sold to Capt John (Job?) Fuller, who kept it at least 10 years more (tavern license, 1821); license also to an M. M. Fuller, 1823, location unknown;

c. 1812:   a tavern, Azaubah Davis; kept by her while her husband John was away at war; acquired by Daniel Bow Jr by 1817; Bow was Pittsfield's first PM, from 1824-41; this is the present (i.e., 1988) Wilson house; the stand originally contained all the land between the cemetery and the Methodist church;

c. 1819:   first tavern in the village, Capt Elisha Holt; for a short time, on the site of Mr Dingman's house in 1880 (Child); 100 feet north of the Methodist church; became a store by 1835, burned in 1903;

c. 1835:   (a) Vose House, Caleb Sparks; followed by Asa Gaines until about 1838; the Rutland Herald (1/29/1839) says Caleb Sparks has sold his "mostly new" tavern, and that stages from Rutland, Montpelier and Hanover stop there; Penuel Child for 12-15 years; James Furman for about one year; Lyman Gibbs for about 15 years; George Orcutt a short time; Albert Vose, and later his daughter Nellie; next to the church on the village green. It burned in 1903, was replaced and is now operating as the Pittsfield Inn; closed for several years at one point in Vose's tenure; A24 on the Pittsfield Village Historic District map; (3)

c. 1840:   a tavern, James Eggleston; just south of the cemetery; probably A18 on the map cited immediately above;

1849:   (a) --, P. Child (NEMU Dir; became the Vose House);

1854:   (a) --, J. Furman* (Scott map);

1855:   (a) --, L. Gibbs;

1869:   (a) --, L.Gibbs* (Beers);

1870:   (a) --, Lyman Gibbs (Vt Dir);

1870:   (a) --, George Orcutt (Walton);

c. 1870:   (b) Green Mountain House, Rufus Holt; built as a private home by Daniel Bow Jr about 1830; after Holt, Justin Spaulding had it for 2 years; James Fletcher for 6; Holt again, briefly; then William Sherburne; there was a large dance hall over the horse barn, and this was a center of social activity in the latter part of the 19th century; later converted to tenements and shops;

1873, '75:   (b) <u>Pittsfield House</u>, Rufus Holt; same as the <u>Green Mountain House</u>;

1879, '80:   (b) <u>Green Mountain House</u>, J. C. Fletcher;

(?):   (c) <u>Ranney Hotel</u>, --; on the east side of the park, just north of the Methodist parsonage; photo, ref 2;

1881:   (a) <u>Vose House</u>, Albert Vose (Child);

1883:   (a) as above; (b) as above;

1887, '90, '92, '95:   (a) as above;

1898:   (a) as above; (c) --, H. G. Ranney (presumably this is <u>Ranney's Hotel</u>, see above);

1903:   State Board of Agriculture booklet lists the <u>Vose House</u> and the <u>Mountain View House</u> (presumably the <u>Green Mountain House</u>);

1901, '05:   (a) as above; the <u>Vose House</u> burned in 1903; was rebuilt by Albert Vose; followed by his daughter, Miss Nellie Vose, until c. 1925, became the <u>Pittsfield Inn</u>; (c) as above;

1908:   (a) 2nd <u>Vose House</u>, -- (see photo); (b) <u>Green Mountain House</u>, --;

2nd Vose House

1911, '13, '15: (a) --, Nellie Vose (shown on 1915 Sanborn); (c) --, H. G. Ranney; this place burned in 1915;

1920, '25:   (a) <u>Vose House</u>, --; later owned by Vaughan Griffin, Clifton Merrill, became the <u>Pittsfield Inn</u>, still operating.

Note: the assistance of Mrs Catherine S. Davis and Barbara A. Balzano, Town Clerk, is gratefully acknowledged.

* * *

References

(1) History of Rutland County, Vermont, Henry P. Smith and William S. Rann, 1886.
(2) A Glimpse of the Past: Pittsfield, Vermont, Catherine S. Davis and Dawn D. Hance,

1976.

(3) Historic Architecture of Rutland County, Vermont, Vermont Division of Historic Preservation, 1988.

* * *

(145) **Pittsford** (Rutland).

(145a) East Pittsford, (145b) 1st Florence (formerly Pittsford Quarry), and (145c) 2nd Florence (Fowler, 1902-13), no listings found.

(145d) Pittsford.

c. 1774:   first tavern, Samuel Waters; "before the Revolution...on the west side of the creek, near the military road...until 1777, when Waters fled at the time of Burgoyne's invasion" (Child); almanacs, 1771-1802;

1783:   first tavern after the war, Deacon Caleb Hendee; on the site of old Fort Vengeance, until 1808 (Child); almanacs, 1796-1829; now a bed-and-breakfast known as the Fort Vengeance Inn;

1786:   a tavern, Nathan Webster; on the site of the later Otter Creek House; bought by Augustine Hibbard in 1792, then Stephen Hopkins in 1794 (almanac, 1796), Capt Kimball in 1796, Abraham Anthony in 1798 (almanacs, 1802, '07). Bought by Reuel and Abigail Keith about 1800, who moved it and built a larger inn on the site, "continued as a public house to the present time" (i.e., 1872, ref 1; almanacs, 1817-22); subsequent owners and/or proprietors include: Oliver Keith, 1807; William Baxter, 1808; Isaac Wheaton, 1812; Dr K. Winslow, 1814; Luther Hurlbut, 1815; Haywood and Chapin, 1818; Asher Southworth, 1819 (tavern license, 1822); Isaac Hayden, 1823 (license); Hendee and Perry, 1824; Whipple Spooner, 1827; Elijah Brown Jr, 1828; A. W. Titus, 1838; H. G. Sessions, 1839; Elijah Wood, 1842; Thomas McLaughlin, 1843; J. C. Harmon, 1844; Milo June, 1845; Elisha Orcutt, 1848; D. P. Bartlett, 1849; Edward Mallory, 1852; J. V. Sheldon, 1854; R. H. Mead, 1857; J. V. Sheldon, 1858; Julius Scofield, 1865; Lewis F. Scofield, 1868; the building burned in 1931, now the site of Kamada's Super Market (1979);

1789:   Ewings Tavern, James Ewing; almanac, 1802, '07; a little south of E. B. Rand's home in 1872, kept as a tavern until 1795 when Ewings built the larger place that later became the Rand House; owners/proprietors of this latter place were: James Ewing, 1795; Abraham Anthony, 1800; Eli Keeler, 1804; Jonathan Kendall, 1807 (almanac, 1817-22; tavern license, 1817); John Barnes, 1810; Cary Allen, 1814; Gilbert Evans, 1816; Ebenezer Brooks, 1817, '26; David Hall, Jr, 1819, '22, '23; Rufus Frost, 1837; Ebenezer B. Rand, 1840; Rand died in 1851, not kept as a tavern since. The Rand House is B27 on the Pittsford Village Historic District map. (2) Volunteers for the War of 1812 were organized here when John Barnes had the place, before departing for Plattsburg; (3)

c. 1790:   a tavern, Thomas Hammond; on what became the town farm, until 1796, when Hammond was succeeded by Vinton Barnes; he moved away in 1805, and the place was not kept again as a tavern;

1796:   a tavern, John Penfield; in what was Virgie Fish's home in 1979; Allen Penfield replaced his father in 1811, kept it until 1817, no longer used as a tavern; Allen Penfield continued until 1828 (see entry under Pittsford Mills, below);

c. 1798:   a tavern, Hammond Ladd; on the farm owned in 1872 by Royal Hall; kept until 1804, sold to Stephen Mead, who gave it up in 1810;

c. 1804:   a tavern, Abraham Drury; in what was the residence of F. B. Barnes in 1872 (1); kept until 1816, sold to Timothy Boardman, whose son Charles G. became landlord (tavern license, 1823); he kept it until 1837, moved away, not used since as a tavern; Everest photo, 1950s;

1849:   (a) --, Milo June (NEMU Dir; this is Webster's, later the Otter Creek Inn); (b) --,

B. Rand (NEMU Dir; presumably this is the Rand House);

    1854:   (a) --, E. Mallery* (Scott; the Otter Creek Inn);

    1855:   (a) --, J. V. Sheldon;

    1869:   (a) Otter Creek House, L. F. Scofield* (Beers);

    1870, '73, '75: (a) as above;

    1879:   (a) as above, Mrs B. J. Gorham;

    1880:   (a) as above, E. E. Rich;

    1883:   (a) as above, H. Parker;

    1887:   (a) as above, J. Gosselin;

    1890:   (a) as above, J. Poro;

    1892, '95:   (a) as above, --;

    1898:   Riverside Inn, Mrs J. Poro (probably same as the Otter Creek Inn); Mountain View House, C. E. Scofield; same listing in the Rutland Railroad guide for 1897;

    Note: There is a small difficulty here. The Otter Creek Inn was also known at one time as the Pittsford Inn (see photo), and there was also at one time a second place with the same name. This second Pittsford Inn was originally a private home, built in 1832, on the east side of Rte 7, south of the bridge at Pittsford Mills. It was operated as the Pittsford Inn in later years by two successive owners, Mrs Emmie Ostheimer (1929-44) and Mr Fred Wenton (1944-61).

Pittsford Inn

    1901:   (a) Otter Creek Inn, S. Manley and son;

    1905:   (a) as above, W. S. Tarble;

    1911:   (a) as above, --; Kimball's Hotel, --;

    1913:   (a) as above, --;

    1915:   (a) as above, --* (Sanborn); Swift Cottage, Mrs Gould;

    1916, '20:   (a) as above, G. T. Dolan;

1925: (a) as above, -- (the Otter Creek Inn burned in 1931); Green Mountain Motor Inn, the Misses Pye;

1931: a house built in 1894 was operated as the Leonard Hotel from about 1931 until 1936; later as Rolling Acres Inn, and later still, the Telemark Ski Club.

(145e) Pittsford Mills.

1796: there is a 1950s Everest photo of the "Penfield-Shaw house," said to have been a tavern, 1796-1809; probably same as Penfield's tavern, under Pittsford;

(?): Pittsford Inn, --; see Note under Pittsford, above.

* * *

References

(1) A. M. Caverly, Town of Pittsford, Vermont (Rutland: Tuttle, 1872), (reprinted 1976).
(2) Vermont Div. of Historic Preservation, Historic Architecture of Rutland County, Curtis B. Johnson, ed., Elsa Gilbertson, asst ed. (Montpelier: 1988).
(3) Rilla F. Kitson, "Pittsford in Rutland County," Vermont History 24 (April 1956): 121-131.

* * *

(146) **Plainfield** (Washington).

(146a) Plainfield.

c. 1800: first tavern in town, Isaac Washburn Jr; who lived with his father at the Four Corners, near L. C. Batchelder's residence (c. 1882, Hemenway); this place is shown on the 1873 Beers; a large 2-story house "that was never entirely finished"; the Washburns left in 1812;

c. 1805: first tavern in the village, Silas Williams (Jr?); tavern license, 1817-30; south part of S. B. Gale's house, c. 1882 (Hemenway); building shown on the 1873 Beers, became an apartment building, burned 1962;

Note: tavern licenses to Shubael B. Flint, 1830, '33, and Stephen Sanborn, 1833, locations unknown;

1849: --, N. Bancroft (NEMU Dir);

1855, '56: --, S. (?) Wells, Jr

1858: --, J. Wells, Jr* (Walling);

1870: --, J. B. Wells (B. J. Wells in Vt Dir);

1872: (a) Plainfield House/Inn, Solomon Wells; built c. 1835;

1873: (a) as above, B. P. Young* (Beers);

1875, '78: (a) as above;

1880, '87: (a) as above, A. C. Slayton;

1889: (a) as above, George F. Nutting;

1890: (a) as above, N. Hamell;

1892:   (a) as above, Hamel and Ryan;

1895:   (a) as above, Nelson Shory (?);

1898:   (a) as above, Nelson Hamel;

1901:   Pleasant Valley House, George Raymond (see photo); listed as Pleasant View House in the 1903 State Board of Agriculture booklet;

1905:   (a) Plainfield House, S. W. Beaulac (see photo);

1911, '13:   (a) as above, C. M. Hawes; Plainfield House burned on New Year's Eve, 1914, rebuilt by Fred Bancroft as the Bancroft Inn; but sometimes referred to as the Plainfield House in directories;

1914:   no hotel on Sanborn map;

1915:   (b) 2nd Plainfield House (Bancroft's), F. J. Bancroft (see photo);

Pleasant Valley House

1st Plainfield House

409

1920: Bancroft Inn, F. J.Bancroft; became the T. R. Trail House; listed in 1916 VPB, J. J. Gardner proprietor, 1923 VPB, Gretchen Sibley, closed in 1936; used by Goddard College, now a furniture/antique store;

1925: T. R. Trail House, S. B. Sibley; Greeley Inn, Mrs Alice Greeley.

(146b) Plainfield Springs (PO from 1874-80).

1858: (a) Mountain Springs Hotel, Lamson and Moore* (Walling); later the Plainfield Spring House; built c. 1845;

1872: (a) Plainfield Spring House, Burridge Marsh;

1873: (a) as above, James Morse* (Beers);

1873, '75, '78: (a) as above, James Morse;

1879, '80: (a) as above, E. H. Holmes;

1883: (a) as above, N. D. Page; said to have burned before 1880 (on a legend on the back of a stereo view in the Vermont Historical Society museum) but to have been operating in 1849.

Note: the assistance of Cora Copping, Plainfield Historical Society, is gratefully acknowledged.

Bancroft Inn

* * *

(147) **Plymouth** (Windsor).

(147a) Plymouth (including Plymouth Notch).

1849: Notch House, R. P. Pollard (NEMU Dir, location unknown);

1855: R. P. Pollard's hotel* (Hosea Doten map).

(147b) Plymouth Union (Unionville, locally).

c. 1853: (a) a hotel, Levi J. Greene;

1869: (a) Union House, L. J. Green* (Beers);

1873, '75, '79, '80, '83, '87, '90, '92, '95, '98: (a) as above; became a store, then a store and PO, and then the Salt Ash Inn, still operating, 1988 (see photo); present owners believe that the original building, much altered, was built c. 1830;

1875, '79, '80, '83, '87: (b) Wilder House, D. P. Wilder (see photo); built c. 1830, still operating at the turn of the century; (1) one part was taken down in the 1940s, and another in the 1950s, but the main building still stands (1988); used as a state-owned hospitality center; once the home of Coolidge's mother;

1883: (a) as above (Child); (b) as above, Norris D. Wilder (Child).

(147c) Tyson (Tyson Furnace, including Echo Lake);

1799: (a) Tyson House, Frank Josslyn; built this year, according to a leaflet from the Echo Lake Inn, which eventually replaced it. The original building was at the rear of the present structure; it was on a main stage line, and prospered so that a larger inn was built about 1840. (VDHP says the Tyson House was built by the iron company in the 1860s.) The original building served as an antique shop in recent years, collapsed during a storm in the 1970s;

Salt Ash Inn

c. 1837: (a) a hotel, --; (1)

1849: A. Page's Inn, -- (NEMU Dir; an ad for this place is reproduced in ref 1);

Wilder House

411

1869: (a) <u>Tyson House</u>, J. W. Moore* (Beers; later the <u>Echo Lake Inn</u>); there is a <u>Prior Cottage Inn</u> in the same general location on the 1855 Hosea Doten map;

1870: (a) as above;

1873, '75: (a) as above, G. L.Cass;

1879: (a) as above, A. F. Hubbard;

1880: (a) as above, W. F. Miner; replaced by the <u>Echo Lake Hotel</u> in the late 1880s, according to VDHP; VDHP 1412-7;

1883: (a) as above, D. H. Fuller; --, Webster Addison (Child, location unknown);

1887: (a) as above, William Parker (also PM, 1886-97);

1890, '92: (a) <u>Echo Lake Hotel</u>, A. F. Hubbard (same as <u>Tyson House</u>);

1895, '98: (a) as above, Charles Knight;

1901, '05, '11: (a) as above, D. C. Fen (Fenn);

1913, '15: (a) as above, -- (R. A. Chase in 1916 VPB); the <u>Echo Lake Hotel</u> is still operating (1988); see photo.

(147d) <u>Outside the Villages</u>.

c. 1830: an inn, --; in the "Plymouth Kingdom", in the southeast corner of the town;

1878: <u>Glen House Hotel</u>, --; at "Five Corners"; there is an 1896 photo of this place in ref 1; no longer standing.

Echo Lake Hotel, Tyson

Note: the assistance of Maria Rebideau, of the Calvin Coolidge Memorial Foundation, and of Mrs Dorothy Stillwell, Woodstock, is gratefully acknowledged.

* * *

References

(1) Eliza Ward, Barbara Mahon and Barbara Chiolino, A Plymouth Album: A Pictorial History of Plymouth, Vermont (Randolph Ctr: Greenhills Books, 1983).

* * *

(148) **Pomfret** (Windsor).

Several early taverns are listed in Vail, but with one exception, it is hard to know where they were. (1) The exception is Winslow's Tavern, which was just west of South Pomfret village (see below); another one may have been on what became the Town Farm (also see below). It would seem likely that another one of these early taverns would have been in North Pomfret, which was an active settlement early on, known as Snows Store, with the first PO in the town.

(148a) North Pomfret (Snows Store until 1866).

1902: Farm House, O. Whipple (CVRR Dir; probably only summer boarding).

(148b) Pomfret (Center).

1778: a tavern, Abida Smith; "in the present poor house" (1); there is a Town Farm shown on the 1869 Beers, somewhat west of Pomfret village; but Lewis Smith, of the Pomfret Historical Society, has a somewhat different view of things. He says that Abida kept a tavern in his original log house in the 1770s, and in 1782 built the first frame house in Pomfret with the tavern in an ell at the rear. This was located about one-half mile east of Pomfret (Center), on the road known as the King's Highway (an estate known as Galaxie Hill now occupies the site). The old Smith tavern is listed in the 1796 Vermont Almanac and Register;

1781, '83, '86: taverns, Abida Smith and Capt Edmond Hodges (town licenses);

1793: taverns, Abida Smith and Ebenezer Winslow (for Winslow's, see South Pomfret, below);

1795: an inn, Rev Elisa Hutchinson; in the house built for him as first settled minister; apparently closed about 1801; and another inn, Jonathan Reynolds, "on the road from Woodstock to Barnard and Royalton"; (1)

1802: five taverns in town: Abida Smith, who moved to the "Red House" (location unknown); his son Elisha at the old stand (the later Town Farm location); also Jesse Smith, Ebenezer Winslow (see below) and Jonathan Reynolds;

1902: Farm House, M. E. Adams (CVRR Dir; location unknown).

(148c) Snows Store. No listings found under this name.

(148d) South Pomfret.

When the county road was finished in the early 1800s, the traffic past Smith's in Pomfret became so slight that it closed. The original tavern sign stayed there until the early 1900s, when a photo was taken (see Appendix B); the sign itself is in the possession of the Pomfret Historical Society.

The turnpike went past the Winslow Tavern (below), which flourished until the railroad came through. The prohibition law of 1850 also had a negative effect on it. Its exact date of closing is uncertain; it was still operating in 1869 (Beers) and a place called the Winslow Inn is listed in 1906. Mr Smith and the Pomfret Historical Society, however, are of the opinion that it closed soon after the 1850 prohibition law took effect, and since it isn't listed in the directories through all of the 1870s-80s-90s, it is likely that the 1906 Winslow Inn is a different place. The original Winslow's Tavern site is marked with a Historical Society plaque.

1849: --, Gardner Winslow; (NEMU Dir; established in 1793, see under Pomfret);

413

almanacs, 1807-16;

1855:   --, G. Winslow* (Hosea Doten map);

1856:   --, Gardner Winslow;

1869:   G. Winslow's Hotel* (Beers);

c. 1906:   Winslow Inn, -- (VHS photo).

Note: the assistance of Lewis Smith, North Pomfret, is gratefully acknowledged.

* * *

References

(1) Henry H. Vail, Pomfret, Vermont, Emma C. White, ed. (Boston: Cockayne, 1930).

* * *

(149) **Poultney** (Rutland).

(149a) East Poultney. Business center of the town until the railroad came through in 1852.

(?):   (a) Eagle Tavern, before 1800; a tavern frequented by the Green Mountain boys was rebuilt c. 1790 as the Eagle Hotel (B19 on the East Poultney Historic District Map, ref 1); according to a 1951 booklet, the original Eagle Tavern dated back to the Colonial era, but was "too primitive for prosperous post-Revolutionary Poultney," and was razed and replaced by the present building (no date provided); (2)

* * *

It was in this tavern that Capt William Watson of the Revolutionary forces proposed the famous toast: "The enemies of our Country! May they have cobweb breeches, a porcupine saddle, a hard-trotting horse and an eternal journey!"

Horace Greeley boarded here in the late 1820s, when Harlow and Sarah Hosford were proprietors; he gave his first political speech in the Academy across the Green. Hosford made the place a temperance inn in 1838 (as did Joel Beaman in Poultney). (3)

* * *

There were two taverns in East Poultney in the "early days" (c. 1812). Judge Thompson, an ardent Democrat, kept the Eagle; while Daniel Parsons, Federalist, kept the Rising Sun, diagonally across the street. The Rising Sun became the Neal House, was later converted to apartments, and burned in 1954. Thompson sold the Eagle to Harlow Hosford; other proprietors included a Kellogg; George Dye; his daughter Emma, who married Frank Buckingham, and ran it with him.

* * *

c. 1775:   a tavern, Deacon Silas Howe; Howe is said to have come in 1772, and built a two-story house where he kept tavern for many years. He died in 1810, and the building was replaced about 1854 by what was known as the Howe-Pallmerine house in 1951;

c. 1790:   Rising Sun Inn, Daniel Parsons; who built it, and ran a store and inn there; Henry J. Neal, who married Parson's adopted daughter Julia, added a large wing and ran it as the Neal Place (1); tavern license, 1817;

1849: --, Abner Pember (NEMU Dir);

1854: (a) <u>Eagle Tavern</u>, --* (Scott);

1869: (a) as above, H. Potter* (Beers; same site);

1872: (a) as above;

c. 1873: <u>Neal Tavern</u>, Stephen Scott; originally the <u>Rising Sun</u>, on the corner opposite the <u>Eagle Tavern</u> "in later years" (4); Daniel Samson kept tavern here earlier;

c. 1880: (a) <u>Eagle Tavern</u>, Alexander Murdock;

1873, '75, '78, '80: (a) as above;

1904, '09: (a) as above, --* (Sanborn; see photo; not operating in 1922, according to Sanborn); but the <u>Eagle Tavern</u> is operating now (i.e., 1988) as a bed-and-breakfast place.

Eagle Tavern

(149b) <u>Lake St Catherine</u> (St Catherine PO, 1913-16; see also under Wells).

1880: (a) <u>Lake View House</u>, P. J. Griffith; built in 1876, about 3 miles from Poultney; on the western shore of the lake, torn down long ago; the PO was in this hotel from 1913 to 1916, but its popularity declined after World War I;

1881: (a) as above (Child);

1887, '92: (a) as above (also known as <u>Lake-View-in-the-Pines</u>); see photo;

1888: (a) <u>Lake-View-in-the-Pines</u>, I. H. Francisco; (Boston and Maine travel guide);

1890, '92: <u>Oakdale</u>, E. J. Brown; on Lake St (summers);

1897: the Rutland Railroad guide lists both the <u>Lakeview House</u> and the <u>Oakdale House</u>;

1916: (a) as above, I. H. Francisco (VPB); <u>Maple Lodge</u>, Mrs John R. Jones (VPB);

(149c) <u>Poultney</u>.

"At one time, ten distilleries were in operation here" (i.e., the township); "The business began to decline by 1830, and in a few years was known only as a thing of the past; (5);

1785:   Brookins Tavern, --; almanac, location unknown;

1798:   a tavern, Daniel Sprague (a blacksmith);

(?):   a tavern, Samuel Hyde; tavern license, 1817; almanac, 1812; "in the early days," on the farm now part of the Pomeroy Wells estate (i.e., 1886, ref 5);

Lake St Catherine House (Special Collections, UVM)

c. 1805:   Stanley's Hotel, John Stanley; became Beaman's Hotel; Stanley built a 2-story house in 1794, opened a tavern a few years later; sold to Joel Beaman in 1809 (tavern license, 1817, '21, '22), who kept it until he died in 1846; his son J. D. took over until 1849, then another son, C. C. Beaman; rebuilt several times, this place could accommodate about 30 guests in the 1880s; on the northwest corner of Main St and Beaman Place. It was the halfway stop on the Albany-Burlington stage, which ran until the railroad came through in 1852 (4); (A112 on the map of the Poultney Historic District, ref 2);

Note: tavern licenses to Henry G. Neal, 1817, and Isaac Fuller, 1821, locations unknown;

(?):   a hotel, Timothy Chittenden; at the west end of present Main St (c. 1875, ref 4); on what became the Troy Conference grounds in 1834; a school was kept here for a while; occupied in 1875 by Elias Whitcomb; on the north side of Main St; according to Smith and Rann, a tavern on "the school house site on the main road" was the first hotel in town, run by Thomas Ashley (5); it seems likely that this is the same as Chittenden's; the building was moved to South Poultney and used as a law office;

1849:   (a) --, J. D. Beaman (NEMU Dir); this is Beaman's Tavern, listed in an 1812 almanac; (b) --, J. W. Austin (NEMU Dir);

1854:   (a) Beaman's Hotel, --* (Scott); (b) Austin's Hotel, --* (Scott; this place became Hyde's Hotel by 1869 (Beers) and the Poultney House later; it was on the southwest corner of Main and Grove Sts at this time, across from Beaman's;

1868:   (b) Poultney House, --; according to Joslin et al., this place was built as a store

416

about 1840, then a commercial college, and only became a hotel as of this year (4); but this account is in conflict with map and directory evidence, and with Smith and Rann, who say it was built about 1834 by Henry Stanley, and say nothing about earlier use as a store or college. (5) A. H. Brown is said to have kept it longer than anyone else, and he was the predecessor of the "present" incumbent (i.e., a Mr Joselyn in 1886, ref 5);

1869: (a) as above, C. C. and J. D. Beaman* (Beers); (b) --, N. C. Hyde* (Beers; formerly Austin's);

1870: (a) as above, Collin C. Beaman; (b) Poultney House, D. B. Bartlett (formerly Hyde's, Austin's);

1872: (a) as above; (b) as above, Abram Thompson;

1873: (a) as above; (b) as above, E. G. Dyer;

1879, '80, '83, '84: (a) as above; (b) as above, A. H. Brown;

1887: (a) as above; (b) as above, E. O. Joslyn; by 1892, according to Sanborn maps, the Poultney House had moved, to a location further west on Main St, a little east of Maple St, and the old building was gone; it moved again later (see below);

1895: (a) as above; (b) Hotel Poultney, D. E. O'Brien; Parker House, G. Parker (location unknown); by 1897, according to Sanborn, the Poultney House/Hotel Poultney had moved again, further east on Main St; and somewhat later the Arcade (see below) was occupying the 1892 Poultney House location;

1898: (a) as above; (b) as above;

1901, '05: (a) as above; (b) as above, George Gilfeather;

1908: (a) as above; Beaman's became a home for the elderly; (b) as above, --; Arcade (in the former Poultney House location);

1907: according to the Sanborn map for this year, Beaman's and the Hotel Poultney are as above; the Arcade is as above; and the Cottage Hotel is operating a little east of the Poultney House (now Arcade) location on Main St;

1911: (b) as above; (c) Cottage Hotel, M. McCarty;

1913, '15: (b) as above; (c) Cottage Hotel, --; (both also in 1916 VPB);

1920: (b) as above, --; (c) as above, --; The Dorms, -- (summers, location unknown, listed in 1916 VPB);

1922: (b) as above, -- (Sanborn); (c) Cottage, -- (as above, Sanborn); Arcade building now gone;

1925: (b) as above, -- (still listed in 1968); (c) as above, --; the Cottage is now an apartment house (Sanborn); Colonial Inn, -- (summers, "near center of village," 1923 VPB, exact location unknown; same as The Dorms).

(149d) South Poultney, and (149e) West Poultney, no listings found.

Note: the assistance of Mr Charles Parker, Poultney Historical Society, is gratefully acknowledged.

* * *

References

(1)   East Poultney, Chartered 1761: Vermont's Cradle of Culture in the Wilderness (Poultney: Journal Pr., 1951).

(2) Vermont Div. of Historic Preservation, Historic Architecture of Rutland County, Curtis B. Johnson, ed., Elsa Gilbertson, asst ed. (Montpelier: 1988).

(3)   Walter E. Johnson, "We came to Vermont for the rest of our lives,"   Vermont Life 7 (Summer 1953): 20-25.

(4)   Joseph Joslin, Barnes Frisbee and Frederick Ruggles, A History of the Town of Poultney, Vermont (Poultney: Journal Pr., 1875; Univ. Microfilms).

(5)   Henry P. Smith and William S. Rann, History of Rutland County, Vermont (Syracuse: D. Mason, 1886).

* * *

(150) **Pownal** (Bennington).

(150a) North Pownal.

1849:   --, Andrew J. Whipple (NEMU Dir); tavern license, 1822;

1855:   --, A. Whipple;

1856:   --, A. Whipple and Son* (Rice and Hardwood map); building now gone;

(?):   a tavern, --; VDHP 0208-4, #21, now a private home;

1869:   (a) North Pownal Hotel, W. Burrington* (Beers; at a different site than Whipple's, above; at the intersection where Richard Champney's house was in 1977 (1); burned in 1928;

1870, '73, '75: (a) as above, John S. Eldred;

1880:   (a) as above, Byron M. Eldred (Child);

1883:   (a) as above, Roland Taylor;

1887:   --, Henry A. Tainter;

North Pownal Hotel

1888:   Glenwood Cottage, A. C. Peckham; Green Mountain House, D. C. Gardner (Boston and Maine guide);

1892, '95, '98: (a) as above, D. J. Pratt;

418

1901:   (a) as above, H. H. Packer (see photo);

1915:   Glenwood, --* (Sanborn; different location than the North Pownal Hotel, above);

1923:   Green Mountain House, Mrs D..C. Gardner (VPB);

(150b) Pownal (South village).

c. 1763:   a tavern, Charles Wright; "where the "low road to Bennington branched off the River Road" (1); the oldest house in town;

Note: tavern licenses to Henry Lyman, Willard Bates, Timothy Ware, Abel B. Wilder, Jonathan B. Norton, and Solomon Wright, Jr, 1822, locations unknown;

1785:   Jewett tavern, --; almanac, location unknown; a Perry Jewett had a tavern license, 1822;

c. 1813:   a tavern, Josiah Wright; also the first post office in town; Wright was a veteran of the Battle of Bennington;

1849:   Keyes Tavern, --; at the "south corner" (1); location unknown, but "south corner" probably refers to Williamstown and the Massachusetts line;

1849:   --, Josiah Wright (NEMU Dir; see above);

1864:   a tavern, Levi Burlingame; a license to run an inn in his house; later, L. and B. Burlingame ran the Exchange Hotel (see below);

1869:   (a) Exchange Hotel, L. and G. (?) Burlingame* (Beers); a large building at the Depot St corner, became the Wayside Inn; this was the last hotel in town, closed about 1900 for liquor law violations, burned under suspicious circumstances soon after (1); on the site of the present Country Glen Tourist Cabins (i.e., 1977, ref 1);

1872, '73:   (a) Exchange Hotel, L. Burlingame;

1878:   (a) as above, Adelbert Brown;

1880:   (a) as above, S. W. Scott; (b) American House, Thomas Clark;

1883:   (a) as above, T. A. Clark;

1884:   (a) as above, George Peoples;

1887:   (a) as above, William Bates (listed as W. H. Moran in Vt Dir); (b) as above, E. W. Barber; Swift says that Addison and Sullivan Barber "owned the store and hotel in Pownal village in 1880"; (2)

1890:   (a) as above, H. E. Kent; (b) as above, Mrs. E. W. Barber;

1892:   (a) as above, Frank Donahue; (b) as above;

1895:   (a) as above, C. J. Murphy; (b) as above;

1898:   Pownal House, George Pratt; not known if this is the Exchange Hotel, the American House, or an entirely different place;

1908:   Green Mountain , -- (unidentified);

1915:   no hotel on Sanborn.

(150c) <u>Pownal Center</u>.

(?):   <u>Munson Tavern</u>, --; near today's Pownal Elementary School (i.e., 1977, ref 1); this is on the east side of "new" Rte 7; place torn down about 1908 after long use as a home by the Mallory family;

1855:   --, J. W. Mallory; location unknown, could be North Pownal, Pownal or outside the villages;

1855:   --, Nelson Myers; later known as <u>Kimball's</u>, <u>Lampman's</u> and the <u>Union House</u>, see below;

1850s: (a) <u>Kimball House</u>, --; also known as the <u>Union House</u>, and <u>Lampman's</u>; shown on a map in Park's book (1); operated in 1856 by Nelson Myers, by Daniel W. Kimball in 1865; Mrs Kimball was town clerk and PM, and had a store in the front of the hotel; Kimball died in 1877, and the widow married Myron Lampman; the place became <u>Lampman's Hotel</u>;

1869:   --, Daniel W. Kimball* (Beers);

1870, '73, '75: (a) <u>Union House</u>, Daniel W. Kimball;

1880:   (a) as above, W. E. Russell;

1884:   (a) as above, M. E. Lampman;

1887:   (a) as above, --;

1908:   <u>Mountain View</u>, --; probably on old Rte 7, near the Town Clerk's office; established by the Clyde Peckham's, became <u>Bartel's Inn</u>.

Note: the assistance of Margaret Lillie and the Pownal Historical Society is gratefully acknowledged.

* * *

<u>References</u>

(1) Joseph Parks, Pownal: A Vermont Town's Two Hundred Years and More (Pownal: Pownal Bicentennial Comm.; Hoosick Falls, N.Y.: A-B Graphic Arts, 1977).
(2) Esther M. Swift, Vermont Place-Names: Footprints in History (Brattleboro: Stephen Greene Pr., 1977).

* * *

(151) **Proctor** (Rutland).

Sutherland Falls was a village lying partly in Rutland and partly in Pittsford originally. It had its name changed to Proctor in 1882, in honor of Redfield Proctor, who was responsible for reorganizing and revitalizing the marble industry in that place; and the town of Proctor was created by an act of the Vermont legislature in 1886, in response to efforts of Proctor and his associates, with land from Rutland and Pittsford. No tavern or hotel listings for Sutherland Falls have been found.

(151a) Proctor.

1905:   (a) <u>Proctor Inn</u>, W. H. Spier (also known as the <u>Marble Town Inn</u>; see photo); this place had been the Proctor Hospital until 1904, located at 21 South St; it was operated as an inn until 1968, later razed.

Proctor Inn

1911, '13, '15: (a) as above, N. B. Ladabouche;

1922: (a) as above, --* (Sanborn; also 1929, shown as <u>Marble Inn</u> by 1934; listed until at least 1968; oddly enough, no inn is shown on the 1910 Sanborn).

Note: the assistance of Mr Sanborn Partridge, Proctor Historical Society, is gratefully acknowledged.

* * *

(152) **Putney** (Windham).

(152a) <u>East Putney</u> (Cornton, from 1864-82). No listings found.

(152b) <u>Putney</u>.

c. 1766: a tavern, <u>Lt Leonard Spaulding</u>; "in the period 1766-1771"; (1)

c. 1770: first tavern (?), and store, <u>Peter Wilson</u>; (listed as Wetson in Child); a little west of the house of Deacon S. W. Houghton (i.e., c. 1871, Hemenway); shown on the 1869 Beers;

(?): an inn, <u>Moses Johnson</u>; early town meetings held there; he built the first 2-story house in town, now (1988) owned by Robert Wilcox; shown on the 1869 Beers at the north end of District 2 as G. Hooper;

1785: <u>Luther tavern</u>, --; almanac, location unknown;

1796: <u>Goodwin's tavern</u>, --; listed in Vermont Almanac and Register as a stage stop on the Windsor to Hartford, Conn., road; also 1797, 1802, '03;

Note: tavern licenses to David Leavitt, 1817-24; Isaac Grout, 1820-22; Minot and Parker, 1824, '25; Leavitt and Haven, 1825, '26; Minot and Brown, 1826; and Haven and Goddard, 1828, locations unknown;

1801: a tavern, <u>Samuel Wheat</u>; on Tavern Hill Road, at the north end of town; this road is shown on the Vermont Road Atlas, Northern Cartographic; shown on the 1869 Beers in District 4 as J. Joslin, who was related or connected to Samuel Wheat; extensively remodeled in 1877, now owned by George and Elizabeth Carow; there is a floor plan and detailed description of this place in ref 1;

1802: <u>Stowers tavern</u>, John Stowers; almanac; until at least 1829; tavern license, 1817; on the southwest corner of High and Main Sts, now an apartment building owned by Craig and Elizabeth Stead (1988); Asa Houghton, 1818-30 (tavern license, 1817-28; also a license to a Sally Houghton, 1830-33); John Black and James Keyes later; also known as <u>Farmer's Hotel</u>, on a Putney map of 1856, later the <u>Putney Tavern</u>; #26 in the Putney Historic District (VDHP 1313-3);

1838: (a) a hotel, <u>Russell Perry</u>; tavern license, 1827-33; near or in front of the present Town Hall (see below);

1849: (a) --, Russell Perry (NEMU Dir); --, J. Block's <u>Stage House</u> (NEMU Dir);

1855: (a) --, Russell Perry; --, Seth W. Hogekins and S. L. Merritt (probably the <u>Union House</u>, see below);

1856: (a) as above;   --, I. P. Day (probably the <u>Union House</u>);

1856: (a) a hotel, <u>R. Perry</u>* (McClellan); (b) <u>Union House</u>, --* (McClellan); on this map, these two places stand side by side on the west side of Main St, a little north of the Methodist church, the <u>Union House</u> further north; both are now gone; the <u>Union House</u> was about where the present (1988) Town Hall is, right next to <u>Houghton's Tavern</u> (<u>Stower's</u>);

1869: (a) <u>Vermont House</u>, J. P. Day* (Beers; probably this was <u>Perry's Hotel</u>, although it is hard to be sure from the map); (c) <u>Farmer's Hotel</u>, --* (Beers; same as Asa <u>Houghton's</u>, see above; later, this was <u>Kendrick's</u>, and the <u>Putney Tavern</u>;

1870: (c) as above, H. A. Green;

1873, '75: (c) as above, Dudley H. Kendrick (<u>Kendrick's Hotel</u>, later the <u>Putney Tavern</u>);

1879, '80: (c) as above, William M. Moore;

1883: <u>Gilson House</u>, C. P. Gilson; now Mt Paul's Market, a little north on Rte 5 (photo, Putney Historical Society);

1884: (c) <u>Kendrick's Hotel</u>, D. H. Kendrick (Child);

1887: (c) as above, Mrs A. O. Kendrick (listed as G. S. Cook in Walton); <u>Lewis House</u>, F. M. Lewis (unknown);

1890, '92: (c) as above, Mrs A. Kendrick;

Putney Tavern

422

1895:   (c) as above, John McNulty;

1898:   --, C. E. Blood; --, Charles Miller;

1901:   (c) Kendrick's House, C. Davison;

1905:   (c) as above, C. S. Willard;

1915:   (c) Putney Hotel, --* (Sanborn; see photo);

1925:   (c) Putney Tavern, E. W. Parker (formerly Kendrick's); listed until c. 1940, later a motel.

(152c)   Putney Falls (formerly Slab Hollow). No listings found.

Note: the assistance of Laura Heller and the Putney Historical Society is gratefully acknowledged.

* * *

References

(1) Edith DeWolfe et al., The History of Putney, Vermont, 1753-1953 (Putney: Fortnightly Club; Ann Arbor: Edward Bros., 1953).

* * *

(153) **Randolph** (Orange).

East Randolph was the principal village in the township in the beginning, partly because the turnpike passed through (as it also did North and South Randolph). Randolph (the "Center") benefited from being both the geographical and political center of the town. When the railroad came, however, it went through West Randolph, and things changed. West Randolph became 2nd Randolph, postally, in 1895, and Randolph became Randolph Center, while East Randolph died away as the commercial center of the town.

(153a)   East Randolph.

1849:   --, L. Kingsley (NEMU Dir);

1856:   --, George W. Graves; this is VDHP 0909-50, #7, built c. 1820; just north of the Union Church, and said to be a predecessor of the Blodgett Tavern (see below), which burned;

1858:   hotel (and PO), G. W. Graves* (Walling);

(?):   four early taverns are mentioned in Child: Shubael Converse; John Wheatley; Samuel Blodgett (who also ran stages; almanac, 1825, '29); and Samuel Fish, "where W. R. Holden now lives" (i.e., 1888, Child; see note below about almanac listing);

* * *

In the East Randolph Historic District (VDHP 0909-50), building #18, owned by Peter Kawecki in 1980, is said to have been an inn at one time, built c. 1850. This site appears to be the same as a place owned by R. Holden on the 1877 Beers, and hence is probably the Samuel Fish tavern above (where W. R. Holden lived in 1888, according to Child).

* * *

Note: two other tavern-keepers are listed in almanacs, unidentified, could be in any of the villages: Holmes (1816, '23); and Fisk (1807, '16, but this is probably Fish, see above);

Note: two other taverns mentioned in ref 2 as being in East Randolph, not identified, are "Goodrich's" and "Talbot's";

(?): Village Inn, --; built c. 1830, stood next north of the Blodgett tavern site; still standing (1988) but not in use; photos, refs 1,2; see photo;

1870: (a) East Randolph Hotel, Darius Goodrich (Darwin in Hemenway);

1873, '75: (a) as above, D. A. Talbert;

1877: (a) as above, J. Z. Sprague* (Beers; different site from the 1858 Graves site);

1879, '80: (a) Revere Hotel, J. Z. Sprague (formerly the East Randolph);

Village Inn, East Randolph
(Early Photographs of Randolph, 1986, Wes Herwig)

1883: (a) as above, C. Hovey;

1887: (a) as above, Jerome Chesley (Walton);

1887, '90: (a) Revere House, Clarence Hayward; (b) St Clair House, Frank St Clair (Vt Dir);

1888: (a) as above, Jerome Chesley (Child); (b) as above (Child);

1892: (a) as above, Albert B. Emery;

1895: (a) as above, George Raymond;

1898: (a) as above, Charles Pearson;

1901: (a) as above, --;

1905: (a) as above, C. P. Rogers;

c. 1915: Boston House, -- (photo, ref 2); PO was in this building when Elva Savage was PM, for some time after 1930;

1923: Boston House, H.H. Curtis (VPB).

(153b) North Randolph.

1798: Carpenter's Tavern, Jonathan Carpenter; on the road from Randolph Center to Brookfield (2); it burned in 1930, now the Warren Preston farm (photo, ref 2);

1879, '87: Traveler's Home, James M. Ryder (Vt Dir);

1888: Traveler's Rest, J. M. Ryder (Child);

1901: Traveler's Home, -- (Vt Dir).

(153c) Randolph (Center).

1810: Brackett Tavern, Capt Charles Brackett; almanac, 1825, '29; in stage coach days. Took the name The Maplewood much later, when the larger place with this same name, standing just north, burned in 1893. Lafayette addressed assembled citizens from its porch in 1825; became the first dormitory for the Vermont School of Agriculture in 1911, replaced by a new building in 1918;

1849: Green Mountain House, A. B. Perno (NEMU Dir); there is an early advertisement referring to Perno's Temperance House;

1856: --, Thomas Welch; --, Carlos Newton (presumably the Randolph House);

1858: (a) Randolph House, G. Carpenter* (Walling); --, T. Welch* (Walling);

1870, '73: (a) as above, Gilman Tarbell;

1875: (a) as above, G. W. Davis;

1877: (a) as above, G. W. Davis and Mrs Tarbell* (Beers);

1878: Ryder's Hotel, --; upstairs in the Austin Smith block, built in 1878, which escaped the big fire of 1884; rebuilt after fire damage in 1893; building now in commercial use (1988); photo, ref 2;

1879, '80, '83: (a) as above, Elijah Blodgett;

1885: the Normal School boarding house closed, and it became a summer hotel, the "new" Maplewood (see below);

* * *

The Maplewood Hotel at Randolph Center was built about 1876 by a Civil War hero, Col J. B. Mead. Of massive proportions, it stood opposite the present Herwig house (i.e., 1978, ref 1); it housed Normal School students and summer guests, lasted only 17 years before burning in 1893 (see photo).

1887: (a) as above, C. S. Murphy (L. S. in Vt Dir);

1888: (a) as above, Samuel S. Murphy (Child);

1890, '92, '95: (a) as above; (b) The Maplewood, Thatcher Stone;

1898: (a) as above, Nett Murphy; (c) The Maplewood; second place with this name, originally Brackett's (see above) since the first Maplewood burned in 1893;

Maplewood Hotel
(Early Photographs of Randolph, 1986, Wes Herwig)

1901: (a) as above, --; (c) as above, --;

1902: (c) as above (CVRR booklet);

1905: (a) as above, William L. Hebard; (c) as above;

c. 1906: The Colonial, --; primarily a boarding-house for Normal School students, but also a summer hotel;

1908: (c) as above, Mrs Thatcher Stone;

1911: (a) as above, W. L. Hebard;

1913: (a) as above;

1920, '25: (a) as above; the Randolph House gradually fell into decay after closing in 1939, and burned in 1967.

(153d) South Randolph.

1792: a tavern, Samuel Benedict; Vermont Almanac and Register; built in 1792, first building in South Randolph, a toll house and tavern on the turnpike which came through about 1800; "It was the same size and style as the old Haraden house on the South Randolph road. Imagine the crowded conditions one night in February 1804 when 70 horses and 40 lodgers 'filled every part of the house and barn and shed'." (3) Not clear if it was a tavern between 1792 and 1800. Sold to Samuel Paine Jr in 1803; "its most famous guest was Edward, Duke of Kent, the father of Queen Victoria" (2); taken down in 1961 and re-erected in Fairfield, Connecticut; a busy place in its day, with 40-50 teams sometimes putting up here in one night (Hemenway); the site is shown as #1 in the South Randolph Historic District (VDHP 0909-5); they say that the sale to Samuel Paine occurred in 1798. (See photo).

(153e) West Randolph (2nd Randolph, 1895).

1806: (a) Egerton's Tavern, Asa Egerton; at the northeast corner of Main and Central Sts, also operated by Amplius Blake and Peter Bates, and others; President James Monroe stopped here

426

in 1817, when it was <u>Bailie's Tavern</u>; it burned in 1853, was replaced by the <u>West Randolph Inn</u> until about 1870, when its name was changed to the <u>Mansion House</u>, under which name it operated for many years; also the <u>Randolph House</u>; dance hall attached (see photo, next page); a tenement in later years, damaged by fire in 1923, repaired, torn down in 1968, now the site of the Mini-Mart Store;

* * *

"The 4th of July came on Sunday, and was celebrated on Tuesday. It is not known what the interval was between toasts at the first table, but the number must have been sufficient for a glorious Fourth, if the worthy gentlemen who issued the following notice were able to pay for their dinners after the fifteenth bumper to fair Columbia's daughters. It did appear that more tickets were sold than Mr Egerton could supply seats for at the table.

Toasts prepared for the occasion will be given on the field and afterwards drunk at table. A separate table will be provided for the ladies, who will be waited upon in the genteelest manner by a committee appointed for that purpose. Gentlemen of both political parties from this and neighboring towns are cordially invited to attend the celebration, as the committee pledge themselves there will be no invectives or personalities whatever on the occasion.

A subsequent notice states that the bill for the liquors, etc, will be made up after dinner, and paid jointly by those gentlemen who dine at the first table. Toasts were given to, American Independence, The People, The American Farmer, The Mechanic Interest, Thomas Jefferson, The Federal Constitution, A well Regulated Militia, The American Navy, Our Sister, Massachusetts, Vermont ('a political paradox, may the first Tuesday of September next furnish an explanation,') The State of New York, The Vermont State Bank, Columbus, George Washington, Literature, and The fair Daughters of Columbia."(4)

Benedict Tavern, South Randolph
(Early Photographs of Randolph, 1986, Wes Herwig)

1849: (a) --, J. W. Bates (NEMU Dir; this is the precursor of the <u>Mansion House</u>, see above);

1856: --, Holden Hatch;

1858: (a) --, L. Fish* (Walling; this is the <u>Mansion House</u>);

427

1870:   --, B. F. Chadwick; (b) Cottage Hotel, W. and J. W. Gabrielle; near the present junction of Main and Pleasant Sts (i.e., 1978, ref 1);

* * *

The Cottage Hotel was opened by A. H. Beedle, who bought Dr Philander Bradford's Main Street home, added a story, and re-opened it as the Cottage Hotel in 1868. A favorite stopover for the drummers, it burned in 1884. See photo.

* * *

1873:   (b) Cottage Hotel, W. and J. W. Gabrielle; Chadwick Hotel, R. F. Chadwick (photos, ref 2);

Egerton's Tavern, West Randolph
(Early Photographs of Randolph, 1986, Wes Herwig)

1875:   (b) as above, Strong and Chadwick;

1877:   (a) as above, H. M. Nichols* (Beers; appears to be the same location as the Mansion House in 1858);

1878:   (a) Mansion House, --; (b) Cottage Hotel, E. D. Strong;

1879, '80:   (b) as above, W. and J. Gabrielle;

1880:   (a) Mansion House, H. H. Bean; later converted to apartments, razed in 1968;

1883:   (b) as above, Mrs H. S. Langdon;

1887:   (c) Red Lion Inn, Beedle Bros (Vt Dir; W. B. Nichols in Walton); this place opened in 1886, operated until 1936, in a new block built at the corner of Main and Merchant's Row after the big fire of December, 1884 (shown on an 1886 birdseye view, ref 5; Farmer's Hotel, H. R. Sulhan (location unknown);

1888:   (d) Newton House, James V. Newton (South Main St, Child); (c) as above, Beedle Bros (Main St, corner of Merchant's Row, Child);

1890, '92, '95: (c) as above, J. L. Battles (K. W. Morse in Vt Dir); (d) Newton House, James

428

Newton;

1898: (c) as above, F. I. Church; (d) as above;

1901: (c) as above; (d) as above, --;

1902: (c) as above, J. W. Brown (CVRR booklet);

1905: (d) as above, Mrs James Newton; (e) Randolph Inn, W. C. Hayward (the Red Lion Inn until 1903);

Cottage Hotel, West Randolph
(Early Photographs of Randolph, 1986, Wes Herwig)

1908: The Manchester, A. B. Manchester ("no consumptives or children taken");

c. 1910: Green Mountain Inn, --; built as a private home in 1887 (R. J. Kimball); Randolph Country Club briefly after his death in 1903, then an inn until c. 1950, now a nursing home; PC photo;

1911: (b) Cottage Hotel, --; listed in Walton this year, but said to have burned in 1884; presumably an error, or a short-lived place with the same name; (e) as above, C. W. Hayward;

1913: (e) as above, --; The Washburn, -- (became the Maples, see below); listed as Hotel Maples, H. M. Smith, 1916 VPB.

* * *

Hotel Maples (The Maples), on South Main St (VDHP 0909-87, at the northeast corner of the intersection of Rte 66 and the Rte 12 cutoff). Built c. 1870, taken over by Alfred Chandler during World War I. The main place in Randolph for more than 35 years. The building was moved in 1955, Mr and Mrs Henry Batchelder were the last operators. It was the Washburn Hotel earlier, in 1912, for example, and its name was changed to Mid-State Villa in 1927, later Windover House. Listed as The Maples 1930, '35, '40, Hotel Maples in 1955. See photo, next page.

* * *

429

c. 1916:   photo of a proposed luxury hotel, never built, to be built at the <u>Windover House</u> site; (2)

c. 1920:   <u>The Greystone</u>, Sawyer sisters; built by Col. Chandler as a home for his son, Albert E. Chandler (see below);

1923:   <u>Stedman Inn</u>, Albert E. Chandler; who bought the Burt place and opened it as the <u>Stedman Inn</u>, the name coming from his mother's family. This was the <u>Windover House</u> in 1986, originally built as the Thomas Hayden home in 1808, later the Henry Stedman farm (photo, ref 2); (e) <u>Randolph Inn</u>, Patrick Muldoon (VPB); <u>The Maples</u>, VPB;

Note: the assistance of Mr Wes Herwig and the Randolph Historical Society is gratefully acknowledged.

Hotel Maples
(Early Photographs of Randolph, 1986, Wes Herwig)

* * *

References

(1) Harry H. Cooley, Randolph, Vermont--Historical Sketches (Randolph: Town History Committee, 1978).
(2) Wes Herwig, Early Photographs of Randolph, Vermont, 1855-1948 (Randolph Ctr: Greenhills Books, 1986).
(3) Miriam Herwig, Randolph's Beginnings (Randolph Ctr: Greenhills Books, 1981).
(4) The Illustrated Historical Souvenir of Randolph, Vermont (Randolph: Nickerson and Cox, 1895).
(5) J. Kevin Graffagnino, Vermont in the Victorian Age (Bennington: Vermont Heritage Press, 1985).

* * *

(154) **Reading** (Windsor).

Reading is difficult because the name has been used for three different places by the Post Office Department over the years. A post office was established at Bailey's Mills, near Reading Center, from 1818 to 1832, and this was the 1st Reading. A post office was established at Hawkinsville in 1830 which became the 2nd Reading in 1832 when the 1st Reading closed. Hawkinsville was also known as Hammondsville, and is shown as such on the 1869 Beers map. This office lasted until 1903, and when it closed there was no Reading office until 1922, when the name was imposed, over the objections of the residents, on what had been Felchville since 1830. Felchville is now the 3rd Reading. There was also a village at Reading Center (no post office by that name) and one at South Reading (PO, 1832-1903).

(154a) Felchville (became 3rd Reading in 1922).

(?):   a hotel, Joel Holden; born in town in 1804, he kept a hotel both in Felchville and Hammondsville (probably not concurrently, although Child doesn't say) and died in 1850; said to be a performer on the organ, banjo and guitar, and a ballad singer as well;

1815:   Amsden Tavern, Abel Amsden; who built it on the northeast corner of the intersection of present Vt 106 and 44; VDHP 1414-17, now a private home;

1827:   (a) a tavern, William Felch; founder of the village, and a man of many talents; he built and kept the first store, tavern and factory; he served as a mail-carrier, state representative, justice of the peace, selectman, lister and PM (1859-61); he also built houses and mills (1); (Felchville House, later the Merrill House and the Valley House, see below);

1849:   Felchville House, H. Dow (NEMU Dir);

1869   (a) Merrill House, S. R. Kendall* (Beers; formerly the Felchville House, later the Valley House);

1870:   (a) as above, J. F. Kendall;

1871, '72:   (a) as above, Aaron T. Kendall;

1873:   (a) as above, Trask and Co;

1878:   (a) Felchville Hotel, Horace Willis;

1875, '87:   (a) Hotel Felchville, L. G. Coolidge;

1879, '80:   (a) as above, S. A. Brock;

1883:   (a) as above, G. W. Race (Child); it is Isaac Rice in Vt Dir;

1887:   (a) Valley House, H. O. Bingham (formerly the Merrill House);

1890:   (a) as above, L. G. Coolidge; Maple Grove House, I. Howard Newall;

1892: --, E. J. Johnson;

1895, '98: --, E. E. Cross;

1901: Maple Grove House, --;

1901, '02: (a) Valley House, W. L. (or W. B.) Pratt; also the Hotel Marion at one time; burned in 1907; (photo, cover of 1989 town report);

1911, '13: --, C. M. (or N.) Hook;

1915: no hotel on Sanborn, only a boarding-house.

(154b) Hawkinsville. (2nd Reading PO, Hammondsville on 1869 Beers map).

1822: (a) a hotel, William L. Hawkins; burned in 1836, rebuilt and kept for 20 more years by Hawkins, who came in 1789; he was the leading citizen (and namesake) of Hawkinsville, holding many offices, including that of PM (1830-32, when the place was called Hawkinsville; and 1832-35, 1836-39 and 1851-59); see 1869 entry below;

1855: --, Mrs Hapgood;

1856: --, Samuel H. Taylor;

(?): a hotel, Joel Holden (see under Felchville);

1869: a hotel, --* (Beers); this hotel was also the PO, according to Beers; Buck is listed in Post Office Dept records as the Reading PM from 1871 to 1876, when it was at Hawkinsville; place known as the Forest House at one time; Hammond's Hall on the top floor well known for its dances, an important tavern in the freighting days; building (except for the ell) moved to Quechee some years ago;

(154c) Reading (at Bailey's Mills). No listings found.

(154d) Reading Center (no post office).

1782: a tavern, Moses Chaplin (another record says 1812, according to local historians); later run by Rufus Forbush; on Eastman Road, a little north of Reading Center village, shown as A. Eastman on the 1869 Beers;

Note: there are two other early taverns in this same area: the Tim Collins tavern ("which had a floating dance floor which would spring with the rhythms of the dance"), a little south of the Chaplin tavern; and the Sherwin tavern, still further south, just below E. Hammond on the 1869 Beers (shown on a 1961 map prepared by the Reading Historical Society);

1786: a hotel, Capt David Burnham ; opened a hotel at the Center, first hotel in town, shown as "AB" on the 1869 Beers, on the west side of the village; "much frequented for many years" (Child);

1855: hotel, J. B. Collins* (Hosea Doten); there is a photo of this place, the Collins tavern, in the VHS collection; used as the town hall, c. 1910; there is a T. Collins, apparently at the same site, on the 1869 Beers.

(154e) South Reading.

c. 1780: the Sawyer stand, Benjamin Sawyer; kept a hotel that was carried on by his son, Benjamin Jr., 1827-34 and 1840-43 (Child); this place was a stage stop on the Windsor-Rutland turnpike, until the railroad put it out of business; west of South Reading, shown on the 1869 Beers as E. M. North; also on the 1961 Reading Historical Society map.

Note: the assistance of the Reading Historical Society is gratefully acknowledged.

* * *

<u>References</u>

(1) Gilbert A. Davis, History of Reading, Windsor County, Vermont, Vol II, (Windsor, 1903).

* * *

(155) **Readsboro** (Bennington).

(155a) <u>Heartwellville</u>.

(?):   <u>Old Coach Inn</u>, --; said to be near a mill illustrated in ref 1; in Heartwellville, on the Bennington-Brattleboro (Windham County) Turnpike; this is the present name of VDHP 0209-2; VDHP gives no date for construction, but built 1783 according to present owners (also ref 3); at the intersection of Rtes 8 and 100 in Heartwellville; also the <u>Canedy Tavern Stand</u>, the <u>Heartwellville Inn</u>, <u>Britton's Inn</u>, see below;

1797: <u>Heartwell's Tavern</u>, --; listed in Thomas's New England Almanack, on the Bennington-Brattleboro turnpike, presumably same as above; a second tavern is listed, but with no name, probably in Readsboro or Readsboro Falls; <u>Hartwell</u> listed in almanacs until at least 1829;

1856:   --, - Windell;

1856:   a hotel, --* (Rice and Hardwood);

1869:   --, E. L. Fuller* (Beers; but not the same site as 1856, above; F. E. and J. G. Thayer are shown as the proprietors on the inset, Fuller on the town map); later the <u>Canedy Stand</u>, <u>Old Coach Inn</u>, see below;

1873:   --, Fuller and Toby; --, Thayer and Bros; (which is the <u>Canedy Stand</u>?);

1880:   --, Milo Canedy; --, E. P. Fuller;

1883:   (a) <u>Heartwellville House</u>, Thomas Canedy (Child);

(?):   <u>City Hotel</u>, Charles E. Cutler (road 5, Child, unidentified;

1887:   (a) as above; (b) <u>Canedy's House</u>, Thomas Canedy (Vt Dir; apparently Canedy had two places at the same time for a while); but it is puzzling that the <u>Heartwellville House</u> disappears from the directories until 1901;

1888:   (d) <u>Maple Row Inn</u>, L. M. Canedy (Boston and Maine guide);

1890:   (b) <u>Canedy House</u>, Thomas Canedy; (c) <u>Crawford House</u>, E. Crawford; (location of this second place unknown);

1892:   (b) --, Thomas Canedy; (c) --, E. Crawford;

1895:   (b) <u>Canedy House</u>, Thomas Canedy; --, Edward Leray;

1898:   (b) as above;

433

1901:   (a) as above, Brittan and Morgan; (c) as above;

1903:   (a) Morgan Inn, -- (SBA guide; presumably this is the Heartwellville House/ Canedy's);

1905:   (a) as above, A. Brittan; (c) as above;

1911:   (a) as above, A. Britton; (c) Crawford House, T. Canedy;

1913, '20:   (a) as above, --; (c) as above, --; (d) Maple Row Inn, -- (burned in the 1970s);

1925:   (a) as above; (b) Canedy House,--; (d) as above.

(155b) Readsboro (also known as Readsboro City at one time).

c. 1782:   a tavern, Asalph White; authorized to build a toll bridge by the General Assembly, and granted a license to keep a tavern there; (2)

1822:   tavern licenses to Jonathan Houghton, Solomon Eddy and Bethuel Finney, locations unknown;

1856:   --, J. W. Goodell;

1856:   Smith's Hotel, --* (Rice and Hardwood);

1869:   --, George Carpenter* (Beers; same site as in 1856);

1870:   --, George Carpenter;

1873:   --, Carpenter and Faulkner;

1875:   --, M. E. Pettee; --, T. N. Stevens;

1879, '80:   (a) Deerfield Valley House, E. A. Cutler; Stowe House, M. E. Pettee (location unknown);

1883:   (a) as above; Davenport House, Drury and Goodnow;

1884:   Davenport House, Tyler D. Goodell; bought the hotel from Charles N. Davenport, ran it for more than 21 years; sold to Frank Allen in 1905, and it burned the next year; not rebuilt, but a cottage on the property survived the fire and served as a hotel from 1920 to at least 1936 (2); and a boarding-house into the 1970s (see Cottage Hotel, below);

1887, '92, '95, '98, 1901, '05, '08:   Davenport House (sometimes listed as Goodell House); see photo, next page;

1909:   Cottage Hotel, --* (Sanborn);

1911, '13:   Cottage House, Mrs C. F. Snow;

1920, '25:   as above, Mrs Carl Perry; also on Sanborn for 1919, '27, still listed 1968 VPB; now a private residence.

(155c) Readsboro Falls. No listings found.

Note: the assistance of Mrs Barbara L. Coe is gratefully acknowledged.

* * *

434

<u>References</u>

(1) Tyler Resch, Shires of Bennington (Bennington: Bennington Museum, 1975).
(2) Frank S. Ross, Down Through the Years at Readsboro, Vermont (Readsboro: The Town; Williamstown, Mass.: McClelland Pr, 1936).
(3) Bernice Barnett and Lucie Sumner, Border to Border: Along the Windham Turnpike, Cracker Barrel (Fall-Winter, 1987-88).

Davenport House (Goodell House), Readsboro

(156) **Richford** (Franklin).

(156a) <u>East Richford</u>.

1890: <u>Riverside Hotel</u>, Sisco Brothers;

1901: --, A. L. (?) Miltimore;

1904, '09: <u>Missisquoi House</u>, --* (Sanborn); this was the <u>Line House</u>, partly in Canada, partly in the US; (see below);

1920: <u>Green Mountain House</u>, --* (Sanborn); formerly the <u>Missisquoi</u>; vacant in 1930;

* * *

The <u>Missisquoi House</u> (also known as the <u>Riverside</u> and the <u>Line House</u>) had a checkered history. Not known when it was built, first listed in 1890, when it was owned by the Sisco brothers. They sold to Eugene Miltimore in 1893, and bought it back in 1898. Sold again very soon to R. W. Hadlock, and transferred again almost at once to L. M. Miltimore, a nephew of Eugene; soon taken over by Horace Miltimore, L. M.'s father, and sold again to Bert L. Wilson in 1909. Wilson carried out extensive renovations, with a grand opening in January, 1910, but the place burned on March 15, 1911. (1)

The site with its ruins was purchased by one Lillian Miner ("Queen Lill," see photo, next page). Miss Miner was originally from Stevens Mills, and had become the madam of a Boston brothel, but ran afoul of the law, and managed to re-establish herself here in what one might have thought would be the unpromising environment of East Richford. She built a 3-story hotel on the old site, and won her first legal victory when she managed to convince the court that she had not violated a Federal law against building places on the international line, because she was merely repairing an old one. There is a fascinating account of this colorful period in Salisbury's book, portions of which have been used in Chapter III. (2) There is also a photo of Queen Lill's "hotel" in Salisbury's book.

* * *

(156b) <u>Richford</u>.

435

c. 1796:   a hotel, <u>Joseph Stanhope</u>; who came in 1796, and soon after settling (on a farm owned by H. and S. Stanhope in 1882, Child) built a framed house, kept the first hotel;

c. 1804:   a hotel, <u>Nathaniel Rains</u> (Raines); at the lower end of present Main St (2); shown on a sketch map of Richford in 1807 in Salisbury; (2)

(?):   a hotel, <u>John Powell;</u> customs officer, who kept the only hotel at the "falls" (i.e., Richford; this information comes from Aldrich, but is confusing, because Child mentions Daniel Powell, early settler, as a customs officer; he died in 1810, no mention of a hotel, nor of a John Powell in Child;

"Queen Lill", of the East Richford Line House
(Richford, Vermont: Frontier Town, 1987, Salisbury)

Note: tavern license to Stephen Blasdill, 1819, '20-26, location unknown;

1831:   (a) <u>Union House</u>, Alden Sears; tavern license, 1827-32; for 35 years, at the corner of Troy and Main Sts (photo, ref 2); Sears was PM, 1837-39 and 1840-44); sold in 1866 to Albert Clement, who sold almost at once to Park Goddard; also known as the <u>Richford House</u>, still operating in 1893, but moved in 1901 and became a rectory when the new Roman Catholic church was built on the site;

* * *

"Park Goddard had been the stage driver on the run from St Albans to Richford for a long time. He was a keen sportsman, and the hotel became a center of great interest in horse racing when he purchased the big island in town and transformed it into a trotting park and the site of the Franklin County Agricultural Society's annual fairs.

Mr Goddard's large brass kerosene lantern...hung for many years on the porch of the Union House and was a beacon for pedestrians walking on Main Street at night. People would sit on the wide verandas of his hotel in the evenings and exchange news and gossip brought by travelers on stage lines." (2)

* * *

1849:   (a) --, Alden Sears (NEMU Dir; this is the <u>Union House</u>);

1855: --, G. N. Powell; --, L. P. Draper;

1857: (a) <u>Richford House</u>, --* (Walling; same as the <u>Union House</u>); a hotel, J. Campbell* (shown on a sketch map of Richford in 1857, in ref 2); on River St; it became the <u>Royce Hotel</u> a little later (photo, ref 2). It is not shown on the 1873 sketch map of Richford, but is on the 1871 Beers); now a private residence;

1871: (a) <u>Union House</u>, J. P. Goodland* (Beers); (b) <u>American House</u>, J. B. Sweatland* (Beers; photo, ref 2);

1870, '73: (a) as above; (b) as above;

1875: (a) as above; (b) as above, M. P. Andrews;

1879: (a) as above; (b) as above, McKenzie W. Rounds (PM, 1865-72 and 1881-85);

1880: (a) as above; (b) as above; both visible in an 1881 birdseye view, ref 4;

1882: (a) as above; (b) as above, Jerome F. Hale;

1883: (a) as above, I. P. Goddard; (b) as above;

Note: there is a small problem here, since Child says that there were 4 hotels in Richford c. 1882, without naming them. The contemporary directories list only the two shown above; <u>Royce's</u>, which never made the directories, makes three...what was #4, the <u>Riverside</u> in East Richford?

1887: (a) as above, L. G. Green; (b) as above;

"The Union House and the American House were thriving competitors in the 1880s. MacKenzie W. Rounds started the many alterations to the American House with a new mansard roof in 1881. By 1883 J. F. Hale was the new owner and, in that year, added a new veranda at the hotel's north end. Dances were held occasionally and were often all-night affairs, with a concert first, dancing, then a midnight dinner, followed by dancing until dawn. The partygoers would leave for home at daylight by horse and buggy, some with many miles to travel. A ball put on by Mr Hale in 1885 was the grandest occasion ever held in town. It featured a seven-piece band from Concord, New Hampshire...The owner built a 40' x 90' addition ...in 1886 to take care of his ever growing guest list." (2) (See photo, next page).

* * *

Hale sold the <u>American</u> by the end of the decade, and it was leased to Leman Greene, who ran it in addition to the <u>Union House</u>. It was Greene who "built the pagoda and picnic tables at the area on Loveland Brook known as Powder Springs, where many picnics and outings were enjoyed during the summer months..." (2)

It was Hale who said, in the course of a controversy over the city's construction of a municipal water system, that he had had only one bath in the six years he had been in Richford, and that was when he fell in the mill pond.

1890, '92: (a) and (b), both managed by L. G. Greene; and both shown on the 1892, '97 Sanborn;

1895, '98: (a) as above; (b) as above, J. F. Kelley;

* * *

437

Kelley built a large addition to the American House, to provide the service needed when the Union House closed (in 1901); but the place was nearly destroyed by fire in 1904. It was rebuilt the following year.

* * *

1901, '05, '08, '13:   (b) as above (also on 1904, '09 Sanborn); Union House replaced by the Roman Catholic church;

1916:   (b) as above, F. N. and M. L. Pike (VPB); (closed during the winter of 1917-18 because of fuel shortages and the high price of food);

1920:   (b) as above, Pike and Pike (also on Sanborn);

1925:   (b) as above, H. A. Dunbar (also on 1930 Sanborn); New American House listed until at least 1940; razed in the 1950s to make way for a gas station.

(156c) Stevens Mills.

No listings, but there is a postcard in the VHS collection showing a place here called the Adams House.

Note: the assistance of William R. Rowley is gratefully acknowledged.

* * *

References

(1) Rhoda Berger, "Once Upon A Time...," County Courier, August 6, 1987.
(2) Jack C. Salisbury, Richford, Vermont: Frontier Town (Canaan, N.H.: Phoenix Publ, for the Richford Historical Soc., 1987).
(3) Lewis C. Aldrich, History of Franklin and Grand Isle Counties, Vermont (Syracuse: D. Mason, 1891).
(4) J. Kevin Graffagnino, Vermont in the Victorian Age (Bennington: Vermont Heritage Press, 1985).

American House

* * *

(157) **Richmond** (Chittenden).

(157a) Fays Corners. No listings found.

(157b) Jonesville.

(?):   a tavern (and store), Nathaniel Alger; "in the last house in Richmond, on south side of river near Bolton"; (1)

c. 1810:   a stage hotel, --; in a house later occupied by Joseph Whipple, who leased the place from Ransom Jones, and ran it until the railroad came through in 1849, when it apparently went out of business; on the old stage route, two miles south of the village on Rte 2; the existence of two taverns at this time is confirmed, ref 2;

* * *

"Hemenway recounts an incident involving an emotional meeting between General Winfield Scott and his former orderly sergeant which took place...in front of the tavern. General Scott, passing through Vermont, stopped at Whipple's. It so happened that it was muster day and all of the militia in the western part of the state had been ordered to assemble in Richmond...for a muster on the training ground in front of the hotel. Scott inspected the troops, and inquired if any soldiers belonged to the 11th Regiment of infantry which fought with him at Lundy's Lane or Bridgewater. One soldier--Orderly Sergeant William Humphrey, a Richmond resident--stepped forward. General Scott gave a rousing speech praising the men who had fought so valiantly under his command. After the speech, Humphrey remarked, 'One name you forgot.' 'Who?' asked Scott. 'General Winfield Scott!,' shouted Humphrey, whereupon thunderous cheers arose from the spectators." (3)

* * *

c. 1815:   Hunt's Hotel, Roswell Hunt; who built it on the old stage route (Rte 2) in what is now Jonesville; it became a tenant house after Hunt's time, but was bought and repaired by Ransom Jones (for whom Jonesville was named) in 1843. Run as a hotel with C. Stevens as landlord until the railroad came in 1849; Jones continued to operate a tavern at one end of the building, with a PO at the other, until he died in 1858; various proprietors until 1886, when it was made into a store (Quinn's store in recent years); VDHP 0411-31, burned in 1980; also known as the Jones Hotel, Jonesville Hotel/House, and the Forest House (see below);

1849:   --, R. Jones (NEMU Dir);

1855, '56:   --, R. Jones;

1869:   (a) Jonesville Hotel, E. R. Morse* (Beers);

1870:   (a) as above;

1872:   (a) Forest House, E. R. Morse (same as Jonesville Hotel);

1873, '75:   (a) as above, A. B. Cooper;

1878:   (a) Forest House, C. C. Stevens;

1879, '80, '81: (a) as above, F. P. Hunt;

1882:   (a) as above, William M. Bruce (Child);

1920:   --, C. M. McGaughan (unidentified);

c. 1920:   Duck Inn, --; on Snipe Ireland Road.

(157c) Richmond.

Richmond's tavern history is complex. The town lay on a major stage route, and there were five or six early taverns, several of uncertain location. Also, there is not always complete agreement between the accounts provided by different sources. Rann mentions 5 taverns in Richmond, listed immediately below. (1)

1798:   a tavern, William Church; first in town, according to Rann (1); on the "farm" owned in 1882 by John Mason (location uncertain); there were Masons near the meeting house (Old Round Church);

1796-1814:   a tavern, John Russell; "back of present store of Jacobs and Woodworth" (i.e., 1886, ref 1); just beyond the store on the northwest corner of the Main and Bridge Sts intersection; almanacs, 1796-1814 (but it is possible that the almanac "Russell" is really Robert Russell (see below); John Russell died in 1814;

c. 1800:   a tavern, Benjamin Farnsworth; "on the old turnpike road (i.e., the Winooski Turnpike) at the upper end of Richmond village" (i.e., west of the village), exact location unknown; (1)

c. 1812:   a tavern, Thomas Whitcomb; "about three-quarters of a mile west of the village"; (1)

* * *

Levi Woodbury, who was a lawyer and a justice in the New Hampshire Superior Court, spent a week traveling through Vermont in 1819, and described his travels in detail in a journal kept for his fiancee. He spent one night in a Richmond tavern, described as follows: "The Meeting house is on the West bank of the river (i.e., the Onion) and opposite to the Tavern, where I now write. It was painted white, was in a circular form with sixteen sides...(i.e., the Old Round Church)...My landlady...contrived to have a bar room, parlour, kitchen, two chambers and a garret in a one story house of no large size." It seems likely that this place was either Church's or Whitcomb's. (4)

* * *

Note: other almanac listings are Spicer, 1816; Stearns, 1823; and Bosworth, 1825, '29; a Nathaniel Stearns 2nd is also mentioned in the Vermont State Archives as a licensed tavern-keeper in 1821;

pre-1838:   the "old brick hotel," Robert Russell; built by him "at an early day" (c. 1835) on the southwest corner of the Main and Bridge Sts intersection; Rann says that Charles M. Huntington was first to keep this tavern (1); there exist orders for a component of the Vermont militia to muster at the Charles M. Huntington Inn in October, 1838. Many owners, including, Daniel Goodrich Jr (1848), Daniel Barber (1851), and Alanson B. Shepard (1851-57). Leased by Shepard to Barney and Ransom for a hotel (Barney and Ransom Hotel, see 1857, below); sold to Horace M. Bruce in 1857, who renamed it the Richmond Hotel, first of several places with that name. Bought by Saul Bishop in 1863, then Julius Ransom (now the Richmond House, then Leonard Love (1870), again the Richmond Hotel. Capt. R. J. Coffey took over in 1880, and was proprietor when it burned, some time before 1886.

1840:   an inn, Joseph Smith; the same militia unit mentioned above in connection with Huntington's was ordered to report at Smith's in September, 1840; unidentified, probably corresponds to the Farmer's Hotel, the Stage Hotel in Jonesville, or one of two places listed in the 1849 NEMU Dir also not identified (see 1849, below); the Farmer's Hotel (also known as Freeman's) was west of the village, dates of operation unknown, but there was a hotel there for 60 years (building burned in 1891, Freeman's home at the time);

1849:   --, Daniel Goodrich; --, B. R. Jones; Farmer's Hotel, W. S. Freeman (all NEMU Dir);

1855, '56:   --, A. B. Shepard; this is the "old brick hotel";

1857: (a) a hotel, <u>Barney and Ransom</u>* (Walling);

1869: (a) 1st <u>Richmond House</u>, J. H. Ransom* (Beers; same site as Walling, 1857, above);

1870: (a) as above;

1872, '73, '75, '79, '80:   (a) as above, Leonard Love;

1882: 2nd <u>Richmond House/Hotel</u>, R. J. Coffey; Coffey was proprietor at Russell's earlier, is referred to by Rann as first proprietor of this place; this inn is also referred to by Rann (c. 1886) as the"present hotel"; Coffey followed in 1884 by George W. Orcutt, G. E. Barnum in 1887, '90, last listed in 1890; on the northeast corner of the Main and Bridge Sts intersection, apparently adapted from a store owned by Salmon Green;

(?):   <u>Chequered (Checkered) House</u>, --*; dates of operation uncertain, probably early 1800s (this is VDHP 0411-51, who say it was an inn before the 1820s); on the north side of Rte 2, a little west of Richmond village, just west of the Rte 117 intersection; shown on Beers, 1869; purchased by Giles Howe in 1876, "after it had been a stage coach tavern," now a restaurant; described in detail in ref 3;

1889: (b) <u>Bellevue House</u>, G. W. Mandigo; also known as the <u>Bostwick</u>; from 1889 until 1908, when it burned, but not in use as a hotel at that time; on the southeast corner of the Main and Bridge Sts intersection; the <u>Tourist Hotel</u> opened on this site in 1923 (see below);

1892-1901:   (b) as above, Charles Bostwick; M. D. Downey, 1904, '05;

1902: (b) as above, Charles Bostwick; (c) <u>Park House/Cottage</u>, J. W. McGarghan (also known as <u>McGarghan's</u>); on Depot St, on the site of a funeral home; also burned in the 1908 fire, not rebuilt;

(?):   3rd <u>Richmond Hotel</u>, --; also known as <u>Hotel Richmond</u>, <u>The Richmond</u>, and listed in Walton in 1917 as the <u>Colgrove Inn</u>, R. W. Douglas; from at least 1917 until c. 1940, in a house dating from at least 1857; proprietors included Mrs Fred Berry, Mr and Mrs A. L. Carpenter, Mr and Mrs L. P. Hart, Mrs Emma Buley, and John Baker; on Main St, diagonally opposite the Catholic church, VDHP 0411-1, #24; building now in use as an apartment;

1905: <u>Richmond House</u>, C. Degue (?), see Note below; ; (b) <u>Bellevue House</u>, M. D. Downey; (c) <u>Park</u>, J. W. McGarghan;

1908: (c) as above, --; no hotels listed in 1911-12, '13, '15;

Note: confusion is created by the existence of still another <u>Richmond House</u>, which it has not been possible to locate definitely. This place is listed in Walton in 1903 and 1904 with Richard Burke as proprietor, and for two more years (1905, C. Degue; and 1906, no proprietor.) Also, in 1904, the magazine Expansion referred to three hotels in Richmond, describing the <u>Bellevue House</u> in detail but not naming the other two, which must have been the <u>Park House</u> and the <u>Hotel Richmond</u>, although this does not help with identification. It is possible that this fourth <u>Richmond</u> was at an entirely different location, lasting for only 4 years (1902-06). It is also possible that it was the <u>Richmond House</u> of the 1880s, unlisted for some 12 years (1890-1902); or somewhat more probably, that it was the <u>Hotel Richmond</u> of the 1920s, again with a long gap in directory listing (1905-16). This problem has not been resolved.

1920, '25:   <u>Hotel Richmond</u>, --; see photo;

1923: <u>Tourist Hotel</u>, E. B. Gannon; on the site of the old <u>Bellevue</u>;

1926: <u>Hotel Richmond</u>, --* (Sanborn); still operating in 1939; <u>Tourist's Hotel</u>, --* (Sanborn; until c. 1940);

Note: places more in the nature of boarding-houses than inns include the <u>Maple Inn</u> and the <u>Hotel Bradley</u> (later the <u>Richmond Inn</u>), a boarding-house for women employees of the Richmond Underwear Company.

Note: the assistance of Harriet W. Riggs, Richmond Historical Society, is gratefully acknowledged.

* * *

References

(1) William S. Rann, History of Chittenden County, Vermont (Syracuse: D. Mason, 1886).

(2) Z. Thompson, History of Vermont, Natural, Civil and Statistical (Burlington: The Author, 1853; Part 2, Gazetteer): 149.

(3) Lilian B. Carlisle, ed., Look Around Chittenden County, Vermont (Burlington: Chittenden County Historical Soc., 1976).

(4) H. B. Fant, "Levi Woodbury's Week in Vermont, May 1819," Vermont History <u>34</u> (January 1960): 54.

Hotel Richmond

* * *

(158) **Ripton** (Addison).

(158a) <u>Bread Loaf</u>.

1866:   <u>Bread Loaf Inn</u>, Joseph Battell;

* * *

Battell was a wealthy philanthropist with a variety of interests who raised Morgan horses on a farm in Weybridge which he ultimately gave to the US government; the state of Vermont took it over in 1951. He also bought large tracts of land in the mountains east of Middlebury which he gave to the people of the state of Vermont, held in trust by Middlebury College. The inn that he built (and where he served several terms as postmaster) has served the Middlebury College summer school and the Bread Loaf Writer's Conference in recent times. Battell is listed as proprietor in Walton through 1915. (See Chapter V, Resorts, for a description of this place and a photo, and Battell's "summit house," <u>Lincoln Lodge</u>).

* * *

1871:   Bread Loaf Inn, Joseph Battell* (Beers);

1870, '75, '80, '87, '91, '95, '98, 1905, '08, '13, '15:   as above;

1916:   Bread Loaf Inn, -- (Vermont Publicity Bureau);

1920, '25:   Bread Loaf Inn (summers), --; owned by Middlebury College; listed in Walton until at least 1940.

(158b) Ripton.

(?):   a tavern, Abraham Lackey; "very nearly on the turnpike...in the house now owned by Albert Whitcomb" (i.e., 1886, ref 1);

Note: the village's origins go back to the re-routing of the Center Turnpike in 1825, from its original hillside location to what is now, approximately, Rte 125 (VDHP);

(?):   a tavern (the second), Ethan Owen; on the site of George A. Baker's store, "when the town was young"; Benjamin Hale Jr bought it years ago, also run by Seaver Fletcher, Elias Matteson and his son Elias H. Matteson; the latter had charge when the place (then called the Green Mountain House, see below) burned in May 1877;

1849:   Green Mountain House, A. J. Church (NEMU Dir);

1856:   --, S. S. Fletcher* (Walling; this is surely the Green Mountain House);

1905, '11, '13: Maple Inn, Napoleon La France.

* * *

References

(1) Henry P. Smith, History of Addison County, Vermont (Syracuse: D. Mason, 1886).

* * *

(159) **Rochester** (Windsor).

(159a) Robinson. At West Rochester, a PO from 1904-18 called Robinson, still the local name for the area. No listings found during the time it was called Robinson.

(159b) Rochester.

An anecdote about an early hostelry in Rochester is presented in Whitney et al. (1) A woman named Granny Way once had a place for travellers near the top of the mountain road to Bethel, with a sign that said: Oats and Beer and Lodging Here. According to the legend, those who stopped did not always continue their journey; robberies, especially of peddlers, were followed by murders and night burials. Granny Way is said to have been helped by a giant, one-eyed runaway slave, and both are said to have fled after the local authorities investigated. Some maps of the area still show Granoway Mountain, and rabbit hunters talk of a Granny Way swamp.

* * *

1783:   a tavern, Timothy Clements; first in town (1); "nearly opposite where the lower mill school house now stands"; still standing in 1975, occupied by Mansil Parmenter;

c. 1790:   a tavern, Cephas Sheldon; "near the southwest corner of the common on the west side" (1); building no longer there; a part of this tavern served as the first store in 1792, and the first post office was also here then (Child); the first PM, officially, was John Flint, from 1816-

22, in Sheldon's Tavern (2); became the E. P. Briggs tavern later (see below);

(?):   a tavern, Dr Retire Trask; who came in 1790 and later built "the old Webber house, at the top of the hill, at the south part of the village" (Child); he kept tavern "awhile";

1811:   a tavern, E. D. Briggs; (there is an 1812 almanac listing for "Grigs," probably a garbled version of Briggs; in his house and store on the common where the Rochester Inn now stands (i.e., 1988; see map in ref 1); originally the Cephas Sheldon tavern; there is a reproduction of a drawing of Briggs' tavern sign, dated 1811, in ref 1; there is an E. D. Briggs at this location on the 1855 Hosea Doten map, and he apparently ran the place until 1869; remodelled from time to time, became a private home, burned in 1914 and rebuilt; became an inn again in 1935, see Parker's Inn, below;

1832:   a tavern, Elijah Wyman; in "Jerusalem," an area bordering Bethel, at the south end of town;

1849:   --, H. Cheney (NEMU Dir; see below); --, R. H. Tupper (NEMU Dir; there is an R. H. Tupper on the 1855 Hosea Doten map on the Center Turnpike, south end of town, just barely in Rochester); --, P. L. Goss (NEMU Dir);

1855:   a hotel, H. Cheney* (Hosea Doten); later the Nichols Inn, on the site of the present Gulf Station (i.e., 1975, ref 1; see map there);

1856:   --, F. Fales (Walton; location unknown);

1869:   Nichols Hotel, H. F. Nichols* (Beers, on the Cheney site);

1869:   (a) Rochester House, Caleb Eaton; a 50-room hotel built by Eaton, the main hotel in town for many years; later owners and/or managers included Timothy Eaton, H. O. Peabody (when it was known as Peabody's Hotel; see 1877 photo), R. M. Hemenway, Mr Pettengill, M. L. Faulkner, Quincy M. Ford, F. W. Johnson, C. H. Stoddard and William McCray (McCray House, see below); stopped operating soon after 1914, torn down years later; lithograph in Child;

1870:   (a) as above, C. and A. Eaton;

1873:   (a) as above, T. M. Eaton;

1875:   (a) as above, E. T. Bugbee;

1878:   (a) as above, H. O. Peabody;

1879, '80:   (a) as above, R. M. Hemingway (sp?);

1883, '87:   (a) as above, M. F. (?) Faulkner;

1890, '92, '95: (a) as above, Q. M. Ford;

1898:   (a) as above, C. H. Stoddard;

1901, '02, '05, '08:   (a) as above, Q. M. Ford;

1905:   McCray House, William McCray; manager of the Rochester House at the time, McCray bought a large house north of the present Charles Andrews house (i.e., 1975, see map in ref 1). He used it first as an annex for the Rochester House, later ran it as the McCray House/Rochester Inn, the only place in town for some time after the old Rochester House closed. Bought by Edson J. and Florence Parker in 1930, became the first Parker's Inn. Five years later they converted a large house on the south corner of the common (a building that had replaced the old Briggs Tavern, and which was known as the Pierce House) into the second Parker's Inn (see photo, next page), which was renamed the Rochester Inn when it was sold in

1952; still operating (1988); this is #8 in the Rochester Village Green Historic District, VDHP 1415-1;

Peabody House
(Rochester, Vermont: Its History, 1780-1975)

Rochester Inn
(Rochester, Vermont: Its History, 1780-1985)

1911:   <u>Rochester House</u>, W. M. McCray;

1913, '20:   --, W. McCray;

1925:   Rochester Inn, W. M. McCray;

(?):   White River Valley Inn and Golf Club, --; no further information.

(159c) Talcville.   No listings found.

2nd Parker's Inn

(159d) West Rochester. A PO with that name from 1848-74, later site of the Robinson PO (see above).

(?):   Bliss Hotel, --; shown as C. G. Bliss on the 1855 Hosea Doten map; became O. R. Blodgett's Tavern by at least 1869 (Beers); on the stage road to Goshen and Brandon (present Rte 73), owned by the King family since 1899. (1)

Note: the assistance of Earl and Mary Davis, Rochester Historical Society, is gratefully acknowledged.

* * *

References

(1) E. E. Whitney et al., Rochester, Vermont: Its History 1780-1975 (Rochester: The Town, for the Rochester Town History Comm.; Burlington: Queen City Pr., 1975).
(2) Wendell W. Williams, History of the Town of Rochester, Vermont (Montpelier: Eli Ballou, 1869).

* * *

(160) **Rockingham** (Windham).

(160a) Bartonsville (1st LaGrange, 1835-37; Bartonsville established postally on the same site in 1842).

pre-1840:   two taverns at the hamlet of LaGrange, which became Bartonsville a short time later; where the town farm was located in 1907 (1); one kept by "Squire" Willard, known as Willard's Tavern (almanac, 1825, '29); and the other in a brick house opposite (occupied by J. A. Liddle in 1907), managed successively by John R. Gibson (tavern license, 1820-27), Levi and Elijah Beeman (license, 1832, '33), Peter Willard (license, 1816-27), and Carlton H. Roundy;

Note: the 200th Anniversary Pictorial booklet of the town of Rockingham (1953) says Jeremiah Barton built the "old tavern," c. 1840 (no other information);

* * *

There are two old houses now standing in the Town of Rockingham that were taverns in years gone by. One is in the village of Rockingham, now owned by Mr and Mrs Robert Avery Smith (i.e., 1969); built by Jehiel Webb, who occupied it many years as a tavern; he came in 1774, built a log house, the present house was built later...The other old tavern building is at LaGrange (Bartonsville), a two-story brick house standing at the intersection of what was the G r e e n Mountain Turnpike and the road to Cambridgeport, probably built prior to 1817. (2)

* * *

Note: Jehiel Webb above is probably the Webb listed in almanacs, 1785, '96, 1802; hard to distinguish from the Webb of Webb's Hotel in Bellows Falls, see below; there are also almanac listings for 1817, '20, '22, '25.

1869:   a hotel, B. Snow Jr* (Beers);

1907:   reference to Arthur Day's new store in the hotel (unnamed, but probably the Parker House, see photo, next page); this building also contained the PO, and burned on Dec 13, 1914 (3);

(160b) Bellows Falls.

1796:   Sanderson's tavern, --; almanac, unidentified; not necessarily in Bellows Falls village;

pre-1798:   Morgan Tavern, Quartus Morgan; who came in 1798 and bought an existing hotel, which he said in later years was "a very old building when I bought it" (1); almanac, 1812, '13; known as the Frost Block in 1907, with a store below and tenements above, on the west side of Rockingham St just north of the Central House (photo, ref 1; its location is shown on an 1808 sketch of Bellows Falls, reproduced in ref 6). Morgan ran it until 1810, and his widow Lorana until 1814 (there is a photo of the tavern sign in Hayes, ref 1). Used as a hotel for some time after this before being made into tenements. It was the main stage house until Robertson's Tavern was built in 1816 (see below), and the oldest building in the city in 1907, but it is now gone;

* * *

"Bellows Falls has, in the greater part of its history, been fortunate in the quality of its hotels. In number, the high water mark seems to have been reached in 1823, when a directory of the state credits it with "seven taverns." The low water mark was reached in 1860, when for a few months subsequent to the burning of the old Bellows Falls Stage House, the village had no hotel, and the citizens opened their houses in many instances to travelers. L. D. Hurd, who was then proprietor of the depot restaurant, furnished meals and lodging to strangers. The hotel was burned in March, 1860, and the first hotel to be opened thereafter was in the Harris Block on Canal Street. It was opened the next February by L. P. Bowker and continued for several years as the only public house of the place." (1)

c. 1801:   Cold River House, Deacon Samuel Wightman; almanac, 1807 until at least 1829; about a mile south of Bellows Falls, at the south end of Mount Kilburn; Wightman came in 1801 and lived for a while in a tavern on the site of the "present" (i.e., 1907) Keyes place, a tavern which burned about 1867.

* * *

"During stage coach times it (i.e., the Cold River House) was one of the noted hostelries of this part of New England." (1) The Cheshire Railroad acquired the property when it came to Bellows Falls about 1850, and continued to run it as a hotel.

447

Parker House (Bartonsville)

1816:   (a) <u>Webb's Hotel</u>, Col E. B. Webb and Solomon Snow; Webb had a tavern license, 1816-21; he built a large 2-story frame building on the site of the <u>Hotel Windham</u> of later years, at a cost of $3,000; sold to John Robertson in 1821, becoming <u>Robertson's Tavern</u>; almanac, 1825, '29; tavern license, 1821-33; its name was changed again a few years later to the <u>Bellows Falls Stage House</u>, a name which was retained until the place burned on March 14, 1860. Col Russell Hyde bought it in 1834 and added a 3rd story; all the Bellows Falls stages stopped there; other proprietors included Davis and Russell, 1839-41; Wells W. Felt, 1854, 1855; Solan S. Finlay, 1856, 1857; Sanderson, 1857; M. W. Merrill, 1858; and Charles Towns, who bought it in 1859, a few months before the fire; there is an 1834 daguerrotype photo in ref 1, and a photo in the Pictorial History in which several Bellows Falls citizens sitting on the porch are identified (3);

* * *

"One Fourth of July some representatives of Young America, in celebrating at a very early hour in the morning, had an old cannon which they were causing to 'talk' in front of Mammoth block across the Square. The patrons of Robertson's Tavern, being unable to sleep, were many of them sauntering about the house. A guest of the house, who had been lying on an old haircloth sofa in the 'sitting-room' on the south side, had just risen and sauntered out to the piazza. He stood leaning against the second pillar from the east when the boys in their excitement, forgetting to remove the iron ramrod from the cannon, fired it toward the hotel. The ramrod passed between the post and the guest, and through the side of the building into the sitting-room, lengthwise through the lounge from which the guest had just risen, and buried itself in the opposite wall of the room, without doing further damage."

* * *

pre-1817:   <u>Mansion House Hotel</u>, Fred W. Geyer; built originally as an elaborate private home, the Tucker mansion, at the east end of the toll bridge. This place had been used "for some time" as a hotel before Fred Geyer advertised it for rent in 1817; (1)

448

1825, '29:   Hitchcock Tavern, --; almanac, unidentified; tavern license to Amos Hitchcock, 1820-33, and Hitchcock and Evans, 1817;

1825, '29:   Hoyt tavern, --; almanac, unidentified; tavern license to a Levi Hoit (sic) 1817, '20-22;

pre-1826:   Mansion House, James I. Cutler and Co; almanac, 1812; on the west side of the square, extending south towards the School St stairs...the front piazza stood where the front of the present (i.e., 1907) Chase Furniture Co block is; later the American House. It burned on Nov 17, 1867. (1)   The first proprietor was Solomon Mann (tavern license, 1826); Capt Theodore Griswold was manager in 1840 when Daniel Webster made his historic trip to Stratton Mountain; he was a guest at the Mansion House, and "addressed a great throng... from the top of the piazza" (1); this is apparently the second Mansion House, different from the Geyer place described above);

* * *

"For some years the hall over the horse sheds was the principal public hall of the village...At the south end, over the last horse shed, were two anterooms or 'dressing rooms'...One year a number of well known business men became so interested in playing cards, and gambling therewith, that they neglected both their business and their wives at home. At last a number of the staid matrons of the village investigated, and one night looking through the windows of these rooms from the high bank in the rear saw their husbands engrossed in an interesting game. They quietly summoned a number of other women who also had husbands there, and the party arming themselves with sticks and stones approached the rear and stormed the citadel, demolishing the windows and driving out the men, who later straggled home, somewhat discomfited, not knowing who had committed the deed. This assault had the effect of breaking up the practice." (1)

* * *

Note: tavern licenses to Jonas Parker, 1816, '17; George Willson, 1817-32; Hiram Morgan, 1820; Coleman Cooke, 1817, '20; John Clark, 1820-32; Stephen Wales, 1821, '27-30; Benjamin Gates, 1824, '25; Levi Stone, 1825; Gilbert Evans, 1826, '27; Levi and Willard, 1825, '32, '33; William Merritt (Merrill?), 1827-32; Thomas G. Hayden, 1828; Alpheus Willard, 1827; Abraham Ingraham, 1829; Benjamin Smith, 1832; Ora M. Burk, Henry Harris, and James I. Cutler and Co, 1833; and Billings Carpenter, 1830, all locations unknown;

1836:   Valley House, --; a large 2-story frame building on the island, south of the railroad station, on the site of the Vermont Farm Machine Co office in 1907; a boarding-house at times in connection with the cotton factory, also known as Gage's Hotel; it burned in 1852; the manager in 1851 was Charles F. Sawyer;

1849:   (a) Bellows Falls Hotel, Russell Hyde (this is the Bellows Falls Stage House);

1851:   Island House, Col Roswell Shurtleff; on the north side of Bridge St. Shurtleff was converting a fine old frame house into a hotel, but it burned just before completion. He at once began building a new and larger brick building, which until the time of the Civil War was one of the most successful and popular summer resort hotels of New England, catering especially to wealthy southerners. The hotel owned most of the "island," and went to great lengths to provide excursions and entertainment: bowling alleys; an entertainment hall (the building occupied by the Fall Mountain House in 1907); stables, gardens, greenhouses and parks; a carriage road to a picnic house on top of Mount Kilburn; and trips to the Abenaqui mineral springs in Walpole, New Hampshire (see below). There was even a popular song of the day, "The Island House Polka" (see illustration, next page).

Business declined sharply during the Civil War, and never recovered; land had to be sold, industries and the railroad expanded around the inn, and it closed as a hotel in 1887. Partly destroyed by fire in 1907, rebuilt, served as a warehouse, and burned to the ground in 1965. Managers included Col Shurtleff until 1854; he sold in 1859 to E. D. Page, S. Chase and I. M. Questen; C. R. White; E. G. Ball; Edmund Jones, 1861; Stephen Taft, 1862; S. C. Fleming in the

1870s; Charles Towns was the last manager. President Grant was a guest of the hotel, and spoke to a crowd on August 7, 1869; and Gen W. T. Sherman visited in 1869.

* * *

The Abenaqui mineral spring in Walpole, New Hampshire, was well known to the Indians, but not much developed until shortly before the Island House was built. In 1849 one Algernon S. Baxter bought the site, and invested a lot of money in improvements: "It was substantially walled in, making a large reservoir...and a pavilion was erected over it. Pipes led from the spring into a large granite fountain for drinking, from which the bottled water was sold in bulk. From this fountain the waters were conducted into the top of a building in which were bath tubs, and also shower baths, which were patronized by thousands.

The grounds were artistically laid out, the spring being so far up on the hillside as to admit of several terraces...Another building contained a bowling alley, and lunch rooms, and there was a dancing pavilion...Public teams were run on pleasant days during the summer season once in two hours between the Island House and the spring, and less frequently to the Mountain House on Table Rock on Mount Kilburn." (1)

When the tourist business fell off, interest in the springs also slackened; the buildings fell into decay, with the last one disappearing about 1870.

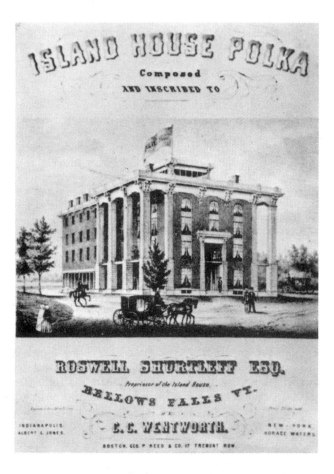

The Island House Polka
(Rockingham: A Pictorial History, 1776-1976)

1856:   (a) as above, W. W. Felt* (McClellan map); (b) Mansion House, Nathan Adams*

(McClellan; the second place with this name, shown as the American House on the map; see above); (c) Island House, Roswell Shurtleff* (McClellan);

1861: a hotel, L. P. Bowker; on Canal St, first place opened after the Stage House burned;

c. 1860: Star Hotel, --; on the east side of the square; (photos in ref 3);

1869: (c) as above, Charles Towns* (Beers);

1870: (c) as above;

* * *

Principal Bellows Falls Hotels

(a) Webb's Hotel (later Robertson's Tavern, Bellows Falls Stage House);
(b) 2nd Mansion House (also known as the American House);
(c) Island House;
(d) Town's Hotel (later the Hotel Windham);
(e) Commercial House (later the Central House);
(f) The Rockingham;

* * *

1873: (d) Town's Hotel, Charles Towns; on the site of the Bellows Falls Stage House, after a 13-year interval; a brick, 3-story building, partly destroyed by fire on April 12, 1899. The place was restored to 4 stories, and continued operating as Town's Hotel until 1902, when it became the Hotel Windham, F. F. Shepard, proprietor. F. C. Wills followed in 1912; then W. P. E. Doyen and John A. Rowell in 1912, and Jay Greaves in 1920. It burned in a major fire on March 28, 1912, and was rebuilt and burned yet again in 1932, being re-opened in 1933.

1873: (c) as above, S. C. Fleming (Vt Dir; also on 1874 Sanborn); (d) Towns House, Charles Towns (Vt Dir, also on 1874 Sanborn);

1875: (c) as above; (d) as above;

1879, '80: (c) as above; (d) as above; Farmer's Hotel, G. F. Colcord (location unknown);

1883: (d) as above (also shown on 1885, '91 Sanborns);

1884: (c) as above, C. W. Towns (also on 1885 Sanborn); (d) as above, C. W. Towns (Child);

1885: Avalon House, --* (Sanborn; on Rockingham St, east side; not operating by 1891, became the Rockingham); VDHP 1314-5, unoccupied in 1971;

1885: (e) Commercial House, A. P. Pollard; built this year by Henry S. Frost, on the west side of Rockingham St, next north of the opera house; the Central House by 1907; site of the Army-Navy Store in 1975; photo, ref 3;

1887: (c) as above; (d) as above; (e) Commercial House, A. P. Pollard;

1890: (c) as above; (d) as above, A. R. Mason; (e) as above, Ladd and Nims (all three on the 1891 Sanborn); Fall Mountain House, C. G. Moore;

1892: (d) as above, J. D. Lawrence; (e) as above, D. E. Ladd;

1895: (d) as above, D. E. Ladd; (e) as above, O. F. Knowlton;

1895:　(f) Hotel Rockingham, L. T. Lovell; who built it, between Rockingham and Canal Sts; A. P. Pollard and L. T. Moseley were the first managers (but Lovell and Lovell say it was built in 1889); they also say that L. T. Lovell himself ran it until his death in 1913, followed by David Cushion until 1919, and Will Patterson, 1922-25; the place was derelict in 1975 (photo, ref 3). The PO was also located here for 3 months in 1925 after a fire that destroyed the town hall building which contained it; and it was then moved to the Central House for a short time;

1896:　(c) Sanborn's still shows the Island House, but it cannot have been operating at this time; (d), (e) and (f) the Rockingham also shown;

1898:　(d) as above, W. S. Dunham; (e) as above, A. P. Pollard; (f) The Rockingham, L. T. Lovell 2nd; all three on the 1901 Sanborn;

1899:　(d), (e), (f), as above; Fall Mountain House, C. S. (G?) Moore, Depot St (Bellows Falls Business Directory);

1901:　(e) Commercial House, Mrs J. W. Leech; Falls Mountain House, C. S. Moore (operating in 1896);

1905, '08:　(d) Hotel Windham, F. T. (F.?) Shepard (on the 1906 Sanborn; see photo); (e) Central House, -- (former Commercial House, on the 1906 Sanborn); (f) as above;

1906:　Burnet Hotel, --* (Sanborn; east side of Westminster St, two buildings before the square);

Hotel Windham

1909:　Burnet House; Phelps House, Frank B. Phelps, 10 School St; Fall Mountain House, W. D. Stevens; (d) Hotel Windham, F. F. Shepard (Bellows Falls Business Directory);

1911:　(d) as above, W. J. Willis; (e) Central House, C. C. Frost; (f) as above, Nichols and Annabel;

1913:　(d) as above, W. J. Willis; (f) as above, --;

1920:　(d) as above, F. C. Willis; (f) as above; (d), (e) and (f) on Sanborn; Burnet Hotel now the Westminster House (Sanborn); also, the Royal Lunch and Hotel, on the west side of the square, on the old Mansion House site, on the 1920 Sanborn;

1925:　(d) as above, Jay Greaves; (f) as above (rooms only), W. N. Patterson* (on the 1927 Sanborn);

452

1927: (d), (e) and (f) on Sanborn; <u>Westminster House</u> (former <u>Burnet</u>) now the <u>Bellows Falls House</u>; there is also a <u>Bellows Falls Inn</u>, on the east side of Atkinson (Sanborn), listed until c. 1935;

1956: Sanborn update: (d) and (f) still operating; (e) <u>Central</u> and <u>Bellows Falls House</u> gone; the <u>Bellows Falls Inn</u> now a rest home; (d) <u>Hotel Windham</u> ceased operating in the early 1980s, now vacant; (f) <u>Rockingham</u> closed in the 1950s, converted to apartments in the late 1970s.

(160c) <u>Cambridgeport</u>.

1814: a tavern, <u>Simeon Evans</u>; tavern license, 1820-30; with "a spring dance floor which attracted many gay parties fifty years ago" (i.e., before 1907, ref 1); torn down in 1949; photo, ref 3).

1856: a hotel, <u>I. Bolls</u>* (McClellan);

1869: <u>George Washington Hotel</u>, I. Bolls* (Beers; same site as in 1856);

1870: --, John N. Blake;

1872: --, - Spaulding;

1873: --, B. L. W. Bissell (Vt Dir);

1878: --, J. Blake;

1883, '87, '90: (a) <u>Cambridgeport Hotel</u>, John L. Wilder (Vt Dir);

1901, '11: (a) as above, -- (see photo, next page).

(160d) <u>Rockingham</u>.

(?): a log cabin inn, first in Rockingham, built by David Pulsipher near the meeting house; (5)

c. 1774: a tavern, <u>Jehiel Webb</u> (see note under Bartonsville);

1849: --, D. Smalley (NEMU Dir);

1869: (a) <u>Rockingham Hotel</u>, L. C. Lovell* (Beers);

1870: --, S. (?) C. Lovell;

1870: (a) <u>Rockingham Hotel</u>, L. C. Lovell (Vt Dir);

1873, '75: --, L. C. Lovell;

1883, '87, '90: <u>Lovell's Hotel</u>, --;

1901: <u>The Rockingham</u>, L. T. (?) Lovell (Vt Dir); <u>Lovell's Hotel</u> burned in 1908 in a fire that essentially destroyed the old village; it was not rebuilt.

(160e) <u>Saxtons River</u>.

1817: <u>Saxtons River Hotel</u>, Capt Jonathan Barron; he built the ell first, and ran out of money. It was completed 6 years later by Col Carter Whitcomb, who at one time had a store where the parlor was (tavern license, 1829). Always the principal hotel of the village, and a familiar landmark, especially because of two lions painted on the gables. Abel K. Wilder became owner and proprietor in 1856, and the place stayed in his family until 1903, when it was torn down to make room for a modern building, built by a group of local people. Owners since that time have been Harry Kimball; Frank F. Shepard, 1909 (also in the Hotel Windham); Anthony Turcolt, 1912; G. T. Alexander, 1914; Geraldine E. Ainsworth, 1919; Mrs N. B. Law, 1922-24; Fay S. Fuller, 1926. As the Hotel Kimball, it was closed for a while. Owned by the Campbell family in 1975, still operating;

Cambridgeport Hotel
(Rockingham, Vermont: A Pictorial History, 1776-1976)

1835:   Old Yellow Tavern, --; "on Main Street, some distance west of the Saxtons River Hotel, where is "now" (i.e., 1907) the photograph studio of E. P. Taft." (1) James McAfee an early proprietor; then George Wilson, Thomas Heaton, John Goodell. It became a tenement house and was finally razed.

1849:   (a) Saxton's River Hotel, C. Dickinson (NEMU Dir);

1856:   --, A. D. Schollay;

1856:   (a) as above, --* (McClellan);

1869:   (a) as above, M. A. Wilder* (Beers); an Abel K. Wilder was manager and proprietor from 1852, succeeded by his son, Marshall A., in 1861; (5)

1870, '75, '80, '83, '87, '92, '98, 1901: (a) as above (also on 1885, 1894 Sanborn);

1905:   (b) Saxton's River Hotel, C. H. Woolley (the second Saxton's River Inn, presumably; see photo); also on the 1909, 1928 Sanborn;

Note: it is not clear why the building in the photo has the date 1859; the 1st Saxton's River Hotel was much older, and the 2nd not built until 1903;

1913:   (b) Hotel Kimball, A. Turcott (same as Saxton's River Inn; Kimball and Turcott were both early owners); listed as The Inn in 1916, '23 VPB; apparently used as a dormitory for Saxton's River Academy students in the fall, winter;

1920:   (b) as above, J. W. Bryant;

1925:   (b) as above, Vermont Academy now the proprietor.

Note: the assistance of James Managan, Bellows Falls Historical Society, is gratefully acknowledged.

* * *

References

(1) Lyman S. Hayes, History of the Town of Rockingham, Vermont (Bellows Falls: The Town; Lynn, Mass.: Frank S. Whitten, 1907).

(2) George F. Webb, Rockingham Historical Notes (Bellows Falls: Bellows Falls Historical Soc., Model Pr., 1969).

(3) Rockingham: A Pictorial History, 1776-1976; Robert D. Warner, ed. (Bellows Falls: Pictorial History Committee, A/G Pr., 1975).

(4) Frances S. Lovell and Leverett C. Lovell, History of the Town of Bellows Falls, Vermont, 1907-1957 (Bellows Falls: The Town, 1958).

(5) Ruth M. Buxton and Ethel Wiley Hill, Days of Old: the history of the Wileys and other early settlers of Saxtons River, Vt., 1783-ca 1850 (Bellows Falls: A/G Pr., 1980).

(6) Vermont Landscape Images, 1776-1976, William C. Lipke and Philip N. Grime, editors (Burlington: Fleming Museum, 1976).

Old Hotel and Main St. looking North, Saxtons River, Vt.

Saxton's River Hotel

(161) **Roxbury** (Washington).

(161a) East Roxbury.

(?):   a tavern, kept (apparently successively, according to Hemenway) by Stillman Ruggles, E. B. Pride, Samuel P. Wales, Shubael Wales (license, 1830, '33), and Alpheus Kendall; "on the Samuel Edwards place" (i.e., c. 1882, Hemenway);

1849:   --, Samuel Wales (NEMU Dir).

(161b) Roxbury.

c. 1810:   a tavern, Dr John Stafford;   where L. A. Rood was living about 1882 (Hemenway); first tavern in town;

Note: tavern license to Bille (?) Woodward, 1822, '25, '26;

(?):   a tavern, Darius Spaulding; the second in town, where Frank Snow lived (c. 1882);

c. 1820:   an inn, --; on the west side of Town Hwy 23, one-half mile north of Rte 12A;

VDHP 1215-2, the William Hulse house in 1980;

1822: a hotel, John Spaulding and wife; (Spaulding had a tavern license, 1823-33); where Julius Kent was living in 1882; opposite the home (at that time) of Mr Pearsons "on the mountain road"; Spaulding built the Summit House in 1830 (see below) where he stayed until a few years before he died in 1864 (Hemenway)...or "until the railroad was built" (Child; about 1850);

1830: (a) Summit House, John Spaulding; kept later by Stephen Fuller, Chester Clark, Page J. C. Rice, E. G. Sanborn, Van Ness Spaulding, Thomas Wilson, E. N. Spaulding, Spaulding and Nichols, Warner and Spaulding, Mrs J. P. Warner, and D. A. Spaulding (apparently not in order);

1849: (a) as above, M. (?) Spaulding (NEMU Dir);

1858: (a) --, E. N. Spaulding* (Walling; with S. G. Fuller as proprietor);

1869: (a) as above, J. P. W.* (Beers; this would be Warner);

1870: (a) --, Van Ness Spauldng;

1873: (a) as above, James P. Warner;

1875: (a) --, Thomas Wilson;

1879: (a) as above, Spaulding and Nichols;

1880: (a) --, Spaulding and Warner;

1883: (a) as above, E. S. Whitcomb;

1887: (a) as above, M. E. Yarington (Vt Dir; M. S. Davis in Walton);

1889: (a) as above, Merrill E. Yarington (Child);

1890: (a) as above, Mrs J. P. Warner;

1892: (a) as above, Martin N. Hanlan;

1895: Columbian House, S. H. Kent; Dickinson House, C. Dickinson; one of these places is presumably the old Summit House);

1898: Columbian House, C. L. Dickinson;

1901: Stanwix Hall, F. C. Fletcher;

1902: Stanwix Hall, F. C. Fletcher, M.D. (CVRR booklet);

1911: --, Cora A. Cleveland;

1908, '13: --, F. W. Barber;

Note: there is an undated postcard photo of a "hotel" in Roxbury (see photo), said to have burned in December, 1912; probably the Summit House in its later years, under a different name (Columbian House, Dickinson House, Stanwix Hall?);

1914: Spaulding House, --* (Sanborn map; next to the Union Church, not the same site as the Summit House);

1920: --, Harry Spaulding.

Roxbury Hotel (see text, above)

* * *

(162) **Royalton** (Windsor).

(162a) Royalton.

c. 1795: a tavern, Elkanah Stevens; first landlord in the village of whom there is a record (1); listed in the 1796 Vermont Almanac and Register as a stage stop on the Windsor-Burlington road; Stevens came in 1791; not very successful, perhaps because of the Gilbert Stand in South Royalton. Stevens' Tavern was the forerunner of the Cascadnac House (see below for more on this place);

1818: Fox's Stand (and store), Jacob Fox; "a fine brick inn," built by Amasa Dutton Jr in District IX at the north end of the village (really North Royalton, but that settlement never got a PO). This place was a tavern from 1811, according to Nash, who includes detailed maps with precise locations of buildings, numbered by school districts, and detailed histories of buildings in an appendix (2); also a photo of the building in recent times). Became a private home in 1850 when the stages stopped; VDHP 1416-1, operating today as the Fox Stand Inn;

* * *

"The coming of the railroad had brought a fever of speculation and rivalry. North Royalton got a station first, but not for long; Royalton soon after, but it did not bring in business. It wrecked the pleasant village; buildings lucky enough to be left untouched had trains running just in front or in back. The stage quit and the inn was no longer busy...The busy people were just down the river" (i.e., South Royalton, see below, ref 2);

* * *

1806: Stevens Tavern/Cascadnac (continued); Stevens was followed by David Waller, 1806; Dr J. Gallup, 1808; Stafford Smith, 1810, who built the main part of the Cascadnac House and entertained Lafayette in 1825 (almanac, 1815-29); Smith leased the place to Moses Cutter in 1826, "who had a store and could give little personal attention to running a hotel"; Simeon T. Stone was landlord in 1828; sold to Amos Bosworth in 1829; Samuel Blodgett a half-interest soon after, and also landlord; other proprietors were John M. Alexander (1843); Benjamin and Harrison Alexander; Alden W. Titus, 1845; William Skinner; Chester Baxter; Frederick Washburn, 1855; Pearl D. Blodgett and William Skinner, 1856; Alden Chamberlin, 1856; Mr Chamberlin was an experienced landlord, having served in that capacity in Gaysville and East Randolph;

"Mrs Chamberlin was a famous housekeeper, cook and manager, and he was genial and courteous to his guests. The hotel in those days entertained many parties, and was a favorite place for lovers of Terpsichore. Its hall was also devoted to charitable works, and there the Soldiers' Aid Society met in those trying days of the Civil War. If its walls could speak, they would rehearse the scenes when men and women gathered there, and with busy fingers scraped lint, plied the needle, knitted stockings, and eagerly discussed news from the front, while many hearts were aching with anxious thoughts of loved ones, or with the consciousness that the soldier boy would nevermore return to the home next. They could tell, too, of the mazy whirl, as the squeaky violins ground out 'Money Musk' for tripping feet of maid and youth."

* * *

1863-1901:   Cascadnac, --; Chamberlin sold to Bryan G. Conant and Stephen Freeman in 1863; then George Gilson; Ira P. Thatcher; Horace White; Alden B. Crapo, 1872; Arthur P. Brown, 1876; Henry A. Brown; Herbert H. Taylor, 1884; David C. Stearns, 1884;

* * *

"The hotel had led a precarious and varied life in the last twenty years before its occupancy by Mr Stearns. When he assumed control of it, a new period of prosperity began...It now began to be sought as a delightful place in which to spend a summer vacation, and guests once enjoying the quiet and kindly hospitality of the host and hostess, were eager to come again."

* * *

1901-44:   Cascadnac, --; Caspar P. Abbott, 1901; George D. Harrington less than a year later; he left for the larger hotel in South Royalton a few years later; James M. Boyd; J. H. Zottman; sold to George L. Moore in 1910, with Albert E. Emery as manager (there is a photo of this period in ref 2); Raymond Greenbank, 1920s to c. 1936; stood empty for a while, the "low point for Royalton village arrived when all three floors of the Cascadnac Inn (which had been standing empty) were given over to chickens. It was almost a relief when the old inn burned down in 1944 with the chickens inside"; (2)

1807:   Williams tavern, --; almanac, unidentified (also 1810, '13);

(?):   "the old hotel", Minot Wheeler; "at an early date... for a long time" (Child; Wheeler moved away in 1849; was this the Cascadnac? Wheeler is not one of the landlords listed above);

1849:   --, A. W. Titus (NEMU Dir; this is the Cascadnac); Royalton House, J. M. Currie (NEMU Dir);

1855:   --, Alden Chamberlin;

1856:   --, Fred Washburn;

1856:   a hotel,--* (Hosea Doten map);

1869:   --, W. E. White* (Beers; same site as in 1856);

1870:   --, Horace White;

1873:   (a) Cascadnac House, A. B. Cross (Vt Dir); Royalton House, H. E. White (Vt Dir);

1875:   (a) Cascadnac House, George Jeffords;

1879, '80:   (a) as above, H. A. Brown;

1883: (a) as above, G. (?) A. Brown (Child);

1887: (a) as above, D. C. Stearns;

1890, '92, '95, '98: (a) as above;

1900: (a) as above, --* (Sanborn map);

1901: (a) as above, G. D. Harrington (Vt Dir);

1902: (a) as above, Charles Clapp (CVRR booklet);

1905, '08: (a) as above, G. D. Harrington; also on 1906 Sanborn;

1911, '13: (a) as above, A. E. Emery;

1929: (a) as above, --* (Sanborn).

(162b) <u>South Royalton</u>.

1792: <u>Gilbert Stand</u>, Capt David Gilbert; "the busy inn all alone at the corner of the Tunbridge road near the river above the Fort fordway" (2); the <u>Gilbert Stand</u> was red, later as the <u>Pierce Stand</u> it was white. Replaced by "Mrs Martin's brick castle about 1900"; other proprietors were Willard Pierce, 1811; Asahel Cheney, 1818; Phineas Pierce, 1827; a tavern sign was painted by John Marshall in 1833; P. Pierce, 1855; P. and P. D. Pierce, 1869; Phineas D. Pierce, 1884; taken down in the late 1890s;

* * *

"In 1848 the site of South Royalton was still just a grassy field, but Daniel Tarbell...and Lyman Benson were about to change all that." These enterprising gentlemen built a bridge in 1848, "leading the Chelsea road across the river to the new railroad. Then they built a combination store and station by the tracks and had a train stop: South Royalton. Tarbell built a hotel by the tracks (the <u>South Royalton House</u>, see below), a church and school, and more houses; the new village came up like a mushroom." (2)

* * *

1849: --, P. Pierce (<u>Pierce's Stand</u>, formerly <u>Gilbert's</u>, see above; NEMU Dir);

1850: (a) <u>South Royalton House</u>, Daniel Tarbell; who brought in Harvey H. Woodward to run it (known locally as <u>Woodward's</u> for a while); Woodward died in 1878, and his son Charles carried on; Charles Woodward sold to George Harrington, 1902; the place was enlarged about 1909; Webb Thrasher, 1911, "who catered to traveling salesmen"; in 1914, Harrington again, who sold to Charles Woodbury; George Raymond rented it in 1918; traded by Woodbury in 1922 for a farm, with William and Clayton Curtis; in 1924, Dr E. H. Stearns, who sold to Karl Hilton; the last person to operate it as an inn was Anthony Doria, in the late 1960s, who later ran a restaurant there (2); #21 in the Depot Square Historic District, VDHP 1416-4; see photo, Chap IV;

* * *

1855, '56: --, H. H. Woodward;

1856: --, H. H. Woodward* (Hosea Doten);

1869: (a) <u>South Royalton House</u>, H. H. Woodward* (Beers); Mr Woodward gave a free meal and a free night's lodging to every Union soldier passing through;

1872: <u>Central Vermont House</u>, --; also built by Daniel Tarbell, south of but close to the

459

<u>South Royalton House</u>; burned about 1887;

    1873, '75, '79: (a) as above;

    1880, '83: (a) as above, Charles H. Woodward; <u>Central Vermont House</u>, A. R. Pike;

    1887: <u>Central Vermont House</u>, D. C. Jones;

    1890: (a) as above;

    1892: (a) as above; <u>Park Hotel</u>, H. V. Whipple;

    1895: (a) as above, E. G. Brown;

    1898: (a) as above; <u>Brightwood Hotel</u>, J. W. Bright;

Note: according to Lovejoy, the <u>Brightwood</u> was "not strictly speaking a hotel, but furnished entertainment...for transients and regular boarders for several years"; (1)

    1902:   (a) as above, C. H. Woodward; <u>Brightwood</u>, J. W. Bright (CVRR booklet);

    1905, '08:   (a) as above;

    1911: (a) as above, G. H. Harrington;

    1913: (a) as above, -- (summer boarding); also 1916 VPB, Charles L. Woodbury;

    1920: (a) as above, G. H. Raymond;

    1923, '25:   (a) <u>South Royalton House</u>, Flora B. Raymond; property acquired by the Vermont Law School in 1977; public restaurant still operating, guest rooms now used by law school students.

Note: the assistance of Hope Nash, South Royalton, is gratefully acknowledged.

* * *

References

(1) Mary E. W. Lovejoy, History of Royalton, Vermont, 1769-1911 (Royalton: The Town and the Royalton Woman's Club; Burlington: Free Press Pr., 1911).
(2) Hope Nash, Royalton, Vermont (Royalton: The Town, South Royalton Woman's Club, Royalton Historical Soc.; Lunenburg: Stinehour Pr., 1975).

* * *

(163) **Rupert** (Bennington).

Reference is made in Fisher et al. to several early taverns in the town, without specifying where they were located. (1) They are listed immediately below.

    c. 1770:   an inn, <u>Jonathan Eastman</u>; early proprietors' meetings held here, near the present (i.e., 1976) Roger Leach house;

    (?):   an inn, --; there is a turn-of-the-century photo in ref 1 of a building said to have been an inn, now (i.e., 1976) the home of Mrs Jessie Harwood;

    c. 1790:   an inn, --; photo, ref 1, of a derelict building built by James Moore in 1786, said to have become an inn soon after, until about 1850; restored, owned in 1976 by Mrs Wilma

460

Batease;

Note: tavern licenses to Harrison Elwell, Jedediah Freeman, Abner Wright, and Timothy Ladd, 1822;

Note: early taverns are also referred to in Hibbard: a reference to a meeting in 1773 at Daniel Smith's, innkeeper; Jonathan Eastman as one of the first innkeepers (he is also listed above); and to Amos Curtis, innkeeper, who also came about 1767, died in 1795 (but an Amos Curtis (son?) had a tavern license in 1822). (2)

(163a) East Rupert.

Note: two early taverns on the West Road from Dorset were Manley's and Farwell's (present Bea Jackson Humphreys, ref 3);

1849:   --, George Jenks (NEMU Dir); this is VDHP 0210-4, Jenks Tavern in the late 1700s, still a hotel in the 1970s; at the intersection of Rtes 30, 315 and Dorset West Road; built c. 1815; however, according to Fisher et al., George Jenks, who died in 1873, was the last operator, and it was a private home in 1976 (ref ; Mrs Roger Beach; see photo); this discrepancy has not been resolved;

Jenks Tavern
(Rupert, Vermont: A Pictorial History, 1976, Raymond Fisher)

1855:   --, George Jenks;

1856:   --, G. Jenks* (Rice and Hardwood map);

1869:   East Rupert Hotel, G. Jenks* (Beers);

1870, '72:   as above;

(163b, c and d) North Rupert, Rupert and West Rupert, respectively. No listings found.

References

(1)   Raymond G. Fisher et al., Rupert, Vermont: A Pictorial History, 1776-1976

461

(Rupert: Telescope Pr. for the Rupert Bicentennial Comm., 1976).

(2) George S. Hibbard, Rupert, Vermont: Historical and Descriptive, 1761-1898 (Rutland: Tuttle, 1899).

(3) Tyler Resch, Dorset: In the Shadow of the Marble Mountain (West Kennebunk, Me.: Phoenix Publ. for the Dorset Historical Soc., 1990).

* * *

(164) **Rutland** (Rutland).

(164a) Center Rutland.

1771:   James Mead tavern; in a 3-room log house on the Crown Point Road (W. Proctor Road), between Butler's Tavern in Clarendon and Water's Tavern in Pittsford; almanac, 1773-74;

c. 1782:   2nd James Mead Tavern; on the northeast corner, intersection of Rte 4 and (old) East Proctor Road; run by John Hopson Johnson c. 1780; tavern license to Mead, 1782; sold to Elisha Clark in 1795 (who had a license, 1799);

(?):   a tavern (and store), Ralph Paige; "the old Page Tavern," also a distillery (1); on the old section of Rte 4, building still stands;

1856:   Center Rutland House, -- (Walton);

* * *

There is an oil painting by James Hope of a hotel in Center Rutland in 1852. The picture shows Mead's tavern (on the East Proctor Road, see above) as being replaced by a brick store, and an unidentified hotel just east of this. According to Rutland historian Dawn Hance, this is probably the Center Rutland House.

* * *

1887:   as above, - Eggleston;

1895:   Blake House, --; South (?) Rutland House, --; (Walton, probably an error, this is presumably the Center Rutland House);

1898, 1905:   Blake House, --.

(164b) Eureka (PO, 1885-87) and (164c) Glen (PO, 1894-1901), no listings found.

(164d) Rutland.

1782:   John Smith Tavern (tavern license); on the site of the Park Pharmacy parking lot, north side of West St; operated by Nathan Perry, c. 1787;

1784:   David Tuttle Tavern; west side of S. Main St on Gouger's Hill; also a brewery, 1799; on the site of a double house that is not that old;

Note: tavern licenses in 1782 to William Barr (north corner of N. Main and North Sts; William Post before him, Barr died in 1813); Col James Claghorn (east side of S. Main St, a little north of Allen St); and in 1800 to E. A. Sherwood, Lombard Hart and William Barnes, locations unknown;

c. 1787:   Nathan Perry Tavern; later owned by Dr James Porter, who moved it to Woodstock Ave, c. 1831;

1788:   Eleazer Wheelock's Tavern; an early settler, at 76 South Main St; enlarged, bricked in 1805, third story added in 1858, became <u>Huntoon's</u>, later the <u>Brock House</u> (see below); major stage stop; building still standing, 1989;

1788: (a) <u>Huntoon House</u>, --; originally <u>Wheelock's Tavern</u>; acquired by Josiah Huntoon in 1849 or '50 from Cynthia Page; he added a 3rd story; place later became the <u>Brock House</u> (S. A. Brock) on S. Main St, east side; also known at one point as the <u>Railroad House</u>, the <u>Wickham House</u> (in 1880);

(?): <u>Gove tavern</u>, --; a little north of the old Court House on S. Main St; torn down about 1810, another building built on site; known as <u>Government House</u> in the 1790s, operated by Issacher Reed before he built <u>Reed's Tavern</u>;

c. 1790: <u>Page's Tavern</u>, Abel Page; tavern license, 1817; early settler, kept tavern for a long time on the north side of West St, a little east of present Nichols St; kept by Elias Buel, 1794, as <u>Tontine Coffee House</u> (sign of the "Bull's Head"); Grafton Ingalls, 1796; then Rev Heman Ball, probably as a private home; sold to Abel Page (whose granddaughter married George A. Custer!), who opened it as <u>Page's Tavern</u>; Alanson Dyer, 1852, as the <u>Washington House</u>, name changed to <u>American House</u> in 1856; burned in 1857; 1857 photo in "Rutland in Retrospect" (2); also known as the <u>Village Tavern</u> in 1849; there is an A. Dyer on the 1854 Scott map, and a "hotel" at the same site on the 1852 Presdee and Edwards map;

1793: <u>Munn's Tavern</u>, Joseph Munn; kept by him until 1797 as <u>Rutland Hotel</u> at sign of the "Federal eagle"; Oliver Wyman until 1800, then Henry Gould (<u>Gould's Tavern</u>); tavern license, 1817; near the old Court House, eventually became the <u>Franklin House</u> (see below);

c. 1795: a hotel, --; on the northwest corner of Main and West Sts, used as a hotel "a long time" (Child); this is the <u>Corner House</u>, a well-known place, built c. 1786 by Nathaniel Gove and John Eliot; Nathaniel Gove, Simeon Lester had it in the 1790s as <u>City Tavern</u>, sign of the "golden ball"; probably kept by William Lee (tavern license, 1800); "Capt Lester's Corner Tavern" in Smith and Rann; (1)

c. 1795: a tavern, <u>Elijah Taylor</u>; who opened the tavern "lately" occupied by Major Buell (Child); this is the later <u>American House</u> (see below);

c. 1795: a tavern, <u>Daniel Greeno</u>; on N. Grove St; Greeno came before the Revolution, later kept a tavern where Amasa Greeno lived c. 1881 (Child; A. A. Greeno on the Beers map); building still standing, Denards Farm;

1802, '07: <u>Finton's Tavern</u>, --; almanac; tavern license, 1800; northwest corner of Field Ave and N. Main St (Mrs Lester on 1869 Beers); building gone;

c. 1802: a tavern, <u>Gershom Cheney</u>; (almanac, 1812); on Cheney Hill, well north of Rutland, in a building labeled R. E. Patterson on the 1869 Beers; until 1813; building gone; Cheney died in 1855 (Child); a nephew of the same name later managed the <u>Franklin House</u>;

1803: <u>Samuel Gordon's Tavern</u>; until 1810, when he apparently moved to West Rutland, to the <u>West Rutland House</u>, which see; building still standing at 18 S. Main St;

(?): (b) <u>Reed's Hotel</u> (<u>Rutland Coffee House</u>), Issacher Reed; tavern license, 1800, '17, '21-23; almanacs, 1802-1822; on the east side of N. Main St, just north of Terrill St, about where present Grand Union is; burned in 1845, when Elisha Warner had it; Reed came about 1794, kept it a long time, place later operated by his son, Willard; Issacher died in 1838;

Note: there is a lithograph representing Rutland in 1840 that shows the <u>Reed House</u> on Main St, across from the intersection with West St, several buildings north of the old Court House; (3)

Note: tavern licenses to Daniel Ford, 1817 (East Rutland, at Mill Village, probably on site of present Farm and Home Co); J. A. Graham, 1817 (who leased the <u>Franklin</u> or the <u>Gould Tavern</u>

463

that year); Nathan Cushman, 1817, '21; Royal H. Gould, 1821, '22; and Moses Lester, 1821, locations unknown;

1829:   (c) Franklin House, --; originally Munn's Tavern (see above); run by Henry Gould in the early 19th century (tavern license, 1800, '17; Gould's Tavern; almanacs, 1812-1829); acquired by Nathaniel Gould, his son, in 1829, who renovated it and renamed it the Franklin House; remodeled again in 1833 by Robert Temple; on Main St, east side, just south of the old Court House; the leading Rutland hotel of the stagecoach era; acquired by Gershom Cheney two years before it burned on April 13, 1868, "from the bursting of a lamp in the middle of the night," not rebuilt;

* * *

"The proprietor at one time entertained a whole circus, horses and all, and that during court week. He divided the dancing hall annexed to the tavern into rooms, and had another barn for the animals...This famous hostelry had many proprietors...Among the most prominent were George H. Beaman, 9 years until about 1843; then George R. Orcutt, and after him Pratt and Ira C. Foster. Then came Putnam and Bryant and in 1854 John C. Parke...afterwards Foster and Morris. Morris withdrew and Gershom Cheney bought of Foster about 2 years before the house was burned." (3)

* * *

1825, '29:   Butman's Tavern, --; almanacs; tavern license to William Butman, 1817, '21, '31; this building was the old State Police barracks on S. Main St, opposite Howard Johnson's (B. Hayward on 1869 Beers), building gone;

Note: innkeepers licensed in 1831 were N. Gould, W. Reed, W. Butman, R. Paige and A. Mead;

1842:   (b) Reed's, Elisha Warner; (c) Gould's, George H. Beaman; (d) American House, Alanson Dyer; the American House is described as being where the Armory was in 1922 (4); all in Walton; (b) and (c) are also listed in 1843, the latter as the Franklin House with G. R. Orcutt;

1849:   (a) --, Josiah Huntoon (the Wheelock/Huntoon/Brock, acquired by Huntoon in 1849; (c) Franklin Hotel, Putnam and Bryant (kept in 1851 by Pratt and Foster); (d) Village Tavern, A. Dyer (the American, Alanson Dyer, originally Page's Tavern); (NEMU Dir);

Note: Smith and Rann list four hotels in 1850: the Huntoon Hotel, the Franklin House, the Reed Hotel, and the Grove House (this is almost certainly Dyer's American House, which lasted until 1857, since the list omits it, and it was in operation at the time; also, the Reed burned in 1845).

1851:   Landon's Hotel, W. C. Landon; (see under Central House, 1867);

Note: the 1852 Presdee and Edwards map shows (a) Huntoon Hotel and (c) Franklin House; also a place labeled "hotel" at the Alanson Dyer site (the American see above);

1853:   Allen House, Dr H. D. Allen; built by him on the northeast corner of Elm and West Sts, a 4-story wooden building, burned in 1860 while being operated by Caleb B. Hall;

1854:   Note: the Scott map shows (a) Huntoon Hotel, (c) Franklin House, and (e) Bardwell House; the Bardwell was built in 1852 by Otis Bardwell and kept by his son-in-law, E. Foster Cook, on the corner of Merchant's Row and Washington St (see photo, Chapter IV); bought by John W. Cramton in 1864, who enlarged it in 1869; "Jay Gould made his home here when he obtained his first railroad holdings, and it was at this hotel he made the acquaintance of Jim Fisk" (3); a new section of the Bardwell burned in 1917 and was apparently rebuilt;

1856:   (a) Huntoon Hotel, -- (also called the Railroad House here); (c) Franklin House, --;

(d) Washington Hall (American House), --; (e) Bardwell House, --; (Walton);

1866: (h) 1st Bates House, Daniel Kellogg Jr; built by A.C. Bates on the north side of Center St this year; managers included A. C. Bates, M. Quinn, Paige and Marston, Paige and Tolhurst, and W. F. Paige alone; burned in 1876, re-opened in 1877; then A. C. Bates and son for 4 years; J. M. Haven and Dr (later Governor) John A. Mead; W. H. Valiquette until 1885, when Morse and Quinn became landlords; then Albert H. Tuttle until it ceased business as a hotel (3); burned again in 1906;

1867: (a), (c), (e) as above; (f) Central House, --; on the west side of Merchant's Row, at Evelyn St, mostly a boarding-house in later years, eventually burned; referred to as "new" in 1858, owned then by W. C. Landon, who opened it in 1851 as Landon's Hotel, leased to Louis D. Turrell in 1859, scheduled to be called the Rutland House, but became the Central House instead; (1) Union House, -- (west side of Freight St);

1868: (a), (c), (e) and (f) as above (Walton);

Note: the 1869 Beers map shows (a) Huntoon Hotel, (e) Bardwell House, (f) Central House and (g) Stevens House (the Berwick by at least 1873); this latter place was built in 1868 by C. F. Richardson, managed for him by Mr Stevens until 1885 when his son, F. H. Richardson, and D. N. Hayner, took over; 1868 photo in ref 3; on the northwest corner of Center and Wales Sts; burned in 1973;

1870: (a) Huntoon House, Edward Boutelle; (e) Bardwell, John W. Cramton; (f) Central House, J. A. Salsbury; (g) Stevens House, Pierce and Edson; (h) 1st Bates House, Daniel Kellogg Jr;

* * *

"Dr Allen, having removed his boarding place, may hereafter be found During the Night at the Bates House. Office as heretofore, in the drugstore, Allen and Higgin's, under the Bates House." (from the Rutland Herald, Dec 1, 1870).

* * *

Principal Rutland Hotels

(a) Huntoon House (Wheelock's Tavern, later the Brock House; also Railroad House, Wickham House)
(b) Reed's Hotel (Rutland Coffee House)
(c) Franklin House (Munn's Tavern, Gould's Tavern)
(d) American House (originally Page's Tavern; also Village Tavern, Washington Hall/House)
(e) Bardwell House
(f) Central Hotel/House (originally Landon's Hotel)
(g) Stevens (later the Berwick)
(h) Bates (1st and 2nd)
(i) Farmer's Hotel (also Freight House)
(j) Valiquette House
(k) Continental (later Globe, St James and Morris Inn)
(l) Union House
(m) Brunswick House (later the Hotel Oxford)
(n) Belmont
(o) Banquet House/Hotel Banquet (later Hotel Hamilton)
(p) Elmore
   Gove Tavern
   Commercial House
   Feeley House
   Grandview (also the Glenwood)

Holland House (The Holland)
Sycamore Inn
Watkins Inn
American (later the Lenox)

* * *

1873:   (e) as above; (f) as above; (g) <u>Berwick House</u>, M. K. Hotchkiss (but the <u>Stevens</u> is still listed this year, with C. F. Richardson, presumably in error); (h) as above, Paige and Tolhurst; (i) <u>Farmer's Hotel</u>, J. E. Johnson (on Evelyn St, across from the <u>Central</u>); (j) <u>Valiquette House</u>, B. Valiquette;

1875:   (e), (f) as above; (g) as above, C. F.Richardson; (h) as above; (i) as above;

1878:   Rutland Directory lists (e), (g), (h), and (i) as above;

1879:   (a) <u>Wickham House</u> (formerly <u>Huntoon's</u>), R. C. Wickham (Main St); (e) as above; (f) as above, Julius J. Scofield; (g) as above; (h) 2nd <u>Bates House</u>, Paige and Tolhurst; (i) as above, Mrs J. E. Johnson;

1879:   Note: the Sanborn map shows (e) <u>Bardwell</u>, (f) <u>Central</u>, (g) <u>Berwick</u>, (h) <u>Bates</u>, and (i) <u>Freight House</u> (same as <u>Farmer's Hotel</u>);

* * *

"Proctor was...a marble town...It took us all day to go to the big metropolis of Rutland, taking the 11 o'clock train in the morning to ride the six miles, and then coming back on the 6 o'clock, when drunks were put off at the Double Roads junction. When we arrived in Rutland, there were two men, always fat, beating on tin pans, one yelling, 'Come to the Bardwell!' while the other tried to drown him out with, 'Come to the Berwick!' Such a din." (5)

* * *

1880:   (a), (e), (g), (h) and (i) as above; (f) as above, L. F. (?) Scofield;

1880:   Rutland Directory lists (e), (g) as above; (h) as above, J. M. Haven; (i) as above; (j) <u>Valiquette House</u>, B. Valiquette (61 West St); (f) <u>Central</u>, J. J. Scofield (55 West St);

1880:   <u>Killington House</u>, Vincent C. Meyerhoffer; outside Rutland, of course, but much frequented by Rutland visitors; a road to the top of Killington Mountain was opened in 1860; the first building was a small rustic cottage intended for the use of the owner (1879), but it was expanded into a summer hotel next year, with accommodations for 40 guests (see Chapter V, Resorts);

1881:   (a) as above, S. A. Brock (<u>Brock's Hotel</u>), 145 Main St; (e), (f), (g) as above; (h) as above, Joel M. Haven, prop, W. F. Paige, mgr; (i) <u>Freight House</u>, Mrs J. E. Johnson; (Child);

1883:   (e) <u>Bardwell</u>, Cramton and Carpenter; (f), (g), (h) and (i) as above;

1884:   Rutland Directory lists: (a) <u>Brock House</u>, S. A. Brock; (e), (f), (g) and (h) as above; (i) as above, J. M. Ballou; and (j) <u>Valiquette House</u>;

1885:   Note: Sanborn lists (e) <u>Bardwell</u>, (f) <u>Central</u>, (g) <u>Berwick</u>, (h) <u>Bates</u>, (i) <u>Farmer's</u>, and (k) <u>Continental</u>, on West St, north side, between Church and Elm Sts; later the <u>Globe</u>, <u>St James</u> and <u>Morris</u>, in that order);

1887:   (a) <u>Brock House</u> (formerly the <u>Huntoon Hotel</u>, <u>Wickham House</u>), S. A. Brock; (e) as above; (f) as above, J. M. Ballou; (g) as above, W. H. Valiquette; (i) as above; (k) <u>Globe</u> (former <u>Continental</u>), --; (l) <u>Union House</u>, F. B. Gorham;

1890:   (a) as above; (e) as above; (f) as above, Leon Pomeroy; (g) as above; (h) as above, A. H. Tuttle; (i) as above, Edward Pomeroy; (j) Valiquette House, B. Valiquette; (k) as above, J. C. Burpee; (l) as above, M. Lovejoy;

1890:   Note: the Sanborn shows (e) Bardwell, (f) Central, (g) Berwick, (h) Bates, and (i) Farmer's;

1892:   (e), (f), (g), (h) and (i) as above; (k) as above, Stephen French; (m) Brunswick House, B. H. Wooley (on Merchant's Row, across from the depot) Commercial House, Joel Todd; Feeley House, Thomas Feeley;

1895:   (a), (e) as above; (f) as above, Leon Pomeroy; (g), (h) as above; (k) as above, C. W. Mason; (m) as above; (n) Belmont, --; Commercial House,-- (on the northeast corner of Wales and Strang);

1895:   Note: Sanborn shows (e) Bardwell, (f) Central, (g) Berwick, (h) Bates, and (k) Globe; also Commercial Hotel; (i) Farmer's is now a grain and feed store; (m) Brunswick House; (o) Hotel Banquet (Banquet House), on the southwest corner of Freight and West Sts;

1898:   (a), (e) as above; (f) as above, Clayton Chase; (g) as above; (k) St James, E. D. Kennedy (formerly Globe, Continental; became the Morris Inn, later razed for the telephone company annex); (m) as above, J. J. Kelley; (n) as above, Edward Pomeroy; (o) Banquet House, C. A. Clifford; (p) The Elmore, J. P. Rounds, southeast corner of Edson and West Sts (see photo);

The Elmore

1900:   Note: Sanborn shows (e) Bardwell, (g) Berwick, (k) St James, (m) Brunswick, (o) Hotel Banquet; (h) Bates is apparently not operating, but building seems to be the same on the map;

1901:   (a), (e), (f), (g), (k) as above; (m) as above, John Barrett; (n) as above; (o) as above, Frank Duffy; (p) as above;

1905:   (a) as above; (e) as above, Lalor Brothers; (g) as above; (o) as above, J. F. Kelly; (p) as above, Mrs M. H. Cook; Grand View, - Pomeroy (Strangs Ave and Main St);

1905:   Note: Sanborn shows (e) Bardwell, (g) Berwick, (k) St James, (o) Hotel Banquet; also the American House, on Wales between Center and Washington Sts, west side;

1908:   (e), (g) and (o) as above;

1910:   Note: Sanborn shows (a) Brock (see photo, next page), (e) Bardwell, (k) St James (see photo, next page), (l) Union House (just north of the American House); (m) Hotel Oxford (former Brunswick), and (o) <u>Hotel Banquet</u>; also the <u>American House</u> and the <u>Grandview House</u> (on Strangs Ave and South Main St);

Brock House (Rutland Historical Society)

1913:   (a), (e), (g) as above; (k) as above, G. E. Pool; (m) <u>Hotel Oxford</u>, F. C. Wilson (former <u>Brunswick</u>); <u>Grandview</u>, --; (p) as above;

St James Hotel (Vermont Historical Society)

1916:   Note: Sanborn shows (a) <u>Brock</u>, (e) <u>Bardwell</u>, (g) <u>Berwick</u>, (k) <u>St James</u>, (p) <u>Elmore</u>; also the <u>Holland House</u> (see photo; on Merchants Row); the <u>Hamilton Hotel</u> (see photo; formerly the <u>Hotel Banquet</u>, declined in its later years, closed in 1977, razed in 1986; on the southwest corner of West and Freight St); the <u>American</u> has become the <u>Lenox</u>, a boarding-house; the <u>Sycamore Inn</u> (southeast corner of South Main and East Center St); and the <u>Grandview</u>;

1920:   (a) as above, --; (e) as above, N. G. Nicklaw; (g) as above, A. J. Boynton; (k) as above, C. E. Pollard; (m) <u>Hotel Oxford</u>, F. C. Wilson; (p) as above, --; <u>The Hamilton</u>, O. S.

Bergstrom (corner of West and Evelyn Sts); The Holland, J. J. Brohel, east side of Merchant's Row; Sycamore Inn, G. L. Gilbert; and Watkins Inn, --;

Holland House (Vermont Historical Society)

Hamilton Hotel

1925:   (a) as above, H. S. Parker; (e) as above; (g) as above; (k) as above, --; (p) as above; The Hamilton, as above; The Holland, as above; Watkins Inn, Miss M. A. Morris;

1925:   Note: Sanborn shows (a) Brock, (e) Bardwell, (g) Berwick and (p) Elmore; also the Glenwood (former Grandview), the Hamilton and the Holland;

Note: the 1951 Sanborn update shows (a) Brock, (e) Bardwell, (g) Berwick and (k) Morris Inn (same site as the former St James, Globe, and Continental); the Glenwood building is gone (e) and (g) are listed until at least 1968, the Bardwell now provides housing for the elderly.

(164e) West Rutland.

c. 1799:   a tavern, Ephraim Blanchard; tavern license, 1800; at the intersection of Rte 4 and Clarendon Ave; followed by Charles Wells, 1813; Jacob Gates (tavern license, 1817 until 1830), Elijah Corbet (1822, '23); and Jonathan C. Thrall (tavern license, 1831); Thrall had it from 1830-38, it burned 11/23/1838;

1809:   reference (Rutland Herald, 3/25/1809) to a meeting of the "Ohio Company" at Benjamin Pratt's Tavern;

1809:   West Rutland House; there are several references in early Rutland Heralds to

469

taverns, most of which were probably the <u>West Rutland House</u> with different proprietors: Medad Sheldon (Oct 7, 1809 and Feb 13, 1811); Samuel Gordon's tavern Oct 10, 1810 and March 11, 1812); John Herring (Jan 19, 1816); and N. Cushman (March 5, 1817; also tavern licenses, 1817, '21).

The place was built by Medad Sheldon before October 1809, as a 2-story house on the south side of Rte 4 in West Rutland (southeast of Pleasant St). He advertised it for sale in 1809 as being ideally situated for a tavern, and it was leased to Samuel Gordon, 1810-12, sold to William Fairchild and William B. Harmon in 1812. Subsequent owners were Nathan Cushman, 1814-27; Abner Mead, 1827-33; Reuben Smith, 1833-36; Leonard Blanchard, 1836-40; and Daniel S. Ewings, later. Also called the <u>Clement House</u> after William R. Clement who ran it in the 1840s (Walton, 1842). Elisha Warner ran it in 1846 after his place burned. Leased by Prentiss L. Goss as the "well known West Rutland House on the Rutland-Troy Railroad." Shown on the 1854 Scott map, now gone.

1843: <u>Gershom Cheney 2nd Tavern</u>; (Walton, precise location unknown); advertised for sale in the Rutland Herald (Jan 2, 1846) as a tavern stand now occupied by James Everson, in operation for 5 years;

1849: --, John C. Harris; --, Jarris Larned (NEMU Dir);

1856: <u>West Rutland House</u>, -- (Walton);

1869: (a) <u>Barnes House</u>, Hazelton and Thompson* (Beers); built in 1857, leased to Prentiss L. Goss;

1870, '73, '75, '80, '83, '87, '92:   (a) <u>Barnes House</u>, --; (William Barnes developed the marble industry in West Rutland); M. J. Olivette is listed as proprietor in Vt Dir in 1890; G. W. Peck in Rutland Directory, 1880;

1878: <u>Marsh Valley Hotel</u>, C. H. Campbell (Rutland Directory);

Note: the 1890 Sanborn map shows the <u>Barnes Hotel</u>, on the north side of Barnes St near the depot, but the building is gone by 1905 (there was a major fire in 1903); the 1900 and 1905 Sanborns show the <u>Rutland(West Rutland) House</u>, on the east side of Marble St;

1901: <u>Douglas House</u>, P. F. O'Neill (Vt Dir);

1905: <u>West Rutland House</u>, H. G. Odell;

1908, '13, '15:   <u>West Rutland House</u>, --.

Note: the assistance of Dawn Hance, author of a forthcoming history of Rutland, is gratefully acknowledged.

* * *

<u>References</u>

(1) Henry P. Smith and William S. Rann, History of Rutland County, Vermont (Syracuse: D. Mason, 1886).
(2) Robert E. West, Rutland in Retrospect (Rutland: Rutland Historial Soc. and Academy Books, Sharp Offset Pr., 1978).
(3) F. E. Davison, Historical Rutland: 1761-1911, Souvenir Edition (Rutland: Philip H. Brehmer, Tuttle Pr., 1911).
(4) Edward L. Temple, Old Rutland: Side Lights on Her Honorable and Notable Story (Rutland: E. L. Temple; A. J. Novak, Pr., 1923).
(5) Postscript: An extract from the correspondence of Mrs Wing, Vermont History <u>22</u> (1954): 151.

(165) **Ryegate** (Caledonia).

Most of the early taverns listed below were on the old "county road" (the Bayley-Hazen road) that passed through the town from Newbury to Danville, and not in Ryegate Corner (Center) village, although most of them are listed there for convenience.

(165a) East Ryegate.

c. 1832:   a stage stop, --; on present Rte 5, about 2 miles north of Wells River, on the east side of the road; built originally as a stagecoach inn, later the Longmeadow Inn; (VDHP 0310-13);

Note: tavern licenses to William Gray, 1824-27; Robert Whitcomb, 1822-27; and Jabez Bigelow Jr, 1825-27, locations unknown.

(165b) Ryegate (Corner, Center).

c. 1780:   a tavern, John Gray; "for some years the only one in town, the only one between Newbury and Canada"; (1)

c. 1780:   a tavern, Deacon Andrew Brock; first house built for a tavern, "a little north of the brick house at the Corner" (1); described in the Bicentennial Booklet as being a little north of the old brick tavern cellar hole opposite the present (i.e., 1963) PO (2); known as "the old Red Tavern"; Samuel Peters had this place a long time, following Jabez Bigelow (who was "approbated" in 1798, see below); it was then let to William Morrill and Joshua Bailey, and burned while they had it; Morrill then built a tavern a little south of the village (see below); "the old brick tavern was built later";

1796:   four tavern-keepers "approbated" by the town: Josiah Page (almanac listing, 1802, '05); Andrew Brock; Samuel and Hugh Johnson (almanac, 1805); and Capt John Gray; Miller and Wells then list other tavern-keepers approbated in subsequent years; 1797, Nathan Barker Page; 1798, Jabez Bigelow; 1800, Alexander McDonald; 1803, James Esden; 1805, Eri Chamberlin (tavern license, 1822); 1808, Robert Brock; 1810, Nathaniel Smith; (1)

* * *

"The earlier taverns were along the 'county road,' as the main road from Newbury to Danville was called...Danville was made the county seat (when Caledonia county was organized in 1792), making it for many years the most important place between Haverhill and Canada, and the stage center for a large section of the country, so that most of the business and travel was along this road. There was no road along the river above Barnet till some years after the Revolutionary war...Consequently the Hazen road...was the main highway of travel and business, numbers of loaded teams passed along it daily, and, according to old people, at one period, there were seven inns along that road in this town." (1)

* * *

(?):   Morrill Stand, William Morrill; "south of the Corner, under the great elm, of which there were formerly two" (1); Josiah Page also kept tavern there, as did his son, Nathan Barker Page (see list of approbated tavern-keepers, above); Ebenezer Morrill came about 1820 (tavern license, 1822-27), and it was continued by him and his sons during many years; they were stage owners and mail contractors. Henry F. Slack also kept tavern at the Corner in the 1840s;

(?):   a tavern, Robert Whitelaw; tavern license, 1822; on his farm for many years, "only a depression in the ground is all that marks the site of the old stand"; (1)

* * *

"It will be understood that in the early years, before 1800, this country was new, and the roads were bad at the best, and people traveled on foot and on horse back, so it was only the strong and vigorous who could travel at all, except, perhaps, in winter. People generally travelled with their own teams and it was not until about a century ago (i.e., c. 1810) that roads were good enough for wheeled vehicles, and there began to be a class of people who were willing to pay for being carried from place to place. About 1809, Silas May, who was then the mail carrier between Concord and Haverhill, began to convey it in a wagon, and any chance passenger as well." (1)

* * *

c. 1808:   a tavern, Andrew Warden; tavern license, 1822-27; on the turnpike in Ryegate, where A. A. Miller has long lived (1); there was another tavern along this turnpike operated by Thomas Nelson;

1849:   -, A. J. Morrill (NEMU Dir; presumably this is the Morrill stand, see above);

1870:   --, John Gibson;

1872:   Blue Mountain House, John Gilson (?);

1883:   --, W. H. Page.

(165c) South Ryegate.

c. 1850:   (a) a hotel (and store), R. F. Carter; set up in connection with the Ryegate Granite Works, when the opening of the railroad (1848) led to development of the granite business, and the arrival of merchants;

1883:   --, Mrs M. J. Bailey;

1887:   (a) Ryegate Granite Works Hotel, A. H. Noyes (Child);

1887, '90, '92, '95, '98:   --, Mrs Charles Bailey;

1901:   (a) as above, Charles Oakley.

* * *

References

(1) Edward Miller and Frederic P. Wells, History of Ryegate, Vermont, 1774-1912 (St Johnsbury: Caledonian, 1913).
(2) Celebrating 200th Anniversary, Town of Ryegate, Vermont. Bicentennial, (Ryegate: Bicentennial Comm.; Littleton, N.H.: Courier Pr., 1963?).

* * *

(166) **St Albans** (Franklin).

(166a) Lake View House.

1871:   Lakeview House, C. E. Wilson* (Beers); built by Wilson in 1870 on Lapan Bay, enlarged by his son-in-law, H. L. Samson; also known as Samson's; however, Child says that H. S. Samson built it, sold to Wilson in 1871, re-purchased it in 1877, and then enlarged and renovated it;

1870, '79, '82, '87, '90, '92, '95, '98:   (a) Lake View House, H. L. Samson (summers; see photo; Samson was PM for many years, with the post office in the hotel);

472

Lake View House (St Albans Historical Society)

1902, '11, '13, '20:   (a) as above, J. W. Samson (W. J. in Vt Dir and VPB).

(166b) <u>St Albans</u>.

"In the early history of the town Distils and Hotels were more numerous than churches and schools. Of the former there was one at the foot of Howard Hill, another near the residence of Judge Bedard, and one at the foot of the hill on Congress Street, called "The Devil's Tea Kettle." The Potter House was a hotel about 1793...". (1) The taverns referred to are listed below (1793-1810).

* * *

1793:   a tavern, <u>Silas Hathaway</u>; tavern, residence and court-house, building still standing at 255 N. Main St, the home of Mrs E. F. Lucas in 1925; sold to Asa Fuller in 1800; (2)

1793:   <u>Potter's Tavern</u>, --; still standing at 229 S. Main St (i.e., 1925, ref 2);

1797:   a tavern, <u>William Nason</u>; "south end of town," until 1810 (2); almanacs, 1807-13;

1796:   "the <u>Blaisdell House</u>"; (1)

1796:   "the large house that stood where is now the house of H. Brainerd" (1889, ref 1);

1797:   a tavern, <u>Alfred Hathaway</u>; on the corner of Hoyt and North Main Sts;

Note: Royce also mentions the <u>Danforth House</u>, before 1800, at the head of Center St; (3)

c. 1796:   a tavern, <u>John Gilman</u>; just north of the Greenwood Cemetery;

1798:   "the <u>Kendall House</u>" (1); there was also a "distil" called the "Devil's Teakettle," before 1802, at the foot of Congress St;

473

1800: "the Branch Farm House"; (1)

1802: Adams also refers to a section of St Albans once known as Parsonville ("from Nason Street to Johnny-cake Hill"--Nason Street extends west from South Main St) as having a tavern in 1795, and two in 1802;

1810: "the hotel that stood opposite the Brainerd store as early as 1810"; (1)

Note: other early tavern-keepers listed in almanacs, but unidentified, are: Jones, 1807, 1810; Keith, 1812-23 (tavern license to a Ruel Keith, 1821); Mansfield, 1813; and Gage, 1812.

Also, tavern licenses to Warren Munson and Joseph H. Munson, 1815; Keith Barlow, 1817; Widow Mary Fuller, 1816, '19, '21; Barlow Thatcher, John R. Phelps and Thomas H. Campbell, 1817; John Ball and Samuel Merritt, 1819; Jonathan R. Danforth, 1817, '20, '21; Franklin Fuller (Tuller?), 1822-28; William Fuller, 1824, '25; Samuel Campbell, 1824-29; Zeno Campbell, 1833; John Ball, 1819, '21; James S. Merritt, 1819; Reuben Wood, Elijah Danton, 1822; Henry Follett, Zedediah Tracy, 1830; Locke Catlin, 1825-30; Parker Ingalls, 1826; William H. Wilkins, 1827-32; Richard Sackett, 1827, '28; Heziah Sackett, 1829, '30; Samuel Maynard, 1832; Abel Smith and Henry Wood, 1833, all locations unknown;

1815: (a) Phoenix Hotel, --; still standing at the northwest corner of Main and Lake Sts (map location #1); known later as the Bliss House, briefly, and then the American House;

1842: (a) as above, Samuel Barlow (tavern license, 1820-32); (b) St Albans House, F. A. Potter (once called Pierce's Hotel);

1843: (b) as above, Bradley and Loveland; --, M. Ladd; --, R. Lasell;

1849: (b) as above, Thomas Campbell; --, Samuel H. Barlow; --, Ralph Lasell; --, Mrs Danforth (all NEMU Dir);

1853: (a) Phoenix Hotel, --* (Presdee and Edwards map); (c) Barber's Hotel, --* (Presdee and Edwards; on the same site as the Tremont in 1857, which it presumably became);

1855, '56: --, V. Adams; --, C. Pierce (probably the St Albans House); --, W. M. Hosmer;

1857: (a) Bliss House, O. S. Bliss* (Walling; formerly the Phoenix); (b) St Albans House, C. Pierce* (Walling); (c) Tremont House, J. L. Sanderson* (Walling; formerly Barber's; this place was built in the 1830s where City Hall now is, was in other use by the 1880s, burned in 1894);

1870: (a) American House, Hiram Pierce (formerly the Bliss House, see photo); (b) as above, Rice and Olmstead (Willard Pierce in Vt Dir); (c) as above, S. S. Skinner; (d) Welden House, W. McDonald;

* * *

The Welden House was built in 1864-65, and burned in 1897. It was replaced by the Colonial Inn in 1910 (see below), which later became The Tavern. "Supported by the pleasure travel," listed in Appleton's Railway Guide, 1866. Four stories, 200 rooms, "largest country hotel in New England" (Hemenway).

1871: (a) American House, Hiram Pierce*; (b) St Albans House, Willard Pierce*; (c) Tremont House, Martin and Osborn*; (d) Welden Hotel, Thomas Lavender* (all Beers);

Principal St Albans Hotels

(a) Phoenix Hotel (Bliss House, American House)
(b) St Albans House (Pierce's, earlier)
(c) Barber's Hotel (Tremont, Stevens House)

(d) Welden House
(e) Union House
(f) Central House
(g) Park House (Exchange)
(h) Franklin House (Stratton, Park View)
(i) Colonial Inn/Tavern (Jesse Welden)
(j) Spenser House (Hotel Kelly)

* * *

American House (St Albans Historical Society)

1873:   (a) as above; (b) as above; (c) <u>Stevens House</u>, Gilman Stevens (formerly the <u>Tremont</u>); (d) <u>Welden House</u>, Thomas Lavender; (e) <u>Union House</u>, Albert Jones (at the corner of Welden and Allen Sts); <u>Haywood House</u>, J. W. Haywood (unidentified); <u>Lake House</u>, L. C. Mann (unidentified);

1875:   (a) as above; (b) as above; (c) as above, T. Brenan; (d) as above; <u>Lake House</u>, Mrs S. L. Mann;

1879:   (a) as above, S. I. Stroud; (b) as above; (d) as above; (e) <u>Union House</u>, Albert Jones; (f) <u>Central House</u>, George W. Cushman (on Lake St, between Catherine and Main);

1880:   (a), (b), (d) and (f), as above;

1882:   (a), (b), (d) and (f), as above; <u>Lake House</u>, Joseph Doyle;

1883:   (a), (b), (d), (e) and (f), as above; <u>Lake House</u>, R. Jenkins;

1884:   (a) <u>American</u>, (b) <u>St Albans House</u>, (d) <u>Welden</u>, (f) <u>Central</u> and (g) <u>Park House</u> shown on Sanborn; (see photo of <u>Park House</u>, next page);

1887:   (a) as above; (b) as above (J. H. Stratton in Vt Dir); (d) as above, A. A. Merrifield; (f) as above, Granville Shedd; (g) <u>Park House</u> (later the <u>Exchange</u>), on Lake St between Catherine and Main, F. C. Johnson; (h) <u>Franklin House</u>, W. W. White (Main, corner of Fairfield; probably "John White's old place," later the <u>Stratton</u>, <u>Park View</u>);

1889:   (a), (b), (d), (f), (g) and (h) on Sanborn;

1890:   (a) as above; (b) as above, Owen Marron; (d) as above, W. H. Johnson; (f) as above, listed as <u>Grand Central</u> in St Albans Directory; (g) as above, Tom Keough; (h) <u>Stratton House</u>, J. H. Stratton (formerly the <u>Franklin</u>);

1892:   (a) as above; (b) as above; (d) as above, John Greenway; (f) as above, E. J. Taylor; (g) <u>Exchange Hotel</u>, C. W. Reagan (formerly <u>Park House</u>); (h) <u>Stratton House</u>, J. H. Stratton;

Park House (St Albans Historical Society)

1895:   (a) as above, J. J. Thompson; (b) as above; (d) as above, W. Landon; (f) as above; (g) as above; (h) as above, J. A. Labeau; all of these on 1895 Sanborn map;

1898:   (a), (b), (g), as above; (h) <u>Park View</u>, Eugene Girard (formerly <u>Stratton</u>); <u>Lenox Hotel</u>, James Purcell; <u>Elm Tree House</u>, T. C. Brennan;

1896:   (a), (b), (d), (f), (g), and (h) all on the 1896 Sanborn; so is the <u>Elm Tree House</u> (above), in the same block as the <u>Exchange</u>, on the northeast corner of Lake and Water Sts; Water St must have been renamed, not shown on a current map of St Albans;

1901:   (a) as above, Lynch and Claflin; (b) as above; (h) <u>Park View</u>, R. Nulty; (a), (b), (d), (f), (g), and (h) all on 1901 Sanborn; <u>Elm Tree House</u> not operating;

1905:   (a) as above, M. F. Spencer; (b) as above; (f) as above, A. W. Gilmore; (g) as above; (h) as above, William Landon;

1906:   (a), (b), (f) and (h) on Sanborn; (g) <u>Exchange</u> is no longer operating;

1908:   (a), (b), (f), (h), as above (no managers listed);

1910:   (i) <u>Colonial Inn</u>, built on the <u>Welden</u> site; sold to Henry Carlisle and became <u>The Tavern</u> in 1919;

1911:   (a) as above, H. A. Dunbar; (b) as above, Owen Marron; (f) as above, W. H. Larry;

476

(h) as above, John Barrett;

1912: (a), (b), (f), (h) and (i) on Sanborn; so is (j) <u>Spenser House</u>, on the west side of Main St, a little north of the present PO;

1913: (a) as above, H.A. Dunbar; (b) as above; (f) as above, W. H. Larry; (h) as above, John Barrett;

1916: (a), (b), (f), (h), (i) and (j) all listed in VPB booklet;

1920: (a) as above, W. H. Larry; (b) as above, --; (h) as above, F. A. Stebbins; (i) <u>The Tavern</u>, H. D. Carlisle; formerly the <u>Colonial</u>; sold to George St Laurent in 1924, renamed the <u>Jesse Welden</u> in 1941, and burned in 1948; (j) <u>Spenser House</u>, Mrs M. F. Spenser; all of the above are shown on the 1920 Sanborn; (f) the <u>Central</u> is shown as not operating;

1925: (a) as above, I. J. Wry; (i) as above, --; (j) <u>Spenser House</u>, Kelley and Petrie;

1926: (a), (b), (h), (i) and (j) on Sanborn; so is a place called <u>Crawford House</u> (probably a boarding-house) on the east side of Federal St, between Lake and Kingman; (b) <u>St Albans House</u> listed until at least 1940;

1959: Sanborn update: <u>Spencer</u> has become the <u>Hotel Kelly</u> (listed in VYB as late as 1968); the <u>American House</u>, the <u>St Albans House</u>, and the <u>Park View</u> are still shown; but the <u>Tavern</u> is gone; however, local historians say the <u>Park View</u> was not operating as late as this; it is listed in 1930, not in 1935.

(166c) <u>St Albans Bay</u>.

1828: a reference to the <u>Wilkins Inn</u> in Adams; (1)

1849: --, W. S. Meach (NEMU Dir);

1857: --, A. M. Brooks* (this is the <u>Brooks House</u>; Walling; see photo, next page);

1871: --, G. Younger* (Beers, different site than Brooks, 1857);

1887: <u>New York House</u>, James McDonald (unidentified);

1890: <u>Rocky Point Hotel</u>, W. H. Johnson; on Hathaway Point, became Kamp Kill Kare, apparently also known as <u>Balmaqueen</u>, see photo;

Note: the assistance of George Beebe, St Albans Historical Society, is gratefully acknowledged.

* * *

References

(1) Henry K. Adams, A Centennial History of St Albans, Vermont (St Albans: Wallace Pr., 1889).

(2) D.A.R., Bellevue Chapter, Sketches of Early Life in St Albans, Vermont (n.p, 1925).

(3) Edmund A. Royce, Highlights in the History of St Albans, Vermont (St Albans: E. H. Royce, 193(?)).

* * *

(167) **St George** (Chittenden). Smallest town in the state.

(167a) <u>St George</u>.

1828:   Sunrise Tavern, Silas Isham; a stagecoach stop on the Essex Junction-Hinesburg (Boston to Montreal) route; a large, 2-story building built by Isham at the intersection of Rte 2-A and Ayer Road. There is an S. Isham at this location on the 1871 Beers; Silas Isham died in 1882. This is VDHP 0412-2.

* * *

Brooks House (St Albans Historical Society)

Balmaqueen (St Albans Historical Society)

* * *

(168) **St Johnsbury** (Caledonia).

(168a) East St Johnsbury (East village).

(?):   a tavern, Josiah Gage; tavern license, 1821-'27; built before 1830, "some distance up the river, where the road turns following Gage's brook to Lyndon" (1); building now part of Don's Wayside Furniture;

478

1828:   a tavern, Silas Hibbard; on the west side of the street, four buildings north of the cemetery; same location as E. J. Stiles' hotel on the 1858 Walling map (see below);

1849:   --, George Aldrich (NEMU Dir);

1856:   --, E. J. Stiles;

1858:   a hotel, E. J. Stiles* (Walling);

1870:   --, G. E. Goodall and Sons;

1875:   --, Asa Hurlburt; a private residence soon after.

(168b) St Johnsbury (the "Plain").

c. 1790:   Lord's Inn, Dr Joseph Lord; "open for the housing of strangers...as early as 1790... later it was enlarged and known as Lord's Inn" (1); listed in the 1796 Vermont Almanac and Register; later kept by Seth Ford, who was an original grantee; this place was at the south edge of the Plain, first place seen as one came up the road from Barnet; the site of Joseph P. Fairbanks' home in 1841; and it is possible that Lord's "red tavern" became part of the Academy clubhouse; (2)

1799:   a tavern, Maj Thomas Peck; Willard Carleton's Tavern in 1810, later the Cross bakery, c. 1867; razed in 1897 to make way for the St Aloysius church;

(?):   Hoffman's Tavern, Henry Hoffman; tavern license 1824; who came in 1790; in the vicinity of the Court House in 1914 (1); a Capt John Barney built a new tavern on the site "some time after 1810"; Barney sold to Presbury West, who sold in turn to Abel M. Rice (tavern license, 1824-27); there is reference to an 1830 meeting at "Rice's Hotel";

* * *

"On a high standard in front of the house hung and swung on creaking hinges the sign--A RICE HOTEL. Prominent on entering its hospitable doors was the indispensable bar, adorned with a wealth of decanters which invitingly contained a plentiful supply of good cheer, running thro' the gamut of beverages from potato whiskey to French brandy...These were the brave old days when it was counted a good joke for an honest man to lose his way home of an evening, or to mistake his neighbor's home for his own. Abel mixed toddies with a mild satisfied air, and stabled horses in a determined way; while the ample and jolly landlady beguiled the traveler with fried sausage and gossip."

* * *

Rice sold to Ezra Ide, 1836; then A. H. Wilcox, 1838; Joseph Hutchinson, 1841; Hull Curtis, 1847; Curtis sold to a syndicate who built the St Johnsbury House in 1850, with the old tavern being incorporated into the rear of the new house;

Note: tavern licenses to Alpheus Bugbee, 1823, John Barney, 1822, and John Barnes, 1822, locations unknown;

1847:   George Ely's hotel, and a Union Temperance celebration held there; (1)

1849:   (a) --, Hull Curtis (NEMU Dir); this is Rice's Hotel; the NEMU Dir says he was managing the St Johnsbury House, but that wasn't built until 1850, according to Fairbanks; (1)

1850:   (a) St Johnsbury House, -- (incorporating Rice's Hotel); built by a syndicate as the entry of the railroad led to increased demand for hotel space; on the Plain (1858 Walling, 1875 Beers, see below; there is also a lithograph of the place on the Walling map); managers/proprietors included A. C. Jennings, until 1853; Col Carter for 2 years; A. M. Watson in 1854 for 8 years; then

479

Hiram Hill, E. A. Parks, Emery Thayer, Gilmore, Jerry Drew, George B. Walker, E. E. Bedell, S. B. Krogman, Landlord Chase, B. G. Howe; the place was badly managed at times, and went bankrupt in 1887, with the bank holding the mortgage until 1900; it continued to operate, but not successfully, and was entirely rebuilt in 1913; operated until c. 1973, converted into apartments;

1850: (b) Passumpsic House, Russell Hallett; at the corner of Railroad St and Eastern Ave, near the depot, at a cost of approximately $4,000; managers/proprietors included: Horace Evans in 1854; Clough and Downing, 1856; Col O. G. Harvey, 1860-62; S. K. Remick, who made extensive changes, and opened a bar which got him into serious difficulties with the local authorities, since by then Vermont was operating under a prohibition law (see below, and Chap III); Remick subsequently converted the place to a temperance hotel and began to make money; sold to Jonathan Farr in 1867; then Bela S. Hastings; O. G. Hale, 1869-75, who greatly enlarged it; Morrison and Howe in 1875, who changed the name to Avenue House (see photo); B. G. Howe was the proprietor for about 22 years. The place burned in 1896, with one death, and was immediately rebuilt as the New Avenue House (fire photo in ref 2);

* * *

"The hotel was a huge structure, especially for a small village of that day. It was probably too ambitious a project for the times, and the first few owners lost money. It remained for a Mr S. K. Remick to change this. He felt that a hotel was not properly caring for its guests unless liquor was served and he opened a bar. In the lily white town that St Johnsbury was, this was about the worst thing he could have done. It was perfectly legal to get your weekly jug at the express office if you ordered it from Boston but drink in a hotel was sinful. He was apprehended several times and paid over a thousand dollars in fines. The last conviction came with a warning that he would have to go to jail on the next offense. He promised to conduct a temperance house and, instead of losing money, he made twenty thousand dollars." (3)

1852: (c) Cottage Hotel, Richard B. Flint; who put up a small house on a lot he got in exchange for a horse, later enlarged it into the Cottage Hotel; on the site now occupied by the Green Mt Supermarket (i.e., 1987, ref 2); a temperance house with a family atmosphere, it lasted into the 1920s, but more of a boarding-house by then; the Hotel Sheldon at one point (see below), now the Green Mountain Super Market;

Avenue House (Special Collections, UVM)

480

1855, '56:   (a) --, W. S. Watson; Fairbanks says that one A. M. Watson had the St Johnsbury House at this time (1); (b) Passumpsic House, Clough and Downing;

1858:   (a) St Johnsbury House, W. S. Watson* (Walling); (b) Passumpsic House, --* (Walling; became the Avenue House);

* * *

The St Johnsbury Caledonian reported in January, 1869 (quoted in ref 2): "A. N. Bryant and J. F. Laducer were talking about swapping horses. Laducer got into the sleigh to try out Bryant's horse, which started quickly and threw Mr Laducer out, in front of the Passumpsic House, breaking his leg. The horse ran between the Passumpsic House and Brigham's store, went through the door into the Passumpsic House, bolted down the stairs into the office, and was found lying on its back with the sleigh on top. The encumbrances were removed and he was led through the hotel and out the east side, unhurt. The sleigh, however, was badly demoralized!"

* * *

1870:   (a) as above, H. Hill; (b) as above, Hale and Hastings; (the Caledonian reported in March, 1869 that Hale planned to add to the west wing and raise the whole building another story, but there were objections because the structure was so close to the street; the townspeople overruled the village trustees at a special meeting, and the Passumpsic House (renamed the Avenue House this year) became the largest building in town; --, N. J. Johnson (Vt Dir; on Railroad St; not identified, Cottage or Union);

1873:   (a) as above, T. B. Lyford; (b) as above, Aldrich and Miles;

1875:   (a) as above, G. L. Gilmore; (b) Avenue House, G. H. Aldrich (formerly the Passumpsic);

1875:   (a) as above, --* (Beers); (b) as above, B. G. Hale* (Beers);

1879, '80:   (a) as above, G. B. Walker; (b) as above, Benjamin G. Howe; (c) Cottage, R. B. Flint (82 Railroad St);

1884:   (a) St Johnsbury, (b) Avenue, and (c) Cottage, all on Sanborn map;

1887:   (a) as above, W. A. Little; (b) as above; (c) as above;

1888:   (a) St Johnsbury House, H. E. Moore; (b) Avenue House, E. J. Healey; Sheldon Hotel, B. C. Sheldon; Burton House, Rebecca Burton (Boston and Maine guide);

1889:   (a) and (b) on Sanborn; Cottage not shown, but a place called Willow House, also on Railroad St, appears on Sanborn, probably the same;

1890:   (a) as above, W. L. Krogman; (b) as above; (c) as above;

1892:   (a) as above, S. B. Krogman; (b), (c) as above;

1894:   "...and Dr Truman Stiles' house, where Caplan's is now located, was turned into a hotel and livery stable--the Union House" (1); the Union House is shown on the 1895 Sanborn (see below), just up the street from the Cottage, across from where Portland St intersects; it is mistakenly listed in St Johnsbury Center by Walton; (see also ref 5);

1895:   (a) as above, H. S. Chase; (b) as above, G. V. Frasier (the Avenue House burned in 1896, and was rebuilt immediately as (d) the New Avenue House (see below; see photo, next page); (c) as above, Higgins and Houghton; (a), (b) and (c) all shown on the 1895 Sanborn, also the Union, which got electric lights in 1897;

481

1898:   (a) as above, --; (c) as above, R. O. Lindsay; (d) New Avenue House, H. L. Doyle (went on the telephone exchange this year); (e) Union House, --; 92 Railroad St (Walton);

1900:   (a), (c) and (d) on Sanborn, also (e) Union House;

New Avenue House

1901:   (a) as above, B. G. Howe (Vt Dir); (c) as above, R. B. Flint; (d) as above, F. M. Black; (e) Union House;

1905:   (a) as above, F. N. Keeler; (c) as above; (d) as above, J. J. Caldbeck; Atheneum House (a boarding-house), Misses Burton; (e) as above; (a), (c), (d) and (e) on Sanborn;

1908:   (a), (d) as above;

1911:   (a) as above, --; (b) as above, E. J. Healey; Sheldon's Hotel (former Hotel Cottage);

1912:   (a), (d) on Sanborn; (c) Cottage is now the Sheldon Hotel; Union (now Caplan's) not operating;

1913:   (a) as above, --; (d) as above, E. J. Healey; the St Johnsbury House was extensively renovated in 1913, reopened in 1914;

1916:   (a) as above, H. E. Moore; (d) as above, W. L. Palmer; (c) Sheldon's Hotel, -- (formerly the Cottage);

1919:   (a), (d) on Sanborn; (c) Sheldon's has changed its name back to Cottage;

1920:   (a) as above, H. E. Moore; (c) Sheldon's Hotel, --; (d) as above, W. L. Palmer;

1925:   (a) as above, Mrs H. E. Moore; (c) as above, --; (d) as above, T. J. Murphy; St Johnsbury Inn, B. R. Jones;

1927:   (a), (d) on Sanborn; (c) Cottage, shown as not operating on Sanborn; (converted to a store in 1920, according to Johnson, ref 4); (a), (d) listed until at least 1955;

Note: the New Avenue House still stands, not operating, with a ground floor restaurant as the only occupant.

(168c) St Johnsbury Center.

Originally North St Johnsbury; known as "Center Village."

c. 1792:   a tavern, <u>Eleazer Sanger</u>; "tho not advertised as a tavern, became a favorite stopping place for teamsters, and for men who brought their wives in to the village on town meeting days, when great suppers were served" (1); at Sanger's Mills, in Center Village;

1797:   <u>Edson's Tavern</u>, Nathaniel Edson; "tho not generally advertised as such" (1); a mile south of present village center; town meetings held here, and mail left by post riders;

c. 1812:   a tavern, <u>Capt Samuel French</u>; tavern license, 1821; "the bridge builder" who built "on the edge of the bog at the north end of the street" (1); <u>C. Sherman's hotel</u> on the 1858 Walling (see below) appears to be in about the right location;

* * *

"Business increased and some years later French put up a new two story building; on the first floor was the bar room with a well furnished bar, also parlor and dining room; upstairs were sleeping rooms and a dance hall... French's Tavern was for many years a famous hostelry; it became noted as a good place for holiday functions, on Training days, Fourth of July and Thanksgiving...". (1)

* * *

"Judging from the Grand List records, a good many of the younger men...were considered to be members of the militia...Their main requirement was to appear on June training day...for inspection and drill, an effort made less arduous by the passing of the rum jug (captain's treat) down the line, after inspection, and the general holiday atmosphere which prevailed at these drills. Usually these were held at the Center--Edson's Tavern or French's Tavern, which was just south of Green Mountain Mall, (dismantled recently ...)." (2)

* * *

1820:   a tavern, <u>Capt Walter Wright</u>; "near the lower bridge," still standing in 1914; (1)

(?):   a hotel, <u>Ira Armington</u>; "an ornament to the village with fine hall attached" (1); on the corner opposite the Universalist church; an I. Armington building fitting this description is found on the 1858 Walling and 1875 Beers maps; burned in 1876;

1849:   --, Samuel French (NEMU Dir);

1856:   --, G. Sherman;

1858:   --, C. (?) Sherman* (Walling);

1875:   <u>Union House</u>, Mrs Winter* (Beers; approximately the same site as the 1858 hotel on Walling);

1875:   --, L. C. Farnham;

Note: Walton erroneously lists the <u>Union House</u> for 1898, 1901, '05 (at 92 Railroad St) under St Johnsbury Center instead of St Johnsbury city.

(168d) <u>Summerville</u>.

Now part of St Johnsbury city; east of the plain, where the Moose River joins the Passumpsic; this settlement had a post office from 1883-91. No listings found.

Note: the assistance of Claire D. Johnson, St Johnsbury Historical Society, is gratefully acknowledged.

<u>References</u>

(1) Edward T. Fairbanks, The Town of St Johnsbury, Vermont (St Johnsbury: Cowles Pr., 1914).

(2) Claire D. Johnson, I See by the Paper: An Informal History of St Johnsbury (St Johnsbury: Cowles Pr., 1987).

(3) Edward D. Asselin, "The Passumpsic House," Vermont Historical Society News and Notes <u>14</u> (April 1963): 57-58.

(4) Claire D. Johnson, I See by the Paper: An Informal History of St Johnsbury, Volume II, 1920-1960 (St Johnsbury: Cowles Pr., 1989).

(5) E. Donald Asselin, "Grandmother Bought a Hotel," Vermont Historical Society News and Notes <u>12</u> (1961): 49-51.

* * *

(169) **Salisbury** (Addison).

Includes Lake Dunmore (most of which lies in Salisbury, with the rest in Leicester), Salisbury and West Salisbury. Villages that never got POs, and are now hard to locate, are East Salisbury (Branbury State Park area); Salisbury Plains; and Salisbury Station, a stop on the Rutland Railroad for farmers and guests at the summer hotels on Lake Dunmore.

(169a) <u>Lake Dunmore</u> (with a PO from 1901-64).

1832: a tavern, --; at the "glassworks" on the shores of the lake, where glass-making was resumed at this time after the first company failed in 1817. This second operation lasted until 1839, and the property stood vacant until purchased by the Lake Dunmore Hotel Co in 1849; (1)

* * *

The old glass factory tavern was used as a small hotel until the new hotel was finished about 1854; various other glass company buildings were converted to use as cottages, etc.

"The new, three-story Lake Dunmore Hotel was completed about 1854. Its main front, facing the lake, was 75 feet long and contained wide halls and large airy rooms. A two-story wing on the back featured a dining room and dance hall, each 75 feet long by 36 feet wide." It came to be one of the most popular resorts in northern New England in the mid-1800s. Destroyed by fire in July, 1877, when John Dyer had it. Replaced by a new three and a half story hotel, the <u>Lake Dunmore House</u>, capable of accommodating 200 guests. Some of the cottages are still in use by Camp Dunmore for Boys, but this second hotel also burned, in 1906. (ref 1, which also has a photo of the second hotel; see photo, next page, of 1st <u>Lake Dunmore Hotel</u>).

* * *

1856: (a) <u>Lake Dunmore House</u>, Ellery Howard;

1857: (a) as above, --* (Walling; also a lithograph);

1870: (a) as above, John Cloyes;

1871: (a) as above, Dyer, Travers and Cameron* (Beers); at the north end of the lake, west side;

1873, '75, '79: (a) as above, E. P. Hitchcock and W. M. Porter;

1880: (a) as above, J. M. Dyer;

1881: (a) as above, Frederick Kooper, proprietor, Robert Dinwiddie, manager (Child); (b)

Cascade House, Loyal J. Kelsey; a modest 2-story hotel near what is now the main entrance to Branbury State Park, building now gone; according to Petersen, this place was not built until about 1895 (1); see photo;

1887:   (a) as above, W. H. Merritt (John Higgins in Vt Dir);

1st Lake Dunmore Hotel (Special Collections, UVM)

Cascade House

1892:   (a) as above, Coxe and Hack;

1895:   (a) as above, F. M. Coxe; (c) Mountain Spring Hotel, E. G. Town;

485

The Mountain Spring Hotel and Cottages, built for J. K. Parsons in 1892; renamed the Lake Dunmore Hotel and Cottages later, after the second Lake Dunmore House, farther up the lake, burned in 1906 (see photo). Built in a swampy area that had been filled with stumps, trash, etc, the building shifted later, and was finally declared unsafe by the state about 1957. Parsons died soon after the hotel was built. His mother sold it to Frank J. Quinn who ran it until 1912; then Karl Kimpton and Solomon Duckwitz; C. A. Coles in 1916; Abraham Shapiro; and from 1920-29, the Marvel Hotel Corp, Roscoe A. Marvel. From then until it closed, it was operated by Walter Bean and then his son Gregory.

Mountain Spring Hotel/Lake Dunmore Hotel

1898:   (a) as above, Pierce and Capen; (c) as above, F. J. Quinn;

1901:   (a) as above, Charles A. Dunn; (c) as above

1905:   (a) as above; (b) Cascade House, --;

1908:   (a) as above, --; (still listed in Walton, but burned in 1906); (b) as above, --; (c) as above, --;

1911:   (c) as above, I. Shapiro

1913:   (b) as above, --;

1916:   (c) as above, H. E. Bissell (VPB);

1920:   (b) as above, --; (c) Lake Dunmore Hotel and Cottages (former Mountain Springs Hotel);

1923:   Moosalamoo Inn, Mrs A. T. Worden (listed in 1935 VPB, 1955, '68 VYB);

1925:   (c) as above, -- (listed until at least 1940); Higgins Tavern, -- (on the west shore, about a mile from the old hotel; became Camp Dunmore; also 1923 VPB; listed until at least 1940).

(169b) 1st Salisbury.

Its PO closed in 1907, and the name was transferred to the former West Salisbury in 1909, still shown that way on maps.

c. 1783:   a tavern, Col Thomas Sawyer; a millwright, blacksmith and carpenter; first public house, "on site of Carl Whitney's home near the village bridge" (i.e., 1976, ref 1); this place

486

was bought by John Deming, a prominent Middlebury tavern-keeper, in 1795, and lasted until 1906, when it burned. Other proprietors were Patrick Johnson (almanacs, 1817 until at least 1829, but there were several Johnsons who served as tavern-keepers in Salisbury, see list below), Corey Allen, Ellery Howard, T. W. Kelar and Rollin T. Howard;

* * *

"Chittenden and a party of about 30 legislators were on their way to Rutland for the 1786 session of the legislature. Hearing that his old friend, the governor, was in the area, Col Sawyer prepared food and drink for the official party.

During the excitement, two of Sawyer's sons and an employee dragged the Colonel's old swivel gun to a concealed spot, loaded it and stood by to fire a salute. When the party of riders arrived and started to dismount, the cannon went off with a roar. The frightened horses bolted, throwing the Governor and several legislators into the dust...The party was uninjured except for its pride, but that too was soothed later when the Governor reportedly laughed about the incident over a pint of grog." (1)

* * *

1788:   a tavern, <u>Sam Bigelow</u>; "in the village";

1789:   a tavern, <u>Eleazer Claghorn</u>; "on the west side";

* * *

"Although the west part of town was settled first, the falls area (i.e., Salisbury village) was the business center...There appears to have been at least two taverns or public houses in the village, as well as one in the north part of town and another in the southwest section, to serve travellers on the early north-south road along the creek (i.e., Otter Creek) and the later post road through the village. A survey of business in town in 1823 (Zadock Thompson) listed four taverns and noted that a tavern license cost 34 cents." (1)

* * *

Table of Tavern Keepers, and Time When Each Went Into Business (2)

Solomon Bigelow, 1788	Jacob Linsley, 1812
Eleazer Claghorn, 1789	(almanac, 1812)
Hamlin Johnson, 1798	P. and A. Johnson, 1813
Lorin Lakin, 1795	Isaac Hill, 1813
Stephen Hard (Heard), 1795	Ellery Howard, 1814
(Hard's tavern in almanacs,	Moses Hitchcock, 1815
1796, 1802, '07)	Ruel Smith, 1818
Reuben Saxton, 1799	Elnathan Darling, 1826
Christopher Johnson, 1800	Carey (Corey) Allen, 1818
Elias Kelsey, 1801	Abiel Manning, 1829
Solomon Everts, 1803	P. G. Alden, 1831
William Kilburn, 1804	Lucius Barker, 1832
Patrick Johnson, 1808	James Cook, 1836
Johnson and Brooks, 1810	Nehemiah Pray, 1836
Brooks and Kilburn, 1811	T. W. Kelar, 1840
(Brooks in almanacs, 1813)	Rollin T. Howard, 1846

The foregoing is made with reference to the time each tavern keeper took out his license. It may not show the exact time when each commenced keeping a public house.

* * *

487

1797: a tavern, <u>John Deming</u>;

1801: a tavern, <u>Elias Kelsey Sr</u>; near the junction of Rte 7 and "the road leading to the plains"; burned in mid-1800s, replaced by a home occupied by Mrs Nina Mudge in 1976; (1)

1820s: a public house, <u>Lucius Barker</u>; "in the southwest part of town, on the old main highway that parallels the creek" (1); known as Barker's Assembly Hall, the scene of numerous social gatherings. Originally in Salisbury, but later in Leicester (the "Jerusalem" part) because of a boundary change;

1825, '29: <u>Child tavern</u>, --; almanac, location unknown;

(?): (a) <u>Howard Hotel</u>, Ellery Howard; on the north side of the river; built and kept many years by Ellery Howard and his sons, burned in 1875; the building "where Keros Howard now keeps tavern" (i.e., 1886, ref 3); also on the north side of the stream is one of the oldest buildings in town, taken by Howard when the other place burned; long used as a public house (see below); other operators (not clear if the first or second Howard establishment is meant) were R. T. Howard, Elnathan Darling, Abiel Manning, Thomas W. Kelar, and James Cook;

1849: (a) --, R. T. Howard; --, N. Pray; --, E. Howard (NEMU Dir);

1855: (a) --, K. K. Howard; --, E. D. Barber;

1870: (b) --, K. K. Howard (2nd <u>Howard's</u>);

c. 1875: (b) 2nd <u>Howard Hotel</u>, Keros K. Howard; on the corner just north of the village bridge; "this small hotel provided food, drink and rooms as well as dancing in an upstairs ballroom from about 1860 to 1892" (1); Luther Harrington was apparently the last operator, from 1879; it burned c. 1907, site now occupied by Whitney building (VDHP 0117-30, #38);

1871: (b) hotel, K. K. Howard* (Beers);

1873, '75: (b) <u>Howard House</u>, K. K. Howard;

1879, '80: <u>Belvue House</u> (sic), Charles C. Lamorder;

1881: (b) as above (Child); <u>Bellevue House</u>, C. W. Lamorder (Child); VDHP talks of a house, built c. 1815, that was remodeled in the late 19th century to make a hotel (VDHP 0117-30, #40); may be this place, owned in 1977 by Bernard Gale;

1883: (b) as above; <u>Maple Grove House</u>, A. L. Sawyer;

1887, '92, '95: (b) as above;

1905: <u>Hyde Park</u>, -- (Walton; location unknown);

Note: there is a VHS postcard photo of the <u>Winona Inn</u>; apparently a tourist inn, and probably 1930s.

(169c) <u>West Salisbury</u>. (2nd Salisbury postally, West Salisbury until 1909).

No listings found as such; however, see Eleazer Claghorn, tavern, 1789, under Salisbury, described as being "on the west side"; there is also an Everest photo, 1950s, of a tavern called the "<u>Kelly place</u>," no other information.

Note: the assistance of Virginia Cameron, Salisbury-Leicester Historical Society, is gratefully acknowledged.

* * *

References

(1) Max P. Petersen, Salisbury: from Birth to Bicentennial (South Burlington: Offset House, 1976).
(2) John M. Weeks, History of Salisbury, Vermont (Middlebury: A. H. Copeland, 1860).
(3) Henry P. Smith, History of Addison County, Vermont (Syracuse: D. Mason, 1886)

* * *

(170) **Sandgate** (Bennington).

(170a) Sandgate.

1822:   tavern licenses to Joseph Tuttle, John H. Sanderson;

1849:   --, Mrs Tuttle (NEMU Dir).

* * *

(171) **Searsburg** (Bennington).

(171a) Searsburg.

(?):   a hotel, Freeman Clark; on the Searsburg turnpike (Wilmington to Bennington), near the bridge; a busy road, built in the 1830s, until the Troy and Boston railroad came through; on what was the "Robinson place" in 1889 (1); it burned in 1871. Child refers to the "Green Mountain House" as the only hotel ever built in the town, by Freeman Clark, undoubtedly the same place; later proprietors were Solomon Rich and Sherman Robinson. Wolter says that Solomon Rich lost his life in a wagon accident in 1848, "many years before the hotel burned," and that there was still a marker at the site of the accident (i.e., 1960, ref 2);

1856:   a hotel, S. Robinson* (Rice and Hardwood); there is an S. Robinson, no hotel indicated, on the main road through Searsburg on the 1871 Beers;

1856:   --, Sherman Robertson (probably Robinson); Walton.

* * *

References

(1) Lewis C. Aldrich, History of Bennington County, Vermont (Syracuse: D. Mason, 1889).
(2) Carlo Wolter, "Searsburg," Vermont Historical Society News and Notes 11 (January 1960): 33-35.

* * *

(172) **Shaftsbury** (Bennington).

Geographically, there are, or have been, three Shaftsburys: Shaftsbury Center; Shaftsbury Depot (North Shaftsbury on recent maps); and South Shaftsbury. Postally, things are more complicated. Shaftsbury (Center) was the 1st Shaftsbury PO, from 1804-1904; the name was then transferred to the Depot, which had its own PO from 1897-1904. This office was discontinued in 1943, but the Shaftsbury designation was shifted once more, to South Shaftsbury, making it the third Shaftsbury. South Shaftsbury had also had its own PO from 1831-1961, and is still shown as South Shaftsbury on most maps.

(172a) Shaftsbury Center (first Shaftsbury).

1765:   Waldo Tavern, --; built by Abiatha Waldo, an original settler; demolished in 1905, it stood on the west side of old US 7 in Shaftsbury Center; photo in Levin, ref 1;

1787: (a) David Galusha Inn, David Galusha; a tavern and stagecoach stop in Shaftsbury Center on the west side of old US 7 (now 7A); almanacs, 1785, 1796; shown as building #26 on the excellent map in Levin's book. (1) The inn was visited by Timothy Dwight, president of Yale University, in one of his Vermont tours (quote in Levin, ref 1); now a private home (VDHP 0213-8);

1849: (a) --, D. G. Cole (NEMU Dir);

1855: (a) --, D. E. (?) and H. A. Cole;

1856: (a) a hotel, D. Cole* (Rice and Hardwood map; the old David Galusha Inn); it has not been established when this place stopped operating;

1908: Lyon's, --; probably an error in Walton; no other listing for Shaftsbury Center around this date, and a W. M. Lyons is listed as managing the Hastings Hotel in South Shaftsbury for several years around this time; also, postcard photos show that the Hotel Lyons and the Hotel Lawrence (in South Shaftsbury, see below) are the same.

(172b) Shaftsbury Depot (2nd Shaftsbury, North Shaftsbury).

(?): Babcock Tavern, --; just off Rte 7A, west side, a little south of North Shaftsbury Depot; it was the R. Matteson place in 1978, shown on the Levin map but without a number. (1)

(172c) South Shaftsbury (3rd Shaftsbury PO).

(?): Hastings Hotel, Charles E. Hastings; on the southeast corner at the four corners in South Shaftsbury; photo in ref 1;

c. 1779: a tavern, Amaziah Martin; for many years; shown as building #37 on the map in Levin, on old Rte 7 (now 7A) (1); Levin says that this place was operating in 1769; Amaziah died in 1819, and his son carried on the business until 1856;

1812: Huntington tavern, --; almanac, location unknown, not necessarily South Shaftsbury; a Henry Huntington had a tavern license in 1822;

1869: (a) --, C. E. Hastings* (Beers);

1870, '75, '79, '87, '92, '95: (a) --, Charles E. Hastings;

1901: (a) Hastings Hotel, W. M. Lyons (Vt Dir);

1898, 1900, '05, '06: --, W. H. (?) Lyons;

1908: Hasting's, --;

1911, '13, '20, '25: Hotel Lawrence, Oliver L. Lawrence (see photo);

1921: Hotel Lawrence, --* (Sanborn; on the southeast corner at the four corners in South Shaftsbury, formerly the old Hastings Hotel; same building?

(172d) Outside the Villages.

1777: a tavern, Peter Matteson; one of the oldest buildings in the state, operated as a stage coach inn for nearly 100 years by the Mattesons, but closed when business declined in the 1850s with the advent of the Western Vermont Railroad (2); sold to Lady Beatrice Gosford of Ireland in 1926, who left it to the Bennington Museum when she died 40 years later; now a museum, it was Lady Gosford who named it the Topping Tavern; on East Road, between Shaftsbury Center and Shaftsbury Depot; #32 on the map in Levin's book (1); VDHP 0213-12;

Hotel Lyons/Lawrence

Note: tavern licenses to David Andrews and Jonathan Draper, 1822, locations unknown;

1849:   --, William Matteson (NEMU Dir);

(?):   State Line House, --; built by Capt David Mathews in 1802, a Revolutionary War veteran; became a tavern after his death; on the New York-Vermont state line, on Rte 67; (VDHP 0213-14, still operating in 1974); operated as a nightclub in the 1970s, closed when it was damaged by fire in 1984; see John Spargo. (3)

Note: the assistance of Helen H. Clawson and Marjorie Galusha, Shaftsbury Historical Society, is gratefully acknowledged.

* * *

References

(1) Ruth Levin, Ordinary Heroes, the Story of Shaftsbury (Shaftsbury: Shaftsbury Historical Soc., 1978).
(2) James D. Sage, "The Old Topping Tavern," Vermont Life 25 (Spring 1971): 42-47.
(3) John Spargo, The True Story of Captain David Mathews and his State Line House (Rutland: Tory Pr., 1930).

* * *

(173) **Sharon** (Windsor).

(173a) Sharon.

1849:   --, Alvan Tucker; --, J. Morrill, Jr; --, A. Gray; --, J. Roberts; United States Hotel, B. B. Brown (all NEMU Dir);

1855:   hotel, S. Morrel* (Hosea Doten map; probably a misspelling of J. Morrill, see below);

1856:   --, Joseph Morrill;

1869:   (a) Williamson Hotel, A. E. Williamson* (Beers; same site as Hosea Doten, above);

1870, '75, '80: (a) as above;

1883: (a) <u>Sharon House</u>, Albert E. Williamson (Child; same place with a new name);

1887: --, C. A. Williamson;

1890, '92, '95, '98, 1902: <u>Manley's Hotel</u>, F. M. Manley (presumably still the same place);

1905: (a) <u>Sharon House</u>, Patten Brothers;

1908: (a) as above; eventually converted to a tenement building, burned in July, 1935;

1911, '13: --, G. B. Drown;

1916: (a) as above, G. H.Raymond (VPB);

1920, '25: --, F. W. Byers (also 1923 VPB).

Note: the assistance of Mrs Sarah G. Donahue is gratefully acknowledged.

* * *

(174) **Sheffield** (Caledonia).

(174a) <u>Sheffield</u>.

1802, '05: <u>Miles Tavern</u>, --; almanac, location unknown;

1823: tavern license to John Green, location unknown;

1832: first hotel, <u>Sewall Bradley</u>; but taverns as early as 1800 (Hemenway, no names given);

1858: --, N. C. Folsom* (Walling);

1870, '75, '80: --, N. C. Folsome (sp?); listed as <u>Sheffield House</u> in Vt Dir;

1875: --, N. C. Folsome* (Beers);

1887: --, W. C. McNeal.

* * *

(175) **Shelburne** (Chittenden).

(175a) <u>Shelburne</u>.

early 1800s: two taverns, Samuel and Simon Blin(n); a <u>Blin</u> tavern listed in an 1812 almanac; the Samuel Blin place still stands as VDHP 0413-15, the Evans home (1976); the <u>Samuel Blin tavern</u> has been described (1); there are said to have been four public houses in the township; with the two Blin taverns and <u>Harrington's</u> (below), there is one unaccounted for;

1796: <u>Parson's (Pearson's) tavern</u>; almanacs, location unknown; until at least 1829;

1796: (a) a tavern, <u>Benjamin Harrington</u>; on the main road from Middlebury to Burlington, on Rte 7 in Shelburne village; kept by his descendant, Cornelius H. Harrington, became the <u>Shelburne Inn</u>; other proprietors were Levi Comstock, 1835; George H. Isham, 1857; O. J. Baldwin and W. A. Weed, 1869 (when it was known as the <u>La Platte Hotel</u>, after a small river of that name running into Shelburne Bay); William McNeil, 1890; William Gadue, 1895; Edward Lawrence, 1897; Dr Bettinger, 1903; now operated by the Shelburne Inn Corp, it appears to have been operated continuously since 1796 (VDHP 0413-1, #6); only the Walloomsac Inn, in Bennington, now closed, and the Dorset Inn, have had longer runs; also served as the PO at one time; there is an old photo in the lobby of the inn;

1812: Geer tavern, --; almanac, location unknown;

1825, '29: Burritt tavern, --; almanacs, location unknown;

1849: (a) --, George B. Isham (NEMU Dir);

1855, '56: (a) as above;

1857: (a) --, George B. Isham* (Walling);

1869: (a) La Platte Hotel, William A. Weed* (Beers);

1870, '73, '75: (a) as above;

Note: it is odd that there are no listings at all for inns in Shelburne in Walton for 25 years or so, from about 1875-1900;

1900, '01: (a) as above, Fred LaRose;

1905, '11, '13: (a) --, E. D. Lawrence;

1916: Hotel Shelburne, L. D. Bettinger (VPB); this may be VDHP 0413-7, built in 1910 as a home for Clarence Morgan, then an inn; a retirement home in 1977, The Pillars;

1920, '25: --, L. D. Bettinger; this is the Shelburne Inn, still operating.

* * *

References

(1) Lilian B. Carlisle, ed., Look Around Chittenden County (Burlington: Chittenden County Historical Soc., 1976).

* * *

(176) **Sheldon** (Franklin).

Many Vermont towns had mineral spring hotels, and participated in the remarkable popularity these places enjoyed in the latter part of the 19th century; but no town had so many hotels or went through the cycle so quickly as Sheldon.

In Sheldon, the boom began with the apparently miraculous cure of a cancer patient, one C. Bainbridge Smith, a wealthy New York lawyer. He quickly developed the first of the springs (the Missisquoi; there were five, eventually, within a few miles of each other) near Sheldon Junction, and began selling bottled water. He also built the first and largest of the hotels, the Missisquoi Springs Hotel, in 1867. Within a very short time, there were eleven hotels distributed over four of the five villages in the township. Some were new, others simply enlarged and renovated private homes. Most of them either burned, went out of business or were carrying on marginally within five years or so. None of the original hotels are left, although the New Portland House, built to replace the original after a fire in 1901, is now in use as a nursing home. It has been estimated that nearly 300,000 people visited Sheldon during the boom era that lasted no more than five years.

(176a) <u>East Sheldon</u>. No listings found.

(176b) <u>North Sheldon</u>.

(?):   <u>Fish Hotel</u>, Benjamin Fish; the PO was in this place at one time; a Daniel Fish had a tavern license, 1819, '22, '24;

c. 1840:   a hotel, Benjamin S. Gallop; on Rte 105 near the old Missisquoi Camp Grounds; once known as <u>Halfway House</u>, because it was halfway between St Albans and Richford; the second floor had movable partitions so that the bedrooms could be transformed into a dance hall; now a private home; (1)

1855: --, R. S. Gallup; probably Gallop's <u>Halfway House</u>, see above;

1871: <u>Fish Hotel</u>, Benjamin Fish, Jr* (Beers);

1870, '73, '75, '79, '80, '83:   as above.

(176c) <u>Sheldon</u> (Village, or Creek).

1803:   first tavern (and PO), Dr Hildreth;

Note: tavern licenses to Josiah Peckham, 1815; Samuel White, 1817, '20, '21; John Ganson, 1817-33; Augustus Burt, 1819; John Ellithorp (?), 1822; Samuel B. Hulbert, 1832, '33; Abel Fairbanks, Cyrus Keith, 1826; Benjamin Ganson, 1827; Oliver A. Keith, 1828, '29, '32; F. W. Hudson, 1829; and Jonathan Keith, 1836, locations unknown;

1849: --, M. T. Darwin (NEMU Dir; location unknown, could be anywhere in the township);

1855, '56:   --, Joseph Mitchell (location unknown, same comment as above);

1857:   (a) --, D. Wright* (Walling; same site as the <u>Central House</u> in 1871); (b) --, J. C. Kittell* (Walling; same site as <u>Traveler's House</u> in 1871);

(?):   (a) <u>Central House</u>, S. Vandenberg; "where Lena Stephenson lives" (i.e., 1979, ref 1); enlarged from a private home; see photo;

c. 1868:   (b) <u>Traveler's Home</u>, J. C. Kittell and daughter Helen; later another daughter and son-in-law, Charlotte and William Buck, until it burned in 1883;

c. 1868:   (c) <u>Vermont House</u>, John Fish;

1867:   (d) <u>Bellevue House</u>, Alfred Keith; opposite the present home of Ida Bocash (i.e., 1979, ref 1); opened as the <u>Keith House</u>, renovated soon after and became the <u>Bellevue</u>; sold to the St Johnsbury and Lake Champlain Railroad about 1880, who moved it in sections to the Maquam shore (on Lake Champlain in Swanton), where it operated for many years as the <u>Champlain Hotel</u>, with C. F. Smith manager into the 1920s; it closed 2-3 years after Smith left, and burned on Oct 2, 1926;

(?):   (e) <u>Portland House</u>, -- (see photo, next page); its name came from the Portland and Ogdensburgh Railroad, one of two lines that intersected at Sheldon Junction; 3 stories high with 30 guest rooms, this bustling place was not built specifically for the mineral springs business, but served the normal needs of Sheldon over a considerable period of time. It burned on Thanksgiving Day, 1901, rebuilt immediately on a smaller scale as the <u>New Portland House</u>; declined in the 1920s, still operating as late as 1955, now the Napoli Home for the Aged; VDHP 0614-2, #21;

Central House (St Albans Historical Society)

1870: (a) as above, S. Vanderburgh (Vandenberg); (b) as above; (c) as above, Fish and Eldred; (d) as above, A. Keith;

1871: (a), (b), (c), (d) and (e) all on Beers;

1873: (a), (b), (d) and (e) as above;

Portland House (St Albans Historical Society)

1875:   (d) and (e) as above;

1879:   (e) as above;

1880:   (e) as above, Frank Brown;

1882:   (b) as above, J. W. Buck; (e) as above, William Chadwick;

1883:   (b) and (e) as above;

1887, '92, '95: (e) as above, Arthur Marvin;

1898, 1901, '05:   (e) as above, G. H. Thomas; burned in 1901, rebuilt as <u>New Portland House</u>;

1908, '11, '13, '16, '20, '25:   <u>New Portland House</u>, G. H. Thomas.

(176d) <u>Sheldon Junction</u> (the Depot).

1857:   (a) <u>Missisquoi Valley House</u>, J. Mitchell* (Walling); on the north side of the "plank road" from St Albans, between present Sheldon Springs and the toll bridge across the river;

c. 1868:   (b) <u>Goodspeed's Hotel</u>, A. Jones;

c. 1868:   (c) <u>Riverside Hotel</u>, W. Landon (also known as <u>Landon House</u>);

1867:   (d) <u>Missisquoi Springs Hotel</u>, C. B. Smith; an elegant place (see lithograph, ref 1) with a hundred rooms and spring water piped to every one of them (2); the place burned in July 1870 in a fire allegedly set by a discharged female chef, and not rebuilt; not shown on the 1871 Beers, but the Missisquoi Spring is, as well as two other buildings marked "C. B. Smith";

c. 1868:   (a) <u>Missisquoi Valley Hotel</u> (<u>Valley Hotel</u>), A. C. Wheeler; near the old depot; the "plank road" from St Albans and the first railroad both passed nearby;

1870:   (a) <u>Missisquoi Valley House</u> (<u>Valley House</u>), A. C. Wheeler; (b) <u>Goodspeed's House</u>, F. L. Goodspeed; (c) <u>Landon House</u> (<u>Riverside</u>), William Landon; (d) <u>Missisquoi Springs Hotel</u>, C. B. Smith;

1871:   (b) as above* (Beers);

1873:   (b) as above, A. Jones; (a) and (c) as above;

1875:   (b) as above, R. J. Ashton; (c) as above, Lemuel Adams;

1879, '80:   (e) <u>Junction House</u>, J. A. Shedd (location unknown, probably <u>Goodspeed's</u>;

1892, '95:   (c) as above, H. B. Thomas;

1898:   (c) as above, C. Skeels;

1905:   (e) as above, L. E. Willard;

1908:   (c) as above, --;

1911:   (e) as above, L. E. Willard;

1913, '20:   (c) as above, Harry Hopkins; (e) as above, L. E. Willard;

1925:   (c) as above, L. E. Willard and wife; (e) as above, A. L. Doner; both listed in 1930, not 1935.

(176e) <u>Sheldon Springs</u> (Olmsead Falls until 1884).

1868:   (a) <u>Congress Hall</u>, S. S. F. Carlisle and Dr S. S. Fitch; where St Anthony's church now stands (i.e., 1979, ref 1); 4 stories high, with water pumped by a windmill from the Kimball Spring; it burned on Dec 19, 1908; see photo, Chapter IV;

1870:   (a) as above, S. S. F. Carlisle;

1871:   (a) as above, Dr Fitch* (Beers);

1873:   (a) as above;

1879, '83:   (a) as above, A. McLean (McLane);

1887, '90:   (a) as above, William West.

* * *

References

(1) Dorothy H. Ashton, Sheldon, Vermont (St Albans: Regal Art Pr., 1979).
(2) Enna Bates, "A Vermont Spring and a Cure for Cancer," Vermont Historical Society News and Notes <u>3</u> (March 1952): 49-52.

* * *

(177) **Sherburne** (Rutland).

(177a) <u>North Sherburne</u>.

(?):   a tavern, <u>Ichabod Johnson</u>; before the Stockbridge to Rutland turnpike was opened in 1808 (which probably ran over Elbow Road); on what was the George Frink farm in 1886 (1); Note: the Elbow Road was the old turnpike road, that went all the way from Sherburne to Rutland, via North Sherburne and Mendon; no longer a through road past North Sherburne, according to the Vermont Road Atlas;

c. 1818:   an inn, <u>Royal Turner</u>; tavern license, 1822;

1833:   <u>Coffee House</u>, Reuben Thrall; built by Thrall, used as a tavern until 1883, with Dudley Estabrook, occupant in 1886, as last proprietor; Francis Giddings, first PM in North Sherburne, had this place in 1849, when it was known as <u>Giddings Tavern</u>; operated by Eli D. Estabrook, 1865-83, last tavern proprietor; also the North Sherburne PO, 1872-1919; a mail stage stop until 1927 (2); in Chittenden Gore, a stopover at the intersection of the Rutland-Bridgewater turnpike and the North Road, #4 on the Town of Sherburne map in ref 3;

1854:   hotel (and PO), --* (Scott map);

1856:   --, R. D. Estabrook (probably the <u>Coffee House</u>);

1869:   (a) <u>Coffee House</u>, --* (Beers);

1870, '75, '80, '83:   (a) <u>Coffee House</u>, E. D. Estabrook (PM listed as R. D. Estabrook);

1873, '79:   (a) as above, Joseph Segar (Vt Dir).

(177b) <u>Sherburne</u> (Killington, Sherburne Center).

1794: reference to a meeting to organize the town at <u>Nathan Eddy's</u>, "inn-holder" (2); listed in the Vermont Almanac and Register as a stage stop on the Rutland-Windsor road;

1817: first hotel, <u>Josiah Wood</u>; tavern license, 1820-23; shown on the 1869 Beers as the Wood homestead, north of Sherburne village; across the road from the present day Mission Church (i.e., 1988), on the old Rutland-Bridgewater turnpike; #21 on the Town of Sherburne map, ref 3;

Note: tavern license to Nathaniel Fuller, 1821, '22;

c. 1832: <u>Richardson's Hotel</u>, Rufus Richardson Jr; built by his father near what was Harley Gifford's home in 1972; referred to as the "lower" of two hotels in 1834, burned on July 7, 1862 when Loren E. Atwood had it (Rutland Herald);

c. 1832: a hotel, <u>William Lewis</u>; kept only 2 years, building later used as a store by Frank Spaulding; location unknown;

1843: <u>Stone tavern</u>, --; lately occupied by Edwin Clement, burned; (Rutland Herald, 6/8/1843);

1854: hotel, <u>R. Richardson</u>* (Scott);

1855: --, Rufus Richardson; --, John Hoyt (location unknown);

1856: --, Rufus Richardson;

c. 1863: a hotel, <u>Bradford Chase</u>; built as a home c. 1840 by Albert Wilson, who occasionally accommodated wayfarers (1); expanded by Chase, then A. D. Estabrook very briefly; and Benjamin Maxham in 1865, who had it for 18 years; it became the <u>Hotel Sherburne</u> at some point. Maxham established "an imperishable reputation for jocularity" (1); sold to Jerome Taylor in 1884; the PO was in the hotel at least part of the time when Maxham had it; Mrs Augusta Taylor owned it in 1889 (relationship to Jerome unknown), she leased it to various parties; called the <u>Traveler's Home</u> at one point; amongst the leasees were John and Artie Morse, when he was a stage-driver, c. 1890; and Ida Perkins, who married Horace Wilder, in 1891, for 7 years; it closed in 1898, and eventually collapsed;

1869: (a) hotel, <u>B. Maxham</u>* (Beers);

1870, '73, '75, '80: (a) --, Benjamin Maxham (also PM; listed as the <u>Sherburne House</u> in 1879);

1881: (a) --, Benjamin Maxham (Child);

1883: (a) <u>Trout House</u>, Benjamin Maxham (Vt Dir; apparently another name for the place);

1887: (a) --, Jerome Taylor;

1890: (a) --, John J. Morse;

1901: (a) <u>Traveler's Home</u>, H. E. Wilson; this is in disagreement with Fleming, who says the place closed in 1897;

1923: <u>Long Trail Lodge</u>, --; given to the Green Mountain Club by the Proctor family, burned in 1968, name transferred to a second building across the road. The <u>Inn at Long Trail</u> now operates on the site.

(177c) <u>South Sherburne</u> (West Bridgewater).

1869: hotel, <u>F. Madden</u>* (Beers); according to Fleming, this place was built before 1833, and was <u>Ellis Madden's hotel</u> from 1855-1900s (2); stood next to the <u>Val Roc Motel</u> (1972); Sherburne town meetings held in the second floor dance hall in the 1920s; building now gone;

1880:   <u>Killington House</u>, --; room for 40 guests, at 4100 feet elevation, accessible by a carriage road off the Wheelerville Road, now a hiking trail; hotel gone by 1915; not quite at the summit; the road is shown on the Vt Road Atlas; listed in Child in 1881 with V. C. Meyerhofer as manager; Oscar Wilde stayed here in 1882, signing the register with an acrostic poem (2); originally <u>Pico Lodge</u> (3); see also Chapter V, Resorts, and under Rutland.

* * *

References

(1) Henry P. Smith and William S. Rann, History of Rutland County, Vermont (Syracuse: D. Mason, 1886).

(2) Madeline C. Fleming, An Informal History of the Town of Sherburne, Vermont (Rutland: Sharp Offset Pr., 1972).

(3) Vermont Div. of Historic Preservation, Historic Architecture of Rutland County, Curtis B. Johnson, ed., Elsa Gilbertson, asst ed. (Montpelier: 1988).

* * *

(178) **Shoreham** (Addison).

(178a) <u>Cream Hill</u>.

(?):   a tavern, <u>Timothy Chipman</u>; "for many years" (1); according to Everest (1950s photo), this place dates from c. 1790, was on Cream Hill Rd;

Note: Goodhue says there were 5 taverns in the vicinity of Cream Hill: Major and Nathaniel Callender's (see below under Shoreham); Philemon and Jesse Wolcott's (unidentified); and Gen. T. T. Chipman's (see above) (2); see also quote below under Larabees Point;

(178b) <u>East Shoreham</u>. No listings found.

(178c) <u>Larabees Point</u>.

(?):   a tavern, <u>Samuel Beeman</u>; in a log house before the Revolutionary War, until 1783;

1783:   a tavern, <u>Thomas Rowley Jr</u>; Green Mountain boy and poet; until 1787, when he sold to John S. Larabee. Larabee kept the tavern and a store, and established a ferry; the tavern burned in 1838 and operations were shifted to a small house opposite the original site until 1847, when the <u>United States Hotel</u> was built (see below); on Basin Harbor Rd; there is an Everest photo (1950s) of what must be the second <u>Rowley</u> tavern;

* * *

"The amount of transportation in former years made many taverns, and these modified the social habits of the country. Information came by travelers, and a knowledge of the world was got in long journeys in the carriage of produce. All this was by teams, and chiefly in winter. Seventy teams a night are spoken of as stopping at the Larabee House (sic) by the Lake, and an equal number at one of the taverns about Cream Hill of which there five in the same vicinity" (ref 2).

* * *

1847:   (a) <u>United States Hotel</u>, Samuel H. Holley and Benjamin B. Brown; on the original <u>Rowley tavern</u> site; sold soon after to Charles W. and Olive L. Larabee ; then Horatio N. Baldwin, 1852; Henry S. Gale, 1866; Sheldon S. Baker, 1866; John Cushing, 1867; Ambrose Graves and Stillman P. Marsh, 1869; Isaac Stebbins, 1872; Almon C. Farr and Frederick Kimball, 1873; Farr alone, 1876. Name changed to <u>Larabees Lake House/Point House</u> when Farr died, with K. W. King manager. The place burned in 1917 and was never rebuilt; the Larabees Point PO was in the hotel, as long as the PO existed, with the innkeepers often serving as PMs;

1849: (a) <u>United States House</u>, A. Davis (NEMU Dir);

1856: (a) as above, H. S. Gale* (Walling);

1870: (a) as above, Cutting and Graves;

1871: (a) as above, A. P. Cutting* (Beers);

1873: (a) as above, --;

1875: (a) as above, Fred Kimball (also PM);

1879, '80, '83, '87: (a) as above, Almon C. Farr;

1890, '92, '95: (a) as above, Mrs Jane Farr;

1898: (a) as above, Robert Abegg;

1905: (a) as above, K. W. King;

1913, '16: (a) <u>Larabees Point House</u>, Frederick Ives (also PM); see photo; listed as <u>Lake House</u> in 1916 VPB.

(178d) <u>Shoreham</u>.

1774: <u>Moore's Tavern</u>, --; almanacs, until 1802; on the Crown Point Rd; it is odd that this place, which apparently lasted 30 years or so, is not mentioned in the various histories;

HOTEL LARRABEE'S POINT, VT.

Larabees Point House

* * *

1793: a tavern, <u>Amos Callender</u>; "...brick...for many years...the most elegant in this part of the country" (Hemenway); on the southwest corner of the intersections of Lapham's Bay Rd and Basin Harbor Rd; razed in 1988, being reconstructed in Brandon; there is a 1950s Everest photo;

Callender came c. 1793, fled when the Revolutionary War began, and returned in 1783. In 1793, he built the brick house now occupied by R. H. Holmes (i.e., c. 1886) and kept a "noted hostelry for many years." His farm included the place known as the Cream Hill Stock Farm in 1886. (1)

* * *

1795:   a tavern, <u>Ebenezer Turrill</u>; "a large house...for many years" (2); commonly known as <u>Hill House</u>; near the site of the Catholic church (i.e., 1886, ref 1). His son, Truman Turrill, began to keep the old tavern about 1810, then others until 1849;

1800:   (a) a tavern, <u>Joseph Miller</u>; a large place in the village, sold to T. J. Ormsbee in 1802, who used it as residence and store; became a tavern again with Robert R. Hunsden, who kept it from 1828 until his death in 1845 (<u>Hunsden Hotel</u>, became the <u>Shoreham Hotel</u>, see below); Col F. M. Wilcox followed Hunsden, then Mr Ensign, George L. Deming, and A. J. Bennett until 1880, when the present landlord, D. J. Wright, took over (i.e., 1886, ref 1);

Note: there is a 1950s Everest photo of the "Doolittle tavern," on Rte 22A, said to date from the 1830s; probably <u>Turrill's</u> or <u>Miller's</u> (see above) but not identified;

1849:   --, E. Hill (NEMU Dir);

1855:   (a) --, F. M. Wilcox;

1856:   (a) --, - Sloan;

1857:   (a) --, P. Hamsden* (Walling; probably Hunsden, see above);

1873:   (a) --, Bennett and Jones;

1875, '79:   (a) <u>Shoreham Hotel</u>, A. J. Bennett;

1880, '83:   (a) as above, D. J. Wright;

1881:   (a) as above, E. J. Severance (Child);

1887, '90:   (a) as above, A. H. Smith;

1892:   (a) as above, K. W. King;

1895:   (a) as above, H.E. Bissell (also called the <u>Hotel Bissell</u>);

1898:   (a) as above, Paul Cornell;

1901:   (a) <u>Hotel Bissell</u>, H. Bissell (Vt Dir);

1905, '11, '13, '20, '25:   (a) as above, A. Dudley (also on 1915 Sanborn); closed as an inn c. 1930, but became a bed-and-breakfast place (<u>The Shoreham Inn</u>) in 1973, still operating.

(178e) <u>Shoreham Center</u> (formerly Richville).

1799:   a tavern (and store), <u>Charles Rich</u>; "in his old house next east of the grist mill," until 1811. (2)

Note: the assistance of Mrs Susan H. MacIntire, Shoreham, is gratefully acknowledged.

References

(1) Henry P. Smith, History of Addison County, Vermont (Syracuse: D. Mason, 1886).
(2) Joseph F. Goodhue, History of the Town of Shoreham, Vermont (Shoreham: The Town, 1861; reprinted, Platt Library, Shoreham (Middlebury, Addison Pr.) in 1975).

* * *

(179) **Shrewsbury** (Rutland).

Most of the information below on Shrewsbury's early taverns comes from the very detailed account in Dawn Hance's excellent book, which includes a remarkable map prepared by the Shrewsbury Historical Society, showing the locations of all eleven of Shrewsbury's taverns; there are also photos of many of them. (1) Most of these places were located on main roads outside the villages. The Crown Point road passed near Shrewsbury Center, but the Green Mountain turnpike (1799) bypassed it in favor of Cuttingsville, as did the railroad in 1849 (see also ref 2).

(179a) Cold River (PO, 1889-1904), no listings found.

(179b) Outside the Villages.

(?):   a tavern, Lemuel White; by at least 1776, on what is now Lincoln Road (site #1 on the Hance map); White died in a typhoid epidemic in 1813, as did two other local inn-keepers, Nathan Finney and Phinehas Page, probably catching the disease from travelers. White was the first settler and first town representative, although he could neither read nor write; he is described by Smith and Rann as "illiterate, eccentric but intelligent"; (3)

c. 1792:   Finney's Tavern (first), Nathan Finney; "Perhaps the most prominent of all the early settlers, and certainly the one most clearly remembered (3); near the first turnpike, a little north of Cuttingsville (later the railroad right of way, site #2 on the Hance map, ref 1); the turnpike was moved about 1806, and Finney's Tavern was no longer on the road, but he bought land nearby on the second turnpike, and opened the second Finney Tavern (see below);

* * *

"Father (i.e., Nathan Finney)...built the first framed house in town...it was painted red. He afterwards built on additions and opened a public house--being constantly pressed to give entertainment to travelers--so many used to drop in and ask to stay overnight, he and Mr Robinson (see below) who lived above us both concluded to put up their sign. Father got prosperous right off" (this quotation is from Finney's daughter, Lydia Finney Meech, in Hemenway).

* * *

"This was a famous place in its day, as the following...from the Vermont Tribune...illustrates. The author is Mr L. Dawley, a resident of Cuttingsville:

"There is probably no place in town where so much convivial enjoyment has been indulged in as at what was once known as the old Finney Tavern. We remember over half a century ago the sign with the square and compass and other emblematical designs glittering in the sunshine of this ancient hostelry. The place was known from the Canadian provinces to Boston, and was a home for the weary traveler, and a resort for pleasure seekers and invalids in search of health. Colonel Finney, the proprietor, was far above the mediocrity of men, affable, jovial, of fine physique, a man of full habits and liberal indulgences, which called around him a large circle of friends. Two or three four-horse coaches called daily at the door, the stables afforded room for at least one hundred horses, and were often filled.

502

Immense droves of cattle were driven over the road from Northern New York, and the lake towns to Boston markets, and, stopping over night at this old stand, would litterly (sic) cover the meadows and hill sides with lowing herds. But those 'good old times' are gone. Mails, passengers, freights and live-stock are now rushed by like the wind by steam. The old inn has been demolished (at least portions of it) and a commodious farm-house stands in its place. The worshipers of Bacchus no longer assemble there, the jovial song and the merry raps of the toddy-stick are heard no more. This valuable old farm is now owned by Amos Pratt...It is one mile below the village." (3)

* * *

1809:   Finney's Tavern (second), Nathan Finney; almanacs, 1812-at least 1829; near the first tavern, site #3, Hance (1); Nathan died in the typhoid epidemic of 1813, and his sons Alvin (tavern license, 1817) and Levi took over; Levi carried on alone for a long time after Alvin died in 1821, and the tavern was in its heyday while he was proprietor (tavern license, 1821, '23). The tavern was probably larger than the portion still standing, now occupied by D. R. Kelley (i.e., 1980, ref 1); there was a livery with space for 100 horses in the old days, and a store and blacksmith shop. Levi Finney was also PM here from 1825-38; when he died in 1847, the tavern went to his son, Hannibal H. Finney, and later to Levi's daughter Caro and her husband, William H. Barker; sold in 1866 to Amos Pratt;

c. 1792:   a tavern, Ichabod Robinson; on the "shunpike" (Old South Road, a little south of Cuttingsville, site #4 on the Hance map); property passed to Calvin Robinson in 1798, but not clear if he kept the tavern; probably discontinued by 1806 due to relocation of the turnpike; listed in the Vermont Almanac and Register as a stage stop on the Rutland-Boston road, 1796, 1802, '07;

1808:   a tavern, Jeffrey Barney; on Rte 103 a little north of Cuttingsville (site #7, ref 1); only information on this tavern comes from a passing reference in the Rutland Herald of 1808; (1)

1821:   a tavern, Daniel Foster; tavern license, 1821-23; until 1824, at the foot of Lincoln Hill (site #9, ref 1); Foster sold to William Lincoln, and the property passed to his daughter Sally and her husband Otis Webb later;

c. 1836:   a tavern, Russell Lincoln; built either by Jonathan Onion or John Willoughby, near the foot of Lincoln Hill (site #10, Hance); owned by Abel Willoughby in 1817, and by Russell Lincoln in 1836, but not clear when he opened it as a tavern; Lincoln was fined in 1848 for selling liquor without a license; descendants of the Lincolns remember dances being held there in the early 1900s, but the building is no longer there.

(179c) Cuttingsville (Finneysville from 1825-38).

c. 1830:   a tavern, Charles Cutting; later named the Union House (see photo, next page); an early settler for whom the town was re-named in 1838 (it is a curious fact that he later gave his name to towns in both Indiana and Iowa, according to Smith and Rann, ref 3); at site #11 in Cuttingsville. (1) He sold out to William Barnes when he left town in 1838; Barnes sold a few years later to Jeremiah Dow; then Horace Todd in 1866; Dow also leased the place while he had it, to P. G. Alden in 1850, and Lawson Dawley, 1860-65 (known also as Todd's Hotel); Todd sold to Dan Butterfield in 1877, who made improvements the place burned in 1903. Liquor was sold at a nearby tent or shed while a new inn was being built, but the town went dry in the interval and the new inn was never used as such. (1) Now owned by John C. Stewart and Son, Inc;

1849:   (a) Union House, P. G. Alden (NEMU Dir);

1854:   tavern, S. Dow* (Scott map; on the Union House site);

1855:   --, J. Starkey;

1869:   (a) hotel, H. Todd* (Beers; same site as the Union House on the Hance map);

Union House
(Shrewsbury, Vermont: Our Town As It Was, 1980, Dawn D. Hance)

1870, '73, '75: (a) <u>Todd's Hotel</u> , Horace Todd; same as the <u>Union House</u>;

1879, '80, '81 (Child), '87, '92, '95, '98:   (a) as above, D. K. Butterfield.

(179d) <u>North Shrewsbury</u>. No listings found.

(179e) <u>Shrewsbury</u> (the Center).

c. 1800:   a tavern, <u>Phinehas Page</u>; at site #5, ref 1; Page died in the 1813 typhoid epidemic, but there is a tavern license in his name in 1817;

c. 1817:   a tavern, <u>Stephen Gleason</u>; tavern license, 1817, '21, '22; the tavern may be earlier, since he acquired the land from Page in 1808, but his first license is 1817; see photo of the tavern sign; operated until at least 1837, but may have been only a place where drinks were served, without accommodations for guests; B11 on the Shrewsbury Center Historic District map, #6, ref 1;

1820: a tavern, <u>John Buckmaster</u>; until the 1840s, on the Woodstock Rd (#8, ref 1); Buckmaster was PM in 1846; tavern license, 1820-23; see photo, next page;

1856: --, J. Billings;

Note: the present <u>Shrewsbury Inn</u> did not open until the 1980s.

Note: the assistance of Dawn Hance, Rutland, is gratefully acknowledged.

* * *

<u>References</u>

(1) Dawn D. Hance, Shrewsbury, Vermont: Our Town As It Was (Rutland: Academy Books, 1980).

(2) Vermont Div. of Historic Preservation, Historic Architecture of Rutland County, Curtis B. Johnson, ed., Elsa Gilbertson, asst ed. (Montpelier: 1988).

(3) Henry P. Smith and William S. Rann, History of Rutland County, Vermont (Syracuse: D. Mason, 1886).

Gleason Tavern sign
(Shrewsbury, Vermont: Our Town As It Was, 1980, Dawn D. Hance)

* * *

(180) **Somerset** (Windham).

Somerset had a post office from 1870 to 1916, but the town was disenfranchised by the state legislature in 1937, becoming an official wilderness.

(180a) <u>Somerset</u>.

1901:   <u>River View House</u>, -- (Vt Dir).

* * *

(181) **South Burlington** (Chittenden).

(181a) <u>South Burlington</u>.

Two stage roads came through what is now South Burlington: the main road from Vergennes (the Lake Road, now Rte 7, more or less); and the Hinesburg-Middlebury route (along old Fourth Street, now the Hinesburg Road, Rte 116); this road intersects the old Winooski Turnpike (present Williston Road, Rte 2) within present South Burlington.

c. 1788:   a tavern, <u>Nathan Smith 2nd</u>; a "Minute Man" in the Revolution; near Mr Van Sicklen's on Fourth St until 1822 (2); Everest photo, 1950s;

John Buckmaster Tavern, Shrewsbury
(Shrewsbury, Vermont: Our Town As It Was, 1980, Dawn D. Hance)

* * *

c. 1800: a tavern, John Eldredge; on the north side of Williston Road, corner of Hinesburg Road, until his death in 1813 in a typhoid epidemic which hit inn-keepers especially hard;

c. 1815: a tavern, --; built for John Van Sicklen Jr; at 2000 Hinesburg Road, now known as Star-Thru Ranch Corp (i.e., 1979); VDHP 0414-16;

c. 1830: a tavern, --; present Rollin Tilley home, 700 Hinesburg Road, near the interstate overpass (VDHP 0414-8); allegedly this tavern-owner bribed a gang of workmen with a keg of rum to move the road in his direction when it was being repaired in the early 1800s; (1)

1923: Allenwood Inn, E. P. Woodbury (VPB); south of Queen City Park (1); owned and operated for many years by Col E. P. Woodbury, last listed in 1961.

* * *

References

(1) Lilian B. Carlisle, ed., Look Around Chittenden County (Burlington: Chittenden County Historical Soc., 1976).
(2) William S. Rann, History of Chittenden County, Vermont (Syracuse: D. Mason, 1886).

* * *

(182) **South Hero** (Grand Isle).

(182a) Keeler's Bay.

1811: a tavern, Issi Fletcher; tavern license, 1825-30; "on the inlet, south end of Keeler's Bay. (1) Sold by Fletcher in 1840, now the Charles Tracy home (i.e., 1980; VDHP 0705-66);

1868: (a) <u>Iodine Spring House</u>, Frederick Landon; owner of a farm on the west shore of Keeler's Bay, including a well-known mineral spring; Landon built a handsome spring-house, and a boarding-house nearby, and started doing business with city folk; he also shipped bottled water, but went broke and sold to Capt Warren Corbin in 1871; the place continued to flourish; leased briefly to J. W. Morey (1890), but Mrs Corbin was proprietor from 1892 until she died in 1896; then George W. Squier until his death in 1925 (place also known as <u>Squier's Spring House</u>); it burned about this time, and was rebuilt on a smaller scale by Frank Robeyor; known as <u>Hotel D'Gomond</u> for a while, with C. L. Gomo proprietor; listed in 1930, not in '35;

* * *

"He (i.e., Corbin) was an enterprising and successful owner-operator, and his Iodine Spring House became famous for its hospitality and beautiful location. To ensure the convenience of guests...(he) bought half interest in the Stage line from Burlington to Grand Isle, making sure that passengers would find his place. Also he was captain of the steamer 'A. Williams' from 1869-1873. This steamer...made regular stops at the Iodine Spring House dock in Keeler's Bay." (1)

* * *

1871: (a) <u>Iodine Spring House</u>, --* Beers);

1873, '75, '79, '80, '82, '87, '90: (a) as above, W. Corbin;

1892, '95: (a) as above, Mrs W. Corbin;

1898, 1901, '05, '08, '13, '16, '20: (a) as above, G. W. Squier.

(182b) <u>South Hero</u>.

1783: a tavern, <u>Col Ebenezer Allen</u>; first cousin of Ira and Ethan, and a hero of the French and Indian, and Revolutionary, Wars; kept a public house and ferry at the south end of the island (now Allen's Point) until 1800, when he moved to Burlington and opened a tavern there (1); his son Timothy may have carried on for a while; Swift says that he was "in many ways...the direct antithesis of Ethan Allen. The two were great friends, however, and it was Ebenezer whom Ethan had been visiting in South Hero the night he became ill and died" (2); Allen also entertained Prince Edward, later Duke of Kent, "with a numerous suite" in 1793; (1)

c. 1795: a tavern, <u>Thomas Dixon</u>; on the southwest corner at the "Corners" in South Hero (where South St intersects Rte 2), until his death in 1823; the place burned shortly before 1800, but was rebuilt "a bit further south from the 'corner'" (1); his widow kept the place a few more years after he died; it became the <u>Island House/South Hero Inn</u>, in continuous use until the present time (see below); National Register of Historic Places;

"...Dixon hoped to cater to the travelers crossing by way of the Sand-Bar on their way to Montreal and Quebec...His Tavern also held a distinctive place in the community. It was a place of hospitality, warmth and good cheer...a gathering place for the exchange of outside news and local gossip...a place for the cold and tired traveler, to the driver with his herd of cattle or team going to market... and much rum was consumed to ward off the 'evil spirits'...however drunkenness was much disapproved and rarely seen." (1)

* * *

1807: a tavern, <u>Alexander Phelps</u>; (licenses issued, 1807-18, according to Stratton, (1) who searched for the years 1806-21); location unknown;

1808: a tavern, <u>Richard Mott</u> (licenses issued for the years 1808-21, see above; also 1825, '26, '28, State Archives);

Note: tavern licenses also to Lewis Mott, 1830; Horace Lamphear, 1826; and Eli B. Hungerford, 1829, locations unknown;

1829: (b) Island House; a blacksmith, Helmer Kent had built a large stone building, of Isle La Motte marble, on the Dixon site at the "Corners"; this was "a famous halting place for many years" (1); tavern license, 1826, '30; became the South Hero Inn about 1915, continued until very recently (i.e., until nearly 1980); longest continuously operating inn in the Islands; this is #1 in the South Hero Village Historic District, VDHP 0705-47;

* * *

"In the early days...much trading was done with the Montreal market. The farmers...when the lake froze...would load their wagons and start on perhaps a month's trip to and from Montreal. ...the Island House became a popular stopping over place for these travelers. To accommodate them, bunks were built against the downstairs walls and the men used their own fur robes for covering. If no bunks were left for late arrivals, they rolled themselves in covers and slept on the floor. There was a huge box stove for heat. Later as the Stages took to running between Plattsburgh and Burlington across the ice, they would meet at the Island House for dinner." (1)

* * *

Place sold to James Conro in 1844; owners since then are: Gideon H. and H. I. Rice, 1850-70; Clark S. Keeler, 1870-93; Frederic F. Allen, 1893-1914; Lillian Axtell, 1914-19; Mina Griswold, 1919-25; Raymond Mooney, 1925-46; John M. Rooks, 1946-47. Of these, Mrs Axtell made many improvements and added cottages, and the name was changed to the South Hero Inn in this period; (1)

1855, '56: (a) --, H. I. Rice and Co;

1857: (a) hotel, G. H. and H. I. Rice* (Walling; this is the Island House);

1870: (a) Island House, C. S. Keeler;

1871: (a) as above* (Beers);

1873, '75, '79, '80, '82, '87: (a) as above;

1890, '92, '95: (a) as above, Mrs Kibbe;

1898, 1901, '05, '08, '11, '13: (a) as above, F. F. Allen;

1900: Phelps House, Benajah Phelps; built next to the old toll-house at the Sand Bar Bridge, South Hero, close to the present Sand Bar Restaurant, by Phelps, who had been toll-keeper since 1890, before that PM at Keeler's Bay; Phelps died in 1919, place sold in 1923 to Mr and Mrs George Phelps, who changed the name to Sand-Bar Inn; see photo; building moved and renovated in 1938; this is VDHP 0705-1; still operating as Sand Bar Motor Inn and Restaurant;

1916, '20: (a) South Hero Inn, Robinson and Axtell (former Island House); see photo, next page;

1925: (a) as above, Ashley Hoag; (b) Sand Bar Inn, George Phelps (former Phelps House); both still listed in 1968.

* * *

References

(1) Allan L. Stratton, History of the South Heroe Island being the towns of South Hero and Grand Isle, Vermont (Burlington: Queen City Pr., 1980).

508

Greene Pr., 1977).

Sand Bar Inn

South Hero Inn

* * *

(183) **Springfield** (Windsor).

Springfield's tavern history is complicated, partly because there were a great many taverns here; and partly because there are available five sources (see references). Each of these is useful, of course, but there are contradictions; and in addition, taverns are sometimes described in terms which make it difficult to match them up (especially for someone not a native, writing in 1988).

(183a) <u>Black River</u>. (shown on most later maps as Goulds Mills; PO from 1866-67).

According to Baker, there were two early taverns here: "A hostelry of much repute...at Morris Mills, afterwards Gould's Mills, at an early date by Jotham White...Oliver Fairbanks kept a tavern about 1793 at the same settlement. He also had a sawmill and gristmill. A tavern at this place was carried off by high water...". (1)

* * *

(183b) <u>North Springfield</u>.

It is very difficult to match up the places mentioned in Baker with those found in the other sources. This section will therefore start with two quotations from Baker's book, followed by the list of places established from the other sources, with comments as appropriate.

* * *

"There was always at least one hotel in North Springfield. The building known as the D. J. Boynton house was the first tavern in the village; it formerly stood on the corner where Will Fuller now lives (i.e., 1922, ref 1). It was built about 1800 and here the Indians used to stop and have their dances before the immense fireplace in the dining room.

In 1821 a house was built by Joel Griswold on the corner of Main street and the road to Kendrick's Corners over the plain. This was kept as a tavern, was burned and rebuilt by Abel Brown, and was burned a second time when occupied by Isaac Gregory, who also kept a store there. The famous Joel Griswold tavern, now standing, a large brick house afterwards occupied by Wayland Bryant, was built about 1839. It was kept as a strictly temperance house." (1)

* * *

"July 4, 1844, in which year the town voted not to license any house of public entertainment to sell intoxicating liquor, there was held a large temperance celebration at the Griswold tavern. In 1816 the town's population was about 2,700 and there were six taverns in operation. A few years later than this it was told as an evidence of the prosperity of the town that 16 hogsheads of rum were sold in one year from the old Springfield House, besides brandy and other liquors. Every store at one time sold drams and the other hotels were by no means kept on temperance principles." (1)

* * *

c. 1800:   a tavern (and store), <u>John Griswold</u>; in the first framed house in town, occupied by Mrs Knight in 1883 (Child); a little north of the center of the village; (a Mrs I. Knight is shown on the 1869 Beers at the appropriate location);

(?):   a tavern,--; first in North Springfield, "on the corner where Sylvanus Newhall lived" (i.e., 1895, ref 2); there is an S. Newhall on the 1869 Beers;

1849:   --, <u>Isaac Gregory</u> (NEMU Dir; mentioned in Baker as occupying the original <u>Joel Griswold</u> tavern); --, Joel Griswold (NEMU Dir; a temperance house; this is presumably the second ("famous") <u>Joel Griswold</u> tavern referred to by Baker, ref 1);

1855:   hotel, --* (Hosea Doten).

(183c) <u>Outside the Villages</u>.

c. 1762:   a tavern, <u>Simon Stevens</u>; who came in 1762, died in 1817; one of the first two taverns in town, on the "present" poor farm site (i.e., 1895, ref 2); the town farm is shown in School District 3, north of Springfield, on the 1869 Beers; almanac listings, 1771-1822;

1777:   a tavern (and store), <u>Roger Bates</u>; a Scotsman who came in this year, bought a farm long known as the Christopher Ellis place, in the Eureka district, from Joseph Little, an old pioneer; (1) Bates kept this tavern until 1797, selling then to Joseph Ellis;

(?):   a tavern, <u>Phineas White</u>; where Henry Burr now lives (i.e., 1895, ref 2) in the "Hardscrabble" district, the four corners in School District 10, where the Christadelphia church is now (1988);

c. 1790:   a tavern, <u>Ebenezer Fletcher</u>; at Parker Hill; VDHP 1418-13, the Eldridge home in 1973; about one-half mile north of the two places listed next;

(?):   a tavern, Leonard Walker; at an early day on Parker Hill, in the southern part of town, on the county road from Bellows Falls through Springfield and Weathersfield, to Windsor; area named for Isaac Parker, who settled here about 1790; Walker married his daughter, kept tavern many years; first Masonic lodge meetings held here; still standing;

(?):   a tavern, Leonard "King" Parker; also at an early day, on Parker Hill; Leonard Parker built the house where Leon Cutler lived in 1922, next door to the old Universalist church, kept a tavern for a long time; Luther Hammond was the last landlord here; still standing; (1)

* * *

"For many years the little old bar where they dealt out New England rum at three cents per glass stood in the southeast room of the house. The dance hall was not changed until a few years ago (i.e., a few years before 1922). A daughter of Leonard Parker, named Betsey, married Charles Holt, and they remained with her parents at the tavern for 25 years, when Mr Holt...moved...". (1)

* * *

(?):   a tavern, --; in the Eureka district, on a corner of the Hubbard farm; "the famous Wells and Newell store...was built in 1790 or a bit earlier...Here Ashabel Wells kept store...and a little later it was kept by Joseph Selden. A tavern, a courtroom and a jail were in the same building..."; (1)

(?):   Gaylord Tavern (and store), Capt James Martin; before 1787, at the intersection of Eureka St and the Crown Point Road, in the Eureka district east of Springfield, where the first settlement was made (3); Martin died young, and his widow married Moses Gaylord, with the tavern continuing as the Gaylord Tavern. Her second husband ran off with her money, however, and she died without heirs. The estate came to the town, and the Gaylord Fund has helped the Springfield schools ever since. Part of the old tavern is an ell of a home on Woodbury Road; and the old Springfield House (see below) was a partial reproduction of the Gaylord Tavern, on a larger scale. (Note: certain of these details are contradicted in Baker (1); an excerpt from this book appears below).

* * *

"The building was 40 feet square with a basement and windows in the gable roof. Only one room was completely finished. The upper part was used for dancing. In many of the old taverns the lower floor alone was partitioned off into rooms, and the second story was all one room. Numerous beds were arranged in this apartment and the only privacy granted travelers and guests was afforded by the hanging of sheets and chintz or other convenient things between the beds. Mr Gaylord was known as Captain Esquire. He was town clerk and a Tory at heart. After his death his wife married James Martin, who kept the tavern in 1790." (ref 1, emphasis added).

* * *

1789:   a tavern, Whitford Gill; (almanacs, 1807-1816); in Spencer Hollow on the farm now owned by John R. Gill (i.e., 1895, ref 2); this is the place mentioned by Barney as being on the Connecticut River road, which burned in 1938, Dorr Kendall owner at the time (4); the Dan O. Gill homestead is shown in the appropriate place on the 1869 Beers; operated in 1820 by James Gill Jr (James Whipple Jr, according to Baker, who says that James Whipple Sr and his son leased "of General Morris the farm and tavern so well known as the Dan O. Gill homestead on the Connecticut River. This tavern was built in 1789 by Whitford Gill." (1) Baker also refers to "a tavern in Spencer Hollow on the farm afterwards owned by John R. Gill."

(?):   Note: there are two other taverns referred to in Baker that do not appear to match up with any of those mentioned in the other sources, and these are listed immediately below.

(1) "The house now occupied by Arthur Whitcomb on the Arms farm (i.e., 1922) was a tavern when the Crown Point road ran past the place. The main part of the house was of the original tavern, the old ell having been torn away and rebuilt. The house was built by John Walker..."

(2) "For many years the large building on the farm so recently owned by Allen Brown in West Springfield was kept as a tavern by Moses and Jim Bates. The bar where toddy was passed out was kept intact until Finns, the present owners, purchased the property...".

(183d) Springfield.

(?):   Wales Tavern, --; "previous to 1810, when the first tavern on the present hotel location was erected (i.e., the first tavern on the later Springfield House location), there was kept a tavern in the building just below the library. Mr Sparrow's block was the main building...(tavern) sold separately from the main building about 1832...known generally as the 'Wales Tavern' and was kept by Daniel Darrah as early as 1802"; (1)

(?):   a tavern, Lester Fling; "on the common where Walker Newton's home stands" (i.e., 1895, ref 2); later James McAlister; probably the first hotel in the village; the common is shown on the 1869 Beers, and an M. W. Newton nearby;

(?):   a hotel, --; kept by the "Browns" on Seminary Hill (2); this is Park St Hill, in Springfield village, northwest quadrant; operating in 1816;

(?):   a tavern, Jonathan Williams; in the central village where George O. Henry lived in 1891 (5); building gone;

* * *

"In 1800 Col Jonathan Williams built so much of the tavern house as ran east and west on Main street, so long known as Black River Hotel and Springfield House. Later he built the house on the corner of South and Clinton streets, known as the 'Williams Tavern,' where he and afterwards his son, Luke, kept tavern. The Williams tavern was more sumptuous than most at that time...". (1) Col Moses Fairbanks was proprietor in 1815.

There is disagreement between Hubbard and Dartt (ref 2) and Aldrich and Holmes (ref 5) on the long list of later proprietors and landlords. Aldrich and Holmes have Horace Hall, 1821, who leased it to various, including Justus Brooks, George Kimball, Russell Burke and Edmond Durrin; only the latter two are listed by Hubbard and Dartt, but they have David Oakes; then Benjamin Sawyer in 1835 for 10 years on both lists; D. D. Winchester, H. H. Mason, Frederick Barnet, Jonas B. Spencer, and George O. Henry on the Aldrich-Holmes list;

Hubbard and Dartt have several others between Sawyer and Henry: Hamlin Whitmore, Josiah Spencer, D. C. Gibbs, Fale and Eaton, Moses F. Chase, Edward R. Backus and Francis Long. The place was bought by George O. Henry in 1867, who ran it as a strict temperance house and "clearly demonstrated the fact that a hotel can be kept in the best manner and made to pay without the sale of intoxicating drink" (2); Henry sold to a syndicate in 1884, and the managers in the next few years were - Conrad, Frank Barney Jr and W. F. Milner; the place was torn down in 1891 to make way for the Adnabrown (see below);

1849:   (a) Black River Hotel , H. H. Mason (NEMU Dir);

1855:   (a) as above, --* (Hosea Doten);

1869:   (a) Springfield House, George O. Henry* (Beers; same as the Black River);

1870, '73, '79, '80, '83 (Child):   (a) as above; (see photo, next page);

Springfield House

1887, '90, '92: (a) as above, W. F. Miner; (shown on an 1889 birdseye view of the village, ref 6);

1892: (b) Adnabrown Hotel, Eddy and Davis; built on the site of the old Springfield House, which was razed in 1891, under the leadership of Adna Brown, leading Springfield businessman; a first-class commercial hotel for a number of years, entered into a decline in the 1930s; burned on January 1, 1961, site now occupied by the Vermont National Bank and stores;

* * *

"According to legend there was a very fine, and entirely illegal, bar located in the cellar for many years. Perhaps because of this, but certainly because of the excellent table the hotel set, until the coming of the automobile it was a favorite place for traveling salesmen to tie up for the night or for weekends." (4)

* * *

1895: (b) Adnabrown Hotel, Eddy and Davis;

1898, 1901, '05, '08, '13: (b) as above, J. H. Hart;

1900: (b) Adnabrown Hotel, --* (Sanborn; see photo, next page); a place called the Morrill Hotel, on the east side of Main St near the Square, is also shown;

1905: Windsor Tavern, H. P. Wyman* (Sanborn, in the Tontine block, corner of Main and Summer Sts, on the square); both the Adnabrown and the Morrill are also shown on Sanborn for this year;

1910: (b) Adnabrown, and the Morrill on Sanborn; the Windsor has disappeared; and there is a place called the Hillside Inn, on Summer St near Town Square;

1911: (b) as above, --;

1916: (b) as above, John H. Hart (VPB);

1920: (b) as above, O. C. Miller;

1921: (b) Adnabrown, and the Morrill, on Sanborn; the Hillside has disappeared; and by 1928 the Morrill has become offices;

1925: (b) as above, C. H. Parker; listed in 1955.

Note: the <u>Hartness House Inn</u> operates in a mansion built in 1904 for James Hartness, governor of Vermont (1920-22), industrialist, inventor and pilot (one of the first hundred in the U.S.); the mansion was converted to an inn in 1954, still operating; National Register of Historic Places, VDHP 1418-35.

Note: the assistance of Richard Whitcomb is gratefully acknowledged.

* * *

Adnabrown Hotel

References

(1) M. Eva Baker, Folklore of Springfield, Vermont (Springfield: The Altrurian Club, Springfield Pr., 1922).

(2) Charles H. Hubbard and Justus Dartt, History of the Town of Springfield, Vermont, 1752-1895 (Boston: G. H. Walker, 1895).

(3) Mary W. Ellis, Eureka: the First Village in Springfield, Vermont (Springfield: Historical Committee of Miller Art Ctr; Springfield Pr., 1959).

(4) Keith R. Barney, The History of Springfield, Vermont (Springfield: William L. Bryant Fndn, 1972). 1972.

(5) Lewis C. Aldrich and Frank R. Holmes, History of Windsor County, Vermont (Syracuse: D. Mason, 1891).

(6) J. Kevin Graffagnino, Vermont in the Victorian Age (Bennington: Vermont Heritage Press, 1985).

* * *

(184) **Stamford** (Bennington).

(184a) <u>Stamford</u>.

1780s: a tavern, <u>William Clark</u>; first in town (Hemenway);

1785: <u>Brace tavern</u>, --; almanac, location unknown;

c. 1810: (a) <u>Wilmarth Hotel</u>, --; on the west side of Rte 8 at intersection of Old County Road; known as the <u>Paradise Hotel</u> in the 1890s, now a private home (Paradise Farm, VDHP 0214-17);

1822: tavern licenses to James Millard and Loring Richmond, locations unknown;

c. 1830:   a tavern, --; now an apartment house (VDHP 0214-01);

1849:   --, W. Houghton (NEMU Dir);

c. 1850: an inn, --; "possibly an inn at one time," according to the VDHP (0214-08, the Call home in 1977);

1856:   (a) --, I. L. Wilmarth;

1869:   (a) a hotel, A. W. Wilmarth* (Beers);

1870, '75:   (a) Wilmarth House, A. W. Wilmarth;

1873:   (a) as above (Vt Dir); (b) State Line House, Niles and Belding (see also under Shaftsbury);

1880:   (a) as above, Smith and Robinson;

1880:   (a) as above, Henry L. Smith (Child); (b) as above, Sylvester Sherman (Child; see also under Shaftsbury);

1883, '87, '92, '95:   (a) as above, Fred Paradise; see photo;

Paradise House

1888:   (a) Paradise House, Fred Mather (Boston and Maine guide);

1898, 1901, '05, '08, '13:   (a) Paradise House, Fred Paradise; now offices;

Note: the 1903 State Board of Agriculture guide lists both Paradise House and Stamford House, which is a puzzle.

* * *

(185) **Stannard** (Caledonia).

(185a) Stannard. No listings found.

* * *

(186) **Starksboro** (Addison).

(186a) <u>South Starksboro</u>. PO from 1857-1902.

1871:   --, F. B. Ross* (Beers);

(?):   a hotel, --; in the Jerusalem district, shown on the Vermont Road Atlas as east of South Starksboro; Swift says there was once a hotel here without providing any more information. (1)

(186b) <u>Starksboro</u>.

(?):   a hotel, <u>Elisha Kellogg</u>; in a house owned c. 1882 by D. L. Dike (Child); this place probably corresponds to one of the buildings listed by VDHP, below); Smith describes this place as being on the farm "originally settled by Capt David Kellogg, now Ezra C. Dike"; (2)

(?):   <u>Tavern Stand</u>, Abel Wentworth; now the home of Rena Tobin (i.e., 1975); this is bldg #16 in the Starksboro Historic District, VDHP 0119-1, at the intersection of Rte 116 and Brown Hill Rd;

(?):   a hotel, --; second story added late in the 19th century; now owned by Nora Wedge; VDHP 0119-1, #14;

(?):   an inn, --; off Village Hill Road, north of the village; the "old Asa Fuller homestead"; built in the early 19th century, a stage-coach stop on the road to Richmond; present Harley Brace place; VDHP 0119-24;

(?):   an inn, <u>George Bidwell</u>; he was one of the first two settlers in 1787; his place was open as an inn from about 1795 until about 1820; "east of where the buildings now are"; (2)

1849:   --, R. C. Taft (NEMU Dir);

1855:   --, S. Wentworth;

1856:   --, Mrs S. Wentworth;

1857:   a hotel, <u>S. Wentworth</u>* (Walling); Note: Smith refers to a tavern in the village, kept by Asahel Wentworth, "where the widow Strong now lives" (i.e., 1886) (2); this place (<u>Wentworth's</u>) and the <u>Brooks hotel</u> (below) are thus probably the same place, since the <u>Brooks hotel</u> is also described as being now occupied by a Mrs Sarah A. Strong;

1873, '79:   <u>Green Mountain House</u>, J. Kinsley;

Traveler's Inn

516

1879, '80:   (a) <u>Village Inn</u>, J. L. Brooks; Smith says that this place was opened by Brooks "about nine years ago" (i.e., 9 years before 1886, ref 2); and that for some time before that, there had been no hotel in town; perhaps the Wentworth place closed and was re-opened by Brooks; or burned and was replaced by a new building;

1883:   <u>Starksboro Hotel</u>, Freeman J. James (probably the same place);

1887, '92, '95, '98, 1905, '08:   (a) as above, Mrs F. J. James;

1911, '13, '20, '25:   (a) as above, F. M. Walston; listed as <u>Traveler's Inn</u>, Frank M. Walston, 1916 VPB; also 1923 VPB with Mrs Ella J. Watson (?); see photo.

* * *

References

(1) Esther M. Swift, Vermont Place-Names: Footprints in History (Brattleboro: Stephen Greene Pr., 1977).
(2) Henry P. Smith, History of Addison County, Vermont (Syracuse: D. Mason, 1886).

* * *

(187) **Stockbridge** (Windsor).

(187a) <u>Gaysville</u>.

1849:   --, Daniel Gay (NEMU Dir); --, S. Gilson (NEMU Dir); location unknown, could be Stockbridge, or outside the villages;

1855:   <u>Durkee's Hotel</u>, --* (Hosea Doten map; in the village); a hotel, L. B. Morey* (Hosea Doten; on the main road a little south of Gaysville village); also in Walton for this year;

1856:   --, D. Strong (location unknown);

1870, '75, '79, '83 (Child), '87, '90, '92, '95, '98:   <u>Clay's Hotel</u>, J. M. Clay; he died in 1901, at which time he had run the hotel for 25 years, except for the last three, when he leased it (1); the place burned on April 10, 1910 (fire photo, ref 1).

(187b) <u>Stockbridge</u>.

c. 1800:   a hotel, --; "a hotel through most of the 19th century...on stage road to Rochester" (VDHP 1419-6, now a private home);

1812:   <u>Keys and Stevens tavern</u>, --; almanac, location unknown;

1849:   --, H. D. Morgan (NEMU Dir); shown as store and PO on 1869 Beers;

1855:   (a) hotel, <u>T. S. Hubbard</u>* (Hosea Doten);

1869:   (a) --, J. Whitcomb* (Beers; became <u>Whitcomb's Hotel</u>, same site as 1855 Hosea Doten);

1873, '75, '79, '80: --, D. W. Johnson;

1883:   --, A. W. Chamberlain;

1887, '90, '92: (a) <u>Whitcomb's Hotel</u>, E. H. Whitcomb; (b) <u>Stockbridge House</u>, E. W. Clark (Vt Dir);

1895: --, E. H. Whitcomb (probably Whitcomb's Hotel);

1898, 1901: Sawyer House, J. B. Sawyer; --, E. W. Clark; it is not clear which of these is Whitcomb's, which the Stockbridge House (see photo); Clark probably still has the latter, but managers moved around a lot;

1911: --, P. W. Green;

1913, '20: (b) as above, P. W. Green; who bought it in 1906. (1)

* * *

References

(1) Ramona Blackmer et al., A Picture History of Stockbridge/Gaysville, 1761-1976 (Bethel: Spaulding Pr. for the Bicentennial Committee, 1976?).

Stockbridge House

* * *

(188) **Stowe** (Lamoille).

(188a) Moscow.

1902: Pleasant View House, -- (CVRR booklet; see photo);

1916: as above, O. S. Smith (VPB).

(188b) Mt Mansfield.

1849: Halfway House, Joseph Robinson (NEMU Dir);

* * *

"In 1857 Mr Bingham induced the town of Stowe to construct a road half way up the east side of the mountain. Near a large cold spring...a small building was erected for a caretaker's family and a sizable barn for saddle ponies...called the Halfway House. From this house the summit was reached by riding ponies over a trail. After the completion of a carriage road to the summit, the business at the Halfway House vanished and the buildings were abandoned...

Mr Bingham then realized the necessity of having land on the summit ...and the University

518

deeded him twenty acres..." (he and another large land-owner had previously given the University of Vermont all land above the tree line) "...To construct the Summit House timbers were borne on the backs of men from Stevensville up the west side of the mountain...opened in 1858...at the age of seventy-five years it is still in use as the hotel on the summit." (1)

Note: there seems to be a discrepancy here, between the date given by Bigelow for the construction of the Halfway House (c. 1857, ref 1) and the date given in the New England Mercantile Union Directory. It does not seem likely that the NEMU Dir would list a place that had not yet been built. There was another Halfway House on the west side of the mountain, in Underhill.

A carriage road from Halfway House to the Summit House was finished in 1870; this was converted into an automobile road in the 1920s.

* * *

Pleasant View House (Vermont Historical Society)

1883: (a) Summit House, E. C. Bailey (Child); see photo;

1890: (a) as above, William P. Bailey;

1898: (a) as above, W. F. Churchill;

1905, '08, '11: (a) as above, Walter M. Adams;

1913: (a) as above; Adams also PM;

1916, '20:   (a) as above;

1923: Mt Mansfield House, C. A. Riley (VPB);

1925: (a) as above, Mt Mansfield Hotel Co; this Summit House was the last survivor of a series of "summit houses" in the 1860-90 period: Ascutney, Camel's Hump, Killington, and Snake Mountain among them (see Chapter V).

(188c) Stowe.

c. 1794:   a tavern, Oliver Luce; first settler and first tavern-keeper, his sign a large white ball; (1)

c. 1798:   a hotel, Nathan Robinson; came in 1798, bought from Amasa Marshall "what is now known as the Frank V. Smith place, about a mile above the village toward

519

Morristown" (i.e., 1934, ref 1); for many years";

* * *

Probably the same as a place surveyed by the Vermont Division of Historic Preservation (# 0806-26), said to have been built about 1830, and to have served as a stage stop for most of the 19th century on the route to Morrisville. On the west side of the junction of Rte 100 and TH #4, owned by C. Lovejoy in 1878; a private home in 1981; known only as "The Tavern."

* * *

"That was rather a pretentious house for those times. It was built of logs 40 x 20 feet in dimenson, one story high, and had two rooms. The kitchen had one bed; the 'square room' had three. By climbing a ladder one went 'above,' where there were three more beds. The house was heated by an immense stone fire place which would take in logs six feet long; and before which the guests would nightly gather with the neighbors who always came in to hear the news." (1)

* * *

Summit House (Special Collections, UVM)

1803: a hotel, Maj Nehemiah Perkins; tavern license, 1817-32; kept a hotel in a 2-story brick house that he built, now the town farm (i.e., 1934, ref 1); "In 1820 he exchanged a yoke of oxen for a cookstove, the first one to be used in town";

1811: a tavern, Samuel Dutton; in "center village," expanded to an inn in 1814, by Nathaniel Butts; on the site of the later Mt Mansfield Hotel;

1815: a tavern, Calvin Sartle; tavern license, 1817-25; on the site of the hotel later known as the Isham House in the lower village (see below);

1817: Raymond Hotel, Col Asahel Raymond; in the North village; he ran it as a store and hotel initially; sold the store and ran the hotel until he died in 1849; building later part of the Mt

Mansfield Hotel;

Note: tavern licenses to Daniel Lathrop, 1830, Estey Russell, 1820-23;

1845:   (a) Isham House, Thomas Downer; builder and first landlord, in the lower village; subsequent owners were Daniel Goodrich, Westley Matthews, Edward Isham, and Daniel Isham. After Daniel's death, kept by Mrs Isham and her daughters; Leslie Peterson the last occupant, and the place burned in 1933;

1849:   Union Hall, N. B. Raymnond (NEMU Dir); --, Moses L. Duncan (NEMU Dir);

1850:   (b) Mansfield House, Stillman Churchill; who traded his farm (the house on which was later known as "The Fountain") for Peter Lovejoy's house in the village, built in the late 1820s-early 1830s; Churchill added two brick wings, a dance hall and a double porch, called it the Mansfield House (not to be confused with the Mt Mansfield Hotel, see below); lost the property to W. H. H. Bingham;

1856:   --, George Raymond (this is the old Raymond Hotel, later moved and made into a wing of the Mt Mansfield Hotel); (a) --, Daniel Goodrich (this is the Isham House);

1859:   the Walling map shows two hotels, G. Raymond and Bingham's, both on the south side of Main St in the upper village; and the D. Goodrich Hotel (Isham's) in the lower village;

1864:   (c) Mt Mansfield Hotel, Mt Mansfield Hotel Company (W. H. H. Bingham and 9 others; see photo);

"...the Raymond House was moved and attached as an ell...and by spring (i.e., 1864) a hotel with 200 roooms with a spacious lobby and parlors was complete. The new hotel was dedicated with an opening ball on June 24, 1864. N. P. Keeler was the first landlord and secured the then famous 'Hall's Band' of Boston to furnish music for the opening ball, which undoubtedly was the most brilliant and distinguished society event ever held in Stowe...". (1)

* * *

Visitors would leave the Vermont Central Railroad at Waterbury and proceed 10 miles by stage to Stowe; if one left New York at midday on the Montreal Express, one would arive at White River Junction at midnight and at Waterbury at 3:22 A.M., with the stage ride still ahead.

* * *

Another hundred rooms were added later, guests were attracted from all over the east; sold to Col E. C. Bailey in 1878, who became sole owner of the Mt Mansfield Hotel, the old Mansfield House, the Halfway House, the Summit House, and a small house called the Notch House (see photo) in Smuggler's Notch, at the end of the carriage road into the Notch at that time. Various managers and owners, until Silas Gurney acquired it in 1888; it burned to the ground on Oct 4, 1889.

After the fire, the remaining properties were owned by William P. Bailey, Col E. C. Bailey's son; the Mansfield House became the Brick Hotel, and both this place and the Summit House were run by him for a while; Mark Lovejoy bought the Brick Hotel in 1893, renamed it the Green Mountain Inn; various owners sub- sequently, the only inn in Stowe in 1934; (1) W. F. Churchill bought the Summit House, and sold it a few years later to Walter Adams, who ran it until he sold to the present corporation (i.e., 1934) in 1919; listed in Walton in 1930;

1870, '75:   (a) Isham's Hotel, Daniel Isham; (c) Mount Mansfield Hotel, W. H. H. Bingham (Daniel Hall in Vt Dir);

1878:   (a) Isham's Hotel, --* (Beers); (c) Mt Mansfield Hotel, --* (Beers);

Mt Mansfield Hotel (Special Collections, UVM)

Notch House (Special Collections, UVM)

1879, '80:   (c) as above, E. C. Bailey;

1883:   (a) as above, Mrs F. D. Isham (Child); (c) as above; --, W. A. Foss (Vt Dir);

1887:   (b) <u>Brick Hotel</u>, G. N. Dike (the old <u>Mansfield House</u>; became the <u>Green Mountain Inn</u>); (c) as above, George Doolittle (burned in 1889);

1888:   (b) <u>Green Mountain Inn</u>, E. N. Webster; <u>Summit House</u>, W. M. Adams; <u>Adams House</u>, W. M. Adams (Boston and Maine guide);

522

1890:   (b) as above, George N. Dyke;

1892, '95:   (b) as above;

1898:   (b) Green Mountain Inn, M. C. Lovejoy; also shown on Sanborn map, on the south side of Main St, just past the Mt Mansfield trolley station;

Green Mountain Inn (Vermont Historical Society)

1902:   (b) as above; see photo;

1905, '08:   (b) as above, Walter M. Adams (also on 1905 Sanborn);

1911:   (b) as above, A. H. Currie; Lake Mansfield Trout Club, --; a private fishing lodge, summers only; Oliver Luce first president, place still in operation;

1913:   (b) as above, --;

1916:   (b) as above, L. B. Bamforth; also on Sanborn for 1912, 1926;

1920:   (b) as above, A. A. and D. E. Hunter; (d) Lower Village Hotel, Roy Peterson;

1923:   The Lodge, Joseph T. Lance; at the entrance to Smuggler's Notch on the road to Jeffersonville; main building, and a tent colony for hikers; opened in 1923;

1925:   (b) as above, --; (d) as above;

1927:   The Fountain, Mrs W. C. Norcross; guest house, later operated by Zelta Norcross, now a bed-and-breakfast place; in an 1825 building built by the first couple to be married in Stowe.

Note: the assistance of Doris Hunter, Stowe Historical Society, and Zelta M. Norcross is gratefully acknowledged.

* * *

References

(1) Walter J. Bigelow, History of Stowe, Vermont (from 1763 to 1934) (Hartford, 1934).

* * *

(189) **Strafford** (Orange).

(189a) Copperas Hill. No listings found.

(189b) South Strafford.

1818:   (a) Barrett House, Joseph Barrett; veteran of the War of 1812, bought a small house, kept improving it; kept by his son Hiram, 1835-38;

1849:   --, E. St Clair (NEMU Dir); St Clair had the place until at least 1858; this is the Barrett House;

1870, '73, '75, '80, '87:   (b) Soule's Hotel, J. M. Soule (opened in 1866); this is still the Barrett House;

1877:   (b) as above* (Beers);

1888, '90, '92, '95, '98, 1901, '02, '05: (c) Barrett House, J.E. Kendall;

1910, '13, '16: (c) as above, T. G. (F.?) Dearborn;

1920:   --, H. L. Stamford;

1925:   Cottage Inn, Mrs Amelia Root; (boarding-house).

(189c) Strafford.

(?):   a hotel,--; kept for many years by the son of Lt Frederick Smith, an original settler, Revolutionary War veteran, who came in 1768 (Child);

* * *

When Fred Smith became convinced that handling rum was an evil, he emptied all the kegs of liquor, kept a temperance house (aided by his son-in-law). (1)

* * *

1849:   --, F. Smith (NEMU Dir); location unknown;

1870, '73, '75, '80, '87, '88, '90:   (a) Hazelton's Hotel, H. C. Hazelton;

(?):   a hotel, Lucius Carpenter; Child says he kept it "for twelve years," dates not given; this is Hazelton's;

1877:   (a) as above* (Beers);

1892, '95, '98: (a) as above, Fred B. Hazelton;

1901:   Strafford House, Frank P. Merrill (Vt Dir); see photo, next page; probably the same as Hazelton's, above;

1902:   Strafford House, H. Silloway (CVRR booklet); he bought the place in 1901, ran it for many years; also stage driver until 1925;

1905:   --, Bert Silloway;

1911, '13, '20: --, H. B. Silloway.

Note: the assistance of Mrs Carrie R. Judd, Strafford Historical Society, is gratefully acknowledged.

* * *

References

(1) "Strafford Village Many Years Ago," Vermonter <u>25</u> (February 1920): 24-25.

Strafford House

* * *

(190) **Stratton** (Windham.

    (190a) <u>Stratton</u>.

      c. 1785:   first tavern, <u>Joseph Patch</u>;

      c. 1820:   <u>Torrey's Tavern</u>, Luther Torrey; came in 1820, died in 1851; tavern license, 1826-33;

* * *

On the road from Arlington to Stratton there was a stretch once known as "Nine Mile Woods," between the last settlers on the west side of the mountains and <u>Torrey's Tavern</u>, the first house near the road on the east. When liquor began to be preached against as sinful, "he (i.e., Torrey) laid aside his glass, took down his bar and sign and became thenceforth a farmer and lumberman." (Hemenway).

Note: tavern licenses to Jonathan Phillips, 1825-27; Hudson Grout, 1829; and Ebenezer Allen, 1830, locations unknown;

    1849: --, Truman Wyman (NEMU Dir);

    1856: --, Cheselton Allen (location unknown);

    1856: (a) hotel, <u>F. Wyman</u>* (McClellan map);

    1869: (a) hotel, <u>F. Wyman</u>* (Beers; same site as above);

    1870: (a) <u>Stratton Hotel</u>, Freeman Wyman;

525

Stratton Hotel

1873, '75:　　(a) as above, Mrs F. Wyman;

1878:　--, W. Shepherd (Walton);

1879:　Ransom's Hotel, A. B. Ransom (Vt Dir; presumably same place as above);

1880:　Winslow (Hotel), A. B. Ransom;

1883:　(a) Stratton Hotel, Willard Sheppard (Vt Dir);

1887:　(a) as above, E. H. Willis; see photo, above.

* * *

(191) **Sudbury** (Rutland).

Includes Lake Hortonia, which lies partly in Hubbardton.

(191a) Sudbury. On the Crown Point road.

1801:　--, - Mills; first hotel in town, on the site of the later Hyde Hotel, about a mile south of Sudbury village on what was the main stage-coach road; this place was bought in 1801 by Pitt W. Hyde, formerly an inn-keeper in Hyde Park, Vt; (almanac, 1812; tavern licenses, 1817, '20 '22); Hyde was a stageline operator, Hyde Park was named for him; as the Hyde Manor/Hyde Hotel, this became one of the best known inns in New England, first as a stagecoach inn, later as a summer resort;

* * *

"Mr Hyde immediately made improvements, and it soon became, and still is, one of the most popular summer resorts in New England. It is located in a beautiful valley, and is 80 x 150 feet and five stories high, containing about ninety sleeping apartments, with a dining-room capable of seating at family tables, 200 guests...A three-story building, 46 x 60 feet, the lower floor of which is to be used as a concert hall or opera house, furnished with a very fine stage...has been erected this season (1881). The hotel is open from May until November, during which time it is thronged with guests." (Child; this description applies to the second Hyde hotel, see below).

* * *

Pitt Hyde died in 1823, and was succeeded by his son, James K. Hyde (tavern license, 1823); he died in 1870, and was in turn succeeded by his son, Arunah W. Hyde, who then added various recreational facilities, including what is thought to have been the second oldest golf course in the United States; the place burned in 1862 and was rebuilt in 1865; the annex referred to above burned in 1944. The place left the Hyde family ownership in the 1960s, operated until 1973 as "Top of the Season," but is not now operated as an inn; National Register of Historic Places;

c. 1790 (?): Sawyer Stand, John C. Sawyer; on road 4, at the corner of road 5; the "halfway house" from Brandon to Orwell, and a station on the old stage road from Vergennes to Whitehall (Child); there is a hotel shown on both the 1854 Scott map and the Beers at a four corners north of the village, apparently present Rte 30; Everest 1950s photo;

(?): a tavern, --; described as a possible inn, facing Rte 30 north of the village (ref 1, photo); it is possible that this is the Sawyer Stand, above;

Note: tavern license to H. T. Wheeler (Harry), 1817, '20-22, location unknown;

c. 1830: a tavern, --; became a store and PO by mid-century as a result of the temperance movement; #19 on the Town of Sudbury map, ref 2;

(?): a tavern, --; Keefe and Ritter say that this place, the home of the L. F. Smiths in 1978, on Rte 73, once stood in the village between present Noble and MacDonald homes, and was an inn; moved at the turn of the century;

Note: tavern license, Harry Wheeler, 1817, '21, '22, location unknown;

(?): Webster House, --; at the junction of Rtes 73 and 30, once a stage-coach hotel; (1) dance-hall on the second floor; now an apartment house on a farm known as the Rocky Knoll Cattle Company (i.e., 1978; photo, ref 1);

c. 1850: The Hortonia, --; well south of the village on Rte 30, overlooking Lake Hortonia; there is a quotation from a 1912 advertisement in ref 1; the place offered its own milk, butter, eggs, chicken, lamb, maple syrup, honey and vegetables, and was the place for those who put "comfort and rest before dress and display"; also known as the Mallory Inn; now vacant; #32 on the Town of Sudbury map; (2)

Note: Walton sometimes lists The Hortonia (Lake Hortonia, Sudbury) and the Silver Lake House (Leicester) under Brandon;

1849: --, J. K. Hyde (NEMU Dir);

1854: Hyde's Hotel, --* (Scott); hotel, --* (Scott); this second place is north of the village, at the same location as D. Sawyer on the 1869 Beers;

1856: --, James K. Hyde;

1869: hotel, A. W. Hyde* (Beers); --, D. Sawyer* (Beers; at the 1854 Scott hotel location, but no hotel indication here);

1870, '75, '79, '80: (a) Hyde's, A. W. Hyde; (b) Royal House, Royal W. Pitts (also store and PO; Pitts was PM, 1861-80);

1883, '87, '92, '95, '98, 1901, '05: (a) as above;

1903: Silver Lake House, Frank Chandler (SBA); see photo;

1908: (a) as above,--;

1911, '13, '15: (a) Hyde Manor, A. W. Hyde and son; see photo;

527

Silver Lake House

Hyde Manor Inn

1916, '17, '20, '23:   (a) as above; <u>Hortonia</u>, E. A. Mallory; the <u>Hortonia</u> was essentially an abandoned building for many years, but was partly razed recently, and the remainder rebuilt;

1916: <u>Silver Lake House</u>, Frank Chandler;

1925: (a) as above, J. K. Hyde (fourth generation; until 1973); <u>Hortonia</u>, Mrs E. A. Mallory (see photo).

* * *

References

(1)   Arthur Keefe and Josie Ritter, Sudbury, Vermont: A Pictorial Record (Sudbury: Sudbury Bicentennial Comm., 1978).
(2) Vermont Div. for Historic Preservation, Historic Architecture of Rutland County, Curtis B. Johnson, ed., Elsa Gilbertson, asst ed. (Montpelier: 1988).

The Hortonia

* * *

(192) **Sunderland** (Bennington).

(192a) <u>Sunderland</u>.

1777:   a tavern, --; stage-coach stop on the turnpike between the <u>Kelly Stand</u> and East Arlington, on Sunderland Rd north of Chiselville covered bridge, until 1841; probably the same as the <u>Bradley tavern</u>, listed in almanacs for 1785, 1796, as a stage stop on the Rutland-New York road; and listed as <u>Lockwood's tavern</u> in 1812; now the Hayden homestead (1973, VDHP 0215-4);

(?):   <u>Stage Coach Inn</u>, --; now a bed-and-breakfast known as the <u>Sycamore Inn</u>, about one-half mile south of the Sunderland Rd intersection with Rte 7A; may be the same as place above; building said to have been built 1774, by or for Ira Allen; tavern license, 1814; not clear when it became an inn, also known as Ethan Allen Farm, Ethan Allen Motor Lodge, Ethan Allen Inn; see photo;

Ethan Allan Lodge (Sycamore Inn)

1849:   --, E. H. Graves (NEMU Dir; location unknown);

1840s: <u>Kelly Stand</u>, J. W. Kelly/Kelley; built in the 1840s on the road from Stratton through Sunderland to East Arlington; "...(it) remained a place to stay overnight, have a trout supper or attend an occasional dance until near the World War I era, then it was left to deteriorate and hardly a trace can be found today." (1) There is a photo of a ticket issued by Kelley in 1866 which entitles the bearer to "Supper, admission to the Hall and Horse fed to hay during the night and 4 or 6 q'ts of oats at the option of the holder." Resch quotes Arlington historian James McCabe as holding the view that the name "stand" gave the place a better reputation than it deserved. (1) See photo.

* * *

"By noon we had covered twelve miles of the old turnpike and had reached 'Kelley Stand,' one of the old-time taverns, still doing some kind of hotel business in the midst of desolation, which yielded us a dinner excellent beyond our expectations. It seemed that 'Kelley Stand' possessed some little reputation for its unique lonesomeness, which brought a profitable number of summer boarders from even as far away as New York City, and now that the frosty fall mornings had come, another class had arrived to keep the business alive. For the woods for miles around were alive with a busy throng who sought far and wide for the ferns which grew so abundantly, picking them in great armfuls, and carrying them to the roadside to be packed and shipped to the cities... To these workers the deserted houses and barns are a boon, and, for a few weeks each fall, they camp in such as have sufficient roof remaining to shed the rain. A large force were camped in some houses near 'Kelley Stand' and the call for dinner brought them from all directions like hailstones in a summer storm." (2)

Kelly Stand
(Russell Vermontiana Collection, Canfield Free Library, Arlington)

1856: Kelly's hotel,--* (Rice and Hardwood map);

1869: hotel, --* (Beers; same site as above);

1870: --, John H. Lockey (Vt Dir);

1872: --, George Coulton;

1873, '75: (a) Summit House, C. Pratt; location unknown; in later listings, this place has an East Arlington PO address, which see;

1879, '81: (b) Green Mountain House, Lawrence Brothers (East Arlington PO, probably same as the Summit House);

1883: (b) as above, Jack Ross;

1892, '95, '98: (a) Summit House, Robert Lawler;

1887, '90, 1901:   (a) as above, R. Lawler (East Arlington PO);

1908:   (a) Summit House, --; Elmwood, --.

* * *

References

(1) Tyler Resch, Shires of Bennington (Bennington: Bennington Museum, 1975).
(2) Frederic J. Wood, The Turnpikes of New England (Boston: Marshall Jones Co, 1919), 275.

* * *

(193) **Sutton** (Caledonia).

Chartered as Billymead, kept this name postally until 1817.

(193a) Clark. At Sutton Depot, a PO from 1903-21. No listings found.

(193b) Sutton.

c. 1825:   a hotel, Stephen Eaton; tavern license, 1824-27; until 1846; where E. Roundy lived on road 26 about 1887 (Child);

Note: tavern licenses to Daniel Beckwith, 1822-26; Josiah Rawson, 1824-27; Stephen Gillman, James Way, 1822, '23, and Josiah Crane, 1827, locations unknown;

1849:   --, William Hutchinson; --, W. H. Gay; --, S. S. Shaw; --, J. and J. Q. Evans (all NEMU Dir; none of these locations known);

1858:   (a) hotel, C. Holman* (Walling);

1870:   --, Milton A. Campbell;

1873, '75, '80: (a) Sutton Hotel, R. Jenness;

1875:   (a) hotel, R. Jenness* (Beers; same site as on Walling, above);

1879, '83, '87, '90, '92:   (a) as above, Lucius J. Campbell (who was also PM, 1879-88);

1895, '98, 1901, '05: (a) as above, J. E. Wentworth;

1908:   (a) as above, --;

1911:   (a) as above, --.

* * *

(194) **Swanton** (Franklin).

There have been five postal villages in this town, but only Swanton is still operating. The offices were: (a) East Swanton/Greens Corners, both names used postally at different times; (b) Swanton village, also known as the "Falls"; (c) Swanton Center, on the "middle road" from St Albans to Highgate Falls; (d) Swanton Junction, between Swanton and St Albans on present Rte 7; (e) West Swanton, on Hog Island, including the Maquam shore (Maquam Bay) on Lake Champlain.

Hemenway lists taverns on what are referred to as the "east," "west," and "middle" roads. The west road is present Rte 7, more or less, and these taverns are listed below under Swanton Junction. The middle road is the direct road from St Albans to Highgate Falls, before the interstate cut it off a little north of St Albans; taverns on this road are listed under Swanton Center. It is not clear whether the east road is present Rte 105, or a road between Rte 105 and the middle road, but taverns listed in Hemenway for the east road are listed here under East Swanton/Greens Corners.

(194a) East Swanton/Greens Corners ("east road").

c. 1796: a tavern, William Green; until 1803, then Nathan Scofield, 1803; Paul E. Jackson, 1827-29 (tavern license, 1826); Joseph Butler, 1829-31 (tavern license, 1822); Asa Ordway, 1831-33; George Green, 1833-35 (tavern license, 1819, '21-24);

c. 1820: an inn, --; said to have been a stage stop in early days; Justin Smith place in 1982, near the southeast corner of Rte 105 and Fairfield Pond Rd; VDHP 0615-04.

(194b) Swanton (the "Falls").

1793: first tavern, Asa Holgate; listed in almanacs for 1807, 1810; where L. Lasell lived about 1882, near the park (Hemenway); until c. 1798, followed by his widow, 1798-1802; Theophilus Mansfield, 1802-c. 1821 (tavern license, 1817, '20); John R. Phelps, c. 1822; John Capron, 1823; Harrison Stevens, 1824 or 1825; Thomas Webster, 1826 (tavern license, 1824-26);

(?): Stearns Stand, --; (almanacs, 1812-1820); became Turrill's Hotel; stood near the large house built by C. H. Bullard; Ezra Jones about 1805; Nathaniel Stearns, 1812-25 (tavern license, 1817, '19, '21; a Widow Lucy Stearns has a tavern license, 1824); James Brown, 1825-26; Seth Rice, c. 1826-28 (license, 1826); Nelson Bullard, 1828-32 (license 1823); Calvin Perry, 1832-37 (license, 1830, '33); William Cain, 1837-41; Nelson Bullard, 1841-48; L. D. Turrill, 1845-58 (see below); burned in 1858 while Turrill had it;

1823: (a) a hotel, Ira and Erastus Church; tavern license to Ira, 1828; on the west side of the river, near the present Riviere Hotel; Ira Church, 1851-53; Mrs Ira Church, 1854; Stiles Faxon (see also under Eagle Hotel, c. 1825); William Keyes, 1855-65 (Keyes Hotel, see below); - Hammond, c. 1865-69; William Keyes again, 1869-72; J. I. Gibbs, 1872-74; bought by R. L. Barney in 1876, who "moved back the old building," put on additions, named it the Barney House; sold to Charles and William Pease, 1876; then A. Kellogg, 1878; E. A. Soules, who added a third floor in 1881, and named it the American House; J. F. Kelly, 1882 (see below);

1824: three taverns at the "Falls" (Hemenway, unnamed);

Note: tavern licenses, locations unknown, to John Keys, 1818; Samuel Bullard, 1819-24; Orra H. Willard, 1821; Charles Bullard, 1827-32; Abigail Bullard, 1825, '26; and Daniel Meigs, 1826;

c. 1825: (b) Eagle Hotel, Thomas Webster; at the corner of Grand Avenue and First St, where the library now stands; became the Central Hotel in 1866; after Webster, James Brown, c. 1827; Samuel Curtis, c. 1830 (license, 1826); Mrs Samuel Stevens, c. 1831; Lorenzo Perry, c. 1833; Daniel B. Marrin, c. 1835; Thomas Dimon, c. 1835; William Keyes, 1836; Samuel Stevens, 1837; Harry Asselstyne, 1838-41; William Cain, c. 1842; Homer E. Loveland, 1844-47; Mrs Samuel Stevens, 1847; Ward Barney, 1848; Stiles Faxon, 1851; William Keyes, 1852; Horace Stearns, 1853; name changed to Central Hotel in 1866; Erastus C. Jennison, 1855-66; widow Jennison and sons, 1866-69; - Briggs, 1869-70; C. F. Smith, 1870-80; he made many changes, added a story, and sold to J. C. Babbitt; burned on July 16, 1895.

Note: there is a problem here, however, because there seems to be a second Eagle Hall/House; the Vermont Business Directory for 1873, '79, lists both the Central House and the Eagle Hall/Hotel;

c. 1825: an inn, --; said to have been a stage stop, the John Raleigh place in 1982, west side of Rte 7 about one-half mile south of John's Bridge; VDHP 0615-31; (Swanton Junction?);

1849: (b) --, Ward Barney (NEMU Dir; this is the Eagle Hotel); --, Nelson Bullard (NEMU Dir; at the "Falls," probably the Stearns stand, see above);

1855: --, L. D. Turrill (Turrill's Hotel, formerly the Stearns stand); (a) --, Ira A. Church (Keyes Hotel, later the Barney House);

1856: --, L. D. Turrill (see above); (a) --, Stiles Faxon (probably the Keyes Hotel);

1857: hotel, L. D. Turrill* (Walling; on the west side of the park, formerly the Stearns stand); (a) Railroad Hotel, W. W. Keyes* (Walling; the Keyes Hotel);

1870: (a) as above; (b) Central House, C. F. Smith (formerly the Eagle Hotel);

1871: (a) hotel, W. W. Keyes* (Beers; Keyes Hotel, same site as Walling, above); (b) Central House, Charles F. Smith* (Beers; on the corner of Grand Ave and First St, where the library now stands);

1873: (b) as above; Eagle Hall, Charles Mullen (location unknown, see note under Eagle Hotel, c. 1825, above); Commercial House, J. J. Gibbs, location unknown;

1874: (a) Barney House, R. Lester Barney (who bought the Keyes Hotel this year; A. T. Kellogg proprietor in 1877);

1875: (b) as above;

* * *

Principal Swanton Hotels

Stearns Stand (later Turrill's Hotel);
(a) Keyes Hotel (also Railroad House; became Barney House, American House, Adams House, Riviere, River View Hotel);
(b) Eagle Hotel (became Central House);
(c) West Side Inn;
(d) Hotel Swanton (later Swanton Inn, Grand Avenue House);

* * *

1879: (a) Barney House, A. T. Kellogg (on the site of the present Riviere Hotel, later known as the American House, the Adams House and the River View House (b) Central House, Frank Lawrence; Eagle Hall, A. T. Kellogg (see 1873 entry, and note under c. 1825);

1880: (b) as above; Eagle House, A. T. Kellogg (see above);

1882, '83: (a) American House, James F. Kelley (formerly the Barney House); (b) as above, T. S. Babbitt (Child);

1887: (a) as above, E. S. Whitcomb; (b) as above, J. F. Kelley;

1892: (a) as above, E. A. Hill; (b) as above (also shown on Sanborn);

1895: (a) as above, Mrs C. E. Harrington (should be Honsinger); (b) as above, F. E. Pierce;

1897: (b) Central, not shown on Sanborn; the map shows a hotel "to be built" north of the Methodist church, which would be the Hotel Swanton;

1898: (a) as above, Mrs C. E. Honsinger; (c) West Side Inn, Henry Tatro (near the depot on Depot St; now an apartment building); (d) Hotel Swanton, G. A. Best (on Grand Ave, north of the Methodist church; also known as the Swanton Inn and the Grand Avenue Hotel);

1900: (a) as above; (c) as above; (d) as above; (also in 1902 CVRR guide);

1904: (c) and (d) on Sanborn;

1905: (a) Adams House, J. R. Morrill; (c) as above, J. O. Guyette; (d) as above;

1908: (a) as above, --; (c) as above, --; (d) as above, --;

1909: (a) Adams House now the Riviere on Sanborn; (c) is still shown; (d) the Swanton Hotel is now the Grand Avenue; see photo;

Grand Avenue Hotel

1911: (a) Adams House, B. Mullen; (c) West Side, S. Robistow; (d) Grand Avenue, M. A. Hungerford;

1913, '15:   (a) Adams House, S. Robiston (Robistow); (d) Grand Avenue Hotel, M. A. Hungerford;

1920: (a) Riverside Hotel (or River View, Riviere), C. M. Chappell; see photo; also in 1916 VBP; the Riviere listed until at least 1968, but not a hotel in 1990; (d) as above, --;

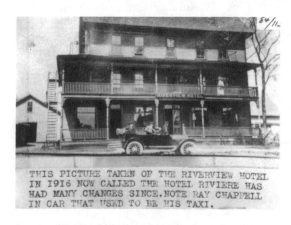

Riverside Hotel (History of Swanton, Vermont, 1988)

1925: (a) as above; (d) <u>Swanton Inn</u>, H. B. Field (razed in 1938); both shown on 1930 Sanborn.

(194c) <u>Swanton Center</u> ("middle road").

c. 1798: a tavern, <u>Clark Hubbard</u>; Jaris Jackson, 1801-07 or -08; Ora Willard, 1815-20; David Chappell, 1818-25 (tavern license, 1819, '21-24); Daniel O. Meigs, 1825-27 (license, 1825); Seth W. Hathaway, 1827-31 (license, 1827);

c. 1835: an inn, <u>A. Honsinger</u>; Norman Tarte house in 1982, on the west side of the Highgate road about one mile north of the Bushey road; said to have been an inn, VDHP 0615-13.

(194d) <u>Swanton Junction</u> ("West road," Fonda Junction).

c. 1797: a tavern, <u>Levi Hathaway</u> (there is a <u>Hathaway's tavern</u> in an 1812 almanac); near C. H. Bullard's wagon shop; there is a C. H. Bullard, wheelwright, on the west road a little south of the Rice Hill road, on the 1857 Walling; Hathaway was followed by Nathaniel Stearns, John R. Phelps, Adam Andros; John A. Keys, c. 1823 (tavern license, 1820);

* * *

"It was customary for the citizens to meet at these houses every Saturday to learn the news, to spend time in sport and frolic, to transact business, and, too often, simply to have a day of dissipation." (Hemenway).

* * *

c. 1819: tavern (and store), <u>Samuel Bullard</u>; tavern license, 1819, '22, '24; until 1825, followed by Widow Bullard and son Charles, 1825-32 (Hemenway); possibly the same place as <u>Hathaway's</u>, above.

(194e) <u>West Swanton</u> (Maquam shore).

1880: <u>Bellevue House</u>, O. M. Gallup (probably became the <u>Hotel Champlain</u>);

1882: (a) <u>Hotel Champlain</u>, Reuben Parker; on the Maquam shore, at the western terminus of the St Johnsbury and Lake Champlain railroad; this building was moved from Sheldon; see photo, next page;

1883: (a) as above, C. F. Smith;

1887: (a) as above, W. W. Hill (C. F. Smith in Vt Dir);

1888: (a) as above, C. W. (?) Smith (Boston and Maine guide);

1892, '95, 1900, '05: (a) as above, C. F. Smith;

1908: (a) as above, --;

1911, '13, '15: (a) as above; said to have burned in 1920 (ref 1), but listed in the 1923 VPB.

* * *

References

(1) Rodney R. Ledoux, ed., The History of Swanton, Vermont (Barre: Northlight Studio Pr., for the Swanton Historical Society, 1988).

Hotel Champlain (Jim Murphy photo)

* * *

(195) **Thetford** (Orange).

(195a) East Thetford.

c. 1780: a tavern, Capt William Heaton; where the depot stood (c. 1869, Hemenway); town meetings held there for some time, and first session of the Orange County court in 1781;

1796: Childs Tavern, --; listed in the Vermont Almanac and Register as a stage stop on the Windsor-St Johnsbury road, location unknown;

c. 1860: (a) a hotel, Fred S. Slack; in his home; he was also PM, 1861-84 and 1885-87;

1870, '73: (a) Slack's Hotel, E. F. (?) Slack;

1875: (a) as above, F. S. Slack;

1877: (a) as above* (Beers);

1879, '80, '83, '87, '88: (a) as above;

1892: --, Mrs Ranlett;

1901. (a) Selleck's Hotel, B. A. Turner (presumably same as Slack's); burned;

1920, '25: Thetford Inn, -- (unidentified; is this the same as Slack's?).

(195b) North Thetford (Lyme Bridge).

(?): a tavern, Eben Cummings (E. Cummings is listed as an inn-keeper in 1849 NEMU Dir);

536

c. 1850:   a hotel, --; when the railroad came through (1); this place burned;

1855, '56:   --, E. Cummings;

1901:   (a) Jaquith's Hotel, A. W. Jaquith;

1916:   (a) Hotel Jaquith, Arthur W. Jaquith (VPB);

1920:   (a) as above; this place burned in 1930;

1925:   --, R. Wilson (probably still Jaquith's).

(195c) Post Mills (Post Mill Village).

On Lake Fairlee, which lies partly in Thetford and partly in West Fairlee.

1869:   Commodore House, Commodore T. H. Chubb; on Main St just north of the junction with the road to Lake Fairlee; Chubb was a southerner, and his place "attracted a largely Southern clientele, especially from Baltimore" (1); other proprietors were Will Church, Harry Davidson and Llewellyn Miller, who owned it when it burned in 1910; see photo; known as the Green Mountain House at that time;

Commodore House

1865:   (a) Lake House, Nathan Davis; at the northwest corner of the lake, now a bed-and-breakfast operated by Ralph and Len Easton; (VDHP survey, 1979; 0911-30);

(?):   Lake House, Isaac Guild; second place with the same name, at the other end of the lake, near present Camp Norway (i.e., 1972, ref 1); Guild also operated a steamboat landing and boat livery; "one of the incidental services provided by a boat livery was a license to sell spirits, so that these areas often had a very convivial flavor";(1)

1873:   (a) Lake House, Nathan Davis; (b) Lake View Hotel, William Knight;

1875:   (a) as above, - Double (?);

1878:   (a) as above, N. Davis; (b) Lake View Hotel, --;

1880:   (a) as above; (b) as above;

1887:   (a) as above;

1892, '95, '98: (a) as above; (b) as above, G. W. Comstock;

1901: (b) as above, W. H. Church;

1905: (a) as above; (b) as above;

1908: <u>Commodore House</u>, --;

1911, '13: (a) as above, B. Smith; Nathan Davis died in 1917; place closed, re-opened in the 1920s, now a bed-and-breakfast, still the <u>Lake House</u>, Mrs Elizabeth Pemberton;

1920s-30s: a hotel, Mr and Mrs George Colby; in the house where the Wrights lived in 1978; (2) now apartments.

(195d) <u>Thetford (Thetford Hill)</u>.

1797: an inn, <u>Jesse Hawley</u>; first town meetings held here, later the <u>Thetford Tavern</u>, Lyman Fitch; at the southeast corner of the crossroads at Thetford Hill;

1849: --, P. M. Swift (NEMU Dir; location unknown, could be any of the villages, or outside them);

1916: <u>Burton Hall</u> (<u>Hanoum Inn</u>), Mrs H. F. Emery (VPB); a dormitory for Thetford Academy students in the winter, a residence for visiting parents of Camp Hanover girls in summer; burned in 1942.

(195e) <u>Thetford Center</u>.

c. 1780: a tavern, --; in the house owned by Mrs Marthedith Stauffer in 1979, VDHP 0911-50; original use as a tavern, established as such by 1784; later a store and stage stop operated by Mrs George Harvey; by 1858 it was a hotel and store, B. Lang (see below); and it was the Lucas (and Wesley Sayre) store and PO in the late 1870s; on Rte 113, west side, in Thetford Center; also cited in ref 1;

1855: --, A. Ashley;

1858: hotel (and store), <u>B. Lang</u>* (Walling);

1870: (a) <u>St James</u>, Joseph Allen (also PM, 1869-70);

1873, '75, '80, '83: (a) as above, C. D. Lucas.

(195f) <u>Union Village</u> (originally Lockes Mills; lies partly in Norwich, on the Ompompanoosuc River).

1849: <u>Union House</u>, David Hall (NEMU Dir);

1855: --, D. Hall;

1859: --, L. S. Hutchins* (Walling);

c. 1867: <u>Union Village Hotel</u>, Daniel B. Turner; PO also here at one time; on the Boston-Montreal stage road;

1875, '80, '83, '87, '88, '92: (a) <u>Turner's</u>, Daniel B. Turner;

1898, 1901, '05, '11, '13: (b) <u>Cottage Inn</u>, E. M. Fullington (also known as the <u>Village Inn</u>);

538

1920, '25:   (b) Village Inn, Mrs. E. M. Fullington.

(195g) Rice's Mills.

(?):   a tavern, Page George; on present Rte 132, an old stage road; present Gene Ilsley place (i.e., 1978, ref 2).

Note: the assistance of Mrs Marian Fifield and the Thetford Historical Society is gratefully acknowledged.

* * *

References

(1)   Charles Latham Jr, A Short History of Thetford, Vermont, 1761-1870 (Thetford: Thetford Historical Society, 1972).
(2)   Helen S. Paige, Tales of Thetford (Hanover, N.H.: X-Press, 1978).

* * *

(196) **Tinmouth** (Rutland).

(196a) Tinmouth.

c. 1781:   Bingham's Tavern, Solomon Bingham; Tinmouth was the county seat at one time, and courts held here for several years, in one room of this large log house, while Bingham and his family kept their inn in the other (Hemenway); the jury would retire to a long barn a few rods away;

c. 1800:   an inn, --; near the site of the old court house, #10 on the Town of Tinmouth map, ref 1;

c. 1800:   a tavern, --; in the southwest corner of town, a stop on the Salem, N.Y.-Rutland stage route; modified c. 1845, #25 on Town of Tinmouth map; (2)

Note: tavern licenses to Daniel (David?) Mosher, 1821, and Charles Phillips, William Vaughan, 1822, locations unknown;

1849:   --, Z. Lewis (NEMU Dir).

* * *

References

(1) Vermont Div. of Historic Preservation, Historic Architecture of Rutland County, Curtis B. Johnson, ed., Elsa Gilbertson, asst ed. (Montpelier: 1988).

* * *

(197) **Topsham** (Orange).

(197a) Topsham (Topsham postally, but known as East Topsham locally and on maps).

c. 1800:   a tavern, --; it was still a tavern under James "Mountain" Carter, who died in 1852; present Norman McLam house (#11 in the East Topsham Historic District, VDHP 0912-23, surveyed in 1979); on a stage route, at the northeast corner of the intersection of Hart's Road and Galusha Hill Road;

1905, '11, '13, '20: --, E. Hood.

(197b) <u>Topsham Four Corners</u> (no PO).

c. 1830-40:   an inn, --; surveyed by VDHP in 1979 (0912-15), at the northeast corner at Topsham Four Corners; on a stage road, supposedly a stagecoach inn at one time; shown as belonging to H. Butterfield on the 1858 Walling map, Mrs H. Butterfield on the 1877 Beers, now a private home.

(197c) <u>Waits River</u>.

1840s: (a) <u>Waits River Hotel</u>, H. S. Swift; on the old stage road, outside the village; burned in 1879;

1855, '56:   --, E. C. Swift;

1858: (a) as above, C. P. Simpson* (Walling);

1870: (a) --, A. J. Worthin (Vt Dir);

1872, '73:   (a) as above, A. J. Worthen (sp?);

1877: (a) as above, C. P. Simpson* (Beers);

1880: (a) as above;

1901, '05:   --, D. S. Folsom (PM, 1889-93 and 1897-1909);

1911, '13:   --, B. G. Miles (building burned in 1953, VDHP).

(197d) <u>West Topsham</u>.

1822: (a) <u>Jenness House</u>, Jonathan Jenness (the "father of West Topsham"); on the old stage road across the state; probably became the <u>West Topsham Hotel</u> (see below), burned in 1892; the PO was in the hotel when George Jenness was PM, 1827-39;

1849: --, S. Jenness (NEMU Dir);

1855, '56:   --, J. Smith;

1858: (a) --, A. J. Wallace* (Walling);

1877: (a) <u>West Topsham Hotel</u>, A. J. Wallace* (Beers);

1873, '75, '80, '83, '87, '88:   (a) --, Andrew J. Wallace; he was also PM, 1854-65 and 1872-82;

1890: --, C. H. Beede;

1905, '13:   --, George Rice.

* * *

(198) <u>Townshend</u> (Windham).

(198a) <u>Townshend</u>.

c. 1770:   first tavern, - <u>Butterfield</u>; tavern license to a Zatter Butterfield, 1817;

(?):   a tavern, <u>Capt James Taggart</u>; tavern license, 1822-33; "who kept a good house in the brick building, long after known as the Ranney residence" (Hemenway); there is a reference to the 'old brick tavern on the common'(and a photo) in ref 1; this place lasted until the mid-1800s; owned by Chapin Howard in 1810; Mr Chapin's daughter, Clarina, was an early feminist, who edited a newspaper and scandalized Brattleboro by wearing bloomers on Main St; probably VDHP 1317-7, present Hinkle home; according to Phelps, "Chapin Howard kept the tavern now occupied by Ransel Frost" (i.e., 1880s, ref 2); original building and back kitchen built 1810 by Timothy Burton; Daniel Cobb made an addition in 1823, Chapin Howard other changes in 1828, Timothy W. Boynton in 1845;

* * *

"The house had a ballroom on the second floor with a cave ceiling...There was stencilling in the hall and under the wallpaper, and under paint in the taproom on the south side of the house is a wall painting of a soldier. The west side of the house was moved across the ditch in 1820 to become the wooden house now owned by R. Dexter and Shirley Greenwood..." (i.e., 1979, ref 1); tavern building owned in 1988 by D. J. Papale;

* * *

(?):   a hotel, <u>Chester Rand</u>; who later apparently took over <u>Taggart's tavern</u>, above;

c. 1840:   (a) <u>Union Hall</u>, Capt James Taggart (later the <u>West River House</u>); built the "present hotel now kept by O. F. Coombs (i.e., c. 1890, Hemenway) after he sold the original tavern to Rand"; "Taggart had just finished his new hotel when Daniel Webster spoke on the issues of the day in 1840, on Stratton Mountain"; Webster spent the previous night at <u>Taggart's</u>; later proprietors were Abner Johnson, - Allen, Taggart again, Thomas Evans (1855-60), R. M. Flint, Holbrook and Burke, C. H. Willard, and O. F. Coombs; burned in 1894, rebuilt as the <u>Townshend Inn</u>, which also burned in 1918 (then owned by Frank McLean); fire photo, 1894, in ref 1;

1839:   <u>Blandin Tavern</u>, John Blandin; who kept hotel for 20 years in this place, which he built; became the <u>Cedar Post Inn</u> later after serving as the home of C. Q. Standish; on Rte 30;

1849:   <u>Traveller's Home</u>, John Blandin (<u>Blandin Tavern</u> , see above); NEMU Dir; shown as J. Blandin on McClellan map, 1856; and as the "old Blandin Tavern stand" on Beers, 1869;

1856:   (a) hotel, <u>T. Evans</u>* (McClellan);

1869:   (a) hotel, <u>C. H. Willard</u>* (Beers; the <u>West River House</u>); approximately same location as on the McClellan map, 1856;

1870:   (a) <u>West River House</u>, C. H. Willard;

1873, '75, '80, '83, '87, '90:   (a) as above, Osman F. Coombs;

1892:   (a) as above, Thomas Evans; burned in the "big fire" of 1894, replaced after some delay;

1895:   --, Julian C. Taft;

1901:   (b) <u>Townshend Inn</u>, M. P. Corser; see photo;

1905, '08, '11: (b) as above, H. M. Burk;

1913:   (b) as above, L. J. Strong; burned in 1918, not replaced;

1916:   (b) as above, G. W. Powers (VPB);

(?):   <u>Maple Dell</u>, --; a summer boarding place on Windham Hill;

(?):   <u>Cedar Post Inn</u>, --; see photo, next page.

Townshend Inn

(198b) <u>West Townshend</u>.

* * *

"Before the present tavern building was erected, the traveling public were entertained under licenses granted at various times to Gen Fletcher, Ezekiel Ransom, Amariah Taft, Thomas Sumner, Lemuel Marsh, John Putnam and possibly other persons...Timothy Burton built...the house, where, with a single exception, the only hotel of the place has ever since been kept...we have prepared the following list of innkeepers at West part of the town.

* * *

1789, '90, '92:   Samuel Fletcher; 1789: Amariah Taft; 1793: Thomas Sumner; 1799, 1800: Ezekiel Ransom; 1811-13: Benjamin Rider; 1813-15: Eleazer H. Ranney; 1815-17: Elisha Taft; 1817-19: Simeon Leland; 1819-20: John Adams; 1820-21: Benjamin Low; 1821-22: Solomon Willard; 1822-24: Asa Farnsworth; 1824-28: Jonathan Melendy; 1829-32: Chapin Howard; 1829: license to Abiel Stoddard, who kept a hotel in the brick house now (i.e., 1880s) occupied by J. H. Fullerton; 1832-40: Zadock Sawyer; 1840-42: Timothy W. Boynton; 1842-48: Theodore Phelps; 1848-51: F. D. and E. Sawyer; 1851-53: no hotel; 1853-54: Orison H. Kimball; 1854-58: no hotel; 1858-59: Jay S. Gates; 1859-60: Benjamin B. Burroughs; 1860-67: Barton B. Cook; 1867-68: Archibald L. Allen; 1868-69: Mrs A. L. Allen; 1869-70: Josephus Dunham; 1870-72: Osmon F. Coombs; 1872-74: Josephus Dunham and son; 1874-77: Marshall M. Martin; 1877-83: Ransel Frost."

Of this group, John Adams, Benjamin Law, Solomon Willard, Jonathan Melendy, Chapin Howard, Abiel Stoddard and Zadock Sawyer are also listed in the State Archives; Silas Brown (1820, '21) and Jacob Allen Jr (1827, '28, '30) are in the archives but not on the Phelps list.

1849:   --, F. D. and E. Sawyer (NEMU Dir; also Phelps list, see above);

1869:   <u>Dunham's Hotel</u>, J. and C. H. Dunham* (Beers; also Phelps list, see above);

1870:   --, - Dunham;

1873:   --, J. Dunham and Sons;

1875:   --, Marsh Martin; (also Phelps list);

1879, '80, '83: <u>Valley Hotel</u>, Randall Frost; same place as above; also Phelps list, see above;

1884:   --, A. D. Ayer;

1887:   <u>Holden's</u>, E. W. Holden; burned 1915, a garage now on the site;

1888:   <u>Maple Hill</u>, Charles Jones (Boston and Maine guide).

Note: the assistance of Charles Marchant, Townshend, is gratefully acknowledged.

* * *

References

(1) Townshend: The Way It Was Till Now (Townshend, 1979).
(2) James H. Phelps, Collections relating to the history and inhabitants of the town of Townshend, Vermont (Brattleboro: George E. Selleck, 1877-1884).

Cedar Post Inn
(Townshend, The Way It Was 'Till Now, 1979)

* * *

(199) **Troy** (Orleans).

   (199a) <u>North Troy.</u>

1849:   --, Curtis Elkins (NEMU Dir);

1856:   --, C. Elkins;

1858:   <u>Troy Hotel</u>, --* (Walling);

1868:   a hotel burned and was rebuilt in this year, according to Child; not clear if this was in North Troy, or Troy (South);

1870, '72:   (a) <u>Frontier House</u>, H. W. Baker; same site as <u>Troy House</u>, above; burned in 1918;

* * *

"The Old Frontier Hotel, built before 1878, stood on the present site of the Chittenden Trust Company bank. It was a large three story square building with a large entrance hall, dining room, office and display room in the main part of the house, with large kitchen space, pantries and storage rooms in the rear of the main part, and, over the entire kitchen area was a large assembly hall with an auditorium, stage, dressing rooms, and a spring dance floor, especially enjoyed by the many couples who attended the various special balls...For these formal dances, the ladies were resplendent in their beautiful evening gowns, long kid gloves and ornate fans. In those days, such dances were very formal, attended by the townspeople and many couples from up and down the Missisquoi Valley.

Besides dances, the hall was used for plays...minstrel shows, school graduations...Usually during a year several Traveling Road Companies, such as a series of melodrama plays, a glass blowing company, variety shows and a Kick-a-poo Indian Company, who entertained by skits, etc., meantime selling bottles of medicine...Charles A. Ramsdell was the popular proprietor during those early years...The display room which was on the main floor was used by the commercial travelers, who came into town on the trains with their huge trunks of samples and used this room in which to display their wares, consisting of clothing, shoes, hats; in fact, a great variety of articles. The merchants could see and select the things they wished to buy, and the orders were shipped to them later by freight or express.

The office was a large room and could accommodate the men who wished to play cards if the day was too cool to sit on the large front porches...These chairs were filled on all pleasant days, as the sitters could enjoy the day watching the many activities on Main Street...The idle sitters found it very entertaining and often retained their favorite seat far into the evening when the North Troy Frontier Band gave a concert in the old bandstand." (1)

* * *

1873, '75, '79, '83, '87, '90:   (a) as above, C. A. Ramsdell;

1878:   (a) as above* (Beers);

1892:   (a) as above, George Boyden; (b) <u>Cottage House</u>, George Martin (also known as <u>Ladd's Hotel</u>); on Railroad Street;

1895:   (a) as above, R. Cutler;

1898:   (a) as above, George Shepard;

1901:   (a) as above, E. W. Farnham; (b) <u>Ladd's Hotel</u>, C. R. Ladd;

1905:   (a) as above, G. A. Curry; (b) as above;

1908, '13:   (a) as above; burned in 1918;

1916:   (a) as above, Mrs B. B. Gilbert; (b) as above, C. C. Smith;

1920, '25:   <u>New Troy Hotel</u>, Lucy E. Ladd;

1923:   <u>Valley House</u>, O. A. Benoit (VPB); continued until c. 1940, <u>Hotel Reba</u> in 1955.

(199b) <u>Troy</u>.

(Troy postally, but at South Troy, which was the principal village until the railroad came to North Troy in 1871).

Note: tavern licenses to Ralph Chamberlin, 1824-30; Charles Hard, 1822, '23, '25; Leonard P. Walker, 1826, '27; Isaac Grant, 1827; Oliver Chamberlin, 1827; Ezra Sanger, 1830; Levi M. Parkhurst, 1832; and James Craigie, 1833, locations unknown;

1837: a tavern, <u>Ezra Johnson</u>; who apparently bought an existing tavern stand, kept it several years, went bankrupt in 1848 (Hemenway);

1849: <u>Pavilion</u>, E. Johnson (NEMU Dir);

1855: --, Arad Hitchcock;

1858: hotel, <u>F. Flint</u>* (Walling);

1870: (a) <u>Missisquoi House</u> (<u>Missisquoi Valley House</u>), Portus Smith (Porter in Vt Dir); see photo;

Missisquoi Valley House (Special Collections, UVM)

1873: (a) as above, P. H. Smith;

1878: (a) <u>Waumbec House</u>, A. Hodsden* (Beers); the <u>Waumbec</u>, <u>Missisquoi</u> and <u>Troy Houses</u> are almost certainly the same place; but apparently not on the same site as <u>Flint's</u> on the 1848 Walling, above; perhaps an 1868 fire referred to in Child destroyed the Flint place;

1875, '79, '80, '83: (a) <u>Waumbec House</u>, Albert Hodsden;

1883: (a) <u>Missisquoi House</u>, Augustus Boyden (Child);

1887: (a) <u>Missisquoi House</u>, -- (Vt Dir);

1887: (a) <u>Troy House</u>, A. Boyden (Walton);

1890, '92: (a) <u>Missisquoi House</u>, W. Y. Hadlock;

1895, '98, 1901, '05: (a) as above, George Boyden;

1908: (a) as above, --;

1911: (a) as above, George Boyden;

1913: (a) as above, --; Wayside Inn, --; see photo;

1916: Wayside Inn, W. E. Brock (VPB); also, Sanborn for this year shows the Wayside Inn as burned, and the Missisquoi House, on Church St.

(199c) Troy Furnace. (PO, 1841-51). No listings found.

* * *

References

(1) Anne H. Butterfield, Memories of the Early Days in the Town of Troy, Vermont (n.p., 1977).

Wayside Inn

* * *

(200) **Tunbridge** (Orange).

(200a) North Tunbridge. No listings found.

(200b) South Tunbridge.

c. 1850:   an inn, --; a stagecoach stop, later a store and PO in the 1870-1900 period; owned by Mrs Harold Chamberlin in 1988. (1)

(200c) Tunbridge. (The "Market," Tunbridge Center).

1849: --, H. H. Woodward;

(?):   --, Orris P. Cilley; who "kept the old hotel here two years, a little south of the present hotel" (i.e., 1888, Child); this would be Woodward's, which burned in 1865;

1858: Woodward's Hotel, D. Woodward* (Walling);

1870: --, J. Tucker;

1877: (a) Tunbridge House, A. N. King; built after the Civil War to replace Woodward's;

the automobile was the ultimate downfall of this place, partly torn down in the 1930s, gone by the 1940s; Cilley's shop, #19 in the Tunbridge Village Historic District (VDHP 0913-83) is on the site;

1877:   (a) as above* (Beers);

1878, '79, '80: (a) as above, C. J. Kenrick;

1883:   (a) as above, Pike and Bennett;

1887:   (a) as above, E. Woodward;

1890, '92, '95: (a) as above, G. W. Stearns;

1898:   (a) as above, G. W. Raymond;

1901, '05, '08, '11, '13, '20:   (a) Tunbridge House, --; see photo;

Tunbridge House

1902:   (a) as above, A. N. King (CVRR booklet).

Note: the assistance of Mr Euclid Farnham, Tunbridge Historical Society, is gratefully acknowledged.

* * *

References

(1)   Euclid Farnham, Tunbridge Past, A Pictorial History of Tunbridge, Vermont (Randolph: Herald Printery, for the Tunbridge Historical Soc., 1981).

* * *

(201) **Underhill** (Chittenden).

(201) North Underhill.

(?):   a tavern, Joseph Robinson; "at the foot of Station Road where it intersects with the Creek Road (Rte 15)" (1); the North Underhill post office was in this building when it opened in 1864, and Joseph Robinson was PM, 1864-1874.

(201b) Underhill Center.

(?): (a) <u>Mountain House</u> (<u>Mansfield Mountain House</u>), --; "the old hotel near the main corner...in operation for nearly one hundred years", ref 1); built c. 1825, but not clear when it started operating as an inn, certainly by mid-century, possibly earlier; a favorite stopping-off place for persons who planned to climb the mountain; last operators were Mr and Mrs Edwin Henry (as the <u>Mansfield Inn</u>); three different Henrys (Carrie F., Henry N., and L. Leora) were postmasters from 1904-1943, with the PO in the hotel part of this time; (VDHP 0415-20, #5); Ralph Waldo Emerson once a guest, according to oral tradition;

1857: (a) <u>Green Mountain Hotel</u>, M. Wires* (Walling; probably same as above);

1858: 1st <u>Halfway House</u>, Mr Gray; on the plateau at the 2300 ft level; not to be confused with the <u>Halfway House</u> on the Stowe side of Mt Mansfield; burned in 1876, rebuilt by Francis Cahall; acquired by Dr W. G. E. Flanders, 1924, who made improvements, including electric lights (the 1878 building was probably replaced at some point, since there are two quite different photos, taken many years apart); "on a clear night when the lights were lit, the illumination on the mountain side could be seen in Burlington" (photo, ref 1); razed c. 1939;

1869: (a) <u>Prouty's Hotel</u>, E. H. Prouty* (Beers; same site as the <u>Green Mountain House</u>, above);

1870, '75: (a) --, E. H. Prouty;

1873: (a) <u>Prouty's Hotel</u>, L. O. Horton;

1879, '80: (a) as above, O. R. Farnham (<u>Farnham House</u> in the Vt Dir for 1879, '83);

1882: (a) as above, Elon H. Prouty (Main St, Child);

1887: (a) <u>Mountain House</u> , G. W. Woodworth;

1890, '92: (a) as above, A. J. Lavigne;

1895, '98, 1901: (a) as above, E. W. Blakey (Blakeley);

1906: (a) as above, W. A. Pollard;

1908: (a) as above, --; <u>Shannon's</u>, Mr and Mrs Shannon; originally a summer boarding house, later a ski center (from 1908-47), now a private home, in the Stevensville section of Underhill;

1911, '13: (a) as above, W. L. Bennett;

1915: (a) as above, F. C. Slater* (Sanborn, where it is listed as "closed"); no Walton listing in 1917;

1923, '25: (a) as above, Mrs. E. W. Henry; until at least 1940; now an apartment building.

(201c) <u>Underhill Flats</u> (Underhill, postally; the main business area).

c. 1800: a tavern, <u>Elijah Benedict</u>; for many years; he was an early settler and a Tory, who came from Canada in 1786, and died in 1811; this is VDHP 0415-13, #12; Lorenzo Dow, a 19th century evangelist, spent two years preaching here because there was no church in town; (2)

c. 1800: <u>Barney Tavern</u>, Martin C. Barney; until 1856, when it became a private home;

* * *

"The house has had an interesting life. Martin C. Barney and Edward Hutchings operated it as a tavern for many years. The tavern bar is still in place...From 1832 to about 1843, residents of Underhill congregated in the tavern for their town meetings. In 1856 it became the home of Dr Hiram G. Benedict, who in addition to his medical work kept an inn here. The house became known locally as the Benedict Tavern House...Dr Hiram died in 1886." (3).

* * *

1802: Birge Tavern, William Birge; on Poker Hill Road, near the stage route to Cambridge; "perhaps the oldest house in town"; just north of the first settlement; VDHP 0415-1; Cyrus Birge was the first PM, 1826-28; tavern license to a James Birge, 1821; place now owned by the Brewers; (3)

1849: --, C. Barney (NEMU Dir; the Barney tavern);

1887, '92, '98, '13:   (a) Custer House, T. S. Whipple; approximately on the site of the Flats post office in 1976; burned in 1915, not rebuilt; proprietors included Thaddeus Whipple and George I. Lincoln; see photo;

Custer House

1901, '92, '05, '13:   (a) as above, George I. Lincoln;

1908:   (a) as above, --;

1911:   (a) as above, George I. Lincoln;

1923, '25:   Sinclair House, Mrs E. S. Sinclair; listed as Fair View Cottage in 1916 VPB; Hotel Sinclair in 1935 VPB; see photo, next page; closed soon after Mr Sinclair's death in 1933, but now a bed-and-breakfast, Sinclair Tavern.

Note: the Bostwick House is just across the town line in Jericho, in the Riverside area.

Note: the assistance of Carol Wagner, Underhill Historical Society, is gratefully acknowledged.

* * *

References

(1) Lorraine S. Dwyer, The History of Underhill, Vermont (Underhill: Underhill Historical Society, 1976).
(2) Esther M. Swift, Vermont Place-Names: Footprints of History (Brattleboro: Stephen

Greene Pr., 1977).

(3) Lilian B. Carlisle, ed., Look Around Chittenden County (Burlington: Chittenden County Historical Soc., 1976).

Hotel Sinclair

* * *

(202) **Vergennes** (Addison).

(202a) Vergennes.

1796: Vaughan tavern, --; listed in the Vermont Almanac and Register as a stage stop; almanacs also list Branson (1812) and Rich (1825, '29) as Vergennes tavernkeepers, locations unknown;

1793: Stevens House, --;

* * *

The Stevens Hotel was built in 1793, according to the Vermont Division of Historic Preservation (#0120-13). It is one of the oldest hotel buildings in the state, and also one of the oldest in terms of continuous use as a hotel. It has been extensively altered and remodeled over the years. Original building owned by one Jesse Hollister (Hollister Tavern) in 1795 (almanacs, 1796, 1802, '07), then rented to Azariah Painter; known as Painter's Tavern until 1816 (almanacs, 1812-at least 1829). It was a meeting place for "patriots and politicians" after Vermont became a state, and MacDonough took his meals there, with an office across the street, while his fleet was under construction in the War of 1812. It became the Stevens Hotel in 1840 (see photo). A stage stop until the railroad came in 1849. John Brown's body lay in state in the parlor here after his execution, before being taken to Basin Harbor, and across the lake to its final resting place in North Elba, New York. Became the Vergennes Inn in 1927, now houses Painter's Tavern (a restaurant) and stores (refs 1, 2, and VDHP survey).

1842, '43: (a) Stevens House, --; American House, M. Crane (but according to Child, the American House of later years wasn't built until 1870, so this is apparently a different place, location and fate unknown);

1848: (b) Franklin House, Hiram Adams;

* * *

Adams built the Franklin House in 1848 when the railroad came through, and offered free shuttle service to all trains. "Fifteen bays wide, three and a half stories high, with double parapeted chimneys, its massive brick facade still dominates the downtown district. It survived Vergennes's

550

wavering fortunes and hosted guests for nearly forty years, but in 1886, it underwent a metamorphosis." It has since housed commercial space on the ground floor, and apartments above (the Ryan block, VDHP 0120-9). Also known as the <u>Hollister Hotel</u> at one time. (See photo, Chapter IV).

* * *

Stevens Hotel

1849:   (a) <u>Stevens Hotel</u>, C. T. and C. O. Stevens;

1853:   (a) as above, --* (Walling); hotel, E. W. Chapman* (Walling; probably the <u>Franklin House</u>, see above);

1855, '56:   (a) --, C. T. and C. O. Stevens; --, C. C. Everest (probably the <u>Franklin</u>);

1870:   (a) as above; (b) <u>Franklin House</u>, Foster and Prentice; (c) <u>American House</u>, Edward C. Everest; (at the corner of Main and Monkton Rd, built by Everest; became the <u>Norton House</u> by 1910);

1871:   (a) as above* (Beers); (b) as above, Adams and Foster* (Beers); (c) as above* (Beers);

1873:   (a) as above, D. McBride; (b), (c) as above; <u>Cataract House</u>, Hayes and Wright (Vt Dir, location unknown);

1875:   (a) as above, S. S. Gaines; (b), (c) as above;

1879, '80:   (b) as above, T. B. Smith and Son; (a), (c) as above;

1881:   (a) as above, Samuel S. Gaines; (b) as above, John W. Jackson; (c) as above;

1883:   (a), (b) as above; (c) as above, L. A. Holmes;

1887:   (a) as above, G. W. Peck; <u>Grand Union</u>, -- (Walton; not identified);

1887:   (a) as above; (c) as above, C. H. Colson (Vt Dir);

1890:   (a) as above; (c) as above, E. W. Train;

1892:   (a) as above, S. S. Gaines; (c) as above, --;

1895:   (a), (c) as above; <u>Wheeler House</u>, E. W. Train;

1898: (a) as above; (c) as above, C. H. Colson; <u>Wheeler House</u>, E. Hallock; (d) <u>Prospect House</u>, George E. Stone;

1901: (a), (c), (d) as above;

1905: (a), (d) as above; (c) as above, John Perkins;

1908: (a) as above, --; (c) as above, --; <u>Hotel Lenox</u>, -- (unidentified);

1911: (a) as above, Mrs S. S. Gaines; (c) as above, W. H. Norton;

1913: (a) as above; (c) <u>Norton House</u>, -- (formerly the <u>American House</u>; shown on Sanborn as the <u>American House</u> in 1897, but the <u>Norton House</u> in 1910, 1920, 1927, not shown after that);

1916: (a) as above, George F. Daniels (VPB);

1920: (a) as above, --; (c) as above, --;

1925: (a) as above, --; became the <u>Vergennes Inn</u> by 1927 (Sanborn) but much reduced in size; first shown on Sanborn as <u>Stevens House</u> in 1885. Still listed as <u>Stevens House</u> in Walton until c. 1940, <u>Vergennes House</u> in 1955, ceased operating as an inn in the 1960s.

* * *

References

(1) C. A. G. Jackson, "Vergennes," Burlington Free Press (Feb 9, 1922).
(2) Nancy P. Graff, "At Christmas Vergennes Lights Up Its Landmarks," Vermont Life (Winter 1982): 50.

* * *

(203) **Vernon** (Windham).

(203a) <u>Dummer</u>. (PO from 1895-1910, became 2nd Vernon postally in 1910). No listings found under Dummer.

(203b) <u>South Vernon</u> (no PO, village is partly in West Northfield, Massachusetts).

1869: hotel, <u>C. Merrill</u>* (Beers; there is a slight problem here, because Child says that the <u>South Vernon House</u> wasn't built until 1872);

1870: --, Charles Merrill;

1872: (a) <u>South Vernon House</u>, Priest Brothers; built in this year, according to Child;

1873, '75, '79, '80: (a) as above, D. S. Priest;

1883, '84: (a) as above, R. T. (or F.) Smith;

1887: (a) as above, George A. Wright (Vt Dir; but Walton lists two places this year, neither of them operated by Wright, and one cannot tell which is South Vernon, which Vernon; they are --, Fred T. Davis and --, Hawkins and Ripley);

1890, '92, '95, '98, 1901, '02, '05, '08, '11, '13: (a) as above, George E. Alderman; see photo.

South Vernon House

(203c) <u>Vernon</u> (now Central Park on the Northern Cartographic Vermont Road Atlas).

Note: there are two hotels listed for many years in Vernon; it is entirely possible that one of them was in Dummer, which became 2nd Vernon in 1910.

c. 1820:   (a) hotel (and store), <u>Marshall Whithed</u>; tavern license, 1823, '24; the only one in town for years; also PM, 1828-52 and 1852-60; "a commodious hall occupied from time to time by the different societies for public worship" (Child);

Note: tavern licenses to Jonah Titus, 1817; Apollos Root, 1820-23; Royall Tyler, 1820; and William Stebbins, 1821;

1849:   (a) --, M. Whithed (NEMU Dir);

1850:   (b) <u>Burrows House</u>, Jarvis F. Burrows (known later as the <u>Vernon House</u>); Burrows built it, kept it for 25 years; represented Vernon in the state legislature, held most of the town offices;

1869:   (a) hotel, store and PO, <u>A. Whithed</u>* (Beers; Addison Whithed was PM from 1860 until 1901);

1870, '73, '75: (a) --, A. Whithed; (b) --, J. F. Burrows (this is the <u>Burrows House</u>);

1879:   (a) as above; (b) <u>Vernon House</u>, T. E. Stockmore;

1880:   (a) as above; (b) --, T. E. Stockwell (?);

1883:   (a) as above; (b) <u>Vernon House</u>, T. L. Johnson;

1884:   (b) as above, W. A. Squires (Child);

1887:   (b) as above, William A. Squires; --, R. A. Smith (Vt Dir);

1887:   (a) --, A. Whithed (see comment for this date under South Vernon);

1890:   (b) as above, Loughman and Robbins;

1892:   --, George H. Barrett;

1895, '98:   --, George B. Read;

1901:   --, T. L. Johnson.

Note: a J. F. Burrows is shown on the 1869 Beers near a depot at a hamlet a little north of Vernon. This may be Dummer (second Vernon), and may be the site of Burrow's Hotel, later the Vernon House. It is perplexing that Burrows is listed in the Business Directory portion of this Beers only as a farmer, however.

* * *

(204) **Vershire** (Orange).

(204a) Copperfield. (PO, 1892-1906).

c. 1860:   a tavern and dance-hall established originally to serve the employees of the Ely Copper Mines (VDHP 0914-4); at the intersection of Beanville and Miller Pond Rds; may not have accommodated overnight guests, now a private residence.

(204b) Ely (PO, 1871-89, at the copper mines; there is also an Ely in Fairlee). No listings found.

(204c) Vershire.

c. 1785:   first tavern, Jonathan Maltby; an early settler; on the place owned by Danford Blanchard, c. 1888 (Child); he died in 1801, his widow kept the tavern "many years after";

1849:   --, Alden Church; this is the Davenport Tavern, according to VDHP (0914-26); built about 1820 on north side of Rte 113, near the corner of North Road in Vershire village; present Wesley Parker residence (i.e., 1980);

1855, '56:   --, P. M. Swift;

1858:   hotel (and PO)* (Walling); surveyed by the VDHP in 1980 (0914-24); on the north side of Rte 113, corner of North Road, in Vershire village; built c. 1790, present Earl Sleeper home;

1883:   --, P. M. Swift (Vt Dir);

1887, '90:   Traveller's Home, J. H. Gilman (Vt Dir);

1895, '98:   --, J. Woodstock; --, L. L. Robinson;

1901, '05, '11, '13:--, L. L. Robinson.

* * *

(205) **Victory** (Essex).

Three settlements in this town achieved post office status: Damon's Crossing (1884-96); Gallup Mills (1887-1925); and Victory (1858-1952). Gallup built a hotel and store at Gallup Mills about 1880 (see below), and it seems likely that this was the only hotel in the township; but Child says it was in Damon's Crossing, almost surely an error.

(205a) Damon's Crossing. No listings found.

(205b) Gallup Mills.

c. 1880:   a hotel, O. M. Gallup; who came this year, built mills, a hotel and store, and a railroad;

1887:   Hotel Victory , A. F. Kellogg (Child, attributed to Damon's Crossing, probably an

554

error);

1887:   Hotel Victory, O. H. (?) Kellogg (Vt Dir);

1890:   Victory Hotel, John E. Estabrooks (Vt Dir);

1892:   --, W. L. Buzzell (Walton);

1895:   --, F. S. Seavey (Walton);

1900:   --, Thomas Mitchell (Walton).

(205c) Victory. No listings found (but see note at the beginning of this section).

* * *

(206) **Waitsfield** (Washington).

(206a) Waitsfield.

c. 1802:   a tavern, Capt John Campbell; tavern license, 1833; on road 32, on the farm where John Waterman lived c. 1889 (Child); died 1852;

1805:   a tavern, Gilbert Wait; in a home built earlier by Ezra Wait, of which no trace exists (1); the old sign is still preserved;

c. 1825:   a tavern, Garinter Hastings; tavern license, 1826, '27, '30; "along the old highway...on a farm occupied by Walter C. Joslyn" (i.e., in 1909, ref 1); there is a W. Joslyn on the road southeast out of Waitsfield on the 1873 Beers;

Note: tavern licenses to - Robinson and James Baldwin, 1817; Elias Taylor Jr, 1820-25; Edward Rice, 1823; George T. Kidder, 1826; and Julian Dumans, 1830, '32, locations unknown;

c. 1840:   a tavern, William McAllister; in Waitsfield village, for several years;

1849:   --, Moses J. Johnson (NEMU Dir);

1851:   (a) Waitsfield Hotel, Roderick Richardson; Richardson had a tavern license in Waitsfield, 1817-32; this building was built in Irasville, date unknown, by Elisha Foster, near the foot of the "Dugway," moved by Richardson to the south corner of the square in 1851; other managers were William McAllister (see c. 1840, above), John McDermid, J. Monroe Joslin, Richard F. Carleton, William Simonds, Calvin C. Richardson, Robert J. Coffey, Francis C. Lamb, Andrew W. Bigelow, and H. E. Brewster;

1858:   (a) --, J. McDermid* (Walling); this is the Waitsfield Hotel;

(?):   a tavern,--; in a brick house, now gone, built by Roderick Richardson for his son, Dan, and kept as a tavern by "Uncle Julie" Dumas and "Colonel" John S. Campbell (1); south of the Mad River, more or less across from where the Congregational parsonage stood in 1873 (Beers);

1870:   (a) Waitsfield Hotel, E. Ainsworth;

1873:   (a) as above, William Dodge* (Beers; same site as above);

1875:   (a) as above, C. C. Richardson;

1879, '80, '83: (a) as above, F. D. Lamb;

1887:   (a) as above, Noble Irish (Vt Dir);

1887: --, F. D. Lamb; --, A. W. Bigelow (Walton; not identified);

1889: (a) as above, Andrew W. Bigelow (Child);

1890: (a) as above;

1892: --, J. J. Kelly;

1895: --, H. E. Brewster;

1898: --, R. E. Denton;

1901, '02, '05: (a) as above, J. A. Carpenter;

1908: (a) Waitsfield House, --; see photo;

Waitsfield House (Vermont Historical Society)

1911, '13: --, C. D. Gibbs;

1914: Sanborn map shows the Waitsfield House closed;

1925: --, R. H. Downer.

Note: the assistance of Mr J. B. Joslin and the Waitsfield Historical Society is gratefully acknowledged.

* * *

References

(1) Matt B. Jones, History of the Town of Waitsfield, Vermont, 1782-1908 (Boston: Geo. E. Littlefield, 1908).

* * *

(207) **Walden** (Caledonia).

(207a) North Walden. (PO, 1871-1904). No listings found.

(207b) South Walden. (PO, 1833-1922).

1799: Farrington Stand, Nathaniel Farrington; kept the only place in town, on the Bayley-

Hazen Road, where it intersects Rte 15, where Roy and Jennie Goodenough now live (i.e., 1986, ref 1); a public house there until about 1900, became Dutton's (see below); other owners were Jaros and Lucy Dutton, Alonzo and Elizabeth Dutton, and Edmond Goodenough; an Abner Farrington had a tavern license, 1822-26;

Note: tavern licenses to Daniel Johnson, 1822, '24; Hiram Babbitt, 1825, '26; and Samuel Kittredge Jr, 1822-26, locations unknown;

1849: --, L. Farrington (NEMU Dir);

1855: --, Dutton and Kimball;

1858: (a) hotel, J. Dutton* (Walling);

1870: --, J. M. Bradford;

1873: (a) Dutton's Hotel, A. E. Dutton (Vt Dir);

1875, '80, '83, '87: (a) --, A. E. Dutton;

1892, '95, '98, 1908: --, E. T. Goodnough.

(207c) Walden (known locally as Noyesville at one time).

1808: a hotel, Adam Amsden Jr; tavern license, 1822-26; for 30 years, where I. T. Farrow lived c. 1887 (Child); in the southeast corner of town, on the old County Road over Haviland Hill, from Danville through Walden; across the road from the present I. John Farrow home; building gone, land still in the Farrow family (personal communication, Mrs Elizabeth P. Hatch);

c. 1848: a hotel, Abijah Jennison; on road 32 (County Road) until his death in 1883;

1855: --, A. Jennison;

1858: hotel, A. Jennison*; (Walling; on the road from Noyesville to Hardwick);

c. 1865: Noyesville Hotel, Jason F. Dow; with an ell containing a spring dance floor; John Batchelder, Dow again, and then Augustine and Hannah Rogers in 1869, for 10 years; other owners were Norman Perkins; his widow and her second husband, Amos Scott; Carl and Eva Perkins; Thomas and Ada Greene; Edmund and Carrie Woodard; Philippe and Alphonse Audet; and Hugh and Ella Merrill, who run it now as a restaurant (i.e., 1986);

1870, '75: --, Augustine Rogers;

1873: --, B. A. Rogers (Vt Dir);

1890: Walden House, S. V. Meader (Vt Dir);

1900, '05: --, S. V. Meader.

(207d) Walden Heights (also Walden Station, Depot and Summit, with a PO from 1916-54).

c. 1820: a hotel, Hanson Rogers; tavern license, 1821, '22, '26, '27; at Walden Depot for many years (Child); on the hill road from Danville.

Note: the assistance of Mrs Elizabeth P. Hatch, West Danville, is gratefully acknowledged.

* * *

References

557

(1) History Committee, A History of Walden, Vermont (Randolph Ctr: Greenhills Books, for the Walden Public Library, 1986).

* * *

(208) **Wallingford** (Rutland).

(208a) East Wallingford (no village here until the Central Vermont railroad came through).

1863:   (a) East Wallingford Hotel, E. A. Cutler; built by him this year, burned in 1888; also known as Todd's Hotel; kept for 2-3 years by Cutler, who was followed by H. E. Sawyer, Daniel Ensign, Charles Allen, H. L. Warner, Alson Ahite, J. B. Powell and Joel Todd, who began in 1879; "his dancing hall, it is claimed, is the largest one connected with a hotel in the State"; A. W. Duval built a smaller hotel to replace it after the fire (see below);

1869:   (a) as above, H. L. Warner* (Beers);

1870, '73:   (a) --, H. L. Warner;

1875:   --, E. W. Warner;

1878:   --, J. B. Powell;

1879:   (a) as above, Joel Todd (Todd's Hotel);

1880, '81, '83, '87:   --, Joel Todd;

c. 1889:   a hotel, A. W. Duval; opposite the depot, after the East Wallingford House burned; but moved to old Todd site next to the church when the road was relocated in 1911; this place also burned, and the fire house now stands on the site;

1892, '95:   --, J. F. Eggleston;

1898:   --, M. M. Furman;

1901:   --, H. N. Hill;

1905, '11, '13, '20, '25:   --, Alfred W. Duval.

(208b) South Wallingford (on the Rutland-Bennington railroad).

1792:   a tavern, --; on present Rte 7, on the stage road from Bennington to Rutland on West Hill; the Green Mountain Tea Room in recent years, but not operated as an inn between 1957-73 (1); also known as Scott's Hotel, Miller's Hotel, Crapo Hotel (see below);

(?):   a tavern, Moseley Hall; tavern license, 1817; about a mile north of South Wallingford on a farm occupied in 1886 by Lewis Stafford (3); described by Thorpe as being "between the two villages" (i.e., Wallingford and South Wallingford), "near where Mr George Stafford lives in Hartsborough..." (ref 4, also an engraving of the tavern sign); the place was falling into disrepair in 1911;

1796:   Hall tavern, --; almanac, location unknown;

(?):   a hotel, Jarvis Andrus; across from the church site in railroad days (3); kept by various, last being Joseph Edgerton, who left c. 1875;

1869:   hotel, F. E. Crapo* (Beers);

1873, '75:   --, Joseph Edgerton;

558

1913, '20:   --, G. Holt.

(208c) <u>Wallingford</u> (North village, on the Rutland-Bennington railroad).

c. 1773:   first tavern, <u>Abraham Jackson Jr</u>; for 8 years, on a bend of Otter Creek, just east of P. G. Clark's place in 1881 (Child); a P. G. Clark is shown south of town on the 1854 Scott map;

c. 1775:   a tavern (and store), <u>Abraham Ives</u>; a high sheriff who had to sell out and leave town because of his role in an irregular land sale; "near the Meachem place"; (4)

1784:   a hotel, <u>Lent Ives</u>; almanac, 1796; a Revolutionary War veteran; near the residence of the late Isaac Munson (i.e., 1881, Child); this place was moved to its "present" (i.e., 1881) location in 1855; Ives kept the place a long time, was also PM, 1810-26; there is an I. Munson on the 1854 Scott map (and the Beers) just south of P. G. Clark (see above);

(?):   a tavern, <u>Jonathan Thompson</u>; almanac, 1812; about two miles east of Wallingford on the Samuel Rogers place near the Tinmouth line (i.e., c. 1886, ref 3);

c. 1814:   a tavern (and store), <u>Eliakim Johnson</u>; there is a Rutland Herald reference (2/19/1828) to Johnson and his son selling this place; and an 1827 reference (7/17/1827) to <u>E. H. Johnson's Inn</u>;

c. 1824:   a hotel, <u>John Ives</u>; described as the "only" hotel in 1886; built by Ives as a tavern but soon converted to other uses; in 1835 Chester Spencer kept it for a short time as "first temperance hotel in the world," but it only lasted 2-3 years as such; other proprietors were Almerson Hyde, Arnold Hill, J. H. Earle, Elmer C. Barrows, L. J. Vance, and others. Known as the <u>Tavern House</u> and the <u>Wallingford Hotel</u> at various times (see photo, next page). Bought by W. D. Hulett in 1877, who remodeled it extensively in 1892, renamed it the <u>New Wallingford</u>; also E. Shaw, A. J. Gardiner and J. K. Ford. Became the <u>True Temper Inn</u>, in the Treadway Real New England Inn chain, in 1926. President Theodore Roosevelt spoke from the front porch during the 1912 campaign. Became the <u>Wallingford Inn</u> in 1949.

Note: tavern licenses, locations unknown, to O. and S. Hyde, 1817; and Johnson and Marsh, 1822, '23;

* * *

"Between the one at South Wallingford opposite the church (i.e., the <u>Andrus tavern</u>, see above) there was Deacon Hall's (i.e., <u>Moseley Hall's tavern</u>, see above); one where Mrs J. Westcott lives, one where A. W. Andrews house is--that in mid-1800s was known as the Beehive--one on site of present hotel in Wallingford; and one where L. S. Congdon lives, known as Marm Hull's tavern." (4)

* * *

(?):   an inn, --; north of the village in the present Albert Kelley home (i.e., 1976, ref 1);

1849:   --, A. L. Hyde (NEMU Dir);

1854:   <u>Hyde's Hotel</u>, --* (Scott);

1869:   --, J. H. Earle* (Beers);

1870:   as above;

1873:   --, J. H. Earle; (a) <u>Wallingford House</u>, E. C. Barrows;

1875, '78:   (a) --, L. Vance;

559

1879, '80, '83: (a) --, William D. Hulett;

1887:   --, A. D. Fletcher (James Connally in Vt Dir);

Hotel Wallingford

1895:   (a) Hotel Wallingford, S. H. Otis;

1898:   (a) as above, G. W. Wallis; but the Rutland Railroad guide of 1897 lists the New Wallingford;

1901:   (a) as above, Miss Knight;

1905:   (a) New Wallingford Hotel, F. H. Higgins;

1911, '13:   (a) as above, --; (with H. R. Leffingwell in 1916 VPB);

1920:   (a) as above, W. H. Snow; --, W. D. Clark (summers, location unknown); Maple Grove Farm, W. D. Clark, in 1916 VPB;

1925:   (a) as above, --; the True Temper Inn from 1926 until at least 1940, Wallingford Inn in the 1960s, converted to apartments in 1986; --, W. D. Clark;

Note: the assistance of William Dolt, Wallingford Historical Society, is gratefully acknowledged.

* * *

References

(1) Julian Klock, ed., A History of Wallingford, Vermont (Rutland: Academy Books, for the Hart Library, 1976).
(2) Vermont Div. of Historic Preservation, Historic Architecture of Rutland County, Curtis B. Johnson, ed., Elsa Gilbertson, asst ed. (Montpelier: 1988).
(3) Henry P. Smith and William S. Rann, History of Rutland County, Vermont (Syracuse: D. Mason, 1886).
(4) Walter Thorpe, History of Wallingford, Vermont (Rutland: Tuttle, 1911).

* * *

(209) **Waltham** (Addison)

"The town came about through an unusual set of circumstances," having to do with the

560

creation of the city of Vergennes. (1) Always lightly populated, it has never had either a village or a post office.

(209a) Waltham.

(?): a tavern, - Manchester; according to Smith, one Polly Barton, a widow, married Manchester, who kept a "country tavern on the Barton farm," known as the Manchester Inn; (2)

(?): a tavern, Isaac Hobbs; almanac, 1812; who was the first to occupy the Hobbs Farm on "East Street" and kept a tavern there (2); Hobbs lived to "a great age," farm now (i.e., 1886) the property of Mrs E. A. Hulburd;

Note: there is a 1950s Everest photo of a building said to have been the Daniel Chipman tavern, c. 1820; later George Fisher place, Harold Morcomb in the 1950s.

* * *

References

(1) Esther M. Swift, Vermont Place-Names: Footprints of History (Brattleboro: Stephen Greene Pr., 1977).
(2) Henry P. Smith, History of Addison County, Vermont (Syracuse: D. Mason, 1886).

* * *

(210) **Wardsboro** (Windham).

(210a) South Wardsboro. Postally, this was Wardsboro from 1817-53, when it became South Wardsboro. This PO closed in 1933. Known locally and on Beers as Wilder Hollow.

(210b) Wardsboro. North Wardsboro, 1832-92, when it became the second Wardsboro, postally. Known locally as Wardsboro City, according to Child. It is assumed here that a Wardsboro listing in Walton refers to this place.

Note: tavern licenses to Nathaniel Ward, 1820-24; Jonathan Robinson, 1819-21; Leland Fairbank, 1823, '24; William Kelly, 1822; Jason Sprague, 1817; Fairbank and Crosby, 1825; Wales A. Bridges, 1832, '33; Ira P. Hayward, 1833; Solomon Higgins, 1833; Jonathan Converse, 1826-30; and Reuben Killbury, 1832, locations unknown;

1849: --, J. G. Higgins (NEMU Dir);

1856: hotel, --* (McClellan map);

1869: (a) Wardsboro House, A. Watson* (Beers, same site as in 1856);

1870, '73: (a) --, Asahel Watson (who had it from 1861-81);

1875, '80: (a) as above; (b) --, Dexter Wait;

1883: (a) Wardsboro House, Mrs Watson; damaged by a major fire in the village in 1882; (b) Elmwood, Dexter Wait;

1884: (a) as above, Fred Underwood (Child); who took over management after marrying Ella Watson, whose mother had been operating the place;

1887, '90, '92, '95, '98, 1901, '08, '11, '13: (a) as above; Underwood died in 1918, his widow carried on briefly;

1920: (a) as above, B. G. Wilder;

1925:   (a) as above, W. W. Hodgman; building razed in 1939.

(210c) <u>Wardsboro Center</u>. No listings found.

(210d) <u>West Wardsboro</u> (Hammonds Mills, 1832-46).

1825:   (a) <u>West Wardsboro Hotel</u>, Justice Knowlton; later the <u>Green Mountain House</u> (see below); at the end of the Stratton-Arlington post road; on Stratton Road, just west of the intersection with Rte 100; Knowlton sold a parcel assumed to contain the hotel because of its description to Jackson and Solomon Newell for $900 (the tavern must have existed prior to 1835; ref 1); then Joseph Knowlton a year later, and Levi Fitts in 1841, who kept it 19 years; then Alured Newell, 6 years; Chester Briggs, one year; John N. Glazier; and Henry Waite in 1873, who kept it until he died in 1914 (see below); the last four transactions were all for the same amount, $1,000; VDHP 1319-2, still operating in 1971, burned in 1979;

c. 1830:   a hotel, --; just east of the <u>Green Mountain House</u> (above); VDHP 1319-3, last operated as <u>"Rest-a-While</u>," vacant in 1971;

1849:   (a) <u>Green Mountain House</u>, F. G. Kapp (NEMU Dir);

1856:   hotel, --* (McClellan map);

1869:   (a) <u>Green Mountain House</u>, J. N. Glazier* (Beers); it is hard to be certain, but this seems to be close to, but not exactly on, the 1856 McClellan map site;

1870:   --, Alonzo Smith;

1873:   (a) <u>Green Mountain House</u>, Henry Waite; who also ran the stage from West Wardsboro to Arlington until 1880, when the West River Railroad began running from Brattleboro to South Londonderry, and mail was sent from Wardsboro to East Jamaica; Waite then ran this route, carrying mail, freight and passengers, for the benefit both of the community and his <u>Green Mountain House</u>; his daughter Hattie carried on for a few years after he died; place burned in 1979; see photo;

Green Mountain House

1911:   (a) --, H. A. Waite;

1916:   as above, -- (VPB); summer board until at least 1930;

Note: the assistance of Janet LeBlond, Wardsboro, is gratefully acknowledged.

* * *

References

(1) C. S. Streeter, Return to Yesterday, A History of Wardsboro, Vermont (Canaan, N.H.: Phoenix Pr., 1980).

* * *

(211) **Warren** (Washington).

(211a) East Warren.

c. 1824:   a tavern, Richard Sterling; tavern license, 1833; on the place owned by George W. Cardell (i.e., c. 1889, Child); Child places this in the west part of town, but according to Mrs Katherine Hartshorn (personal communication) it was in East Warren, on the road south from East Warren to Granville, about one mile south of the intersection with the road from Warren village to Roxbury Mountain; probably VDHP 1217-7, present Thomas Blair house (1983); local authorities say it was built in 1812 by James Eldridge, first PM; VDHP says c. 1830.

(211b) Warren.

c. 1820:   a tavern, William Cardell; tavern license, 1830, '33; in "South Hollow"; Cardell also kept the toll-gate and "made the mountain road to Lincoln" (Hemenway);

* * *

"Samuel Austin ran a distillery in early times when 'toddy' was considered a necessity in every family. It was then used to keep out cold and to keep out heat. It was necessary at raisings, quiltings, parties, weddings, neighborly visits, funerals, sheep washing, butchering, and to entertain the minister when he called to inquire of the spiritual welfare of his parishioners." (Child).

* * *

c. 1850:   Pitcher Inn, --; built about 1850, but probably not an inn until well after 1915; #39 in the Warren Village Historic District, VDHP 1217-58;

1849:   (a) Union House, R. C. Perkins (NEMU Dir; became the Warren Hotel, see below); --, J. C. Hamblen; --, G. N. Brigham (both also NEMU Dir);

1855:   --, C. Divol;

1856:   --, S. C. Billings (there is an S. C. Billings on the Lincoln Gap road on the 1858 Walling map);

1858:   (a) hotel, A. Mills* (Walling);

1873:   (a) hotel, H. W. Lyford* (Beers, same site as above);

1870, '73, '75, '80, '87, '89 (Child), '92, '95, '98, 1901, '05, '11, '13:   (a) Warren Hotel, Horace W. Lyford (also known as the Union House and Lyford's Hotel); stopped operating in the 1930s or '40s, now a commercial building (1988); #45 in the Warren Village Historic District, VDHP 1217-58; see photo, next page;

1899-c. 1915:   Lincoln Lodge, --; a "summit house" on Lincoln Mtn, owned by Battell; see Chapter V;

1914:   (a) Warren Hotel, --* (Sanborn);

1915:   --, J. A. Pierce;

563

1920, '25:   --, G. H. Sevior.

Note: the assistance of Katharine Hartshorn, Warren, is gratefully acknowledged.

* * *

References

(1) Katharine C. Hartshorn, ed., Commemoration of Warren's Bicentennial, 1789-1989 (Waterbury: Buy Monthly Publ, 1989).

* * *

(212) **Washington** (Orange).

(212a) South Washington. No listings found.

(212b) Washington.

1801, '02:   Bartholomy tavern, --; almanacs, location unknown;

Warren House
(Warren Bicentennial booklet, 1989, Katharine C. Hartshorn)

1849:   --, H. Godfrey; --, S. G. Fisher (NEMU Dir);

1856:   --, H. H. Welch;

1858:   (a) hotel, J. L. Bowles* (Walling);

1870:   (a) Washington House, Henry Sherman; (b) Lake House, George W. Wason (there is no lake in the township);

564

1873: (a) as above, J. Colburn (Vt Dir); (b) as above;

1875: (a) as above, J. Coburn;

1877: (a) as above, Dr J. Coburn* (Beers, same site as in 1858);

1878, '83: (a) as above, A. C. Winship;

1879, '80: (a) as above, George Stearns;

1887, '88 (Child), '92, '95, '98, 1901: (a) as above, William E. Worthley (also PM, 1874-84);

1905, '08: --, M. R. Bohannon; this place burned in 1970, PO now on the site; VDHP 0915-51; see photo;

1911, '13: --, I. L. Slocum;

1914: no hotel on the Sanborn map;

1920: --, W. F. Turney.

Washington House

* * *

(213) **Waterbury** (Washington).

(213a) Waterbury.

c. 1802: a hotel, Amasa Pride; Pride had tavern licenses in 1821-24, and the fee was cut in half in 1823 "in consequence of fire"; on the southeast corner of Stowe and Main Sts, where Col George Kennan kept tavern at an early day (this must be the second place Kennan kept, see Outside the Villages, below); Pride was also the first successful merchant in town; Pride's Hotel burned in 1822, immediately rebuilt; kept as a public house until after the railroad came, not shown on 1858 Walling; Sayles Hawley, village eccentric, was a later proprietor, kept it in the 1830-50 period (1); almanacs list a Hawley as tavern-keeper from 1825 until at least 1829; also a tavern license to Hawley, 1829; on the site of the present Gulf station (i.e., 1976, ref 2);

1815, '16: Peck tavern, --; almanac, location unknown;

Note: tavern licenses to William P. Spicer, 1817; John Smith, 1820-22; Horace Atkins, 1825, '26; Parmalee and Atkins, 1830; and Lucius Parmalee, 1833, locations unknown;

1849:   --, A. G. Greene; --, Alpheus Robins (NEMU Dir, locations unknown);

1855, '56:   --, Matthews and Crossett; it is not known when Pride's closed, so one can't tell if this place is Pride's in its last days, or the Washington House before the 1858 fire (see below);

1858:   (a) Washington House, --* (Walling);

* * *

"After Franklin Pierce settled in as president (i.e., 1853-57), O. C. Howard, prominent Democrat, proprietor of the Washington Hotel, boasted of his wide acquaintances, including the president, whom he referred to as 'Frank'; and tales of fishing trips in New Hampshire long ago; he had hotel rooms decorated profusely with portraits of his distinguished friend, so great was his admiration for him; Howard went to Washington to advance the cause of Rufus C. Smith, incumbent PM; but upon arrival in the presence, to his dismay etc., Pierce did not recognize him, nor remember the fishing trips; returned home mortified, tore the Pierce photos off the walls, kicked them down into the cellar; and Thomas B. Seagel was made PM." (1)

* * *

1858:   worst fire in town history burned "the spacious hotel of E. and W. Moody" (Hemenway); this would have been the Washington House, rebuilt on the same site as the Waterbury House/Hotel;

1870:   (b) Waterbury Hotel, Bruce and Ladd (Albert J. Starr in Vt Dir, W. H. Skinner in Lewis (1); (c) Village Hotel, J. Brown (Vt Dir);

1873:   (b) as above, Lester S. Hills* (Beers, and Vt Dir); (c) Village Hotel, Mrs Nancy F. Brown* (Beers, and Vt Dir);

1875, '78:   (b) as above, E. H. Hayes; (c) as above;

1879:   (b) Waterbury Hotel, H. H. Bishop (see photo); (c) as above;

Waterbury Hotel (William Orcutt stereo)

1880:   (b) as above; (c) as above, A. B. Stockwell;

1883:   (b) as above, O. Chase; (c) as above, O. Chase (Vt Dir, is this an error?);

566

1884:   (b) and (c) above both shown on a birdseye view, ref 3;

1887:   (b) as above, B. Barrett and Son; (c) as above, Seth Jones (A. R. Pike in Vt Dir); (d) Central House, F. P. Norris (Vt Dir; and on Park Row on the 1884 Sanborn map);

1888:   (b) Waterbury Inn, W. F. Davis (Boston and Maine guide);

1889:   (b) as above; Trotter House, E. J. Ennis (Child, on Main Street; (unidentified, probably the Village Hotel);

1889:   (b), (c) and (d) all shown on Sanborn;

1890:   (b) as above; (c) as above, J. B. Phillips; (d) as above, George Burnham;

1892, '95:   (b) as above; (c) as above, G. B. Evans; became the American House by 1894, Sanborn;

1898:   (b) as above; (c) American House, A. E. Ellis (formerly the Village Hotel); Central not operating in 1899, Sanborn;

1901, '05, '08: (b) as above, B. Barrett and Son; (c) American, C. D. Robinson; both on the 1904 Sanborn, but the American House became the Green Mountain House by 1909;

1911:   (b) Waterbury Inn, W. F. Davis; (c) Green Mountain House, W. H. Goodwin;

1913, '15, '20: (b) as above, W. F. Davis; (c) Green Mountain House, W. K. Goodwin (formerly the American, Village);

1925:   (b) as above; (c) Village Tavern, A. S. Picard (see photo); (formerly the Green Mountain House, etc); Teacup Inn, Mrs Nellie Morse (at 60 South Main St, now an apartment house; this building was originally the Esquire Carpenter house, one of the oldest in town); White Creek Inn, Mrs H. F. Demerritt (unidentified); a White Crest Inn (?) listed in 1930;

Village Tavern (Vermont Historical Society)

Note: The Waterbury House, and all the buildings on Park Row, burned in 1953; the Village Tavern became Clement's Tavern, still operating in 1988).

(213b) Waterbury Center.

c. 1802:   a tavern, --; on the north side of Alder Brook;

1870:   Green Mountain House, William Hudson (H. J. Campbell in ref 1); there is also a

567

<u>Green Mountain Lodge</u>, Elizabeth Colley, listed in 1916, '23 VPB; see photo, next page;

1889: "the village has no hotel, but W. E. Marshall opens his door to the traveler" (Child; there is an E. Marshall on the 1873 Beers).

(213c) <u>Outside the Villages</u>.

c. 1790: a tavern, <u>Jason Cady</u>; a log house "near the arch bridge" (Hemenway);

Green Mountain Lodge (Vermont Historical Society)

c. 1790: a tavern, <u>Stiles Sherman</u>; almanac, 1801, '02; tavern license, 1817-30; a log house, on the Morris Thompson place (i.e., 1882, Hemenway); for many years;

1791: a tavern, <u>Joshua Hill</u>; tavern license, 1823; for many years, near Alder Brook, when the main travel north was over the hill road (Hemenway);

(?): a tavern, <u>Col George Kennan</u>; on this same road, near the south line of the township, precise location unknown (Hemenway);

Note: there is a "<u>Cannon</u>" <u>tavern</u> listed in the 1796 Vermont Almanac and Register, location unknown (could this be "Kennan's", above?); and a "<u>Holden</u>" <u>tavern</u>, 1807-13, also unidentified.

Note: the assistance of Gleason W. Ayers, Waterbury Historical Society, is gratefully acknowledged.

* * *

References

(1) T. G. Lewis, History of Waterbury, Vermont, 1763-1915 (Waterbury: Harry C. Whitehill, 1915).
(2) A. G. Wheeler et al., Waterbury Sketches (Waterbury: Waterbury Historical Society, 1976).
(3) Vermont in the Victorian Age, J. Kevin Graffagnino, Vermont Heritage Press, Bennington, 1985.

* * *

(214) **Waterford** (Caledonia).

(214a) <u>Gaskill</u>. (PO, 1894-1901). No listings found.

(214b) <u>Lower Waterford</u>. (known locally as "Pucker Street," PO still operating).

1795: a tavern (and store), <u>Samuel Hodby</u>; VDHP 0316-9, #3, now a motel, the <u>Briar Patch</u>, owned by <u>Rabbit Hill Inn</u> next door;

1800: a tavern, <u>Asa Grow</u>; first landlord on Pucker Street, flourished in the early part of the century, in a small red house on the meeting house site (i.e., 1941, ref 1); Grow's sign was a kettle hung on an arm of the post;

* * *

The Burlington-Portland stage route was established about 1804, passing through Lower Waterford, and this became a heavily travelled route, with as many as 150 wagons a day passing through. At one time, this place was said to have been as busy as St Johnsbury.

* * *

1805s: <u>Niles tavern</u>, --; almanac, location unknown, could be in the Upper Village;

1822: a tavern, <u>Lyman F. Dewey</u>; tavern license, 1827; at one end of the "long tontine" built by Roswell Shurtleff, who had a store at the other; then Asa Robbins, until 1828 (tavern license, 1824); then Luther Knight, and Abel Goss; fate of this building unknown;

Note: tavern licenses to James Williams Jr, 1822-24; Edward Pickett, 1825; and Abiel Richardson, 1826, locations unknown;

c. 1830:   <u>Waterford House</u>, Jonathan Cummings; who built part of the old <u>Waterford House</u> this year for his home and shop; sold to Nathan Bishop in 1832, then O. G. Hale and F. A. Cross in 1834, when it first became an inn (<u>Fred Cross's Churn</u>); enlarged c. 1840, with two piazzas and an alcove, "all supported by four solid Doric pillars made from pine trees which were cut across the river in New Hampshire, dragged across on the ice by oxen and worked into shape by hand." Hale and Cross leased to Russell Armington in 1844, then William Goss until 1848; Walter Buck; F. D. Beder; Buck again, until 1855; O. D. Hurlburt (Hurburt), until he died in 1870; his widow, briefly, then H. A. Bowman, who sold in 1873 to his nephew (son?), Edwin C. Bowman, who kept it until 1912. An inn until 1919, then a private home, acquired by St Johnsbury Homes Inc in 1957, who converted the ballroom and carriage stalls into motels, reopened the main building as an inn; known variously as <u>Fred Cross's Churn</u>, <u>Traveller's Home</u>, <u>Valley House</u>, <u>Bowman's Hotel</u>, and the <u>Rabbit Hill Inn</u>, according to VDHP (0316-9, #4). Operating in 1991 as the <u>Rabbit Hill Inn</u> (see photo, next page).

* * *

"It was a historic old building guarded by Rabbit Hill behind, commanding a beautiful view of the Connecticut Valley. In the far distance could and can still be seen the outlines of the Franconia and Presidential ranges of the White Mountains.

It was a noted stopping place for farmer's teams, being on the line of traffic from northeastern Vermont to Portland, Maine, especially at the period dating from 1830 to 1860...E. B. Chase of Lyndon...ran a line of freight teams and it is recorded that at one time his outfit stopped there overnight with 30 teams loaded with 30 tons of pork bound for Portland.

Mr Hurlburt named the hotel "<u>The Valley House</u>." Before his time, in the 1840s and '50s, it was the "<u>Traveler's Home</u>." The sign was a plain square on which was painted a picture in color of a chariot, with a man standing up, waving a flag with an inscription on it, "Traveler's Home." The chariot was drawn by six prancing bay horses. The first telephone in Lower Waterford was installed here in July, 1899." (1)

Rabbit Hill Inn, c. 1909

1849:   --, Walter Buck (NEMU Dir); this is the <u>Valley House</u>, see above;

1855, '56:   --, Walter Buck;

1858:   (a) hotel, <u>O. B. Hurlbut</u>* (Walling; the <u>Valley House</u>, see above);

1870:   (a) --, Ozro B. Hurlbutt (also PM, 1863-65);

1873, '79:   (a) <u>Valley House</u>, H. A. Bowman (Vt Dir; which also lists H. A. Bowman in 1883, but see below);

1880, '87, '92, '95, '98, 1901:   (a) <u>Valley House</u>, Edwin Bowman (PM, 1890-1907);

1908:   (a) <u>Valley House</u>, --;

1911:   (a) --, E. Bowman;

1913, '20:   (a) as above, but this is in disagreement with Harris, who says the place was a private home by 1912. (1)

(214c) <u>Waterford</u> (Upper village; PO, 1807-1935; underneath the Moore Reservoir on the Connecticut since 1957).

(?):   first hotel, <u>Warren Call</u>; about opposite the store (Child);

(?):   a tavern, <u>Simeon Hill</u>; tavern license, 1821-27; came c. 1808, kept it until 1810; this is VDHP 0316-2, on the east side of Rte 18 just before the St Johnsbury town line; building extensively remodeled later;

c. 1800:   a tavern, <u>Stephen Hadley</u> (location unknown);

1823:   <u>Pike-Streeter Tavern</u>, Nathan and Dennis Pike; tavern license, 1825, '27; who kept it many years (Child; the date is given as 1820 by Asselin, ref 2); <u>Pike's Hotel</u> is listed in the Badger and Porter Stage Register, 1828; once on the main coach road from the White Mountains to Boston, much travelled in the first half of the 19th century; a landmark for over 125 years.

* * *

Built when <u>Call's</u> tavern became inadequate, by adding two two-story additions and an

570

overall roof to an existing farmhouse, making a rambling structure with floors at various levels inside, and other irregularities (photo, and detailed description, ref 3).

After the Pikes gave it up, J. Hosmer; Warner Ross; the Jennisons; and John Morse, who sold it in 1864 to Timothy Streeter. Streeter "kept the house open for some years after the village began to decline on account of the building of the railroads, which put an end to teaming and staging. Its reputation... brought some transients and city guests in the summer but by 1874 traffic had ceased to such an extent that hotel keeping was no longer profitable and the tavern was closed to the public. Mr Streeter continued to live there, as did his family after his death." (3) (Note: there is a problem here, since Walton continues to list this place until at least 1898).

* * *

1849:   --, J. Hosmer (NEMU Dir);

1855, '56:   (a) --, Jefferson Hosmer (this is the Pike-Streeter Tavern);

1858:   (a) hotel, W. Buck* (Walling);

1875:   (a) Waterford House, T. R. Streeter* (Beers);

1870, '73, '79, '80, '83:   (a) Waterford House, T. R. Streeter;

1880, '87, '92, '95, '98:   (a) --, T. R. Streeter; in disagreement with Walter, who says the place was closed to the public by 1874; (3)

1905, '11, '13: (a) --, N. Kinne.

(214d) Waterford Hollow (no PO).

On Stiles Pond on present Rte 18 in the northern part of town; originally a sawmill town, but a summer hotel there by mid-19th century. (4)

(214e) West Waterford. (PO, 1857-1905). No listings found.

* * *

References

(1) Charles E. Harris, A Vermont Village, 1941.
(2) Edward D. Asselin, "Not Even a Ghost Town," Vermont Historical Society News and Notes 13 (April 1962): 58-59.
(3) Mabel H. Walter, "The Pike-Streeter Tavern, Waterford, Vermont," Old-Time New England 22 (July 1931): 15-22.
(4) Esther M. Swift, Vermont Place-Names: Footprints of History (Brattleboro: Stephen Greene Pr., 1977).

* * *

(215) **Waterville** (Lamoille).

(215a) Waterville.

Note: tavern license to Joseph Rowell, 1826-36, location unknown;

1849:   --, J. M. Hotchkiss; --, J. T. Matthews; (NEMU Dir);

1854:   a hotel, Moses McFarland; he "went away to the Civil War" (Chlild);

571

1856: --, R. T. Call;

1858: (a) <u>Mountain Spring House</u>, Charles Wilbur and Cephus Boutell; a "fine hotel on Bakersfield Road, near Bear's Den Rock" to commercialize a mineral spring (1); near a small pond, Lake of the Woods; place burned in 1873, nothing left; there is a minuscule body of water called Saddle Pond off Bakersfield Road in Waterville on the Vermont Road Atlas; this place cannot be the same <u>Mountain Spring House</u> as (b) below (shown in the village on Beers);

1870: (b) <u>Mountain Spring House</u>, Moses McFarland; (b) <u>Central House</u>, R. Darah;

* * *

Note: there are problems here, because Hemenway says (c. 1871) that there were two hotels in town, the <u>Mountain Spring House</u> and the <u>Union House</u>, and one planned near the Green Mountain Spring; but no place named the <u>Union House</u> ever shows up in Walton or elsewhere. Perhaps there were two different Mountain Spring Houses, one in the village and one outside (see below); and perhaps the <u>Union House</u> and the <u>Central House</u> are the same place). There is an undated UVM Sanborn map showing a place called the <u>Mountain Spring House</u> across the street from the town hall in the village, and a little north.

* * *

1873: (b) <u>Mountain Spring House</u>, Moses McFarland;

1875, '79, '80, '83, '87:   (b) as above, S. R. Miller;

1878: (b) as above* (Beers);

1883: (b) as above (Child); (c) as above, F. W. Darrah (Child);

1890, '92, '95, '98:   (b) as above, J. M. Parker;

1901: (b) as above, F. E. Brown; (c) <u>Central House</u>, F. W. Darrah; this is VDHP 0809-4, east side of Rte 109, north of the village and south of East Hill Road; built c. 1840, now apartments;

1902: (b) as above, F. B. Brown (CVRR booklet);

1905: (b) as above, E. M. Thomas;

1908: (b) as above, --;

1911: (b) as above, C. L. Westcott;

1913: (b) as above, J. W. Stevens;

1916: (b) as above, Edward Shattuck (VPB);

1920: (b) as above, Martha Parrington.

* * *

References

(1) Mary C. Westcot, Log Cabin Days of Coit's Gore and Waterville (Waterville: 1941; Essex Jct: Roscoe Pr., 1975).

* * *

(216) **Weathersfield** (Windsor).

(216a) <u>Amsden</u> (formerly Greenbush, Upper Falls).

c. 1820:   an inn, <u>George Potwine Jr</u>; at the southwest corner of Tarbell Hill and Little Ascutney Rds; north of Downer's; Potwine was the Greenbush PM, 1819-29;

(?):   a tavern, <u>Nathaniel Staughton</u> (or one of his sons); at the same intersection as above, a little earlier (1); the building still standing at this intersection is either <u>Staughton's</u> or <u>Potwine's</u>;

1830:   <u>Downer's Hotel</u>, Samuel Downer; at what is now the intersection of Rtes 131 and 106; Downer died in 1838 and his son Roswell took over in 1843; "for the next 57 years established a reputation for his inn that had no equal"; he died in 1900, and his son Frederic succeeded; the place burned on December 24, 1916; (there was apparently a later building at this corner that served as a hotel, but the corner is clear of all buildings now); for years a stuffed panther, shot in 1867, stood above the mail-boxes in the post office in the hotel; Roswell Downer was PM, 1868-75;

Note: for a remarkable account of a ball at <u>Downer's</u> in the old days, written in 1902 by an elderly woman then living out of state, and a photo, see Chapter II;

1849:   --, R. Downer (NEMU Dir);

1855:   <u>Downer's Hotel</u>, --* (Hosea Doten map);

1856:   --, R. Downer;

1869:   (a) <u>Downer's Hotel</u>, R. Downer* (Beers);

1870, '73, '75, '79, '83, '87, '90, '92, '95, '98:   (a) as above;

1901:   (a) as above, Fred Downer;

1905, '11, '13:   (a) as above, C. E. Parker;

1908:   (a) as above, --;

1916:   (a) as above, A. L. Saxton (VPB);

1920:   (a) as above, John Olson; this cannot be the original <u>Downer's</u>, since it burned in 1916;

1925:   (a) as above, George Robinson (same comment as above); still listed in 1930, not 1935.

(216b) <u>Ascutney</u> (formerly Corners, Ascutneyville).

c. 1792:   a tavern, <u>Paul Cook</u>; on Rte 131, building 35 in school district 9 on an elegant map contained in Hurd's book; (1)

c. 1792:   a tavern, <u>Benajah Dean</u>; also on Rte 131, building 30 in school district 9, the John Wright place in 1975; (1)

c. 1800:   <u>Colston's Tavern</u>, - Colston; a large hotel and dance hall; "the center of the commercial and social life of the community...The taproom...was the meeting place for the flatboat men and the freight teamsters. Here, over mugs of toddy, they dickered and closed the deals for the transfer of freight from water to wheels. The Corners was the starting point of the teamster's journeys, westward into the dust and ruts of the turnpike, or down to the river for the slow passage on Sumner's Ferry" (1); VDHP 1420-4, now the Chateau; there is also a photo in Congden's book of a place apparently known as "South Farm" in 1946, said to have been a tavern frequented by boatmen on the Connecticut River in the old days; (2)

(?): a tavern, Zebedee Beckley; a brick building still standing (i.e., 1975) between Thrasher Road and the Mountain Road (building 24 in school district 10, the Corners District on the Hurd map, ref 1);

1849: --, William G. Colston (NEMU Dir);

1887: --, F. O. Pitts;

1890: (a) Maple Cottage, Andrews Brothers;

1892, '95: (a) as above, --;

1898: (b) Acorn Inn, Edward Ayers;

1901: (b) as above, --.

(216c) Perkinsville (once known locally as Lower Falls, Lower Village, and Duncansville).

(?): first tavern (and store), Nathan Duncan; on the hill where George S. Alford now keeps a hotel; (3)

(?): Hawks Mountain House, --; a hotel for a number of years, then closed and used as a private home; later opened by David F. McIntire, who ran it until his death, finally closed in 1891;

(?): a hotel, Samuel Alford and sons; Alford came in 1836, "later" built a hotel near his home, probably at the southeast corner of the crossroads; (1)

1849: --, H. A. Thayer (NEMU Dir);

1855: hotel, --* (Hosea Doten map);

1869: (a) Hawks Mountain House, T. H. Proctor* (Beers; same as 1855);

1870: (a) as above, --;

1879, '80, '83: (a) as above, David M. McIntire;

1887: (a) as above, A. J. Billings; Alford House, George J. Alford;

1890, '92: Alford House, George S. (?) Alford;

1901, '05, '11, '13: (a) Hawks Mountain House, J. C. Barton and Sons; (ballroom known as Barton Hall).

(216d) Weathersfield (the "Bow," where first settlement in town occurred at a convenient Connecticut River crossing).

Note: almanacs list three Weathersfield tavern-keepers, all unidentified: Jennison, 1807; Copeland, 1815, '16; and Spafford, 1771-1822; it is odd that this last place, in business for fifty years, is not noted in the town history;

c. 1780: Lyman's Tavern, Gideon Lyman; near Ashley's ferry; first two-story frame building in Weathersfield (building 16 in school district 4 on the Hurd map, ref 1); still standing in 1975; this is #1 in the Weathersfield Bow Historic District (VDHP 1420-24); VDHP says it was built by Elias Lyman, not Gideon; place also contained a store and the first PO between

Rockingham and Windsor; Joseph Danforth acquired the place in 1801, and it became a stage stop when the stage route was established; property stayed in the family until 1853;

1849:   --, J. Danforth (NEMU Dir); (J. Danforth Jr, 1818-53);

1853:   hotel, --*; on the northeast corner at the intersection, next to the Union church;

Note: the Inn at Weathersfield (formerly Weathersfield Lodge) is in a building built c. 1796 by Thomas Prentiss; according to Hurd, it may have been an inn once, but there is no real evidence for this; its first known use as an inn was in 1963. (1)

(216e) Weathersfield Center.

(?):   a tavern, Horace Cook; near the meeting-house in district 6; sold to James Goldsmith in 1832, now the museum of the Weathersfield Historical Society (i.e., 1975, ref 1); c. 1821, according to Aldrich and Holmes; (3) Cook was also a blacksmith;

(?):   a tavern, Carlos Cole (ref 3, no further information).

Note: the assistance of Dorothy Stankovich, Weathersfield Historical Society, is gratefully acknowledged.

* * *

References

(1)   John L. Hurd, Weathersfield Century One (Canaan, N.H.: Phoenix, for the Weathersfield Historical Soc., 1975).
(2)   Herbert W. Congdon, Old Vermont Homes (N.Y.: Knopf, 1946).
(3)   Lewis C. Aldrich and Frank R. Holmes, History of Windsor County, Vermont (Syracuse: D. Mason, 1891).

* * *

(217) **Wells** (Rutland).

Lake St Catherine (once known as Lake Austin) lies partly in Wells and partly in Poultney. The short-lived St Catherine PO was in the lobby of Lake View In The Pines, in Poultney. Lakeside hotels (or those apparently so from their names) are listed in Walton under both Wells and Poultney, and that is how they are shown here, as listed.

(217a) Wells.

(?):   a tavern, Davis Amidon; in the west part of town on the turnpike road; (1)

c. 1835:   a tavern, --; at the crossroad in the village (A2 on the Wells Village Historic District map, ref 2);

1841:   the Rutland Herald of Aug 17 reports a murder at John Howe's Inn;

1849:   --, Joseph B. Smith (NEMU Dir);

1859:   Lake House (Lake St Catherine House), Merritt Lewis; who built a summer hotel this year "on the west bank, 10 rods from the water, on a rise" (Hemenway); bought by Charles W. Potter who rebuilt it in 1867 (Child), kept it until 1878, then leased to Oliver Reynolds until 1911; then Irving Wood; (see also Poultney);

* * *

"The Lake St Catherine Hotel, an attractive four-story building, was erected in 1859 and by 1880 had become a popular attraction for prominent social, political and theatrical leaders from the New York City area.

A large dining room contained 2500 square feet of floor space and charges to guests ranged from ten dollars a week up...

The popularity of the Lake St Catherine Hotel, usually called the Lake House, is evidenced by the names of some of the guests who registered there. They included Lillian Russell, the world-famous beauty and Broadway actress, DeWolf Hopper, one of the great actors of the American stage, Lew Dockstader of the famous minstrel troupe, and the noted Ott family.

William K. Vanderbilt registered at the hotel on September 10, 1883, and requested to be furnished with fourteen horses for his party for an outing. In the summer of 1884 Jay Gould, the railroad magnate and reputed millionaire, registered, as did Charles Delmonico, well-known restaurateur, and Pierre Lorillard, the tobacco tycoon.

Probably the hotel's most famous guest was President Grover Cleveland who came during his first term in office...Benjamin Harrison also vacationed here, but before he was elected to the presidency.

The popularity of the Lake House was of short duration, mainly between 1880 and 1890. This was partly due to the fact that transportation began to be revolutionized about that time, with the introduction of gasoline driven automobiles imported from Europe, very expensive at first but within the reach of the wealthier class. Then in 1908 Henry Ford came out with his Model T which took the country by storm. The horse and buggy days were at an end. Families took to the road and expensive hotels in summer resorts went out of business. The Lake House, which stood on the site of the present cottage No. 114 (i.e., 1979) was torn down in 1909" (ref 3; another source indicates 1912).

* * *

Note: there is a place called the Lake St Catherine Inn, built 1926 and still operating, not to be confused with the old Lake St Catherine House;

1869:   (a) Lake St Catherine House, C. W. Potter* (Beers); (b) Union Hall, H. C. Thompson* (Beers);

Note: it has been suggested by a Wells historian that the Union Hall was not a hotel, but a meeting room over a store; however, it is listed in Walton as a hotel; and the proprietor of the Union Hall in 1873, '75 and '78, one H. W. Lewis, is the proprietor of Lewis House in 1880, probably the same place under a new name;

1870:   (a) as above; (b) Union Hall, Chauncey Gilford;

1873, '75, '78:   (a) as above; (b) as above, H. W. Lewis;

1880:   (a) as above, O. Reynolds; (b) Lewis House, H. W. Lewis (presumably the same as the Union Hall);

1881:   (a) as above, Irving Wood; (b) as above (Child);

1887:   (a) as above; (b) as above, L. Bushee;

1890:   (a) as above; (b) as above, S. Kinner (Vt Dir);

1892:   (a) as above; (b) as above, George Barrows;

1895, '98:   (a) as above; (b) as above, J. S. Wilcox;

1901:   (a) as above; (b) as above, Charles Clifford;

1905:   (a) as above; (b) as above, John Kalahan; (c) <u>Forest House</u>, Herman Smith;

* * *

"The first Forest House, a large two-story structure, was built by William Munson about 1900. It was a combination rooming house, dance hall, grocery store and amusement area, with boats for rent. The dining room offered fine cuisine and was a popular place for 'eating out.' This building was torn down, or partly torn down, about 1913, it is believed, and was replaced by a one-story structure which featured a dance hall, bowling alley and snack bar. The second <u>Forest House</u>, after years of great popularity, was also demolished several years ago (i.e., prior to 1979) and the St Catherine Cottages now stand on the site." (3)

* * *

1908:   (a) as above, --; (b) as above, --;

1911:   (a) as above, G. Barrows; (b) as above, E. J. Smith; <u>Forest House</u>, W. Munson;

1913:   (a) as above, --; (b) <u>Lewis House</u>, --; became a boarding-house, and finally an apartment for senior citizens, still standing in 1988; (c) as above, --;

1920:   (c) as above, J. A. Jones; <u>Idylwild Park</u>, Walter Brown; built in 1914, this was a recreation center with a picnic area, bathing beach, boats, etc; torn down in 1969;

1923:   <u>Forest House</u>, John A. Jones (VPB); on Lake St Catherine;

1925:   (c) as above, --; <u>Idylwild Park</u>, --.

Note: the assistance of Mrs Iris H. Read, Wells Historical Society, is gratefully acknowledged.

* * *

References

(1) H. Paul and R. Parks, History of Wells, Vermont (Rutland: Tuttle, 1869).
(2) Vermont Div. of Historic Preservation, Historic Architecture of Rutland County, Curtis B. Johnson, ed., Elsa Gilbertson, asst ed. (Montpelier: 1988).
(3) Iris Hopson Read, "Lake St Catherine, A Historical Scrapbook," (Wells: I. H. Read, 1979).

* * *

(218) **West Fairlee** (Orange).

See Post Mills in Thetford for Lake Fairlee, the northern part of which lies in West Fairlee town. West Fairlee flourished in the 1860s and '70s because of the Ely copper mines.

(218a) <u>West Fairlee</u>.

1828:   first inn, <u>A. B. Southworth</u>; who kept it for 30 years, also PM for most of this time (1829-53); probably stood on the northwest corner of the crossroads in the village, where a store has long been located (W. Whitney on Beers, Paul's store more recently);

c. 1835:   a hotel, <u>Capt Comstock</u>; where the hotel stood c. 1888 (Child; this would be the <u>Eagle Hotel</u>, but whether the same building or not is not known); sold to a Mr Joseph; successive proprietors were E. Kimball, Noble Thompson, William Kimball, Steward Brown (who died in 1871), and Fred Farnham (see below);

1849: --, A. B. Southworth; --, G. B. Jessup (NEMU Dir);

1855, '56: --, A. B. Southworth;

1858: (a) Kimball's Hotel, E. P. Kimball* (Walling; became the Eagle Hotel, see below); --, C. C. Knapp* (Walling; also on the west side of Main Street, but north of the four corners, where W. Whitney lived in 1877);

1870: (a) Eagle Hotel, Stewart D. Brown (same site as Kimball's, above);

1872: (a) as above, Mrs Brown;

1875, '79, '80, '83, '88: (a) as above, F. W. Farnham;

1877: (a) as above, F. W. Farnham* (Beers; same site as above);

1890, '92: --, W. H. Church;

1895, '98, 1901: (a) Eagle Hotel, W. C. Gilman;

1905, '08: (a) as above, Fred W. Manley; the Eagle burned in 1908;

1914: there is no hotel on the Sanborn map of this date.

(218b) West Fairlee Center (Middlebrook PO, 1852-55). No listings found.

Note: the assistance of Mrs Doris O. Honig, West Fairlee Historical Society, and Collamer Abbott, White River Junction, is gratefully acknowledged.

* * *

(219) **Westfield** (Orleans).

(219a) Westfield.

1827;
Note: tavern licenses, locations unknown, to Jere Hodgkins, 1823, and James G. Bernard,

1849: --, H. Richardson; --, H. Hulbert (NEMU Dir);

1856: --, Henry Richardson;

1878: (a) Westfield House, Calvin Reed* (Beers);

1879, '80, '83 (Child), '87, '92, '95: (a) as above;

1883: (a) as above, Mrs C. Reed (Vt Dir);

1887: (a) as above, H. D. Reed (Vt Dir);

1890: (a) as above, C. Reed;

1901: (a) as above, --;

1898, 1901: (a) --, B. E. Gilman;

1908: (a) as above, --; no longer standing, but precise fate of the Westfield House not established.

(220) **Westford** (Chittenden).

(220a) <u>Brookside</u>. (PO, 1893-1910). No listings found.

(220b) <u>Westford</u> (Westford Center).

Note: tavern licenses to Ebenezer Bowman, Henry Bowman, and Samuel Calhoon (sic), 1821, locations unknown;

c. 1830:   "<u>Old Hotel</u>," Danforth Wales; on the northeast corner of the green in Westford; Wales was followed by William Parker, 1836; J. R. Halbert, 1838; this is VDHP 0416-54;

Note: ref 1 says the <u>Brick Tavern</u> (below) and the "Old Hotel" are the same, but this is an error;

c. 1835:   <u>Brick Tavern</u>, Thompson Beach; on the northwest corner of the green; meals, entertainment only, no rooms; Daniel Douglas, 1848; Harminius Halbert, 1852 (shown on the 1857 Walling map); and the Henry Stones, in the 1880s; now known as the Fay house (VDHP 0416-52); Everest photo, 1950s;

1855, '56:   --, E. Hard;

1857:   hotel, <u>E. Hard</u>* (Walling);

1869:   hotel, <u>E. Grow</u>* (Beers; on the northeast corner of the green, i.e., the "<u>Old Hotel</u>" site); same site as the 1857 hotel, above;

1870, '73:   as above;

1878, '80:   --, T. N. Rogers;

1882:   (a) <u>Westford Hotel</u>, Thomas N. Rogers (Child); the "<u>Old Hotel</u>" lasted into the 20th century;

1883:   (a) <u>Eagle Hotel</u>, T. N. Rogers (Vt Dir; probably same as above);

1887:   (a) <u>Westford Hotel</u>, N. C. Dimick (also PM, 1889-93);

1890:   <u>Eagle Hotel</u>, H. N. Macomber; Everest photo, 1950s;

1892, '95, '98, 1901:   --, H. N. Macomber.

Note: the assistance of Mrs Suzanne Foss, Westford, is gratefully acknowledged.

* * *

<u>References</u>

(1) Lilian B. Carlisle, ed., Look Around Chittenden County (Burlington: Chittenden County Historical Soc., 1976).

* * *

(221) **West Haven** (Rutland).

(221a) <u>West Haven</u> (westernmost town in Vermont).

c. 1783:   a tavern, <u>Ichabod Mitchell</u>; on what was Mrs Adelaide Mitchell's place c.

1877, "at the corner of the road" (Hemenway);

1795: a tavern, Charles Rice; near where Nathaniel Fish lived c. 1877 (Hemenway); until 1799; there is an N. Fish on the 1869 Beers, near the Fair Haven line;

1814: a tavern, Apollos Smith; tavern license, 1817, 1821-23; also PM, 1814-39; first PO in town was in the old Smith tavern, according to Smith and Rann, "where Ransom Wood now lives" (i.e., 1886); (1)

Note: tavern licenses to Samuel W. Fellows, 1817, and Alexander Jennings, 1821-23, locations unknown;

1821: Gleason Stand, Oliver Hitchcock; Child says he became landlord here in this year; an Enoch Gleason had a tavern license in 1817; in the eastern part of town, #22 on the West Haven map in ref 2, on Stage Rd just north of the Main Rd intersection, east side;

1849: --, R. S. Armstrong; --, H. C. Rowell (NEMU Dir); (a Ransom Armstrong kept the PO for about 15 years);

1854: hotel, --* (Scott map); at the four corners in the village;

1869: a tavern, R. Wood* (Beers); very near the Fair Haven line, in the southeast corner of West Haven;

1870, '73, '75, '79, '80, '83, '87, '90, '92, '95: Wood's Hotel, Ransford Wood.

* * *

References

(1) History of Rutland County, Vermont, Henry P. Smith and William S. Rann, 1886.
(2) Historic Architecture of Rutland County, Vermont, Vermont Division of Historic Preservation, 1988.

* * *

(222) **Westminster** (Windham).

(222a) Westminster.

c. 1755: Whig tavern, William Gould; who came in 1751, kept a tavern in Revolutionary times on the "lower street" (Hemenway); place kept later by his son, John, who died in 1809, and by the grandson, Jonathan; it stood just north of the present Westminster motel, in the village on the same side of the street, replaced long ago by a private home; (close to O. Whitman on the Beers map); originally on the opposite side of the street; oldest tavern of record in Vermont (see Appendix C, Hotel Longevity);

c. 1760: Norton Tavern, John Norton; (almanac, 1785); on the "upper street" in 1775; there is an F. Brigham on Beers in this general area, with the added notation, "formerly known as Tory Tavern"; it was here that the New York party met before the Westminster massacre; it was in this tavern also, according to Child, that Gen Ethan Allen and Mrs Buchanan were married; "Mrs Buchanan, strange to say, being the daughter of the arrant Tory, Creen Brush"; torn down in the 1870s, a home built on the site which is #22 in the Westminster Historic District, VDHP 1320-1;

(?): a tavern, Capt Michael Gilson; came after the war, kept a tavern for 20 years on the "old stage road" (Hemenway; at another point, Hemenway says it was from 1765-85, "at the south part"); this place is still standing, on Rte 5, just north of the road to East Putney; the B. P. Page place in District 9 on the Beers map;

c. 1800:   a hotel, <u>Asahel Southard</u>; (almanac, 1802); in the building occupied by R. S. Safford's store, c. 1891 (Hemenway), for several years (this store is shown on Beers); then Aaron Wales for about 10 years (almanac, 1815, 1816); Joseph Willard (tavern license, 1820-32), John Foster (license, 1821-24), and Joel Aldrich (see 1849 entry below);

(?):   a tavern, <u>Joseph Erwin</u>; "on the Hunt place at the south part about the same time" (Hemenway); probably in the present Kissell home (1988) on Pine Bank Rd (shown as J. and J. S. Hunt on the Beers map);

(?):   a tavern, <u>Samuel Cone</u>; opposite the "brick store"; then a Mr Brown, c. 1810; and much later, Mr Danforth (1868, Hemenway);

Note: tavern licenses to Ellery Allbee, 1817-33; Joseph Hamblin, 1819; Joseph Hamblin and B. W.Hamblin, 1833; Simon Goodell, 1827-29; William King, 1824; and David Hardy, 1825, locations unknown;

1849:   --, Joel Aldrich (NEMU Dir; this was Southard's, above);

1855:   --, Allen Wells (see below);

1869:   a tavern, <u>A. Wells</u>; so described in the directory portion of Beers, and an A. Wells place is also shown on the map of the village, but not designated as a hotel; referred to as the only tavern in town, c. 1891, Hemenway; it appears to be this place that Child refers to as the "People's Tavern"; burned in 1915 or 1916;

1925:   <u>Westminster Inn</u>, Mrs Lottie B. Miller; next to the Westminster Institute, burned in the 1940s.

(222b) <u>Westminster Station</u>.

(?):   a tavern, <u>Ephraim Ranney Sr</u>; above John Norton's at a later date (Hemenway); in the east parish but closer to Westminster Station than Westminster village; precise location uncertain;

(?):   a tavern, <u>Eliakim Spooner</u>; (almanacs, 1796-at least 1829); "where Mr Lord now lives...about two miles below Bellows Falls" (c. 1891, Hemenway); there is an E. W. Lord there on the Beers map, in the vicinity of Westminster Station (which didn't get a PO until 1882); this is thought to be the present Morse home, at the foot of the Exit 5 ramp from I-91, near the Allen Brothers vegetable stand (1988).

(222c) <u>West Westminster</u>.

(?):   a hotel, <u>Joseph Ide</u>; "near the top of the hill on the old military road, that runs from E. R. Goodell to George A. Goodell" (Hemenway); George A. Goodell is on the Beers map, in the southwest corner of the town; (the military road is shown on a map of Putney prepared in 1947 by C. E. Cory and M. C. Carpenter, that also shows the southwest part of Westminster as it was in 1800); "a log house, did a large business in toddy...a necessity to meet the wants of the traveling community as early as 1790...That log house was witness to many a fight to let off the fire of New England rum on the brain. The proprietor was often obliged to fall back on his large physical organism to keep control...";

(?):   a hotel, <u>Joseph (Josiah?) Hendee</u>; before 1800, in the old house in the village now used as a shop by F. O. Dunham (i.e., c. 1891, Hemenway; this shop is shown on Beers); from 1802-08, Gideon Warner was landlord in the same place;

1804:   a hotel, <u>Ebenezer Goodhue</u>; in house now used by Warren Peck (i.e., c. 1891, Hemenway); there is a sketch of the Goodhue tavern in Simonds (1); near the grist mill in District 1 in the west parish (Beers);

* * *

At the installation of the Rev Timothy Field in 1807 (pastor of the Westminster West Congregational church) the place was opened as an ordination hall, which Hemenway said showed the tastes and habits of the times; "it was not certain which had the most attention, the fiddle or the toddy-stick. The heels kept time to the fiddle, the heads to the toddy-stick."

* * *

c. 1805: a tavern, <u>Benjamin Smith</u>; in place now used by Ephraim Wilcox for a store, for a few years; then David Johnson; place was known as <u>Abel Edgell's Hotel</u> for a while, famous for toddy and horse-trading. Then Ephraim Ranney, Gideon Warner. The Wilcox store is shown on Beers; now a private residence, #10 in the Westminster West Historic District, VDHP 1320-22;

(?): <u>Wheat Tavern</u>, - Wheat; in the the Windmill Hill area, in the southwest corner of the township; in Revolutionary times, on the old military road;

1802: <u>Brown Tavern</u>, --; almanac, location unknown;

c. 1830: a tavern, W. Field; in district 3, no further information;

(?): a tavern, <u>Ephraim Ranney</u>; son of Ranney Sr, tavern-keeper near Westminster Station;

1870: --, E. Wilcox (Vt Dir).

Note: The help of Mr Robert Haas of the Westminster Historical Society is gratefully acknowledged.

* * *

References

(1) M. Elizabeth M. Simonds, History of Westminster (Westminster: The Town, 1st ed., 1941, revised 1983).

* * *

(223) **Westmore** (Orleans).

(223a) <u>Long Pond</u>. (PO for seven months in 1884, a sawmill settlement).

1895: <u>Arcadia Retreat</u>, Floyd Varis; on a farm in the Long Pond area; "this imposing hotel always was remote from the life of the town...rumors that it was a retreat for artists, for those recuperating from tuberculosis or from nervous diseases, for gamblers, even for a sort of pre-1900 "love-in" (1); never a paying proposition, changed hands often, closed in 1912, abandoned, and finally burned about 1923.

(223b) <u>Westmore</u>. No listings found.

(223c) <u>Willoughby Lake</u> (PO, 1853-72) and <u>Willoughby</u> (PO, 1884-1904, same location).

There was a second Willoughby PO, in South Barton, 1909-27. Access to Lake Willoughby only became possible with Peter Gilman's road, finished in 1852.

1852: <u>Lake House</u>, Alonzo Bemis and Company; a four-story building with front verandas at each floor, on the south end of the lake; "help lived in a farm house across the road, as did the Bemis family in the winter when the Lake House was closed" (1); there was a boat, and guests were brought from the West Burke depot in luxurious horse carriages; burned in 1903, the farm house

582

became <u>Pisgah Lodge</u>, which also burned, in 1973; the Willoughby Lake PO was in the hotel, and when the Richardsons acquired the place in 1884 and renovated it, so was the Willoughby PO; see photo;

* * *

An excellent description of this place in the old days, written from the perspective of a young boy traveling there with his parents from New York City, appeared in Vermont History (2); an extended quotation from this article will be found in Chapter III. Reproduction of a lithograph and an old photograph appear in ref 3; see also ref 4.

* * *

c. 1852:   <u>Gilman's Tavern</u>, Peter Gilman; same man who built the road on the east side of the lake; also known as <u>Willoughby House</u>, and <u>New Willoughby Hotel</u>; burned in 1941;

1870, '72:   (a) <u>Willoughby Lake House</u>, Alonzo Bemis; (b) <u>Willoughby House</u>, Harry Cheney;

1873:   (a) as above, A. C. Denison; (b) as above;

1878:   (a) as above, C. C. Thurber* (Beers); (b) --, H. Cheney* (Beers);

1880:   (a) as above, F. and W. A. Richardson; (b) as above, C. C. Thurber;

1883:   (a) as above, S. Richardson; (b) as above, E. M. Atkins;

1883:   (a) as above, Francis Richardson; (b) as above, Hall and Atkins (Child);

1887:   (a) as above; (b) as above, H. H. Gilman;

Willoughby Lake House (Special Collections, UVM)

1890, '92, '95, '98, 1901:   (a) as above, Naomi Richardson; (b) as above, H. H. and E. M. Gilman;

1905:   (a) as above, Mrs N. R. Richardson; (b) <u>Gilman's Tavern</u>, H. H. and E. C. (?) Gilman;

1908:   (a) as above, --; <u>Ben Hur</u>, --;

1911:   (b) <u>Willoughby House</u>, -- (see photo): (c) <u>Evergreen Park</u>, G. W. Conley; (d) <u>Foster's Grove</u>, G. Myers; (e) <u>Lakeside Park</u>, J. W. Hyde;

1913:   (b) <u>Willoughby House</u> (<u>Gilman's Tavern</u>), --; (c) <u>Evergreen Park</u>, G. W. Cawley (sp?); (d) <u>Foster's Grove</u>, G. Myers; (e) <u>Lakeside Park</u>, J. W. Hyde;

1916:   (b) as above, W. F. Richardson (VPB);

1920:   (b), (c), (d) and (e) as above; <u>Pisgah Lodge</u>, Clemma Seaver;

1925:   (b) as above, Mrs L. M. Hubbard; (c) as above, R. M. Wells; <u>Pisgah Lodge</u> and <u>New Willoughby Hotel</u> listed until at least 1940; the former, and <u>Willoughby Lake Inn</u>, in 1955;

Note: one or another of the Richardsons was PM here from 1884 until 1904; and Alonzo Bemis was PM, 1860-72.

New Willoughby House (Vermont Historical Soc)

<u>References</u>

(1) The Westmore Story (Westmore: Westmore Assoc'n, 1977).
(2) Cecil B. Dyer, "Willoughby Lake Sixty Years Ago," Vermont History <u>24</u> (July 1956): 240-242, 247-250.
(3) J. Kevin Graffagnino, Vermont in the Victorian Age (Bennington: Vermont Heritage Press, 1985).
(4) Harriet F. Fisher, Willoughby Lake, Legends and Legacies (Brownington: Orleans County Historical Soc., 1988).

* * *

(224) **Weston** (Windsor).

    (224a) <u>Weston</u>.

    1770s: first inn, <u>Frederick Rogers</u>; on the "Old Colonial Road" that led from Andover to the "Island" in the southern part of Weston, and west; (Weston was created from the western part of Andover in 1799);

    (?): a tavern, <u>Alvin Simons</u>; at the bend in the West River, present Cranshaw place (i.e., 1982, ref 1); late 1770s;

    (?): <u>Tavern Stand</u>, George White; in operation by at least 1843, when White bought it as a "tavern stand"; he was also a shoemaker; sold to Henry Clay in 1844, then James Taylor, 1845; leased to Stillman White (when it was known as the <u>Union Hotel</u>), sold to Horace B. Allen in 1850; then Alonzo Farley, who ran it until he died of "camp fever" in the Civil War; then Hiland H. Pease and Lorin Pease, 1865-76; Charles Sprague after Pease's death, until 1885; Amaziah French; and Lizzie H. Wilkinson in 1892. It had apparently ceased operating as a tavern during French's ownership, perhaps before; this place became the Vermont Country Store;

    1797: an inn, <u>Oliver Farrar</u>; a hospitable taproom, a big L-shaped kitchen, and seven fire places, one in each room; bought by Franklin Mansur in 1857 as a private home; the building was given to the Weston Community Club in 1932, now a historical museum, the Farrar-Mansur House;

    (?): a hotel, - <u>Blodgett</u>; in a big store building built by Ambrose Pease in the "Charleston" section of town, west of the West River; the building backed up to a hill and could be entered at different levels; first known as the "Beehive," later the "Ark" (see photo, next page); Blodgett kept a hotel on the second floor "at one time" (1); it is said that his sign was made of large letters cut from newspapers and pasted to a board displayed in the window; later a tenement, now gone;

    1849: <u>Union Hotel</u>, Stillman White (NEMU Dir); this is <u>White's Tavern Stand</u>, see above;

    1855: (a) <u>Green Mountain Hotel</u>, J. G. Cragin* (sp?); (Hosea Doten map);

    1869: (a) --, A. H. Drury* (Beers, same site as 1855 Hosea Doten);

    1870: --, L. H. Lincoln; probably same place as above;

    1872: --, W. P. Tenney;

    1878: --, A. A. Smith;

    1879, '80: (a) <u>Weston House</u>, D. J. Pratt (Vt Dir calls it <u>Weston House</u> during this period, Walton doesn't list it);

    1883: (a) <u>West River Hotel</u>, W. E. Gates (Gale in Vt Dir); at the corner of Park and Charles Streets, Child; this is the same location as on the Beers and Hosea Doten maps, above;

    1887: --, C. J. Winship (William Holland in Vt Dir);

    1890: (a) <u>Weston House</u>, F. A. Rowell;

    1892, '95: --, J. C. Barton;

    1897: <u>Hotel Weston</u>, -- (Rutland Railroad guide);

    1898: --, E. C. Wood;

    1901: <u>Park View Hotel</u>, J. M. Harwood;

1908: Park View, --;

1915: no hotel on the Sanborn map for this year;

1916: Mt Wyanview, Mrs Theron Turner (VPB);

1925: Simonds House, F. A. Simonds.

* * *

References

(1) Ernestine D. Pannes, Waters of the Lonely Way (Canaan, N.H.: Phoenix, for Weston Chronicles, 1982).

The Ark
(Waters of the Lonely Way, 1982, Ernestine D. Pannes)

* * *

(225) **West Windsor** (Windsor).

(225a) West Windsor.

This town was created from Windsor in 1848; the PO was West Windsor from 1828-32, then Brownsville.

1773: a tavern (?), Steele Smith; who was one of the four licensees to sell "spirituous liquors"; a town meeting held here; presumably this was in the "West Parish;" (1)

(?): a tavern (and still), Gad Orvis; early 1800s;

(?): a hotel, Rufus Root; tavern license, 1811; "for many years" (Child, no other information);

1836: a hotel, Return B. and Betsy Brown; (Return was also PM, 1836-41, tavern license to a Briant Brown, 1811); sold to his niece, Amanda Sherman, in 1843; then Frederick A. Gale, 1845; Joel Hale, 1848; Samuel Parker, 1849, who ran it for 14 years (as tavern and PO); Fred Robinson, 1865; Reverend Zenas Kingsbury, 1866; C. O. Upston, 1897, for 17 years, with the Rev

586

Kingsbury being cared for at the hotel by Upston until the death of the former in 1906 (2); George Swallow bought the hotel in 1914; then George Wait, 1915-19; Ernest Sykes in 1919; it became a Sykes home in 1959; used as a dormitory by brick-layers from Boston working on the Story Memorial Hall in the early 1900s.

It is odd that this place is never listed in Walton or the Vermont Directory. There is a detailed description of the building in Fenn (1); the building is #9 in the Brownsville Historic District, VDHP 1422-7; VDHP says the place grew up around the town poor farm, built by Return Brown in 1827;

(?):   Turner's Tavern, --; in the Sheddsville section of town, at the southwest corner of Sheddsville and Sheddsville Cemetery Rds.

* * *

References

(1) Mary B. Fenn, Parish and Town, the History of West Windsor, Vermont (Taftsville: Countryman Pr. for West Windsor Historical Soc., 1977).
(2) Erla B. Scull, The Heritage of West Windsor (Barre: Northlight Studio Pr. for the West Windsor Historical Soc., 1980).

* * *

(226) **Weybridge** (Addison).

Weybridge Lower Falls, 1832-82, when it became plain Weybridge; PO closed in 1905.

(226a) <u>Weybridge</u>.

(?):   a hotel, <u>Enoch Sprague</u> ; a veteran of the War of 1812, who built the hotel soon after the war; kept it many years, followed by Charles Moody, others;

1812:   two tavern-keepers listed in an almanac, neither site identified: Smith and Phippany;

1870, '72:   (a) -, H. Tyler (Walton);

1870:   (a) <u>Otter Creek House</u>, -- (Vt Dir); also known as the <u>Old Tavern</u>, still standing in 1988, much modified; on the site Beers shows as H. Tyler;

1871:   "old tavern site," --* (Beers); on Otter Creek at the north end of town, this probably refers to an older tavern than the <u>Otter Creek House</u>;

1873, '83:   (a) as above, H. Tyler (Vt Dir);

1887:   (a) as above, C. L. Tyler (Vt Dir);

1890:   (a) as above, -- (Vt Dir).

Note: the assistance of Mr Edward Bowdish, Weybridge Historical Society, is gratefully acknowledged.

* * *

(227) **Wheelock** (Caledonia).

(227a) <u>South Wheelock</u> (PO, 1871-1905).

(?):   a tavern, <u>Joseph Venen</u>; an original lessee, near the Danville line;

(?):   a tavern, <u>Jesse Leavenworth Jr</u>; tavern license, 1822-27; near the millsite in South Wheelock; Leavenworth was also PM for Wheelock, 1824-30, presumably in his tavern.

(227b) <u>Stannard</u> (PO, 1871-1912). No listings found.

(227c) <u>Wheelock</u> (Wheelock Hollow).

1793:   first hotel, <u>Col John Bean</u>; almanacs, 1802, '05; outside the village, in his home; town meetings held there before the meeting-house was built, 1794-1801; conveyed to his son-in-law, Col Edward Fifield, in 1806, who ran it as <u>Fifield's Tavern</u>; Fifield was PM, 1812-1815, moved away after the War of 1812, when it became Elijah Bagley's tavern (the <u>Bagley Stand</u>), later the Buckley farm; Bagley too was PM, 1830-35; this place was on the old county road over which stages ran from Concord, New Hampshire to Derby Line. The route was through Barnet, Peacham, Danville, North Danville, South Wheelock, over the hill by the Red Schoolhouse to Ramsay Corner (see below), past the Stephen Morgan place and on to Sheffield, Glover, Barton, Brownington and Derby Line.

* * *

"These taverns or stands were on one of the main lines of travel from "Down Below" into this north country. A century and more ago they were well patronized by travelers. They were the scene of many good times in the old days...When the stage route was changed from Danville Green to South Wheelock and on to Wheelock on the present road, the old tavern must have ceased doing any regular business. Its site is marked by a bronze tablet erected by the late Ferd Chase...". (1)

* * *

(?):   a tavern, <u>Thomas Mathewson</u>; on the county road which ran through Squabble Hollow in Lyndon, past the David Renneff House and on over Vail Hill, "A favorite stopping place for teamsters when Mathewson kept open house in the early days of the last century. It had a huge fireplace in the Men's room and a 'still' nearby for making potato whiskey. One can almost feel the comfort and smell the good cheer of a cold wintry night." (1)

(?):   <u>Ramsay Hotel</u>, --; at Ramsay Corners, a settlement in the early 1800s when there were two hotels there; it is said that the proprietors of the <u>Ramsay Hotel</u> owned 1,000 acres of land and at one time ran as many as 6,000 sheep. One of the owners, Bob Ramsay, was a fiddler of considerable talent and was in great demand for every party held within miles;

(?):   a tavern, <u>John Chase</u>; tavern license, 1822-27; first in the village; Chase had a mill on the lower fall, with a house in front in which he kept a tavern for many years (2); place finally moved across the street to where it now stands (i.e., 1956, ref 1), marked with a bronze tablet donated by Ferd Chase, whose grandfather ran it;

* * *

Eleazar Wheelock founded Dartmouth College in Hanover, New Hampshire with a land grant from Benning Wentworth, in 1770. The General Assembly of the Republic of Vermont "adopted" Dartmouth in 1778, but Wheelock died in 1779, with the college in deep financial trouble. His son John became president, and in 1785 the Vermont General Assembly granted him a tract of land which became Wheelock a few years later. Lease monies were paid to Dartmouth by the town. There was a troubled relationship between the residents and Dartmouth for many years, which eased starting in the 1830s. In 1832, President Lord revived John Wheelock's custom of traveling to Wheelock each January to receive the land rent, setting up an office in a downstairs room at the <u>Brick Tavern</u> (see below, ref 3).

* * *

Note: tavern licenses to John Curtis, 1824; Philip B. Swazey, 1821-25; Elijah Sargeant, 1822; and Mason Thurston, 1825, locations unknown;

c. 1830: Brick Hotel, Samuel Avery (Ayer?); became the Caledonia Spring House (see below); built by Avery, who kept a tannery opposite; originally two-story, remodeled into a three-story building c. 1872 by Adolphus Winter (Royal Winter, in other accounts) who attempted to make it into a fashionable summer resort, taking advantage of a sulfur spring in back of the hotel;

* * *

The mineral spring was located a half-mile behind the hotel, some 50 or 60 feet from the tiny Sulliway Brook. Winter brought the water to the hotel in pump-logs, and erected a small spring-house nearby. The water came up in a cement block in the spring house as a bubbling fountain. There were convenient seats all around the inside of the building. Winter...enlarged the old hotel, put on a French roof and built a double veranda...Then he named the enterprise "The Caledonia Mineral Springs Hotel", and was ready for business. Meanwhile, local people redecorated a spare room or finished off a new one...in preparation for the influx of summer boarders and patients...Winter had a promotional brochure printed advertising the remarkable cures made...

Winter and company invested more than $15,000 to improve the hotel and develop the spring, but, alas, they were at the tail end of the mineral water cure craze. During the few years of operation not enough guests came to "take the waters" in Wheelock Hollow. The bottled water did not retain its curative powers, and leftover bottles were destroyed or stored here and there...Winter rented the hotel to various parties until he sold it in 1886. (4) The place was finally restored to its original lines by John Sanborn, and retains them to the present time (i.e., 1957, ref 1; photo, ref 3).

* * *

1856: --, Calvin Blake;

1858: (a) hotel, --* (Walling);

1870, '72, '73: (a) Caledonia Spring House, Royal Winter;

1875: (a) Caledonia Mineral Spring Hotel, R. Winter (J. Sanborn, proprietor)* (Beers, same site as the 1858 Walling);

1873: White's Tavern, Willey Holmes (Vt Dir);

1875, '78: Jerusalem House, M. B. Dike; (not known if this place, and White's, above, are the Caledonia under another name or not);

1887: Wheelock Hotel, Jesse G. Gray (Child);

1887, '90: Wheelock House, J. G. Gray;

1898: (a) as above, H. E. Colby;

1901, '05, '08, '11, '20: (a) as above, A. J. Rennie.

* * *

References

(1) O. D. Mathewson, "Hotels in Wheelock," Vermont History 25 (January 1957): 20-21.
(2) Ferdinand W. Chase, "Early Days of Wheelock, Vermont," (Troy, N.Y.: Times Art Pr., 1915).
(3) Eleanor J. Hutchinson, "Town of Wheelock, Vermont's Gift to Dartmouth College,"

(Rochester: Emerson Publ., 1961).

(4) Tennie G. Toussaint, Burlington Free Press, May 20, 1971.

* * *

(228) **Whiting** (Addison).

1780s: Marshall Stand, --; on the old Crown Point Road; (1)

Note: the present town clerk of Whiting agrees that there was a place on the Crown Point Road, but says it was known as the Parker House, not the Marshall Stand;

c. 1795:   a hotel, Luther Drury; in the northern part of town, first hotel in the township (Child); a Luther Drury is shown on a map of Whiting in 1800, prepared by Harold Webster, former town clerk for Whiting, in the northwest corner of the town;

1800:   Walker Stand, James O. Walker; almanac, 1812; who built it this year; now owned by George S. Walker (i.e., 1886, ref 2);

1800:   Pierce's Tavern, --; became the Pierce Hotel and later the Collin's Hotel (see below); still standing on the northeast corner of the main four corners in the village, the Coakley residence;

Note: two other tavern-keepers listed in an almanac, at unidentified sites: Curtis and Rich;

1849:   --, L. Pond (NEMU Dir);

1856:   (a) --, H. W. Pierce;

1857:   (a) Pierce Hotel, --* (Walling);

1871:   (a) hotel, --* (Beers; same site as 1857 Walling);

1872:   --, L. E. McAllister;

1900:   Collin's Hotel, Elmer Collins; became a boarding-house.

Note: the assistance of Grace E. Simonds, Town Clerk, is gratefully acknowledged.

* * *

References

(1) Allan S. Everest, "Early Roads and Taverns of the Champlain Valley," Vermont History 37 (Autumn 1969): 247-255.
(2) Henry P. Smith, History of Addison County, Vermont (Syracuse: D. Mason, 1886).

* * *

(229) **Whitingham** (Windham).

(229a) Davis Bridge. PO, 1892-1913; now under the waters of Whitingham Lake; and (229f) Surge Tank, no listings found.

(229b) Jacksonville (Point Pleasant from 1826-34).

c. 1837:   a hotel, Willard Foster; one of a handful of buildings here at the time, but "very soon the village began to grow rapidly" (ref 1; see also ref 2); Whitingham Center declined from about 1838, while Jacksonville grew; this hotel was on the site of one kept later by R. Q. Wilcox;

1840s: --, Ellis F. and Elliott F. Chase; twins, kept the hotel in Jacksonville for a short time;

1849: Village Hotel, Josiah French (NEMU Dir);

1856: (a) Stafford's Hotel, --* (McClellan map; Ira Stafford was PM here, 1856-57);

1869: (a) Glen House, N. B. Hall* (Beers; same site as Stafford's in 1856); (b) Daniel Lake and Miles Wilcox Hotel, D. Lake and M. Wilcox* (Beers; on the west side of the road leading south out of town); private residence for many years, now Engel House, a bed-and-breakfast;

1870: (a) --, N. B. Hall; (b) --, Lake and Wilcox;

1873: Brown House, - Briggs (Vt Dir); unidentified, probably the Glen House;

1875: --, H. C. Lynde; --, T. A. Hicks (probably an error, should be Sadawga);

1879, '80: (a) Glen House, H. C. Barker (formerly Stafford's);

1884: (a) as above, R. Q. Wilcox (Child);

1883, '87, '90, '92, '95:   (a) as above, R. Q. Wilcox;

1898, 1905:   (a) as above, D. M. Canedy;

1908, '11, '13: (a) as above, --;

1916: (a) Glen House, N. E. Adams (VPB); building gone now, date unknown;

1920, '25:   Maple Inn, (The Maples), Mrs Agnes Cross.

(229c) Sadawga (and second Whitingham at Sadawga).

PO, 1861-82, at the village of Sadawga Springs, on Sadawga Lake, a resort area in the latter part of the 19th century. Became Whitingham postally in 1882, and Sadawga Springs is now Whitingham.

1869: (a) Sadawga House/Hotel, H. N. Hix* (Beers); built in 1869 across the road from the old spring; now apartments and a woodworking shop, but it operated until at least 1915 or so; built by H. N. Hix (2); not to be confused with the Sadawga Lake House;

1870: (a) --, Tyler A. Hix (sp?); who drowned while swimming in the mill-pond at Jacksonville in 1874;

1873: (a) as above, T. A. Hicks (Vt Dir);

1875: (a) --, William H. Hicks;

1879: (a) Sadawga House, William Robinson and Son (Vt Dir); Sadawga became the second Whitingham, postally, in 1882;

1880: (a) --, Robinson and Son; --, E. J. Temple;

1883: (a) as above, E. A. Cutler (?):

1884: (a) Sadawga House, Charles E. Cutler; (b) Spring Hotel, Edward A. Cutler;

Note: this is a problem; there was a "spring house" associated with the Sadawga Hotel, but that was simply a shelter for the mineral spring; and the second hotel in Sadawga, known as

591

the <u>Sadawga Lake House</u>, wasn't moved there until 1889. This date may be in question, and it seems likely also that one of the two places must have been known for some years as the <u>Spring Hotel</u>;

1887: (a) as above, D. Huntley; (b) <u>Spring House</u>, E. A. Cutler (Walton; see Note above);

1888: <u>Sadawga Springs Hotel</u>, M. J. Anderson (Boston and Maine guide);

1887: as above, H. D. Huntley (?);

1889: <u>Sadawga Lake House</u>, --; built in Whitingham Center in 1840 (see below), moved to present location on shores of Lake Sadawga, on Rte 100, in 1889, known at that time as the <u>Charles Putnam House</u>; still operating, Lillian Jennings; VDHP 1321-5;

1890: <u>Sadawga Springs Hotel</u>, Dan Wilson;

1892, '95, '98: <u>Spring House</u>, E. A. Cutler;

1905: <u>Spring House</u>, J. E. Morris (see Note above);

1908: <u>Mountain Spring</u>, --;

1911, '13: --, Mrs F. E. Kent;

1916: VPB lists both <u>Sadawga Springs Hotel</u>, L. H. Tyler, 50 guests; and <u>Sadawga Lake House</u>, C. E. Putnam, 20 guests; latter still operating; see photos;

1920: --, M. J. Anderson.

Sadawga Springs Hotel

(229d) <u>Sherman</u>. PO, 1886-1902, in the southwest corner of the township.

1920: --, T. D. Goodell; summers; listed under Readsboro in Walton.

(229e) <u>South Whitingham</u>. PO, 1890-1907. A neighborhood on Route 18A, south of Jacksonville. No listings found.

(229g) <u>Whitingham</u>. First PO in town, 1816-82, at what was sometimes called Whitingham Center.

c. 1772: first hotel, <u>Silas Hamilton</u>; on the Addison Eames place (3); Hamilton was an early settler in the northeast corner of town, near the Marlboro line;

Sadawga Lake House (Vermont Historical Society)

* * *

"Silas Hamilton was the first representative for the town of Whitingham to the General Assembly in Windsor in 1778. He was also town treasurer, and used his log cabin as a hotel when travelers came to Whitingham. For the first few years of Whitingham's history, he must have been a very important man.

Then it was discovered that Silas Hamilton was using the money of the town, which he held as treasurer, as his own. Mr Hamilton was asked to leave town, and to turn over to the town his land in Whitingham to replace the money he had taken." (1)

* * *

(?):   first hotel, Jacob Porter; an early settler, on road 38 (the road leading south from Whitingham Center; Child); this account conflicts with Butterfield, who says that Silas Hamilton's hotel was the first (see above); (3)

Note: tavern licenses to Ephraim Smith, 1817, '20, '21; Emery Greenleaf, 1823; Greenleaf and Houghton, 1824-26; Robert Riddle, 1833; Josiah S. Allen, 1821, '22; and Austin and Caldwell, 1830, '33, locations unknown;

c. 1824:   a hotel (and store), Eli Higley and Asahel Booth; tavern license, 1827, '28; "a new store and hotel near the old one" (Hemenway); not clear what is meant by "the old one," probably Jacob Porter's, above; changed hands several times, not clear how long the hotel continued; location shown on a map in Graves; (1)

1840:   Sadawga Lake House, Capt Reuben Winn; moved to Sadawga in 1889;

1849:   Stage House, Ira Stafford; --, Timothy Puffer;

1856:   hotel, --* (McClellan);

1869:   hotel and PO, J. Gates* (Beers);

1870:   --, R. A. Stafford (PM, 1869-70);

Note: the Whitingham name moved to Sadawga in 1882, with Whitingham becoming known locally as Whitingham Center, or Town Hill Common.

Note: the assistance of Ronald E. Hadley, Whitingham Historical Society, is gratefully acknowledged.

* * *

References

(1) Marjorie W. Graves, Stories of Whitingham (n.p., 1975).
(2) Leonard Brown, History of Whitingham (Brattleboro: Frank E. Housh, 1886; 2nd edition, North Adams, Mass.: Lamb Pr., 1986).
(3) A. A. Butterfield, Some Facts About the Early History of Whitingham, Vermont (Brattleboro: Vermont Pr., 1916).

* * *

(230) **Williamstown** (Orange).

(230a) East Williamstown/2nd Williamstown. PO as East Williamstown, 1820-42, when it became the second Williamstown.

(?): (a) first hotel, David Watson; "at an early date"; there have been three hotels on this site, now occupied by a garage (1989), all of which burned: Watson's Hotel, from an unknown date until 1874 (also known as the Williamstown Hotel, Traveler's Home); Hibbard House, 1878-1889; and Monument House, 1892-1935 (also known as the Williamstown Inn); see below;

Note: almanacs list two other Williamstown tavern-keepers, sites unidentified: Jones (1816,'23) and Wright (1825, '29);

c. 1820: Flint Tavern, --; on the northeast corner of Flint and George Roads intersection; according to VDHP (#0917-38) this was a stage inn in the early 19th century; Flint Road used to connect to the Paine Turnpike, but is now a dead-end road; the William Werneke home in 1989;

1824: David Gale Inn, --; on the east side of Rte 14, about one-third of a mile south of the Barre town line; the Cathrew home in 1988; operated as a tourist home in the 1920s and 1930s; VDHP (0917-95) says the original use was as an inn;

1847: (b) Gulf Spring House, Porter Flint; acquired by Thomas Saunders in 1884, managed by E. F. Dunham; near a mineral spring in the "gulf" about three miles south of town, on present Rte 14; the first Gulf Spring House must have burned or been razed (date unknown), because there was a second;

1849: (b) as above, Larned and Flint; --, Ebenezer Bass (NEMU Dir); the Bass house, a large house at the south end of the village, became known as the Carpenter farm, recently converted into apartments;

1855: --, G. Conner;

1856: --, Alfred Bigelow;

1858: (a) --, C. M. Patterson* (Walling); same as Watson's Hotel; (b) Gulf Spring House, --* (Walling);

1870: (a) Williamstown Hotel, Ezra D. Bennett (this appears to be Watson's Hotel); (b) Gulf Spring Hotel, George W. Lange;

1873: (a) as above, Fifield Bohannon; (b) as above, George W. Jeffords;

594

1875:   (b) as above, --;

1877:   (a) Traveler's Home, W. F. Levings* (Beers; on the same site as Patterson's on the 1858 Walling, i.e., Watson's Hotel);

1880:   (b) as above, Fred Martin; (c) --, George W. Lang; this is probably the Hibbard House, built after Watson's burned in 1874;

1883:   (b) as above, George W. Lang (?); (c) Hibbard House, Charles E. Peters;

1887:   Springs House, E. D. Barnes (?); (c) Hibbard House, C. E. Peters (Vt Dir);

1888:   (b) Gulf Spring House, Elbridge F. Dunham; (c) Hibbard House, Charles E. Peters (Child); the Hibbard House burned in November, 1889; boarders were temporarily accommodated in the Methodist parsonage across the street;

1890:   (b) as above;

1892:   (d) Monument House, George Clark and Son; built to replace the Hibbard House; became the Williamstown Inn (visible in an 1894 birdseye view, ref 3);

1895:   --, A. S. Winchester;

1898:   --, J. W. Brown;

1901:   (d) Monument House, W. L. Towne;

1902:   Gulf House, E. J. Gale (CVRR booklet); this may be the second Gulf (Springs) House; the first was razed, date unknown; there is now a restaurant on about the same site known as the Gulf House; (d) Monument House, L. Town;

1905:   (d) Monument House, J. K. Lynde;

1908:   Gulf House, --; (d) Monument House, --;

1911, '13:   Gulf House, --; (d) Williamstown Inn, --; (see photo; same as Monument House);

Williamstown Inn

1916:   (d) Monument House, C. H. Corliss; and Williamstown Inn, William F. Morgan; this listing of both the Monument House and the Williamstown Inn is almost certainly an error in the

595

Vermont Publicity Bureau pamphlet, since everything else suggests that these two places are the same;

1920: (d) <u>Williamstown Inn</u>, --;

1925: (d) <u>Williamstown Inn</u>, F. A. Bruce; listed in 1930, not 1935.

(230b) 1st <u>Williamstown</u>.

In the western part of town, where the first settlement was made; PO as such, 1798-1842, when it became West Williamstown for four months before being discontinued.

1792: a hotel, <u>Josiah Lyman</u>; first framed house in town, could be same as one referred to in Hemenway (below); the first school was in Mr Lyman's "decaying log house" (Child) and it moved to the "new" hotel where it was often disturbed by travelers calling for refreshment;

1792: a tavern, --; referred to as a "new" tavern in the western part of town by Hemenway;

(?): a tavern, --; referred to as the "Cornelius Lynde house, used as a Rooming House and Stage Stop", in ref 1; almanac listings, 1796-1815; at the corner of Northfield and Stone Rds, burned in the 1930s; Lynde was PM, 1804-07;

(?): a tavern, --*; <u>Judge Elijah Paine's</u> home was used as a hotel (and PO, stage stop) at one time, still standing in 1916, but burned subsequently (2); shown on the 1858 Walling map on Stone Road near I-89; Paine was also PM from 1815-42, and US senator;

* * *

Elijah Paine was born in Brooklyn, Connecticut, in 1757, started law practice in Windsor, and began a settlement in the western part of Williamstown. He was state representative, 1787-91; state supreme court, 1791-95; and US senator, 1795-1801. He resigned and became a U.S. judge of the Vermont district until his death in 1842. Also PM in Williamstown, 1815-42.

* * *

Note: The assistance of Mrs Janice M. MacAskill, Williamstown Historical Society, is gratefully acknowledged.

* * *

References

(1) Williamstown Historical Soc., Williamstown Through the Years, 1781-1981 (n.p., 1981?).
(2) Percy J. Jeffords, "History of Williamstown," Vermonter <u>21</u> (January 1916): 40-43.
(3) J. Kevin Graffagnino, Vermont in the Victorian Age (Bennington: Vermont Heritage Press, 1985).

* * *

(231) <u>**Williston**</u> (Chittenden).

Williston had a lot of taverns (and distilleries) because it was on a main turnpike, and the center of a number of stage lines.

(231a) <u>North Williston</u>. PO in 1865, no village here until the railroad came in 1848. No listings found.

(231b) <u>Talcott</u>. PO, 1897-1903.

c. 1786:   first tavern, <u>Deacon David Talcott</u>; in his large frame house "on top of the hill" (i.e., Talcott Hill; ref 1) until Talcott died in 1810; this is Oak Hill, according to Moody and Putnam. (2)

(231c) <u>Williston</u> (including taverns outside the villages).

c. 1787:   a tavern, <u>Thomas Chittenden</u>; described as a friend and contemporary of David Talcott's (ref 2, see above); "(Chittenden) also operated in his home a tavern for the few travelers that passed his farm on the Winooski"; this is Vermont's first governor and one of its most eminent citizens;

* * *

"Mr Pennoyer, one of His Majesty's Justices of the Peace at Missiskoui (sic) Bay, states in a letter to a friend the dire effects he feels tavern-keeping may have had on Governor Chittenden. 'A few days before he died, he was fined One Hundred and Eighty Dollars for selling Liquors by small measure without License. This is no more laughable than true, whether the Fine killed him or not, I can't say' ." (2)

* * *

(?):   a tavern, <u>Calvin Morse</u>; tavern license, 1821; an early settler; at the Four Corners on the turnpike in the southwestern corner of town, until at least 1825 (1); this is Taft's Corner, now the intersection of Rtes 2 and 2A;

c. 1800:   a tavern, <u>Isaac French</u>; on the opposite side of the street from Morse's, above (i.e., the north side) until at least 1825; according to Rann, French bought this land from Ira Allen about 1800, and his place soon became a regular stagecoach stop;

c. 1804:   a tavern, --; the Mackey house in 1976 (VDHP 0417-78, on Rte 2 in Williston village, on the north side); according to tradition, this place was built by a young man's parents to keep him from leaving home;

Note: two other Williston tavern-keepers, neither identified, are listed in almanacs: Atwater (1807, '10, '13) and Parker (1815, '23); also, tavern licenses to Nehemiah Saxton, 1820, and Leonard Hodges, 1821;

c. 1825:   a tavern, <u>Epaphras Hull</u>; at the west end of the village; (1)

c. 1825:   a tavern, <u>Mr Arnold</u>; (almanac, 1816); also at the west end;

c. 1825:   <u>Eagle Hall</u>, Benjamin Going; a large tavern on the site of the later Methodist church (now the Federated church); later kept by David French (c. 1830), Eli Chittenden, and others; burned in 1850 when James Hurlburt was proprietor, not rebuilt, as a result of the railroad's effect on turnpike traffic; almanacs list a <u>Going tavern</u>, 1825, '29;

* * *

It was for many years one of the best hotels in the county. Four and six horse teams and stages passed very frequently along the turnpike road, and the passengers and drivers were accustomed to stay over night at Eagle Hall.

* * *

c. 1825:   a tavern, <u>Isaac Morton</u>; on the road to Hinesburg, in the southwest part of town;

597

c. 1840: a hotel, <u>William Brown</u>; in the house occupied by George Brownell (i.e., c. 1886, ref 1);

1840: a hotel, <u>Capt Lathrop</u>; in the house occupied by Mrs John Forbes c. 1886, ref 1;

c. 1845: a tavern, --; at Tafts Corner; but it is not certain if the present building (the Blair house, VDHP 0417-70), on the southwest corner, was this tavern;

1849: <u>Eagle Hall</u>, Stephen Seaford (NEMU Dir);

1887: --, M.W. Bidin (? name illegible, Vt Dir).

* * *

References

(1) William S. Rann, History of Chittenden County, Vermont (Syracuse: D. Mason, 1886).

(2) F. K. Moody and F. D. Putnam, The Williston Story, 1763-1961 (Essex Jct: Roscoe Pr., 1961).

* * *

(232) <u>**Wilmington**</u> (Windham).

(232a) <u>East Wilmington</u>. (PO, 1884-94). No listings found.

(232b) <u>Mountain Mills</u>. (PO, 1910-24, now under Whitingham Lake). No listings found.

(232c) <u>Wilmington</u> (including Lake Raponda).

1785: two taverns are listed in almanacs, neither identified: Cook's and Thompson's, both until at least 1829; a Samuel Thompson has a tavern license in 1817;

(?): first hotel, Capt Gooding Lincoln (<u>Lincoln Hotel</u>); "east of the wheelwright shop" (1); on Main St just west of the bridge, Rte 9; "drinking habit universal but drink was the "pure quill"--home-made potato whiskey, New England and West Indian rum unmixed with river water, or the villainous compounds of today. It required a good consignment of rum to raise a meeting house." This place burned, c. 1885;

Note: tavern licenses to Stephen Hubbard, 1820-22; Elijah Bowker, 1820; Lucius Field, 1817, '20, '21; Russell Fitch, 1820; William Goodnow, 1821, '22; John Thomson, 1823, '27; Thomas Wilson, 1821; Otis Alvord, 1825-27; Luther Spears, 1817; Elnathan Lincoln, 1828-32; James Averell, 1832; Nathan Briggs, 1830, locations unknown;

1820: <u>Averill Tavern</u>, -- (1); tavern license to a Benjamin Averill, 1820-26, and to a Stephen Averill, 1829 (see photo); at the intersection of Rtes 9, 100, east of town, midpoint on the Windham County turnpike, Bennington to Brattleboro, in the old days; an apartment building at one time, a bed-and-breakfast operating as the <u>Averill Stand</u> since 1979;

1849: <u>Village House</u>, L. J. Childs; --, G. W. Lamb (NEMU Dir);

1855: --, John Patch;

1856: --, J. Patch* (McClellan); the <u>Patch House</u>, built c. 1850, became the <u>Vermont House</u> (see below); still standing, a restaurant/bar below, apartments above;

1869: (a) <u>Vermont House</u>, Wilder and Kidder* (Beers; same site as the <u>Patch House</u>, 1856); VDHP 1322-7, on Rte 9, west of the junction with Rte 100;

Averill Tavern

1870: (a) as above; <u>Gulf Spring House</u>, --; (Vt Dir, no other information; this is probably an error in the directory; the only Gulf Springs House known is in Williamstown, and this place is unknown to local historians);

1870, '73, '75: (a) --, Wilder and Kidder;

1879, '80: (a) as above, J. H. Kidder;

1883: (a) as above, P. G. Wilder;

1884: (a) as abve, Paxton G. Wilder (Child; on West Main St);

1887: (a) as above, Burr and Ames;

1888: <u>Child's Tavern</u>, F. S. Crafts (Boston and Maine guide); first opened in 1903, according to the VDHP, but listed in this guide; operated later intermittently as a winter inn, now a time-sharing resort called <u>Crafts Inn</u> (VDHP 1322-9), on Rte 9 at the Deerfield River; on the 1906 Sanborn, the <u>Vermont House</u> is shown as an annex to <u>Child's Tavern</u>, a new building;

1889: (b) a hotel, --; at Lake Raponda; enlarged in 1892, burned in 1896; a new hotel was built in 1899, a little east of the original site, near the island; razed in the 1930s;

1890: (a) as above, Burr and MacClellan; (b) <u>Raponda House</u>, R. Q. Wilcox;

1891: (a) <u>Vermont House</u> and (b) <u>Raponda House</u> shown in lithograph, ref 2, also an 1889 photo of <u>Hotel Raponda</u>;

1892: (a) as above; (b) <u>Raponda and Silvan Lake Park Association</u>, George R. Whipple;

1895: (a) as above; (b) as above, M. C. Wilcox; (c) <u>Forest and Stream Club</u>, H. R. Barber, pres;

* * *

This latter place was a private club, located just east of Haystack Mountain; started in 1893 by Wilmington natives who had "made good" in New York City and wanted to vacation in Vermont; golf course, several buildings, became a summer camp in 1924; finally ceased operating, and the last building burned in 1967.

1898: (a) as above, F. L. Allen; (c) as above, H. R. Barker (Barber?);

599

1901:   (a) <u>Vermont House</u>; also shown on 1901 Sanborn, same location as 1869 Beers (see photo); the <u>Forest and Stream Club</u> is also shown on the same Sanborn;

VERMONT HOUSE, WILMINGTON, VT.

Vermont House

1905:   (a) as above, Mrs F. S. Crafts; (c) as above, A. H. Watson; <u>Raponda Pavilion</u>, C. C. Abbey (is this the <u>Raponda House</u>?); (d) <u>Childs Inn</u>, F. W. Childs (see under 1888, above);

1908:   (a) as above, --; (b) as above, --; (d) as above, --;

1911:   (a) <u>Childs Tavern</u>, and <u>Vermont House</u>, F. S. Crafts; (b) as above, V. L. Adams;

1913:   (a) as above, F. S. Crafts; (b) <u>Lake Raponda Hotel</u>, V. L. Adams;

1920:   (a) as above; (b) as above, Antonia Treupel;

1925:   (a) as above; (b) as above, -- (also 1930); by this year, according to Sanborn, the <u>Childs Tavern</u> had become <u>The Tavern</u>, annex not in use; listed until at least 1955.

Note: the assistance of Mrs Margaret Greene, Wilmington, is gratefully acknowledged.

* * *

References

(1) John H. Walbridge, Wilmington, Vermont (Supplement to The Deerfield Valley Times, Aug 17, 1900).
(2) J. Kevin Graffagnino, Vermont in the Victorian Age (Bennington: Vermont Heritage Press, 1985).

* * *

(233) <u>**Windham**</u> (Windham). Created from the eastern part of Londonderry in 1795.

(233a) <u>South Windham</u>. No listings found.

(233b) <u>Windham.</u>

(?):   first hotel, <u>John Woodburn</u>; where early settlers stayed until they could build a cabin; where L. S. White's house stood, c. 1884 (Child);

Note: tavern licenses to Zadock Sawyer, 1817; John Aiken, 1819, '20; Simeon Hartwell,

1822; and Niles Aldrich, 1820, '25, '26, '30, locations unknown;

1849: --, William Harris (NEMU Dir);

1888: Mountain Grove House, M. H. Ingalls; Maplewood Farm, M. P. Fales (Boston and Maine guide);

1908: Mountain Grove, --.

Note: North Windham is in the town of Londonderry.

* * *

(234) **Windsor** (Windsor).

(234a) Windsor.

1772: in this year, the Cumberland County court (New York) issued tavern licenses to Benjamin Wait and Col Nathan Stone, tavern-keepers; and in 1773, to Hezekiah Thomson;

1777: Constitution House, Elijah West (tavern license, 1790); in existence by at least this date, because the Vermont constitutional convention met there that summer; "the welcome resort of weary travelers, brave patriots, valiant soldiers and distinguished statesmen" (Child); originally on the east side of Main St, just south of the road to the depot, moved later, became a state historic site; Elijah West was "the host of those glorious heroes, the Allens, Chittenden, Fay, Bowker, and others, who convened at Windsor...to complete the organization of the first Independent State Republic on the American continent" (Child); then Samuel Patrick Sr (almanacs list a Patrick tavern, 1803-25; tavern licenses to Samuel Patrick, 1800, '01, '06, '11), Samuel Patrick Jr, Thomas Boynton, c. 1840; it was at about this time that the Patrick Inn became the Constitution House; a series of managers, but the place was running down; Hadley, Durgin, S. R. Fitch, Thomas Emsworth, Albert Tuxbury; converted to other uses from about 1850, later moved and restored;

1786: Parmelee House, --; at the south corner of Main and Durkee Sts, south end of town; tavern licenses to an Alexander Parmelee, 1798; Elizabeth Parmelee, 1799; Josiah (Joseph?) Parmelee, 1799, 1802, '06; became the Ascutney House, and burned in 1881, site now occupied by a Cumberland Farms building;

1797: Conant's tavern, --; tavern license to a Stephen Conant in 1790, 1800; listed in Thomas's New England Almanack as a stage stop this year, also 1802;

1800: Pettes Hotel, Capt Joseph Pettes; tavern license, 1801, '06, '11; on the site of the Windsor House; it burned, rebuilt by 1801 as the "New Coffee House"; (almanacs, 1802-at least 1825); Pettes moved away in 1835; the Badger and Porter Stage Register lists a Frederick Pettis in 1828;

1807: Dean tavern, --; almanac, location unknown;

Note: other early tavern-keepers "approbated" (i.e., licensed) by the town were: 1790, Briant Brown; 1798, Gershom West, Robert Grandy, Joseph Allen, Willard Dean, Isiah Burk, Allen Hayes, John Gill, Gad Langdon, Jabesh Hunter, Samuel Root, Phineas Hemingway; 1799, Joel Dickinson; 1800, John Gill, Gad Langdon, Z. P. Smead, Samuel Root, Ezekiel Pearson, Willard Dean, Gershom West, Thomas Hunter; 1801, Z. Smead, John Gill, Gad Langdon, Oscar Townsend, Thomas Hunter, W. Dean, G. West, Perez Cady, Ezekiel Pearson; in 1802, remove Gill, Townsend, Hunter and Pearson; 1806, G. Langdon, Oliver Marcy, P. Cady, Winslow and Dean; 1811, Dean, David Orvis, Nathan Perkins, Rufus Root, Perez Cady; (Rufus Root and Briant Brown are West Windsor);

1842, '43   (a) Constitution House, T. Emsworth; (b) Windsor House, J. H. Simons (Simonds); built in 1840 on the site of Pettes Coffee House; (c) Mansion House, A. and E. Tuxbury

(Walton, location unknown);

1843: --, M. McKensee (Walton);

1849: (b) as above; (c) --, Albert Tuxbury; Armory House, J. A. Davis; Farmer's Hotel, N. E. Perkins (all NEMU Dir);

1853: (b) as above, --* (Presdee and Edwards map);

1855: (b) --, J. H. Simonds;

1855: (b) as above, I. W. Hubbard* (Hosea Doten map); Armory House, T. P. Shepherd* (Hosea Doten; on the east side of Main St, a little north of Bridge); became a tenement, razed in the 1930s to make way for a filling station;

1856: (b) as above; --, J. H. Cross;

1858: the first Summit House on Mt Ascutney was built this year; destroyed by vandals, rebuilt in 1903, and dedicated on Labor Day, 1904, when hundreds gathered; a shelter for climbers;

* * *

"Those in this vicinity--farmers, lawyers, mechanics and merchants--who... are not averse to a little sport now and then, will turn out 'bright and early' on Friday morning next, and repair to the 'field of action' near the foot of the mountain (i.e., Mt Ascutney), where a ROAD is to be opened to the top...

Every man will bring his own tools...and luncheon, spirits, etc, to last 'til sundown...when they will be conducted to a house (comfortably furnished, all things considered) near the top of the mountain, where will be supplied provisions and lodgings for not less than one hundred, it is expected, and for more should it be necessary."

This advertisement appeared in a Windsor newspaper on June 6, 1825 (ref 2); the purpose being to build a road to enable the aging Gen Lafayette to view the whole Connecticut valley from the top of the mountain. Lafayette did visit Windsor late in June, and attended a banquet at Pettes Coffee House, but did not make the trip to the top of Ascutney, and it is not clear from the paper's account (ref 2) whether the road was built then, or whether there was a house on the summit at that time.

* * *

1869: (b) as above, J. H. Simonds* (Beers);

1870: (b) as above, J. H. Simonds; Armory House, B. F. Hemenway; (d) --, Mrs Dudley (Vt Dir); built by Shubael Wardner in 1830 on Main St, now (1988) a private home;

1873: (b) as above; (d) Dudley House, Mrs George Dudley; (e) Ascutney House, W. H. and Charles O. Durkee (formerly the Parmelee House; see photo, next page);

1875: (b) as above (shown on Sanborn map for this year); (d) as above; (e) as above, C. O. Durkee (also on Sanborn);

1879, '80: (b) as above; (d) as above, Seymour Ashley; (e) as above;

1883: (b) as above, R. J. Coffey; (d) as above;

1883: (b) as above, R. J. Coffee (Child); (d) Ashley House, Mrs Ashley (formerly Dudley House; Child); the Ascutney is missing from the Sanborn for 1884 (it burned in 1881), Windsor still shown;

Ascutney House (Special Collections, UVM)

1887:   (b) as above, D. S. Simons; (d) as above, Seymour Ashley;

1890, '92:   (b) as above, A. J. Smith; (f) McCarty House, John McCarty; this place was once a one-story house where the Seal of Vermont was cut by Reuben Dean in 1778; rebuilt into a two-story house after a fire; on South Main St, now a tenement;

1895:   (b) as above, A. Wolfskiel; (f) as above;

1898:   (b) as above, O. F. Knowlton; (g) Ascutney House, --; (f) as above;

Note: there is a problem with this 1898 listing of the Ascutney House. The old Ascutney House (formerly the Parmalee House) burned in 1881, and it disappears from Walton (and the 1884 Sanborn map); but an Ascutney House is listed in 1898, and until 1913, unidentified and not known to the Windsor Historical Society;

1901:   (b) Windsor House, H. W. Bishop (see photo); the Windsor House is shown on Sanborn for this year, also 1906, '17, '25 and the 1951 update; (g) as above, A. M. Tenney;

1905:   (b) as above, Harvey Clark; (f) as above; (g) as above, John Monahan;

1908:   (b) as above, --; Windsor Inn, -- (?);

1911:   (b) as above, F. H. Chester; (f) as above, J. W. McCarthy; (g) as above, B. S. Brannock;

1913:   (b) as above, --; (f) as above, --; (g) as above, --;

1920:   (b) as above, --; (with Fred H. Chester in 1916 VPB);

1925:   (b) as above, --; still listed in 1968, became a National Historic Site (and crafts center) in 1971; Buena Vista Lodge, --; closed in the 1930s.

603

Note: the assistance of Katherine E. Conlin, Windsor Historical Society, is gratefully acknowledged.

* * *

References

(1) Katherine E. Conlin, Windsor Heritage: Birthplace of Vermont's Constitution and Industry (Taftsville: Countryman Pr. for the Windsor Bicentennial Comm., 1975).
(2) Frank H. Clark, Ascutney Summit Houses, Inter-State Journal 6-11, 1903-05.

Windsor House

* * *

(235) **Winhall** (Bennington)

(235a) Bondville.

Note: tavern licenses to Asa Thatcher, Jr, Oliver Beebe and Francis Kidder, 1822, locations unknown;

1849: --, Eli Hubbard (NEMU Dir);

1856: --, E. A. Hubbard;

1856: (a) hotel, E. Hubbard* (Rice and Hardwood map);

1869: (a) hotel, F. Morgan* (Beers; same site as 1856);

1870,'73, '80: (a) Morgan's Hotel, Frederick Morgan;

1880: (a) as above, Mrs J. S. Morgan (Child);

1887, '92, '95: (a) as above, Mrs J. F. (?) Morgan;

Note: the 1911 Walton lists "Morgan's, C. A. Styles" for Bondville; puzzling, since Styles is listed several times in the early 20th century as proprietor of the Green Mountain House, Winhall (see below); the 1916 VPB also has C. A. Styles at the Morgan House in Bondville.

1925: Monte-Verde House, S. Monteverde (also 1930,'35); same as Morgan's.

(235b) North Winhall. PO for four months in 1888-80. No listings found.

(235c) <u>Winhall</u>.

1849:   (a) --, Beriah Wheeler; --, John Brooks (NEMU Dir);

1856:   (a) <u>Wheeler's Hotel</u> (and PO), --* (Rice and Hardwood map; William T. Wheeler was PM in Winhall, 1854-56);

1856:   --, T. S. Gates;

1869:   (a) <u>Green Mountain House</u>, E. Amsden* (Beers; same site as <u>Wheeler's</u> in 1856, in the northwest corner of town);

1870:   (a) as above;

1873:   (a) <u>Green Mountain Temperance House</u>, W. F. Mills;

1875:   (a) <u>Green Mountain House</u>, P. Billings;

1880:   (a) as above, Charles King (listed as Bondville in Child, presumably an error);

1898:   (a) as above, L. B. Benson;

1905, '13, '16, '20:   (a) <u>Green Mountain House</u>, C. A. Styles (see photo);

Green Mountain House, Winhall

* * *

(236) **Wolcott** (Lamoille).

(236a) <u>North Wolcott</u>.

1872:   --, H. Holton; --, N. Boynton;

1873:   --, H. and A. B. Pike;

1875:   --, H. Holton; --, A. B. Pike;

1878:   a hotel, A. B. Pike* (Beers).

(236b) <u>Wolcott</u>.

(?):   (a) Wolcott Hotel, Ira Woodbridge; built by him at an early date, bought by L. A. Tillotson in 1874 (Child);

(?):   a hotel, Hezekiah Whitney; an early settler, kept a hotel more than 20 years (Child); tavern license, to a Jesse Whitney, 1825-32;

Note: tavern licenses, locations unknown, to Gideon M. Taylor, 1825,'27; Gamaliel M. Taylor, 1826; and Paul Davis, 1833;

1849:   --, P. Hutchins (tavern license to a Parley Hutchins, Jr, in 1833); --, Nathaniel Jones (NEMU Dir; locations unknown, one of these could be North Wolcott);

1855, '56:   --, S. S. Hutchins (same comment as above);

1870:   (b) Hubbell House, Justus Hubbell; --, Noah Boynton; --, John Patterson; one of these latter two is probably the Wolcott House, the other is probably in North Wolcott;

1873:   (a) Wolcott House, B. G. Pike (Vt Dir); (b) as above;

1875:   (a) as above, R. (?) G. Pike; (b) as above;

1878:   (a) as above, L. A. Tillotson* (Beers);

1879, '80, '83, '83 (Child):   (a) as above;

1887:   (a) as above, A. B. Pike;

1890, '92:   (a) as above, Dow Brothers;

1895, '98:   (a) as above, C. E. Clark; also on the 1897, 1904 Sanborn map;

1901:   (a) as above, D. D. Morgan;

1905, '08:   (a) (Wolcott House), Gordon Austin; burned about 1909, missing from the 1909 Sanborn map;

1911, '13:   --, M. A. Barter and Son; place known as the Foster House locally.

Note: VDHP lists a place outside the village, built about 1825, as Martin's Hotel; on Town Hill Road, the stage road to Craftsbury, about 1.7 miles north of Rte 15; VDHP 0810-32, now (i.e., 1983) the Russell Martin home.

Note: the assistance of Mr C. F. Reed, Wolcott, is gratefully acknowledged.

* * *

(237) **Woodbury** (Washington).

(237a) South Woodbury.

1889:   Lake View House, Abraham H. Holt; proprietor of this place, on his farm on Woodbury Lake, formerly Sabin Pond (Child); last operated by the Swain family in the 1930s;

c. 1915:   White Rock Inn, --; VDHP 1219-3, on Woodbury Lake, now a seasonal dwelling;

1920:   (a) Woodbury Lake House, A. G. Nelson; a hotel and farm, also a dance hall, and offering boat rentals (see photo); the old Lake House became a PO and private home in later years;

Woodbury Lake House (Vermont Historical Society)

1925: (a) <u>Woodbury Lake House</u>, A. E. Thompson; until at least 1940.

(237b) <u>Woodbury</u>.

Note: tavern licenses to Joel Cilley, 1822-24, '26, '27;

1849: --, S. Britten; --, B. Wells (NEMU Dir, locations unknown);

1855, '56:   (a) --, E. Town; --, E. Wells;

1858: (a) hotel, E. Town* (Walling);

1873: (a) <u>Town's Hotel</u> (and PO), E. Town* (Beers, same site as 1858); Abner Town was PM, 1852-54; Albert P. Town was PM, 1870-75 and 1881-84; and Orwell D. Town was PM, 1875-81, with the PO presumably being in the hotel during these periods; the relationships between the various Towns not established; this is VDHP 1219-26, built c. 1830, the home of Henry Wilcox in 1983;

1872, '75, '79: (a) as above;

1880: Walton has E. Town at South Woodbury for this year, almost certainly an error;

1887, '90, '92: (a) as above, R. F. Drenan;

1895: (a) as above, R. F. Carter;

1898, 1905:   (a) as above, R. F. Drenan;

1901: <u>Granite House</u>, R. F. Drenan (presumably this was originally <u>Town's Hotel</u>); a boarding-house for quarry workers at one time;

1911, '13:   --, J. Lepp.

Note: the assistance of Mr Glenn A. Sulham is gratefully acknowledged.

* * *

(238) **Woodford** (Bennington).

For a town with few inhabitants and only one road (present Route 9; the old Windham

607

County turnpike ran south of Rte 9 here, and intersected it in Wilmington), Woodford has a remarkably complicated hotel history.

Note: for an excellent description of this road, see an article by Bernice Barnett and Lucie Summer (ref 3); the first stop after leaving Bennington on this road was at a tavern at "The Elbow" in Woodford.

(238a) Woodford (City).

Hemenway says there were two taverns on the old turnpike in this town (the Windham County turnpike, chartered c. 1800). Almanacs list Scott's tavern (1797-at least 1829) and Lawrence's (1785). The Searsburg turnpike opened in 1832 (probably taking over and rebuilding the western part of the Windham Turnpike) and led quickly to two "new" taverns, one in the City (William Park, Jr's, see below); and the other in the Hollow (Elisha Lyon's, see below under 238b). There was a third tavern several miles east of Woodford City (Luther Wilson's), and still another for 6 or 7 years, H. P. Noyes; these are also listed below under Woodford City.

1822:   tavern licenses to Ichabod Woodward, Hepsibah Perry and C. Hull, locations unknown;

c. 1832:   a hotel, William Park Jr; who built it, later sold to Alonzo Fox; said to be a temperance tavern, at least originally (Hemenway); same place kept by Ezra Crawford, c. 1881 (Child, the Crawford House);

(?):   a tavern, Luther Wilson; in the eastern part of the town, near Adam's sawmill in 1881 (Child); closed for many years; there are a couple of sawmills on what is now Rte 9, well east of Woodford City, on Beers;

1849:   --, Alonzo Fox (NEMU Dir; this is Park's place, above);

1869:   (a) hotel, A. Fox* (Beers);

1870:   (a) Mount Prospect House, A. Fox (Vt Dir; probably a different name for Fox's Hotel); (b) Railroad House, S. R. Boardman (Vt Dir, location unknown; probably refers to the Bennington and Glastenbury Railroad, which ran into Woodford Hollow);

1873:   (a) Fox's Hotel, Alonzo Fox (Vt Dir); (b) as above;

1879:   (a) Crawford House, Ezra Crawford (still Fox's Hotel);

1880:   (a) Crawford House, Ezra Crawford (Child); (b) Railroad House, S. R. Boardman (Child); Glen Brook House, E. N. Fisher (Child, location unknown);

1883:   (b) as above, James F. Smith;

1887:   (a) Mt Pleasant (Prospect?) Hotel, James Higgins; (b) as above; (c) Cutler House, Cornelius W. Cutler (Vt Dir; probably the same as the Summit House, below);

1890:   (a) as above, G. W. Knapp; (b) as above; (c) Summit House, C. W. Cutler (see photo);

1895, '98:   (a) as above; (b) as above; (c) as above, W. W. Bowles; Little Pond Hotel, Mrs Trenor Harbour (summer, location unknown);

1901:   (a) as above; (c) as above;

1905:   (a) as above; (b) as above; (c) as above; Little Pond Hotel, --;

1911: (a) as above; (c) as above,--; <u>White Crow Inn</u>, --;

1913: (a) as above; (c) as above, -- (summer); <u>White Crow Inn</u>, -- (locaton unknown).

Woodford Summit House (Weichert-Isselhardt Collection)

(238b) <u>Woodford Hollow</u>.

(?): a hotel, <u>Elisha Lyon</u>; who built it; then Alva Hawks, Simeon Morse, and others; kept by Amos Aldrich c. 1880;

1849: --, John Collard (NEMU Dir, location unknown; possibly Woodford City, or east of it);

1855: --, A. Hawks (this is <u>Lyon's</u>, above);

1869: saloon, D. Crawford* (Beers; not clear if this was the old Lyons place, or if it provided sleeping accommodations);

1895, '98: <u>Camp Comfort Hotel</u>, O. E. Joslin (summer); this is "upstream" from the main part of the Hollow. (1)

* * *

"A new summer resort...opened to the public in 1890, consisting of two hotels, barns, a clubhouse, and 17 cottages, this resort was on the railway but could also be reached by a team...". (2)

* * *

1911, '13: <u>Camp Comfort</u>, --.

* * *

References

(1)   Esther M. Swift, Vermont Place-Names: Footprints of History (Brattleboro: Stephen Greene Pr., 1977).

(2) Tyler Resch, Shires of Bennington (Bennington: Bennington Museum, 1975).

(3) Bernice Barnett and Lucie Summer, "Border to Border: Along the Windham County Turnpike," Cracker Barrel (Fall-Winter 1987-88).

* * *

(239) **Woodstock** (Windsor).

(239a) Prosper. PO, 1896-1903. No listings found.

(239b) Taftsville. No listings found.

(239c) South Woodstock.

1829: a tavern, Richard Ransom; the National Hotel, became the Kedron Tavern, the Colonial Inn, the South Woodstock Hotel, and the Kedron Valley Inn; built in 1829 by Richard Ransom (1822, according to Curtis and Lieberman, ref 3); #14 in the South Woodstock Historic District, VDHP 1424-2;

1838: the Rutland Herald (May 1) reports that Levi Fay's tavern burned (location unknown);

1849: --, S. C. Taylor; --, D. Ransom (NEMU Dir);

1855, '56:   --, Samuel Taylor; --, S. C. Taylor;

1855: hotel, --* (Hosea Doten);

1869: hotel, D. A. Gifford* (Beers, same site as 1855);

1870: --, Azro Gifford (Vt Dir);

1873: (a) South Woodstock Hotel, B. S. Morgan;

1875, '79, '80: (a) as above, D. A. Gifford;

1883: (a) as above, R. J. Coffey;

1883: (a) National Hotel, T. D. Gilson (Child);

1887: --, Frank Rood

1901, '05:   (a) Kedron Tavern, Melvin J. Holt; also PM, 1900-11; Will H. Rood, Jack Conway had it a little later; the old dance hall was torn down, and it was renamed the Colonial Inn (listed as such in 1916 VPB, John C. Conway, and 1923 VPB, Mrs S B. P. Snell); later the Kedron Valley Inn, still operating. See photo, next page.

(239d) West Woodstock. No listings found.

(239e) Woodstock.

1772: a tavern, Joab Hoisington; on the site of the later Eagle Hotel, in a log cabin; Hoisington was an original settler, died 1780;

1789: Eagle Hotel, Capt Israel Richardson; moved the building a little north, c. 1792; listed in the Vermont Almanac and Register, 1796; originally a two-story building, facing the park; Titus Hutchinson added a brick wing for dining room and hall in 1822; Col Cutting added a third floor and piazzas in 1828 or '30; (a J. Cutting is listed in the Badger and Porter Stage Register, 1828); Calvin A. Fairbanks added a fourth floor in 1867; the brick addition burned in 1885, rebuilt by F. B. Merrill; the Eagle was the ancestor of the Woodstock Inn, which replaced it in 1892; the gilded eagle was carved in 1830 by Moody Heath; also known as the Church Hotel at one time, ref 3;

Kedron Valley Inn

* * *

1793:   a hotel, --; on the common where the Churchill house stood in 1891 (1); used only a short time as a tavern;

1796:   Cottle's tavern, --; (almanac);

1796:   Village Hotel, Elisha Taylor (almanacs, 1807-16); at the corner of Elm and Central Streets; Robert Barker, 1819 (almanacs, 1823-29); Samuel Whitney, 1835; Gilman Henry, 1856; burned in March, 1867, replaced by a business block; also known as Barker's Hotel, Henry's Hotel, ref 3;

1842, '43:   (a) Eagle Hotel , G. P. Alden; (b) Whitney's Hotel, Samuel Whitney; Globe, Uriah Hays (location unknown); (all Walton);

1849:   (a) as above, J. Hutchinson; (b) as above, Palmer and Whitney); (NEMU Dir);

1855, '56:   --, G. F. Whitney; --, T. B. Stevens (presumably one of these is the Eagle, the other Whitney's--same as Barker's/Henry's/Village, see photo, c. 1860, next page;

1855:   (a) Eagle Hotel, --* (Hosea Doten);

1869:   (a) as above, C. A. Fairbanks* (Beers);

1870, '73, '75, '79, '80, '83, '83 (Child):   (a) as above;

1884:   (c) Park Cottage Hotel, --; became a hotel this year, in a small brick house built in 1807; on the north side of the green, later became part of the White Cupboard Inn;

1885:   Eagle Hotel shown on Sanborn map for this year;

1887:   (a) as above, F. B. Merrill; (c) Park Cottage, C. A. Fairbanks;

1890:   (a) as above, A. B. Wilder; Eagle razed this year to make way for the Woodstock Inn; (c) as above, H. Fale;

611

Barker's (Henry's, Whitney's, Village)
(Times Gone By, Woodstock, 1976, Curtis, Curtis and Lieberman)

1892:   (d) Woodstock Inn, --; built by local people; Arthur Wilder was manager from 1897-1935; luxurious, four-story building "resembling a fashionable Newport "cottage"; open only in the summer until individual radiators were added, then became "Vermont's first winter-sports center for tourists, and for two decades its riotous winter parties were the talk of Boston and Montreal sportsmen"; originally it was not unusually expensive (2); replaced by the New Woodstock Inn in 1969; see Chapter V for a more extensive description;

1892:   (c) as above, F. H. Baldwin; Woodstock Inn shown on the Eagle site on Sanborn map for this year;

1894:   (c) as above; (d) Woodstock Inn, A. M. Mills; (e) Central House, R. E. Proctor; (f) College Hill House, O. E. Taylor (created from the old medical school, razed in the 1950s);

1895:   (d), (e) and (f) as above;

1897:   Central, Cottage and Woodstock on Sanborn;

1898:   (c) as above, J. L. Buttles; (d) as above; (e) as above, Delber and Deso; (f) as above;

1901:   (d), (e) and (f) as above;

1904:   Central became the Adams House (Sanborn); the New Park and the Woodstock also shown (see photo);

1905:   (d) as above, A. B. Wilder; (e) as above, M. A. Dickinson; (f) as above, --; New Park Hotel, Walter L. Wood;

1908:   (d) as above, --; (e) as above, --; (f) as above, --;

1910:   the Adams has become the Commercial House (Sanborn); New Park, Woodstock also shown;

1911   (d) as above; <u>New Park</u>, F. Brannock; (g) <u>Commercial House</u>, F. S. Atwood;

1913:   (d) as above; (g) <u>Commercial House</u>, F. S. Atwood; (d) and (g) the same in 1916 VPB, (g) also listed in 1923 VPB, A. S. Dutton; <u>New Park</u>, F. Brannock;

1920:   (d) as above; (g) as above, F. B. Dutton; <u>White Cupboard Inn</u>, --;

1925:   (d) as above, still operating; (g) as above, until c. 1935; <u>White Cupboard</u>, --, until at least 1955.

Note: the assistance of Deborah Haynes, Woodstock Historic Society, is gratefully acknowledged.

* * *

References

(1) Lewis C. Aldrich and Frank R. Holmes, History of Windsor County, Vermont (Syracuse: D. Mason, 1891).

(2) Peter S. Jennison, The History of Woodstock (Woodstock: Countryman Pr. for the Woodstock Foundation, 1985).

(3) Will and Jane Curtis, and Frank Lieberman, Times Gone By, Woodstock: Views of an Early Vermont Village (Hartford, Vt: Imperial Pr., 1976).

* * *

Woodstock Inn

* * *

(240) **Worcester** (Washington).

(240a) <u>Worcester</u>.

1816:   a tavern, <u>Amasa Brown</u>; tavern license, 1821, '22, '25, '26; the only family left in town after several hard years, about halfway between Montpelier and Elmore; many "applications from travellers for refreshments" (Hemenway), so Brown opened his log house as a tavern; his sign was a smooth board with letters in red chalk saying "Good cider for sale here"; he built a large two-story house in 1824 or '25, still standing in 1882 (Hemenway);

Note: tavern licenses to Artemas Richardson, 1823; Amos Spaulding, 1833; and Milton Brown, 1827, '30, locations unknown;

1855:   --, E. S. Kellogg; --, O. A. Stone;

613

1856: --, E. S. Kellogg;

1858: --, <u>E. S. Kellogg</u>* (Walling); burned about 1890;

1870: <u>Eagle House</u>, --;

1873: (a) <u>Worcester House</u>, A. A. Bliss* (Beers; not the same site as <u>Kellogg's</u> in 1858);

1872, '73, '75, '78: (a) as above;

1879: (a) as above, William H. Bowen;

1883: (a) as above, Harvey Willey (Vt Dir; spelling?);

1887: (a) as above, Harvey Miller (Vt Dir);

1889: (a) as above, L. H. Keith (Child);

1890: (a) as above;

1901: (a) as above, G. F. Jones;

1908: (a) as above,--; became an Order of Foresters Hall, a private dwelling in 1987.

Note: the assistance of Mr Hiram M. Witham, Worcester, is gratefully acknowledged.

* * *

Indexes

Index A lists all "named" taverns, inns and hotels. There is no problem with most of the entries (places like the Bardwell, the Memphremagog House, and the like) but when it comes to taverns carrying the name of the tavern-keeper, some rather arbitrary decisions have been made. In general, the taverns included in this index are those which clearly were known in their day by the name of their keeper, and also those which were probably so known (because of the length of the proprietorship, for example). Doubtless there are some taverns included here which were not really widely known by the name of the proprietor; and there are also sure to be some that should be here, but which will turn up only under the name of a tavern-keeper in Index B.

Certain problems encountered in creating Index B require comment. The first of these has to do with consecutive name entries that the reader might well think referred to the same individual (e.g., Samson, J. W. and Samson, John W., or Sawyer, D., and Sawyer, Daniel). It is, of course, possible that in many of these cases, the two names do in fact refer to the same person; but it is also possible that they do not, and unless the two names turn up for the same town, at about the same time, they have not been combined into a single entry.

A temptation arises in creating an index, which is to provide extensive cross references (e.g., when listing a given hotel, to follow the entry with all the other names it was known by). Because the indexes are already quite lengthy, this temptation has been resisted insofar as possible, and the indexes tend to be rather compact, with little cross-referencing.

Spelling is also a fairly common problem, usually due to difficulty in deciphering hand-written names in the archive records, or to the fact that Walton (and the Vermont Business Directory) will sometimes spell an innkeeper's name differently from one year to the next. A second version of a name is sometimes entered after the first, but these alternate versions do not have entries of their own in the index. Also, in the course of writing this book, names were sometimes encountered without an initial; these have been included in the manuscript (e.g., - Wilson, etc) but are not included in the index.

* * *

Index A

Taverns, Inns and Hotels

Douglas House, W. Rutland, 470
Douglass Tavern, Isle La Motte, 295
Dow Tavern, Cuttingsville, 503
Downer's Hotel, Amsden, 13, 14, 89, 573; photo, 14
Drake Hotel, Milton, 346
Driscoll Hotel, Fairfield, 235
Drury Tavern, Pittsford, 406
Drury Hotel, Whiting, 590
Dry Pond Hotel, Glover, 251, photo, 251
Duck Inn, Jonesville, 439
Dudley House, Windsor, 602
Dunbar's Hotel, Colchester, 197
Mrs Dunbar's Hotel, Fairfax, 233
Duncan Tavern, Perkinsville, 574
Dunham Hotel, W. Townshend, 542
Dunn's Hotel, Lake Bomoseen, 176, 177
Durkee Hotel, Gaysville, 517
Dutton Hotel, E. Braintree, 130
Dutton House, Cavendish, 77, 89, 179
Dutton Hotel, Hyde Park, 291
Dutton Tavern, Stowe, 520
Dutton Hotel, S. Walden, 557
Duval Hotel, E. Wallingford, 558
Dyer's Hotel, Ludlow, 314

-E-

Eagle Hotel, Cambridge, 83, 168
Eagle, Proctorsville, 180
Eagle, Chester, 190
Eagle, E. Corinth, 201
Eagle, Craftsbury, 205
Eagle, Danville, 209
Eagle, Enosburg Falls, 226
Eagle, Grafton, 254
Eagle, Marshfield, 332
Eagle Tavern, Milton, 345
Eagle Hotel, Montpelier, 84, 353, 354, 355
Eagle Inn/Hotel, Orwell, 394; photo, 395
Eagle Tavern, E. Poultney, 10, 11, 30, 414, 415; photo, 415
Eagle Hotel, Swanton, 532, 533
Eagle, W. Fairlee, 577, 578
Eagle, Westford, 579
Eagle Hall, Williston, 89, 597, 598
Eagle Hotel, Woodstock, 52, 610, 611
Eagle, Worcester, 614

Eagle Mtn Inn, Milton, 345
Eaglewood, Middletown Sprgs, 343
Earle House, Manchester Ctr, 328
East Arlington Hotel, 100
East Bethel House, 125
East Charleston Hotel, 181
East Dorset Hotel, 216
East Fairfield Hotel, 235
East Hardwick Hotel, 273
East Haven Hotel, 221
Eastman Hotel, Rupert, 460, 461
East Randolph Hotel, 424
East Rupert Hotel, 461
East Wallingford Hotel, 558
Eastwood Home, Bethel, 124
Eaton Hotel, Charlotte, 184, 185
Eaton Tavern, Montpelier, 352, 354
Eaton Hotel, Sutton, 531
Echo Inn, E. Charlotte, 182
Echo Inn, Charlotte Ctr, 184
Echo Lake Farm, Brandon, 135
Echo Lake Hotel, Tyson, 412
Eddy's Inn, Sherburne, 88, 498
Eden House, Eden, 224
Eden Pond House, Eden, 224
Edgell Hotel, Westminster, 582
Edge Water Park Hotel, Lowell Lake, 311
Edie's Hotel, Arlington, 99
Edmunds House, Burlington, 161
Edson Tavern, Brookfield, 150
Edson Tavern, St Johnsbury Ctr, 483
Egerton Tavern, W. Randolph, 426, 427; photo, 428
Eggleston Tavern, Pittsfield, 404
1811 House, Manchester, 323
Hotel Elder, W. Derby, 214
Hotel Elder, Newport, 378
Eldredge (Eldrigh) Stand, Burlington, 89, 156, 159, 506
Eldredge Tavern, S. Burlington, see Eldredge Stand, 155
Elgin Spring House, Panton, 61, 92, 396
Elkins Tavern, Peacham, 85, 400; photo, 400
Hotel Elliott, Cavendish, 179, photo, 67
Ellis Park, Lake Bomoseen, 175, 176
Elm House, Danville, 34, 53, 209, 210
Elm House, Eden, 224

Elm House, Manchester, 325, 326
The Elmore, Rutland, 465, 467, 468, 469; photo, 467
The Elms, Mount Holly, 364
Elm Tree House, Bennington, 117, 118
Elm Tree House, Milton, 344
Elm Tree House, St Albans, 27, 476
Elmwood, Burlington, 161, 164
Elmwood, Sunderland, 531
Elmwood, Wardsboro, 561
Ely's Hotel, St Johnsbury, 479
Emerson Hotel, W. Dummerston, 220
Hotel Emery, Bethel, 124; photo, 125
Empire House, N. Bennington, 119
Engel House, Whitingham, 591
England Hotel, Fairfax, 232
English Tavern, Marshfield, 331
Epson Springs House, Chimney Point, 92
Equinox House, Manchester, 49, 50, 51, 61, 82, 323, 324, 325, 326, 327; photo, 327
Equinox Jr, Manchester, 50, 323, 324
Erwin Tavern, Westminster, 581
Essex House, Island Pond, 146, 147; photo, 147
Essex House, Canaan, 171
Essex House, Guildhall, 265, 266
Essex Ctr House/Hotel, 229
Eureka House, Brandon, 132, 133
Eusty House, Fair Haven, 237
Evans Tavern, Cambridgeport, 453
Evans Hotel, Townshend, 541
Evarts House, Burlington, 161, 162
Evarts Inn, Lakeside, 83, 248
Everest Tavern, Addison, 82, 83, 91
Hotel Everett, Johnson, 28, 303; photo, 303
Evergeen Park, Willoughby, 584
Evmar House, Barre, 108
Ewings Tavern, Pittsford, 406
Exchange Hotel, Burlington, 158, 159, 161, 162
Exchange Hotel, Montpelier, 352, 353, 356, 357

637

Clement, William R.. 470
Cleveland, Cora A., 456
Cleveland, Pres Grover (as guest), 42, 576
Cleveland, Pearl, 353
Cleveland, W., 248
Clifford, C. A., 467
Clifford, Charles, 577
Clifford, Mrs James, 364
Clifford, Timothy, 176
Clifford and Means, 163
Clisbee, Charles, 267
Clough, Daniel, 318
Clough, John, 222
Clough and Downing, 480, 481
Clowe, Andrew, 282
Cloyes, John, 484
Cobb, A. H., 196
Cobb, Daniel, 541
Cobb, David A., 71, 72
Cobb, Ellis, 110
Cobb, Silas W., 358
Cobb, Willard, 396
Coburn, Elihu F., 166
Coburn, W. G., 212
Cochran, Ira, 216
Codding, J. B., 151
Codding, Joel, 151
Coe, David, 154
Coffee, C. M., 175, 176, 177
Coffey, R. J., 356, 440, 441, 602, 610
Coffey, Robert J., 555
Coit, William, 156
Colburn, J. , 565
Colburn, W., 173
Colby, A. B., 155
Colby, George (and Mrs), 538
Colby, H., 154
Colby, H. E., 589
Colby, I. A., 307
Colby, John, 112
Colby, M. K., 155
Colchester, 83, 197-199
Colcord, G. F., 451
Cold River, 502
Cole, D. G. (D. E.?), 490
Cole, G. W., 203
Cole, George, 181
Cole, George H., 190, 314
Cole, H. A., 490
Cole, N. C. and A. J., 377
Cole, L. C., 165
Cole, Winthrop, 181
Coleburn, Ebenezer, 352
Coleman, W. E., 276
Coles, C. A., 486
Collard, John, 609

Colley, Eliz., 568
Collins, A. B. (Ansel), 218, 219
Collins, Mrs Aurelia, 242
Collins, C. B., 96
Collins, Cyrus, 242
Collins, Edmond T. , 289, 290
Collins, Elmer D., 348
Collins, J. H., 96
Collins, James (J. Lee), 96
Collins, L., 117, 133, 134;
Collins, Lucius, 118
Collins, T., 432
Colson, C. H., 551, 552
Colston, William G., 574
Colton, C. P., 192, 314, 315
Colton, David B., 236
Colton, Moses, 236
Colvin, C. D., 119
Comes family, 271
Comstock, G. W., 538
Comstock, Levi, 492
Conant, Bryan G., 458
Conant, Charles L., 260
Conant, N., 268
Conant, Stephen, 601
Conant, William J., 92
Concord, 199, 200
Concord Corner, 199
Concord coach, 8, 106
Cone, G. W., 276
Cone, John, 220
Cone, John 2nd, 220
Congdon, L. S., 559
Conger, George, 290
Conger, Gershom, 290
Conley (Cawley?, G. W., 584
Conn, George, 145
Connally, James, 560
Connecticut River Tpk, see Turnpikes, and Appendix D
Conner, G., 594
Conro, James, 508
Converse, F. G., 144
Converse, Jerome, 311
Converse, Jonathan, 561
Conway, Jack (John C.), 610
Cook, A. C., 133
Cook, Anson B., 260
Cook, Capt A. S., 132
Cook, Barton B., 542
Cook, E., 253
Cook, E. Foster, 464
Cook, G. S., 422
Cook, Hiram, 289
Cook, James, 487, 488
Cook, Jesse, 369
Cook, John, 289

Cook, Mrs M. H., 467
Cook, Stephen, 144
Cooke, A. P., 201
Cooke, Coleman, 449
Cooke, Daniel, 200
Cookin, George, 274
Cookman, R. C., 241
Cookman, Robert, 240
Cookville Castleton), 175
Cooley, Theodore, 276
Coolidge, L. G., 431
Coombs, O. F., 541, 542
Coon, H. R., 163
Coon, Simon, 350
Cooper, A. B., 439
Copp, C. S., 181
Copperas Hill, 524
Copperfield, 554
Copping, Wilt, 77
Corbet, Elijah, 469
Corbin, Capt Warren (and Mrs), 47, 507
Corinth, 200-202
Corinth Center, 201
Corinth Corners, 201
Corliss, C. H., 595
Corliss, Frank, 317
Cornell, P. C., 118
Cornell, Paul, 501
Corners (Ascutney), 573
Cornforth, Samuel, 352
Cornton (East Putney), 421
Cornwall, 202, 203
Corse, Orville, 218
Corser, M. P., 541
Cory, C. E., 581
Cotton, M. L., 126
Cottrill, Mahlon, 351, 352, 353, 355
Coulton, George, 530
Courser, M. R., 276
Courser, N. P., 111
Coutier, L. , 146
Couture, George, 126
Coventry, 203, 204
Coventry Center, 203, 204
Coventry Falls, 203
Coventry Station (East Coventry), 203, 204
Cowles, Frank, 106
Cox, L. O., 313
Coxe, F. M., 133, 485
Coxe and Hack, 133, 134, 485
Crafts, F. S. (and Mrs), 599, 600
Craftsbury, 84, 204-206
Craftsbury Common, 204, 205
Craigie, James, 545
Cragin, J. G., 585

Newfane, 69, 371, 372
Newhall, Sylvanus, 510
New Haven, 374; temperance
    house in, 30
New Haven Jct, 374
New Haven Mills, 374
Newman, Albert J., 316,
    317
Newman, J. V., 326
Newport, 16, 32, 40, 84, 211,
    375-381
Newport Center, 380, 381
Newton, Albert, 103
Newton, Carlos, 124, 425
Newton, Horace, 364
Newton, James V. (and Mrs),
    428, 429
Newton, M. W., 512
Newton, Mrs Maude Baker, 207
Newton, Walker, 512
Nichols, A. N., 317
Nichols, Charles, 126
Nichols, George, 337
Nichols, H. F., 444
Nichols, H. M., 428
Nichols, Homer, 340
Nichols, Israel, 229
Nichols, John, 27
Nichols, O. F., 151
Nichols, W. B., 428
Nichols and Annabel, 452
Nicholson, Arnold, 207
Nicklaw, N. G., 468
Niles, E. S. (E. J.?), 269
Niles, Elmer, 381
Niles, William, 348
Niles and Belding, 515
Niles and Hovey, 95
Nilsson, Christine (as guest),
    105
Nisun, Frank, 144
Nixon, Artemus, 336
Nolan, Cornelius (and Mrs), 117
Noonan, Frederick, 396
Norcross, Mrs W. C., 523
Norcross, Zelta, 523
Norman and Drew, 109
Norris, F. P., 567
Norrisville (Barnet), 106
North, E. M., 433
North Bennington, 114, 115, 118
North Calais, 167
North Cambridge, 170
North Chester, 86, 189, 192
North Clarendon, 194, 196
North Concord, 200
North Craftsbury (Craftsbury
    Common), 204, 205
North Danville, 210
North Derby, 213
North Dorset, 217

North Duxbury, 57, 221
North Enosburg, 227
North Fairfax, 233, 234
North Fayston, 241
North Ferrisburg, 185, 242, 244
Northfield, 37, 87, 381-386;
    fire equipment, 65;
    prohibition enforcement, 27
Northfield Falls, 381, 385, 386
North Greensboro, 262
North Hardwick, 272
North Hartland, 281
North Hero, 10, 386-388
North Hyde Park, 292, 293
North Landgrove, 304, 305
North Londonderry, 308
North Montpelier, 223
North Orwell, 393
North Pawlet, 396
North Peacham, 400
North Pomfret, 413
North Pownal, 418
North Randolph, 423, 425
North Royalton, 39, 457
North Rupert, 461
North Shaftsbury (Shaftsbury
    Depot), 489, 490
North Sheldon, 494
North Sherburne, 497
North Shrewsbury, 504
North Springfield, 510
North Thetford (Lyme Bridge),
    536
North Troy, 543, 544
North Troy Frontier Band, 40
North Tunbridge, 546
North Underhill, 547
North Walden, 556
North Wardsboro, 561
North Williston, 596
North Windham, 310, 601
North Winhall, 604
North Wolcott, 605
Norton, Mrs A. L., 145
Norton, Elihu, 187
Norton, Jeremiah, 250
Norton, John, 580
Norton, Jonathan B., 419
Norton, Nathan, 250
Norton, W. H., 182, 552
Norton, 66, 388-390
Norton Mills, 389
Norwich, 86, 390-391
Noyes, A. H., 472
Noyes, David P., 360
Noyes, George L., 358
Noyes, Joseph, 360
Noyes, L. N., 291
Breed Noyes and Co, 291
Noyesville (Walden), 557
Nulhegan (Bloomfield), 126

Nulty, R., 476
Nulty, Robert, 159, 161
Nutt, Col Samuel, 278
Nutting, David A., 121
Nutting, S. E., 279
Nye, George, 152, 294, 408
Nye, H. (Horatio), 111, 383
Nye, J. J., 150
Nye, Norman, 110
Nye, S. Jr, 108

-O-

Oakes, David, 512
Oakland (Georgia), 247
Oakley, Charles, 472
Oatley, Donald, 348
Obermaier, J. L., 215
O'Brien, Albert, 224
O'Brien, D. E., 417
O'Connell, J. J. (and Mrs), 337,
    338, 339
O'Connor, John, 134
O'Connor, Thomas H., 99
O'Dell, E. B., 155
Odell, H. G., 470
O'Dell, William J., 159
O'Donnell, Daniel, 117
Offensend, David, 236
O'Keefe, J., 146
Olcott, 279
Old Bennington, 82, 83, 114, 115
Old Father Peter, 394
Old Round Church (Richmond),
    440
Old South Wharf, 231
Olivette, M. J., 470
Olmstead, Montgomery, 157
Olmstead, Samuel N., 225
Olmstead Falls (Sheldon
    Springs), 497
Olson, John, 573
O'Neill, P. F., 470
O'Neill, R. J., 165
Onion, Jonathan, 503
Orange, 392
Orcutt, Elisha, 406
Orcutt, George, 361, 404
Orcutt, George R., 337, 464
Orcutt, George W., 441
Orcutt and Boynton, 361
Ord, John, 294
Ordway, Asa, 532
Ordway, G. D., 180
Ordway, S. R., 108
Oren, Paul, 186
Orleans, 84, 112
Ormsbee, Benjamin, 151, 371
Ormsbee, T. J., 501
Orr turn, 12, 263
Orris, John M., 220

Orvis, Anna Simonds, 50, 51, 325

Orvis, Charles F., 324, 325, 326, 329

Orvis, David, 601

Orvis, Edward (E. C.), 50, 324, 326

Orvis, Franklin H., 50, 324, 325

Orvis, George, 50, 51, 324, 325

Orvis, Levi C., 50, 324

Orvis, R. J. and A. C., 326

Orvis family, 324

Orwell, 392-395

Osborne, D. F., 170

Osborne, J., 283

Osborne Brothers, 147

Osgood, H. M., 210

Osgood, O. C., 272

Osgood, William H., 371, 372

Osier, Lewis, 348

Osmer, Frank J., 277

Ostheimer, Mrs Emmie, 407

Otis, S. H., 560

Otter Creek (Leicester), 306

Owl's Head (Newport), 379

-P-

Packer, H. H., 419

Packers Corners (Guilford), 269

Paddock, James, 107

Page, Abel, 463

Page, Ansel, 248

Page, B. P., 580

Page, Cynthia, 463

Page, E. D., 449

Page, Dr E. H., 241

Page, G. O. (G. H. Paige?), 165

Page, James and Marta, 227

Page, Jesse, 264

Page, Josiah, 471

Page, Leverett H., 264, 265

Page, Nathan B., 471

Page, N. D., 410

Page, Phineas, 375, 377

Page, Phinehas, 502

Page, Seneca, 101

Page, Thomas, 248

Page, W., 122

Page, W. H., 472

Page's Corner (Essex), 228

Paige, R., 464

Paige, W. F., 464, 466

Paige, Willis, 102

Paige and Marston, 465

Paige and Tolhurst, 464, 466

Paine, Amasa, 312

Paine (Payne), Benjamin, 92

Paine, Charles (Governor), 37, 381, 382

Paine, Elijah, 382, 596

Paine, Samuel Jr, 426

Deacon Paine place, 178

Painesville (Essex Jct), 228

Paine Turnpike, see Turnpikes, and Appendix D

Painter, Azariah, 550

Palmer, George, 242

Palmer, H. P., 287

Palmer, Seneca, 136

Palmer, W. L., 482

Palmer and Whitney, 611

Panton, 61, 92, 395, 396

Papale, D. J., 541

Paquette, Robert, 346

Paradise, Fred, 515

Parke, John C., 464

Parker, A. E., 101

Parker, C. E., 573

Parker, C. H., 513

Parker, D. A. (Barker?), 342

Parker, E. W., 423

Parker, Edson J. and Florence,, 444

Parker, F. C. and F. S., 287

Parker, G., 417

Parker, H., 407

Parker, H. S., 469

Parker, Henry, 160

Parker, Isaac, 511

Parker, J. M., 572

Parker, J. N., 387, 388

Parker, Jonas, 449

Parker, Joshua, 218

Parker, Leonard ("King"), 131, 511

Parker, Marvin, 133

Parker, N. L., 155

Parker, O. D., 309

Parker, O. H., 296

Parker, Reuben, 535

Parker, Samuel, 586

Parker, Wesley, 554

Parker, William, 412, 579

Parker, Wyman, 104

Parker, Lake, 250

Parker Hill (Springfield), 510, 511

Parkerstown (Mendon), 333

Parkhurst, Levi M., 545

Parks, E. A., 480

Parks, Levi P., 106

Parlin, F. J., 113

Parmalee, Lucius, 565

Parmalee and Atkins, 565

Parmelee, Alexander, 601

Parmelee, Eliz., 601

Parmelee, Josiah (Joseph?), 601

Parmenter, C. L., 357

Parmenter, Mansil, 443

Parmenter house, 65

Parrington, Martha, 572

Parvis, J. G., 133

Parris, L. (Levi Paris?), 215

Parsons, C. F., 159

Parsons, Daniel, 360, 414

Parsons, J. K., 486

Parsonville (St Albans), 474

Partch, Frederick M., 374

Partch, William M., 374

Partch and Post, 148

Partridge, Mrs Mary, 391

Partridge, Ora B., 106

Partridge, Vernon D., 130

Passumpsic, 87

Passumpsic Tpk, see Turnpikes, and Appendix D

Patch, John, 598

Pate, Mr and Mrs James, 132

Patrick, Samuel Jr and Sr, 601

Patten Brothers, 482

Patterson, George M., 349, 350

Patterson, I. T., 205

Patterson, John, 606

Patterson, R. E., 463

Patterson, Will, 452

Patterson, W. N., 452

Paul, Dick W., 122

Pawlet, 33, 396-399;

Peabody, Mrs H. M., 98

Peabody, H. O., 191, 444

Peabody, Col H. O., 98, 311

Peabody Station (Groton), 263

Peach, B., 92

Peacham, 19, 85, 399-401

Peacham Hollow, 400

Pearl, Timothy, 344

Pearl (Grand Isle), 256, 258

Pearson, Charles, 424

Pearson, Ezekiel, 601

Pearsons, John, 128

Pease, Allen C., 276

Pease, Ambrose, 585

Pease, Charles W., 276

Pease, Charles and William, 532

Pease, E. J., 233

Pease, George, 242

Pease, Hiland H., 585

Pease, Horace C., 276

Pease, Lorin, 585

Pease, Luther, 276

Peaseville (Andover), 97

Peaslee, E. S., 128

Peck, G. W., 399, 470, 551

Peck, H. A., 108

Peck, Warren, 581

Peckham, A. C., 418

Ranney, J., 115
Ranney, Luther B., 117
Ransom, A., 94
Ransom, A. B., 526
Ransom, D., 610
Ransom, Ezekiel, 542
Ransom, J. H., 299, 383, 441
Ransom, Julius, 440
Ransom, Robert, 94
Ransom (Rawson)?, S. E., 297
Ranta, Julia, 313
Raponda, Lake, 598
Rawson, Grace, 205
Rawson, Josiah, 531
Rawson, Rufus W., 136
Rawsonville (Jamaica), 298
Ray, L. C., 286 (Lewis? 287)
Ray and Boyden, 136
Ray and Brooks, 160
Raymond, Col Asahel, 520
Raymond, Flora B., 460
Raymond, G. H., 315, 383, 460, 492
Raymond, G. W., 547
Raymond, George, 409, 424, 459, 521
Raymond, Joshua, 323
Raymond, N. B., 521
Read, George B., 553
Reading, 431
Reading Ctr, 431
Readsboro, 32, 433, 434
Readsboro City, Falls, 434
Reagan, C. W., 476
Reagan, M. J., 180
Rebek, Andrea B., 44
Redding, Mrs Abbie L., 284
Redfield, H. M., 177
Red House, 397
Red Village, 318, 322
Redway, A., 355
Reed, Calvin (and Mrs), 578
Reed, Curtis, 396
Reed, David, 220, 371
Reed, F. E., 136
Reed, H. D., 578
Reed, Issacher, 463
Reed, J. W., 281
Reed, John, 267
Reed, Jonas, 120
Reed, Paul A., 337
Reed, W. H., 119
Reed, Willard, 463, 464
Reid, J. W., 281
Reid Hollow, see Halifax
Remick, S. K., 25, 480
Renneff, David, 588
Rennie, A. J., 589
Reniff, Daniel, 318
Rescue, Lake (Ludlow), 313, 316
Resorts, see Chap V; Railroads,

effects of on;
Examples of: Bomoseen, 175-177;
   Bread Loaf, 55, 56, 442, 443;
   Equinox, 50, 51, 324, 325; Island
   House, 449; Lake Dunmore, 484;
   Lake St Catherine, 41, 576; New-
   port, 40, 375, 379; N. Hero, 387;
   Sadawga, 591; Willoughby, 56, 57,
   582; Woodstock, 51-53, 612;
Growth of village hotels as, 3, 53;
Mineral Springs, list of, 60, 61;
Spas, as first Vt resorts, 45; see
   Spas;
Summer boarders, 53; at hotels in
   Danville, 53, Greensboro, 54;
Summit Houses, 57; examples of:
   Ascutney, 602; Camel's Hump, 57,
   221; Grandview (Addison), 60, 91;
   Killington, 59, 466; Lincoln Lodge,
   59; Mt Mansfield, 58, 59, 518, 519,
   520; Woodford, 609;
Reuter, Harry, 182
Reynolds, C. P., 262
Reynolds, Dan. 170
Reynolds, Jonathan, 413
Reynolds, Oliver, 575, 576
Rhode, George W., 159
Rice, Abel M., 479
Rice, Alpheus, 394
Rice, Edward, 555
Rice, George, 540
Rice, Gideon H. and H. I., 508
Rice, Isaac, 431
Rice, Liberty, 136
Rice, Page J. C., 456
Rice, Seth, 532
Rice's Mills (Thetford), 539
Rice and Olmstead, 474
Rich, Charles, 345
Rich, E. E., 407
Rich, John, 167, 352
Rich, Samuel, 223
Rich, Solomon, 489
Rich's Hollow (North Montpelier), 223
Richards, Charles F., 261
Richard, Ira, 182, 375
Richards, George E., 140
Richardson, Abiel, 569
Richardson, Artemas, 613
Richardson, Benjamin, 232
Richardson, C. F., 465, 466
Richardson, Calvin C., 555
Richardson, E. (and Mrs), 253
Richardson, Evelyn, 200
Richardson, F. H., 465
Richardson, Francis and W. A., 155, 199, 583
Richardson, G. R., 314
Richardson, George, 403
Richardson, H., 108

Richardson, Helen, 271
Richardson, Henry, 578
Richardson, Capt Israel, 52, 610
Richardson, John, 232
Richardson, Johnson, 333
Richardson, Lester, 277
Richardson, M. L. (C.?), 244
Richardson, Naomi, 584
Richardson, Roderick, 555
Richardson, Rufus, 333, 498
Richardson, Rufus Jr, 498
Richardson, S., 583
Richardson, W. A., 146
Richardson, W. F., 584
Richford, 435-438
Richmond, Loring, 514
Richmond, 89, 438-442
Richville (Shoreham Ctr), 501
Rickard, Mr and Mrs L. A., 212
Rickcord, Edward, 341
Ricker's Mills, 263, 264
Ricker's Pond, 263
Rickett, J. D., 256
Rickett, Judson, 254
Riddle, Robert, 593
Rider, Benjamin, 542
Rider, Darwin, 337
Rider, Hiram, 374
Ridley, G. B., 148
Ridley, J. J., 148
Ridley, Samuel Jr, 57, 221
Ridley's Station (North Duxbury), 57, 221
Riggie, L., 147
Riggs, Franklin, 314
Riley, C. A., 519
Ring, Henry, 201
Ring, J. M., 337
Ring, John, 306
Ripley, Gen Edward H., 334
Ripley, William (W. Y.), 334
Risdon, Alvah, 208
Ripton, 55, 85, 442, 443
Ritchie, James, 295
Ritchie, Thomas, 234, 235
Riverside, 300, 301
Riverton (Berlin), 123
Roach, Israel, 324
Roads
   Organized system of, 5;
   First in Vt, 5;
   Improvements in, 6, 12;
   see Crown Pt Rd, Bayley-Hazen
   Rd; also Turnpikes, and Appendix
   D;
Robbins, A. D., 224, 303
Robbins, A. J., 101, 383
Robbins, Asa, 569
Robbins, Charles, 173
Robbins, D. B., 224
Robert, Hector, 227

Strickland, W. R., 221
Strobridge, L., 401
Strong, D., 517
Strong, E. D., 428
Strong, E. G., 355
Strong, Elijah, 151
Strong, L. J., 311, 541;
  and Mrs, 142
Strong, Mrs Sarah, 516
Strong, Timothy, 396
Strong, William, 275
Strong and Chadwick, 428
Stroud, S. I., 475
Stuart, Walter, 400
Sturtevant, Dr Friend, 281
Sturtevant, W. R., 281
Sudbury, 9, 36, 86, 526-528
Style (Stile?), A. F., 196
Styles, C. A., 604, 605
Sulhan, H. R., 428
Summerville (St Johnsbury), 483
Summer, D. H., 280
Summer, George A., 375
Summit (Walden Heights), 557
Summit houses, see Resorts
Sumner, John T., 297
Sumner, Salem, 136
Sumner, Thomas, 542
Sunderland, 88, 100, 529-531
Surge Tank (Whitingham), 590
Sutherland Falls (Proctor), 420
Sutton, 531
Sutton Depot (Clark), 531
Swallow, George, 587
Swanton (Falls), 55, 531-535
Swanton Center, 531, 535
Swanton Junction, 531, 535
Swazey, Philip B.. 589
Sweat, John, 208
Sweatland, J. B., 437
Sweet, A. P., 313
Sweet, Jennie B., 290
Swezey, Christopher, 323
Swift, E. C., 540
Swift, H. S., 540
Swift, P. M., 538, 554
Sykas, William J., 356
Sykes, Ernest, 587
Sylvester, L., 225

-T-

Tabor, Edward C., 365
Taft, Amaniah, 542
Taft, Caleb, 220
Taft, Elisha, 542
Taft, E. P., 454
Taft, Josiah, 220
Taft, Julian C., 541
Taft, R. C., 516
Taft, Ransom, 148

Taft, Stephen, 449
Tafts, Horace W., 267
Taft's Corner (Williston), 597
Taftsville, 610
Taggart, Capt James, 541
Tainter, Henry A., 418
Talbert, D. A., 424
Talbot, F., 146
Talcott (Williston), 597
Talcville (Rochester), 446
Tallman, Carl and Linda, 225
Taplin, Mansfield, 200
Taplin, M. J., 200
Tarbell, Daniel, 39, 187, 459
Tarbell, Gilman (and Mrs), 425
Tarbellville (Mount Holly), 363
Tarble, W. S., 407
Tatro, Henry, 534
Tarte, Norman, 535
Taverns
  As courthouses, 1, 187, 323,
    386, 536, 539;
  As post offices, 10, 11, 313;
    see also Post offices;
  As social centers, 1, 11, 12,
    13, 22, 218, 231, 252, 263,
    304, 386, 427, 479, 483, 499,
    502, 507, 520;
  Early primitive ones, 1, 6, 7,
    10, 511;
  See Chapter II; effects of rail-
    roads on, 2, 35, 36; also Rail-
    roads, effects of on (various
    towns);
Tavern-keepers
  As militia leaders, JPs, etc, 7,
    11, 22, 110, 136, 187, 219,
    295, 371, 431;
  As proprietors of stage lines,
    6, 304, 423, 471, 498, 562
Tavern signs, 15; list of,
  Appendix B, 77-80; law
  requiring, 15
Taylor, A. E., 315
Taylor, Mrs Augusta, 498
Taylor, C. H., 91
Taylor, D. F., 298
Taylor, E. J., 476
Taylor, Elias Jr, 555
Taylor, Elisha, 611
Taylor, Gamaliel, 291
Taylor, Gamaliel M., 606
Taylor, Gideon M., 606
Taylor, Gordon, 289
Taylor, Herbert H., 458
Taylor, James, 585
Taylor, Jerome, 498
Taylor, O. E., 612
Taylor, Mrs Rama, 271

Taylor, Roland, 418
Taylor, S. C., 610
Taylor, S. S., 268
Taylor, S. W., 158
Taylor, Samuel, 610
Taylor, Samuel H., 432
Temperance
  Issue in 1902 gubernatorial
    campaign, 28;
  Organizations, 22, 25, 26;
  Temperance houses, 23, 24,
    25, 212, 512, 524, 525, 559;
    list of, 29, 30;
  Temperance movement, 3, 23,
    24, 28, 229, 320, 510;
    origins of, 21, 22;
  See also Chap III; Pro-
    hibition; Liquor;
Temple, E. J., 591
Temple, Robert, 464
Tenney, A. M., 603
Tenney, Ames C., 200
Tenney, Truman, 360
Tenney, W. P., 585
Thatcher, Asa, 604
Thatcher, Barlow, 474
Thatcher, Ira P., 458
Thayer, Adin, 220
Thayer, Emery, 480
Thayer, F. E. and J. G., 433
Thayer, H. A., 574
Thayer, I., 124, 125
Thayer, Isaac, 125
Thayer, J. S., 125
Thayer, L. D., 141
Thayer, M., 106
Thayer, Proctor, 106
Thayer, S. E., 328
Thayer and Brothers, 433
Thetford, 536-539
Thetford Center, 538
Thetford Hill, 538
Thomas, David, 121
Thomas, E. M., 572
Thomas, G. H., 496
Thomas, H. B., 496
Thomas, Henry, 203
Thomas, I., 154
Thomas, Mrs Orson, 343
Thomas, R., 317
Thomas, Stephen, 110
Thomas, Thomas, 248
Thomas, William B., 324
Thompson, A., 341, 399
Thompson, A. E., 607
Thompson, Abram, 417
Thompson, Benai, 244
Thompson, D. M., 267
Thompson, Dorothy, 102
Thompson, E. D., 321
Thompson, Fred, 372

West Woodstock, 610
Weybridge, 587
Weybridge Lower Falls, 587
Wheat, Samuel, 421
Wheatly, Major Nathaniel, 150
Wheaton, Isaac, 406
Wheeler, A. A., 401
Wheeler, A. C., 496
Wheeler, Absalom, 244
Wheeler, Beriah, 605
Wheeler, C. B., 281
Wheeler, C. J., 117
Wheeler, Daniel, 179
Wheeler, Frank P. (and Mrs), 277
Wheeler, George, 353, 356
Wheeler, Harry T., 527
Wheeler, John, 242
Wheeler, N. P., 278
Wheeler, Nathan, 255
Wheeler, Nathaniel, 279
Wheeler, Phineas, 152, 167, 182
Wheeler, Robert, 182
Wheeler, R. D., 345
Wheeler, Shubael, 167
Wheeler, Solomon. 107
Wheeler, William T., 605
Wheelock, E., 371
Wheelock, Eleazer, 588
Wheelock, Emory and Asa, 372
Wheelock, Henry, 371, 372
Wheelock, J. S., 223
Wheelock, John, 588
Wheelock, Peter, 367
Wheelock, 46, 61, 587-589
Wheelock Hollow, 588
Whipple, A. S., 294
Whipple, A. S. and M. S., 273, 361
Whipple, Andrew J., 418
Whipple, George R., 599
Whipple, H. V., 460
Whipple, James, Sr and Jr, 511
Whipple, Joseph, 439
Whipple, O., 413
Whipple, Parley, 218
Whipple, Thaddeus S., 168, 549
Whitcomb, Albert, 443
Whitcomb, Arthur, 512
Whitcomb, Col Carter, 453
Whitcomb, Elias, 416
Whitcomb, Elmer A. and Augusta E., 371
Whitcomb, E. H., 517, 518
Whitcomb, E. S., 456, 533
Whitcomb, Harold, 228
Whitcomb, J., 517
Whitcomb, James, 126, 132
Whitcomb, Robert, 471
White, C. C., 192, 314
White, C. R., 449
White, Mrs and Mrs Charles, 368

White, E. E. (and Mrs), 363
White, Frank, 103
White, G. P., 168
White, George, 585
White, H. K., 329
White, Horace (H. E.?), 458
White, John, 364
White, Jotham, 509
White, Miss Julia R., 317
White, L. S., 600
White, Samuel, 494
White, Stillman, 585
White, W. E., 458
White, W. R., 119
White, W. W., 475
White, William A. (and Mrs), 317
Whitelaw, Robert, 78
White Mountains, 3, 44, 140
White River Junction, 32, 37, 52, 56, 277, 278
Whitesville (Cavendish), 178
Whitford, William, 91
Whithed, Addison, 553
Whiting, 5, 86, 590
Whitingham, 61, 590-594
Whitingham Center, 592
Whitingham Lake, 590
Whiting Station (Leicester Jct), 306
Whitman, O., 580
Whitmore, Hamlin, 512
Whitney, A. W., 188
Whitney, C. L., 139
Whitney, Carl, 486
Whitney, D. H., 259
Whitney, G. F., 611
Whitney, Jazaniah, 104
Whitney, Jesse, 606
Whitney, John, 174
Whitney, Jonas, 330
Whitney, Lemuel, 136
Whitney, Samuel, 331, 611
Whitney, W., 577, 578
Whitney and Lyman, 330
Whittier, Rinaldo, 271
Whittier, William P., 165
Wicher (Witcher?), A. and C. R., 273
Wickes, B. P., 394
Wickes, John, 394
Wickes, John, Plinny and Ira, 144
Wickham, R. C.. 466
Wickware, Reuben, 287, 348
Wiggin, B. F., 204, 260
Wiggin, Steven, 321
Wightman, Henry, 396
Wightman, Deacon Samuel, 447
Wilbur, Charles, 572
Wilcox, A. H., 479
Wilcox, C. F., 117

Wilcox, Cushman, 267
Wilcox, Ephraim, 582
Wilcox, Col F. M., 501
Wilcox, Henry, 254, 607
Wilcox, J. S., 576
Wilcox, M. C., 599
Wilcox, P. E. (and Mrs), 120, 121
Wilcox, R. Q., 590, 599
Wilcox, Robert, 421
Wilde, Oscar (as guest), 499
Wilder, 279
Wilder Hollow (S. Wardsboro), 561
Wilder, Abel B., 419
Wilder, Abel K., 453, 454
Wilder, Arthur B., 53, 611, 612
Wilder, B. G., 297, 298, 561
Wilder, D. P., 411
Wilder, Ezra, 297
Wilder, Frank, 181
Wilder, Frederick, 53
Wilder, Horace, 498
Wilder, John L., 453
Wilder, Marshall A., 454
Wilder, Norris D., 411
Wilder, Paxton G., 599
Wilder and Kidder, 598, 599
Wilkins, Martin, 293
Wilkins, William H., 474
Wilkinson, Lizzie H., 585
Willard, Alpheus, 449
Willard, C. H., 541
Willard, C. S., 423
Willard, Charles H., 326
Willard, Daniel, 148
Willard, H. C., 133, 134
Willard, Joseph, 581
Willard, Josiah, 371
Willard, L. E. (and Mrs), 496
Willard, Nelson, 220
Willard, Orra H. (Ora?), 532, 535
Willard, Peter (Squire?), 446
Willard, Salmon, 308
Willard, Solomon, 542
Willey, Bernard, 107
Williams, Alvin, 130
Williams, Bartlett, 205
Williams, C. F., 329
Williams, Channing, 277
Williams, Dwight J., 229
Williams, F. C., 217, 326
Williams, Hosea, 206
Williams, James Jr, 569
Williams, John P., 278
Williams, Col Jonathan, 512
Williams, Lucy, 130
Williams, Luke, 512
Williams, Merrill, 352
Williams, Robert, 203
Williams, Scott,229
Williams, Solomon, 130
Williams, T. C., 185

683

ILL
M 76 C
12/6/95

WITHDRAWN